# The Steps in the Research Process

**1. Find a Research Idea**
Identify a general topic that you would like to explore,
and review the background literature to find
a new idea for a research study.

**10. Refine or Reformulate Your Research Idea** ⟶ **2. Convert the Idea into a Hypothesis**
Use the results to modify, refine, or expand your                    Use your idea to generate a specific, testable hypothesis.
original research idea or to generate new ideas.

**9. Report the Results**                                       **3. Define and Measure Variables**
Use the established guidelines for format and style              Identify the specific procedures that will be used
to prepare an accurate and honest report that also protects     to define and measure all variables. Plan to evaluate
the anonymity and confidentiality of the participants.          the validity and reliability of your measurement procedure.

**8. Evaluate the Data**                                        **4. Identify Participants or Subjects**
Use the appropriate descriptive and inferential                 Decide how many participants or subjects
statistics to summarize and interpret the results.              you will need and what characteristics they should have.
                                                                Also plan for their ethical treatment.

**7. Conduct the Study**                                        **5. Select a Research Strategy**
Collect the data.                                               Consider the relative importance of internal and
                                                                external validity, and decide among an experimental
                                                                (cause-effect), descriptive, correlational, or
                                                                quasi-experimental strategy.

**6. Select a Research Design**
Decide among between-subjects, within-subjects, factorial,
or single-subject designs.

# www.wadsworth.com

# Research Methods
# for the
# Behavioral Sciences

# Research Methods for the Behavioral Sciences

Frederick J Gravetter
*State University of New York College at Brockport*

Lori-Ann B. Forzano
*State University of New York College at Brockport*

THOMSON
™
WADSWORTH

Australia • Canada • Mexico • Singapore • Spain • United Kingdom • United States

# THOMSON
™
## WADSWORTH

Publisher: Vicki Knight
Editorial Assistant/Assistant Editor: Dan Moneypenny
Technology Project Manager: Darin Derstine
Marketing Manager: Lori Grebe
Marketing Assistant: Laurel Anderson
Advertising Project Manager: Shemika Britt
Signing Representative: Tim Kenney
Project Manager, Editorial Production: Paula Berman
Print/Media Buyer: Nancy Panziera

Permissions Editor: Elizabeth Zuber
Production Service: Vicki Moran, Publishing Support Services
Text Designer: Kim Rokusek
Copy Editor: April Wells-Hayes
Cover Designer: Laurie Albrecht
Cover Image: Judith L. Harkness
Cover and Text Printer: Phoenix Color Corp
Compositor: Thompson Type

Printed in the United States of America
1  2  3  4  5  6  7  06 05 04 03 02

For more information about our products, contact us at:
**Thomson Learning Academic Resource Center**
**1-800-423-0563**
For permission to use material from this text, contact us by:
**Phone:** 1-800-730-2214
**Fax:** 1-800-730-2215
**Web**: http://www.thomsonrights.com

Library of Congress Control Number: 2002109839

ISBN 0-534-54911-X

**Wadsworth/Thomson Learning**
10 Davis Drive
Belmont, CA 94002-3098
USA

**Asia**
Thomson Learning
5 Shenton Way #01-01
UIC Building
Singapore 068808

**Australia**
Nelson Thomson Learning
102 Dodds Street
South Melbourne, Victoria 3205
Australia

**Canada**
Nelson Thomson Learning
1120 Birchmount Road
Toronto, Ontario M1K 5G4
Canada

**Europe/Middle East/Africa**
Thomson Learning
High Holborn House
50/51 Bedford Row
London WC1R 4LR
United Kingdom

**Latin America**
Thomson Learning
Seneca, 53
Colonia Polanco
11560 Mexico D.F.
Mexico

**Spain**
Paraninfo Thomson Learning
Calle/Magallanes, 25
28015 Madrid, Spain

# Author Biographies

**Frederick J Gravetter** is a Professor of Psychology at the State University of New York College at Brockport. Dr. Gravetter has taught at Brockport since the early 1970s, specializing in statistics, experimental design, and cognitive psychology. He received his bachelor's degree in mathematics from M.I.T and his Ph.D. in psychology from Duke University. In addition to publishing several research articles, Dr. Gravetter has co-authored *Statistics for the Behavioral Sciences* and *Essentials of Statistics for the Behavioral Sciences*.

Frederick J Gravetter

**Lori-Ann B. Forzano** is an Associate Professor of Psychology at the State University of New York College at Brockport, where she has taught since 1992. She earned a Ph.D. in experimental psychology from the State University of New York at Stony Brook in 1992, where she also received her B.S. in psychology. Dr. Forzano's research interests are in the area of conditioning and learning. Specifically, she studies self-control and impulsiveness in adults and young children. Her research has been published in the *Journal of the Experimental Analysis of Behavior* and *Learning and Motivation* and is regularly presented at the annual conference of the Association for Behavior Analysis.

Lori-Ann B. Forzano

# Preface

For years we have watched students come into psychology Research Methods courses with a fundamental fear of science. Somewhere along the way, these students seem to have developed the idea that psychology is interesting and fun but science is tedious and difficult. Many students even resent having to take a Research Methods course: "After all, I want to be a psychologist, not a scientist."

As the semester progresses, however, most of these students begin to lose their fears, and many actually begin to enjoy the course. Much of this change in attitude is based on a realization that science is simply the technique that psychologists use to gather information and to answer questions. As long as the questions are interesting, then the task of answering them should also be interesting.

When people watch a magician do an amazing trick, they often ask, "How was that done?" In the same way, when you learn something interesting about human behavior, you ought to ask, "How do they know that?" The answer is that most of the existing knowledge in the behavioral sciences was gathered using scientific research methods. If you are really curious about human behavior, then you should also be curious about the process of studying it.

This textbook has been developed from years of teaching Research Methods. During that time, we have tried different examples and explanations in the classroom and watched the students' responses. Over the years, the course has evolved into a less intimidating, more interesting approach that seems to be very effective in getting students involved in research. Our students have been most helpful in this evolutionary process. Their feedback has directed our progress in the development of the research methods course and the writing of this book. In many respects they have been our teachers.

## OVERVIEW OF THE TEXT

*Research Methods for the Behavioral Sciences* is intended for an undergraduate Research Methods course in psychology or any of the behavioral sciences. We have organized the text according to the research process, making it appropriate for use in a lecture-only class or a class with a lab component. The text discusses in detail both experimental and nonexperimental research strategies. We use an informal writing style that emphasizes discussion and explanation of topics. Pedagogical aids include preview outlines, learning checks throughout each chapter, a running glossary, chapter summaries, a list of key words for quick review at the end of each chapter, end-of-chapter exercises, and end-of-chapter InfoTrac® College Edition exercises.

## ORGANIZATION OF THE TEXT

The book's organizational framework is the research process—from start to finish. This step-by-step approach emphasizes the decisions researchers must make at each stage of the process. The chapters are grouped into five sections. Chapters 1 through 3 focus on the earliest considerations in the research process and include tips for finding new ideas for research and developing hypotheses, pointing out the ethics that must govern all further decisions in research. Chapters 4 through 6 focus on the preliminary decisions in the research process and include information on measuring variables, selecting participants, and choosing a valid research strategy. Chapters 7 through 9 provide details of the different research strategies. Chapters 10 through 13 provide details of specific experimental designs. Chapters 14 and 15 focus on decisions in the final stages of the research process and include information on evaluating, interpreting, and communicating research results.

## WRITING STYLE

We have used an informal, conversational style of writing that emphasizes discussion and explanation of topics, instead of a "cookbook" presentation of facts. This style has been successful in our own classes and in Gravetter's coauthored textbook, *Statistics for the Behavioral Sciences*. Students find this style readable and unintimidating; it is particularly useful for material that students perceive as difficult.

## PEDAGOGICAL AIDS

We have paid particular attention to pedagogical aids. In each chapter, there are many opportunities for students to engage the material rather than passively being exposed to it. Learning checks, end-of-chapter exercises, and end-of-chapter InfoTrac College Edition exercises can be used by the instructor as prepackaged assignments.

Each chapter contains:

1. *Chapter Outline:* Each chapter begins with an outline of the material presented in the chapter, to help students see the organization of the material.
2. *Chapter Overview:* A brief summary of the chapter's contents at the beginning of the chapter prepares students for the material to come.
3. *Multiple sections:* Multiple, clearly defined sections and subsections break the material down into manageable chunks.
4. *Definitions:* Each key word is boldfaced upon its first use in the text. A clearly identified, concise definition is provided at the end of the paragraph that contains the new key word.
5. *Examples:* Numerous examples illustrate concepts presented in the text. Some examples are hypothetical, and some are selected from current or classic studies in psychology.
6. *Boxes:* Boxed material, separate from the regular text, offers additional interesting information to help demonstrate certain key points.

7. *Figures:* Where appropriate, diagrams and graphs are included to illustrate important points.
8. *Tables:* Tables are used to present information best conveyed in a list format.
9. *Margin notes:* Brief notes in the margins of the text offer reminders or cautions to students.
10. *Learning Checks:* At the end of major sections within each chapter, a set of questions helps students test how well they have learned the material.
11. *Chapter Summaries:* A general summary at the end of each chapter helps students review the main points of the chapter.
12. *Key Words:* A list of the key words used in the chapter is presented at the end of each chapter. The list is in order of the key words' appearance in the chapter so that related terms are grouped together and so that students can spot parts of the chapter they need to review.
13. *Exercises:* A list of questions and activities appears at the end of each chapter. The exercises help students test how well they have learned the material by applying what they have learned. The instructor can also use the exercises as assignments.
14. *InfoTrac College Edition Exercises:* InfoTrac College Edition Exercises appear at the end of each chapter. These exercises provide students with an additional, unique learning opportunity to apply information presented in the text.

## ACKNOWLEDGMENTS

We appreciate the careful reading and thoughtful suggestions given by the reviewers of this text:

Rudy Hatfield
*University of Michigan at Dearborn*

LouAnne Hawkins
*University of North Florida*

Gary Starr
*Metropolitan State University*

Mark Nagy
*Xavier University*

William Langston
*Middle Tennessee State University*

Michelle Miller
*Northern Arizona University*

Charles Pierce
*Montana State University*

Alfiee M. Breland
*Michigan State University*

Germain Ludwig
*Palm Beach Atlantic College*

Carl Scott
*University of Saint Thomas*

Page Jerzak
*Trinity University*

Kathleen Donovan
*University of Central Oklahoma*

Annette Taylor
*University of San Diego*

Virginia Gregg
*SUNY College at Oswego*

Wayne Mitchell
*Southwest Missouri State University*

We appreciate the hard work provided by the staff at Wadsworth in the production of this text:

| | |
|---|---|
| Vicki Knight | Publisher |
| Darin Derstine | Technology Project Manager |
| Jennifer Wilkinson | Assistant Editor |
| Dan Moneypenny | Editorial Assistant/Assistant Editor |
| Lori Grebe | Marketing Manager |
| Laurel Anderson | Marketing Assistant |
| Paula Berman | Production Project Manager |
| Vernon Boes | Creative Director |

We also would like to thank Vicki Moran for assistance in production and April Wells-Hayes for copy editing. Other professional thanks go to Larry Wallnau for his contributions to an earlier manuscript.

Finally, our most heartfelt thanks go out to our spouses and children: Charlie Forzano, Ryan Forzano, Debbie Gravetter, Justin Gravetter, Melissa Burke, and Megan Burke. This book could not have been written without their unwavering support and patience.

## TO CONTACT US

Over the years our students have given us many helpful suggestions, and we have benefitted from their feedback. If you have any suggestions or comments about this book, you can write to us at the Department of Psychology, SUNY College at Brockport, 350 New Campus Drive, Brockport, NY 14420. We can also be reached by e-mail at:

lforzano@brockport.edu      and      fgravett@brockport.edu.

*Lori-Ann B. Forzano*                    *Frederick J Gravetter*

# Brief Contents

# Contents

CHAPTER 3

## ETHICS IN RESEARCH   58

CHAPTER 4

## DEFINING AND MEASURING VARIABLES   82

CHAPTER 7

## DESCRIPTIVE AND CORRELATIONAL RESEARCH STRATEGIES   161

CHAPTER 8

## EXPERIMENTAL RESEARCH STRATEGY   188

## CHAPTER 9

### QUASI-EXPERIMENTAL STRATEGY: NONEQUIVALENT GROUP, TIME-SERIES, AND DEVELOPMENTAL DESIGNS  214

## CHAPTER 10

### EXPERIMENTAL DESIGNS: BETWEEN-SUBJECTS DESIGN  240

## CHAPTER 11

# EXPERIMENTAL DESIGNS: WITHIN-SUBJECTS DESIGN   266

## CHAPTER 12

# FACTORIAL DESIGNS   291

CHAPTER 13

SINGLE-SUBJECT
RESEARCH DESIGNS   323

# Introduction, Inquiry, and the Scientific Method

## CHAPTER OVERVIEW

In this chapter we introduce the topic of this textbook—research methodology. To help you see the relevance of this material to your life, we begin with some comments about the usefulness of understanding research methodology. Then we discuss the many ways of acquiring knowledge or finding answers to questions, including the scientific method. Next we provide a thorough discussion of the scientific method. The chapter ends with an outline of the research process—the way the scientific method is applied to answer a particular question. The research process provides the framework for the rest of the textbook.

## 1.1   INTRODUCTION TO RESEARCH METHODOLOGY

Consider the following questions.

Are children of divorced parents less likely to commit to romantic relationships?

Do large doses of vitamin C prevent people from getting the common cold?

In general, who has higher self-esteem, a first-born child or a last-born child?

Which city gets more snow during a typical winter, Anchorage, Alaska, or Buffalo, New York?

Are left-handed people more artistic than right-handers?

In this book our goal is to examine some of the methods people can use to obtain answers to questions like these. More specifically, we focus on the method typically used by scientists—the scientific method. The scientific method is considered basic, standard practice in the world of science; we believe that students should understand how this process works and have some appreciation of its strengths and weaknesses.

Before we launch into our discussion of the specifics of research methods, we make a few preliminary comments about why an understanding of research methodology may be important to you. We hope these remarks will pique your interest and at minimum open your mind to the idea that learning about research methodology will be useful.

### WHY TAKE A RESEARCH METHODS COURSE?

Why are you taking this course? Reading this textbook? The most straightforward answer is probably, "Because it's required." Nationwide, students take research methods courses because they have to. Most majors contain one or two relatively difficult, required courses that students tend to look upon as academic hurdles and see as largely irrelevant to their education and career goals. Typically, students majoring in one of the behavioral sciences (psychology, sociology, criminal justice, etc.) are required to take two courses: Statistics and Research Methods. Most students do not look forward to either course.

As we see it, it is perfectly natural for psychology majors not to want to take Statistics and Research Methods courses. Students choose to major in psychology because they want to learn about people; however, Research Methods is not about people, and it is not really even psychology. It's about science. Similarly, Statistics is not psychology; it's the mathematics used by scientists.

### HOW IS UNDERSTANDING RESEARCH METHODOLOGY USEFUL?

Now consider some of the ways in which understanding research methodology can be useful to you.

#### Psychology Is a Science

The basic reason for learning about research methods is that these are the methods psychologists use to answer questions. Psychology is a science, which means that psychologists use the methods of science to gather and interpret information.

For example, suppose that a psychologist wanted to determine the effect of divorce on adolescent children. To answer the question, the psychologist would need to observe some adolescents in families that are experiencing divorce. The psychologist would need to decide exactly what characteristics to observe. Self-esteem, depression, academic performance in school, relationships with friends, eating habits, and sleeping patterns would be sensible choices. And, rather than relying on memory, the psychologist would need to record the observations so that the information could be recovered later. For other people to understand what had been observed and recorded, the psychologist would need to make sure that the observations were accurate and objective, avoiding subjective interpretations such as "To me, John seemed a bit depressed today." Nor would it be sufficient simply to examine adolescents who are experiencing divorce. Suppose, for example, that the psychologist found these individuals to be moderately depressed, with huge swings (highs and lows) in self-esteem, strange relationships with friends, and weird eating habits. Although these characteristics may be associated with divorce, it is also possible that they are simply "normal" for all adolescents. To avoid this problem, the psychologist would need to observe a comparison group of similar adolescents whose families were not experiencing divorce.

This scenario is a simplified overview of scientific research. Our point is that science provides a carefully developed system for answering questions so that the answers we get are as accurate and as complete as possible. Psychologists rely on the methods of science; to understand psychology and to fully appreciate what psychologists have discovered about people, you need a basic understanding of research methods.

## Conducting a Study

A course in research methods will be most useful if you actually conduct a research study at some time in the future. Some of your undergraduate courses, including independent study and honors thesis classes, may involve conducting a study. In addition, if you plan to continue your education in psychology beyond the undergraduate degree, you will certainly be expected to conduct research in graduate school. Incidentally, conducting your own research as an undergraduate enhances your marketability for admittance to a graduate program. Further, you may pursue a job that involves conducting studies, perhaps as a research assistant.

Admittedly, however, most students are not planning to conduct research studies in the immediate future and therefore do not see a research methods course as meeting their immediate needs. In addition, many students do not intend ever to conduct a study. Many psychology majors are interested in securing a position within the human services field after they complete their degrees. For this reason many students do not see a research methods course as relevant to their career aspirations. However, a course in research methods can still be useful. To keep up to date in your profession, you will need to read and understand the most recent research publications.

## Reading and Evaluating Other People's Studies

A grasp of research terminology and logic will allow you to read and understand research articles. Rather than reading a summary of someone else's research in a magazine, newspaper, or textbook, you can read the original article yourself and draw your own conclusions. A research methods course will help you read and critically evaluate journal articles detailing research studies. Many occupations use research findings; for example, if you were a clinical psychologist trying to decide which treatment is best for your client, you might review research articles that examine the effectiveness of different treatments. Similarly, if you were an elementary school teacher trying to decide which teaching method is best for your students, you might review research articles that examine the effectiveness of different teaching methods. Reading and evaluating these articles would help you to determine which treatments might work best with your client's set of symptoms and which teaching method might work best with your students. In addition, reading original sources of research is often required in other classes.

Understanding research methodology will also help you critically evaluate the research presented in journal articles. Many research articles jump from the results section (the section of the article that tells the reader what was found out in the study) to the discussion section (the section of the article where the author interprets the results and draws conclusions). You must be able to analyze and evaluate that jump. You will need to determine to what extent the evidence supports the conclusions. A research methods course will therefore help you to evaluate the research of others.

### Understanding Brief Descriptions of Studies

A research methods course will also help you understand abbreviated descriptions of studies. In most of your other psychology courses and psychology textbooks, you are given abbreviated descriptions of studies as evidence supporting some conclusion or theory. For example, you may be told that a between-subjects design using a placebo control group was conducted with type of treatment as the independent variable and number of cigarettes smoked as the dependent variable, and that the researchers found that the nicotine patch significantly reduced the number of cigarettes smoked by heavy smokers. As you can see in this example, when a textbook or professor describes someone else's study, you are not told everything about the study. Instead there is a style (a lingo or vocabulary) that psychologists use to describe research. That style is determined by the principles of research methodology.

Some principles you will learn about in this textbook are so well known and basic that any research study would follow them. Because all studies follow these principles, assuming that the reader knows they were followed shortens the description. Therefore, a research methods course will help you fill in the gaps in typical descriptions of studies. In addition, if you do not understand research methods, some features of experiments will seem strange, even nonsensical. For instance, in the above example, why was it necessary for the study to include a group of smokers who wore patches that did not contain nicotine (the placebo control group)? A research methods course will help you better understand and remember studies. You will then be better able to master the material in your other courses.

### Making Decisions in Our Daily Lives

You needn't be a researcher or a psychology major to find understanding the research process useful. To be an effective, participating member of our society in the twenty-first century, you must understand and appreciate the role and capabilities of science and experimentation so that you can evaluate and act on research results.

For example, today's paper contained an ad for a hypnosis-based weight-loss program. To demonstrate the effectiveness of the program, the ad describes three satisfied customers: Tania, who changed her eating habits and lost 72 pounds; Carol, who shed 95 pounds; and Tila, who appears in before-and-after pictures showing the effects of losing 35 pounds in four easy months. Is this science? Is this a convincing demonstration that the program works? The answer is, Probably not. If Tania, Carol, and Tila are actually representative of the program's clients, then their results are at least a step in the right direction. On the other hand, if the program directors searched through their client records to find examples of unusual success, then this is definitely not scientific research. Suppose, for example, that we looked through the client records to find individuals who became ill or had serious accidents after starting the program. (Only 2 months after beginning our weight-loss program, Mary fell off a ladder and broke her leg. After 6 short weeks of hypnosis training, Carla suffered acute appendicitis and was hospitalized for 5 days.) After reading three or four of these stories, would you be convinced that the weight-loss program is hazardous to people's health? We hope not.

Every day, you are inundated with research claims. Newspapers, magazines, television, and radio flood us with statements such as "Researchers have found . . . ," "Research shows that . . . ," for example, "Oral contraceptive use increases women's risk for breast cancer," "Echinacea use decreases cold symptoms," "Drinking a glass of wine a day decreases a person's risk of heart disease," "High-carbohydrate diets are effective for weight reduction."

What are we to do with this information? Take it to heart and change our behavior—stop using oral contraceptives and start consuming echinacea, a glass of wine, and lots of bread and pasta every day? Or do we ignore the claims we read about and hear, and hope for the best? We need to be educated consumers of research claims. An understanding of research methodology will enable you to find and evaluate the original research (if indeed there is any evidence for the claim) that supposedly supports the claim. A layperson who can think critically and logically can point out flaws in data collection and flaws in logic. A course in research methods will make you aware of the logical constraints that apply to the conducting of research and the interpretation of data, so that you can tease apart the truth from the data on your own and will not be dependent solely on a supposed expert to do it for you. A research methods course will help you make educated decisions about the research claims you encounter in everyday life.

### Being a Better Thinker

Finally, understanding research methodology—or, more generally, the scientific method—will also improve your thinking. As we discuss later, the scientific method is a method of inquiry, a method that can be used to obtain answers. It is a logical and objective method of critical thinking. This way of thinking is not specific to psychology but can be applied to all aspects of life. A research methods course will teach you to think like a scientist, which—we hope you will see—need not be restricted to the laboratory.

**Summary**

By discussing some of the ways a course in research methods can be of use to you, we have pointed out an alternative way to see the course—as worthwhile in itself, not as just a course you have to take. We hope you are more open to the possibility that this course can be useful, interesting, and perhaps even enjoyable.

Learning
Checks

Briefly summarize the different ways in which understanding research methodology can be useful.

Describe how you can use an understanding of research methodology when reading research claims in the newspaper.

## 1.2   METHODS OF INQUIRY

As we indicated at the beginning of this chapter, this textbook focuses on the use of the scientific method to answer questions. However, the methods used in scientific research are not the only methods available for answering questions, and they are not necessarily the best methods. In general, the different methods that people use to answer questions (or to acquire knowledge) are referred to as **methods of inquiry.** In this chapter we examine several common methods of inquiry. Eventually we describe the scientific method, the general approach used by the scientific community to obtain answers.

Terms printed in bold-face are defined in the glossary. Key words are also defined in the text.

Definition

**Methods of inquiry** are ways in which a person can acquire knowledge or find answers to questions.

The rest of this chapter examines several established methods of inquiry: the method of authority, the method of intuition, the method of tenacity, the rational method, and the method of empiricism. We conclude with a more detailed discussion of the scientific method. As you will see, the scientific method combines elements from each of the other methods to produce a general question-answering technique that avoids some of the limitations or pitfalls of other methods. Although the scientific method tends to be more complicated and more time consuming than the other methods, the goal is to obtain better-quality answers or at least a higher level of confidence in the answers. Finally, we warn that the scientific method outlines a general strategy for answering questions; the specific details of applying the scientific method to particular problems forms the content of the remainder of the book.

### THE METHOD OF AUTHORITY

In the **method of authority,** a person finds answers by seeking out an authority on the subject. This can mean consulting an expert directly or going to a library to read the works of an expert. In either case, you are relying on the assumed expertise of another person. Whenever you consult books, people, television, or the newspaper, you use the method of authority. Some examples of experts are physicians, scientists, psychologists, professors, stockbrokers, and lawyers.

Definition

In the **method of authority** a person relies on information or answers from an expert in the subject area.

For many questions the method of authority is an excellent starting point; often it is the quickest and easiest way to obtain answers. Much of your formal education is based on the notion that answers can be obtained from experts (teachers and textbooks). However, the method of authority has some pitfalls. It does not always provide accurate information.

One limitation of this method is that we assume, by virtue of the person's status as an authority, that expertise can be generalized to include the question we are asking. For example, advertisers often use the endorsements of well-known personalities to sell their products. When a famous athlete appears on television telling you which soup is more nutritious, should you assume that being an outstanding football player makes him an expert on nutrition? The advertisers would like you to accept his recommendation on authority. Similarly, when Linus Pauling, a Nobel Prize-winning chemist, claimed that vitamin C could cure the common cold, many people accepted his word on authority. His claim is still widely believed, even though numerous scientific studies have failed to find such an effect.

Authorities can be biased. We have all seen examples of conflicting testimony by "expert witnesses" in criminal trials. Sources are often biased in favor of a particular point of view or orientation. For example, parents who are having a problem with their child's temper tantrums could seek help from an expert. If they were to ask a psychodynamic psychologist why their child was displaying this behavior, they would probably hear an explanation that involved a failure to meet the child's oral needs. In contrast, if the parents were to consult a behavioral psychologist, the child's tantrums might be explained as the result of the parents' reinforcing of the behavior by giving in to the demands of the child.

Another limitation of the method of authority is that the answers obtained from an expert may represent subjective, personal opinion rather than true expert knowledge. For example, one "expert" reviewer gives a movie a rating of "thumbs up," while another expert gives the same movie "thumbs down." Box 1.1 discusses a historical example of conflict between "expert" authorities.

Another pitfall of the method of authority is that an expert's statement is often accepted without question. This acceptance can mean that people do not check the accuracy of their sources or even consider looking for a second opinion. As a result, false information is sometimes taken as truth. In some situations, the authority is accepted without question because the information appears to make sense, so there is no obvious reason to question it. Other times, we are simply too lazy to double-check or too gullible to realize that we may be hearing lies. (We would all like to believe it when the sales clerk says, "That jacket really looks good on you.")

People sometimes accept the word of an authority simply because they have complete trust in the authority figure. In this situation, the method of authority

BOX 1.1          Conflict Between Science and Authority

The method of authority has a long and at times colorful history in defining truth and disseminating knowledge. History is filled with instances of clashes between official authorities and scientists. Sometimes theological authorities were involved, and scientific pursuit was viewed as a threat to religious doctrine. Scientists were branded as heretics. For example, religious doctrine once held that Earth was at the center of the universe—that all heavenly bodies revolved around Earth. On the other hand, the seventeenth-century astronomer Galileo supported the view of a predecessor, Copernicus, that Earth revolved around the Sun (the heliocentric view). When Galileo discovered, with the aid of a new telescope, that Jupiter has its own moons that revolve around it, he knew that the religious doctrine was faulty. That is, not all objects revolve around Earth and therefore Earth was not the center of the universe. Needless to say, he continued to support the view of Copernicus. Consequently, in 1616 Galileo was condemned by the authorities of the Catholic Church and threatened with imprisonment if he ever espoused the heliocentric view again. Galileo's viewpoint was so opposed to the religious dogma of the time that many of his peers would not even look through his telescope. Lest you worry about Galileo's reputation, the Pope vindicated Galileo in an official statement—in 1992, more than 300 years after his condemnation. Although this is not a commentary on religious doctrine, it is an example of how differing values and differing views of truth and knowledge can clash. Resistance to scientific inquiry often results when science ventures into areas traditionally explained by other methods (authority, intuition, logic, and so on). It is also important to note that different methods of acquiring knowledge can lead to vastly different conclusions about the nature of the universe. Nor is conflict between science and authority limited to events that occurred 300 years ago. For example, today there is considerable debate in science and society about the possible application of cloning.

is often called the **method of faith** because people accept on faith any information that is given. For instance, young children tend to have absolute faith in the answers they get from their parents. Another example of faith exists within religions. A religion typically has a sacred text and/or individuals (pastors, imams, priests, rabbis) who present answers that are considered to be the final word. The problem with the method of faith is that it allows no mechanism to test the accuracy of the information. The method of faith involves accepting another's view of the truth without verification.

Definition

The **method of faith** is a variant of the method of authority in which people have unquestioning trust in the authority figure and therefore accept information from the authority without doubt or challenge.

As a final pitfall of the method of authority, realize that not all "experts" *are* experts. There are a lot of supposed "experts" out there. Turn on the TV to any daytime talk show. During the first 45 minutes of the show, in front of millions of viewers, people haggle with one another—women complain about their boyfriends, estranged parents and teenagers are reunited, two women fight over the same boyfriend. Then in the final 15 minutes, the "expert" comes out to discuss the situation and everyone's feelings. These "experts" are often people who lack the credentials to make the claims they are making. Just being called an expert does not make someone an expert.

Describe how to use the method of authority to find answers.

Learning
Check

## THE METHOD OF INTUITION

The method of intuition is an approach to knowledge acquisition that is not based on inference or reason. In the **method of intuition,** information is accepted as true because it "feels right." With intuition, a person relies on hunches and "instinct" to answer questions. Whenever we say we know something because we have a "gut feeling" about it, we are using the method of intuition. For many questions, this method is the quickest way to obtain answers. When we have no information at all and cannot refer to supporting data or use rational justification, we often resort to intuition. The predictions and descriptions given by psychics are thought to be intuitive.

The problem with the method of intuition is that it has no mechanism for separating accurate from inaccurate knowledge.

In the **method of intuition,** information is accepted on the basis of a hunch or "gut feeling."

Definition

Describe how one uses the method of intuition to find answers.

Learning
Check

## THE METHOD OF TENACITY

The **method of tenacity** is based on habit or superstition. Habit leads us to continue believing something we have always believed. Therefore, tenacity describes a willingness to accept an idea as valid because that idea has been accepted for a long time. For example, you've probably heard the clichés, "You can't teach an old dog new tricks" and "Opposites attract." These statements have been presented over and over again, and they have been accepted as true. In general, the more frequently we are exposed to statements, the more we tend to believe them. Advertisers successfully use the method of tenacity, repeating their messages over and over, hoping consumers will accept them as true. An ad featuring milk-mustachioed celebrities is currently appearing in magazines everywhere—in the sponsor's hope that we get the message and "get milk."

In the **method of tenacity,** information is accepted as true because it has always been believed or because superstition supports it.

Definition

The method of tenacity also involves the persistence of superstitions, which represent beliefs reacted to as fact. For example, everyone "knows" that breaking a mirror will result in 7 years' bad luck and that you should never walk under a ladder or let a black cat cross your path. Many sports figures will only play wearing their lucky socks or jersey, and many students will not take an exam without their lucky pencil or hat.

One problem with the method of tenacity is that the information acquired may not be accurate. With regard to the statement about old dogs not being able to learn new tricks, the elderly can and do learn. Further, with regard to the statement that opposites attract, research shows that people are attracted to people who are like them. In addition, milk is not "the one" for most people; many adults are lactose intolerant. Another pitfall of the method of tenacity is that there is no method for correcting erroneous ideas. Even in the face of evidence to the contrary, a belief that is widely accepted solely on the basis of tenacity is very difficult to change.

Learning Checks

Describe how to find answers using the method of tenacity.

Think of another cliché, and describe how it can be used to explain a person's behavior.

## THE RATIONAL METHOD

The **rational method** involves seeking answers by logical reasoning. We begin with a set of known facts or assumptions and use logic to reach a conclusion. A simple example of reasoning that might be used by a clinical psychologist is as follows:

> All 3-year-old children are afraid of the dark.
>
> Amy is a 3-year-old girl.
>
> Therefore, Amy is afraid of the dark.

In this **argument,** the first two sentences are **premise statements.** That is, they are facts or assumptions that are known (or assumed) to be true. The final sentence is a logical conclusion based on the premises. If the premise statements are in fact true and the logic is sound, then the conclusion is guaranteed to be correct.

Definitions

The **rational method** seeks answers by the use of logical reasoning.

**Premise statements** are sentences used in logical reasoning that describe facts or assumptions.

An **argument** is a set of premise statements that are logically combined to yield a conclusion.

The preceding example (Amy and the dark) demonstrates the rational method for answering questions, and it also demonstrates some of the limitations of the rational method. Although the logic may be sound, it is possible that the real-world child Amy is *not* afraid of the dark. In this case, our logical conclusion is not true even though the logic is perfectly correct. One obvious problem comes from the absolute expressed in the first premise statement, "All 3-year-old children are afraid of the dark." Although this statement may be accurate for *most* 3-year-olds, there is good reason to doubt that it is absolutely true for *all* 3-year-olds. Unless the premise statement is absolutely true, we cannot draw any conclusion about Amy. Also, it is possible that we have been misinformed about Amy's age. If she is actually 4 years old, then we cannot draw any logical conclusion about her fear of the dark. In general, the truth of any logical conclusion is founded on the truth of the premise statements. If any basic assumption or fact is incorrect, then we cannot have any confidence in the logical conclusion.

A common application of the rational method occurs when people try to think through a problem before they try out different solutions. Suppose, for example, that you have an exam scheduled, but when you are ready to leave for campus you discover that your car won't start. One response to this situation is to consider your options logically:

a. You could call the Auto Club, but by the time they arrive and fix the car you probably will have missed the exam.
b. You could take the bus, but you don't have the schedule, so you are not sure if the bus can get you to campus on time.
c. You could ask your neighbor to loan you her car for a few hours.

Notice that, instead of actually doing something, you are considering possibilities and consequences to find a logical solution to the problem.

The following example is one of our favorite demonstrations of the rational method. As you read through the example, keep in mind that the entire process of trying to answer the question is based on logical reasoning.

Imagine that you are standing in the doorway of one building on campus and need to get to another building 100 yards away. Unfortunately, it is pouring down rain, and you have no raincoat or umbrella. Before you step out into the storm, let's take a minute to try to figure out the best strategy to help you keep as dry as possible. Specifically, should you (a) run as fast as you can from one building to the next, or (b) walk at a slow and steady pace?

Logically, as you move through the rain there are two sources of getting wet:

1. the rain that is falling down on your head and shoulders
2. the rain in the air in front of you that you walk into as you move forward

Logically, the first source of wetness depends entirely on how long you are out in the rain. The more time you spend exposed, the more water will fall on you. On the other hand, the second source is independent of the length of time you are exposed. If you imagine the rain as suspended in the air, it is easy to see that your body will sweep a path or tunnel through the rain as you move from one shelter to another. The amount of rain contained in this tunnel determines how wet you will get as you move forward. However, this amount will be the same whether you zip along at 100 miles per hour or walk slowly at 1 mile per hour.

We can now construct a logical argument based on these facts to answer the original question:

The faster you move, the less rain will fall on you (source 1).

The amount of rain you walk into (source 2) will be the same whether you run or walk.

The total amount of rain that hits you is the sum of the two sources.

Therefore, your best bet for keeping as dry as possible is to run as fast as you can.

In addition to demonstrating an application, the preceding example illustrates another limitation of the rational method. In the example, we assumed that there were only two sources of wetness. In fact, when you run through the rain, it is possible to get wet from splashing in puddles or slipping on a wet surface and falling. Because these possibilities were not considered, our conclusion may not be correct. In general, a logical conclusion is only valid for the specific situation described by the premise statements. If the premise statements are incomplete or do not totally represent the real-world situation, then the conclusion may not be accurate.

Finally, people are not particularly good at logical reasoning. Consider the following argument:

All psychologists are human.

Some humans wear glasses.

Therefore, some psychologists wear glasses.

Many people would view this as a sound, rational argument. However, the conclusion is not logically justified by the premise statements. In case you are not convinced that the argument is invalid, consider the following argument, which has exactly the same structure but replaces psychologists and glasses with apples and oranges:

All apples are fruits.

Some fruits are oranges.

Therefore, some apples are oranges.

This time, it should be clear that the argument does not logically support the conclusion. The simple fact that most people have difficulty evaluating a logical argument means they can easily make mistakes using the rational method. Unless the logic is sound, the conclusion may not be correct.

 Learning Check

Describe how to find answers using the rational method.

## THE METHOD OF EMPIRICISM

The **method of empiricism** attempts to answer questions by direct observation or personal experience. This method is a product of the empirical viewpoint in philosophy, which holds that all knowledge is acquired through our senses. Note that when we make observations we use our senses: seeing, hearing, tasting, and so on.

---

The **method of empiricism** uses observation or direct sensory experience to obtain knowledge.

Definition

---

Most of you know, for example, that children tend to be shorter than adults, that it is typically warmer in the summer than in the winter, and that a pound of lobster costs more than a pound of catfish. You know these facts from personal experience—from observations you have made.

Many facts or answers are available simply by observation of the world around you—that is, you can use the method of empiricism. For example, you can check the oil level in your car by simply looking at the dipstick. You could find out the academic major of each student in your class just by asking or by handing out a questionnaire. In many instances, the method of empiricism provides an easy, direct way to answer questions. However, this method of inquiry also has some limitations.

It is tempting to place great confidence in our own observations. Everyday expressions, such as "I will believe it when I see it with my own eyes," reveal the faith we place in our own experience. However, we cannot necessarily believe everything we see—or hear and feel, for that matter. Actually, it is fairly common for people to misperceive or misinterpret the world around them. Figure 1.1 illustrates this point with the horizontal-vertical illusion. Most people perceive the vertical line to be longer than the horizontal line. Actually, they are exactly the same length. (You may want to measure them to convince yourself.) This illustration is a classic example of how direct sensory experience can deceive us.

It also is possible to make accurate observations but then misinterpret what you see. For years people watched the day-to-day cycle of the Sun rising in the east and setting in the west. These observations led to the obvious conclusion that the Sun must travel in a huge circle around Earth. Even today, people still speak of the "sun rising" instead of saying "Earth is turning toward the Sun."

Although direct experience seems to be a simple way to obtain answers, your perceptions can be drastically altered by prior knowledge, expectations, feelings, or beliefs. As a result, two observers can witness exactly the same event and yet "see" two completely different things. For most students, the following example provides a convincing demonstration that sensory experience can be changed by knowledge or beliefs:

> Suppose that you are presented with two plates of snack food and asked to sample each and then state your preference. One plate contains regular potato chips, and the second contains crispy, brown noodles that taste delicious. Based simply on your experience (taste), you have a strong preference for the noodles. Now suppose that you are told that the "noodles" are actually fried worms. Would you still prefer them to the chips? The problem here is that your *objective experience* (the method of empiricism) is in conflict with your *subjective belief* (people do not eat worms).

Finally, the empirical method is usually time consuming and sometimes dangerous. When faced with a problem, for example, you could use the empirical

Figure 1.1   The Horizontal-Vertical Illusion
To most people, the vertical line appears to be longer,
even though both lines are exactly the same length.

method to try several possible solutions, or you could use the rational method and simply think about each possibility and how it might work. Often it is faster and easier to think through a problem than to jump in with a trial-and-error approach. Also, it may be safer to use the rational method or the method of authority rather than experience something for yourself. For example, if I wanted to determine whether the mushrooms in my back yard are safe or poisonous, I would rather ask an expert than try the empirical method.

Learning Check

Describe how to find answers using the method of empiricism.

## 1.3   THE SCIENTIFIC METHOD

The **scientific method** is an approach to acquiring knowledge that contains many elements of the methods previously discussed. By combining several different methods of inquiry, we hope to avoid the pitfalls of any individual method used by itself. The scientific method can be described as a never-ending spiral or a circle of steps (see Figure 1.2). Following, we describe the series of steps that make up one cycle of the scientific method.

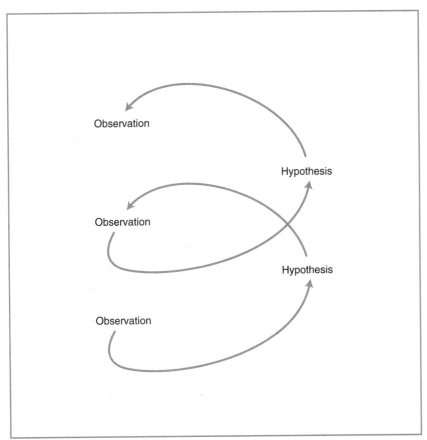

Figure 1.2    The Circle of Scientific Inquiry
The scientific method can be viewed as a circle or a spiral of steps.
Initial observations lead to a hypothesis, which leads to more
observations and then to a new hypothesis. This never-ending process
of using empirical tests (observations) to build and refine our current
knowledge (hypothesis) is the basis of the scientific method.

## THE STEPS OF THE SCIENTIFIC METHOD

### Step 1: Observe Behavior or Other Phenomena

The scientific method often begins with casual or informal observations. Notice that it is not necessary to start with a well-planned, systematic investigation. Instead, simply observe the world around you until some behavior or event catches your attention. The initial observations may be your own personal experience (method of empiricism) and may involve watching the behavior of other people or monitoring your own behavior. For example, you may notice a group of strangers carefully avoiding eye contact as they share an elevator. Or, you may sit in the back row of class one day and notice that you are surrounded by students who don't seem to be paying attention. Based on your observations, you begin to wonder why people don't look at each other in elevators or whether it is true that the better students tend to sit in the front of the class.

Perhaps your attention is caught by someone else's observations. For example, you may read a report of someone's research findings (the method of authority), or you may hear others talking about things they have seen or noticed. In any event, the observations catch your attention and begin to raise questions in your mind.

At this stage in the process, people commonly tend to generalize beyond the actual observations. The process of generalization is an almost automatic human response known as **induction** or **inductive reasoning.** In simple terms, inductive reasoning involves reaching a general conclusion based on a few specific examples. For example, suppose that you taste a green apple and discover that it is sour. A second green apple is also sour, and so is the third. Very soon you reach the general conclusion that all green apples are sour. Notice that inductive reasoning reaches far beyond the actual observations. In this example, you tasted only three apples, and yet you reached a conclusion about the millions of other green apples that exist in the world.

Definition

**Induction** or **inductive reasoning** involves using a relatively small set of specific observations as the basis for forming a general statement about a larger set of possible observations. For example, every rosebush that I have seen has thorns, and from these observations I make the general conclusion that all rosebushes have thorns.

The following scenario combines observation and induction to demonstrate how the first stage of the scientific method can actually work. Suppose that it is the third straight day of dark, cold, and dreary weather in late October, and you notice that you are feeling a bit depressed. It's not a serious clinical depression; you simply have realized that the carefree days of summer are definitely over and you are now facing several long months of cold and overcast winter. As you mope through the day, you begin to wonder if others are sharing your feelings, and so you start watching your friends and colleagues. Very soon you have reached the general conclusion that people seem to become sadder and more depressed during the winter than in the summer. If you are at all curious about this observed phenomenon, you are ready for the next step in the scientific method.

### Step 2: Form a Tentative Answer or Explanation (Hypothesis)

The next step in the process is to form a hypothesis or tentative explanation for your observations. For example, you might hypothesize that people become depressed in the winter because the weather is literally dark and depressing. The hypothesis may come from common sense, or it may be developed from other scientists' theories (the method of authority), or the hypothesis may appear to be the only logical explanation (the rational method). Whatever method generates the hypothesis, the important point is that the hypothesis is not considered to be the final answer. Instead, a hypothesis is a tentative answer that is intended to be tested and critically evaluated.

Usually a scientist attempts to generate several different hypotheses (at least two). The goal is to identify every possible (but sensible) answer to the original question. Eventually, the scientific method attempts to provide support for at least one of the hypotheses and demonstrate that the others are probably wrong.

### Step 3: Use the Hypothesis to Generate a Testable Prediction

Usually this step involves simply taking the stated hypothesis and applying it to an observable, real-world situation. For example, if your hypothesis states that winter depression is the result of a darker environment, then the hypothesis would predict that decreased lighting should impair peoples' moods. A hypothesis that left-handed people are more artistic than right-handed people predicts that you would find more left-handers in a group of successful artists than in a similar group of non-artists. Notice that we are using logic to make the prediction. This time the logical process is known as **deduction** or **deductive reasoning.** We begin with a general (universal) statement and then make specific deductions. In particular, we use our hypothesis as a universal premise statement and then determine the conclusions that must logically follow if the hypothesis is true.

**Deduction** or **deductive reasoning** uses a general statement as the basis for reaching a conclusion about specific examples. For example, if I know that all rosebushes have thorns, then I can conclude that the five rosebushes in my backyard must have thorns.

Induction and deduction are complementary processes. Induction uses specific examples to generate general conclusions, and deduction uses general conclusions to generate specific predictions. This relationship is depicted in Figure 1.3.

Also notice that the predictions generated from a hypothesis must be testable—that is, it must be possible to demonstrate that the prediction is either correct or incorrect by direct observation. Either the observations will provide support for the hypothesis, or the observations will refute the hypothesis. For a prediction to be truly testable, both outcomes must be possible.

### Step 4: Evaluate the Prediction by Making Systematic, Planned Observations

After specific, testable predictions have been made, the next step is to evaluate the predictions using direct observation (the empirical method). This is the actual "research" or "data collection" phase of the scientific method. The goal is to provide a fair and unbiased test of the hypothesis by observing whether or not its predictions are accurate. The researcher must be careful to observe and record exactly what happens, free of any subjective interpretation or personal expectations.

### Step 5: Use the Observations to Support, Refute, or Refine the Original Hypothesis

The final step of the scientific method is to compare the actual observations with the predictions that were made from the hypothesis. To what extent do the observations agree with the predictions? Some agreement indicates support for the original hypothesis and suggests that you consider making new predictions and testing them. Lack of agreement indicates that the original hypothesis was

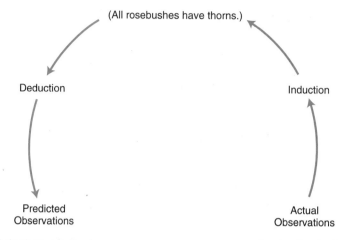

Hypothesis or Premise: Typically a General Statement
about the Relationship between Two Variables

(All rosebushes have thorns.)

Deduction

Induction

Predicted
Observations

Actual
Observations

If I check my neighbor's
rosebushes, I should find
that they all have thorns.

I notice that the five
rosebushes in my
backyard all have thorns.

Figure 1.3   An Example of Induction and Deduction
The process of induction uses a limited set of observations to generate
a general hypothesis. The process of deduction uses a general hypothesis
or premise to generate predictions about specific observations.

wrong or that the hypothesis was used incorrectly, producing faulty predictions. In this case, you may want to revise the hypothesis or reconsider how it was used to generate predictions. In either case, notice that you have circled back to Step 2; that is, you are forming a new hypothesis and preparing to make new predictions. The scientific method continues the same series of steps over and over again: Observations lead to a hypothesis, which leads to more observations, which lead to another hypothesis, and so on.

Definition

The **scientific method** is an approach to acquiring knowledge that uses observations to develop a hypothesis and then empirically tests the hypothesis by making additional, systematic observations. Typically, the new observations lead to a new hypothesis, and the cycle continues.

Learning
Check

Describe the five steps of the scientific method.

## OTHER ELEMENTS OF THE SCIENTIFIC METHOD

In addition to the basic process that makes up the scientific method, a set of overriding principles governs scientific investigation. The three important principles of the scientific method are: It is empirical, it is public, and it is objective.

## Science Is Empirical

As you know, when we say science is empirical, we mean that answers are obtained by making observations. Although preliminary answers or hypotheses may be obtained by other means, science requires empirical verification. An answer may be "obvious" by common sense, and it may be perfectly logical, and experts in the field may support it, but it is not scientifically accepted until it has been empirically demonstrated.

However, unlike the method of empiricism we previously examined, the scientific method involves *structured* or *systematic* observation. The structure of the observations is determined by the procedures and techniques that are used in the research study. More specifically, the purpose of the observations is to provide an empirical test of a hypothesis. Therefore, the observations are structured so that the results either will provide clear support for the hypothesis or will clearly refute the hypothesis. Consider the following question:

Do large doses of vitamin C prevent the common cold?

To answer this question, it would not be sufficient simply to ask people if they take vitamin C routinely and how many colds they get in a typical season. These observations are not structured, and, no matter what answers are obtained, the results will not provide an answer to the question. In particular, we have made no attempt to determine the dosage levels of the vitamin C that individuals have taken. No attempt was made to verify that the illnesses reported were in fact the common cold and not some type of influenza, pneumonia, or other illness. No attempt was made to take into account the age, general health, or lifestyle of the people questioned (maybe people who take vitamin C tend to lead generally healthy lives). We have made no attempt to reduce the possible biasing effect of people's beliefs about vitamins and colds on the answers they gave us. We have made no attempt to compare people who are receiving a specified daily dose of the vitamin with those getting a phony pill (a placebo). We could elaborate further, but you get the general idea.

In the scientific method, the observations are systematic in that they are performed under a specified set of conditions so that we can accurately answer the question we are addressing. That is, the observations—and indeed the entire study—are structured to test a hypothesis about the way the world works. If you want to know if vitamin C can prevent colds, there is a way to structure your observations to get the answer. Much of this book deals with this aspect of research and how to structure studies to rule out competing and alternative explanations.

## Science Is Public

The scientific method is *public*. By this, we mean that the scientific method makes observations available for evaluation by others, especially other scientists. In particular, other individuals should be able to repeat the same step-by-step process that led to the observations so that they can replicate the observations for themselves. **Replication,** or repetition of observation, allows verification of the findings. Note that only public observations can be repeated, and thus only public observations are verifiable.

**Replication** is repetition of a research study, using the same basic procedures used in the original. The intent of replication is to test the validity of the original study. Either the replication will support the original study by duplicating the original results, or it will cast doubt on the original study by demonstrating that the original result is not easily repeated.

The scientific community makes observations public by publishing reports in scientific journals. This activity is important because events that are private cannot be replicated or evaluated by others. Research reports that appear in most journals have been evaluated by the researcher's peers (other scientists in the same field) for the rigor and appropriateness of methodology and the absence of flaws in the study. The report must meet a variety of standards for it to be published. When you read a journal article, one thing you will note is the level of detail used in describing the methodology of the study. Typically, the report has a separate "Method" section that describes in great detail what type of people or animals were studied (the participants or subjects of the study), the instruments and apparatus used to conduct the study, the procedures used in applying treatments and making measurements, and so on. Enough detail should be provided so that anyone can replicate the same study exactly to verify the findings. The notions of replication and verification are important. They provide the "checks and balances" for research.

As we shall see, there is a multitude of ways, by error or chance, in which a study can result in an erroneous conclusion. Researchers sometimes commit fraud and deliberately falsify or misrepresent the outcome of research studies. As scientists, it is important that we scrutinize and evaluate research reports carefully and maintain some skepticism about the results until more studies confirm the findings. By replicating studies and subjecting them to peer review, we have the important checks and balances against errors.

### Science Is Objective

The scientific method is *objective*. That is, the observations are structured so that the researcher's biases and beliefs do not influence the outcome of the study. Science has been called "a dispassionate search for knowledge," meaning that the researcher does not let personal feelings contaminate the observations. What kind of biases and beliefs are likely to be involved? Often, bias comes from belief in a particular theory. A researcher may be trying to find evidence to support his or her own theory. Because the researcher typically is testing a theory, he or she may have an expectation about the outcome of the study. In some cases, expectations can subtly influence the findings. Influence of the experimenter's beliefs or expectations on the results or observations is called **experimenter bias.**

**Experimenter bias** has occurred when the findings of a study have been influenced by the experimenter's expectations or personal beliefs.

In a classic example of experimenter bias, Rosenthal and Fode (1963) had student volunteers act as the experimenters in a learning study. The students were given rats to train in a maze. Half of the students were led to believe that their rats were specially bred to be "maze bright." The remainder were told that their rats were bred to be "maze dull." In reality, both groups of students received the same type of ordinary laboratory rat, neither bright nor dull. Nevertheless, the findings showed differences in the rats' performance between the two groups of experimenters. The "bright" rats were better at learning the maze. The student expectations influenced the outcome of the study. How did their expectations have this effect? Apparently there were differences in how the students in each group handled their rats, and the handling in turn altered the rats' behavior.

One way to reduce the likelihood of experimenter bias is to keep the people who are making the observations uninformed about the details of the study. In this case, we sometimes say the researcher is "blind" to the details of the study. We discuss this type of procedure in detail later.

Describe the overriding principles of the scientific method, and explain why each of these principles is important.

Learning Check

## 1.4   THE RESEARCH PROCESS

The process of planning and conducting a research study involves using the scientific method to address a specific question. During this process, the researcher moves from a general idea to actual data collection and interpretation of the results. Along the way, the researcher is faced with a series of decisions about how to proceed. In this section we outline the basic steps or decision points in the research process. The complete set of steps is also shown in Figure 1.4. Reading this section should give you a better understanding of the scientific method and how it is used, as well as an overview of the topics covered in the rest of the book. As a final note, remember that, although research requires a decision about what to do at each stage in the process, there are no absolutely right or wrong decisions. Each choice you make along the way has disadvantages as well as advantages. Much of the material in the remainder of the book focuses on the kinds of decisions that need to be made during the research process and examines the strengths and weaknesses of various choices.

### STEP 1: FIND A RESEARCH IDEA

The first step in the research process is to find an idea for a research study. This task, discussed in detail in Chapter 2, typically involves two parts: selecting a general topic area (such as human development, perception, social interaction, etc.) and reviewing the literature in that area to find a new idea for research. You may decide, for example, that you are interested in elementary education and want to examine factors that contribute to academic success or self-esteem. Ideas for research questions can come from a variety of sources, including everyday experience, books, journal articles, or class work. It is important that a researcher be honestly interested in the chosen topic. The research process can be a long-term, demanding enterprise. Without intrinsic interest to sustain motivation, it

**1. Find a Research Idea**
Identify a general topic that you would like to explore,
and review the background literature to find
a new idea for a research study.

**10. Refine or Reformulate Your Research Idea**
Use the results to modify, refine, or expand your
original research idea or to generate new ideas.

**2. Convert the Idea into a Hypothesis**
Use your idea to generate a specific, testable hypothesis.

**9. Report the Results**
Use the established guidelines for format and style
to prepare an accurate and honest report that also protects
the anonymity and confidentiality of the participants.

**3. Define and Measure Variables**
Identify the specific procedures that will be used
to define and measure all variables. Plan to evaluate
the validity and reliability of your measurement procedure.

**8. Evaluate the Data**
Use the appropriate descriptive and inferential
statistics to summarize and interpret the results.

**4. Identify Participants or Subjects**
Decide how many participants or subjects
you will need and what characteristics they should have.
Also plan for their ethical treatment.

**7. Conduct the Study**
Collect the data.

**5. Select a Research Strategy**
Consider the relative importance of internal and
external validity, and decide among an experimental
(cause-effect), descriptive, correlational, or
quasi-experimental strategy.

**6. Select a Research Design**
Decide among between-subjects, within-subjects, factorial,
or single-subject designs.

Figure 1.4  The Steps in the Research Process

is very easy for a researcher to get tired or bored and give up before the research is completed.

Bear in mind that your general idea is simply a starting point that eventually will evolve into a very specific research question. Your final question or research hypothesis will develop as you read through the research literature and discover what other researchers have already learned. Your original idea will guide you through the literature and help you decide which research studies are important to you and which are not relevant to your interests. Eventually, you will become familiar with the current state of knowledge and can determine what questions are still unanswered. At this stage you will be ready to identify your own research question. In Chapter 2 we discuss the task of searching through the research literature to find a research idea.

## STEP 2: CONVERT YOUR RESEARCH IDEA INTO A SPECIFIC RESEARCH HYPOTHESIS

Before a research idea can be evaluated, it must be transformed into a research hypothesis. A **hypothesis** is a statement about the relationship between two (or more) variables.

---

A **hypothesis** is a statement describing the relationship between two variables.    Definition

---

Although it is possible to form a hypothesis from logic or from pure speculation, a good hypothesis usually is founded on established theories or developed from the results of previous research. Specifically, a good hypothesis should be the logical conclusion of a logical argument. Consider the following example:

*Premise 1:* Academic success is highly valued and respected in society (at least by parents and teachers).

*Premise 2:* Being valued and respected by others contributes to high self-esteem.

*Conclusion or hypothesis:* Higher levels of academic success are related to higher levels of self-esteem.

In this argument, we will assume that the two premise statements are "facts" or research results that have been demonstrated and reported in the scientific literature. Typically, these facts would be obtained from extensive library research. Library research will acquaint you with the relevant knowledge that already exists—what other researchers have done and found. By knowing the basic facts, theories, predictions, and methods that make up the knowledge base for a specific topic area, you gain a clearer picture of the variables being studied and their relationships. The logical argument provides a rationale or justification for your research hypothesis and establishes a connection between your research and the research results obtained by others.

In addition to being logical, a good hypothesis must be **testable;** that is, it must be possible to make observations that will either support the hypothesis or refute it. In particular, the hypothesis must involve real situations, real events, and real individuals. You cannot test a hypothesis that refers to imaginary events or make-believe situations. For example, you might speculate about what might happen if the heat from the sun were gradually to increase over the next 25 years, or you could debate what might have happened if JFK had not been assassinated. However, neither of these two propositions leads to a testable hypothesis. The propositions cannot be observed and therefore are inappropriate as scientific hypotheses.

A second characteristic of a testable hypothesis is that it must make a positive statement about the existence of something, usually the existence of a relationship, a difference, or a treatment effect. The following are examples:

Hypothesis 1.  There is a relationship between intelligence and creativity.

Hypothesis 2.  There is a difference between the verbal skills of 3-year-old girls and the verbal skills of 3-year-old boys.

Hypothesis 3.  The new therapy technique has an effect on depression.

On the other hand, a hypothesis that denies existence is untestable. The following are examples of untestable hypotheses:

Hypothesis 4.  There is no relationship between age and memory ability.

Hypothesis 5.  There is no difference between the problem-solving strategies used by females and those used by males.

Hypothesis 6.  The new training procedure has no effect on students' self-esteem.

The reason that a testable hypothesis must make a positive statement affirming existence is based on the scientific process that is used to test the hypothesis. Specifically, the basic nature of science is to assume that something does *not* exist until there is enough evidence to demonstrate that it does. Suppose, for example, that we want to test the hypothesis that there is a relationship between creativity and intelligence. In this case, the goal of our study is to gather enough evidence (data) to convincingly demonstrate that a relationship does exist. You may recognize this process as the same system used in jury trials: The jury assumes that a defendant is innocent until enough evidence is presented to prove guilt. The key problem with this system occurs when convincing evidence has not been obtained; if the prosecution fails to produce enough evidence, the verdict is "not guilty." Notice that the defendant has *not* been proved innocent; rather, there simply is not enough evidence to say he or she is guilty. Similarly, failure in a research study means that we simply did not find enough evidence. Thus, the research process is structured to test for the existence of treatment effects, relationships, and differences. It is *not* structured to test a hypothesis that *denies* existence. For example, suppose that we begin with the hypothesis that there is no relationship between creativity and IQ. (Note that this hypothesis *denies* existence and therefore is untestable.) If we conduct a study that fails to find a relationship, have we proved our hypothesis? It should be clear that we haven't proved anything; we have simply failed to find any evidence. We cannot conclude that something does not exist simply because we failed to find it.

Finally, a good research hypothesis must also be **refutable;** that is, it must be possible that the results will *not* show the predicted relationship. A refutable hypothesis is a critical component of the research process. Remember, the scientific method requires an objective and public demonstration. A nonrefutable hypothesis, one that cannot be demonstrated to be true or false, is inappropriate for the scientific method. For example, people occasionally claim to have miraculous or magical powers. However, they often add the stipulation that these powers can be seen only in the presence of "true believers." When the miracles fail to occur under the watchful eyes of scientists, the people simply state that the scientists are nonbelievers. Thus, it is impossible to prove that the claims are false. The result is a claim (or hypothesis) that cannot be refuted.

A **testable** hypothesis is one in which all of the variables, events, and individuals are real and can be defined and observed.

A **refutable hypothesis** is a hypothesis that can be demonstrated to be false. That is, the hypothesis allows the possibility that the outcome will differ from the prediction.

Consider the following hypotheses, which are not testable or refutable:

Hypothesis:  The more sins a person commits, the less likely he or she is to get into heaven.

Hypothesis:  Abortion is morally wrong.

Hypothesis:  If people could fly, there would be substantially fewer cases of depression.

Hypothesis:  The human mind emits thought waves that influence other people but cannot be measured or recorded in any way.

Although you may find these hypotheses interesting, they cannot be tested or shown to be false and therefore are unsuitable for scientific research. In general, hypotheses that deal with moral or religious issues, value judgments, or hypothetical situations are untestable or nonrefutable. However, this does not mean that religion, morals, or human values are off limits for scientific research. You could, for example, compare the personality characteristics or family backgrounds of religious and nonreligious people, or you could look for behavioral differences between "pro-life" individuals and "pro-choice" individuals. Nearly any topic can be studied scientifically if you take care to develop testable and refutable hypotheses.

## STEP 3: DETERMINE HOW YOU WILL DEFINE AND MEASURE YOUR VARIABLES

To scientifically evaluate a hypothesis, we must first translate the hypothesis into a specific prediction about the outcome of empirical observations. Consider, for example, the hypothesis that watching violence on television is directly related to aggressive behavior of preschool children. This hypothesis predicts that, if we observe a group of preschool children, we should see that those who watch more TV violence are more aggressive than those who watch less TV violence. Before we can evaluate this prediction, however, we need to decide exactly how we will define and measure "TV violence" and exactly how we will define and measure "aggressive behavior." The variables identified in the research hypothesis must be defined in a manner that makes it possible to measure them by some form of empirical observation. These decisions are usually made after reviewing previous research and determining how other researchers have defined and measured their variables.

By defining our variables so that they can be observed and measured, we transform the research hypothesis (from Step 2 of the research process) into a specific, well-defined prediction that can be tested by making empirical observations. We are now ready to evaluate the hypothesis by actually observing the variables to determine whether or not they are really related. The key idea is that the hypothesis is now in an *empirically testable* form.

Note that the task of determining exactly how the variables will be defined and measured often depends on the individuals to be measured. For example, you would certainly measure the aggressive behavior of a group of preschool children very differently from the aggressive behavior of a group of adults. The task of defining and measuring variables is discussed in Chapter 4.

### STEP 4: IDENTIFY THE PARTICIPANTS OR SUBJECTS

Before you can begin data collection, you must decide exactly what individuals will participate in the research study. If the individuals are human, they are called **participants.** Nonhumans are called **subjects.** It is the responsibility of the researcher to plan for the safety and well-being of the research participants and to inform them of all relevant aspects of the research, especially any risk or danger that may be involved. The issue of ethical treatment for participants and subjects is discussed in Chapter 3.

In addition, you must decide whether you will place any restrictions on the characteristics of the participants. For example, you may decide to use preschool children. Or you may be more restrictive and use only 4-year-old boys from two-parent, middle-income households who have been diagnosed with a specific learning disability. You also must determine how many individuals you will need for your research, and you must plan where and how to recruit them. Different ways to select individuals to participate in research are discussed in Chapter 5.

Definitions

The individuals who take part in research studies are called **participants** if they are human and **subjects** if they are nonhuman.

### STEP 5: SELECT A RESEARCH STRATEGY

Choosing a research strategy involves deciding on the general approach you will take to evaluate your hypothesis. General research strategies are discussed in Chapters 7, 8, and 9. The choice of a research strategy is usually determined by one of two factors:

1. *The type of question asked:* The simplest kind of research question asks only about the *existence* of a relationship. You may, for example, want to know whether or not there is any relation between academic success and self-esteem. A more sophisticated question would concern *why* there is a relation: what causes the relation between academic success and self-esteem? Questions about *causes* typically require a different strategy from questions about *existence*.

2. *Ethics and other constraints:* Often ethical considerations, which are discussed in Chapter 3, or other factors such as equipment availability limit what you can or cannot do in the laboratory. These factors can often force you to choose one research strategy over another.

## STEP 6: SELECT A RESEARCH DESIGN

Selecting a research design involves making decisions about the specific methods and procedures you will use to conduct the research study. Does your research question call for the detailed examination of one individual, or would you find a better answer by looking at the average behavior of a large group? Should you make a series of observations of the same individuals over a period of time, or should you compare the behaviors of different individuals at the same time? Answering these questions will help you determine a specific design for the study. Different designs and their individual strengths and weaknesses are discussed in Chapters 10 through 13.

## STEP 7: CONDUCT THE STUDY

Finally you are ready to collect the data. But now you must decide whether the study will be conducted in a laboratory or in the field (in the real world). Will you observe the participants individually, or in groups? In addition, you must now implement all your earlier decisions about manipulating, observing, measuring, controlling, and recording the different aspects of your study.

## STEP 8: EVALUATE THE DATA

Once the data have been collected, you must use various statistical methods to examine and evaluate the data. This involves drawing graphs, computing means, and using inferential statistics to help generalize the results from your specific subjects to the general population. Statistical methods are reviewed in Chapter 14.

## STEP 9: REPORT THE RESULTS

One important aspect of the scientific method is that observations and results must be public. This is accomplished in part by a written report describing what was done, what was found, and how the findings were interpreted. In Chapter 15 we review the standard style and procedures for writing research reports. Two reasons to report research results are: (1) the results become part of the general knowledge base that other people can use to answer questions or to generate new research ideas, and (2) the research procedure is public so it can be replicated or refuted by other researchers. At this stage, the researcher must ensure the anonymity and confidentiality of the research participants to protect them from any embarrassment or emotional stress that may result from the public disclosure of their participation. Anonymity and confidentiality are discussed in more detail in Chapter 3.

### STEP 10: REFINE OR REFORMULATE YOUR RESEARCH IDEA

Most research studies generate more questions than they answer. If your results support your original hypothesis, it does not mean that you have found a final answer. Instead, the new information from your study simply means that it is now possible to extend your original question into new domains or make the research question more precise. Typically, results that support a hypothesis lead to new questions by one of the following two routes:

1. *Test the boundaries of the result:* Suppose your study demonstrates that higher levels of academic performance are related to higher levels of self-esteem for elementary school children. Will this same result be found for adolescents in middle school? Perhaps adolescents are less concerned about respect from their parents and teachers and are more concerned about respect from peers. Perhaps academic success is *not* highly valued by adolescents. In this case, you would not necessarily expect academic success to be related to self-esteem for adolescents. Alternatively, you might want to investigate the relation between self-esteem and success outside academics. Is there a relation between success on the athletic field and self-esteem? Notice that the goal is to determine whether or not your result extends into other areas. How general are the results of your study?

2. *Refine the original research question:* If your results show a relationship between academic success and self-esteem, the next question is, "What causes the relationship?" That is, what is the underlying mechanism by which success in school translates into higher self-esteem? The original question asked, "Does a relation exist?" Now you are asking, "Why does the relation exist?"

Results that do not support your hypothesis also generate new questions. One explanation for negative results (results that do not support the hypothesis) is that one of the premises is wrong. Remember, for this example we assumed that academic success is highly valued and respected. Perhaps this is not true. Your new research question might be, "How important is academic success to parents, to teachers, or to elementary school students?"

Notice that research is not a linear, start-to-finish process. Instead, the process is a spiral or a circle that keeps returning to a new hypothesis to start over again. This never-ending process of asking questions, gathering evidence, and asking new questions is part of the general scientific method. There are no final answers. Consider, for example, the theory of evolution: After years of gathering evidence, evolution is still called a "theory." No matter how much supporting evidence is obtained, the "answer" to a research question is always open to challenge and eventually may be revised or refuted.

Learning Check

Identify the 10 steps of the research process.

## CHAPTER SUMMARY

Most students enroll in research methodology courses because it is required. We hope, however, that you now see that understanding research methodology can be useful. For example, perhaps at some point in your future you will conduct a study. In addition, understanding research methodology will help you understand and evaluate journal articles and descriptions of research. Further, with so many research findings bombarding us daily, you'll be able to make more informed decisions about those findings and how they may affect your life. Finally, the type of thinking that a scientist does can be used anywhere and at any time.

Although this textbook is devoted to discussing the scientific method, there are other ways of finding answers to questions. The methods of authority, intuition, tenacity, and empiricism and the rational method are different ways of acquiring knowledge. Each method has its strengths and limitations. The scientific method combines the various methods to achieve a more valid way of answering questions. The scientific method is empirical, public, and objective. The scientific method consists of five steps: (1) Observation of behavior or other phenomena; (2) Formation of a tentative answer or explanation, called a hypothesis; (3) Use of the hypothesis to generate a testable prediction; (4) Evaluation of the prediction by making systematic, planned observations; (5) Use of the observations to support, refute, or refine the original hypothesis.

The research process is the way the scientific method is used to answer a particular question. The 10 steps of the research process provide a framework for the remainder of this book.

## KEY WORDS

methods of inquiry
method of authority
method of faith
method of intuition
method of tenacity
rational method
premise statements

argument
method of empiricism
scientific method
induction or inductive reasoning
deduction or deductive
    reasoning
replication

experimenter bias
hypothesis
testable hypothesis
refutable hypothesis
participants
subjects

## EXERCISES

1. Go through a current newspaper or magazine and cut out one article that describes the results of a study. Summarize the finding according to this article. Do you have any reason to doubt that this information is accurate?

2. Describe one way in which understanding research methodology will be useful in your life. Be specific.

3. Suppose that, after reading about a recent murder in your town, you want to learn more about what causes people to kill. You go to the library and check out a book written by an ex-

pert in the field. Explain which method of inquiry you are using here.

4. Describe a situation in which you or someone you know used the method of intuition to answer a question.

5. Pessimists commonly claim that, if you drop a piece of buttered bread, it will probably land butter side down. Identify the mode of inquiry (authority, rational, empirical) you would use to evaluate this claim, and briefly explain how you would go about it.

6. A European car company claims that their car provides greater protection from rear-end collisions than any other manufacturer's car. Identify the mode of inquiry (authority, rational, empirical) you would use to evaluate this claim, and briefly explain how you would go about it.

7. Identify the six different methods of inquiry introduced in this chapter, and describe the limitations of each.

8. Make up an example of induction or inductive reasoning. In inductive reasoning, if the premises or initial observations are true, does this guarantee that the conclusion is true? Explain why or why not.

9. Make up an example of deduction or deductive reasoning. In deductive reasoning, if the premises or initial observations are true, does this guarantee that the conclusion is true? Explain why or why not.

10. Determine whether each of the following hypotheses is testable and refutable; if not, explain why.
    a. The color red as it is seen by males is different from the color red as it is seen by females.
    b. A list of three-syllable words is more difficult to memorize than a list of one-syllable words.
    c. The incidence of paranoia is higher among people who claim to have been abducted by aliens than in the general population.
    d. If the force of gravity doubled over the next 50,000 years, there would be a trend toward the evolution of larger animals and plants that could withstand the higher gravity.

# Research Ideas

## CHAPTER OVERVIEW

In this chapter we discuss in detail the first two steps of the research process: finding a research idea and converting a research idea into a specific research hypothesis. To get you started, we present some general pointers. To help you find a general topic area, we discuss sources of ideas and common mistakes to avoid. Next, we discuss how to find background literature on your topic, why a literature search is important, and how to conduct a literature search. Finally, we include pointers for using background literature to find new research ideas and for converting your research idea into a specific research hypothesis.

## 2.1 GETTING STARTED

Simply getting started is often a problem for researchers. The research process often appears to be a mysterious, exotic ritual, and the presence of quantities of previously published research can seem overwhelming. Every year, however, thousands of people begin the research process for the first time. Following are a few suggestions that should help make your start a little easier.

### PICK A TOPIC IN WHICH YOU ARE INTERESTED

Developing and conducting a research study involves work and definitely takes time. Working in an area of interest to you will help you stay motivated, avoid burnout, and greatly increase your chances of seeing the research project through to the end.

There are several different ways to define an interest area. Here are a few possibilities:

- A particular population or group of individuals, for example, pre-school children, cats, single-parent families, grandmothers, police officers
- A particular behavior, such as language development, adolescent dating, math anxiety, honesty, overeating, color preferences
- A general topic such as job stress, child abuse, aging, personality, learning, motivation

The key is really wanting to learn more about the topic you select. Preparing, planning, and conducting research will provide you with a lot of information and answers. If the task is important to you personally, gathering and using this information will be fun and exciting. If not, your enthusiasm will fade quickly.

### DO YOUR HOMEWORK

Many people think of research as collecting data in a laboratory, but this is only a small part of the total process. Long before actual data collection begins, most of your research time probably will be devoted to preparation. Once you have identified a research topic, collecting background information is the next essential step. Typically, this involves reading books and journal articles to make yourself more familiar with the topic: what is already known, what research has been done, and what questions remain unanswered. No matter what topic you select, it will soon become clear that there are hundreds of books and probably thousands of journal articles containing relevant background information. Don't panic; although the amount of printed material may appear overwhelming, keep these two points in mind:

1. You do not need to know everything about a topic, and you certainly do not need to read everything about a topic before you begin research. You should read enough to gain a solid, basic understanding of the current knowledge in an area, and this is fairly easy to attain. Later in this chapter (Section 2.4), we provide some suggestions for doing library research.

2.  An equally important goal of your background reading is to home in on a single, sharply focused research idea. For example, in reading a book on developmental psychology, one chapter on social development may capture your attention. Within that chapter, you become interested in the section on aggressive behavior, and in that section you find a fascinating paragraph on the relation between aggressive behavior and television violence. Notice that you have substantially narrowed your interest area from the broad topic of human development to the much more focused topic of aggression and TV violence. You have also greatly reduced the amount of relevant background reading.

### KEEP AN OPEN MIND

The best strategy for finding a research idea is to begin with a general topic area and then let your background reading lead you to a specific idea. As you read or skim through material, look for items that capture your attention; then follow those leads. You needn't start with a specific research idea in mind. In fact, beginning with a specific, preconceived research idea can be a mistake; you may find that your specific question has already been answered, or you may have difficulty finding information that is relevant to your preconceived notion. You may find that you don't have the necessary equipment, time, or subjects to test your idea. So your best bet is to be flexible and keep an open mind. The existing knowledge in any topic area is filled with unanswered questions, untested predictions, and countless hints and suggestions for future research. Also, be critical; ask questions as you read: Why did they do that? Is this result consistent with what I see in my own life? How would this prediction apply to a different situation? Do I really believe this explanation? These questions, expanding or challenging current knowledge, can lead to good research ideas.

### FOCUS, FOCUS, FOCUS

Developing a single, specific research idea is largely a weeding-out process. You probably will find that 1 hour of reading leads you to a dozen legitimate research ideas. It is unlikely that you can answer a dozen questions with one research study, so you will have to throw out most of your ideas (at least temporarily). Your goal is to develop one research question and to find the background information that is directly relevant to that question. Other ideas and other background material may be appropriate for other research but at this stage will only complicate the study you are planning. Discard irrelevant items, and focus on one question at a time.

### TAKE ONE STEP AT A TIME

Like any major project, planning and conducting research can be a long and difficult process. At the beginning, contemplating the very end of a research project may lead you to feel that the task is impossibly large. Remember that you don't need to do the whole thing at once; just take it one step at a time.

As you move through the project, maintain a degree of flexibility. You may discover a new journal article or get a suggestion from a friend that causes you to revise or refine your original plan. Making adjustments is a normal part of the research process and usually improves the end result.

Learning
Checks

Discuss the five suggestions given in the text to make beginning research easier.

Explain why it is not the best strategy to begin with a specific research idea.

## 2.2   SOURCES OF IDEAS

### FINDING A GENERAL TOPIC AREA

All research begins with an idea. Ideas for research can come from many different sources. Unfortunately, beginning students often believe that getting an idea is very difficult, when, in fact starting points for research are all around us. All that is really necessary is that you see the world around you from an actively curious perspective. Ask yourself *why* things happen the way they do or *what if* things were different. Keep your eyes open! Any source can generate legitimate research ideas.

### COMMON SOURCES OF IDEAS

#### Personal Interests and Curiosities

Feel free to generate ideas for research based on your own interests and concerns. What are you interested in? What are you curious about? One way to find out is to think about the psychology courses you have taken. What courses were your favorites? Within courses, what were your favorite units or classes? Think about the people and behaviors that interest you. Think about the issues that concern you. A research project can be about anything, so choose a topic you would like to learn more about.

#### Casual Observation

Watching the behavior of people or animals you encounter daily can be an excellent source of ideas. If you simply watch, you will see people getting angry, laughing at jokes, lying, insulting each other, forming friendships and relationships, eating, sleeping, learning and forgetting. Any behavior that attracts your attention and arouses your curiosity can become a good research topic. In addition, you can monitor your own behavior, attitudes, and emotions. Although casual observation probably will not lead to a precise research question, you can certainly identify a general topic for study, and you may develop your own hypotheses or ideas about why people act the way they do.

#### Practical Problems or Questions

Occasionally ideas for research will arise from practical problems or questions you encounter in your daily life, such as issues from your job, your family relationships, your schoolwork, or elsewhere in the world around you. For example, you may want to develop a more efficient set of study habits. Should you concentrate your study time in the morning, in the afternoon, or at night? Should you spend a 2-hour block of study time working exclusively on one subject, or should you distribute your time so that each of five different courses gets some attention? Or suppose that you want to reduce pilot error in airplanes. What is the best placement of dials and levers on the dashboard of a cockpit to minimize the chances of pilot error? Any of these problems could be developed into a research study.

### Vague and Fleeting Thoughts

Occasionally ideas for research begin with flashes of inspiration. Your initial ideas may emerge at odd times and in a fleeting way. You may get a flash of creative thought while you are in the bathroom, in the midst of a conversation with a friend, crossing the street, or dreaming. For some people, research ideas just spontaneously "pop" into their minds. The history of science is filled with stories of famous researchers whose ideas first appeared as flashes of insight. For example, Archimedes (287–212 B.C.E.) is said to have discovered the law of hydrostatics (buoyancy) while stepping into his bath. The story also claims that he then ran down the street shouting *"Eureka!"* (Greek for "I have found it") still dressed for the bath. According to legend, Isaac Newton (1642–1727) first conceived of universal gravitation when he saw an apple fall to the ground. We do not suggest that you wait for something like this to happen to you. However, we do suggest that you actively use one of the other potential sources for ideas, keeping your mind open to the possibility that, along the way, this could happen to you.

    We don't want to leave you with the impression that research ideas are always found in such unsystematic, creative, haphazard ways. Most research ideas are generated in a highly systematic fashion by using the research of others and theories.

### Reading Reports of Others' Observations

The written reports of observations made by other people are another good source of research ideas. These can include informal sources such as newspaper and magazine reports and television programs. Nor must research ideas come exclusively from "factual" reports. Gossip columns, personal ads, comics, political cartoons, and advertising can stimulate research questions. Keep in mind the fact that published information, especially in nonscience sources, is not necessarily true and does not always tell the whole story. Remember, you are looking for ideas—so read critically and ask questions.

    Although informal sources can stimulate research questions, you are more likely to find good ideas in the formal research reports published in books and professional journals. In this same category is material you have encountered in previous academic courses or textbooks. These scholarly sources are definitely the best ones for identifying questions that researchers are asking and the techniques they use to find answers. As always, read critically and ask questions: Why did the study examine only 4-year-old boys? What would happen if the task were made more difficult? Would the scores have been higher if the participants had been motivated to try harder? Questions like these can lead to a modification or extension of an existing study, which is one pathway to creating new research.

### Behavioral Theories

Watch for theories that offer explanations for behavior or try to explain why different environmental factors lead to different behaviors. In addition to explaining previous research results, a good theory usually predicts behavior in new situations. Can you think of a way to test the explanations or evaluate the predictions from a theory? Look closely at the different variables that are part of the theory (the factors that cause behavior to change), and ask yourself what might happen if one or more of those variables were manipulated or isolated from the others. Testing the predictions that are part of a theory can be a good source of research ideas. Occasionally, you will encounter two different theories that attempt to explain the same behavior. When two opposing theories make different predictions, you have found a good opportunity for research.

Learning
Check

Describe the six common sources of ideas identified in the text.

## COMMON MISTAKES IN CHOOSING A RESEARCH TOPIC

Over the years, we have seen beginning students make many mistakes in trying to find a research topic. We mention these mistakes in the hope that you will either avoid them altogether or recognize when you are making one and quickly shift gears.

### Topic Doesn't Interest the Student

One very common mistake is choosing a topic that is not of interest to you. This seems like an easy enough mistake to avoid, so how do you think it could happen? Through procrastination! This mistake is often the result of putting off thinking about a choice of topic until the latest possible date. When pressed for time to select a topic, students often pick a topic that is only of marginal interest. Because interesting topics don't just pop into one's mind, allow yourself plenty of time to discover a topic. As noted earlier, developing and conducting a research study involves work and time. Unless you are somewhat interested in the topic you pick, you will find this task extremely laborious. As a result, you are likely to lose motivation, and your research project will no doubt reflect this. Start looking for ideas now!

### Topic Is Too Safe or Too Easy

Another mistake is to pick a topic that is too safe or too easy. Often students choose a topic with which they are quite familiar. Hoping to save time and effort, a student may pull out a paper written for another class and try to change it into an idea for a research project. However, the purpose of planning and conducting research is not only to teach you about the research process. We also hope that, in your reading, you will learn something about a topic that is of interest to you.

### Topic Is Too Difficult

The opposite of selecting a too-easy topic is choosing one that is too hard. When you begin your library research, you may find that all the articles on your topic are written in complex scientific jargon that you don't understand. If this happens, it is time to be flexible. When most of the literature in your chosen area is over your head, consider changing topics. The task you are taking on is challenging enough; don't bite off more than you can chew!

### Topic Is Too Broad

Choosing a research topic that is too broad is not a mistake if you are still in the early stages of searching for an idea. As we discussed in Section 2.1, the best strategy for finding a research idea is to begin with a general topic area. However, as you skim material, you quickly need to home in on a single, very specific research idea. You can't answer every question about a topic area with one research project. Your ultimate goal in choosing a topic is to let the background reading lead you to a very specific idea for a research hypothesis that can be tested in a research study.

### Sticking with the First Idea That Comes to Mind

Another mistake that beginning research students often make is sticking with the first idea that comes to mind. If you like your first idea for research, that's great. However, don't commit yet; when you read information on your topic, different and more interesting research ideas may come to light. Be open to this possibility. Second and third, sometimes fourth and fifth, research ideas are usually more refined, simpler, and more manageable than first ones. Although you don't want to switch topic areas the day before you begin conducting your study, don't commit too quickly, either; give your ideas time to evolve.

### Inadequate Literature on the Topic

What if, when you try to read for background in a topic area, you find nothing to read. This can occur for several reasons. First, some of the potentially most interesting topics in psychology appear to have been little investigated. You may have stumbled on an area that no one has thought to investigate. On the one hand, you can be proud of yourself for this discovery; on the other, it will be impossible to develop a research project. Second, the topic may not lend itself to scientific investigation. For example, questions such as, "Is there a God?" "Do angels exist?" and "Is there an afterlife?" are very intriguing topic areas. However, as discussed in Section 1.6, some of life's most interesting questions are unsuitable for scientific research because no testable and refutable hypotheses can be developed about them. Third, it may only *appear* that there is no material on your topic, because you are not using the correct terms (key words) to search for information. In Section 2.4 we discuss in detail how to conduct a literature search using key words. And fourth, it could *appear* that there is no material on your topic, because the database that you are using does not include an abundance of psychological material.

---

Describe the six mistakes discussed in the text as most commonly made in choosing a research topic.

Learning
Check

## 2.3   FINDING AND USING BACKGROUND LITERATURE

Once you have settled on a general idea for a research study, the next step is to go to the library to gather background information on the topic you have identified. In addition to gaining general knowledge about your topic area, your goals are to determine the current state of knowledge and to become familiar with current research—in particular, to find a specific research question. Notice that we said "find" a question rather than "make up" or "create" one. Once you are familiar with what is currently known and what is currently being done in a research area, your task is simply to extend the current research one more step. Sometimes this requires a bit of logic, in which you combine two or more established facts to reach a new conclusion or prediction. Often the authors of a research report literally will give you ideas for new research. It is very common for researchers to conclude a discussion of their results with suggestions for future research. You are welcome to turn one of these suggestions into a research question. In Section 2.5 we provide additional hints for finding research ideas. For now, do not try to impose your own preconceived idea onto the literature. Instead, let the literature lead you to a new idea.

In most college or university libraries, the books devoted to psychology will occupy at least 100 feet of shelves. The psychology journals probably will fill even more space. When you add related publications in the fields of education, sociology, criminal justice, social work, and so on, you are facing a vast amount of printed material. This mass of published information is referred to as "the literature." Your job is to search the literature to find a handful of items that are directly relevant to your research idea. This may at first appear to be an overwhelming task; fortunately, however, the literature is filled with useful aids to guide your search. Specifically, all the individual publications are interconnected by cross-referencing, and there are many summary guides providing overviews that can send you directly to specific topic areas. By following the guides and tracing the interconnections, it is possible to conduct a successful literature search without undue pain and suffering.

### PRIMARY AND SECONDARY SOURCES

Before we discuss the actual process of a literature search, there are a few terms you should know. Individual items in the literature can be classified into two broad categories: primary sources and secondary sources. A **primary source** is a first-hand report in which the authors describe their own observations. Typically, a primary source is a research report, published in a scientific journal or periodical, in which the authors describe their own research study, including why the research was done, how the study was conducted, what results were found, and how those results were interpreted. In contrast, a **secondary source** is a secondhand report in which the authors discuss someone else's observations. Some examples of secondary sources include: (1) books and textbooks in which the author describes and summarizes past research; (2) the introductory section of research reports, in which previous research is presented as a foundation for the current study; and (3) newspaper and magazine articles that report on previous research.

A **primary source** is a firsthand report of observations or research results that is written by the individual(s) who actually conducted the research and made the observations.

A **secondary source** is a description or summary of another person's work. A secondary source is written by someone who did not participate in the research or observations being discussed.

Notice that the principal distinction between a primary source and a secondary one is firsthand versus secondhand reporting of research results. Students often confuse this distinction with the notion that anything published in a journal or periodical is automatically a primary source and that all other kinds of publications are secondary sources. This assumption is incorrect on several levels. The following are also possible:

- The journal article is *not* a primary source. Instead, the article may be a review of other work, a theoretical article that attempts to explain or establish relationships between several previous studies, or a historical summary of the research in a specific area. None of these is a primary source, because none is a firsthand report of research results.
- A book or book chapter is a primary source. Occasionally an individual or a group of researchers will publish an edited volume that presents a series of interrelated research studies. Each chapter is written by the individual(s) who actually conducted the research and is therefore a primary source.
- A journal article is a firsthand report of research results, yet sections of the article are actually secondary sources. Specifically, most research reports begin with an introductory section that reviews current research in the area and forms the foundation of the study that is being reported. This review of current research is *secondary* because the authors describe research conducted by others. Remember, to qualify as a primary source, the authors must describe their own research studies and results.

Both primary and secondary sources play important roles in the literature search process. Secondary sources can provide concise summaries of past research. A textbook, for example, will often summarize 10 years of research, citing several important studies, in a few paragraphs. Individual research reports that fill 10 to 15 pages in journals are often summarized in one or two sentences. Thus, secondary sources can save you hours of library research. However, you should be constantly aware that secondary sources are always incomplete and can be biased or simply inaccurate. In a secondary source, the author has selected only bits and pieces of the original study; the selected parts may have been taken out of context and reshaped to fit a theme quite different from what the original authors intended. In general, secondary sources tell only part of the truth and may, in fact, distort the truth. To obtain complete and accurate information, it is essential to consult primary sources. Reading primary sources, however, can be a tedious process, as primary sources are typically long, detailed reports focusing on a narrowly defined topic. Therefore, plan to use secondary sources to gain an overview and identify a few specific primary sources for more detailed reading. Secondary sources provide a good starting point for a literature search, but you must depend on primary sources for the final answers.

Describe how primary and secondary sources differ.

## THE PURPOSE OF A LITERATURE SEARCH

Research does not exist in isolation. Each research study is part of an existing body of knowledge, building on the foundation of past research and expanding that foundation for future research. Box 2.1 and Figure 2.1 explain how current knowledge grows, with each new piece of information growing out of an existing body of previous knowledge. As you read the literature and develop an idea for a research study, keep in mind that your study should be a logical extension of past research.

Ultimately, your goal in conducting a **literature search** is to find a set of published research reports that define the current state of knowledge in an area and to identify a gap in that knowledge base that your study will attempt to fill. Eventually, you will complete your research study and write your own research

---

### BOX 2.1    The Growth of Research

Throughout this chapter we repeat the notion that each research study builds on previous knowledge and attempts to expand that knowledge base. With this thought in mind, it is possible to represent the existing knowledge base (the literature) as a tree-like structure that is continuously growing over time. Figure 2.1 is a graphic representation of this concept, with each point in the figure representing a single research study and the branches representing the growth and development of the "knowledge tree." When you begin a literature search, you will enter this tree and find your way along the branches. Your goal in conducting the search is twofold. First, you must work your way to the very tips of the highest branches and find a cluster of the most recent research studies. Your study will form a new branch coming out of this cluster. Second, you must search backward, down the tree, to identify the historically significant foundations of your work. You probably will find that most of the current research studies in an area will cite the same

"classic" studies as their foundations. These classics usually will provide a broader perspective for your work and will help you understand and explain the significance of your study as it relates to the more general tree of knowledge.

The tree metaphor is only a conceptual guide to help you visualize the process and the goals of a literature search—the concept of a tree greatly oversimplifies the process. For example, many good research studies involve establishing a connection between two previously unrelated branches of research. Nonetheless, the tree metaphor should help direct your literature search activities. You may, for example, find yourself with a cluster of recent articles that seem to be a dead end, offering no prospect for developing new research. If this happens, you can simply work back down the tree to an earlier branching point and branch off in a new direction without completely abandoning your original research topic.

Current Research
(the most recent research studies)

Major Branching Points
(studies that started a new research direction)

Historical Studies
(the foundation of the research area)

Figure 2.1    How New Research Grows Out of Old
The tree-like structure emphasizes the relationships between
research studies and the notion that current research (the tips
of the branches) are always based in previous research.

report. The research report begins with an introduction that summarizes past research (from your literature search) and provides a logical justification for your study. Although we discuss the task of writing a research report later (in Chapter 15), the topic is introduced now as a means of focusing your literature search. Figure 2.2 presents the first paragraph of a journal article (Schwartz, Dodge, & Coie, 1993) as an example of the use of a literature review to introduce a topic area and provide a logical justification for a new study. The paragraph can be condensed into a simple, logical argument:

1.  A small minority of children consistently seem to be victimized or bullied by their peers.
2.  Although other research has looked at the characteristics of the victim children, little has been done to examine their social behaviors prior to becoming victims. (Are these kids doing something that actually helps them to become victims?)
3.  Therefore, we need to examine children's behaviors before they are identified as victims. The goal is to determine whether some children are destined to become victims because they exhibit behaviors that may cause their peers to view them as easy targets for bullying.

Although we have not described the research study, you should be able to predict the purpose of the study and should have some idea of what was done. Notice that the background literature is used to construct a logical argument that

This study is an investigation of the social behavior processes by which children come to be chronically victimized by their peers. There is substantial evidence that a small minority of children are consistently targeted for victimization by their peers (for a review, see Smith, 1991). Researchers have suggested that these chronic victims are at high risk for later maladjustment (e.g., Olweus, in press). Accordingly, investigators have devoted considerable effort to identifying the correlates of peer victimization (e.g., Björkqvist, Ekman, & Lagerspetz, 1982; Lagerspetz, Björkqvist, Berts, & King, 1982; Olweus, 1978) and designing effective prevention programs (e.g., Elliot, 1991; Olweus, 1991; Smith & Thompson, 1991). Researchers have not, however, systematically identified the behavioral antecedents of chronic victimization. As a result, little is known about the social behaviors that precede and potentially contribute to the emergence of chronic peer victimization. Our limited understanding of these behavioral processes is unfortunate because detailed data on the behavior patterns that precede the emergence of chronic peer victimization would facilitate the development of appropriate interventions and greatly enhance current understanding of the mechanisms underlying bully/victim problems in childhood.

Figure 2.2   The Opening Paragraph of a Research Report by Schwartz, Dodge, and Coie (1993)
Notice that the authors use background literature to introduce a topic and to provide a logical justification for the research that follows.

leads the reader directly into the proposed study. The purpose of your literature review is to provide the elements needed for an introduction to your own research study. Specifically, you need to find a set of research articles that can be organized into a logical argument supporting and justifying the research you propose to do.

Explain the purpose of a literature search.

## 2.4   CONDUCTING A LITERATURE SEARCH

### STARTING POINTS

Let's assume that you are starting your literature search with only a general idea for a research topic. Your purpose, therefore, is to narrow down your general idea to a specific research question and to find all the published information necessary to document and support that question. As you will see, there are many different ways to begin a search of the literature. In this section we identify several different starting points and provide some suggestions to help you find one.

One of the best places to start is with a recently published secondary source—for example, a textbook in a content area appropriate for your idea (perhaps a developmental psychology or social psychology textbook). Use the chapter headings and subheadings in the text to help focus your search on a more narrowly defined area. In addition, make notes of the following items, each of which can serve as an excellent starting point when you begin to search for primary sources (journal articles) relevant to your topic:

- *Key Words:* Make a list of the correct terms or **key words** used to identify and describe the variables in the study and the characteristics of the subjects. Researchers often develop a specific set of terms to describe a topic area. It is much easier to locate related research articles if you use the correct terms. For example, you may have trouble finding articles on "duration of memory" unless you use the accepted term, *retention interval.*
- *Author Names:* Commonly a small group of individual researchers is responsible for much of the work being done in a specific area. If you repeatedly encounter the same names, make a note of these individuals as the current leading researchers in the area.

As you develop your list of key word terms and author names, keep in mind that any single secondary source is necessarily incomplete and probably selective. Thus, it is wise to repeat the list-making process with two or three different sources, then combine your lists. When you finish, you should have an excellent set of leads to help you move into the primary source literature.

### USING ONLINE DATABASES

Although there are thousands of research articles in psychology published every year, many tools are available to help you search through the publications to find the few that are directly relevant to your research topic. In the recent past, the primary tool was a publication called *Psychological Abstracts,* which consisted of bound volumes containing:

- A brief summary of every psychology article, chapter, or book published during the year and information about where to find the original publication. These summaries are the actual **abstracts.**

- A subject index that cross-referenced every publication according to the key words or subjects relevant to the publication.
- An author index that cross-referenced every publication according to author.

Thus, one could use *Psychological Abstracts* to look up everything that was published on a particular topic and/or everything that was published by a particular author in any year. The same principle of cross-referencing publications by subject and by author is still used today, but now most of the cross-referencing tools exist as computer databases. There are many different **databases,** with each one focusing on an individual topic area (like psychology, chemistry, or criminal justice). Table 2.1 shows the basic characteristics of three databases that are commonly available through most college or university libraries. The two databases that provide the best coverage of psychology literature are PsycINFO and PsycLIT (see Box 2.2). The databases provide the same basic information that was available in the bound volumes of *Psychological Abstracts*, but the computer provides much faster and easier access to the information.

 Learning Check

What is *Psychological Abstracts*?

We warn that the process of searching the literature using a database like PsycINFO is very different from conducting a search on the Web. Each month the people at PsycINFO look through more than 1,000 periodicals in the field of psychology, as well as a wide range of books and book chapters, to identify references to add to their database. All the references are selected from reputable scientific publications, and most have been edited and reviewed by professional psychologists to ensure that they are legitimate and accurate contributions. This kind of professional screening does not exist on the World

---

BOX 2.2  **Full-Text Databases**

For searching through psychology research articles, we recommend using **PsycINFO** and **PsycLIT** because each of these databases reviews items published in more than 1,000 periodicals, as well as other books and book chapters in the field of psychology. If something is published in the field of psychology, it is almost guaranteed to be included in PsycINFO and PsycLIT. Note, however, that these databases provide only brief summaries of the items they reference. To read the entire item, you must locate the original journal or book.

There are other databases that provide full-text references; that is, they contain the complete item, word for word, as it appeared in the original publication. However, these full-text databases typically do not cover all the publications in any specific topic area. Thus, a full-text database probably covers only a handful of periodicals in psychology. If you use a full-text database to search for psychology publications, you probably will not find many relevant publications, because they are not included in the database.

Before using any database, quickly check the sources it reviews to be sure it provides good coverage of the area you would like to explore.

TABLE 2.1

Information on Three Databases Available for Conducting Literature Searches

| Database | Subjects Covered | Sources | Number of Records |
|---|---|---|---|
| PsycINFO | Psychology and psychological aspects of related disciplines such as:<br>Anthropology<br>Business<br>Education<br>Law<br>Linguistics<br>Medicine<br>Nursing<br>Pharmacology<br>Physiology<br>Psychiatry<br>Sociology | More than 1,400 periodicals<br><br>Current chapter and book coverage<br><br>Adds more than 55,000 references annually | More than 780,000 records from 1984 to the present<br><br>(Other versions go back to 1967 or to 1887.) |
| ERIC | Adult & vocational education<br>Assessment & evaluation<br>Disabilities & gifted education<br>Early childhood education<br>Educational management<br>Elementary education<br>Higher education<br>Information & technology<br>Language & linguistics<br>Reading & communication<br>Teacher education<br>Urban education | Nonjournal material from the monthly *Resources in Education*<br><br>Journal articles from the monthly *Current Index to Journals in Education* | More than 983,000 records from 1966 to the present |
| Social Science Abstracts | Anthropology<br>Economics<br>Geography<br>Law<br>Political science<br>Psychology<br>Sociology | Records for English-language periodicals from the USA and elsewhere<br><br>Includes articles, interviews, obituaries, biographies, and book reviews | More than 600,000 records from 1983 to the present |

Wide Web. Thus, for example, if you enter the key word *amnesia* in PsycINFO, you will get a set of reputable scientific references. If you use the same key word for a WWW search, you could obtain anybody's site with absolutely no guarantees about the quality or validity of the information.

We also warn that the quality of the information you obtain, even on a reputable database like PsycLIT or PsycINFO, depends on the quality of the key word(s) you use. Generally, it is advisable to try several different but related key words and see what results each produces. For example, you could try a series of key words such as

*eating disorder*

*anorexia*

*bulimia*

*body image*

You may find that one of these (or some combination) produces references that fit your interests better than the others. Usually you can find hints for new key words within a database when you are offered options to refine or to limit your search. Also, watch for potential new key words that appear in the titles of the references you find. In general, we encourage you to explore the different search options available with a database to be sure you get the best possible results for your own research interests. In the next section we lead you through an example of a literature search using the PsycINFO database.

## USING PSYCINFO

PsycINFO and PsycLIT differ in how they are accessed (either online or on CD), how often they are updated (monthly or quarterly), and how far back they go (in years of the abstracts). Check with your reference librarian to find out which system your library subscribes to, how to access the system, and how far back the database goes. The precise procedures for doing a search in the PsycINFO database vary from system to system and also depend on how your library has arranged to obtain access to the database. The basic procedure is to identify a list of key words (or search terms), enter them, and let the computer find publications focusing on issues related to those terms.

When conducting a literature search using PsycINFO, it is common to insert a key word or key words into a Keyword, Search, or Find field. Figure 2.3 illustrates an initial screen in PsycINFO (this figure is an example; your screen will look slightly different). Suppose you are interested in the topic of bulimia. You would enter the term *bulimia* in the Search For box. PsycINFO then searches the titles, abstracts, and descriptor lists (lists of descriptor words found at the end of each PsycINFO entry) for instances of your key word.

When the search is complete you will be notified of the number of records (publications) found. Depending on that number, you may want to (1) use a different key word if no records are found; (2) broaden your search with a broader key word if few records are found; or (3) narrow your search if too many records are found. Figure 2.4 shows a screen indicating how many records have been found from your key word search. In this example 5,326 records have been identified. You probably don't want to read through this large number of abstracts.

There are many ways to narrow down the list. As shown in Figure 2.4, for example, you may want to limit the list to items published by a certain author or within a given time period, say, in the past 10 years. Usually the best way to limit the list is to further restrict the topic. This can be done in a number of ways. Again displayed in Figure 2.4, you can select from a list of subject head-

Figure 2.3    An Initial Screen in PsycINFO

ings to limit your results. Another way to limit your list is to go back to the search screen and add an additional key word to your search using the word *and* to join the key words. So for example, if you are interested in bulimia but only in adolescence, you might enter *bulimia and adolescence* in the Search For field.

Once you have narrowed or expanded the search to yield a list of an appropriate size, you can display a list of the records. Figure 2.5 shows a list of the records, which includes for each publication

the title (of the journal article, book chapter, or book)

author (or authors' names)

source (name of the journal or book in which the publication appears)

document type (what type of publication it is)

Reviewing the titles is the first level of screening journal articles. Most articles are discarded at this stage. By reading the titles, you can select those that still appear of interest to you by clicking on the title to see the detailed record, which includes the abstract of the publication.

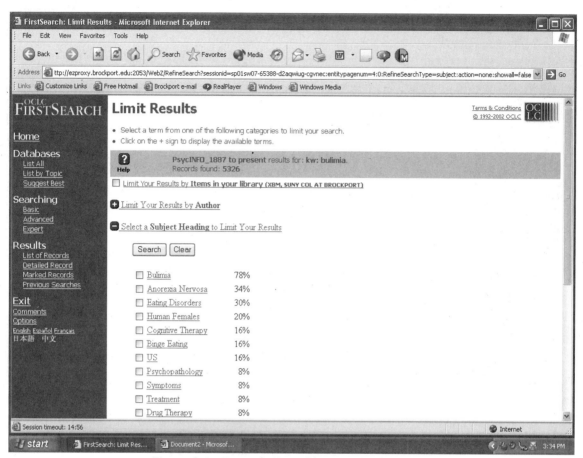

Figure 2.4    Records Found by Keyword Search

Figure 2.6 shows a detailed record. A record contains all of the information about a publication. Within each record are a number of fields, each containing specific information about the publication (author, title, source, and abstract). The full name of each field is included in Figure 2.6, but many systems include abbreviations. For example, in most systems author is abbreviated AU, title TI, source SO, and abstract AB. By reading the abstract, you may find additional key words to use for your search. By reading the abstract you can also get a much better idea of what the article is about and can decide whether you are still interested in reading the whole article. This is the second level of reviewing journal articles. If you are still interested in the article, print out this record, and then locate that journal article, chapter, or book in your library. If your library does not have an item you need, request an interlibrary loan. The procedure for an interlibrary loan is very simple. Often it simply involves clicking some additional keys for an online request, or it may involve completing a form. In either case, your library will get that item for you—usually within days and often for free.

Figure 2.5   A List of Records

## THE PROCESS OF CONDUCTING A LITERATURE SEARCH

In this section we discuss using the library research tools we have described to search the literature for the small number of journal articles that are directly relevant to your research study. The literature search process is likely to uncover hundreds of journal articles. And, although each of these articles is related to your topic, most of them probably are not *directly* related to the research you hope to do. Therefore, as you work through the literature search process, one of your main concerns is to weed out irrelevant material. There are no absolute criteria for determining whether an article is relevant or should be discarded; you must make your own decisions. However, here are some suggestions to help make the selection/weeding process more efficient:

1. Use the *title* of the article as your first basis for screening. You can find a title either in PsycINFO or at the beginning of the article itself. Based only on the titles, you probably can discard about 90% of the articles as not directly relevant.

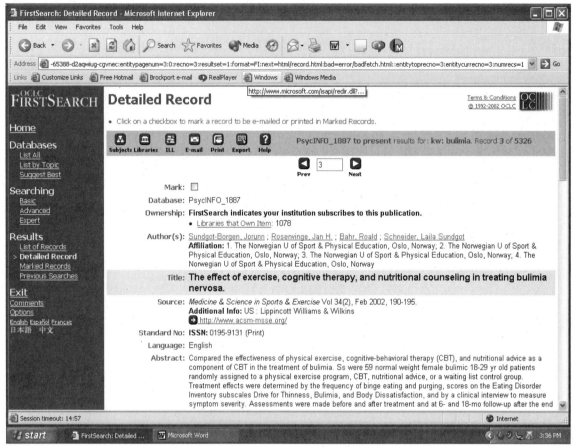

Figure 2.6    A Detailed Record

2. Use the *abstract* of the article as your second screening device. If the title sounds interesting, then read the abstract to determine whether the article itself is really relevant. Many of the articles that seemed interesting (from the title) get thrown out at this stage. You can find an abstract either in PsycINFO or at the beginning of the article itself.

3. If you are still interested after looking at the title and the abstract, go to the appropriate journal to find the article, or request an interlibrary loan if your library does not have that journal. (Incidentally, when you retrieve a journal to look up a specific article, it is often useful to review the contents of the rest of the journal. Occasionally a journal devotes an entire issue to a single topic, and several other relevant works surround your article. Also, the simple fact that the journal considers the topic of your article appropriate for its coverage means that it may publish other articles on the same topic.) Once you find the article, first *skim* it, looking specifically at the introductory paragraphs and the discussion section.

4.  If it still looks relevant, then read the article carefully and/or make a copy for your personal use. When reading a research article, bear in mind that it is customary for an article to be arranged into standard, distinct sections. We discuss in detail how to write these sections in Chapter 15. For now, here is what you can expect to see in each section of a research article and how each section may be of use to you:

*Introduction:* Following the title, authors' names and affiliations, and abstract is the first major section of the article, the introduction. In the **introduction** is a statement of the problem under investigation in the study, where the idea for the research came from (based on previous literature), and what was expected (the hypothesis). The introduction can help you determine whether this article will be useful in the development of your research idea. In addition, the literature review presented will give you possible additional resources. Incidentally, the introduction section is not labeled "Introduction." Instead, the text simply begins after the abstract and continues until the next section, which is entitled, "Method."

*Method:* The second major section of a research article is the **method section.** This section tells you in detail how the study was done, including who participated in the study, what materials were used, and the exact procedures that were followed. You can use the method section of a research article later to help you develop ideas for the methodology of your own study.

*Results:* The third major section of a research article is the **results section.** Here you are told what was found in the study. This section often includes the results of statistical analyses as well as figures and tables of the results.

*Discussion:* The final section of a journal article is the **discussion section.** Here you are told what the author thinks the results mean. Among other things, in this section the author usually discusses ideas for additional research. You may certainly get ideas for a research topic from these suggestions.

*References:* At the end of the article is a complete list of all the publications cited in the article. The list is organized alphabetically by first author's last name and includes the authors, the title, the date of publication, and complete information about the journal or book in which the item was published. The **reference section** can be a good source of new key words or new author names for your literature search.

5.  Use the *references* from the articles that you have already found to expand your literature search. Although the list of references will contain "old"

research studies published years earlier, some of them may be directly relevant to your research idea. In this case, find the relevant articles and add them to your collection. In addition, the titles may contain new terms that you can use for another key word search in PsycINFO. Finally, the authors listed in the references constitute a set of people who are doing research in the same area where you would like to work. You can enter these author names in PsycINFO and find the research reports that they have published recently. If people conducted research in a specific area 5 years ago, there is a good chance that they are continuing to do work in a related area today. In general, "old" references can be a good source for "new" research studies. Theoretically, you should continue using the old references to track down new material until you reach a point where you no longer find any new items. Realistically, however, you must decide when to call off the search. At some point you will realize that you are not uncovering new leads and that you should proceed with the items you have found. Throughout the process, keep in mind that a literature search has two basic goals: (1) to gain a general familiarity with the current research in your specific area of interest, and (2) to find a small set of research studies that will serve as the basis for your own research idea. When you feel comfortable that you are knowledgeable about the topic area and have found a few research studies that are particularly relevant to your own interests, then you have completed a successful search. We are deliberately vague about how many articles form a good foundation for developing a new research idea. You may find two or three interrelated articles that all converge on the same idea, or you may find only one research study that appears to be directly relevant to your interests. In any event, the key criterion is that the study (or studies) you find provide some justification for new research. Even if you have only one study, remember that it cites other research studies that form a basis for the current research question. These same studies should be relevant to your research idea, and you are welcome to include them as part of the foundation for your own research.

Figure 2.7 summarizes the steps of a literature search as detailed in this section.

Learning
Check

List the five sections typically found in a research article, and describe briefly what each should contain.

## 2.5    FINDING AN IDEA FOR A NEW RESEARCH STUDY

Once you have located a set of recent and relevant articles, the final step is to use these research reports as the foundation for your research idea (see Chapter 1, Step 1 of the research process). Earlier we called this task "finding a research idea." When you are familiar with the current research in an area, the idea for the next study involves simply extending the current research one more step. However, discovering this next step may not be as simple as we have implied, and so we list here a few suggestions:

Start with a general idea
of a topic area or a behavior
(such as developmental psychology or anorexia).

Use recently published secondary sources
such as textbooks to narrow your focus and
obtain a list of key words and author names.

Use key words and author names
in an online database (such as PsycINFO)
to locate primary-source journal articles.

Weed out items that are not directly relevant.
Most can be eliminated based on the title;
of those remaining, many can be eliminated
based on the abstract.
Skim the introduction and discussion sections
of the remaining articles to determine their relevance.

Once you have a handful of recent, relevant articles,
use the references from the articles to look for new
key words and author names.

Use the new key words and author names
in an online database search.
Continue until you no longer find new items.

Figure 2.7    The Process
of Conducting a
Literature Search

- The easiest way to find new research ideas is to look for them as explicit statements in the journal articles you already have. Near the end of the discussion section of most research reports is a set of suggestions for future research. In most cases, a research study actually generates more questions than it answers. The authors who are reporting their research results usually point out the questions that remain unanswered. You can certainly use these suggestions as ideas for your own research.
- Another relatively easy way to generate ideas for new research is to ask yourself how an existing study might be modified or extended. Any study uses a specific set of instructions, stimuli, tests, and participants. What might happen if any of these were changed? For example, would a result obtained for 8-year-old boys also be obtained for adolescents? Often this technique involves testing the limits of a theory or a treatment. If one study demonstrates that a treatment is effective under specific circumstances, it is perfectly legitimate to ask whether the treatment would still be effective if the circumstances were changed. Please note that we are not suggesting

that you can create good research ideas by simply changing variables randomly. There should be some reason, based on logic or other research results, to expect that changing circumstances might change results. In general, however, modifying or extending an existing study is a sensible method for creating new research ideas.

- Occasionally it is possible to find a new research idea by combining two (or more) existing results. For example, one study reports that people who experience stressful events tend to have more illness and visit the doctor more often than people with relatively stress-free lives (Rahe & Arthur, 1978). Another study suggests that owning a pet can help people cope with stress (Broadhead et al., 1983). Given these two results, can you generate a hypothesis for a new study? [See Siegel (1990) for one example.] Another possibility is that two research results seem to contradict each other. In this case you could look for factors that differentiate the two studies and might be responsible for the different results.

In general, research is not static. Instead, it is constantly developing and growing as new studies spring from past results. New research ideas usually come from recognizing the direction in which an area of research is moving, then going with the flow.

Learning Check

Describe the three ways identified in the text to find a new research idea.

## CONVERTING AN IDEA INTO A RESEARCH HYPOTHESIS

Typically, a research idea involves a general statement about the relationship between two variables. For example:

- If people use visual images while studying new material, it will improve their memory for the material. (Memory is related to using images.)
- Although providing motivation to people generally improves their performance, too much motivation may create stress and actually lower performance. (Performance is related to motivation.)

To evaluate these ideas in an empirical research study, the idea must be transformed into a specific, concrete research hypothesis that can be tested by direct observation (see Chapter 1, Step 2 of the research process). This transformation usually involves specifying how each of the individual variables will be measured and what individuals will be needed to participate in the study (men, women, children, laboratory rats). Selecting participants and measuring variables are discussed in the following chapters, but for now we provide a brief example of what we mean by a specific, concrete hypothesis.

The first of the two research ideas we have proposed states that memory is related to using visual images. Although this idea could be examined with nearly any group of human beings, it is probably most convenient to use college students as participants in the study. Similarly, the concept of memory can be defined in a variety of different ways, but for this study we choose to measure the number of words correctly recalled from a list of 40 nouns that each participant studies for a period of exactly 2 minutes. Finally, we can define the idea of "using imagery" as "forming a mental image of the object represented by a word." (For example, forming a mental image of a horse when you see the word *horse*.) With these definitions in place, our research hypothesis becomes:

> College students who are instructed to form mental images while studying a list of 40 words for 2 minutes will recall more words (on average) than college students who study the same words for 2 minutes but are not given instructions to form mental images.

Notice that the research hypothesis provides a very specific procedure for testing the research idea. Also note that the same research idea (that memory is related to using images) could produce a variety of different research hypotheses. For example, we could have tested 10-year-old children instead of college students; we could have used a set of 20 items (instead of 40); and we could have manipulated the visual image variable by showing one group a series of words presented on a screen and another group a series of pictures of the same items. The research hypothesis then becomes:

> Ten-year-old children who view pictures of 20 items (for example, a table, a horse, a tree) will recall more items, on average, than 10-year-old children who view a series of words representing the same 20 items (for example, TABLE, HORSE, TREE).

In general, there are many different ways to convert a research idea into a specific research hypothesis. The method you select depends on a variety of factors, including the set of individuals you want to study and the measurement techniques that are available. However, each of the many possible hypotheses should provide a direct test of the basic research idea.

Explain the basic difference between a research idea and a specific research hypothesis.

Learning Check

---

## CHAPTER SUMMARY

Beginning the research process can seem intimidating, but keeping a few points in mind will make the task a little easier. First, pick a topic in which you have some real personal interest to help yourself stay motivated throughout the research process. Second, do your homework on your topic; collect and familiarize yourself with the background information in your area. Third, keep an open mind in settling on a research idea; let your background reading lead you to a specific idea. Fourth, after doing the background reading, focus very specifically on one research question. Finally, break down the planning and conducting of your research into manageable steps, and take them one at a time.

All research begins with an idea, and fortunately there are many places from which ideas can come. Feel free to get ideas for research from your own personal interests, your own casual observations, practical problems, flashes of inspiration, and reports of others' observations and behavioral theories. However you obtain your initial research ideas, be wary of making these common mistakes: choosing a topic that doesn't interest you; picking a topic that is too easy or too difficult; picking a topic that is too broad; sticking with the first idea that comes to mind; choosing a topic for which there is inadequate literature.

Once you settle on a general idea, become familiar with the current research in that area. To find research journal articles, we recommend PsycINFO or PsycLIT because each of these databases provides extensive coverage of psychology literature. Based on their titles and abstracts, discard articles that are not directly relevant. As you read selected articles, you will "find" a new research idea. Finally, convert your research idea into a specific research hypothesis.

## KEY WORDS

primary source
secondary source

##  EXERCISES

1. In addition to the key words, you should be able to define each of the following terms:

   | | |
   |---|---|
   | literature search | PsycLIT |
   | key word | introduction |
   | *Psychological Abstracts* | method section |
   | abstract | results section |
   | database | discussion section |
   | PsycINFO | reference section |

2. Make a list of five general topic areas that interest you. For each, identify the source of ideas you used to come up with that topic.

3. List five behaviors that you could observe in your day-to-day life. For each one, identify one or two variables that might influence the behavior. (For example, falling asleep in class is a behavior that might be influenced by caffeine consumption or amount of sleep the night before.)

4. Find a research article and make a copy of its introduction. In two or three sentences, write out the simple, logical argument for the proposed study.

5. Find the appropriate database at your library for searching the psychology literature. Get background information to determine what kinds of publications the database searches to obtain its references. How many periodicals are searched, and what other kinds of publications are considered? Does your database search the *Journal of Abnormal Psychology*? Does it search *Behavioral Neuroscience*?

6. Using the appropriate psychology database at your library, enter the key word *short-term memory* and see how many references you obtain. Now enter the combination of *short-term memory* and *imagery* as key words. By how much was the number of references reduced with this combination of key words?

7. Using PsycINFO (or a similar database), find five articles on the topic of depression in young children. Print out a copy of the Record List page.

8. Using PsycINFO (or a similar database), find research articles on binge drinking in college students. Print out the Detailed Record (including the abstract) for one research article on this topic.

9. From a research article's discussion section, find a suggestion for a research idea. Make a copy of the discussion section, and highlight the suggestion.

InfoTrac COLLEGE EDITION EXERCISES

The following exercises are intended to introduce you to InfoTrac College Edition, the online library that is available with this text. InfoTrac College Edition gives you access to thousands of articles covering hundreds of topics. To start, simply log on to *www.infotrac-college.com* and enter the pass code that came with your book.

1. Begin by retrieving an article on the subject of personality. As you work through the following steps, keep an eye on the InfoTrac College Edition banner across the top of the page. This banner is always available to offer you options for returning to the previous step in your search or starting a completely new search.

   a. Type *personality* in the box, and then click on Search. You should find a long list of topics related to the subject of personality, including items such as *personality and academic achievement* and *personality and cognition.*

   b. Under each bold heading, you have a variety of options, including different types of publications. Usually we focus on the *periodicals*, which typically present the most recently available reports of individual research studies. (Later we look at the information available under *subdivisions* and *related subjects*.) For now, simply go to the topic of personality, and click on the periodicals.

   c. At this point, you should see a long list of individual publications with title, author(s), journal, date of publication, and so on. At the end of each item, there is a *link* to the actual text of the publication (usually "text with graphics and full content retrieval choices"). Select a title that sounds interesting to you, and click on Text Link.

   d. By now you should be looking at the actual article. In addition to reading the entire publication, you can also select Electronic Delivery or Link. Try each of these options, and in a few sentences describe what each one does. (Remember, you can always go back to the previous step in your search using the options shown in the banner at the top of the page.)

2. Start a new search, again using the subject of personality. Under the general topic personality, you should find 50 to 100 periodical references. In Exercise 1, you simply clicked on periodicals and started reading through the entire list. This time, click on Subdivisions. In a few sentences, describe the purpose of the Subdivisions option.

3. Once again, start a new search using the subject of personality. This time, click on the Related Subjects option under the general category personality. Describe the purpose of the Related Subjects option.

# Ethics in Research

## CHAPTER OVERVIEW

Consideration of ethical issues is integral to the research process. Researchers have two basic categories of ethical responsibility: (1) responsibility to the individuals both human and nonhuman who participate in their research studies, and (2) responsibility to the discipline of science, to be accurate and honest in the reporting of their research. We discuss each of these ethical issues in this chapter.

## 3.1    INTRODUCTION

### ETHICAL CONCERNS THROUGHOUT THE RESEARCH PROCESS

After you have identified a new idea for research and developed a testable hypothesis, you may think, "Great! Now I'm really ready to begin research." We hope you are beginning to feel the excitement of starting a research project; however, we must now consider the fact that the research process includes an element of serious responsibility.

> Caution! Research ethics are not an issue of morality; they concern the proper conduct of researchers. Researchers have observed their own conduct and reached a consensus regarding acceptable conduct for all researchers.

Up to this point your research project has been entirely private and personal. You have been working on your own, in the library and on the Web, gathering information and formulating an idea for a research study. Now, however, you have reached the stage where other individuals will become involved with your research—first the participants whose behaviors and responses you observe and measure during the course of the study, and then the people who will see (and perhaps be influenced by) your report of your study's results. All these individuals have a right to expect honesty and respect from you, and, as you proceed through the following stages of the research process, you must accept the responsibility to behave ethically toward those who will be affected by your research. In general, **ethics** is the study of proper action (Ray, 2000). This chapter is devoted to the subject of **research ethics,** in particular.

Definition

**Research ethics** concern the responsibility of researchers to be honest and respectful to all individuals who may be affected by their research studies or their reports of the studies' results. Researchers are usually governed by a set of ethical guidelines that assist them to make proper decisions and choose proper actions. In psychological research, the American Psychological Association maintains a set of ethical principles for research (APA, 1992).

Consider the following examples:

- Suppose that, as a topic for a research study, you are interested in brain injury that may result from repeated blows to the head, such as those suffered by boxers and soccer players. For obvious ethical reasons (physical harm), you could not plan a study that involved injuring people's brains in order to examine the effects. However, you could compare two pre-existing groups; for example, a group of soccer players, who are regularly hit on the head with soccer balls, and a group of swimmers, who are also athletes but are not routinely hit in the head. [See Downs & Abwender (2002) for a sample study.]
- Suppose that you are interested in sexual behavior as a research topic. For obvious ethical reasons (privacy), you cannot secretly install video cameras in people's bedrooms. However, you could ask people to complete a questionnaire about their sexual behavior. [See Page, Hammermeister, & Scanlan (2000) for a sample study.]

In research, ethical issues must be considered at each step in the research process. Ethical principles dictate (1) what measurement techniques may be used for certain individuals and certain behaviors, (2) how researchers select individuals to participate in studies, (3) which research strategies may be used with certain populations and behaviors, (4) which research designs may be used with certain populations and behaviors, (5) how studies may be carried out with individuals, (6) how data are analyzed, and finally (7) how results are reported. The issue of ethics is an overriding one and must be kept in mind at each step of the research process when you make decisions. Scientists' exploration is bounded by ethical constraints.

## THE BASIC CATEGORIES OF ETHICAL RESPONSIBILITY

Researchers have two basic categories of ethical responsibility: (1) responsibility to the individuals both human and nonhuman who participate in their research studies, and (2) responsibility to the discipline of science, to be accurate and honest in the reporting of their research.

Any research involving humans or nonhumans immediately introduces questions of ethics. The research situation automatically places the scientist in a position of control over the individuals participating in the study. However, the researcher has no right to abuse this power or to harm the participants—physically, emotionally, or psychologically. On the contrary, the relative power of the researcher versus the participant means that the researcher has a responsibility to ensure the safety and dignity of the participants. To assist the researcher in this responsibility, committees such as the Institutional Review Board (IRB) and the Institutional Animal Care and Use Committee (IACUC) examine all proposed research with respect to treatment of humans and nonhumans in research. Safeguarding humans and nonhumans in research is discussed in detail in Sections 3.2 and 3.3.

Reporting of research also introduces questions of ethics. It is assumed that reports of research are accurate and honest depictions of the procedures used and results obtained in a research study. As we discussed in Chapter 1, the scientific method is intended to be a valid method of inquiry. Its goal is to obtain answers in which we are confident. Any reporting decision that jeopardizes this confidence is an ethical issue. Two of these issues, fraud and plagiarism, are discussed in Section 3.4.

## 3.2    ETHICAL ISSUES AND HUMAN PARTICIPANTS IN RESEARCH

### HISTORICAL HIGHLIGHTS OF TREATMENT OF HUMAN PARTICIPANTS

Until the end of World War II, researchers established their own ethical standards and safeguards for human participants in their research. It was assumed that researchers, bounded by their own moral compasses, would protect their participants from harm. However, not all researchers were committed to the ethical treatment of human participants. The major impetus for a shift from individualized ethics to more formalized ethical guidelines was the uncovering of the brutal experiments performed on prisoners in Nazi concentration camps. A variety of sadistic "medical experiments" were conducted on unwilling participants. Some examples include breaking and rebreaking of bones (to see how many times they could be broken before healing failed to occur) and exposure to extremes of high altitude and freezing water (to see how long a person could survive). When these and other atrocities came to light, some of those responsible were tried for their crimes at Nuremberg in 1947. Out of these trials came the **Nuremberg Code,** a set of 10 guidelines for the ethical treatment of human participants in research. It is reprinted here as Table 3.1 (Katz, 1972). The

TABLE 3.1

### Ten Points of the Nuremberg Code

1.  The voluntary consent of the human subject is absolutely essential.

    This means that the person involved should have legal capacity to give consent; should be so situated as to be able to exercise free power of choice, without the intervention of any element of force, fraud, deceit, duress, over-reaching, or other ulterior form of constraint or coercion; and should have sufficient knowledge and comprehension of the elements of the subject matter involved as to enable him to make an understanding and enlightened decision. This latter element requires that before the acceptance of an affirmative decision by the experimental subject there should be known to him the nature, duration, and purpose of the experiment; the method and means by which it is to be conducted; all inconveniences and hazards reasonably to be expected; and the effects upon his health or person which may possibly come from his participation in the experiment.

    The duty and responsibility for ascertaining the quality of the consent rests upon each individual who initiates, directs, or engages in the experiment. It is a personal duty and responsibility which may not be delegated to another with impunity.

2.  The experiment should be such as to yield fruitful results for the good of society, unprocurable by other methods or means of study, and not random and unnecessary in nature.

3.  The experiment should be so designed and based on the results of animal experimentation and a knowledge of the natural history of the disease or other problem under study that the anticipated results will justify the performance of the experiment.

4.  The experiment should be so conducted as to avoid all unnecessary physical and mental suffering and injury.

5.  No experiment should be conducted where there is an *a priori* reason to believe that death or disabling injury will occur; except, perhaps, in those experiments where the experimental physicians also serve as subjects.

6.  The degree of risk to be taken should never exceed that determined by the humanitarian importance of the problem to be solved by the experiment.

7.  Proper preparations should be made and adequate facilities provided to protect the experimental subject against even remote possibilities of injury, disability, or death.

8.  The experiment should be conducted only by scientifically qualified persons. The highest degree of skill and care should be required through all stages of the experiment of those who conduct or engage in the experiment.

9.  During the course of the experiment the human subject should be at liberty to bring the experiment to an end if he has reached the physical or mental state where continuation of the experiment seems to him to be impossible.

10. During the course of the experiment the scientist in charge must be prepared to terminate the experiment at any stage, if he has probable cause to believe, in the exercise of the good faith, superior skill, and careful judgment required of him that a continuation of the experiment is likely to result in injury, disability, or death to the experimental subject.

Nuremberg Code laid the groundwork for the ethical standards that are in place today for both psychological and medical research.

Tragically, even after the development of the Nuremberg Code, researchers have not always ensured the safety and dignity of human participants. Since the late 1940s there have been additional examples of maltreatment of human participants in biomedical research. In 1963, for example, it was revealed that unsuspecting patients had been injected with live cancer cells (Katz, 1972), and in 1972 a newspaper report exposed a Public Health Service study in which nearly 400 men had been left to suffer with syphilis long after a cure (penicillin) was available, just so that researchers could examine the final stages of the disease (Jones, 1981).

Similar examples of the questionable treatment of human participants have been found in behavioral research. The most commonly cited example is the Milgram obedience study (Milgram, 1963). Milgram instructed participants to use electric shocks to punish other individuals when they made errors during a learning task. The intensity of the shocks was gradually increased until the participants were administering what appeared to be dangerously strong and obviously painful shocks. In fact, no shocks were used in the study (the "shocked" individuals were pretending); however, the participants (those who administered the shocks) *believed* that they were inflicting real pain and suffering. Although the participants in Milgram's study sustained no physical harm, they suffered shame and embarrassment for having behaved inhumanely toward their fellow human beings. The participants entered the study thinking that they were normal, considerate human beings, but they left with the knowledge that they could all too easily behave inhumanely.

It is important to note two things about these cases. First, they constitute a very small sample; unfortunately, many examples of questionable treatment exist in research. Second, although cases like these make up a small percentage of all the research that is conducted, it is events like these that shaped the guidelines we have in place today. In the late 1960s the Surgeon General required all institutions receiving federal funding for research from the Public Health Service to review proposed research in order to safeguard human participants. In the mid 1970s, due to the growing concern about research ethics, the Department of Health, Education, and Welfare created a commission to recommend guidelines for safeguarding the rights and safety of research participants. In 1978 the National Commission issued the Belmont Report, a document that detailed criteria for all institutional review board practices and that is still used today.

## AMERICAN PSYCHOLOGICAL ASSOCIATION (APA) GUIDELINES

### Ethical Guidelines for the Use and Treatment of Human Participants in Research

Around the same time that the federal government began to concern itself with protecting human participants in research, the American Psychological Association (APA) prepared its first set of now widely distributed and accepted guidelines (1972). The first APA committee on ethics was set up in 1952; however, it was not until the mid 1960s, in response to major criticisms of Milgram's now famous obedience study, that APA members began to discuss widely a formal code of ethics.

You may have noticed the term "guidelines." Because it is impossible to anticipate every specific research situation, the guidelines are intended to identify general areas in which researchers should be cautious and aware of ethical concerns. The APA guidelines have been updated and expanded several times since they were first developed and are periodically revised. The most recent version was published in 1992. The **APA Ethics Code** contains eight ethical standards, and you should be completely familiar with all of them before beginning any research with human participants. (You can visit APA.org on the Web for more information, or you can go directly to *http://www.apa.org/ethics/code.html* for the complete Ethics Code). According to APA (1992), "The Ethics Code provides a common set of values upon which psychologists build their professional and scientific work. This Code is intended to provide both the general principles and the decision rules to cover most situations encountered by psychologists. It has as its primary goal the welfare and protection of the individuals and groups with whom the psychologists work."

A summary of the most recent ethical guidelines concerning human participants in research (APA, 1992) is presented in Table 3.2. This summary is based on the APA "Ethical Principles of Psychologists and Code of Conduct" (APA, 1992) and includes the elements most relevant to the use and treatment of human participants in research. Table 3.2 is a summary of those sections (parts of Standards 1, 5, and 6) relevant to human participants in research. The APA guidelines are continually reviewed and revised—as are federal, state, and local regulations—so researchers always must check to make sure they are abiding by the current rules.

> The 1992 guidelines were revised, and can be found at http://www.apa.org/ethics.

### Major Ethical Issues

Rather than discussing each of the guidelines point by point, we present in detail a few issues that are the most important for new researchers.

**No Harm (Item 1, Table 3.2)**    The researcher is obligated to protect participants from physical or psychological harm. The entire research experience should be evaluated to identify risks of harm, and when possible such risks should be removed from the study. Any risk of harm must be justified. The justification may be that the scientific benefits of the study far outweigh the small, temporary harm that can result. Or it may be that greater harm is likely to occur unless some minor risk is accepted during the study. (Doctors and their patients face this concern when deciding whether to use a medication that has known side effects.) In any event, participants must be informed of any potential risks, and the researcher must take steps to minimize any harm that can occur. In the behavioral sciences, the risk of physical harm is relatively rare (except in areas where psychology and medicine overlap). Psychological harm, on the other hand, is a common concern. During or after a study, participants may feel increased anxiety, anger, lower self-esteem, or mild depression, especially in situations where they feel that they have been cheated, tricked, deceived, or insulted. Occasionally researchers deliberately create these situations as an integral part of the study; for example, participants may be given an impossible task so the researcher can observe responses to failure. (Note that Item 8 in Table 3.2 allows concealment and deception.) Often

TABLE 3.2

## Summary of the APA Ethical Guidelines Concerning Human Participants in Research

This summary is based on the APA *Ethical Principles of Psychologists and Code of Conduct* (APA, 1992 in revision for Fall 2002) and includes the elements most relevant to the use and treatment of human participants in research. The section numbers correspond to the standards referred to in the APA *Ethical Principles of Psychologists and Code of Conduct*.

1. **No harm (Section 1.14)**
   Psychologists take reasonable steps to avoid harming their research participants and to minimize harm where it is foreseeable and unavoidable.

2. **Maintaining Confidentiality (Sections 5.02–5.05)**
   Psychologists have a primary obligation for and take reasonable precautions to respect the confidentiality rights of those with whom they work.
   Psychologists discuss confidential information only for appropriate scientific or professional purposes and only with persons clearly concerned with such matters.
   Psychologists maintain appropriate confidentiality in creating, storing, accessing, transferring, and disposing of records under their control, whether these are written, automated, or in any other medium.
   Psychologists disclose confidential information only with the consent of the individual or as mandated by law, or where permitted by law for a valid purpose.

3. **Planning Research (Section 6.06)**
   Psychologists design, conduct, and report research in accordance with recognized standards of scientific competence and ethical research.
   Psychologists plan their research so as to minimize the possibility that results will be misleading.
   In planning research, psychologists consider its ethical acceptability under the Ethics Code. If an ethical issue is unclear, psychologists seek to resolve the issue through consultation with institutional review boards, animal care and use committees, peer consultations, or other proper mechanisms.
   Psychologists take reasonable steps to implement appropriate protections for the rights and welfare of human participants, other persons affected by the research, and the welfare of animal subjects.

4. **Responsibility (Sections 1.04 and 6.07)**
   Psychologists conduct research competently and with due concern for the dignity and welfare of the participants.
   Psychologists are responsible for the ethical conduct of research conducted by them or by others under their supervision or control.
   Psychologists conduct research only within the boundaries of their competence.
   Researchers and assistants are permitted to perform only those tasks for which they are appropriately trained and prepared.

5. **Compliance With Law and Standards (Section 6.08)**
   Psychologists plan and conduct research in a manner consistent with federal and state law and regulations as well as professional standards governing the conduct of research, and particularly those standards governing research with human participants and animal subjects.

6. **Informed Consent to Research (Sections 6.11–6.13)**
   Psychologists use language that is reasonably understandable to research participants in obtaining their appropriate informed consent (except as provided under guidelines concerning Dispensing with Informed Consent). Such informed consent is appropriately documented. Psychologists inform participants
   a. of the nature of the research
   b. that they are free to participate, to decline to participate, or to withdraw from the research
   c. of the foreseeable consequences of declining or withdrawing

TABLE 3.2

**Summary of the APA Ethical Guidelines Concerning Human Participants in Research (cont.)**

    d. of significant factors that may be expected to influence their willingness to participate (such as risks, discomfort, adverse effects, or limitations on confidentiality, except as provided under guidelines concerning Deception in Research)

    e. of other aspects about which the prospective participants inquire

When psychologists conduct research with individuals such as students or subordinates, psychologists take special care to protect the prospective participants from adverse consequences of declining or withdrawing from participation.

When research participation is a course requirement or opportunity for extra credit, the prospective participant is given the choice of equitable alternative activities.

For persons who are legally incapable of giving informed consent, psychologists nevertheless (1) provide an appropriate explanation, (2) obtain the participant's consent, and (3) obtain appropriate permission from a legally authorized person, if law permits such substitute consent.

Some planned research (such as that involving only anonymous questionnaires, naturalistic observations, or certain kinds of archival research) may not require the informed consent of research participants. Before determining that informed consent is not required, psychologists should consider applicable regulations and institutional review board requirements, and they should consult with colleagues as appropriate.

Psychologists obtain informed consent from research participants prior to filming or recording them in any form, unless the research involves simply naturalistic observations in public places and it is not anticipated that the recording will be used in a manner that could cause personal identification or harm.

7. **Offering Inducements for Research Participants (Section 6.14)**

Psychologists do not offer excessive or inappropriate financial or other inducements to obtain research participants, particularly when it might tend to coerce participation.

8. **Deception in Research (Section 6.15)**

Psychologists do not conduct a study involving deception unless they have determined that the use of deceptive techniques is justified by the study's prospective scientific, educational, or applied value and that equally effective alternative procedures that do not use deception are not feasible.

Psychologists never deceive research participants about significant aspects that would affect their willingness to participate, such as physical risks, discomfort or unpleasant emotional experiences.

Any other deception that is an integral feature of the design and conduct of an experiment must be explained to participants as early as is feasible, preferably at the conclusion of their participation but no later than the conclusion of the research. (See also Standard 6.18, Providing Participants With Information About the Study.)

9. **Minimizing Invasiveness (Section 6.17)**

In conducting research, psychologists interfere with the participants or milieu from which data are collected only in a manner that is warranted by an appropriate research design and that is consistent with psychologists' roles as scientific investigators.

10. **Providing Participants With Information (Sections 6.18–6.19)**

Psychologists provide a prompt opportunity for participants to obtain appropriate information about the nature, results, and conclusions of the research, and psychologists attempt to correct any misconceptions that participants may have.

If scientific or humane values justify delaying or withholding this information, psychologists take reasonable measures to reduce the risk of harm.

Psychologists take reasonable measures to honor all commitments they have made to research participants.

participants generate their own mental distress from imaginative speculation about the purpose of the research. In either case, researchers should reassure participants by explaining before the study exactly what will be done and why (insofar as possible) and by providing a complete explanation and justification for the research as soon as possible after the study is completed. The goal is for participants to leave the study feeling just as well as when they entered. (Deception and how to deal with it are covered in more detail in a later section.)

A researcher is obligated to anticipate and remove any harmful elements in a research study. During the study, a researcher also must monitor the well-being of the participants and halt the study at any sign of trouble.

Learning Check

When is risk in a study justified?

**Informed Consent (Item 6, Table 3.2)**    The general concept of **informed consent** is that human participants should be given complete information about the research and their roles in it. They should understand the information and then voluntarily decide whether or not to participate. This ideal is often difficult to achieve. Here we consider three components of informed consent and examine the problems that can exist with each.

1.  *Information:* Often it is difficult or impossible to provide participants with complete information about a research study prior to their participation. One common practice is to keep participants "blind" to the purpose of the study. If participants know that one treatment is supposed to produce better performance, they may adjust their own levels of performance in an attempt to satisfy the experimenter. To avoid this problem, researchers often tell participants exactly *what* will be done in the study but not *why*.

    In situations where the study relies on deception, disguised measurement, concealed observation, and so on, informing the participants would undermine the goals of the research. In clinical research, the outcome of an experimental therapy (risks and benefits) may not be known. In this case a researcher might be able to tell the participant what will be done but not what will happen.

2.  *Understanding:* Simply telling participants about the research does not necessarily mean they are informed, especially in situations where the participants may not be competent to understand. This problem occurs routinely with special populations such as young children, mentally retarded people, and psychiatric patients. In these situations it is customary to provide information not only to the participant but also to a parent or guardian who also must consent to the participant's participation. Even with regular populations there may be some question about true understanding. Researchers must express their explanations in terms that the participants can easily understand and should give the participants ample opportunity to ask questions.

3.  *Voluntary Participation:* The goal of informed consent is that participants decide to participate of their own free will. Often, however, participants

may feel coerced to participate or may perceive that they have limited choice. For example, a researcher who is a teacher, professor, or clinician may be in a position of power or control over the potential participants, who may perceive a threat of retribution if they do not cooperate. Suppose, for example, that your professor asked for volunteers from the class to help with a research project. Would you feel a little extra pressure to volunteer just to keep on good terms with him or her? This problem is particularly important with institutionalized populations (prisoners, hospital patients, and so on) who must depend on others in nearly every aspect of their lives. In these cases it is especially important that the researcher explain that the participant is completely free to decline participation or to leave the study at any time without negative consequences.

---

The principle of **informed consent** requires the investigator to provide all available information about a study so that an individual can make a rational, informed decision to participate in the study.

*Definition*

---

The procedure for obtaining informed consent varies from study to study, depending in part on the complexity of the information presented and the actual degree of risk involved in the study. In most situations, researchers use a written **consent form.** A consent form contains a statement of all the elements of informed consent and a line for the participant's signature. The form is provided prior to the study so the potential participants have all the information they need in order to make an informed decision regarding participation. Consent forms vary according to the specifics of the study but typically contain some common elements. Table 3.3 lists the common components of consent forms (Kazdin, 1998).

Although consent forms are very commonly used, in some situations involving minimal risk it is possible to obtain verbal consent without a written consent form. And in some situations (such as the administration of anonymous questionnaires) it is permissible to dispense with informed consent entirely.

---

Explain the role of voluntary participation in informed consent.

*Learning Check*

---

**Deception (Item 8, Table 3.2)**    Often the goal of a research study is to examine behavior under "normal" circumstances. To achieve this goal, researchers must sometimes use **deception.** For example, if participants know the true purpose of a research study, they may modify their natural behaviors to conceal embarrassing secrets or to appear to be better than they really are. To avoid this problem, researchers sometimes will not tell participants the true purpose of the study. One technique is to use **passive deception** and simply withhold information about the study. Another possibility is to use **active deception** and deliberately mislead the participants to think that the study has a particular purpose when, in fact, the real purpose is completely different.

In a classic study of human memory, for example, Craik and Lockhart (1972) presented words one at a time and asked participants to respond to the words in different ways. Some participants were asked to decide whether the word was

TABLE 3.3

## Components of Informed Consent Forms

| Section of the Form | Purpose and Contents |
|---|---|
| Overview | Presentation of the goals of the study, why this is conducted, who is responsible for the study and its execution. |
| Description of Procedures | Clarification of the experimental conditions, assessment procedures, requirements of the participants. |
| Risks and Inconveniences | Statement of any physical and psychological risks and an estimate of their likelihood. Inconveniences and demands to be placed on the participants (e.g., how many sessions, requests to do anything, contact at home). |
| Benefits | A statement of what the participants can reasonably hope to gain from participation, including psychological, physical, and monetary benefits. |
| Costs and Economic Considerations | Charges to the participants (e.g., in treatment) and payment (e.g., for participation or completing various forms). |
| Confidentiality | Assurances that the information is confidential and will only be seen by people who need to do so for the purposes of research (e.g., scoring and data analyses), procedures to assure confidentiality (e.g., removal of names from forms, storage of data). Also, caveats are included here if it is possible that sensitive information (e.g., psychiatric information, criminal activity) can be subpoenaed. |
| Alternative Treatments | In an intervention study, alternatives available to the client before or during participation are outlined. |
| Voluntary Participation | A statement that the participant is willing to participate and can say no now or later without penalty of any kind. |
| Questions and Further Information | A statement that the participant is encouraged to ask questions at any time and can contact one or more individuals (listed by name and phone number) who are available for such contacts. |
| Signature Lines | A place for the participant as well as the experimenter to sign. |

*Source:* From Kazdin, A. E., *Research Design in Clinical Psychology.* Copyright © 1998 by Allyn & Bacon. Reprinted by permission.

printed in uppercase letters or lowercase letters. Others were asked to make judgments about the meaning of each word. After responding to a large number of words, the participants were given a surprise memory test and asked to recall as many of the words as possible. None of the participants was informed that the true purpose of the study was to test memory. In this case, the deception was necessary to prevent the participants from trying to memorize the words as they were presented.

---

**Deception** occurs when a researcher purposefully withholds information or misleads participants with regard to information about a study. There are two forms of deception, active and passive.

**Passive deception** (or omission) is the withholding or omitting of information; the researcher intentionally does not tell participants some information about the study.

**Active deception** (or commission) is the presenting of misinformation about the study to participants. The most common form of active deception is misleading participants about the specific purpose of the study.

---

In any study involving deception, it is not possible for participants to give informed consent. In these situations, a researcher has a special responsibility to safeguard the participants. The APA guidelines identify three specific areas of responsibility (see Item 8 in Table 3.2):

1. The deception must be justified in terms of some benefit that outweighs the risk to the participants. The researcher must consider all alternatives to deception and must justify the rejection of any alternative procedures.
2. The researcher cannot conceal from the participants any significant aspects of the study, such as physical risk, that would affect their willingness to participate.
3. The researcher must debrief the participants by providing a complete explanation as soon as possible after participation is completed.

The first point, justification of the deception, obviously involves weighing the benefits of the study against the rights of the individual participants. Usually the final decision is not left entirely to the researcher but requires review and approval by a group of individuals charged with the responsibility of ensuring ethical conduct in all human research (for example, the IRB, which is discussed shortly). This review group may also suggest alternative procedures not requiring deception, and the researcher must consider and respond to their suggestions. (The review process is also discussed shortly.)

The second point is that researchers definitely cannot use deception to withhold information about risk or possible harm. Suppose, for example, that a researcher wants to examine the influence of increased anxiety on performance. To increase anxiety, the researcher informs one group of participants that they may receive relatively mild shocks occasionally during the course of the study. No shocks are actually given, so the researcher is deceiving the participants; however, this type of deception involves no harm or risk and probably would be considered acceptable. On the other hand, suppose that the researcher wants to examine how performance is influenced by sudden, unexpected episodes of pain. To create these episodes, the researcher occasionally administers mild shocks during the study without warning the participants. To ensure that the shocks are unexpected, the informed consent process does not include any mention of shocks. In this case, the researcher is withholding information about a potential risk, and this type of deception is not allowed.

The final point is that deceived participants must receive a **debriefing** that provides a full description of the true nature of the experiment, including the use and purpose of deception, after the study is completed. The debriefing serves many purposes, including:

- conveying what the study was really all about, if deception was used
- counteracting or minimizing any negative effects of the study
- conveying the educational objective of the research (i.e., explaining the value of the research and the contribution to science of participation in the research)
- explaining the nature of and justification for any deception used
- answering any questions the participant has

---

Definition
| A **debriefing** is a post-experimental explanation of the purpose of a study that is given to a participant, especially if deception was used.

---

Overall, the intent of debriefing is to counteract or minimize harmful effects. Unfortunately, evidence suggests that debriefing may not always achieve its purpose. Although some studies show that debriefing can effectively remove harm and leave no lingering effects (Holmes, 1976a, 1976b; Smith & Richardson, 1983), other studies indicate that debriefing is not effective, is not believed, and may result in increased suspicion (Fisher & Fyrberg, 1994; Ring, Wallston, & Corey, 1970). Most of this work is based on studies in which participants were interviewed immediately after being debriefed. However, some researchers believe that participants may not truthfully reveal their reactions to debriefing, especially when the debriefing informs them of previous deception (Baumrind, 1985; Rubin, 1985). Finally, there is some evidence that debriefing only further annoys or embarrasses participants (Fisher & Fyrberg, 1994)—not only were they deceived during the study, but now the researcher is forcing them to face the fact. Still, the participants deserve a full and complete explanation, and the researcher has an obligation to safeguard participants as much as possible. Some things that seem to influence a debriefing's effectiveness include:

- the participants' suspicions (how likely they are to think the debriefing is merely a continuation of the deception)
- the nature of the deception (whether it was passive or active; debriefing is less effective with active deception)
- the sincerity of the experimenter (the last thing a participant needs is a condescending experimenter)
- the time interval between the end of the study and the delivery of the debriefing (the sooner the better)

In some situations the research design permits a researcher to inform participants that deception may be involved and to ask the participants for consent to be deceived. Drug research, for example, often involves comparison of one group of participants who receive the drug and a second group of participants who are given a **placebo** (an ineffective, inert substitute). At the beginning of the experiment, all participants are informed that a placebo group exists, but no one knows whether they are in the drug group or the placebo group. Thus, before they consent to participate, participants are informed that they may be deceived. This kind of prior disclosure helps to minimize the negative effects of deception—participants are less likely to become angry or feel tricked or abused. On the other hand, when participants know that deception is involved, they are likely to become more defensive and suspicious of all aspects of the research. In addition, participants may adopt unusual responses or behaviors that can undermine the goals of the research. For example, in some studies that examined the effectiveness of experimental AIDS medications, groups of participants conspired to divide and share their medication, assuming that this strategy would ensure that everyone got at least some of the real drug (Melton, Levine, Koocher, Rosenthal, & Thompson, 1988).

Deception can also cause participants to become skeptical of experiments in general. Having been deceived, a person may refuse to participate in any future research or may enter future studies with a defensive or hostile attitude. Deceived participants may share their negative attitudes and opinions with their friends, and thus one deception experiment may contaminate an entire pool of potential research participants.

Explain the difference between passive and active deception.

What factors can influence the effectiveness of a debriefing?

Learning
Checks

**Confidentiality (Item 2, Table 3.2)**    The essence of research in the behavioral sciences is collection of information by researchers from the individuals who participate in their studies. Although the specific information can vary tremendously from one study to another, the different types of information can be categorized as follows:

- Attitudes and opinions; for example, politics and prejudices
- Measures of performance; for example, manual dexterity, reaction time, and memory
- Demographic characteristics; for example, age, income, and sexual orientation

Any of these items can be considered private and personal by some people, and it is reasonable that some participants would not want this information to be made public. Therefore, the APA ethical guidelines require that researchers ensure the confidentiality of their research participants (see Item 2 in Table 3.2). **Confidentiality** assures that the information obtained from a research participant will be kept secret and private. The enforcement of confidentiality benefits both the participants and the researcher. First, participants are protected from embarrassment or emotional stress that could result from public exposure. Also, researchers are more likely to obtain willing and honest participants. Most individuals demand an assurance of confidentiality before they are willing to disclose personal and private information.

Although there are different techniques for preserving confidentiality, the basic process involves ensuring that participants' records are kept **anonymous.** That is, the information and measurements obtained from each participant are not referred to by the participant's name either during the course of the study or in the written report of the research results.

---

**Definitions**

**Confidentiality** is the practice of keeping strictly secret and private the information or measurements obtained from an individual during a research study.

**Anonymity** is the practice of ensuring that an individual's name is not directly associated with the information or measurements obtained from that individual.

---

Instead of using his or her name, each participant is typically assigned a code number or code name, and the code is the only reference used for any individual participant. To ensure the confidentiality of the data, researchers typically avoid any direct connection between the identity of a participant and the reference code that is used for that participant. Usually one of the following two strategies is used:

1. No names or other identification appear on data records. This strategy is used in situations where there is no need whatsoever to link an individual participant to the specific information that he or she provides. Often, a separate list of participants is kept so that they can receive promised payment or extra credit and so the researcher can contact them later if necessary. However, this list is completely separate from the data and is destroyed at the end of the study. There is no way that the researcher or anyone else can connect a specific set of responses to a specific participant.

2. Researchers use a coding system to keep track of which participant names go with which sets of data. This strategy is used in situations where it is necessary to reconnect specific names with specific data at different times during a research study. For example, a study may involve measuring the same participants at different times under different conditions. In this case, the researcher wants to examine how each participant changes over time. When a participant shows up for the third stage of the study, the researcher must be able to retrieve the same participant's responses from the first two stages. Only the code name or code number identifies the actual data, and the researcher keeps a separate, secured list to connect the participants with the codes. Thus, anyone who has access to the data has only the codes and cannot associate a specific participant with any specific data. The secured list is used only to retrieve previous data from a particular participant, and the list is destroyed at the conclusion of the study.

In most research reports, the results are presented as average values that have been collapsed across a large group of individual participants, and there is no mention of any individual participants or even code numbers or code names. In situations where a single participant is examined in great detail, researchers must take special care to preserve anonymity. In these situations, only the code name or code number is used to identify the participant, and any description of the participant is edited to eliminate unique characteristics that could lead to individual identification.

Learning Check

Explain how the enforcement of confidentiality benefits both the participants and the researcher.

## THE INSTITUTIONAL REVIEW BOARD (IRB)

Although the final responsibility for the protection of human participants rests with the researcher, most human-participant research must be reviewed and approved by a group of individuals not directly affiliated with the specific research study. As part of the guidelines for the protection of human participants, the U.S. Department of Health and Human Services (HHS) requires review of all human-participant research conducted by government agencies and institutions receiving government funds. This includes all colleges, universities, hospitals, and clinics—every place that human-participant research takes place.

The review is conducted by an **Institutional Review Board (IRB)** composed of both scientists and non-scientists. The IRB examines all proposed research with respect to seven basic criteria. If the IRB finds that a proposed research study fails to satisfy any one of the criteria, the research project will not be approved. In addition, the IRB can require a research proposal to be modified to meet its criteria before the research is approved. Following is a listing and brief discussion of the seven basic IRB criteria (Maloney, 1984).

1. *Minimization of Risk to Participants.* The purpose of this criterion is to ensure that research procedures do not unnecessarily expose participants to risk. In addition to evaluating the degree of risk in a proposed study, the IRB reviews the research to ensure that every precaution has been taken to minimize risk. This may involve requiring the researcher to justify any component of the research plan that involves risk, and the IRB may suggest or require alternative procedures.

2. *Reasonable Risk in Relation to Benefits.* The IRB is responsible for evaluating the potential risks to participants as well as the benefits that may result from the research. The benefits include immediate benefits to the participants as well as general benefits such as advanced knowledge.

3. *Equitable Selection.* The purpose of this criterion is to ensure that the participant selection process does not discriminate among individuals in the population and does not exploit vulnerable individuals. For example, a researcher recruiting volunteers from the general community can inadvertently exclude the Spanish-speaking population, if all the publicity soliciting participants is in English. The issue for the IRB is not to ensure a random sample (although this should benefit the researcher) but rather to ensure equal opportunity for all potential participants. The concern with vulnerability is that some individuals (children and mentally retarded, psychotic, or institutionalized people) might be easily tricked or coerced into "volunteering" without a complete understanding of their actions.

4. *Informed Consent.* The notion of informed consent is one of the basic elements of all ethical codes and is a primary concern for the IRB. The IRB carefully reviews and critiques the procedures used to obtain informed consent, making sure that the researcher provides complete information about all aspects of the research that might be of interest or concern to a potential participant. In addition, the IRB ensures that the information is presented in a form that participants can easily understand. For example, the information should be in everyday language and should be presented at a level appropriate for the specific participants (the presentation of information for college students would be different from the presentation for 6-year-old children). In addition, the IRB typically looks for a clear statement informing participants that they have the right to withdraw from the study at any time without penalty. The goal is to ensure that participants will receive complete information and will understand the information before they decide to participate in the research.

5. *Documentation of Informed Consent.* The IRB determines whether or not it is necessary to have a written consent form signed by the participant and the researcher.

6. *Data Monitoring.* During the course of the research study, the researcher should make provision for monitoring the data to determine whether any unexpected risks or harm have developed. In some research situations, the researcher should monitor the testing of each individual participant so the procedure can be interrupted or stopped at the first indication of developing harm or danger.

7. *Privacy and Confidentiality.* This criterion is intended to protect participants from the risk that information obtained during a research study could be released to outside individuals (parents, teachers, employers, peers) where it might have embarrassing or personally damaging consequences. The IRB examines all record keeping within the study: How are participants identified? How are data coded? Who has access to participant names and data? The goal is to guarantee basic rights of privacy and to ensure confidentiality for the participants.

To implement the criteria for approval of human-participant research, the IRB typically requires that researchers submit a written research proposal that addresses each of the seven criteria. Often the local IRB will have forms that a researcher must complete. Occasionally the written proposal is sufficient for the IRB to make a decision. However, if the proposed research includes any questionable elements (such as special populations, unusual equipment or procedures, deception, or concealment), the IRB will require that the researcher appear in person to discuss, explain, and answer questions about the research. During the discussion, the IRB members may become active participants in the development of the research plan, making suggestions or contributions that modify the research proposal. Throughout the process, the primary concern of the IRB is to ensure the protection of human participants.

The **Institutional Review Board (IRB)** is a committee that examines all proposed research with respect to its treatment of human participants.

Definition

Describe in your own words the criteria the IRB uses to evaluate proposed research.

Learning
Check

## 3.3   ETHICAL ISSUES AND NONHUMAN SUBJECTS IN RESEARCH

Thus far we've considered ethical issues involving human participants in research. However, much research is conducted with nonhumans—animals—as subjects, and here, too, many ethical issues must be considered.

For many people the first ethical question is whether nonhuman subjects should be used at all in behavioral research. However, nonhuman subjects have been a part of behavioral science research for more than 100 years and probably will continue to be used as research subjects for the foreseeable future. Researchers who use nonhumans as subjects do so for a variety of reasons, including: (1) to understand animals for their own sake; (2) to understand humans (for many processes can be generalized from nonhumans to humans); (3) to conduct research that is impossible to conduct using human participants. Two excellent articles that examine both sides of the animal rights issue appeared back to back in the 1993 *Journal of Social Issues* (Baldwin, 1993; Bowd & Shapiro, 1993). The animal research debate is also presented in a pair of articles in the February 1997 issue of *Scientific American* (Barnard & Kaufman, 1997; Botting & Morrison, 1997).

### HISTORICAL HIGHLIGHTS OF TREATMENT OF NONHUMAN SUBJECTS

To protect the welfare of nonhumans, various organizations have been formed, including the Society for the Prevention of Cruelty to Animals (SPCA), established in the United States in 1866 (Ray, 2000). More recent regulation of the use of nonhumans in research began in 1962 when the federal government first issued guidelines. In 1966, the Animal Welfare Act was enacted; it was most recently amended in 1990. The Animal Welfare Act deals with general standards for animal care. The Public Health Service issued in 1985 and revised in 1996 regulations entitled *U.S. Government Principles for the Utilization and Care of Vertebrate Animals Used in Testing, Research, and Training*. Several organizations, including the American Association for Laboratory Animal Science (AALAS) and the American Association for Accreditation of Laboratory Animal Care (AAALAC), encourage monitoring the care of laboratory animals by researchers.

Today, the federal government regulates the use of nonhuman subjects in research. It requires researchers using nonhuman subjects to follow (1) the guidelines of the local IACUC (the review board for animal research, similar to the IRB, to be discussed shortly); (2) the U.S. Department of Agriculture's guidelines; (3) guidelines of state agencies, and (4) established guidelines within the academic discipline (for example, the APA guidelines in psychology). The U.S. Department of Agriculture's requirements for use of nonhumans in research can be found in the *Guide for the Care and Use of Laboratory Animals* (National Research Council, 1966).

## AMERICAN PSYCHOLOGICAL ASSOCIATION (APA) GUIDELINES

### Ethical Guidelines for the Use and Treatment of Nonhuman Subjects in Research

The APA has prepared a set of ethical guidelines for the use and treatment of non-human subjects that parallels the guidelines for human participants presented earlier. Table 3.4 lists the basic standards of the APA Ethics Code for the care and use of animal subjects (APA, 1992). In addition, the APA's Committee on Animal Research and Ethics (CARE) has prepared even more detailed guidelines for researchers working with nonhuman subjects. This document, *Guidelines for Ethical Conduct in the Care and Use of Animals*, can be obtained from APA's Web site, http://www.apa.org.science/anguide.html. Anyone planning to conduct research with nonhuman subjects should carefully review and abide by these guidelines. As is the case for human participants, the APA guidelines—as well as federal, state, and local regulations—are continually reviewed and revised; researchers should always check to make sure they are abiding by the current rules.

### Major Ethical Issues

The list in Table 3.4 includes many of the same elements contained in the human participants code. In particular, animals must be treated humanely; qualified individuals must conduct research; the research must be justified; and the researcher has a responsibility to minimize discomfort or harm. Because most research animals are housed in a laboratory setting before and after their research experience, the code also extends to the general care and maintenance of animal subjects. In particular, the code refers to federal, state, and local regulations that govern housing conditions, food, sanitation, and medical care for research animals.

## THE INSTITUTIONAL ANIMAL CARE AND USE COMMITTEE (IACUC)

Institutions that conduct research with animals have an animal research review board called the **Institutional Animal Care and Use Committee (IACUC).** Like the IRB, the IACUC is responsible for reviewing and approving all research using animal subjects. The purpose of the board is to protect animal subjects by ensuring that all research meets the criteria established by the code of ethics. Researchers must submit proposals to the board and obtain approval before beginning any research with animal subjects. According to the *Guide for the Care and Use of Laboratory Animals* (National Research Council, 1996), the committee must consist of a veterinarian, at least one scientist experienced in research involving animals, and one member of the public with no affiliation with the institution where the research is being conducted.

Definition

The **Institutional Animal Care and Use Committee (IACUC)** is a committee that examines all proposed research with respect to its treatment of nonhuman subjects.

TABLE 3.4

## 1992 APA Ethical Principles for the Care and Use of Animals in Research

The following ethical standard is reprinted from the *Ethical Principles of Psychologists and Code of Conduct* (APA, 1992).

### 6.20   Care and Use of Animals in Research

a. Psychologists who conduct research involving animals treat them humanely.

b. Psychologists acquire, care for, use, and dispose of all animals in compliance with current federal, state, and local laws and regulations, and with professional standards.

c. Psychologists trained in research methods and experienced in the care of laboratory animals closely supervise all procedures involving animals and are responsible for ensuring appropriate consideration of their comfort, health, and humane treatment.

d. Psychologists ensure that all individuals using animals under their supervision have received explicit instruction in experimental methods and in the care, maintenance, and handling of the species being used, to the extent appropriate for their role.

e. Responsibilities and activities of individuals assisting in a research project are consistent with their respective competencies.

f. Psychologists make reasonable efforts to minimize discomfort, infection, illness, and pain of animal subjects.

g. A procedure subjecting animals to pain, stress, or privation is used only when an alternative procedure is unavailable and the goal is justified by its prospective scientific, educational, or applied value.

h. Surgical procedures are performed under appropriate anesthesia; techniques to avoid infection and minimize pain are followed during and after surgery.

i. When it is appropriate that the animal's life be terminated, it is done rapidly, with an effort to minimize pain, and in accordance with accepted procedures.

## 3.4   ETHICAL ISSUES AND SCIENTIFIC INTEGRITY

Thus far we have discussed the ethical issues that researchers face when they make decisions about the individuals, both human and nonhuman, who participate in their research. Later in the research process, in order to make the research public, the investigator prepares a written report describing what was done, what was found, and how the findings were interpreted (see Chapter 1, Step 9). Ethical issues can arise at this point as well. Here we consider two such issues, fraud and plagiarism. Two APA ethical standards (1992) relate to these issues:

6.21   Reporting of Results

a. Psychologists do not fabricate data or falsify results in their publications.

b. If psychologists discover significant errors in their published data, they take reasonable steps to correct such errors in a correction, retraction, erratum, or other appropriate publication means.

### 6.22  Plagiarism

Psychologists do not present substantial portions or elements of another's work or data as their own, even if the other work is cited occasionally. Copyright © 1992 by the American Psychological Association. Adapted by permission. In revision for Fall 2002. Go to http://www.apa.org/ethics for the revised material.

## FRAUD IN SCIENCE

### Error Versus Fraud

It is important to distinguish between error and fraud. An error is an honest mistake that occurs in the research process. There are, unfortunately, many opportunities for errors to be made in research; for example, in collecting data, in scoring of measures, in entering data into the computer, or in publication typesetting. Researchers are only human, and humans make mistakes. However, it is the investigator's responsibility to check and double-check the data to minimize the number of errors. **Fraud,** on the other hand, is an explicit effort to deceive and misrepresent data. If a researcher makes up or changes data to make it support the hypothesis, this constitutes fraud. As you know, the essential goal of science is to discover knowledge and reveal truth—which makes fraud the ultimate enemy of the scientific process.

| Definition | **Fraud** is the explicit effort of a researcher to deceive and misrepresent data. |
| --- | --- |

### Why Is Fraud in Science Committed?

Although researchers know that their reputations and their careers will be seriously damaged if they are caught falsifying their data, on rare occasions some researchers commit fraud. Why? The primary cause of fraud is the competitive nature of an academic career. You've probably heard the saying, "Publish or perish." There is strong pressure on researchers to have their research published. For example, tenure and promotion within academic departments are based on research productivity. In addition, researchers must obtain significant findings if they hope to receive grants to support their research. Another possible motivator is a researcher's exceedingly high need for success and the admiration that comes along with it. Researchers invest a great deal of time and resources in conducting their studies, and it can be very disappointing to obtain results that cannot be published.

It is important to keep in mind that discussing possible reasons why a researcher may commit fraud in no way implies that we condone such behavior. There is no justification for such actions. We include this information only to make you aware of the forces that might influence someone to commit such an act.

### Safeguards Against Fraud

Fortunately, several safeguards are built into the process of scientific research reporting to help keep fraud in check. First, researchers know that other scientists are going to read their reports and conduct further studies, including replications. The process of repeating a previous study, step by step, allows a researcher to verify the results. Recall from Chapter 1 that replication is one of the primary means of revealing error and uncovering fraud in research. The most common reason to suspect fraud is that a groundbreaking finding cannot be replicated.

A second safeguard against fraud is *peer review*, which takes place when a researcher submits a research article for publication. In a typical peer review process, the editor of the journal and a few experts in the field review the paper in extreme detail. The reviewers critically scrutinize every aspect of the research from the justification of the study to the analysis of data. The primary purpose of peer review is to evaluate the quality of the research study and the contribution it makes to scientific knowledge. The reviewers are also likely to detect anything suspect about the research or the findings.

The consequences of being found guilty of fraud probably keep many researchers honest. If it is concluded that a researcher's data are fraudulent, a number of penalties can result, including suspension or firing from a job, removal of a degree granted, cancellation of funding for research, and forced return of monies paid from grants.

---

What constitutes fraud, and what are some reasons for its occurrence?

Learning
Check

---

## PLAGIARISM

To present someone else's ideas or words as your own is to commit **plagiarism.** Plagiarism, like fraud, is a serious breach of ethics. Reference citations (giving others credit when credit is due) must be included in your paper whenever someone else's ideas or work has influenced your thinking and writing; whenever you use direct quotations or even paraphrase someone else's work, you need to give them credit. If an idea or information you include in a paper is not originally yours, you must cite it. For students, the penalties for plagiarism may include receipt of a failing grade on the paper or in the course, and expulsion from the institution. For faculty researchers, the penalties for plagiarism are much the same as those for fraud.

---

**Plagiarism** is the representation of someone else's ideas or words as one's own; it is unethical.

Definition

---

Plagiarism can occur on a variety of different levels. At one extreme, you can literally copy an entire paper word for word and present it as your own work. In this case, the plagiarism is clearly a deliberate act committed with complete awareness. However, plagiarism can be much more subtle and can even occur without your direct knowledge or intent. For example, while doing the background research for a paper, you may be inspired by someone's ideas or influenced by the phrases someone has used to express a concept. After working on a project for an extended time, it can become difficult to separate your own words and ideas from those that come to you from outside sources. As a result, outside ideas and phrases can appear in your paper without appropriate citation, and you have committed plagiarism.

Fortunately, following these guidelines can help prevent you from plagiarizing (Myers & Hansen, 1997):

1.  Take complete notes, including complete citation of the source: author's name, year of publication, title of the article, journal name, volume number, and page numbers. For books, include the publisher's name and city.
2.  Within your paper, identify the source of any ideas, words, or information that are not your own.
3.  Identify any direct quotes by quotation marks at the beginning and end of the quotes, and indicate where you got the quotes.
4.  Be careful about paraphrasing (restating someone else's words). It is greatly tempting to lift whole phrases or catchy words from another source. Use your own words instead, or use quotes. Be sure to give credit to your source.
5.  Include a complete list of references at the end of the paper. References should include all the information listed in Item 1.
6.  If in doubt about whether a citation is necessary, cite the source anyway. You will do no harm by being especially cautious.

Throughout this book we often use other people's ideas, figures, and passages (including the above guidelines), but note that we always acknowledge and cite the original authors, artists, and publishers.

---

 Learning Check

Explain why plagiarism is unethical.

---

## CHAPTER SUMMARY

Researchers have two basic categories of ethical responsibility: (1) responsibility to the individuals both human and nonhuman that participate in their research studies, and (2) responsibility to the discipline of science, to be accurate and honest in the reporting of their research. Researchers are responsible for ensuring the safety and well-being of their research participants and subjects and must abide by all the relevant ethical guidelines when conducting research. Researchers are also obligated to present truthful and accurate reports of their results and to give appropriate credit when they report the work or ideas of others.

Any research involving humans or nonhumans immediately introduces questions of ethics. Historical incidents in which human participants were injured or abused as part of a research study shaped the guidelines we have in place today. Psychological research using humans and nonhumans is regulated by the APA Ethics Code and by federal, state,

and local guidelines. The primary goal of the APA Ethics Code is the welfare and protection of the individuals and groups with whom the psychologists work. Tables 3.2 and 3.4 provide summaries of the elements of the Ethics Code most relevant to the use and treatment of human participants and nonhuman subjects. In addition, several of the points that are most important for new researchers are discussed in detail, including the issues of no harm, informed consent, deception, and confidentiality. To assist researchers in protecting human participants and nonhuman subjects, IRBs and IACUCs examine all proposed research.

Reporting of research also introduces questions of ethics. It is assumed that reports of research are accurate and honest depictions of the procedures used and results obtained. In this chapter, we considered two reporting issues, fraud and plagiarism.

Ethics in research is an enormous topic. In this chapter we consider the ethical decisions that researchers make when conducting research and when publishing their results. For more on the topic of research ethics, see Rosnow and Rosenthal, 1997; Sales and Folkman, 2000, and Stanley, Sieber, and Melton, 1996. In addition, if you are interested in reading a more detailed history of the development of current ethical standards, we suggest *Encyclopedia of Bioethics* (Reich, 1995).

## KEY WORDS

research ethics
informed consent
deception
passive deception (omission)
active deception (commission)

debriefing
confidentiality
anonymity
Institutional Review Board
   (IRB)

Institutional Animal Care and
   Use Committee (IACUC)
fraud
plagiarism

## EXERCISES

1.  In addition to the key words, you should also be able to define each of the following terms:

    ethics                    consent form
    Nuremberg Code            placebo
    APA Ethics Code           peer review

2.  Describe one historical incident in which human participants were injured or abused as part of a research study. Describe how the injury or abuse would have been avoided if the researchers had followed today's ethical guidelines.

3.  Summarize the major APA Ethical Principles concerning research with human participants.

4.  In your own words define the concept of informed consent and explain its purpose.

5.  Describe the circumstances in which it is acceptable to conduct research without obtaining informed consent from human participants.

6.  What is an IRB, and what is its purpose?

7.  Is it acceptable for researchers to justify the use of human participants in a study simply by saying that they are curious about what might happen? Why or why not?

8.  Under what circumstances is it acceptable for a researcher to use deception in a study with human participants?

9.  What kinds of information must be included accurately as part of the informed consent? (That is, what kinds of information are off limits for deception?)

10. What are some of the purposes of debriefing participants?

11. Describe the two strategies for maintaining participants' anonymity.

12. What are the safeguards against fraud in science?

## InfoTrac COLLEGE EDITION EXERCISES

1.  Locate a journal article that addresses an ethical issue in human research. (Note: Examples of ethical issues are deception, drug research sponsored by drug companies, the healing power of placebos, cloning research, and gene-altering research.) Hint: A good place to start is with a medically related subject term such as *pharmaceutical research* or *placebo effects*, or try using the name of a specific disease or disorder such as *depression, HIV,* or *bulimia*. When you find an article, briefly identify the ethical issue that is discussed, and summarize the arguments made in the article.

2.  Locate a journal article reporting on a research study that used human participants. Check the method section of the article for mention of actions or procedures used to ensure the safety or privacy of the participants.

# 4

# Defining and Measuring Variables

## CHAPTER OVERVIEW

In this chapter we consider how researchers define and measure variables (Step 3 of the research process). Frequently operational definitions are used to define and measure the variables. Two criteria used to evaluate the quality of a measurement procedure—validity and reliability—are discussed. We consider six methods of assessing the validity of measurement and three methods for assessing reliability, and follow with discussion of the scales of measurement and the modes of measuring.

## 4.1   AN OVERVIEW OF MEASUREMENT

As part of the research process (Step 3), a researcher must determine a method for defining and measuring the variables. Although we all measure things from time to time, the process of measurement in research can be complicated; it usually involves a number of decisions that have serious consequences for the outcome of a research study. Two aspects of measurement are particularly important in planning a research study or reading a research report:

1. Often there is a not a one-to-one relationship between the variable measured and the measurements obtained.
2. There are usually several different options for measuring any particular variable. The options chosen can influence the measurements and the interpretation of the variables.

As a more concrete example, suppose an instructor is evaluating a group of students. In this situation, the underlying variable is knowledge or mastery of subject matter, and the instructor's goal is to obtain a measure of knowledge for each student. However, it is impossible for the instructor to look inside each student's head to measure how much knowledge is there. Therefore, instructors typically give students a task (such as an exam, an essay, or a set of problems) and then measure how well students perform the task. Although it makes sense to expect that performance will be a reflection of knowledge, performance and knowledge are not the same thing. For example, physical illness or fatigue may affect performance on an exam, but they probably do not affect knowledge. There is not a one-to-one relationship between the variable that the instructor wants to measure (knowledge) and the actual measurements that are made (performance).

A common way instructors measure students' knowledge is to give exams and record a numerical score or a letter grade as the measurement for each student. This measurement procedure is so familiar that most students (and instructors) accept it without much thought. However, there are many options for administering and scoring exams. For example:

- The instructor may use a 100-question exam or a 10-question quiz.
- The instructor may decide to grade the students on an absolute basis or on a relative basis. Relative grading, for example, could involve ranking the exams from best to worst and awarding As to the top 20%, Bs to the next 20%, and so on. In this case, a grade depends not only on individual performance but also on the performance of all the other students. Absolute grading might involve awarding As to everyone who scores above 90% on the exam. Potentially the whole class can get As under this system.
- The instructor could assign numerical grades based on the number of questions answered correctly, or assign letter grades that group students into broad categories. Or the instructor could use a pass/fail grading system that simply places each student in one of two categories.

Obviously, the instructor has many different options for measuring the students' knowledge or mastery, and these different options have different consequences. For example:

- If each student receives a numerical grade for each exam, it is possible to compute an average for the course. Exam grades of 86, 92, and 74 result in an average score of 84. Letter grades, on the other hand, make determining an average more difficult; for example, what is the average of grades of A, B, and D on three exams?

- Scores from a 100-point exam provide better discrimination between students than a 10-point quiz. On the exam, for example, there is a 4-point difference between scores of 78 and 82. On the other hand, it is reasonable to expect that two students scoring 78 and 82 on the exam would both score 8 on the quiz (assuming that they each have learned about 80% of the material). Is there a real difference between the two individuals, or should they both receive the same grade?

- The measurement (the exam grade) may not be an accurate reflection of the variable (knowledge). A student may learn most of the course material and then encounter an exam that focuses on one small section that he or she did not study. In this situation, the student ends up with a low score despite a high level of knowledge.

Thus the selection of a measurement procedure involves decisions that can have consequences for the outcome of a research study. The remainder of this chapter deals with the general process of measurement, the different measurement options, and some of the consequences of each option.

 Learning Check

Some variables, such as height, can be measured directly, and the measurement procedure is usually quite straightforward. Other variables—for example, hunger, motivation, or attitude about the death penalty—are more difficult to measure.

a. Describe one procedure that might be used to measure hunger.
b. Use the procedure you described in (a) to explain why there may not be a one-to-one relationship between a variable and the procedure used to measure it.

## 4.2   CONSTRUCTS AND OPERATIONAL DEFINITIONS

Occasionally a research study involves variables that are well defined, easily observed, and easily measured. For example, a study of physical development might involve the variables height and weight. Both of these variables are tangible, concrete attributes that can be observed and measured directly. On the other hand, some studies involve intangible, abstract attributes such as motivation or self-esteem. Such variables are not directly observable, and the process of measuring them is more complicated.

### THEORIES AND CONSTRUCTS

In attempting to explain and predict behavior, scientists and philosophers often develop theories that contain hypothetical mechanisms and intangible elements.

Although these mechanisms and elements cannot be seen and are only assumed to exist, we accept them as real because they seem to describe and explain behaviors that we see. For example, a bright child does poor work in school because he has low "motivation." A kindergarten teacher may hesitate to criticize a lazy child because it may injure the student's "self-esteem." But what is motivation, and how do we know that it is low? Do we read the child's motivation-meter? What about self-esteem? How do we recognize poor self-esteem or healthy self-esteem when we can't see it in the first place? Many research variables, particularly variables of interest to behavioral scientists, are in fact hypothetical entities created from theory and speculation. Such variables are called **constructs,** or **hypothetical constructs.**

A **construct** is a hypothetical attribute or mechanism that helps explain and predict behavior in a theory.

Although constructs are hypothetical and intangible, they play very important roles in behavioral theories. In many theories, constructs can be influenced by external stimuli and in turn can influence external behaviors.

External
Stimulus  → Construct  → Behavior
Factors

For example, external factors such as rewards or reinforcements can affect motivation (a construct), and motivation can then affect performance. Thus it is possible for researchers to examine the factors that theoretically influence a construct and study the behaviors that theoretically result from a construct.

## OPERATIONAL DEFINITIONS

Although a construct itself cannot be directly observed or measured, it is possible to observe and measure the external factors and the behaviors that are associated theoretically with the construct. Researchers can measure these external, observable events as an *indirect* method of measuring the construct itself. Typically, researchers identify a behavior or a cluster of behaviors associated with a construct; the behavior is then measured, and the resulting measurements are used as a definition and a measure of the construct. This method of defining and measuring a construct is called an **operational definition.**

An **operational definition** is a procedure for measuring and defining a construct. An operational definition specifies a measurement procedure (a set of operations) for measuring an external, observable behavior and uses the resulting measurements as a definition and a measurement of the hypothetical construct.

Probably the most familiar example of an operational definition is the IQ test, which is intended to measure intelligence. Notice that "intelligence" is a hypothetical construct; it is an internal attribute that cannot be observed directly.

However, intelligence is assumed to influence external behaviors that can be observed and measured. An IQ test actually measures external behavior—responses to questions. The test includes both elements of an operational definition: There are specific procedures for administration and scoring the test, and the resulting scores are used as a definition and a measurement of intelligence. Thus, although an IQ score is really a measure of intelligent *behavior*, we use the score both as a definition of intelligence and as a measure of it.

### USING OPERATIONAL DEFINITIONS

Whenever the variables in a research study are hypothetical constructs, you must use operational definitions to define and measure the variables. Usually, however, this does not mean creating your own operational definition. The best method for determining how a variable should be measured is to consult previous research involving the same variable. Whether or not the variable is an operationally defined construct, reports of previous research will describe in detail how each variable is defined and measured. By reading several research reports concerning the same variable, typically you will discover that a standard, generally accepted measurement procedure has already been developed. When you plan your own research, the best advice is to use the conventional method of defining and measuring your variables. In this way, your results will be directly comparable to the results obtained in past research. However, keep in mind that any measurement procedure, particularly an operational definition, is simply an attempt to classify the variable being considered. Other measurement procedures are always possible and may provide a better way to define and measure the variable. In general, critically examine any measurement procedure, and ask yourself whether a different technique might produce better measurements.

In the following section we introduce the two general criteria used to evaluate the quality of any measurement procedure. In later sections we examine some specific details of measurement that can influence whether a particular measurement procedure is appropriate for a particular research question. As you read through the following sections, keep in mind that the choice of a measurement procedure involves a number of decisions. Usually there is no absolutely right or absolutely wrong choice; nonetheless, you must make these decisions when you develop your own measurement procedure, and you should be aware that other researchers had options and choices when they decided how to measure their variables.

 Learning Check

Briefly explain what an operational definition is and why operational definitions are sometimes necessary.

## 4.3   VALIDITY AND RELIABILITY OF MEASUREMENT

In the previous section we noted that several different methods are usually available for measuring any particular variable. How can we decide which method is best? In addition, whenever the variable is a hypothetical construct, a researcher must use an operational definition as a measurement procedure. In essence, an operational definition is an indirect method of measuring something that cannot be measured directly. How can we be sure that the measurements obtained from an operational definition actually represent the intangible construct? In general, we are asking *how good* a measurement procedure is. Researchers have developed two general criteria for evaluating the quality of any measurement procedure: *validity* and *reliability*.

## VALIDITY OF MEASUREMENT

The **validity** of a measurement concerns the "truth" of the measurement. That is, does it measure the variable that it claims to measure? Although the notion of validity may appear to be self-evident, there are circumstances in which legitimate questions can be asked about what really is being measured when a particular measurement procedure is used.

This problem is especially important whenever an operational definition is used to measure a hypothetical construct. For example, how do we measure intelligence? The answer is, we can't. Intelligence is hypothetical and cannot be directly observed or measured. The best we can do is to measure intelligent behavior or some other external manifestation of intelligence. In the past, researchers have attempted to measure intelligence by measuring brain size (bigger brain equals greater intelligence) and bumps on the skull. Operationally defining intelligence in terms of brain size or bumps probably seems silly, but at one time these were viewed as valid measures of intelligence.

Similarly we could question the validity of a standardized IQ test. Consider, for example, an absent-minded professor who has an IQ of 158 but is incredibly stupid in everyday life (constantly misplacing car keys, forgetting when and where classes are supposed to be, smoking three packs of cigarettes each day, carelessly burning holes in clothes). How intelligent is this person? Has the IQ score truly measured intelligence? Again, this is a question of validity: Does the measurement procedure accurately capture the variable that it is supposed to measure?

---

The **validity** of a measurement procedure is the degree to which the measurement process measures the variable it claims to measure.

Definition

---

Researchers have developed several methods for assessing the validity of measurement. Six of the more commonly used definitions of validity follow.

### Face Validity

**Face validity** is the simplest and least scientific definition of validity. Face validity concerns the superficial appearance or face value of a measurement procedure. Does the measurement technique *look like* it measures the variable that it claims to measure? For example, an IQ test ought to include questions that require logic, reasoning, background knowledge, and good memory. Such questions appear to be appropriate for measuring intelligence and therefore have high face validity. Face validity is based on subjective judgment and is difficult to quantify. In addition, there are circumstances where a high level of face validity can create problems. If the purpose of the measurement is obvious, the participants in a research study can see exactly what is being measured and may adjust their answers to produce a better self-image. For this reason, researchers often try to disguise the true purpose of measurement devices such as questionnaires, deliberately trying to create a measurement technique that has very little face validity.

### Concurrent Validity

Often the validity of a new measurement is established by demonstrating that the scores obtained from the new measurement technique are directly related to the scores obtained from another, better-established procedure for measuring the same variable. This is called **concurrent validity.** For example, if you had developed a new test to measure intelligence, you could demonstrate that your test really measures intelligence by showing that the scores from your test differentiate individuals in the same way as scores from a standardized IQ test. Basically, concurrent validity establishes consistency between two different measures of the same variable, suggesting that the two measurement procedures measure the same thing. However, the simple fact that two sets of measurements are related does not necessarily mean that they are identical. For example, we could claim to measure people's height by having people step on a bathroom scale and recording the number that appears. Note that we *claim* to be measuring height, although we are actually measuring weight. However, we could provide support for our claim by demonstrating a strong relationship between our scores and more traditional measurements of height (taller people tend to weigh more; shorter people tend to weigh less). Although we can establish some degree of concurrent validity for our measurements, it should be obvious that a measurement of weight is not really a valid measure of height. In particular, these two measurements behave in different ways and are influenced by different factors. Manipulating diet, for example, influences weight but has little or no effect on height.

### Predictive Validity

Most theories make predictions about the constructs they contain. Specifically, theories predict how different values of a construct affect behavior. When the measurements of a construct accurately predict behavior (according to the theory), the measurement procedure is said to have **predictive validity.** For example, one characteristic that appears to differentiate people is need for achievement. Theoretically, need for achievement (abbreviated "n-Ach" on tests) is a fundamental motivator that causes individuals to seek success in competitive and challenging situations. According to the theory, individuals with high n-Ach will look for tasks that include reasonable levels of competition and challenge and thus provide an opportunity to satisfy the need for achievement. On the other hand, individuals with low n-Ach will be content with very easy tasks (offering no challenge) or with extremely difficult tasks on which success is very unlikely and probably due to luck if it occurs at all. To evaluate this prediction, McClelland (1958) administered the n-Ach test to a group of kindergarten children and then presented the children with a ring toss game. The goal was to toss a rope ring onto a peg. The children were allowed to choose how far from the peg they wanted to stand, and McClelland measured the distance for each child.

As predicted, children with high n-Ach selected moderate distances that created a reasonably challenging game. The children with low n-Ach showed a tendency to stand very near the peg, where failure was impossible, or to stand very far from the peg, where success was very unlikely. Thus, the scores from the n-Ach test accurately predicted the behavior of the children, demonstrating predictive validity for the n-Ach test.

### Construct Validity

For most variables that you are likely to encounter, numerous research studies probably already have examined the same variables. Past research has studied each variable in a variety of different situations and has documented which factors influence the variable and how different values of the variable produce different kinds of behavior. In short, past research has demonstrated how the specific variable behaves. If we can demonstrate that *measurements* of a variable behave in exactly the same way as the variable itself, then we have established the **construct validity** of the measures. Suppose, for example, that you are examining a measurement procedure that claims to measure aggression. Past research has demonstrated a relationship between temperature and aggression: In the summer, as temperature rises, people tend to become more aggressive. To establish construct validity, you need to demonstrate that the scores you obtain from the measurement procedure are also related to temperature; that is, that the *scores* tend to increase as the temperature goes up. Note, however, that this single demonstration is only one small part of construct validity. To completely establish construct validity, you would need to examine all the past research on aggression and show that the measurement procedure produces scores that behave in accord with everything that is known about the construct "aggression." Obviously, construct validity is difficult to establish and usually requires many research studies that examine the measurement procedure in a wide variety of different situations. In one sense, construct validity is achieved by repeatedly demonstrating every other type of validity.

Earlier, we used the example of attempting to measure height by having people step on a bathroom scale. Because height and weight are related, the measurement that we obtain from the scale would be considered a valid measure of height, at least in terms of concurrent validity However, the weight measurement is not a valid method of measuring height in terms of construct validity. In particular, height is not influenced by short periods of food deprivation. Weight measurements, on the other hand, are affected by food deprivation. Therefore, measurements of weight do not behave in accord with what is known about the construct "height," which means that the weight measurement procedure does not have construct validity.

### Convergent and Divergent Validity

Often researchers attempt to establish construct validity by demonstrating a combination of convergent and divergent validity. In general terms, **convergent validity** involves using two different methods to measure the same construct and then showing a strong relationship between the measures obtained from the two methods. **Divergent validity,** on the other hand, involves demonstrating that we are measuring one specific construct and not combining two different constructs in the same measurement process. The following scenarios illustrate the concepts of convergent and divergent validity.

Suppose that you are interested in measuring aggressive behavior for pre-school children. Your measurement procedure involves observing a group of children on a playground and recording their behaviors. Because you realize that you are observing only a small part of the children's total environment, you decide that you would have more confidence in the validity of your measurements if you also asked the children's teacher to provide ratings of aggression for each child. If there is a strong relationship between your observation scores and the teacher's ratings, you can be reasonably confident that you are obtaining a valid measure of aggression. Using two different methods to measure the same variable and demonstrating a strong relationship (usually a correlation) between the two measures is an example of convergent validity.

Now suppose that you are concerned that your measures of aggression may actually reflect the general activity level of each child. It is possible, for example, that very active children simply appear to be more aggressive than their less active peers. To resolve this problem, you need to demonstrate that the two constructs, "aggression" and "activity," are separate and distinct. Therefore, you now obtain measures of activity level by observing the children on the playground. Once again, you can check the validity of your measurements by asking the children's teacher for a rating of activity for each child. At this point, you have two different measurements (observation and rating) of two different constructs (aggression and activity), and you are ready to evaluate divergent validity.

The first step in establishing divergent validity is to demonstrate convergent validity for both constructs. That is:

- There should be a strong relationship between the observational scores for aggression and the rating scores for aggression.
- There should be a strong relationship between the observational scores for activity and the rating scores for activity.

The second step is to demonstrate that the two constructs are separate and distinct. To accomplish this, you must demonstrate that:

- Relatively little relationship exists between the observational scores for aggression and the observational scores for activity
- Relatively little relationship exists between the rating scores for aggression and the rating scores for activity

By demonstrating that two different methods of measurement produce strongly related scores for the same construct (convergent validity) and by demonstrating that two distinct constructs produce unrelated scores (divergent validity), you can provide very strong and convincing evidence of construct validity. That is, there is little doubt that you are actually measuring the construct that you intend to measure.

| Definition | **Face validity** is an unscientific form of validity demonstrated when a measure superficially appears to measure what it claims to measure. |
| --- | --- |

**Concurrent validity** is demonstrated when scores obtained from a new measure are directly related to scores obtained from a more established measure of the same variable.

**Predictive validity** is demonstrated when scores obtained from a measure accurately predict behavior according to a theory.

**Construct validity** is demonstrated when scores obtained from a measure are directly related to the variable itself.

**Convergent validity** is demonstrated by a strong relationship between the scores obtained from two different methods of measuring the same construct.

**Divergent validity** is demonstrated by using two different methods to measure two different constructs. Then convergent validity must be shown for each of the two constructs and little or no relationship exists between the scores obtained for the two different constructs when they are measured by the same method.

Learning Check

A researcher evaluates a new growth hormone. One sample of rats is raised with the hormone in their diet, and a second sample is raised without the hormone. After six months the researcher weighs each rat to determine whether the rats in one group are significantly larger than the rats in the other group. A second researcher measures femininity for each individual in a group of 10-year-old girls who are all daughters of mothers who work outside of the home. These scores are then compared with corresponding measurements obtained from girls who are all daughters of mothers who work at home. The researcher hopes to show that one group is significantly more feminine than the other. Explain why the first researcher is probably not concerned about the validity of measurement, whereas the second researcher probably is. (Hint: What is each researcher measuring?)

## RELIABILITY OF MEASUREMENT

A measurement procedure is said to be **reliable** if repeated measurements of the same individual under the same conditions produce identical (or nearly identical) values. For example, if we measure a person's IQ today and then repeat the measurement next week under similar conditions, we should obtain nearly identical IQ scores. In essence, reliability is the stability or the consistency of measurement.

The **reliability** of a measurement procedure is the stability or consistency of the measurement. If the same individuals are measured under the same conditions, a reliable measurement procedure will produce identical (or nearly identical) measurements.

On a more theoretical level, reliability includes the notion that each individual measurement has an element of error. Expressed as an equation:

Measured Score = True Score + Error

For example, if we try to measure your intelligence with an IQ test, the score we get is determined partially by your actual level of intelligence (your true score), but it also is influenced by a variety of other factors, such as your current mood, your level of fatigue, your general health, how lucky you are at guessing on questions to which you do not know the answers, and so on. These other factors are lumped together as *error* and are typically a part of any measurement.

It is generally assumed that the error component changes randomly from one measurement to the next and that this causes your score to change. For example, your IQ score is likely to be higher when you are well rested and feeling good, compared to a measurement that is taken when you are tired and depressed. Although your actual intelligence hasn't changed, the error component causes your score to change from one measurement to another.

As long as the error component is relatively small, your scores will be relatively consistent from one measurement to the next, and the measurements are said to be reliable. If you are feeling especially happy and well rested, it may affect your IQ score by a few points, but it is not going to boost your IQ from 110 to 170.

On the other hand, if the error component is relatively large, you will find huge differences from one measurement to the next, and the measurements are not reliable. A common example of a measurement with a large error component is reaction time. Suppose, for example, that we ask you to sit at a desk with your finger on a button and a light bulb in front of you. Your task is to press the button as quickly as possible when the light goes on. On some trials you will be fully alert and focused on the light, with your finger tensed and ready to move. On other trials you may be daydreaming or distracted, with your attention elsewhere so that extra time passes before you can refocus on the task and respond. In general it is quite common for reaction time on some trials to be twice as long as reaction time on other trials. When scores change dramatically from one trial to another, the measurements are said to be unreliable, and we cannot trust any single measurement to provide an accurate indication of an individual's true score. In the case of reaction time, most researchers solve the problem by measuring reaction times in several trials and computing an average. The average value provides a much more stable, more reliable measure of performance.

The inconsistency in a measurement comes from error. Error can come from a variety of sources. The more common sources of error are:

- *Observer error:* The individual who makes the measurements can introduce simple human error into the measurement process. Imagine four people using handheld stopwatches to record the winner's time in a 100-meter dash. In this situation, it is highly likely that the four people will obtain four different times. To some extent, the time that each person records will be influenced by that person's judgment of when the race started and ended and that person's reflex time to push the buttons on the watch. Thus each recorded time includes some error introduced by the observer.

- *Environmental changes:* Although the goal is to measure the same individual under *identical* circumstances, this ideal is difficult to attain. Often there will be small changes in the environment from one measurement to another, and these small changes can influence the measurements. There are so many environmental variables (such as time of day, temperature, weather conditions, and lighting) that it is essentially impossible to obtain two identical environmental conditions.
- *Participant changes:* The participant can change between measurements. For example, a person's mood and even body temperature can change dramatically in just a few hours. Such changes may cause the obtained measurements to differ, producing what appear to be inconsistent or unreliable measurements. For example, hunger probably does not lower intelligence, but it can be a distraction that causes a lower score on an IQ test.

---

Exams given in college classes are intended to measure the knowledge of students.

Learning
Checks

    a.  Identify one way that error might improve a student's exam score.
    b.  Identify one way that error might lower a student's exam score.

Explain how a large error component can make a measurement procedure unreliable.

---

### Types and Measures of Reliability

We have defined reliability in terms of the consistency between two or more separate measures. Thus far, the discussion has concentrated on situations involving successive measurements. Although this is one common example of reliability, it also is possible to measure reliability for simultaneous measurements and to measure reliability in terms of the internal consistency among the many items that make up a test or questionnaire.

- *Successive measurements:* The reliability estimate obtained by comparing the scores obtained from two successive measurements is commonly called **test-retest reliability.** A researcher may use exactly the same measurement procedure for the same group of individuals at two different times. Or a researcher may use modified versions of the measurement instrument (such as alternative versions of an IQ test) for the two different measurements. Typically, reliability is determined by computing the correlation between the two sets of scores.
- *Simultaneous measurements:* When measurements are obtained by direct observation of behaviors, it is common to use two or more separate observers who simultaneously record measurements. For example, two psychologists may watch a group of preschool children and observe social behaviors. Each individual records (measures) what he or she observes, and the degree of agreement between the two observers is called **inter-rater reliability.** This is discussed in more detail in Section 4.5 and Chapter 7.
- *Internal consistency:* Often a complex construct such as intelligence or personality is measured using a test or questionnaire consisting of multiple items.

The idea is that no single item or question is sufficient to provide a complete measure of the construct. A common example is the use of multiple-item exams to measure performance in an academic course. The final measurement for each individual is then determined by summing or averaging the responses across the full set of items. A basic assumption in this process is that each item (or group of items) measures a part of the total construct. If this is true, then there should be some consistency among the different items or different groups of items. To measure the degree of consistency, researchers commonly split the set of items in half, compute a separate score for each half, and then evaluate the degree of agreement between the two scores. This general process results in a measure of **split-half reliability.**

Definitions

**Test-retest reliability** is established by comparing the scores obtained from two successive measurements and calculating a correlation between the two sets of scores.

**Inter-rater reliability** is the degree of agreement between two observers who simultaneously record measurements of the behaviors.

**Split-half reliability** is the degree of consistency of scores from separate items on a test or questionnaire consisting of multiple items.

 Learning Check

Explain how inter-rater reliability is established.

## THE RELATIONSHIP BETWEEN RELIABILITY AND VALIDITY

Although reliability and validity are both criteria for evaluating the quality of a measurement procedure, these two factors are partially related and partially independent. They are related to each other in that reliability is a prerequisite for validity; that is, a measurement procedure cannot be valid unless it is reliable. If we measure your IQ twice and obtain measurements of 75 and 160, we have no idea what your IQ actually is. The huge discrepancy between the two measurements is impossible if we are truly measuring intelligence. Therefore, we must conclude that there is so much error in the measurements that the numbers themselves have no meaning.

A measure cannot be valid unless it is reliable, but a measure can be reliable without being valid.

On the other hand, it is not necessary for a measurement to be valid for it to be reliable. For example, we could measure your height and claim that it is a measure of intelligence. Although there is no validity to this measurement, it would be very reliable, producing consistent scores from one measurement to the next. Thus, the consistency of measurement is no guarantee of validity.

In situations where there is an established standard for measurement units, it is possible to define the accuracy of a measurement process. For example, we have standards that define precisely what is meant by an inch, a pound, a mile, and a second. The *accuracy* of a measurement is the degree to which the measurement conforms to the established standard. Occasionally a measurement procedure produces results that are consistently wrong by a constant amount. The speedometer on a car, for example, may consistently read 10 mph faster than the actual speed. In this case the speedometer readings are not accurate, but they are reliable. (Note that a measurement process can be reliable but not accurate.) When the car is traveling at 40 mph, the speedometer will consistently (reliably) read 50 mph. In the behavioral sciences it is quite common to measure variables for which there is no established standard. In such cases it is impossible to define or measure accuracy. A test designed to measure depression, for example, cannot be evaluated in terms of accuracy because there is no standard unit of depression that can be used for comparison. For such a test, the question of accuracy is moot, and the only concerns are the validity and the reliability of the measurements.

## 4.4    SCALES OF MEASUREMENT

In very general terms measurement is a procedure for classifying individuals. The set of categories used for classification is called the **scale of measurement**. Thus the process of measurement involves two components: a procedure and a scale.

In this section we focus on scales of measurement. Traditionally researchers have identified four different types of measurement scales: nominal, ordinal, interval, and ratio. The differences among these four types are based on the relationships that exist among the categories that make up the scales.

### THE NOMINAL SCALE

The categories that make up a **nominal scale** simply represent *qualitative* differences in the variable measured. The categories have different names but are not related to each other in any systematic way. For example, if you were measuring academic major for a group of college students, the categories would be art, chemistry, English, history, psychology, and so on. Each student would be placed in a category according to his or her major. Measurements from a nominal scale allow us to determine whether or not two individuals are different, but they do not permit any quantitative comparison. For example, if one individual is an art major and another is an English major, we can say that the two individuals have different majors, but we cannot determine the direction of the difference (is art "more than" English?), and we cannot determine the magnitude of the difference.

### THE ORDINAL SCALE

The categories that make up an **ordinal scale** have different names and are organized sequentially. Often an ordinal scale consists of a series of ranks (first, second, third, and so on) like the order of finish in a horse race. Occasionally the categories are identified by verbal labels, such as small, medium, and large drink sizes at a fast-food restaurant. In either case, the fact that the categories form an ordered sequence means that there is a directional relationship between categories. With measurements from an ordinal scale, we can determine whether two individuals are different, and we can determine the direction of difference. However, ordinal measurements do not allow us to determine the magnitude of the difference between two individuals. For example, if Billy is placed in the low-reading group and Tim is placed in the high-reading group, we know that Tim is a better reader, but we do not know how much better.

## THE INTERVAL SCALE

The categories on an **interval scale** are organized sequentially, and all categories are the same size. Thus, the scale of measurement consists of a series of equal intervals like the inches on a ruler. Other common examples of interval scales are the measures of time in seconds, weight in pounds, and temperature in degrees Fahrenheit. Notice that in each case one interval (1 inch, 1 second, 1 pound, 1 degree) is the same size no matter where it is located on the scale. The fact that the intervals are all the same size makes it possible to determine the magnitude of differences. For example, you know that a measurement of 10 inches is larger than a measurement of 7 inches, and you know that it is exactly 3 inches larger.

Another characteristic of an interval scale is that it has an arbitrary zero point. That is, the value 0 is assigned to a particular location on the scale simply as a matter of convenience or reference. Specifically, a value of 0 does *not* indicate the total absence of the variable being measured. For example, a temperature of 0 degrees Fahrenheit does not mean that there is no temperature, and it does not prohibit the temperature from going even lower.

## THE RATIO SCALE

A **ratio scale** consists of equal, ordered categories (like an interval scale), with the series of categories anchored by a zero point that is not an arbitrary location. Instead, the value 0 on a ratio scale is a meaningful point representing none (a complete absence) of the variable being measured. The existence of an absolute, nonarbitrary zero point means that we can measure the absolute amount of the variable; that is, we can measure the distance from 0. This makes it possible to compare measurements in terms of ratios. For example, an individual who requires 10 seconds to solve a problem (10 more than 0) has taken twice as much time as an individual who finishes in only 5 seconds (5 more than 0). With a ratio scale we can not only measure the direction and magnitude of the difference between measurements but also describe differences in terms of ratios.

## SELECTING A SCALE OF MEASUREMENT

One obvious factor that differentiates the four types of measurement scales is their ability to compare different measurements. A nominal scale can tell us only that a difference exists. An ordinal scale tells us the direction of the difference (which is more and which is less). With an interval scale, we can determine the direction and the magnitude of a difference. Measurements from a ratio scale allow us to determine the direction, the magnitude, and the ratio of the difference. The ability to compare measurements has a direct impact on the ability to describe relationships between variables. For example, when a research study involves measurements from nominal scales, the results of the study can establish the existence of only a qualitative relationship between variables. With nominal scales, we can show that a change in one variable is accompanied by a change in the other variable, but we cannot determine the direction of the change (increase or a decrease), and we cannot determine the magnitude of the change. An interval or a ratio scale, on the other hand, allows a much more sophisticated description of a relationship. For example, we could determine that a 1-point increase in one variable (such as drug dose) results in a 4-point decrease in another variable (such as heart rate).

Learning Check

Identify the scale of measurement that allows each of the following conclusions:

  a.  Tom's score is larger than Bill's, but we cannot say how much larger.
  b.  Tom's score is three times larger than Bill's.
  c.  Tom and Bill have different scores, but we cannot say which one is larger, and we cannot determine how much difference there is.

## 4.5   MODALITIES OF MEASUREMENT

Although a construct such as motivation or intelligence is hypothetical and cannot be observed directly, the construct reveals itself in a variety of different external manifestations that can be observed and measured. One major decision for a researcher is which of these external manifestations provides the best indication of the underlying construct. The many different options for measuring a construct are traditionally classified into three categories that define three different types or modalities of measurement. The three categories of measurement are: self-report, physiological, and behavioral. Consider, for example, the hypothetical construct "fear," and suppose that a researcher would like to evaluate the effectiveness of a therapy program designed to reduce the fear of flying. This researcher must somehow obtain measurements of fear before the therapy begins and then compare them with measurements of fear obtained after therapy. The first decision in developing a measurement procedure (an operational definition) is to determine which type of external expression should be used to define and measure fear.

### SELF-REPORT MEASURES

One option is to ask each participant to describe or to quantify his or her own fear. The researcher could simply ask, "Are you afraid to fly?" Or participants could be asked to rate the amount of fear they are experiencing on a scale from 1 to 10. Or they could be given a comprehensive questionnaire about airline travel, and the researcher could use the set of responses to obtain an overall score measuring fear of flying.

The primary advantage of a self-report measure is that it is probably the most direct way to assess a construct. Each individual is in a unique position of knowledge and awareness; presumably no one knows more about the individual's fear than the individual. Also, a direct question and its answer have more apparent validity than measuring some other response that theoretically is influenced by fear. On the negative side, however, it is very easy for participants to distort self-report measures. A participant may deliberately lie to create a better self-image, or a response may be influenced subtly by the presence of a researcher, the wording of the questions, or other aspects of the research situation. One phenomenon observed by clinical psychologists, called the *hello-goodbye effect*, is that patients tend to exaggerate their symptoms at the beginning of therapy and to minimize symptoms at the end, probably in an attempt to please the therapist. When a participant distorts self-report responses, the validity of the measurement is undermined.

Learning Check

What is the primary advantage of self-report measures? What is the primary disadvantage?

## Types of Questions

There are different ways to ask participants for self-report information. Sometimes you may be satisfied with a simple yes or no answer ("Have you ever . . ."), but in other circumstances you may want a quantitative answer (how much, how often). Different types of questions encourage different types of responses. Also, different types of questions permit different degrees of freedom in the participants' answers. For example, a question may severely restrict response options ("Which of the following three flavors of ice cream do you prefer?"), or a question may give each participant complete freedom in choosing a response ("What is your favorite ice cream flavor?"). The wording of a question may introduce bias into participants' answers ("Are you one of those bland, unimaginative people who prefer vanilla ice cream?") Finally, different types of questions permit different types of statistical analysis and interpretation. If answers are limited to values on a nominal scale, for example, you cannot compute a group average.

In this section we consider three general types of self-report questions. Each type has its own individual strengths and weaknesses and is designed to obtain specific information.

**Open-Ended Questions**    An open-ended question simply introduces a topic and allows each participant to respond in his or her own words. For example:

- What do you think about the current availability of food on this campus?
- In your view, what are the most important factors in choosing a college or university?

The primary advantage of an open-ended question is that it allows an individual the greatest flexibility in choosing how to answer. An open-ended question imposes few restrictions on the participant and therefore is likely to reveal each individual's true thoughts or opinions. Although the question may lead the participant in a particular direction or suggest a specific point of view, each individual is free to express his or her own thoughts. However, this can also be a major disadvantage. For example, different participants may approach the question from entirely different perspectives, leaving you with answers that are impossible to compare or summarize. To the question about food on the college campus, for example, one individual may respond with a list of food suggestions, another may suggest new locations for selling food, and a third participant may state simply that the current situation is "OK." All three answers may be useful, but they are clearly not compatible with each other, and they may be very different from the issue you had in mind when the original question was written.

A second disadvantage of open-ended questions is that the answers are often difficult to summarize or analyze with conventional statistical methods. As with the food question, different participants may provide responses that are difficult to group together or to average in any meaningful way. Often the researcher must impose some subjective interpretation on the answer, for example, classifying a rambling response as generally positive or generally negative. Finally, the responses to open-ended questions may be limited by a participant's ability or willingness to express his or her thoughts. An inarticulate or tired person may give a very brief answer that does not completely express the true breadth of his or her thinking.

**Restricted Questions**    A restricted question presents the participant with a limited number of response alternatives, hence *restricting* the response possibilities. Like a multiple-choice question, a restricted question typically asks the participant to select the best or most appropriate answer of a series of choices. For example:

1. If the election were held today, which of the following candidates would receive your vote?

    a. Mr. Jones
    b. Ms. Smith
    c. Mr. Johnson

2. Which of the following alternatives is the best description of your current occupation?

    a. blue collar
    b. white collar (sales/service)
    c. professional
    d. managerial
    e. student
    f. unemployed

Because these questions produce a limited and predetermined set of responses, they are easy to analyze and summarize. Typically, the data are tabulated and reported as percentages or proportions of participants selecting each alternative.

It also is possible to obtain quantitative information from restricted questions by using an ordered set of response alternatives. For example:

1. During a typical week, how often do you eat at a fast-food restaurant?

    a. not at all
    b. once
    c. twice
    d. 3 times
    e. 4 times or more

With this type of question it often is possible to compute some kind of average response for a group of participants.

Finally, an element of open-endedness can be allowed in a restricted question by including a blank category where participants are free to fill in their own responses. For example:

1. Which of the following is your favorite local department store?

    a. Jones & Bederman
    b. Macy's
    c. Marx
    d. McReynold's
    e. Other (please specify) _____

Learning
Check

Briefly identify the relative strengths and weaknesses of open-ended and restricted questions.

**Rating Scale Questions**    A rating-scale question requires a participant to respond by selecting a numerical value on a predetermined scale. Movie critics often use this type of scale to evaluate films with a number from 1 to 10. The numerical scale that accompanies each question typically presents a range of response alternatives from very positive to very negative. A common example uses a 5-point scale on which individuals rate their level of agreement or disagreement with a simple statement:

1. Strongly disagree
2. Disagree
3. Neither agree or disagree
4. Agree
5. Strongly agree

The rating scale is usually presented as a horizontal line divided into categories so that participants can simply circle a number or mark an X at the location corresponding to their response (see Figure 4.1). This type of rating scale question is often called a Likert scale (or a Likert-type scale) after Rensis Likert, who developed the 5-point response scale as part of a much more sophisticated scaling system (Likert, 1932). Notice that the scale is presented with equal spacing between the different response choices. The idea is to simulate an interval scale of measurement; the responses from rating scales are usually treated as interval measurements. Thus, the distance between "agree" and "strongly agree" is treated as a 1-point distance that is equivalent to any other 1-point difference on the scale.

There is no absolute rule for determining the number of categories for a rating-scale question; however, researchers commonly use from 5 to 10 numerical values. This reasoning behind this range of values is based on two observations:

- Participants tend to avoid the two extreme categories at the opposite ends of the scale, especially if they are identified with labels that indicate extreme attitudes or opinions. Thus the actual scale is effectively reduced by two categories.
- Participants have trouble discriminating among more than 9 or 10 different levels. If the scale offers more than 10 options, the participants will usually blend categories and effectively create their own 10-point scale.

Questionnaire

Use the following scale (numbers 1 through 5) to describe how you feel about each of the statements below. For each statement, circle the number that gives the best description of how you feel.

| Strongly Disagree | Disagree | Undecided | Agree | Strongly Agree |
|:---:|:---:|:---:|:---:|:---:|
| 1 | 2 | 3 | 4 | 5 |

1.  I have a natural talent for mathematics.

    1    2    3    4    5

2.  I am a good math student.

    1    2    3    4    5

3.  I like mathematics.

    1    2    3    4    5

4.  Math is easier for me than it is for most students.

    1    2    3    4    5

5.  I probably will use mathematics in my future job.

    1    2    3    4    5

**Figure 4.1    A Likert-Type Rating Scale and a Series of Questions Examining Elementary School Students' Attitudes About Mathematics**

There is no absolute rule for labeling the categories. Typically the opposite extremes are identified with verbal labels called **anchors** that establish the end-points of the scale. In addition, the central category is often labeled, especially if it represents a neutral response. Beyond the endpoints and the middle, however, labeling categories is optional.

One criticism of rating-scale questions is that, whenever questions in a series all have the same choices for responding, participants may tend to answer all (or most) of the questions the same way. This tendency is called a **response set.** With a Likert-type scale, for example, some participants use the neutral (#3) answer for everything. One rationalization is that they really don't feel strongly about any of the items, so they really are neutral. (A more likely explanation is that they simply want to finish quickly.) Another possibility is that a participant may use the "Agree" category for all responses except to those few items where there is serious disagreement. To minimize this problem, it is recommended that the items include a mixture of positive and negative statements, including some alternate phrasing of the same item. For example, one item might be:

Today's teenagers are rude and disrespectful.

Later in the series an alternate item might be:

Today's teenagers are polite and courteous.

The intent is to force respondents to move back and forth between opposite ends of the scale so that they cannot fall into a single response set for answering the questions.

Another common scale, called the **semantic differential,** presents a list of adjectives (such as *helpful, honest, devious*), and asks each participant to use the scale to rate how well each adjective describes a particular individual.

1. Not at all descriptive
2.
3. Somewhat descriptive
4.
5. Very descriptive
6.
7. Describes perfectly

The primary advantage of rating-scale questions is that they produce numerical values that can be treated as measurements from an interval scale. (Recall that an interval scale consists of a series of equal-sized categories, which makes it possible to measure distances on the scale.) Using the five items in Figure 4.1 as an example, each participant receives a total score obtained by adding the responses from the five items. A participant who answered 1 (Strongly disagree) to all five items would have a total score of 5. Someone who answered 5 (Strongly agree) to all five items would have a total score of 25. Thus we can position each individual on a scale that represents attitudes toward mathematics. Not only can we compare different individuals, we can also compute means for different groups of participants and compare mean differences between groups. In general, it is very easy to use standard statistical procedures to summarize and interpret the results from a rating-scale question.

A secondary advantage of rating-scale questions is that participants usually find them easy to understand and easy to answer. Because the scale permits different degrees of response, participants are not forced into an absolute yes or no, all-or-none choice. Instead, they can qualify their answers by indicating degrees of agreement or approval. Also it is easy for participants to breeze through a long series of questions after the rating scale has been introduced at the beginning of the survey. Thus it is possible to collect a lot of data on a variety of different topics in a single, relatively efficient survey.

Learning
Check

What is the primary advantage of using a rating scale, compared to other types of self-report questions?

## PHYSIOLOGICAL MEASURES

A second option for measuring a construct is to look at the physiological manifestations of the underlying construct. Fear, for example, reveals itself by increased heart rate and perspiration (measured by galvanic skin response, GSR). A researcher measuring "fear of flying" could attach electrodes to participants and monitor heart rates as they board a plane and during the flight. Or a researcher could ask participants to imagine a flight experience while GSR and heart rate are monitored in a laboratory setting.

The advantage of physiological measures is that they are extremely objective. The equipment provides accurate, reliable, and well-defined measurements that are not dependent on subjective interpretation by either the researcher or the participant. One disadvantage of such measures is that they typically require equipment that may be expensive or unavailable. In addition, the presence of monitoring devices creates an unnatural situation that may cause subjects to react differently than they would under normal circumstances. A more important concern with physiological measures is whether or not they provide a valid measure of the construct. Heart rate, for example, may be related to fear, but heart rate and fear are not the same thing. Increased heart rate may be caused by anxiety, arousal, embarrassment, or exertion as well as by fear. Can we be sure that measurements of heart rate are in fact measurements of fear?

Describe the strengths and weaknesses of physiological measures.

Learning Check

## BEHAVIORAL MEASURES

Constructs often reveal themselves in overt behaviors that can be observed and measured. The behaviors may be completely natural events such as laughing, playing, eating, sleeping, arguing, or speaking. Or the behaviors may be structured, as when a researcher measures performance on a designated task. In the latter case a researcher usually develops a specific task in which performance is theoretically dependent on the construct being measured. For example, reaction time could be measured to determine whether or not a drug affects mental alertness; number of words recalled from a list provides a measure of memory ability; performance on an IQ test is a measure of intelligence. To measure "fear of flying," a researcher could construct a hierarchy of potential behaviors (visiting an airport, walking onto a plane, sitting in a plane while it idles at the gate, riding in a plane while it taxis on a runway, actually flying) and measuring how far up the hierarchy an individual is willing to go.

Behavioral measures provide researchers with a vast number of options, making it possible to select the behavior(s) that seems to be best for defining and measuring the construct. For example, the construct "mental alertness" could be operationally defined by behaviors such as reaction time, reading comprehension, logical reasoning ability, or ability to focus attention. Depending on the specific purpose of a research study, one of these measures probably is more appropriate than the others. In clinical situations in which a researcher works with individual clients, a single construct such as depression may reveal itself as a separate, unique behavioral problem for each client. In this case, the clinician can construct a separate, unique behavioral definition of depression that is appropriate for each patient.

In other situations the behavior may be the actual variable of interest and not just an indicator of some hypothetical construct. For a school psychologist trying to reduce disruptive behavior in the classroom, it is the actual behavior that the psychologist wants to observe and measure. In this case, the psychologist does not use the overt behavior as an operational definition of an intangible construct but rather simply studies the behavior itself.

On the negative side, a behavior may be only a temporary or situational indicator of an underlying construct. A disruptive student may be on good behavior during periods of observation or may shift the timing of negative behaviors from the classroom to the school bus on the way home. Usually it is best to measure a cluster of related behaviors rather than rely on a single indicator. For example, in response to therapy a disruptive student may stop speaking out of turn in the classroom but replace this specific behavior with another form of disruption. A complete definition of "disruptive behavior" would require several behavioral indicators.

Learning Check

Describe the advantages and disadvantages of behavioral measures.

### Behavioral Observation

The process of behavioral observation simply involves the direct observation and systematic recording of behaviors, usually as the behaviors occur in a natural situation. For example, a researcher may observe children on a playground or tropical birds in a rain forest. This measurement technique, however, introduces two special measurement problems:

1. Because the goal is to observe *natural* behavior, it is essential that the behaviors are not disrupted or influenced by the presence of an observer.
2. Observation and measurement require at least some degree of subjective interpretation by the observer. (If we observe two preschool children bumping into each other, we must decide whether the contact was accidental or deliberate, and if it was deliberate, which child initiated the contact and whether it was aggression or simply play). The fact that the measurements are based in part on a subjective judgment raises the question of reliability; that is, would two different occurrences of the same behavior be judged in the same way?

The first problem can be addressed by concealing the observer so that the individuals do not know that their behaviors are being observed and recorded. As long as we observe public behaviors in public places, there is no ethical problem with this technique. An alternative procedure is to habituate the participants to the observer's presence. **Habituation** requires repeated exposure until the observer's presence is no longer a novel stimulus. For example, an observer might sit in a classroom for an hour every day for a week before the actual observation begins. On the first day or two the observer is a novel event, and the children modify their behaviors. After a few days, however, the children become accustomed to the observer's presence (like a piece of furniture) and return to their normal behaviors.

To address the second problem, subjectivity, researchers typically employ three interrelated devices to help ensure the objectivity of their behavioral observations. First, they develop a list of well-defined categories of behavior; next, they use well-trained observers; and finally, they use multiple observers to assess inter-rater reliability. As noted, the first step in the process is to prepare a list of behaviors called **behavior categories.** Developing a set of behavior categories means that, before observation begins, we identify the categories of behavior we want to observe (such as group play, play alone, aggression, social interaction) and then list exactly which behaviors count as examples of each category. A preexisting list enables observers to know exactly what to look for and how to categorize each behavior. For example, observers do not have to make a subjective decision about whether or not an observed behavior is "aggressive;" they simply need to decide whether or not the observed behavior is on the list. In addition, a set of pre-established behavior categories requires a clear operational definition of each construct being examined. (For example, "aggression" is defined as the occurrence of any of the specific behaviors identified on the list.)

During the observation period, normally only one individual observes and records behaviors, using the set of behavioral categories as a guide. To establish reliability, however, two or more individuals must observe and record simultaneously for some of the observation periods. The degree of agreement between the two observers is then computed (usually as a correlation or proportion of agreement ranging from 1.00 = perfect agreement to 0 = no agreement) as a measure of *inter-rater reliability*.

Behavioral observation also involves converting the observations into numerical scores that can be used to describe individuals and groups. The creation of numerical values is usually accomplished by one of three techniques:

1.  The **frequency method** involves counting the instances of each specific behavior that occur during a fixed-time observation period. (The child committed 3 aggressive acts during the 30-minute period.)
2.  The **duration method** involves recording how much time an individual spends engaged in a specific behavior during a fixed-time observation period. (The child spent 18 minutes playing alone during the 30-minute period.)
3.  The **interval method** involves dividing the observation period into a series of intervals and then recording whether or not a specific behavior occurs during each interval. (The 30-minute observation period is divided into 30 one-minute intervals. The child was observed in group play during 12 of the intervals.)

The first two techniques are often well suited for specific behaviors but can lead to distorted measurements in some situations. For example, a child who spends the entire 30 minutes playing alone would get a *frequency* count of only 1. On the other hand, an aggressive child might spend only 5 seconds each attacking 10 different children and obtain a *duration* score of only 50 seconds. In such situations, the *interval method* provides a way to balance frequency and duration to obtain a more representative measurement.

When an observer is confronted with a complex situation, it can be impossible to observe many different individuals and record many different behaviors simultaneously. One solution is to use videotape, which can be replayed repeatedly to gather observations. A second solution is to take a sample of the potential observations rather than attempt to watch and record everything. The first step in the process of sampling observations is to divide the observation period into a series of time intervals. The sampling process then consists of one of the following three procedures:

1.  **Time sampling** involves observing for one interval, then pausing during the next interval to record all the observations. The sequence of observe-record-observe-record is continued through the series of intervals.
2.  **Event sampling** involves identifying one specific event or behavior to be observed and recorded during the first interval; then the observer shifts to a

different event or behavior during the second interval, and so on for the full series of intervals.

3. **Individual sampling** involves identifying one participant to be observed during the first interval, then shifting attention to a different individual for the second interval, and so on.

Learning Checks

Briefly explain why it is important to determine a set of behavior categories before making behavioral observations

Under what circumstances is it necessary to use sampling (time, event, or individual) during behavioral observation?

### Content Analysis and Archival Research

The same techniques that are used in behavioral observation can be applied to other situations that do not involve the direct observation of ongoing behaviors. For example, it is possible to measure "behaviors" that unfold in movies or books, and it is possible to study documents recording behaviors that occurred long ago. Thus, researchers can measure and record incidences of violence in movies or television programs, and they can look into the pasts of adults with personality disorders to see whether they displayed any evidence of abnormal behavior as children. When researchers measure behaviors or events in books, movies, or other media, the measurement process is called **content analysis.** Recording behaviors from historical records is called **archival research.**

Definitions

**Content analysis** involves using the techniques of behavioral observation to measure the occurrence of specific events in literature, movies, television programs, or similar media that present replicas of behaviors.

**Archival research** involves looking at historical records (archives) to measure behaviors or events that occurred in the past.

To ensure that the measurements are objective and reliable, the processes of content analysis and archival research follow the same rules that are used for behavioral observation. Specifically, the measurement process involves:

1. Establishing behavioral categories to define exactly which events are included in each category being measured; for example, a list of specific examples is prepared to define television violence.
2. Using the frequency method, the duration method, or the interval method to obtain a numerical score for each behavioral category; for example, an observer records how many examples of violence are seen in a 30-minute television program or how many disciplinary actions appear on an individual's school records.
3. Using multiple observers for at least part of the measurement process to obtain a measure of inter-rater reliability.

## 4.6   OTHER ASPECTS OF MEASUREMENT

Beyond the validity and reliability of measures, the scale of measurement, and the modality of measurement, several other factors should be considered when selecting a measurement procedure. The right decisions about each of these factors can increase the likelihood of success of a research study. In this section we consider three additional issues related to the measurement process: multiple measures, sensitivity of measurement and range effects, and participant reactivity and experimenter bias.

### MULTIPLE MEASURES

One method of obtaining a more complete measure of a construct is to use two (or more) different procedures to measure the same variable. For example, we could record both heart rate and behavior as measures of fear. The advantage of this multiple-measure technique is that it usually provides more confidence in the validity of the measurements. However, multiple measures can introduce some problems. One problem involves the statistical analysis and interpretation of the results. Although there are statistical techniques for evaluating multivariate data, they are usually not well understood by most researchers. A more serious problem is that the two variables may not behave in the same way. A therapy program for treating fear, for example, may produce an immediate and large effect on behavior but no effect on heart rate; after therapy, participants are willing to approach a feared object, but their hearts still race. The lack of agreement between two measures is called **desynchrony,** and it can confuse the interpretation of results (did the therapy reduce fear?). Desynchrony may be caused by the fact that one measure is more sensitive than the other, or it may indicate that different dimensions of the variable change at different times during treatment (behavior may change quickly, but the physiological aspects of fear take more time). In general, the problems associated with multiple measures tend to outweigh the advantages unless the multiple measures can be combined into a single score for each individual.

### SENSITIVITY AND RANGE EFFECTS

Typically a researcher begins a study with some expectation of how the variables will behave, specifically the direction and magnitude of changes that are likely to be observed. An important concern for any measurement procedure is that the measurements are sensitive enough to respond to the type and magnitude of the changes that are expected. For example, if a medication is expected to have only a small effect on reaction time, then it is essential that time be measured in units small enough to detect the change. If we measure time in seconds, and the magnitude of the effect is 1/100 of a second, then the change will not be noticed. In general, if we expect fairly small, subtle changes in a variable, then the measurement procedure must be sensitive enough to detect the changes, and the scale of measurement must have enough different categories to allow discrimination between individuals.

One particular sensitivity problem occurs when the scores obtained in a research study tend to cluster at one end of the measurement scale. For example, suppose that an educational psychologist intends to evaluate a new teaching program by measuring reading comprehension for a group of students before and after the program is administered. If the students all score around 95% before the program starts, then there is essentially no room for improvement. Even if the program does improve reading comprehension, the measurement procedure probably will not detect an increase in scores. In this case, the effective range of the measurement scale is constrained, and the measurement procedure is insensitive to changes that may occur in one direction. In general, this type of sensitivity problem is called a **range effect.** When the range is restricted at the high end, the problem is called a **ceiling effect** (the measurements bump into a ceiling and can go no higher). Similarly, clustering at the low end of the scale can produce a **floor effect.**

In general, range effects suggest a basic incompatibility between the measurement procedure and the individuals measured. Often the measurement is based on a task that is too easy (thereby producing high scores) or too difficult (thereby producing low scores) for the participants being tested. Note that it is not the measurement procedure that is at fault but rather the fact that the procedure is used with a particular group of individuals. For example, a measurement that works well for 4-year-old children may produce serious range effects if used with adolescents. For this reason, it is advisable to pretest any measurement procedure for which potential range effects are suspected. Simply measure a small sample of representative individuals to be sure that the obtained values are far enough from the extremes of the scale to allow room to measure changes in either direction.

Definitions

A **ceiling effect** is the clustering of scores at the high end of a measurement scale, allowing little or no possibility of increases in value.

A **floor effect** is the clustering of scores at the low end of a measurement scale, allowing little or no possibility of decreases in value.

 Learning Check

Describe the sensitivity problem of a range effect.

## PARTICIPANT REACTIVITY AND EXPERIMENTER BIAS

The measurement of living organisms, particularly humans, introduces another factor into the measurement process that can affect the validity and the reliability of the measurements. Specifically, living organisms are active and responsive, and their actions and responses can distort the measurements. If we measure an inanimate object such as a table or a block of wood, we don't expect the object to have any response to the measurement, such as "Whoa! I'm being watched. I had better be on my best behavior." Unfortunately this kind of response can happen with human participants.

Participants who are aware that they are being observed and measured may react in unpredictable ways. In addition, the research setting often creates a set of demand characteristics that suggest what kinds of behavior are appropriate or expected. The combination of **demand characteristics** and participant **reactivity** can change a participant's normal behavior and thereby influence the variable or the measurement the researcher is trying to obtain. Although individuals can react to measurement in different ways, problems can occur when they become overly cooperative, overly defensive, or hostile. Cooperative participants may modify their behavior in an attempt to help or to please the researcher. Defensive participants may try to conceal behaviors or attitudes that they consider private or personal. Hostile participants may try to subvert the research study by producing bizarre or unrealistic responses. Any of these reactions will distort the measurements the researcher is trying to obtain.

Although it is essentially impossible to prevent participants from thinking about a research study and speculating about their own performance, there are steps to help reduce the effects of reactivity. Often it is possible to observe and measure individuals without their awareness. Although this strategy is often possible, some variables are difficult to observe directly (for example, attitudes), and in some situations ethical considerations prevent researchers from secretly observing people. An alternative strategy is to disguise or conceal the measurement process. The true purpose of a questionnaire can be masked by embedding a few critical questions in a larger set of irrelevant items or by deliberately using questions with low face validity. Another option is to suggest (subtly or openly) that the participant is performing one task when, in fact, we are observing and measuring something else. In either case, some level of deception is involved, which can raise a question of ethics (see Chapter 3). The most direct strategy for limiting reactivity is to reassure participants that their performance or responses are completely confidential and anonymous, and encourage them to make honest, natural responses. Any attempt to reassure and relax participants helps reduce reactivity.

In addition to the participant's influence on measurement, we must also consider the experimenter's ability to affect measurements. Typically a researcher knows the predicted outcome of a research study and is in a position to influence the results. For example, an experimenter might be warm, friendly, and encouraging while presenting instructions to a group of participants in a treatment condition that is expected to produce good performance, and cold, aloof, and somewhat stern while presenting the instructions to another group in a comparison treatment where performance is expected to be relatively poor. The experimenter is manipulating participant motivation, and this manipulation distorts the measurements. When researchers influence results in this way, the effect is called **experimenter bias.** The experimenter's influence may be very strong or very subtle; it may be a deliberate attempt to control the results, or it may be completely unintentional. The influence may come from tone of voice, body language, enthusiasm, or a variety of factors. Whenever a researcher knows the predicted outcome of a study and has some level of contact with the participants, the potential for experimenter bias exists.

One option for limiting experimenter bias is to standardize or automate the experiment. For example, a researcher could read from a prepared script to ensure that all participants receive exactly the same instructions. Or instructions could be presented on a printed handout, by audiotape, or on video. In each case, the goal is to limit the personal contact between the experimenter and the participant. Another strategy for reducing experimenter bias is to use a "blind" experiment. If the research study is conducted by an experimenter (assistant) who does not know the expected results, then the experimenter should not be able to influence the participants. This technique is called **single-blind** research. An alternative is to set up a study where neither the experimenter nor the participants know the expected results. This procedure is called **double-blind** research and is commonly used in drug studies in which some participants get the real drug and others get a placebo. The double-blind study is structured so that neither the researcher nor the participants know exactly who is getting which drug.

Definitions

A research study is **single blind** if the researcher does not know the predicted outcome.

A research study is **double blind** if both the researcher and the participants are unaware of the predicted outcome.

Learning Checks

Explain (or give an example of) how participant reactivity can influence the measurements obtained in a research study.

Explain how a single-blind study minimizes the potential for experimenter bias.

## SELECTING A MEASUREMENT PROCEDURE

As seen in the preceding sections, the choice of a measurement procedure involves several decisions. Because each decision has implications for the results of the study, it is important to consider all the options before deciding on a scheme for measurement or when reading a report of results from another research study.

The best starting point for selecting a measurement procedure is to review past research reports involving the variables or constructs to be examined. Most commonly used procedures have been evaluated for reliability and validity. In addition, using an established measurement procedure means that results can be compared directly to the previous literature in the area.

If more than one procedure exists for defining and measuring a particular variable, examine the options and determine which method is best suited for the specific research question. In particular, consider which measure has a level of sensitivity appropriate for detecting the individual differences and group differences that you expect to observe. Also decide whether the scale of measurement (nominal, ordinal, interval, ratio) is appropriate for the kind of conclusion you would like to make. Simply to establish that differences exist, a nominal scale may be sufficient. On the other hand, to determine the magnitude of a difference, you need either an interval or a ratio scale. Finally, consider how to deal with potential participant reactivity and the possibility of experimenter bias.

As noted in Chapter 2, criticizing or challenging a published measurement procedure can lead to new research ideas. As you read published research reports, always question the measurement procedures: Why was the variable measured as it was? Would a different scale have been better? Were the results biased by a lack of sensitivity or by range effects? What would happen if the variable(s) were measured in a different way? If you can reasonably predict that the results would be changed by using a different measurement strategy, then you have the grounds for a new research study. Keep in mind, however, that if you develop your own operational definition or measurement procedure, you may need to demonstrate validity and reliability, a task that can be quite tedious.

## CHAPTER SUMMARY

In this chapter we considered how a researcher defines and measures variables in a study. Because many research variables are hypothetical constructs and hence intangible, operational definitions are developed to define and measure the variables. Many measurement procedures are available for each variable. A researcher decides which procedure to use by evaluating the validity and reliability of the procedure. A valid measure truly measures the variable that it claims to measure. The six most commonly used measures of the validity of measurement are face, concurrent, predictive, construct convergent, and divergent validity. A measure is reliable if it results in stable and consistent measurements. Three assessments of reliability are test-retest, inter-rater, and split-half reliability.

The process of measurement involves classifying individuals. The set of categories used for classification is called the scale of measurement. Four different types of measurement scales are nominal, ordinal, interval, and ratio. A major decision faced by researchers is which type or modality of measurement to use. The three modalities of measurement are self-report, physiological, and behavioral; each has certain advantages and disadvantages.

## KEY WORDS

construct or hypothetical
    construct
operational definition
validity
face validity
concurrent validity
predictive validity

construct validity
convergent validity
divergent validity
reliability
test-retest reliability
inter-rater reliability
split-half reliability

content analysis
archival research
ceiling effect
floor effect
single blind
double blind

##  EXERCISES

1. In addition to the key words, you should also be able to define each of the following terms:

| | |
|---|---|
| scale of measurement | duration method |
| nominal scale | interval method |
| ordinal scale | time sampling |
| interval scale | event sampling |
| ratio scale | individual sampling |
| anchors | desynchrony |
| response set | range effect |
| semantic differential | demand |
| habituation |    characteristics |
| behavior categories | reactivity |
| frequency method | experimenter bias |

2. Pick a hypothetical construct. Describe how it serves as an internal mediator, by what external stimuli it can be influenced, and what behaviors it can influence.
3. What is meant by the validity of a measure?
4. Describe how a researcher establishes the concurrent validity of a measure.
5. Describe how a researcher establishes the predictive validity of a measure.
6. What is meant by the reliability of a measure?
7. Describe the three sources of error in a measurement.
8. Describe how test-retest reliability is established.

9. Describe how inter-rater reliability is established.

10. Which scale of measurement would probably be used for each of the following variables?
    a. occupation
    b. age
    c. gender
    d. socioeconomic class (upper class, middle class, lower class)

11. What are the strengths and weaknesses of restricted questions used in a self-report measure?

12. Describe the relative advantages and disadvantages of physiological measures and self-report measures.

13. What are the two measurement problems of behavioral observation?

14. What is the purpose of measuring inter-rater reliability during behavioral observation?

15. How would you use the frequency method to score verbal behavior?

16. A teacher has identified a disruptive child in a third-grade classroom. Your job is to observe the child and obtain a measurement of the child's disruptiveness. After your initial measurement, a psychologist will treat the child, and you will observe again to determine the effectiveness of the treatment. Briefly explain how you might translate your observations into a numerical measurement of disruption.

17. What is the advantage of using multiple measures for a single variable? What is the disadvantage?

18. Briefly explain how a ceiling effect (or floor effect) can affect the outcome of a research study.

19. Imagine that you are a participant in a research study. For each of the following scenarios, describe how you would probably react, and explain how your reactivity would influence your responses.
    a. A researcher tells you that the task you are about to perform is directly related to intelligence. Intelligent people usually find the task to be quite easy and perform very well.
    b. A researcher tells you that the purpose of the study is to measure your attitudes and prejudices concerning race. First assume that the researcher intends to ask you questions in an interview. Then assume that the researcher hands you a questionnaire to fill out privately.

## InfoTrac COLLEGE EDITION EXERCISES

1. Select any subject you want, and use InfoTrac to locate a journal article that reports the results of a research study examining your subject. Specifically, find an article where the researchers obtained a sample of participants and then used some form of measurement. (Note: You are likely to find research articles in psychology journals such as the *Journal of Social Psychology* or in journals that have the word *research* in their titles, such as the *Journal of Advertising Research* or the *Research Quarterly for Exercise and Sport.*) Once you have found your article, answer each of the following questions:
   a. Briefly describe what was measured and how it was measured.
   b. Was the variable measured directly (like height or weight), or did the research use an operational definition to measure a hypothetical construct such as "motivation"?
   c. What scale of measurement was used (nominal, ordinal, interval, or ratio)?
   d. Did the researchers use a physiological, a behavioral, or a self-report measure?

2. Use InfoTrac College Edition to locate an article that examines an issue directly related to the measurement process (for example, an article that addresses the reliability or validity of measurement). Note: Begin with a very general key word such as *learning*, which should lead you to thousands of references or articles. Instead of looking at the items directly, select the Subdivisions option and try to find *measurement* as one of the subdivisions. This should lead you to articles that examine the measurement process.

Identify the issue that your article addresses; briefly summarize why the authors considered this issue important and the suggestions or solutions they provide for resolving it.

3. Using the key word *content analysis*, locate an article that examines the content of a book(s), movie(s), or TV show(s).

a. Identify exactly what types of behaviors or events the authors recorded.

b. Briefly describe how they defined one of the behaviors or events (exactly what did they count as an example?)

c. Briefly summarize the result or conclusion of the study.

# Selecting Research Participants

## CHAPTER OVERVIEW

In this chapter we discuss the selection of individuals for participation in research studies—Step 4 of the research process as outlined in Chapter 1. In any research study, only a small number of individuals actually participate. However, the researcher would like to generalize the results of the study beyond the small group of participants and therefore must develop a plan for selecting participants such that the individuals in the study constitute a reasonable representation of the broader population. The options for selecting individuals are presented.

## 5.1    INTRODUCTION

Beyond the research idea and hypothesis you select and how you decide to define and measure your variables, one of the most critical issues in planning research is selection of research participants (see Chapter 1, Step 4 of the research process). Suppose, for example, that you are interested in conducting a study of high school students' attitudes toward unrestricted searches of their lockers. Who should complete your questionnaire? All the high school students in the nation? Not likely—that would be an enormous and expensive undertaking. Should you use all 5,000 high school students in a local school district? Possibly—but that would still be expensive, and how would you decide what school district or school to use? Perhaps you should use only students in a high school that has reported problems with drugs and weapons; but it is also likely that there are drugs and weapons in high schools not identified as problem schools. The bottom line in any research study is that not *everyone* can participate, and the success of a study depends on the way in which participants are selected.

Each research study is a unique event that involves a specific group of participants. Most research attempts to answer a general question about a large group of individuals, as opposed to a specific question about a few, unique individuals. Therefore, researchers typically want to generalize or extend their results beyond the individuals who participate.

### POPULATIONS AND SAMPLES

In the terminology of research design, the large group of interest to a researcher is called the **population,** and the small set of individuals who participate in the study is called the **sample.** Figure 5.1 illustrates the relationship between a population and a sample. Typically, populations are huge, containing far too many individuals to measure and study. For example, a researcher may be interested in adolescents, or preschool children, or men, or women, or humans. In each of these cases the population is much too large to permit a researcher to study every individual. Therefore, a researcher must rely on a smaller group, a sample, to provide information about the population. A sample is selected from a population and is intended to represent that population. The goal of the research study is to examine the sample and then generalize the results to the entire population.

A **population** is the entire set of individuals of interest to a researcher. Although the entire population usually does not participate in a research study, the results from the study are generalized to the entire population.

A **sample** is a set of individuals selected from a population and usually is intended to represent the population in a research study.

Definitions

Explain the relationship between a population and a sample.

Learning Check

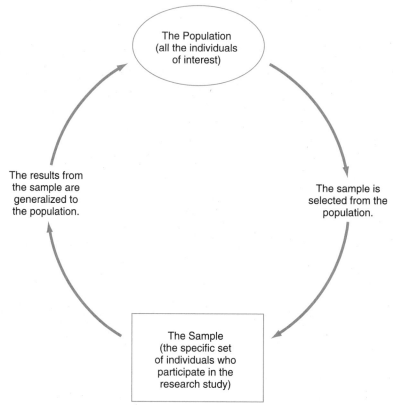

Figure 5.1  The Relationship Between a Population and a Sample

Before proceeding, we need to distinguish among different types of populations. A population is sometimes called a **target population.** A target population is a group that is defined by the researcher's specific interests. Individuals in a target population typically share one characteristic. All children of divorced parents, all elementary school-aged children, and all adolescents diagnosed with bulimia nervosa are examples of target populations.

Usually, target populations are not easily available. For example, for a researcher interested in the treatment of bulimia nervosa in adolescents, the target population would be all of the adolescents in the world who are diagnosed with this disorder. Clearly, the researcher would not have access to most of these people to recruit as participants. However, a researcher would have access to the many local clinics and agencies that treat clients with eating disorders. These local clients (adolescents diagnosed with bulimia nervosa) become the **accessible population** from which to select the sample. Most researchers select their samples from accessible populations. Therefore, we not only need to be cautious about generalizing the results of a study to the accessible population, but, in addition, we must always be extremely cautious about generalizing the results of a research study to the target population. Figure 5.2 depicts the relationship among target populations, accessible populations, and samples. For the remainder of the book, then, we use the term *population* to mean the accessible population.

Figure 5.2   The Relationship Among the Target Population, the Accessible Population, and the Sample

## REPRESENTATIVE SAMPLES

We have said that the goal of a research study is to examine a sample and then generalize the results to the population. How accurately we can generalize the results from a given sample to the population depends on the **representativeness** of the sample. The degree of representativeness of a sample refers to how closely the sample mirrors or resembles the population. Thus, one problem that every researcher faces is how to obtain a sample that provides a reasonable representation of the population. To generalize the results of a study to a population, the researcher must select a **representative sample.** The major threat to representativeness is bias. A **biased sample** is one that has characteristics that are noticeably different from those of the population. If the individuals in a sample are smarter (or older or faster) than the individuals in the population, then the sample is biased. A biased sample can occur simply by chance; for example, tossing a balanced coin can result in heads 10 times in a row. It is more likely, however, that a biased sample is the result of **selection bias** (also called *sampling bias*), which means that the sampling procedure favors the selection of some individuals over others. For example, if the population we are interested in is adults, and we recruit our sample from the people in a university parking lot, we are likely to obtain a sample that is smarter than the population. If we recruit from a health club, our sample is likely to be healthier and more physically fit than the population. Recruiting from the yacht club membership list would probably produce a financially biased sample. The likelihood of the sample being representative depends on which sampling technique is used. In this chapter we consider two basic approaches to sampling and examine some of the common strategies or techniques for obtaining samples.

Definitions

The **representativeness** of a sample refers to the extent to which the characteristics of the sample accurately reflect the characteristics of the population.

A **representative sample** is a sample with the same characteristics as the population.

A **biased sample** is a sample with different characteristics from those of the population.

**Selection bias** occurs when participants or subjects are selected in a manner that increases the probability of obtaining a biased sample.

 Learning Check

Describe why it is important to obtain a representative sample.

### SAMPLING BASICS

The process of selecting individuals for a study is called **sampling.** Researchers have developed a variety of different sampling methods (also called *sampling techniques* or *procedures*). Sampling methods fall into two basic categories, probability sampling and nonprobability sampling.

In **probability sampling,** the odds of selecting a particular individual are known and can be calculated. For example, in a population of 100 people, each individual has a probability of selection of 1/100. Each individual is equally likely to be selected. An important condition of probability sampling is that the exact population size must be known and all the individuals listed. A second condition is that each individual in the population must have a specifiable probability of selection. Finally, the researcher must use an unbiased method for selection. It must be a **random process,** which simply means that every possible outcome is equally likely. For example, each time you toss a coin, the two possible outcomes (heads and tails) are equally likely.

In **nonprobability sampling** the odds of selecting a particular individual are not known because the researcher does not know the population size or the members of the population. In addition, in nonprobability sampling the researcher does not use an unbiased method of selection. For example, a researcher who wants to study the behavior of preschool children may go to a local day care center where a group of preschool children are already assembled. Because the researcher does not ensure that all preschool children have an equal chance of being selected, this sample has an increased chance of being biased. For example, if the day care center includes only White, middle-class children, then the sample will definitely not represent the target population of preschool children. In general, nonprobability sampling has a greater risk of producing a biased sample than does probability sampling.

Notice that probability sampling requires extensive knowledge of the population, which is often unavailable to a researcher. For this reason, nonprobability sampling techniques are more commonly used.

**Sampling** is the process of selecting individuals to participate in a research study.

In **probability sampling,** the entire population is known, each individual in the population has a specifiable probability of selection, and sampling is done by a random process based on the probabilities.

A **random process** is a procedure that produces one outcome from a set of possible outcomes. The outcome must be unpredictable each time, and the process must guarantee that each of the possible outcomes is equally likely to occur.

In **nonprobability sampling,** the population is not completely known, individual probabilities cannot be known, and the sampling method is based on factors such as common sense or ease, with an effort to maintain representativeness and avoid bias.

In the following sections we discuss five probability sampling methods (simple random, systematic, stratified, proportionate stratified, and cluster sampling) and two nonprobability sampling methods (convenience and quota sampling). For each method, the general goal is to obtain a sample that is representative of the population from which it is taken. For different kinds of research, however, the definition of *representative* varies; hence there are several well-defined sampling procedures that attempt to produce a particular kind of representation.

## 5.2    PROBABILITY SAMPLING METHODS

### SIMPLE RANDOM SAMPLING

The starting point for most sampling techniques is **simple random sampling.** The basic requirement for random sampling is that each individual in the population has an *equal* and *independent* chance of being selected. Equality means that no individual is more likely to be chosen than another. Independence means that the choice of one individual does not bias the researcher for or against the choice of another individual.

Suppose a researcher opens a phone book at random, plunks down a finger on someone's name, and selects that person and every fifth name after that to participate in a study. Is this an example of simple random sampling? No, because the requirements of both equality and independence are violated. First, not everyone in the population has an equal chance of being selected. Some people in the population have no chance of being selected, because their names are not in the phone book (for example, people have unlisted phone numbers, phone numbers under other people's names, or no phone at all.) Second, names are not selected independently. Because the researcher picks every 5th person, after a random start, she or he is biased against the 1st, 2nd, 3rd, and 4th people down the list and in favor of the 5th person.

The obvious goal of a simple random sample is to ensure that the selection procedure cannot discriminate among individuals and thereby result in a non-representative sample. The two principal methods of random sampling are:

1. *Sampling with replacement:* This method requires that an individual selected for the sample be recorded as a sample member and then returned to the population (replaced) before the next selection is made. This procedure ensures that the probability of selection remains constant throughout a series of selections. For example, if we select from a population of 10 individuals, the probability of selecting any particular individual is 1/10. To keep this same probability (1/10) for the second selection, it is necessary to return the first individual to the pool before the next is selected.

2. *Sampling without replacement:* As the term indicates, this method removes each selected individual from the population before the next selection is made. Although the probability of being selected changes with each selection, this method guarantees that no individual will appear more than once in a single sample.

Sampling with replacement is an assumption of many of the mathematical models that form the foundation of statistical analysis. In most research, however, individuals aren't actually replaced, because then one individual could appear repeatedly in the same sample. If we conduct a public opinion survey, for example, we wouldn't call the same person 10 times and then claim that we had a sample of 10 individuals. Most populations are so large that, for all practical purposes, the probabilities remain unchanged even when we do not replace individuals. By using large populations, researchers can sample without replacement, ensure that individuals are not repeated in one sample, and still satisfy the mathematical assumptions needed for statistical analysis.

The process of simple random sampling consists of the following steps:

1. Clearly define the population from which you want to select a sample.
2. List all the members of the population.
3. Using a random process, select individuals from the list.

Often, each individual is assigned a number, and then a random process is used to select numbers. For example, suppose a researcher has a population of 100 third-grade children from a local school district, from which a sample of 25 children is to be selected. Each child's name is put on a list, and each child is assigned a number from 1 to 100. Then the numbers 1 to 100 are written on separate pieces of paper and shuffled. Finally, the researcher picks 25 slips of paper, and the numbers on the paper determine the 25 participants.

As noted above, researchers typically use some random process, such as a coin toss or picking numbers from a hat, to guide the selection. But what if, in picking the numbers from a hat, the size of the papers is different or the slips of paper aren't shuffled adequately? The researcher could select individuals with larger slips of paper or individuals at the end of the list whose slips of paper are at the top of the pile. A more unbiased random process involves using the random number table for selection of participants. Appendix A contains a table of random numbers and a step-by-step guide for using it.

The logic behind simple random sampling is that it removes bias from the selection procedure and should result in representative samples. However, note that simple random sampling removes bias by leaving each selection to chance. In the long run, this strategy generates a balanced, representative sample. If we toss a coin thousands of times, eventually the results will be 50% heads and 50% tails. In the short run, however, there are no guarantees. Because chance determines each selection, it is possible (although usually unlikely) to obtain a very distorted sample. We could, for example, toss a balanced coin and get heads 10 times in a row. Or we could get a random sample of 10 males from a population that contains an equal number of men and women. To avoid this kind of nonrepresentative sample, researchers often impose additional restrictions on the random sampling procedure; these are presented later in the sections on stratified and proportionate stratified random sampling.

Explain how it is possible to obtain a biased sample with simple random sampling.

Learning Check

## SYSTEMATIC SAMPLING

**Systematic sampling** is a type of probability sampling that is very similar to simple random sampling. With systematic sampling, a sample is obtained by selecting every $n$th participant from a list containing the total population, after a random start. Systematic sampling is identical to simple random sampling (i.e., follow the three steps) for selection of the first participant; however, after the first individual is selected, the researcher does not continue to use a random process to select the remaining individuals for the sample. Instead, the researcher selects every 4th or 5th, etc., individual after that. The size of $n$ is calculated by dividing the population size by the desired sample size. For example, suppose a researcher has a population of 100 third-grade children from a local school district, from which a sample of 25 children is to be selected. Each child's name is put on a list and assigned a number from 1 to 100. Then the researcher uses a random process such as a table of random numbers to select the first participant; for example, participant number 11. The size of $n$ in this example is 4 (100/25). Therefore every 4th individual after participant 11 (e.g., 15, 19, 23, etc.) is selected (see Figure 5.3).

This technique is truly less random than simple random sampling because the principle of independence is violated. Specifically, if we select participant number 11, we are biased against choosing participants number 12, 13, and 14, and we are biased in favor of choosing participant number 15. However, as a probability sampling method, this method insures a high degree of representativeness.

## STRATIFIED RANDOM SAMPLING

A population usually consists of a variety of identifiable subgroups. For example, the population of registered voters in California can be subdivided into men and women, Republicans and Democrats, different ethnic groups, different age groups, and so on. The different subgroups can be viewed as different layers or strata like the layers of rock on a cliff face (see Figure 5.4). To ensure that each

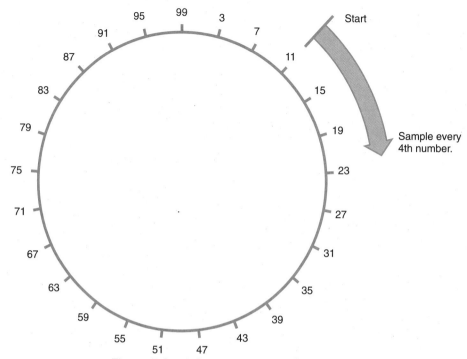

Figure 5.3    A Systematic Sampling Technique
When using systematic sampling, imagine the individuals or
numbers arranged in a circle instead of a straight line. Here,
the numbers 1 to 100 are shown in a circle. The sampling begins with
11 and selects every 4th number. Notice that the sample continues
beyond 100 until the full sample of 25 individuals is obtained.

subgroup is represented equally in a sample, one option is to use **stratified random sampling.** To obtain this kind of sample, we first identify the specific subgroups (or strata) to be included in the sample. Then we select equal random samples from each of the pre-identified subgroups, using the same steps as in simple random sampling. Finally, we combine the subgroup samples into one overall sample. For example, suppose that we plan to select 50 individuals from a large introductory psychology class and want to ensure that men and women are equally represented. First, we select a random sample of 25 men from the males in the class and then a random sample of 25 women from the females. Combining these two subgroup samples produces the desired stratified random sample.

Stratified random sampling is particularly useful when a researcher wants to describe each individual segment of the population or wants to compare segments. To do this, each subgroup in the sample must contain enough individuals to adequately represent its segment of the population. Consider the following example.

A sociologist conducts an opinion survey in a major city. Part of the research plan calls for describing and comparing the opinions of four different ethnic

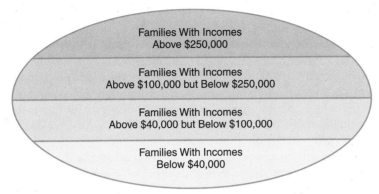

Figure 5.4   The Population of a Major City Shown as Different Layers or Strata Defined by Annual Income

groups: African Americans, Hispanics, Asians, and Whites. If the researcher uses simple random sampling to select 300 individuals, the sample might contain only a few individuals from one (or more) of these groups. With only a handful of representatives of a particular group, the researcher could not make any definite statements about that group's opinion and could not make any meaningful comparisons with other ethnic groups. A stratified random sample avoids this problem by ensuring that each subgroup contains a predetermined number of individuals (set by the researcher). For a total sample of 300, the researcher selects 75 representatives of each of the four predetermined subgroups.

When the focus of a research study is on specific subgroups within a population, a stratified random sample is the best option. That is, this type of random sampling is appropriate when the purpose of a research study is to examine specific subgroups and make comparisons between them. However, if the study focuses on the overall population, then this sampling technique can create problems. For example, the stratified sample just described probably gives a distorted picture of the overall population. Specifically, the four ethnic groups are represented equally in the sample but are probably not equally present in the population. One group, for example, may form only 3% of the city's population but carry a weight equal to 25% in the sample. In the next sampling method, this problem is corrected.

Explain why stratified random sampling is used.

Learning Check

## PROPORTIONATE STRATIFIED RANDOM SAMPLING

Occasionally researchers try to improve the correspondence between a sample and a population by deliberately structuring the sample so that its composition matches the composition of the population. As with a stratified sample, we begin by identifying a set of subgroups or segments in the population. Next we determine what proportion of the population corresponds to each subgroup. Finally, a sample is obtained such that the proportions in the sample exactly match the proportions in the overall population. This kind of sampling is called **proportionate stratified random sampling,** or simply **proportionate random sampling.**

For example, suppose that we want our sample to accurately represent gender in the population. If the overall population contains 75% females and 25% males, then the sample is selected so that it too contains 75% females and 25% males. Proportionate random sampling is used commonly for political polls and other major public-opinion surveys in which researchers want to ensure that a relatively small sample provides an accurate, representative cross-section of a large and diverse population. The sample can be constructed so that several variables such as age, economic status, and political affiliation are represented in the sample in the same proportions in which they exist in the population.

Depending on how precisely we want sample proportions to match population proportions, the proportionate stratified sample can create a lot of extra work. Obviously, we must first determine the existing population proportions, which may require a trip to the library or another research center; then we must find individuals who match the categories we have identified. One strategy is to obtain a very large sample (much bigger than ultimately needed), measure all of the different variables for each individual, and then randomly select those who fit the criteria (or randomly weed out the extras who do not fit). This process requires a lot of preliminary measurement before the study actually begins, and it discards many of the sampled individuals.

When and why is it useful for a researcher to use proportionate stratified random sampling?

## CLUSTER SAMPLING

Usually, samples are obtained by selecting individuals from a population. Occasionally, however, the individuals are already clustered in preexisting groups, and a researcher can randomly select groups instead. For example, a researcher may want to obtain a large sample of third-grade students from the city school system. Instead of selecting 300 students one at a time, the researcher can randomly select 10 classrooms (each with about 30 students) and still end up with 300 individuals in the sample. This procedure is called **cluster sampling** and can be used whenever well-defined clusters exist within the population of interest. This sampling technique has two clear advantages. First, it is a relatively quick and easy way to obtain a large sample. Second, the treatment and measurement of individuals can often be done in groups, which can greatly facilitate the entire research project. Instead of selecting an individual, administering the treatment, and measuring a single score, the researcher can often administer the treatment to the entire cluster, test and measure the entire group at one time, and walk away with 30 scores from a single experimental session.

The disadvantage of cluster sampling is that it can raise concerns about the *independence* of the individual scores. A sample of 300 individuals is assumed to contain 300 separate, individual, and independent measurements; if one individual in the sample directly influences the score of another individual, then the two scores are in fact related and should not be counted as two separate individuals. As an extreme example, suppose one child completes a research questionnaire and then a second child simply copies all the answers. Clearly, the two question-naires should not be treated as two separate individuals. If the individuals within a cluster share common characteristics that might influence the variables being measured, then a researcher must question whether the individual measurements from the cluster actually represent separate and independent individuals.

Describe the problem associated with cluster sampling.

Learning Check

## COMBINED-STRATEGY SAMPLING

Occasionally, researchers combine two or more sampling strategies to select par-ticipants. For example, a superintendent of schools may first divide his or her district into regions (e.g., north, south, east, and west), which involves stratified sampling. From the different regions, the superintendent may then select two third-grade classrooms, which involves cluster sampling. Selection strategies are commonly combined to optimize the chances that a sample is representative of a widely dispersed or broad-based population—for example, in a wide-market sur-vey or a political poll.

## PROBABILITY SAMPLING METHODS SUMMARY

The probability sampling methods have a greater chance of obtaining a repre-sentative sample because of the random selection process involved. However, as noted in the subsection on simple random sampling, these methods do not *guar-antee* a high degree of representativeness. In addition, they are extremely time consuming and tedious (i.e., obtaining a list of all the members of a population and developing a random, unbiased selection process). These techniques also require that the researcher "know" the whole population and have access to it. For these reasons, probability sampling techniques are rarely used except in re-search involving small, contained populations (e.g., students at a school, prison-ers at one correctional facility) or large-scale surveys.

## 5.3    NONPROBABILITY SAMPLING METHODS

### CONVENIENCE SAMPLING

The most commonly used sampling method in psychological research is probably **convenience sampling.** In convenience sampling, researchers simply use as par-ticipants those individuals who are easy to get. People are selected on the basis of their availability and willingness to respond. Examples include people on the street or in a mall who are stopped to be interviewed, people who respond to a maga-zine or television survey or to an advertisement for a study in the newspaper, In-troductory Psychology students who are used in a study, and students who are asked to complete a survey for a class survey project. A researcher who teaches at

Convenience sampling is also known as *accidental sampling* or *haphazard sampling.*

the State University of New York College at Brockport and uses college students as participants is likely to use students enrolled at that college. A researcher at the University of California, Berkeley, is likely to use students enrolled there.

Convenience sampling is considered a weak form of sampling because the researcher makes no attempt to know the population or to use a random process in selection. The researcher exercises very little control over the representativeness of the sample, and therefore there is a strong possibility that the obtained sample is biased. This is especially problematic when individuals actively come forward to participate, as with phone-in radio surveys or mail-in magazine surveys. In these cases the sample will be biased because only those individuals volunteer their time who are inclined to listen to that station or read that magazine and feel strongly about the issue being investigated. These individuals are probably not representative of the general population.

Despite this major drawback, convenience sampling is probably used more often than any other kind of sampling. It is an easier, less expensive, more timely technique than the probability sampling techniques, which involve detailing all members of a population and using a laborious random process to select participants.

Finally, although convenience sampling offers no guarantees of a representative and unbiased sample, do not automatically conclude that this type of sampling is hopelessly flawed. Most researchers use two strategies to help correct most of the serious problems associated with convenience sampling. First, researchers try to ensure that their samples are reasonably representative and not strongly biased. For example, a researcher may select a sample that consists entirely of Introductory Psychology students from a small college in Atlanta. However, if the researcher is careful to select a broad cross-section of students (males and females, different ages, different levels of academic performance, and so on), it is sensible to expect this sample to be reasonably similar to any other sample of college students that might be obtained from other academic departments or other colleges around the country. Unless the research study involves some special skill such as surfing or winter driving, it usually is reasonable to assume that a sample from one location is just as representative as a sample from any other location. The students in a state college in Florida are probably quite similar to the students in a state college in Idaho, and the children in a Seattle day care center are probably similar to the children in a St. Louis day care center. The exception to this simple concept occurs whenever a convenience sample is obtained from a location with unusual or unique characteristics, such as a music school for extremely talented students or a private day care center for child geniuses.

The second strategy that helps minimize potential problems with convenience sampling is simply to provide a clear description of how the sample was obtained and who the participants are. For example, a researcher might report that a sample of 20 children aged 3 to 5 was obtained from a day care center in downtown Houston. Or a research report may state that a sample of 100 students, 67 females and 33 males, all between the ages of 18 and 22, was obtained from the Introductory Psychology class at a large Midwestern state university. Although these samples may not be perfectly representative of the larger population and each may have some biases, at least everyone knows what the sample looks like and can make their own judgments about representativeness.

Describe the advantages and disadvantages of convenience sampling.

Learning
Check

## QUOTA SAMPLING

In **quota sampling,** a researcher first identifies specific subgroups to be included in the sample and then establishes quotas for individuals to be selected from each subgroup. For example, suppose you want to conduct a study with a sample of 30 preschool-age children, and you want 50% males and 50% females in your sample. Rather than simply taking the first 30 children, regardless of gender, whose parents respond to an advertisement for the study, you impose a quota of 15 girls and 15 boys. After the quota of 15 boys is met, no other boys have a chance to participate in the study.

Quota sampling is designed to make a convenience sample more representative of the population. Quota sampling does for a convenience sample what stratified random sampling does for a simple random sample. However, unlike stratified random sampling, in quota sampling a researcher does not randomly select from the population. Finally, there is not 100% agreement about the terminology used to designate the different types of samples. For example, we recently read an article about a study that used "convenience stratified sampling" to create three groups of participants (McMahon, Rimsza, & Bay, 1997). In this study, the groups were obtained by convenience sampling, with the restriction that one half of the participants in each group spoke Spanish only and the other half spoke both Spanish and English. We would call this a "quota sample"—but the term "convenience stratified sample" also provides a sensible description of what was done. In general, you should rely on the description of the sampling technique rather than the name applied to it.

## CHAPTER SUMMARY

The goal of the research study is to measure a sample and then generalize the results to the population. Therefore, the researcher should be careful to select a sample that is representative of the population. This chapter examines some of the common strategies for obtaining samples.

The two basic categories of sampling techniques are probability and nonprobability sampling. In probability sampling, the odds of selecting a particular individual are known and can be calculated. Types of probability sampling are simple random sampling, systematic sampling, stratified sampling, proportionate stratified sampling, and cluster sampling. In nonprobability sampling the probability of selecting a particular individual is not known, because the researcher does not know the population size or the members of the population. Types of nonprobability sampling are convenience and quota sampling. Each sampling method has advantages and limitations and differs in terms of the representativeness of the sample obtained.

## KEY WORDS

| | | |
|---|---|---|
| population | biased sample | random process |
| sample | selection bias/sampling bias | nonprobability sampling |
| representativeness | sampling | |
| representative sample | probability sampling | |

## EXERCISES

1. In addition to the key words, you should also be able to define each of the following terms:
   target population
   accessible population
   simple random sampling
   systematic sampling
   stratified random sampling
   proportionate stratified random sampling
   cluster sampling
   convenience sampling
   quota sampling
2. Explain the difference between target and accessible populations.
3. Dr. Kim wants to conduct a study on memory in nursing home residents. He contacts local nursing homes and selects 50 residents from their resident lists to participate in his study.
   a. What is the target population?
   b. What is the accessible population?
   c. What is the sample?
4. What is the problem with a biased sample?
5. Explain the difference between probability and nonprobability sampling.
6. Explain how the generality of a study's results is affected by the sampling method used.
7. For each of the following scenarios, identify which sampling method is used:
   a. The State College is conducting a survey of student attitudes and opinions. The plan is to use the list of all registered students and randomly select 50 freshmen, 50 sophomores, 50 juniors, and 50 seniors to make up the sample.
   b. A second option for the college survey in Part a is based on the observation that the college accepts a large number of transfer students each year. As a result, the junior and senior classes are twice as large as the freshman and sophomore classes. To ensure that the sample reflects this difference in class size, the alternative plan is to determine the number of students in each class and then select a sample such that the number for each class in the sample is in direct relation to the number in each class for the entire college.
   c. The County Democratic Committee would like to determine which issues are most important to registered Democrats in the county. Using the list of registered Democrats, the committee selects a random sample of 30 for telephone interviews.
   d. A faculty member in the Psychology Department posts notices in classroom building on campus asking for volunteers to participate in a human memory experiment. Interested students are asked to leave their names and phone numbers.
   e. An educational psychologist selects a sample of 40 third-grade children from the local public school, ensuring that the sample is divided evenly, with 20 boys and 20 girls.

## InfoTrac COLLEGE EDITION EXERCISES

1. Use InfoTrac College Edition to locate a journal article reporting the results from a study using either a stratified or a proportionate stratified sample. (Note: The most direct search method is to use the term *stratified sample* as your key word.) Be sure to look for a periodical report that includes *text and retrieval choices* (not simply an abstract). By reading the abstract at the beginning of the article, verify that the study actually collected data from a sample. Then scroll down to the method or subjects section of the article, where the authors describe the participants and how they were obtained.

   a. Give a full citation for your article (title, authors, journal, date, pages).

   b. Describe how the sample was stratified (or proportionately stratified).

   c. Describe the general characteristics of the participants.

2. Use a more traditional key word search (a key word such as *fetal alcohol syndrome* or *color vision*) to locate a research report printed in a periodical. (Go directly to the periodical listing, or look for items that mention a specific journal name.) Read the abstract to verify that the study is a real research report (with actual participants and data collection), then locate the method or subjects section of the article.

   a. Give a full citation for your article (title, authors, journal, date, pages).

   b. Describe how the sample was obtained (recruited from a college class or a newspaper advertisement, etc.)

   c. Describe the general characteristics of the participants.

# Research Strategies and Validity

## CHAPTER OVERVIEW

In this chapter we discuss research strategy selection as well as validity, an issue central to research strategy and design. Both internal and external validity are described, as are the principal threats to each. Research strategies are distinguished from designs and procedures.

## 6.1   INTRODUCTION TO RESEARCH STRATEGIES

After you have identified a new idea for research, developed a testable hypothesis, decided how to measure your variables, and determined what individuals should participate in the study and how to treat them ethically, the next step is to select a research strategy (Step 5 in the research process; see Section 1.4). The term **research strategy** refers to the general approach and goals of a research study. Research strategy is usually determined by the kind of question you plan to address and the kind of answer you hope to obtain—in general terms, what you hope to accomplish. For example, a researcher asking the relatively simple question, Is there a relationship between two variables? would use a different strategy from a researcher asking the more sophisticated question, Why is there a relationship between the two variables? Although there are a number of ways to classify research strategies, we consider four basic categories: the descriptive strategy, the correlational strategy, the experimental strategy, and the quasi-experimental strategy.

A **research strategy** is a general approach to research determined by the kind of question that the research study hopes to answer.

Definition

### DESCRIPTIVE STRATEGY

The goal of the **descriptive strategy** is to describe the state of affairs at the time of the study. A descriptive study typically measures a variable or a set of variables as they exist naturally. Many descriptive studies are numerically descriptive, producing the sort of demographic statistics commonly reported in newspapers and on television. For example, a newspaper might report that only 19% of eligible voters participated in the election last November. Another study could involve distributing an anonymous survey to determine the extent of alcohol use among students at the local high school. The results of the survey would simply describe the current state of affairs at the high school. Other examples of a descriptive approach are illustrated by the following questions: What percentage of Americans support a woman's right to choose abortion? How many hours per week do preschoolers spend watching television? What percentage of senior citizens regularly use the Internet? How many students in a particular high school were absent in a day? The purpose of the descriptive strategy is simply to capture or summarize information or to measure one or more variables.

The purpose of the **descriptive research strategy** is to describe variables as they exist.

Definition

The descriptive research strategy is discussed in greater detail in Chapter 7.

### CORRELATIONAL STRATEGY

The **correlational research strategy** involves measuring two variables for each individual in order to evaluate the relationship between the two variables.

Typically, the two variables are measured as they exist naturally, with no attempt to manipulate or control them. The purpose of the correlational research strategy is to describe the relationship between the two variables and measure its strength. For example, a researcher might find that college students' grade point averages are weakly related to their parents' incomes but strongly related to their SAT scores. A correlational study simply attempts to establish the existence of a relationship and then describe the relationship; it does not attempt to explain the underlying causes.

Definition

The **correlational research strategy** simply measures two variables for each individual in order to describe the relationship between the variables.

The correlational research strategy is discussed in greater detail in Chapter 7.

## EXPERIMENTAL STRATEGY

Caution! Not all research studies are experiments!

The next major approach to research is the **experimental strategy,** also commonly termed the **manipulative strategy.** In this book, we use the terms *experiment* or *true experiment* in a well-defined technical sense. Specifically, a research study is called an *experiment* only if it satisfies a specific set of requirements (which are described in Chapter 8). Thus some research studies qualify as true experiments, and other studies, such as correlational studies, do not. In casual conversation, people tend to refer to any kind of research study as "an experiment." ("Scientists" do "experiments" in the "laboratory.") Although this casual description of research activity is acceptable in some contexts, we are careful to distinguish between experiments and nonexperiments. Therefore, whenever the word *experiment* is used in this text, it is in this more precise, technical sense.

The goal of the experimental strategy is to determine whether a causal relationship exists between two variables. The experimental approach attempts to establish that changes in one variable are directly responsible for changes in another variable; that is, that there is a cause-and-effect relationship. It is possible that two variables are related and yet the relationship is merely coincidental. For example, a child may notice that, every time her father wears a tuxedo, he has a terrible headache the next morning. Although there is a clear relationship between wearing the tux and the headaches, the tuxedo is probably not the *cause* of the headaches.

Definition

The purpose of the **experimental research strategy** is to establish the existence of and demonstrate a cause-and-effect relationship between two variables. An experiment attempts to show that changes in one variable are directly responsible for changes in a second variable.

To establish the existence of a cause-and-effect relationship, the researcher must exert much more control than in a correlational study. The researcher must manipulate one variable (called the **independent variable**) while observing or measuring a second variable (called the **dependent variable**). The goal is to determine whether manipulating the independent variable causes changes to occur in the dependent variable. In addition, all other variables must be controlled to ensure that they do not influence the two variables being examined. In general, an experimental study can be described as having the following four basic components, which are also shown in Figure 6.1:

1. *Manipulation:* The researcher manipulates one variable to create a set of two or more treatment conditions.

2. *Measurement:* A second variable is measured for a group of participants, to obtain a set of scores in each treatment condition.

3. *Comparison:* The scores in one treatment condition are compared with the scores in another treatment condition. Consistent differences between treatments are evidence that the manipulation has caused changes in the scores.

4. *Control:* All other variables are controlled to be sure that they do not influence the relationship between the two variables being examined.

The details of the experimental research strategy are discussed in Chapter 8.

## QUASI-EXPERIMENTAL STRATEGY

Occasionally a researcher would like to use a research study to demonstrate a cause-and-effect relationship between two variables but cannot satisfy all of the strict requirements needed for a true experiment. In this situation, researchers often use the **quasi-experimental research strategy.** A quasi-experimental study is similar to a true experiment except that it contains an unavoidable flaw that prevents the researcher from drawing an unambiguous cause-and-effect conclusion.

The basic distinction between a quasi-experimental study and an experimental study is that the quasi-experimental study uses a nonmanipulated variable or a noncontrolled variable in place of the manipulated variable used in a true experiment. For example, an experiment might manipulate room temperature and then assign people to different temperature conditions to observe how their performance on a problem-solving task is affected by temperature. A quasi-experimental study, on the other hand, might compare how 8-year-old and 10-year-old children respond to a self-esteem program. In this case, the researcher cannot control which children are assigned to each group (the group assignment is already determined by each child's age). Another example of a quasi-experimental study involves comparing the children's self-esteem scores before and after the program. In this case, the research uses a nonmanipulated variable, time (before and after), to define the two groups of scores.

Because quasi-experimental studies do not have the full level of control that exists in an experiment, they cannot produce unequivocal demonstrations of cause-and-effect relationships. Different examples of quasi-experimental designs are examined in Chapter 9.

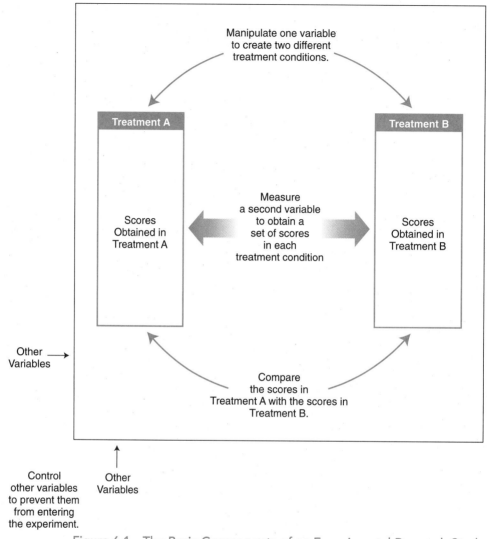

Figure 6.1 The Basic Components of an Experimental Research Study
An experiment involves manipulating one variable, measuring a second
variable, comparing the scores between treatments, and controlling all
other variables.

Definition | Like an experiment, the **quasi-experimental research strategy** compares groups or conditions but lacks one of the critical components, either manipulation or control, that is necessary for a true experiment. A quasi-experimental study typically compares pre-existing groups (such as age groups) or defines the conditions with a time variable (such as before and after treatment).

## SUMMARY

Different research strategies are available to address the variety of questions with which research can begin. See Table 6.1 for a summary of the four categories of research strategies.

Each strategy is directed toward different types of questions, and each strategy has its own strengths and limitations. Although we classify research strategies into four categories, another common method uses only two, experimental research and **nonexperimental** or **nonmanipulative research.** The rationale for this two-way classification is that only experiments can establish the existence of cause-and-effect relationships; nonexperimental strategies cannot.

Before we examine research strategies in detail in Chapters 7, 8, and 9, we discuss the criteria used to judge the quality of any research, regardless of strategy.

TABLE 6.1

### Description and Purpose of the Four Categories of Research Strategy

| Strategy | Description | Purpose |
|---|---|---|
| Descriptive | Measures variables, usually as they exist naturally. | To describe the variables in their current state. |
| Correlational | Measures two variables, usually as they exist naturally. | To describe the relationship between the two variables without attempting to explain the cause of the relationship. |
| Experimental | Manipulates one variable to create treatment conditions. Measures a second variable to obtain scores in each condition. Compares the scores across conditions. Controls all other variables. | To establish a clear cause-and-effect relationship; specifically, to show that manipulation of one variable causes changes to occur in the measured variable. |
| Quasi-experimental | Uses a nonmanipulated variable to define groups or conditions. Measures a second variable to obtain scores in each condition. Compares the scores across conditions. As much as possible, controls other variables. | To obtain evidence in support of a cause-and-effect relationship; however, a quasi-experimental study cannot unambiguously establish a causal relationship. |

What is the fundamental difference between the experimental strategy and the other research strategies?

Is the following research study a true experiment? Explain why or why not.

> Participants are brought, one at a time, into a laboratory and given a self-esteem questionnaire. The results of the questionnaire are used to classify participants into a high self-esteem group and a low self-esteem group. As the participants leave the lab, they encounter another student trying to reach a pay phone from a wheelchair. The researchers record whether or not each participant stops to help. The goal is to compare the helping behavior of the two groups to evaluate the relationship between helping behavior and self-esteem.

## 6.2   VALIDITY

The dictionary defines *validity* as "the quality or state of being true." In the context of a research study, **validity** is concerned with the truth of the research or the accuracy of the results. In general, it is the standard criterion by which researchers judge the quality of research. The concept of validity is a central theme throughout this book and should always be kept in mind when planning a research study or critically reading someone else's research.

**Definition**

The **validity** of a research study is determined by the quality of the research process and the accuracy of the results.

There is some potential for confusion about the use of the word *validity*. In Chapter 4, we introduced the concept of validity as it applies to measurement; the validity of a measurement procedure refers to how well the procedure measures the variable that it claims to measure. Here, however, we introduce the concept of validity as it applies to an entire research study. Specifically, we examine the truthfulness or the quality of the research process and the accuracy of the results. The same word, *validity*, applies to both contexts. Therefore, we are careful to distinguish between the validity of a research study and the validity of measurement, and you should be careful to separate the two concepts in your own mind.

Any researcher's goal is to be able to summarize a research study by stating, "This is what happened, and this is what it means." Any factor that raises doubts about the research results or about the interpretation of the results is a **threat to validity.**

**Definition**

Any component of a research study that introduces questions or raises doubts about the quality of the research process or the accuracy of the research results is a **threat to validity.**

Although there are many approaches to defining validity, questions about the validity of research are traditionally grouped into two categories: questions about internal validity and questions about external validity.

## INTERNAL VALIDITY

**Internal validity** is concerned with factors within the research study that raise doubts or questions about the results or the interpretation. A research study is said to have internal validity if it allows one and only one explanation of the results. Any factor within the study that allows an alternative explanation for the results is a **threat to internal validity.** Typically, the results of a research study show a relationship between two variables; for example, changes in variable X are consistently and predictably accompanied by changes in variable Y. If the study demonstrates unambiguously that changes in variable X are directly responsible for changes in variable Y, then the study has internal validity. On the other hand, any factor (other than variable X) that might be responsible for causing the changes in variable Y is a threat to internal validity.

Definitions

A research study has **internal validity** if it produces a single, unambiguous explanation for the results.

Any factor that allows for an alternative explanation is a **threat to internal validity.**

Note that questions of internal validity focus on the interpretation or explanation of the results. For example, suppose a research study examines the relationship between room temperature and problem-solving ability. Room temperature is varied, and the participants' problem-solving scores are measured in each temperature condition. Suppose that the results show a clear decrease in problem-solving performance as the temperature goes up. The researcher would like to interpret or explain this result by stating that there is a causal relationship between temperature and problem-solving ability: Increases in temperature produce decreases in problem solving. The concern for internal validity is to determine whether any factor in the research study other than temperature could account for the observed decline in problem-solving performance. The issue of internal validity is demonstrated in the following scenario:

> Suppose the research study starts with a group of participants in a 70-degree room; then temperature is increased to 80 degrees and then again to 90 degrees. In each temperature condition the participants are given problems to solve, and their performance is measured. The results show declining performance as the temperature goes up. Although it is possible that the temperature is influencing performance, it also is possible that the participants are just getting tired: They do well on the first set of problems (70 degrees) but are wearing down by the time they get to the second set (80 degrees) and are simply exhausted by the time the third set of problems is presented (90 degrees). In this scenario, the

observed decline in performance may be explained by fatigue. We now have an alternative explanation for the observed result: The decline in problem-solving ability may be due to temperature, or it may be due to fatigue. Although the results of the study are clear, the internal validity of the researcher's explanation is questionable.

Now suppose our researcher tries to eliminate the fatigue problem by using a separate group of participants for each temperature condition. The first 20 people to sign up for the experiment are assigned to the 70-degree condition, the next 20 people are tested at 80 degrees, and the last 20 people to sign up are tested at 90 degrees. Again, the results show a decline in problem-solving performance as temperature increases. However, the decline in performance still may be caused by factors other than temperature; differences among groups of participants might account for the results. Perhaps the first 20 participants were more motivated and more enthusiastic; these people signed up immediately, and they were probably excited about participating in the study and tried to do well. By contrast, the last 20 people to sign up were probably less interested in the study and not highly motivated to perform well. In this scenario, the observed differences in performance may be due to group differences in motivation. Again, there are two possible explanations for the results: The differences in problem-solving performance may be due to temperature, or they may be due to motivation differences between groups. Although the researcher would like to claim that problem solving is related to temperature, the internal validity of this explanation is questionable.

Learning Checks

What does it mean for a research study to be internally valid?

A researcher wants to compare the effectiveness of two methods for teaching reading to first-grade children. One teaching method is used in Mr. Green's class, and the other method is used in Mr. Brown's class. At the end of the year all the students take a reading achievement test, and Mr. Brown's students score higher. In this research study, is the difference between the two teachers (Mr. Brown and Mr. Green) a threat to internal validity? Explain why or why not.

## EXTERNAL VALIDITY

**External validity** concerns the extent to which the results obtained in a research study hold true outside the constraints of the study. Can the results of the study be generalized to other populations, other settings, other measurements? Every research study is conducted at a specific time and place, with specific participants, instructions, measurement techniques, and procedures. Despite the unique nature of the study itself, researchers usually assume that the obtained results are not unique but can be generalized beyond that study.

Definition

**External validity** refers to the extent to which we can generalize the results of a research study to people, settings, times, measures, and characteristics other than those used in that study.

For example, in 1988 Strack, Martin, and Stepper conducted a study showing that people rate cartoons as funnier when holding a pen in their teeth (which forced them to smile) than when holding a pen in their lips (which forced them to frown). Although this study was done in 1988 using undergraduate students from the University of Illinois, it seems reasonable to assume that the results can be generalized outside the limited scope of the study. That is, if other people were tested at other places and at different times, it would be reasonable to expect the same result to be obtained.

For some research, like the preceding smiling-and-frowning example, there is not much question about the validity of generalizing the results. Other research, however, does raise such questions. For example, the diverse structure of the modern family is described in detail in a book entitled *The Family on the Threshold of the 21st Century* (Drèmen, 1997). Clearly, the data presented in this book are intended to describe a specific situation at a specific time. It would be inappropriate to generalize the results to include family structures that existed 50 years ago or in foreign lands.

Some research situations generate doubts about the validity of generalizing results. A common concern is the generalizing of results from a well-controlled laboratory situation to the uncontrolled chaos of the real world. Questions about the validity of generalizing results beyond a specific research study are questions of external validity. Any characteristic of the study that limits the generality of the results is referred to as a **threat to external validity.** The goal of a research study is to produce results that reflect a true relationship between variables. If the results of a study can be generalized to other times, situations, and environments outside the limited scope of the specific study, then the study is said to have external validity. On the other hand, if the results are true only within the limited constraints of the study, then the study lacks external validity.

---

A **threat to external validity** is any characteristic of a study that limits the generality of the results.

*Definition*

---

What does it mean for a research study to have external validity?

*Learning Checks*

To conduct a study examining human memory, Dr. Jones used a group of 10-year-old boys attending a summer computer camp for talented and gifted children. Dr. Smith conducted a similar study using a group of adolescent males and females from the Boston public schools. Which study is likely to have greater external validity? Explain your answer.

---

## 6.3   THREATS TO VALIDITY

The value or quality of any research study is determined by the extent to which the study satisfies the criteria of internal and external validity. The general purpose of a research study is to reveal the true relationship between variables. A well-designed study produces results that accurately reflect the underlying relationship and justify a conclusion that accurately describes the relationship. Any factor that generates doubts about the accuracy of the results or raises questions about the interpretation of the results is a threat to validity.

A good researcher is aware of these threats while planning a research study. Anticipating threats to validity allows a researcher to incorporate elements into a research design that eliminates or minimizes threats to validity before the research is actually conducted. In this section we identify and briefly describe some general threats to internal and external validity. In later chapters we present a variety of different research designs and include a more detailed description of the threats to validity associated with each design. In addition we identify methods of modifying or expanding each design to limit specific threats to validity.

One final caution: It is essentially impossible for a single research study to eliminate all threats to validity. Each researcher must decide which threats are most important for the specific study and then address those threats. Less important threats can be ignored or treated casually. In fact, design changes that eliminate one threat may actually increase the potential for another threat; thus each research study represents a set of decisions and compromises about validity. Although researchers typically try to make the best decisions and produce the best possible studies, most still contain some flaws. This basic "fact of life" has two implications:

1.  Research studies vary in terms of validity. Some studies have strong internal and external validity, and their results and conclusions are highly respected. Other studies have only moderate validity, and some have little or no validity. Never accept a research result or conclusion as true simply because it is said to have been "scientifically demonstrated."

2.  Being aware of threats to validity can help you critically evaluate a research study. As you read research reports, mentally scan the following list of threats and ask yourself whether or not each one applies. A major learning objective of this book is to make you an informed consumer of research, capable of making your own decisions about its validity and quality.

## THREATS TO INTERNAL VALIDITY

### Extraneous Variables

A research study satisfies the criterion of internal validity if the study produces one and only one explanation for the obtained results. Any factor that opens the door to a possible alternative explanation is a threat to internal validity.

Typically a research study concentrates on two variables and attempts to establish the existence of a relationship between them. Earlier we discussed a research study attempting to show that problem-solving ability (the measured dependent variable) is related to room temperature (the manipulated independent variable). Although the study focuses on these two variables, there are countless other elements that vary within the study; that is, there are many additional variables (beyond the two being studied) that are part of every research study. Some of these extra variables are related to the individuals participating. For example, different people enter the study with different personalities, different IQs, different genders, different skills and abilities, and so on. Other variables involve the study's environment—for example, some participants may be

tested in the morning and others in the afternoon; part of the study may be conducted on a dark and dreary Monday and another part on a sunny Tuesday. The
researcher is not interested in differences in IQ or weather, but these factors are
still variables in the study. Additional variables that are part of a research study
but not directly investigated are called **extraneous variables.**

Any variable in a research study other than the two variables being studied is an
**extraneous variable.**

Definition

### Confounding Variables

Occasionally an extraneous variable is allowed to creep into a study in a way
that can influence or distort the results. When this happens, there is a risk that
the observed relationship between the two variables in the study is real but has
been artificially produced by the extraneous variable. Earlier (see page 137), we
demonstrated how a third variable, fatigue, might explain an observed relation
between temperature and problem-solving ability. A third variable of this sort is
called a **confounding variable.**

A **confounding variable** is an extraneous variable (usually unmonitored) that is
allowed to change systematically along with the two variables being studied.

Definition

Whenever three variables all change together systematically, it is impossible
to reach a simple, clear conclusion about the relationship between any two of
them. Thus, whenever a confounding variable exists, internal validity is threatened. One more look at the temperature-and-problem-solving study should illustrate this point. This time, suppose that one group of individuals is given a
problem-solving test in a 70-degree room at 9 o'clock in the morning. A second
group is given the problem-solving test with a room temperature of 80 degrees at
4 o'clock in the afternoon. Finally, suppose that the results show much better performance for the first group than for the second group. Note that this study involves three variables and that all three variables change together systematically.

| Variables | Group 1 | Group 2 |
|-----------|---------|---------|
| Temperature | 70 degrees | 80 degrees |
| Performance | good | bad |
| Time of day | morning | afternoon |

In this example, the time of day is an extraneous variable that has turned
into a confounding variable. The researcher would like to explain the results by
saying that there is a relationship between temperature and performance:

> Increasing the temperature from 70 degrees to 80 degrees caused a de-
> crease in performance from good to bad.

However, the presence of a confounding variable provides an alternative explanation for the results. Specifically, it is possible to explain the results by saying
that there is a relationship between time of day and performance:

A change in the time of day from morning to afternoon caused a decrease in performance from good to bad.

Thus, a confounding variable is a threat to internal validity. Remember, any factor that allows an alternative explanation for the results from a research study is a threat to the internal validity of the study.

Learning
Checks

Suppose that you wake up in the morning with all the symptoms of a head cold. You take a cold pill and then eat a big bowl of your mother's chicken soup. By midday, your cold symptoms are gone and you are feeling much better. Can you conclude that the chicken soup cured your cold? Explain why or why not.

Describe how a confounding variable threatens internal validity.

### General Threats to Internal Validity

The following list identifies some general threats that can undermine the internal validity of a research study. Note that specific threats are usually related to specific research designs. In later chapters, when we present specific research designs, we also introduce the threats to validity related to each design. In addition, we discuss the methods that researchers use to avoid or to minimize threats to validity. For now, we simply want to give you an idea of the kind of problems that limit internal validity. To facilitate discussion, we use the generic terms *treatments* and *scores* to identify the two variables being examined. In a typical, generic study, a researcher creates two or more different treatment conditions (the manipulated independent variable) and then observes and measures another variable (the dependent variable or the scores) in each treatment condition. Figure 6.2 shows the structure of this generic research study. The goal of the research study is to examine the relation between the treatments and the scores. Specifically, the researcher would like to determine whether the change from Treatment A to Treatment B produces a consistent, predictable change in the scores. Any other variable that changes systematically with the treatments and the scores is a confounding variable and threatens internal validity.

1.  *Participant Variables:* Characteristics such as age, gender, and personality are variables that differ from one individual to another and are generally referred to as *participant variables*. These variables can become confounding variables and therefore threats to internal validity. Occasionally the process of assigning participants to treatments results in a situation where the individuals in one treatment have different characteristics from the individuals in another treatment. For example, the individuals participating in one treatment may be faster, smarter, or more motivated than the individuals in other treatments. This problem is called **assignment bias** and is a threat to internal validity because it allows two alternative explanations for any differences observed between the treatments. Specifically, it is possible that the scores in one treatment are higher than the scores in another treatment because:

    a.  There are real differences between the treatments.
    b.  The individuals in one treatment are smarter than the individuals in the other treatment.

| Treatment Condition A | Treatment Condition B |
|:---:|:---:|
| 17 | 12 |
| 19 | 10 |
| 16 | 14 |
| 12 | 15 |
| 17 | 13 |
| 18 | 12 |
| 15 | 11 |
| 16 | 13 |

Variable 1
(The Manipulated or Independent Variable)
Different Treatment Conditions
Created by the Researcher

Variable 2
(The Dependent Variable)
Individual Scores Obtained for the
Participants in Each Treatment Condition

Figure 6.2   The General Structure of a Research Study
Examining the Relationship Between Two Variables
One variable (the manipulated or independent variable) is used to create
treatment conditions, and a second variable (the dependent variable) is
measured to obtain scores within each treatment condition. The goal of
the study is to determine whether the change from Treatment A to
Treatment B produced a corresponding change in the scores.

---

**Assignment bias** occurs when the process used to assign different participants
to different treatments produces groups of individuals with noticeably different
characteristics.

Definition

---

2.  *Environmental Variables:* It also is possible that variables in the general envi-
    ronment, such as size of room, time of day, or gender of the experimenter,
    can become threats to internal validity. If one treatment is administered in a
    large, cheerful room and another treatment is administered in a small, dreary
    room, it is possible that the type of room (and not the treatment) is respon-
    sible for any differences between the scores in the two treatment conditions.
    Another example of this type of problem is a taste-test study that compared
    consumer preference for Coca-Cola versus Pepsi. In this study, individuals
    were presented with two glasses of cola and asked to identify their prefer-
    ences. However, the glass containing Coke was always marked with the let-
    ter $Q$, and the Pepsi glass was always marked with the letter $M$. Although
    the results indicated that people prefer Pepsi, an alternative explanation is
    that people prefer the letter $M$ (Huck & Sandler, 1979). In this study, the
    identifying letter was allowed to vary systematically with the brand of cola,
    so the letters $M$ and $Q$ became a confounding variable. Whenever there is an
    alternative explanation for the results, internal validity is threatened.
        It is also possible for the environment outside the study to influence
    the results and thereby become a threat to internal validity. For example, a
    study might test the effectiveness of a new teen pregnancy prevention pro-
    gram by administering the program in one high school and using another
    high school as a no-treatment comparison. The problem here is that the

students in one high school could be exposed to a completely different environment from the students in the other school. Whenever the participants in one treatment condition have a different background or history of experience from the participants in another treatment, the internal validity is threatened. Specifically, any differences that are found between the two groups could be explained by the different treatments, or they could be explained by the different histories. Influences from the environment or experiences outside the research study are called **history effects.**

Definition

**History effects** occur when the individuals in one treatment condition experience an environment or history that is different from that of individuals in another treatment condition.

3. *Measurement Variables:* Many studies involve repeated measurements of the same group of individuals. The measurements may be repeated over a series of different treatments, or the study may involve a simple pretest measurement (scores before treatment) that is compared with a posttest measurement (scores after treatment). In this situation, the researcher would like to say that any observed change in the scores is due to the change in treatments. However, when people see the same measurement procedure time after time, their scores may improve simply because of **practice effects** or familiarity with the measurement itself, or their scores may deteriorate because of **fatigue.** In this case, testing experience provides an alternative explanation for the results and therefore is a threat to internal validity.

Definitions

**Practice effects** occur when prior exposure to a measurement procedure provides participants with additional skills that produce improved scores.

**Fatigue** occurs when prior participation in a treatment condition or measurement procedure tires the participants so that their scores on subsequent measurements are lower.

Table 6.2 summarizes the threats to the internal validity of a research study.

## THREATS TO EXTERNAL VALIDITY

As discussed previously, external validity refers to the extent to which the results of the study can be generalized to other populations, conditions, experimenters, other measurements, and so forth. When research findings can be generalized outside the confines of the specific study, the research is said to have external validity. Any characteristic of the study that limits the generality of the results is a threat to external validity. The generality of the findings may be limited by virtually any characteristic of the study. Some of the more common threats to external validity follow, grouped into four major categories.

TABLE 6.2

## General Threats to the Internal Validity of a Research Study

| Source of the Threat | Description of the Threat |
|---|---|
| Participant Variables | If the participants in one treatment condition have characteristics that are noticeably different from the participants in another treatment, then the internal validity of the study is threatened. For example, if the participants in one treatment are older than the participants in another treatment, then any difference between the treatments may be explained by age instead of treatment. |
| Environmental Variables | If two treatments are administered in noticeably different environments, then the internal validity of the study is threatened. For example, if one treatment is administered in the morning and another at night, then any difference obtained may be explained by the time of day instead of treatment. |
| Measurement Variables | Whenever the same group of individuals is measured in a series of treatment conditions, there is a potential threat to internal validity. For example, if a group of individuals is measured in one treatment and then measured in a second treatment, their scores in the second treatment may be influenced by prior experience (practice) with the measurement in the first treatment. Thus, any difference obtained between the treatments may be explained by the prior experience instead of treatment. |

### Category 1: Generalizing Across Participants or Subjects

The results of a study are demonstrated with a particular group of individuals. One question of external validity is, To what extent can research results be generalized to individuals who differ from those who actually participated in the study?

**a.** *Subject Selection Bias (Cost-Restrictive Sampling)*    The question of external validity is always raised when a researcher selects participants not in some unbiased way but rather based on convenience. Selection of research participants is discussed in detail in Chapter 5, but for now, consider this common situation. Most researchers are interested in a broadly defined population, for example, adolescents in the United States; however, because of cost considerations, such a researcher is likely to obtain local adolescents. Therefore, a researcher in San Francisco, California, is likely to solicit participants from San Francisco Bay Area high schools, whereas a researcher in Kansas City, Missouri, is likely to solicit participants from Kansas City high schools. The issue here is whether or not the results obtained with West Coast adolescents are generalizable to adolescents in the Midwest or other parts of the country. Research results obtained with participants from one geographic region or setting may contain **subject selection bias** and hence may not generalize to people in other regions or settings (urban, suburban, rural).

**b.** *College Students*    The undergraduate shares with the laboratory rat the status of the most easily available and therefore most favored participant in behavioral research. However, evidence is accumulating to suggest that many of the characteristics of college students limit the generalizability of the results to other adults. For example, Sears (1986) demonstrated that college students are likely to have a less formulated sense of self, a stronger tendency to comply with authority, less stable peer relationships, and higher intelligence than noncollege adults. We need to be cautious about generalizing research results obtained with this highly select group.

**c. *Volunteer Bias***     In most cases, someone who participates in research has volunteered for it. As noted in Chapter 3, the APA guidelines for human research require (in most cases) that research participants be volunteers. This creates a basic problem for researchers, known as **volunteer bias,** because volunteers are not perfectly representative of the general population. The question of external validity is, To what extent can we generalize results obtained with volunteers to individuals who may not volunteer to participate in studies? Evidence suggests that volunteer participants tend to be different from the populations from which they come.

In an extensive study of volunteer participants, Rosenthal and Rosnow (1975) identified a number of characteristics that tend to differentiate individuals who volunteer from those who do not. Table 6.3 presents a list of some of the characteristics they examined. Note that none of the individual characteristics is a perfectly reliable predictor of volunteerism, and some are better predictors than others. After extensive review of previous research, Rosenthal and Rosnow grouped the items into categories indicating the amount of evidence supporting the notion that these characteristics are in fact associated with volunteering.

As you read through the list in Table 6.3, try to classify yourself and determine your own likelihood of volunteering. You probably will find that some of the characteristics describe you perfectly, some are completely wrong, and some do not seem to apply at all. Although you may be educated and intelligent (suggesting that you will volunteer), you may not be an arousal-seeking individual (suggesting that you won't). This is part of the reason that it is impossible to predict perfectly who will volunteer and who will not. Another complicating factor is the type of research being considered. For example, females are more likely to volunteer in general, but for studies involving stress, males tend to be the most likely volunteers. Similarly, high intelligence is related to volunteering in general but not if the research involves unusual experiences such as hypnosis, sensory isolation, or sex research.

Thus, the items in Table 6.3 should be viewed as general characteristics of volunteers; they are not intended to apply to each individual or to every situation. Nonetheless, the data clearly indicate that, on the average, volunteers are different from nonvolunteers—which raises questions about the external validity of research conducted with volunteer participants.

**d. *Participant Characteristics***     Another threat to external validity occurs whenever a study uses participants who share similar characteristics. Demographic characteristics such as gender, age, race, ethnic identity, and socioeconomic status can limit the generalizability of the results. For example, a study done in a suburban preschool with predominately White, middle-class children may not generalize to other populations. You certainly would not expect to gen-

TABLE 6.3

## Participant Characteristics Associated With Volunteering

The characteristics are grouped according to the degree of confidence that the items are indeed related to volunteerism. (From Rosenthal & Rosnow, 1975)

I. Maximum Confidence
   1. Volunteers are more educated.
   2. Volunteers are from a higher social class.
   3. Volunteers are more intelligent.
   4. Volunteers are more approval motivated.
   5. Volunteers are more sociable.

II. Considerable Confidence
   6. Volunteers are more arousal seeking.
   7. Volunteers are more conventional.
   8. Volunteers are more likely to be female than male.
   9. Volunteers are more nonauthoritarian.
   10. Volunteers are more likely to be Jewish than Protestant or more likely Protestant than Catholic.
   11. Volunteers are more nonconforming.

III. Some Confidence
   12. Volunteers are from smaller towns.
   13. Volunteers are more interested in religion.
   14. Volunteers are more altruistic.
   15. Volunteers are more self-disclosing.
   16. Volunteers are more maladjusted.
   17. Volunteers are more likely to be young than old.

eralize the results to urban, Hispanic adolescents. It is always possible that the results of a study may be specific to participants with a certain set of characteristics and may not extend to participants with different characteristics.

**e. *Cross-species Generalizations***    External validity is also in question when research is conducted with nonhumans and presumed to be readily applicable to humans. Before we can consider whether the results obtained with one species can be generalized to another species, we must note the parallels and differences between the two species on the mechanism or process of interest. For example, rats are an excellent species to use for research on eating. Rats' eating is similar to human eating both physically and behaviorally (rats and humans have similar digestive systems, eating patterns, and food preferences). As a result, researchers can confidently generalize the results of research with rats to humans. In contrast, the blowfly is not a good species to use to generalize results to humans' eating because, unlike that of humans, the blowfly's eating behavior is purely reflexive and not learned (Logue, 1991). All of this is not to imply that nonhuman research is worthless and not applicable to humans; many major scientific advances in understanding humans have been made from research conducted with nonhumans. We must be careful not to presume, however, that all nonhuman research is directly applicable to humans.

**Learning Check**

Explain how subject selection bias may limit the external validity of a study's findings.

### Category 2: Generalizing Across Features of a Study

In addition to the fact that each research study is conducted with a specific group of individuals, the results of a study are demonstrated with a specific set of procedures. The question of external validity is, To what extent can the results of the study be generalized to other procedures for conducting the study?

**a.** *Novelty Effect*    Participating in a research study is a novel, often exciting or anxiety-provoking experience for most individuals. In this novel situation, individuals may perceive and respond differently than they would in the normal, real world—called the **novelty effect.** In addition, the treatment(s) being administered are typically clearly defined and unusually salient to the participants. Thus the behavior (scores) of individuals participating in a research study may be quite different from behavior (scores) they would produce in other, more routine, situations.

**b.** *Reactivity*    **Reactivity** refers to the influence of the participant's awareness of participating in an investigation. In most behavioral research, the participants know that they are serving in an investigation. The act of observation or measurement can produce changes in the responses being observed. The issue of external validity is that the results of a study may be influenced by the fact that a participant knows he or she is being studied. Participants are likely to behave differently than they might when not being observed and measured. The external validity question here is whether the same results would be obtained if the participants were not aware of being studied.

Reactivity is particularly a problem in studies conducted in a **laboratory** setting, where participants are fully aware that they are participating in a study. In contrast, in a **field** setting participants are much less likely to know that they are being investigated. Laboratories and fields are discussed in more detail in Chapter 8.

### Definitions

**Reactivity** occurs when participants modify their natural behavior in response to the fact that they are participating in a research study or the knowledge that they are being measured.

A **laboratory** is any setting that is obviously devoted to the discipline of science. It can be any room or any space that the subject or participant perceives as artificial.

A **field** setting is any place that the participant or subject perceives as a natural environment.

In addition to reacting to elements of the research arrangement or environment, participants may also react to the knowledge that they are being measured. For example, to conduct a study on eating disorders, we might measure a participant's risk for eating disorders with a specially designed questionnaire. As the participants are completing the questionnaire, however, they are likely to recognize what is being measured. When this happens, participants may begin to alter the responses to the questionnaire. For example, a participant may lie to conceal embarrassing behaviors. When the act of measurement changes the behavior being observed, the measure is said to be reactive. Whenever possible, nonreactive measures should be used. Nonreactive measures do not alter the participants' responses by virtue of measuring it. One-way mirrors, hidden video cameras or tape recorders, and behavioral measures that include observation are less reactive ways to assess most responses.

Describe why reactivity is more problematic in a study conducted in a laboratory than in a study conducted in the field.

Learning
Check

**c. *Demand Characteristics***    **Demand characteristics** are cues given to participants about how they are expected to behave. More specifically, demand characteristics are any potential cues available to participants regarding the nature and the purpose of the study that may influence the participants' reactions to the experimental treatment by "demanding" that the participant behave a certain way.

The term **demand characteristics** refers to any of the potential cues or features of a study that: (1) make obvious to the participants what the purpose and hypothesis is, and (2) influence the participants to respond or behave in a certain way.

Definition

For example, suppose you participate in a study in which you are first seated at a desk in a well-lit, quiet room and given a questionnaire to fill out that asks questions about how "relaxed" you are feeling. Next, you are escorted into a low-lit room in which soft music is playing; you are seated in a comfortable recliner and asked to complete the same questionnaire. The cues in this situation "demand" that you respond with more relaxed answers in the second half of the study. Any feature of the study, for example the setting or the procedures, can inadvertently lead participants to respond in a certain way.

Participants adopt different ways of responding to these experimental cues based on whatever they judge to be an appropriate role in the situation. These ways of responding are referred to as **subject roles** or **subject role behavior**. Four different subject roles have been identified (Weber & Cook, 1972):

1.  *The good subject role:* Participants taking on the **good subject role** attempt to provide responses that will corroborate the investigator's hypothesis. These participants have identified the hypothesis of the study and are trying to act consistently with the investigator's hypothesis. As good as this may sound, we do not want participants to adopt the good subject role because we then do not know if the results of the study extend to those participants who did not adopt such a role.

2. *The negativistic subject role.* Participants adopting the **negativistic subject role** attempt to refute the investigator's hypothesis. These participants have identified the hypothesis of the study and are trying to act contrary to the investigator's hypothesis. Clearly, we do not want participants in our study to adopt this role.

3. *The faithful subject role.* These are the participants we really want in our study. Participants adopting the **faithful subject role** attempt to follow instructions to the letter and avoid acting on any suspicions they have about the purpose of the study. Two types of participants take on this role: (1) those who want to help science and know they should not allow their suspicions to enter into their responses, and (2) those who are simply apathetic and do not give the study much thought.

4. *The apprehensive subject role.* Participants who adopt the **apprehensive subject role** are overly concerned that their performance in the study will be used to evaluate their abilities, personal characteristics, or opportunities. These participants try to place themselves in a desirable light by responding in a socially desirable fashion instead of truthfully.

**d.  *Multiple Treatment Interference***   When individuals participate in a series of different treatment conditions, it is possible that their responses in one treatment are influenced by their experiences in earlier treatments. This is called **multiple treatment interference.** The question of external validity is, Can the results from the treatment be generalized to individuals who have not received earlier treatments?

Learning Check

What are demand characteristics, and how do they limit the external validity of the results?

## Category 3: Generalizing Across Experimenters

As we have noted, each research study is conducted with a specific group of participants and a particular set of procedures. In addition, the results of a study are demonstrated with a specific experimenter conducting the study. The question of external validity is, To what extent can the results of the study be generalized to other experimenters?

**a.  *Experimenter Bias or Experimenter Expectancy Effect***   As described in Chapter 1, **experimenter bias** or **experimenter expectancy** occurs when the experimenter's beliefs or expectations regarding the outcome of the study influence the results of the study. The experimenter may intentionally or unintentionally influence or bias the behavior or data of the participants in the following ways (Rosenthal & Fode, 1963):

by paralinguistic cues (variations in tone of voice) that influence the participants to give the expected or desired responses

by kinesthetic cues (body posture or facial expressions)

by verbal reinforcement of expected or desired responses

by misjudgment of participants' responses, in the direction of the expected results

by misrecording of participants' responses (errors in recording of data), in the direction of the expected or desired results

Experimenter bias threatens external validity because the results obtained in a study may be specific to the experimenter who has the expectations. The results may not be the same with an experimenter who did not have such a bias.

**b.** *Experimenter Characteristics* Experimenter characteristics are another threat to external validity. The results of a study can be specific to an experimenter with a certain set of characteristics. Both demographic and personality characteristics can limit the generality of the results. Demographic characteristics can include gender, age, race, and ethnic identity; personality characteristics can include degree of friendliness, prestige, anxiety, and hostility. For example, a study conducted by a hostile experimenter is likely to produce different results from a study conducted by a kind experimenter.

Describe how experimenter expectations may threaten the external validity of the research findings.

Learning Check

### Category 4: Generalizing Across Features of the Measures

As we have noted, each research study is conducted with a specific group of participants, a particular set of procedures, and a specific experimenter. In addition, the results of a study are demonstrated with a specific set of measures. The question of external validity is, To what extent can the results of the study be generalized to other ways of measuring in the study?

**a.** *Sensitization* Occasionally the assessment procedure can alter participants so that they react differently to treatment. This phenomenon is called **sensitization** or **assessment sensitization.** Sensitization is a threat to external validity because it raises the question of whether the results obtained in a research study using assessment are different from results in the real world, where the treatment is used without assessment. Assessment sensitization commonly occurs in many studies where participants' behavior is measured, they are given a treatment, and they are measured again. In many studies pretests are given to assess participants' standing before receiving a treatment. The concern with regard to external validity is that the pretest may in some way sensitize the participants so that they are affected differently by the treatment. This threat to external validity is also known as **pretest sensitization.**

Assessment sensitization also commonly occurs with academic exams. Although an exam question is intended to measure a student's knowledge, the question itself can change knowledge. For example, an exam question may cause you to think about relationships that had not occurred to you, or prompt you to look at a topic from a new perspective, or simply crystallize vague, disjointed thoughts about a subject. Note that your test performance (score) is now influenced not only by your previous study but also by the test itself. If the question had not been asked, you would not have thought of the answer.

A similar phenomenon occurs in studies that use self-monitoring as a means of measuring scores. Harmon, Nelson, and Hayes (1980) demonstrated that the process of self-monitoring significantly reduced depression. That is, depressed patients who simply observed and recorded their own behavior showed significant improvement without any clinical treatment or therapy. Again, this is an example of a measurement procedure (not a treatment) affecting scores. You may recognize the self-monitoring effect as a common component of diet plans and smoking cessation programs in which simply observing habits sensitizes people to their behavior and thereby changes it.

**b.** *Generality Across Response Measures*    Many variables can be defined and measured in different ways. The variable "fear," for example, can be defined in terms of physiological measures (e.g., heart rate) or self-report measures or behavior. In a research study, a researcher typically selects one definition and one measurement procedure. In this case, the results of the study may be limited to that specific measurement and may not generalize to other definitions or other measures. For example, a study may find that a particular therapy is effective in treating phobias, where "fear" is defined and measured by heart rate. In actual practice, however, the therapy may not have any effect on phobic patients' behaviors.

**c.** *Time of Measurement*    In a research study the scores for individuals are measured at a specific time after (or during) the treatment. However, the actual effect of the treatment may decrease or increase with time. Thus, the results obtained in a research study in which responses are measured at a specific time may differ from the results obtained when measured at a different time.

Learning Check

Describe two ways in which assessment issues threaten the external validity of research findings.

Table 6.4 provides a summary of the four major categories of threats to the external validity of research results.

## 6.4    MORE ABOUT INTERNAL AND EXTERNAL VALIDITY

The obvious goal of any research study is to maximize internal and external validity; that is, every researcher would like to be confident that the results of a study are true and that the truth of the results extends beyond the particular individuals, conditions, and procedures used in the study. However, it is almost impossible to design and conduct a perfect research study. In fact, the steps taken to reduce or eliminate one threat to validity often increase others. As a result, designing and conducting research is usually a balancing act filled with choices and compromises that attempt to maximize validity and provide the best possible answer to the original research question. As we introduce specific re-

TABLE 6.4

**General Threats to the External Validity of a Research Study**

| Source of the Threat | Description of the Threat |
|---|---|
| Participants | Characteristics that are unique to the specific group of participants in a study may limit ability to generalize the results of the study to individuals with different characteristics. For example, results obtained from college students may not generalize to noncollege adults. |
| Features of the Study | Characteristics that are unique to the specific procedures used in a study may limit ability to generalize the results to situations where other procedures are used. For example, the results obtained from participants who are aware that they are being observed and measured may not generalize to situations where the participants are not aware that measurement is occurring. |
| Experimenters | Characteristics that are unique to the specific experimenter conducting the study may limit ability to generalize the results to situations with a different experimenter. For example, the results obtained in a situation where the experimenter knows the research hypothesis (and can subtly influence the participants) may not generalize to a situation where a researcher does not know the research hypothesis (and cannot influence the participants). |
| Measurements | Characteristics that are unique to the specific measurement procedure may limit ability to generalize the results to situations where a different measurement procedure is used. For example, the results obtained from measurements taken immediately after treatment may not generalize to a situation where measurements are taken 3 months after treatment. |

search designs in later chapters, we discuss in more detail the choices and consequences involved in developing a research study. In particular, we consider the specific threats to internal and external validity associated with specific designs. For now, we outline some of the general constraints on validity to consider when planning or reading research, and discuss some of the necessary trade-offs between internal and external validity.

## BALANCING INTERNAL AND EXTERNAL VALIDITY

To gain a high level of internal validity, a researcher must eliminate or minimize confounding variables. To accomplish this, a study must be tightly controlled so that no extraneous variables can influence the results. However, controlling a study may create a research environment that is so artificial and unnatural that results obtained within the study will not occur outside it. Thus, attempts to increase internal validity can reduce external validity. In general, the results from a tightly controlled research study should be interpreted as demonstrating what *can happen* but not necessarily what *will happen* in an outside environment where other variables are free to operate.

On the other hand, research that attempts to gain a high level of external validity will often create a research environment that closely resembles the outside world. The risk in this type of research comes from the fact that the real world is often a chaotic jumble of uncontrolled variables, especially in comparison with the highly regulated environment of a research laboratory. Thus, striving for increased external validity can allow extraneous variables (potentially confounding variables) into a study and thereby threaten internal validity.

In very general terms, there tends to be a tradeoff between internal and external validity. Research that is very strong with respect to one kind of validity often tends to be relatively weak with respect to the second type. This basic relationship must be considered in planning a research study or evaluating someone else's work. Usually the purpose or goals of a study will help you decide which type of validity is most important and which threats must be addressed.

## ETHICAL CONSTRAINTS

Any research involving human or animal subjects is necessarily restricted in terms of the kinds of treatments and measurements that can be used. As noted in Chapter 3, basic human and animal rights prohibit techniques and procedures that might be dangerous or harmful to the individuals in the study. For example, researchers may have questions about changes in behavior that may be caused by brain injury or dietary deficiency or chemical imbalances; although it is often possible to examine these questions in descriptive research studies, it is usually unethical to conduct true experiments. You cannot have one group of individuals assigned to a brain injury group to be compared with a second set of individuals who do not receive brain injuries. It is unethical to manipulate some variables to examine cause-and-effect relationships.

In addition, researchers occasionally encounter situations in which some potentially confounding variables simply cannot be eliminated. For example, a researcher may conduct a behavior modification study in an elementary school classroom where it is possible to control most of the extraneous variables that might influence behavior. At the end of the day, however, the children are sent home, where they are free to interact with parents, siblings, and friends and where they are exposed to a wide variety of uncontrolled variables. To completely eliminate the threat of confounding variables, it would be necessary to isolate the children during the times they are outside the classroom as well as in the controlled classroom environment. Obviously, isolating research participants in this way would generate serious ethical questions. In general, ethical constraints limit what can be manipulated and controlled in a research study and as a result can compromise validity.

## EXAGGERATED VARIABLES

Most research is undertaken in the hope of demonstrating a relationship between variables. To accomplish this goal, a research study often maximizes the differences for one of the variables to increase the likelihood of revealing a relationship with a second variable. In particular, researchers often exaggerate the differences between treatment conditions to increase the chance that the scores obtained in one treatment are noticeably different from the scores obtained in another treatment. To evaluate the effects of temperature on learning, for example, a researcher probably would not compare a 70-degree room and a 72-degree room. The study has a greater chance of success if it involves comparison of 70 degrees and 90 degrees. Although the larger temperature difference is likely to reveal a relationship between temperature and learning, the researcher should be cautious about generalizing the result to a normal classroom situation, in which 20-degree temperature changes are unlikely.

## 6.5   VALIDITY AND INDIVIDUAL RESEARCH STRATEGIES

Because different research strategies have different goals, they tend to have different levels of internal validity and external validity. For example, descriptive and correlational studies tend to examine variables in their natural, real-world settings and therefore tend to have relatively good external validity. On the other hand, experimental research tends to be rigorously controlled and monitored and therefore has high internal validity. Quasi-experimental studies tend to fall somewhere in between; they attempt to mimic the control of true experiments, which helps internal validity, and they tend to take place in applied, real-world situations, which helps external validity.

### VALIDITY AND THE DESCRIPTIVE STRATEGY

As discussed in Section 6.1, the goal of the descriptive research strategy is to describe variables as they exist. Usually, therefore, a descriptive study observes and records variables as they occur naturally. As a result, descriptive research tends to have high external validity. However, because there is typically no attempt to monitor or control extraneous variables, the causes of the observed behavior cannot be explained. Thus, descriptive research tends to have low internal validity.

### VALIDITY AND THE CORRELATIONAL STRATEGY

Also as discussed in Section 6.1, the goal of a correlational study is to demonstrate the existence of a relationship between two variables without trying to explain the relationship. Usually a correlational study observes and records the two variables as they exist naturally, with no attempt to control, manipulate, or otherwise interfere with them. As a result, correlational research tends to have high external validity. However, the correlational research strategy tends to have relatively low internal validity because extraneous variables (potentially confounding variables) are allowed to enter the study with little or no control or monitoring.

### VALIDITY AND THE EXPERIMENTAL STRATEGY

Again as we discussed in Section 6.1, the goal of the experimental strategy is to establish and demonstrate the existence of a cause-and-effect relationship between two variables. That is, an experiment attempts to show that changes in one variable (the independent or manipulated variable) are directly responsible for corresponding changes in a second variable (the dependent or measured variable). To demonstrate that one specific variable (and no other) is responsible for changes, it is essential that any potentially confounding variables be eliminated. Thus, experimental research studies typically attempt to isolate the two variables being examined, excluding all other variables from the study. As a result, true experiments tend to have high internal validity. In fact, internal validity is a primary concern for experimental research. On the other hand, experiments risk having relatively low external validity. Because experiments must eliminate all extraneous variables, experimental research is usually conducted in highly controlled conditions. The risk for external validity is that the results obtained in the structured, regulated, and monitored environment of an experiment may not generalize to the relatively chaotic real world.

## VALIDITY AND THE QUASI-EXPERIMENTAL STRATEGY

As discussed in Section 6.1, the goal of the quasi-experimental strategy is to provide evidence for a cause-and-effect relationship between two variables. Because quasi-experimental studies attempt to emulate true experiments, they tend to have higher internal validity than descriptive and correlational studies. However, unlike the true experiment, a quasi-experimental study uses a nonmanipulated or noncontrolled variable to define different groups or conditions. Thus, unambiguous cause-and-effect conclusions cannot be formed. As a result, quasi-experimental studies tend to have lower internal validity than true experiments. On the other hand, because quasi-experimental studies often take place in real-world environments and attempt to accommodate real-world restrictions (for example, ethical concerns), they have relatively high external validity.

 Learning Check

Which research strategy is strongest in terms of internal validity? Why?

## 6.6 RESEARCH STRATEGIES, RESEARCH DESIGNS, AND RESEARCH PROCEDURES

The process of developing a research study can be broken down into three distinct stages: Determining a **research strategy,** determining a **research design,** and determining **research procedures.** Although these three terms are often used interchangeably without much regard for precise definitions, we introduce them here as a means of differentiating the separate stages of research development and identifying the choices and decisions that compose each stage.

## RESEARCH STRATEGIES

As discussed in Section 6.1, the term *strategy* refers to the general approach and goals of a research study. Research strategy is usually determined by the kind of question you plan to address and the kind of answer you hope to obtain. The four basic research strategies are the descriptive strategy, the correlational strategy, the experimental strategy, and the quasi-experimental strategy. In general terms, a research strategy is concerned with what you hope to accomplish in a research study. Chapters 7, 8, and 9 provide more details about these four different approaches.

## RESEARCH DESIGNS

The next step, the **research design,** addresses how to implement the strategy. Determining a research design requires decisions about three basic aspects of the research study:

1. *Group versus individual:* Will the study examine a group of individuals, calculating an average for the entire group, or should the study focus on a single individual? Although group studies tend to have higher external validity (results from a large group can be more confidently generalized than results from a single individual), the careful examination of a single individual often can provide detail that is lost in averaging a large group.

2. *Same individuals versus different individuals:* Some research examines changes *within* the same group of individuals as they move from one treatment to the next. Other research uses a different group of individuals for each separate treatment and then examines differences *between* groups. Each design has advantages and disadvantages that must be weighed in the planning phase.

3. *The number of variables to be included:* The simplest study involves examining the relationship between two variables. However, some research involves three or more variables. For example, a researcher may be interested in multiple relationships, or a study may focus on two variables but ask how their relationship is affected by other variables. Thus, one factor in determining a research design is deciding how many variables will be observed, manipulated, or regulated.

A research design is a general framework for conducting a study. Different designs and their individual strengths and weaknesses are discussed in Chapters 10 through 13.

---

A **research design** is a general plan for implementing a research strategy. A research design specifies whether the study will involve groups or individual subjects, whether the study will make comparisons within a group or between groups, and how many variables will be included in the study.

Definition

---

## RESEARCH PROCEDURES

The next stage in developing a research study involves filling in the details that precisely define how the study is to be done. This final, detailed stage is called the **research procedure.** It includes a precise determination of:

Exactly how the variables will be manipulated, regulated, and measured

Exactly how many individuals will be involved

Exactly how the individual participants or subjects will proceed through the course of the study

The procedure contains the final decisions about all choices still open after the general design is determined. The task of defining and measuring variables is discussed in Chapter 4; different ways of selecting individuals to participate in a study are discussed in Chapter 5.

---

A **research procedure** is an exact, step-by-step description of a specific research study.

---

In summary, research strategies are broad categories that classify research according to the type of question the research study addresses. Research designs are general categories that classify research according to how the study is conducted. Notice that several different research studies can all have the same strategy, and different studies can all share the same design. Research procedures, on the other hand, are unique to the specific study being considered. (Occasionally a researcher deliberately copies the procedures from another study. This kind of direct replication is relatively rare and usually is done only when there is some doubt that the two "identical" studies will produce the same results.) Normally, each study has its own unique procedures.

 Learning Check    Explain the difference between the terms *research strategy*, *design*, and *procedure*.

---

## CHAPTER SUMMARY

There are four general categories of research strategies: descriptive, correlational, experimental, and quasi-experimental. The descriptive strategy assesses the variables being examined as they exist naturally. The correlational strategy determines whether there is a relationship or association between two variables. The experimental strategy assesses whether there is a causal relationship between two variables. The quasi-experimental strategy obtains evidence for a causal relationship between two variables, but this strategy cannot unambiguously demonstrate cause and effect.

Central to selecting a research strategy and design is validity, which is concerned with the truth of the research or the accuracy of the results. Any factor that raises doubts about the research results is a threat to validity. Questions about the validity of research are traditionally grouped into two general categories, internal validity and external validity. A

research study has internal validity if it produces a single, unambiguous explanation for the results. Any factor that allows for an alternative explanation of the results of a study is a threat to the internal validity of the research. Confounding variables are the most common threats to internal validity. A study has external validity if the results of the study can be generalized to people, settings, times, measures, and characteristics other than those in the study. The generality of a study's findings may be a function of virtually any characteristic of the study, including characteristics of the participants or subjects, characteristics of the study's procedures, characteristics of the experimenter, and characteristics of the measures.

There tends to be a tradeoff between internal and external validity. Research that is very strong with respect to one kind of validity is often relatively weak with respect to the second type. This basic relationship must be considered in planning a research study or evaluating someone else's work. Research strategies also vary in terms of validity. Descriptive and correlational studies tend to have high external validity and relatively low internal validity; experiments tend to have high internal validity and relatively low external validity. Quasi-experimental studies tend to fall in between.

Research *strategy* refers to the general approach of a research study. Research *design* addresses the question of how to implement the strategy. A research *procedure* is an exact, step-by-step description of a specific research study.

## KEY WORDS

research strategy
descriptive research strategy
correlational research strategy
experimental/manipulative
    research strategy
quasi-experimental research
    strategy
validity
threat to validity

internal validity
threat to internal validity
external validity
threat to external validity
extraneous variable
confounding variable
assignment bias
history effects

practice effects
fatigue
reactivity
laboratory
field
demand characteristics
research design
research procedure

##  EXERCISES

1.  In addition to the key words, you should also be able to define each of the following terms:
    independent variable
    dependent variable
    nonexperimental/nonmanipulative research
    subject selection bias
    volunteer bias
    novelty effect
    subject role or subject role behavior
    good subject role
    negativistic subject role
    faithful subject role
    apprehensive subject role
    multiple treatment interference
    experimenter bias/expectancy
    sensitization/assessment sensitization/pretest
        sensitization
    research strategy
2.  For each of the following scenarios, identify which research strategy is used (descriptive, correlational, experimental, or quasi-experimental).

a.  Dr. Jones conducts a study examining the relationship between viewing violent television and aggressive behavior of 5-year-old boys. Television preferences are obtained by interviewing each child, and aggressive behavior is measured by observing the children during an outdoor play period.

b.  Dr. Jones conducts a study examining the relationship between viewing violent television and aggressive behavior of 5-year-old boys. Television preferences are obtained by interviewing each child. Based on the interview results the boys are divided into two groups: those who prefer violent TV and those who prefer nonviolent TV. Then aggressive behavior is measured by observing the children during an outdoor play period to determine if there is any difference between the two groups.

c.  Dr. Jones conducts a study examining the relationship between viewing violent television and aggressive behavior of 5-year-old boys. A group of boys is randomly separated; half the boys are shown violent TV programs for 30 minutes before play time, and the other half of the boys are shown nonviolent TV programs during the same period. Aggressive behavior is then measured by observing the children during an outdoor play period to determine if there is any difference between the two groups.

d. Dr. Jones conducts a study examining aggressive behavior of 5-year-old boys. Each afternoon for one week, a group of boys in a day care center is observed during a 30-minute period while they watch TV and during a 30-minute period while they play outdoors. Aggressive behaviors are recorded during each 30-minute period.

3. Describe the difference in the goals of the four different research strategies.

4. Develop an example of a research study that contains a confounding variable.

5. Explain how using college students as participants in a study may limit the external validity of a study's research findings.

6. What is the novelty effect, and how does it affect a study's external validity?

7. Describe one way in which the experimenter may threaten the external validity of the results of a study.

8. How does sensitization threaten the external validity of research findings?

9. Obtain a research article from a psychology journal. Discuss the internal validity of the study.

10. Obtain a research article from a psychology journal. Discuss the external validity of the study.

## InfoTrac COLLEGE EDITION EXERCISES

1. Using InfoTrac College Edition, find one research study (periodical article) that involves a comparison between two or more groups. (You could begin with a subject that is likely to produce different groups. For example, terms like *sex differences* or *personality* are likely to be studied using separate groups.) Find the section of your article that describes how the groups were formed or the general characteristics for each group. (Usually this information is provided at the beginning of the *method* section, following the introductory paragraphs.)

   a. Is there reason to suspect that a participant variable such as age or IQ is a threat to internal validity? That is, are the participants in one group older or smarter than the participants in another group?

   b. Explain why (or why not) you think that a participant variable may be a confounding variable in this study.

2. Using InfoTrac College Edition, find one research study (periodical article) that examines a specifically restricted segment of the general population. For example, look for a study that examines only adolescent girls or a study where the participants are all over 65 years old. (You could begin with a subject term identifying a specific type of participant.) Does your study discuss how external validity may be limited by considering only one small segment of the population? (This discussion typically occurs in the *discussion* section at the end of the article and may be presented in the form of a suggestion that future research be done with a different section of the population.)

# Descriptive and Correlational Research Strategies

## CHAPTER OVERVIEW

In this chapter we discuss the details of descriptive and correlational research strategies. The goal of descriptive research is to describe variables as they exist. Three descriptive research designs are considered: observational research design, survey research design, and case study research. The goal of correlational research is to describe the relationship between two variables and to measure the strength of the relationship. Applications, strengths, and weaknesses of this type of strategy are discussed.

## 7.1 INTRODUCTION

In the preceding chapter we identified four basic research strategies—descriptive, correlational, experimental, and quasi-experimental. In this chapter we deal with the details of the **descriptive research strategy** and the **correlational research strategy.** Details of the experimental and quasi-experimental strategies are discussed in Chapters 8 and 9.

Both the descriptive and correlational strategies are nonexperimental approaches to research. In both, there is usually no attempt to manipulate or control or interfere with the variables. More specifically, descriptive research typically involves measuring a variable or set of variables as they exist naturally. The goal of the descriptive strategy is to describe a single variable or, when multiple variables are involved, to obtain separate descriptions for each variable. The correlational strategy involves measuring two (or more) variables as they exist naturally; its goal is to establish that a relationship exists between variables and to describe the nature of the relationship.

Both strategies are extremely useful as preliminary research (i.e., in the early stages of research) and in their own right. The first step in understanding a new phenomenon is to gain some idea of the variable of interest as it naturally exists. It can also be useful to know if a relationship exists between two variables. After establishing that a relationship exists, a researcher may then use the experimental research strategy to investigate underlying causality. In addition, the results from descriptive and correlational research are valuable in their own right: both strategies help us to capture interesting, naturally occurring behavior.

Before we begin our formal discussion of descriptive and correlational research, look briefly at the following items, each of which appeared in our local newspaper around Labor Day in 2001:

> Of children 16 to 24 years old, fewer worked or looked for work in the summer of 2001 than did so in the previous three decades. (8/26/01)

> The results of a survey indicate that a man's appearance matters in the job market. Of those responding, 70% said that looking younger is important for career placement and for promotion. (8/26/01)

> The longer you live with your partner, the more likely you are to sleep on a larger mattress. Of the couples surveyed, 52% slept on a full-size mattress when they first got together. Now, 80% sleep on a queen- or king-size mattress. (8/28/01)

> A study of thousands of Minneapolis high school students found that they behaved better, got better grades, experienced less depression, and were less likely to miss classes when the school changed the starting time to allow students to sleep an extra hour in the morning. (8/29/01)

> A study reports that older people are more likely to be injured or to die in automobile accidents. Drivers aged 70 to 74 who have accidents are twice as likely to die as are drivers between 30 and 59. (9/4/01)

Although none of these reports is particularly earthshaking or insightful (we are not even sure if they are really true), they are good examples of nonexperimental research. In each case the intent of the study is simply to describe a phenomenon. The studies do not try to explain why these things happen or identify the underlying causes. Although these newspaper reports may appear to be somewhat trivial, this kind of research plays a very important role in the behavioral sciences. Much of what we know about human and animal behavior is based on descriptions of variables and their relationships.

In the following sections three descriptive research designs are considered: observational research, survey research, and case study research. In the observational research design, we describe observation of behaviors as they occur in natural settings. In survey research design, we describe people's responses to questions about behavior and attitudes. In case studies, we describe a single individual in great detail. Details of the correlational research strategy are discussed later in the chapter.

Describe the similarities and differences between descriptive and correlational research.

Learning Check

## 7.2   OBSERVATIONAL RESEARCH DESIGN

In the **observational research design,** the researcher observes and systematically records the behavior of individuals for the purpose of describing behavior—for example, the mating behavior of birds, parent–child interactions on a playground, or the shopping behavior of adolescents in a mall. Behavioral observation can be used to measure variables in many other research designs as well. In Chapter 4 we discussed behavioral observation as one measurement technique applicable to the general process of measuring variables, and in Section 4.5, we described how to make behavioral observations objectively. A study using behavioral observation simply for descriptive purposes is classified as an observational research design.

> Caution! Many students assume all research studies that use behavioral observation are observational research designs. But observation is used to measure variables in a variety of different designs. The defining element of an observational research design is that the results are used simply to describe behavior.

In the **observational research design** the researcher observes and systematically records the behavior of individuals in order to describe the behavior.

Definition

What is the difference between observation and observational research design?

Learning Check

### TYPES OF OBSERVATION AND EXAMPLES

Ethologists (researchers who study nonhumans in their natural environment) and researchers interested in human behavior commonly use the observational research design. There are three basic kinds of observation: naturalistic observation, participant observation, and contrived observation.

#### Naturalistic Observation
When a researcher observes and records behavior in a natural setting without intervening in any way, it is called **naturalistic observation** or **nonparticipant observation.** A natural setting is one in which behavior ordinarily occurs and

that has not been arranged in any way for the purpose of recording behavior. In naturalistic observation researchers try to be as inconspicuous and unobtrusive as possible, passively recording whatever occurs.

| | |
|---|---|
| Definition | In **naturalistic observation** or **nonparticipant observation** a researcher observes behavior in a natural setting as unobtrusively as possible. |

Naturalistic observation could be used to describe any behavior, for example, the behavior of children in a classroom, the behavior of protestors in a riot, or the behavior of patrons at a bar. A classic example of naturalistic observation used to describe nonhuman behavior is Jane Goodall's research (1971, 1986). Goodall lived with a colony of chimpanzees in Gombe, Tanzania, for a number of years during the 1960s and observed behaviors in chimps never before recorded—for example, tool use in a nonhuman. She observed chimpanzees stripping leaves off twigs, inserting the twigs into a termite hill, then withdrawing the twigs and licking off the termites that clung to them.

Naturalistic observation is particularly useful in providing insight into real-world behavior. The results of studies using naturalistic observation also have high degrees of external validity because the behavior is examined in real-world settings as opposed to laboratories. Further, naturalistic observation is useful for examining behaviors that, for practical or ethical reasons, cannot be manipulated by the researcher. For example, if a researcher were interested in investigating spanking behavior in parents, he or she obviously couldn't make parents spank their children for the purposes of scientific exploration. A researcher could, however, stroll through public places, such as malls, and watch parents disciplining their children.

One limitation of naturalistic observation is the time needed to conduct this type of research. To observe the mating behavior of a particular species of bird, for example, a researcher would need to wait not only until one member of that species of bird showed up but also until another member of that species' opposite sex appeared. In addition, both birds would need to be sexually ready before a researcher could observe their courtship and mating behaviors. Similarly, using naturalistic observation of parent–child interactions on a playground means waiting for a parent with a child of the appropriate age and gender to arrive at the playground and then engage in the behavior the researcher wants to observe. A second problem with naturalistic observation is that because the goal is to observe natural behavior, the behaviors must not be disrupted or influenced by the presence of the observer. This problem is usually addressed by concealing the observer or accustoming the individuals to the observer's presence. Both techniques are attempts to make the observer as unobtrusive as possible (see Chapter 4).

Learning Check

Describe what a researcher attempts to do in naturalistic observation.

### Participant Observation

In **participant observation** a researcher does not observe from afar, as does a naturalistic observer. In participant observation the researcher interacts with the participants and becomes one of them in order to observe and record behavior.

This type of observation is needed in situations where inconspicuous observation is not possible. For example, researchers certainly couldn't set up observation in the middle of a cult or gang meeting and expect that no one would notice them, that their presence would not alter behavior, or that the behaviors observed would be at all natural.

Definition

In **participant observation** the researcher engages in the same activities as the people being observed, in order to observe and record their behavior.

A great example of participant observation is Rosenhan's (1973) research investigating the experiences of mental patients and patient–staff interactions in psychiatric hospitals. In this research, Rosenhan had eight individuals misrepresent their names and occupations and claim they heard voices, in order to be admitted to various mental hospitals. All eight individuals were admitted. The pseudopatients observed hospital conditions, their own treatment, and the behaviors of staff and patients. The eight researchers were admitted to 12 different hospitals, and apparently no hospital staff realized that they were not real patients.

Participant observation allows researchers to observe behaviors that are not usually open to scientific observation—for example, occult activities—and to get information that may not be accessible to outside observation. Additionally, by having the same experiences as the participants in the study, the observer gains a unique perspective, obtaining insight into behavior not obtainable by observing from afar. The results of participant-observation studies have high external validity because the behaviors are examined in real-world settings, not laboratories.

There are several limitations of this type of observation. It is extremely time consuming; for example, the observers' stays in the mental hospitals in the Rosenhan study ranged from 7 to 52 days. In addition, participant observation is potentially dangerous for the observer. The observer may inadvertently alter participant behavior by directly interacting with them; and, finally, by interacting with the participants and identifying closely with the individuals in the study, an observer may lose objectivity.

Describe the situations in which participant observation may be particularly useful.

Learning Check

### Contrived Observation

Another type of observation is **contrived observation** or **structured observation.** In contrast to observing behavior in natural settings, here the observer sets up a situation so that events can be observed without waiting for them to occur naturally. The purpose of contrived observation is to precipitate a behavior that occurs naturally but infrequently— to create a situation wherein a natural behavior may occur and be observed in a more timely fashion.

Definition

Observation of behavior in settings arranged specifically for observing and recording behavior is known as **contrived observation** or **structured observation.**

Often such studies are conducted in laboratory settings. For example, if a researcher wants to observe parent–child interactions, the parents and children could be brought into a laboratory and given a task to perform while being observed or videotaped. This process is much quicker than waiting for parents and children to show up at a playground and interact with one another, which is how natural observation would proceed. Developmental psychologists frequently use structured observation. The most notable example is Jean Piaget (1896–1980). In many of Piaget's studies a child is given a problem to solve (for example, which cylinder contains more water), and the researcher observes and records how the child solves the problem. These descriptions have provided a wealth of information regarding children's cognitive abilities and are the basis for Piaget's stage theory of cognitive development.

Contrived observation may also take place in a natural but "set up" setting: a field setting (which the participant perceives as a natural environment) arranged by the researcher for the purposes of observing and recording a behavior. For example, to observe the eating behaviors of birds, a researcher could set up a bird feeder. Structured observation is a compromise between the purely descriptive naturalistic observation discussed earlier and manipulative field experiments (discussed in Chapter 8). Ethologists frequently use contrived observation to study animals' responses. For example, Nobel Prize-winning ethologist Konrad Lorenz discovered the phenomenon of imprinting by observing the behavior of graylag goslings. Imprinting is the establishment of a strong, stable preference for or attachment to an object when that object is encountered during a sensitive period in an animal's life; normally a gosling imprints on its parent immediately after hatching. Lorenz discovered imprinting by naturalistic observation, when the goslings pursued him as if he were their parent! He and others then used contrived observation to see if the young goslings would imprint on other models as well. (Indeed they will; graylag goslings will imprint on almost any moving object in the environment.)

An advantage of contrived observation over both natural and participant observation is that there is no waiting for behaviors to occur; the researcher makes them occur by setting up the environment in such a way that they are more likely to occur. However, a disadvantage of contrived observation is that, because the environment is less natural, the behavior may be as well.

**Learning Check**

Why might a researcher use contrived observation instead of another type of observation?

## STRENGTHS AND WEAKNESSES OF OBSERVATIONAL RESEARCH DESIGNS

The strengths and weaknesses of the three types of observation are summarized in Table 7.1. Here we discuss some additional strengths and weaknesses of observational research designs in general. A major strength of observational research is that the researcher observes and records *actual* behavior; in contrast, in survey research design, for example, the researcher relies on the participants' *reports* of their behavior. Participants can distort or conceal the accuracy or

TABLE 7.1

### A Summary of the Strengths and Weaknesses of the Observational Research Design

| | Strengths | Weaknesses |
|---|---|---|
| Naturalistic Observation | • Behavior observed in the real world<br>• Useful for nonmanipulated behaviors<br>• Actual behaviors observed and recorded | • Time consuming<br>• Potential for observer influence<br>• Potential for subjective interpretation |
| Participant Observation | • When natural observation is impossible<br>• Get information not accessible otherwise<br>• Participation gives unique perspective | • Time consuming<br>• Potential loss of objectivity<br>• Increased chance for observer influence |
| Contrived Observation | • Do not have to wait for behaviors to occur | • Less natural |

truthfulness of their responses and thus not reflect their actual behavior. Observational research results often have high external validity as well. With the exception of contrived observation in a laboratory, most observational research is conducted in a field setting; as was mentioned in Chapter 6 (and discussed in more detail in Chapter 8), research conducted in field settings tends to have higher external validity. Another strength of observational research is its flexibility: A researcher can complete a comprehensive observation of antecedents, behaviors, and consequences of the behaviors, whereas other studies examine a single, discrete behavior.

The goal of all observational research designs is to observe natural behavior, and therefore it is essential that the behaviors not be disrupted or influenced by the presence of an observer (the problem of reactivity, discussed in Chapters 4 and 6.) When people know they are being observed, they may respond differently than when unaware of it. Two ways to minimize reactivity (see Chapter 4) are to habituate the participants to the observers and to conceal the observer. Concealed or disguised observation is less reactive than unconcealed or undisguised observation.

Another concern with observational research designs is observer objectivity. Demonstrating interrater reliability (see Chapter 4) is one way to address this problem. A third problem with observational research is the ethical concern about "spying" on people. If participants are not aware that their behavior is being observed, the researcher may be violating a person's privacy and right to choose to participate in the study. (In Chapter 3 we discussed when it may be justified to deceive people for research purposes.) Finally, a weakness of all observational research designs is that they simply describe behavior and do not examine its causes.

## 7.3   SURVEY RESEARCH DESIGN

Surveys and questionnaires are used extensively in the behavioral sciences as relatively efficient ways to gather large amounts of information. By presenting people with a few carefully constructed questions, it is possible to obtain self-reported answers about attitudes, opinions, personal characteristics, and behaviors. The simple notion behind a survey is that it is not necessary to observe directly where people shop or what foods they prefer or how many hours they sleep each night; instead, we simply ask. With a survey, a researcher does not have to wait until a behavior or response occurs; for example, it is not necessary to wait until after an election to discover people's attitudes about candidates or issues; we can ask at any time. Although surveys can be used to obtain scores for a variety of different research designs, a survey often is conducted simply to obtain a description of a particular group of individuals. A study using a survey simply for descriptive purposes is classified as a **survey research design.**

Definition

A research study that uses a survey to obtain a description of a particular group of individuals is called a **survey research design.**

Caution! The survey is used as a measurement technique in a variety of different research designs. Simply because a study uses a survey does not mean that it is a survey research design. The defining element of the survey research design is that the survey is used only to describe the variables being studied.

The goal of the survey research design is an accurate picture of the individuals to be studied. The survey provides a "snapshot" of the group at a particular time. Sometimes survey research focuses on a specific characteristic such as eating behavior or political attitudes; other survey research may seek a more complex picture of a variety of behaviors and opinions. For example, a researcher could use a survey to investigate alcohol use at a local high school. Depending on the questions asked, the results could provide a description of how many students drink alcohol, how much they drink, and when and where. Other questions could yield a description of student attitudes toward alcohol use among their peers.

A common application of survey research is by companies to obtain more accurate descriptions of their customers. When you buy a small appliance, for example, a "warranty registration card" usually accompanies it. In addition to your name and address and the serial number of the product, other demographic questions are usually asked:

What is your age?

What is your occupation?

What is your income?

How did you hear about our product?

Clearly the purpose of these questions is to obtain the demographic characteristics of customers; that is, to put together a description of the people who are likely to buy this product so that the company can do a better job of targeting its advertising.

Conducting survey research presents researchers with three issues that must be addressed for the results to be accurate and meaningful. First, survey construction: the questions must be assembled and organized. Second, a selection process must be developed to determine exactly who will participate in the survey and who will not; survey participants must be representative of the general group to be studied. Finally, administration of the survey: Will participants receive printed surveys through the mail; will the survey questions be read to people over the telephone; will participants complete the questions in person?

## CONSTRUCTING A SURVEY

Once the survey questions are determined, the next step is to organize the questions into a coherent survey that participants can easily understand and complete. The details of constructing a survey are beyond the scope of this text, but there are a few general guidelines for creating a well-organized survey:

1. Demographic questions (such as age, gender, level of education) should be placed at the end of the survey. These items are considered boring, and you do not want participants to quit because they are bored by the first few questions.

2. Sensitive questions or items that may cause embarrassment or discomfort should be placed in the middle of the survey. By the time participants encounter these items, they are more likely to have warmed up to the topic and become committed to completing the survey.

3. Questions dealing with the same general topic should be grouped together. Also, questions in the same format should be grouped together; for example, all rating-scale questions. Grouping questions simplifies the survey so participants do not have to jump from one topic to another or switch from one type of question to another.

4. If participants are going to read the survey, the format for each page should be relatively simple and uncluttered. Questions that are crammed together and seem to fill every square inch of the page create an overwhelming appearance that can intimidate participants.

5. Finally, vocabulary and language style should be easy for participants to understand. A survey with language appropriate for college students probably would not be appropriate for elementary school students.

These guidelines address only a few of the considerations involved in designing a survey. If you plan to construct your own survey, you probably should seek more detailed guidance. Two excellent sources are Converse and Presser (1986) and Dillman (1978).

## SELECTING RELEVANT AND REPRESENTATIVE INDIVIDUALS

Researchers typically want to generalize their results from the study's sample to the target population. (The different techniques for selecting research participants were discussed in Chapter 5.) In addition, the external validity of a research study is limited in part by the representativeness of the sample to the population (see Chapter 6).

A few concerns must be addressed regarding sample selection for survey research. First, many surveys address a specific issue that is relevant to only a small subset of the general population. For such a survey, care must be taken to select survey participants to whom the questions are relevant. For a survey about child care issues, for example, participants should be parents with small children. A sensible strategy might be to hand out surveys to parents as they pick up their children at day care centers around the city. Or you might obtain mailing lists from the different day care centers. Similarly, participants for a shopping survey might be selected from the people in a shopping mall, and participants for an education survey could come from the parents of children in the local school district.

Second, although some surveys focus on a specific topic or group of people, some surveys seek to describe a broad cross-section of the general population. In this case, the sample of survey participants must not be too restricted. For example, administering surveys to the students in a psychology class would not result in an accurate description of the political attitudes of people in the community. A researcher should take some time to identify the group to be described and then make an effort to select individuals who accurately represent the group. This often means that the individuals who participate in the survey are not necessarily the ones who are easiest or most convenient to obtain.

Occasionally individual researchers seek professional help preparing surveys and identifying participants. In most major metropolitan areas there are several research companies that design, administer, and analyze surveys. These companies usually have access to specialized mailing lists that can focus on a specific, well-defined population. Typically, a researcher supplies specific demographic characteristics, and the computer generates a list of individuals who meet the criteria—for example, single mothers between the ages of 20 and 29 who have incomes above $35,000. Focusing a survey in this way can increase the chances of obtaining a reasonable number of useful responses.

## ADMINISTERING A SURVEY

Once you have constructed the survey and identified the participants, the next step is to distribute the survey to the individuals you would like to investigate. There are a number of options for administering a survey, each of which has advantages and disadvantages. In this section we examine three of the most common methods for administering surveys—by mail, phone, and in person. It is also increasingly common to administer surveys on the Internet.

### Mail Surveys

One common method of administration is to mail the survey to a large sample of individuals. For individual participants, a mailed survey is very convenient and nonthreatening. Each individual can complete the survey at his or her own convenience and can be relatively confident that responses are anonymous and confidential. On the other hand, the fact that the survey is anonymous means that a researcher can never be sure exactly who in the household completed and returned the survey.

Mailing surveys is usually a relatively simple and easy process, although printing a large number of surveys, addressing them, and paying postage can be expensive and time consuming. The expense is compounded by the fact that response rates tend to be very low for mailed surveys: A response rate of 10% to 20% is fairly typical. This means that you need to distribute at least five times the number of surveys you hope to have returned.

In addition to the costs of a low response rate, there may be a bias differentiating those who do and those who don't return surveys. One obvious possibility is that people who are most interested in the survey topic (those with the most intense feelings) will be most likely to complete and return the survey. This trend creates what is called a **nonresponse bias** in the sample: The individuals who return surveys are usually not representative of the entire group who receives them. Nonresponse bias can limit your ability to generalize survey results—a threat to the external validity of your study.

Although it is impossible to eliminate nonresponse bias completely, several actions can increase the overall response rate for a mail survey and thereby reduce the bias. First, response rates can be significantly improved if a good cover letter accompanies the survey. A cover letter should not only introduce the survey and ask for participation but also include the following elements:

1.  An explanation of why the topic is important. For a survey on television program preferences, for example, you should point out the major role that TV plays in the entertainment and education of most people.

2.  An explanation of the usefulness of the results. Usually the results of a survey are used in future planning or to help determine a future course of action. This should be explained in the cover letter so that participants know that the information they are providing may actually influence them in the future.

3.  An emphasis on the importance of each individual response. The intent is to encourage all people to respond, whether or not they feel strongly about the issues in the survey. The cover letter should point out the importance of results that represent the entire population (not just a small group with special interests) and that it is therefore especially important that each person respond.

4.  A contact person (name, address, and phone number) participants can call or write to if they have any questions or comments. Participants will rarely contact this person, but a real name and address help personalize the survey.

5.  The signature of a person who is recognized and respected by individuals in the sample. People are more likely to respond if they are asked to by someone they know and like.

A second technique for improving response rates is to include a "gift" or token of appreciation with each survey. Common examples include a pen ("Please use this pen to fill out the survey, then keep the pen as our gift to you.") or money. Some surveys arrive with a dollar taped to the top and a note suggesting that the recipient use the money to buy a cup of coffee ("Sit back and enjoy your coffee while you complete the survey.")

Finally, it is possible to increase response rates by giving participants advance warning of the survey, then providing a follow-up reminder after the survey has been received. Typically, participants are notified by mail or by phone, about one week before the survey is mailed, that they have been selected to participate. The advance warning helps make the individuals feel special (they are a select group) and helps ensure that they will be watching for the survey in the mail. Approximately one week after the surveys have been received, a follow-up call or postcard is used to remind each person to complete and return the survey if they have not done so already and to thank each person for participating. Essentially, the advance notice and reminder provide a polite way to add an extra "please" and "thank you" to the recruitment process and can significantly increase the response rate.

### Phone Surveys

A second method of administering a survey is to contact individuals by telephone. However, administering a survey by telephone can be incredibly time consuming. The obvious problem with a telephone survey is that there is a direct, one-to-one relationship between the time spent by the researcher and the time spent by the participants; to get 100 minutes of survey responses, a researcher must spend 100 minutes on the phone. Therefore, most phone surveys are restricted to situations in which a large number of researchers or assistants can share the telephone assignments.

Administering a survey by telephone does have some advantages. First, the survey can be conducted from home or office. If several people place the calls, and the survey is relatively brief, it is possible to contact a fairly large number of participants in only a few days. If you are considering a phone survey, here are a few important notes for improving your chances for success:

1. Keep the questions short, and use a small number of response alternatives. With a telephone survey the participants do not have a written copy for reference, so you must depend on the listener's memory. If a participant gets confused or lost in the middle of a long, complicated question, you may not get a sensible response.

2. Practice reading the survey aloud. Listening to a question can be different from reading a question. On the telephone, participants cannot see the punctuation and other visual cues that help communicate the content of a written question. A good strategy is to pretest your survey questions by reading them to a set of friends. Be sure that your listeners understand the questions as you intended.

3. Beware of interviewer bias. Whenever a researcher has direct contact with participants, even over the telephone, there is a risk that the researcher will influence their natural responses. On the phone, the primary problem is exerting influence by tone of voice or by rephrasing questions. The standard solutions are to practice reading the survey questions in a consistent, neutral

tone and never to alter a survey question. If a participant does not understand a question and asks for clarification, your only option is to reread the question. If you paraphrase a question or try to explain what it means, then you have changed the question and may have changed the participant's answer. Consider the following two versions of the same question. The first uses neutral wording and focuses on the library hours; the second question is phrased in a leading way—that is, it appears to be an invitation for the participant to join a happy little group (especially if the question is read in a very friendly tone of voice).

> Do you think there should be an increase in the hours that the library is open on weekends?

> Don't you think we should increase the hours that the library is open on weekends?

4.  Begin by identifying yourself and your survey. People are constantly bombarded by "junk" telephone calls and are inclined to hang up whenever a stranger calls. You can help avoid this problem if you immediately identify yourself and your topic and make it clear that you are conducting a survey and not trying to sell anything. Your first few sentences on the telephone are similar to the cover letter for a mail survey and should contain the same elements (see page 171).

Outline the advantages and disadvantages of using telephone surveys as compared to mail surveys.

Learning Check

### In-Person Surveys and Interviews

Probably the most efficient method for administering a survey is to assemble a group of participants and have them all complete the survey at the same time. You can ask people to sign up for predetermined meeting times or simply ask for volunteers to gather at a specific time and place. Another possibility is to approach pre-existing groups such as those in school classrooms or work-place lunchrooms. By having participants volunteer before the survey is presented, you guarantee a 100% response rate. The efficiency comes from the fact that you give instructions once to the entire group and then collect a whole set of completed surveys in the time it takes one participant to finish.

It also is possible to administer a survey in person to a single participant. In this case, the survey becomes a one-on-one interview. Although this may appear to be a very inefficient method of collecting information, an interview can be quite valuable. Usually, interviews are reserved for a very small group of specially selected individuals often called *key informants*. Typically these are people in positions to have unique perspectives on the issues or unique access to information (such as a college president, a chief of police, or a mayor). Interviews are also useful in situations in which you are willing to accept the limitations of a small group of participants in exchange for the in-depth information that can come from a detailed interview. An interview provides an opportunity for follow-up questions, and it is possible to explore complex issues more fully than could be done with a few isolated paper-and-pencil questions. Finally, interviews allow you to gather information from individuals who are unable to read and answer printed questions, such as young children, people who cannot read, and persons with low IQ.

A major concern with the interview is that experimenter bias will distort the results. If the experimenter simply smiles or nods, a participant may perceive a sign of approval or encouragement to continue on the current topic. Thus, the participant's response may be influenced by subtle actions on the part of the experimenter. Although it is impossible to completely eliminate this problem, it can be limited if the interviewer maintains a consistent attitude throughout the entire interview. A common strategy is to adopt a universal, mildly positive response to anything the participant says.

## STRENGTHS AND WEAKNESSES OF SURVEY RESEARCH

Table 7.2 summarizes the strengths and weaknesses of each type of survey. In general, one of the real strengths of survey research is its flexibility. Surveys can be used to obtain information about a wide variety of different variables including attitudes, opinions, preferences, and behaviors. In fact, some of these variables are very difficult to describe in any other way. In addition, surveys typically provide a relatively easy and efficient means of gathering a large amount of information.

We have already noted some of the disadvantages of survey research, such as low response rates and nonresponse bias. Responses to survey questions can also be difficult to analyze or summarize. This problem is especially important with "open-ended" questions, to which participants are allowed to respond in their own words. For example, if you ask students to identify what they consider the "best things" about their college or university, you probably would obtain a wide variety of answers that would be difficult to classify or categorize in any systematic

### TABLE 7.2

**A Summary of the Strengths and Weaknesses of the Survey Research Design**

| | Strengths | Weaknesses |
|---|---|---|
| **Mail Surveys** | • Convenient and anonymous<br>• Nonthreatening to participants<br>• Easy to administer | • Can be expensive<br>• Low response rate and nonresponse bias<br>• Unsure exactly who completes the survey |
| **Telephone Surveys** | • Can be conducted from home or office<br>• Participants can stay at home or office | • Time consuming<br>• Potential for interviewer bias |
| **In-Person Surveys** | • Efficient to administer with groups<br>• 100% response rate<br>• Flexible (groups or individual interviews) | • Time consuming with individual interviews<br>• Risk of interviewer bias |

manner. A final concern about survey research is that the information obtained is always a self-report. Ultimately, the quality of a survey study depends on the accuracy and truthfulness of the participants. It is certainly possible that at least some participants will distort or conceal information or simply have no knowledge about the topic when they answer certain questions. Therefore, if your survey results show that 43% of the high school students use alcohol at least once a month, keep in mind that the results actually show that 43% of the students *report* using alcohol at least once a month.

---

What is the general advantage of using the survey research design instead of the observational design? In the same context, what is the disadvantage of survey research?

Learning Check

---

## 7.4   CASE STUDY DESIGN

Research in the behavioral sciences tends to emphasize the study of groups rather than single individuals. By focusing on groups, researchers can observe the effects of a treatment across a variety of different personal characteristics and form a better basis for generalizing the results of the study. At the same time, however, some fields within the behavioral sciences are more concerned with individual behavior than with group averages. This is particularly true in the field of clinical psychology, in which clinicians concentrate on treatments and outcomes for individual clients. For clinicians, research results averaged over a large group of diverse individuals may not be as relevant as the specific result obtained for an individual client. In fact, it has been argued that intensive study of individuals (called the **idiographic approach**) is just as important as the study of groups (called the **nomothetic approach**) for clinical research (Allport, 1961).

Although it is possible to conduct experimental research with individual participants (see Chapter 13), most individual-participant research studies can be classified as case studies. A **case study** is a report describing a single individual, usually a detailed description of observations and experiences during the diagnosis and treatment of a specific clinical client, including a detailed description of the unique characteristics and responses of the individual. The information that is included in a case study can be obtained in a variety of ways, such as interviews with the client and/or close relatives, observation of the client, surveys, and archival data.

---

The **case study design** involves the in-depth study and detailed description of a single individual (or a very small group). A case study may involve an intervention or treatment administered by the researcher. When a case study does not include any treatment or intervention, it often is called a **case history.**

Definitions

---

Identify the advantages of conducting a research study with a single individual instead of a group of participants.

Learning Check

Caution! Other types of research, too, involve the detailed study of single individuals (see Chapter 13). The defining element of a case study design is that its goal is simply to obtain a description of the individual.

## APPLICATIONS OF THE CASE STUDY DESIGN

The case study design is most commonly used in clinical psychology. However, the case study has a long history of successful application throughout the behavioral sciences. Although group studies probably offer a more direct path to discovering general laws of behavior, it can also be argued that group studies are necessarily limited because they overlook the importance of the individual. By highlighting individual variables, case studies can offer valuable insights that complement and expand the general truths obtained from groups. In some instances, case studies can lead directly to general laws or theories. The developmental theories of Jean Piaget, for example, are largely based on detailed observations of his own children. The following sections identify specific applications of the case study design.

### Rare Phenomena and Unusual Clinical Cases

The case study design is often used to provide researchers with information concerning rare or unusual phenomena—for example, *multiple personality*, a dissociative disorder in which two or more distinct personalities exist within the same individual. Although multiple personality is fairly common in television and popular fiction, it is actually an extremely rare condition. With a disorder this rare it is essentially impossible to gather a group of individuals to participate in any kind of experimental investigation. As a result, most of what is known about multiple personality and its treatment comes from case studies. One of the most famous cases involved a relatively quiet and humble 25-year-old woman, Eve White, who also exhibited a more playful and mischievous personality, Eve Black, as well as a more mature and confident personality, Jane (Thigpen & Cleckley, 1954, 1957). You may recognize this highly publicized case study by the title of the 1957 publication, *Three Faces of Eve*.

Unique or unusual examples of individuals with brain injuries are often used to help identify the underlying neurological mechanisms for human memory and mental processing. A classic example is the case study of a patient identified as H. M. (Scoville & Milner, 1957). In an attempt to control severe epileptic seizures, H. M.'s hippocampus was surgically severed in both the left and right hemispheres of the brain. After surgery, H. M. had normal memory of events that occurred prior to surgery, and his overall intelligence was unchanged. In addition, his immediate memory (short-term memory) also appeared to function normally. For example, he could repeat back a string of digits such as a phone number. However, H. M. had lost the ability to permanently store any new information in memory. You could introduce yourself and talk briefly with H. M., then leave the room while he was occupied with some other task; when you returned to the room after only a few minutes, H. M. would have no memory of ever having met you and no memory of your conversation. In general, H. M. was unable to learn any new information presented to him after the surgery. This remarkable case study completely changed the way psychologists think about memory. Prior to the H. M. case, psychologists tended to view memory as a location in the brain. Now, memory is viewed as a process. H.M.'s injury did not destroy any specific memories; instead it seems to have disrupted a process. As a consequence of the study of H. M.'s case, evidence was provided that the hippocampus appears to play a crucial role in the process by which our current experiences are transformed into permanent memories.

## Case Studies as Counterexamples

Another application of the case study design is to use the detailed description of a single individual to demonstrate an "exception to the rule." Although a single case study is usually not sufficient to demonstrate that a treatment is universally effective, it is possible to use a single case study to show that the treatment does not always work.

One case study used in this manner exposed the flaws in a controversial method of treating phobias. The initial study (Valins & Ray, 1967) claimed to have demonstrated a new therapy technique called cognitive desensitization. The technique essentially tricks the client into thinking that his or her phobia has been cured. The idea is that clients who believe that they are cured develop new thinking patterns that eventually lead to a real cure. The study examined a group of individuals with fear of snakes. The treatment involved having the participants view pictures of snakes while listening to their own heartbeats played over a loudspeaker. However, the researchers actually presented false heart rates that appeared to show participants that they no longer experienced fear when shown the snake pictures. A follow-up study (Kent, Wilson, & Nelson, 1972) disputed the effectiveness of the treatment by clearly demonstrating that the treatment simply did not work. In addition to the experimental demonstration, the follow-up report presented a case study as a clinical addendum. The case study described a 24-year-old woman, Miss H, who had a phobia of spiders. She was given the false-feedback "therapy" using pictures of spiders instead of snakes. After treatment, Miss H stated that her fear of spiders was in no way altered or reduced. Although she accepted the false feedback as her own heart rate, she stated that she was still "paralyzed by fear" and that she would prefer to avoid such therapy sessions in the future.

## STRENGTHS AND WEAKNESSES OF THE CASE STUDY DESIGN

One of the primary strengths of a case study is the intense detail that is typically included. A case study exposes a wide variety of different variables, events, and responses that would probably be overlooked or deliberately eliminated (controlled) in an experiment. Thus, a case study can identify or suggest new variables that might account for a particular outcome, and can thereby generate hypotheses for future research.

As we saw in the false heart-rate study cited earlier (Kent, Wilson, & Nelson, 1972), case studies also can be used to demonstrate "exceptions to the rule." It takes only one negative demonstration, a single counterexample, to show that a general "law" of behavior is not always true. Case studies provide researchers with a good opportunity to identify special situations or unique variables that can modify a general treatment effect. Although this type of case study can be used to destroy or discredit a theory, usually counterexamples serve as constructive criticism. They allow theories to expand and develop by introducing new variables, and they can help establish the boundaries or limitations of a treatment application. There are very few absolute laws of behavior; most have exceptions, limitations, and qualifications, and often the qualifiers are discovered in case studies.

The false heart-rate study (Kent, Wilson, & Nelson, 1972) also demonstrates one final strength of the case study strategy: Case studies can be extremely powerful and convincing. The detailed description in a case study tends to make it more personal, more vivid, and more emotional than the "cold" facts and figures that result from a traditional laboratory study. These factors have all been demonstrated to have a strong, positive effect on memory (Tversky & Kahneman, 1973), suggesting that case studies may be more memorable and have a greater impact than experiments. As an analogy, consider your own response to witnessing an automobile accident versus reading an article on accident statistics. Witnessing one accident usually has more influence than reading a statistical summary of all the accidents across the state during the past year. In addition, case studies are typically descriptions of the everyday work of clinicians. This fact gives a case study a sense of realism that can be lacking in an "artificial" laboratory study. As a result, case studies often have an appearance of credibility and a degree of acceptance that far exceed a more objective evaluation of their true levels of internal and external validity.

Like all descriptive designs, the case study is necessarily limited because it simply describes and does not attempt to identify the underlying mechanisms that explain behavior. For example, a case study can provide a detailed description of the individual participant's characteristics (age, sex, family background, etc.), but it provides no means of determining how these variables influence the participant's response to treatment. A case study can tell *how* a specific individual, with specific characteristics responded to a specific treatment, but it cannot explain *why*. Although a case study may offer an explanation for the observed results, alternative explanations are always possible. In research terminology, case studies lack internal validity.

In addition to lacking internal validity, case studies also tend to be weak in external validity. Because a case study reports results for a single individual in a specific situation, it is difficult to justify generalizing the results to other individuals in other situations. It is always possible that a case study concerns a unique event in the life of a unique person, and there is no reason to expect the same outcome outside the confines of the study. Again, this threat can be tempered by the extent and detail of description within the study. If the study describes a relatively typical client and a relatively straightforward treatment procedure, there is good reason to expect the results to generalize to a broader population. On the other hand, if the case includes odd or unusual circumstances, a strange historical background, bizarre behaviors, or a uniquely individualized treatment program, it is less likely that the results will generalize beyond the specific case being described.

Finally, case studies can suffer from bias that distorts or obscures the results and interpretations. First, there is always a degree of selective bias that determines which cases are reported and which are not. Obviously, a researcher is likely to report the most successful or dramatic case. It is unlikely that a researcher would write a detailed report (and that a journal would publish the report) of an elaborate new treatment that has absolutely no effect. More subtle biases can operate within a reported case study. Remember, a case study consists of observations made by the researcher. These observations are subject to interpretations, impressions, and inferences. In general the reports of participants are filtered through the researcher, who decides what is important and what is not. In addition, the client may provide a biased or falsified report. Clients may exaggerate, minimize, lie about, or simply imagine events that are reported to a clinician/researcher.

Although case studies are exposed to serious threats to both internal and external validity and are subject to bias, many of these problems are reduced by replication. A case study rarely exists by itself but rather is accompanied by several similar reports. Repeated examples of the same basic finding by different researchers with different clients clearly helps bolster the validity and the credibility of the results. Table 7.3 summarizes the strengths and weaknesses of the case study research design.

Discuss how internal validity and external validity are both threatened in a case study design.

Learning Check

## 7.5   CORRELATIONAL RESEARCH STRATEGY

The earlier sections of this chapter focus on different examples of the descriptive research strategy. The general goal of the descriptive strategy is to describe a single variable or, when multiple variables are involved, to obtain separate descriptions for each variable. In this section we turn our attention to the **correlational research strategy.** The goal of the correlational strategy is to examine and describe the associations and relationships between variables. More specifically, the purpose of a correlational study is to establish that a relationship exists between variables and to describe the nature of the relationship. Notice that both the correlational strategy and the descriptive strategy are nonexperimental approaches to research. In each case, there usually is no attempt to manipulate, control, or interfere with the variables.

The data for a correlational study consist of two measurements for each individual, one for each of the two variables being examined. For example, a

| TABLE 7.3 |
| --- |

**A Summary of the Strengths and Weaknesses of the Case Study Research Design**

| Strengths | Weaknesses |
| --- | --- |
| • Not averaged over a diverse group | • Limited generalization |
| • Detailed description | • Potential for selective bias |
| • Vivid, powerful, convincing | • Potential for subjective interpretation |
| • Compatible with clinical work | |
| • Can study rare and unusual events | |
| • Can identify exceptions to the rule | |

researcher might record IQ and measure creativity for each person in a group of college students. Or a researcher could record food consumption and activity level for each animal in a colony of laboratory rats. Measurements can be made in natural surroundings, or the individuals can be measured in a laboratory setting; the important factor is that the researcher simply measures the two variables being studied. The measurements are then examined to determine whether they show any consistent pattern of relationship. The statistical procedures that are used to measure the strength or consistency of a relationship are discussed in Chapter 14 (pages 431–432).

---

Definition

In a **correlational research strategy,** two variables are measured and recorded for each individual. The measurements are then reviewed to identify any patterns of relationship that exist between the two variables and to measure the strength of the relationship.

---

For example, a researcher interested in intelligence and heredity could record the IQ scores and mothers' IQ scores for a group of high school students. Note that the researcher has two scores (own IQ and mother's IQ) for each student. The researcher can then look for patterns of relationship in the scores. For example, the data will probably show a tendency for the students with the highest IQ scores to have the mothers with the highest IQ scores. Similarly, students with lower IQ scores will tend to be associated with mothers who have lower IQ scores.

## APPLICATIONS OF THE CORRELATIONAL STRATEGY

As noted earlier, the correlational design is used to identify and describe relationships between variables. Following are three examples of how correlational designs can be used to address research questions.

### Prediction

One important use of correlation research is to establish a relationship between variables that can be used for purposes of prediction. For example, clinical researchers have established a relationship between specific behaviors and imminent suicide attempts. The relationships that have been demonstrated allow clinicians to watch for warning signs (for example, increased talk about suicide or suddenly giving away prized personal possessions) and take steps to intervene before a client makes a suicide attempt.

The use of correlational results to make predictions is not limited to predictions about future behavior. Whenever two variables are consistently related, it is possible to use knowledge of either variable to help make predictions about the other. Knowing a person's IQ, for example, allows us to make some prediction about the intelligence of his or her parents. Often one of the two variables is simply easier to measure or more readily available than the other. In these situations it is possible to use the available knowledge of one variable to predict the value of the unavailable variable. By establishing and describing the existence of a relationship, correlational studies provide the basic information needed to make predictions.

Within a correlational study, the two variables examined are essentially equivalent. Nonetheless, correlational studies often identify one variable as the **predictor variable** and the second variable as the **criterion variable.** In a correlational study used for prediction, the designation of the two variables is usually quite clear. University admissions offices occasionally use GRE (Graduate Record Exam) scores to predict graduate school success. In this situation, the GRE scores are the predictor variable, and graduate performance is the criterion variable. Clearly one variable, the predictor, is used to predict the other, the criterion. [Incidentally, there are data suggesting that GRE scores are not necessarily good predictors of graduate school success (Nagi, 1975; Kaczmarek & Franco, 1986)].

In situations where a correlational study is not used for prediction, researchers still tend to refer to a "predictor" and a "criterion" variable. In these situations the labels are usually determined by the purpose of the study. Typically, a correlational study begins with one of the two variables relatively well known or well understood, while the second variable is relatively unknown. Thus, the purpose of the study is to gain a better understanding of the "unknown" variable by demonstrating that it is related to an established, "known" variable. In this situation, the "known" variable is designated as the predictor, and the "unknown" variable is the criterion. For example, in a study exploring the relation between IQ and creativity, the goal is probably to gain a better understanding of creativity by determining how it is related to IQ; in this example, IQ would be the predictor variable and creativity would be the criterion.

---

Definition

In a correlational study, a researcher often is interested in the relationship between two variables in order to use knowledge about one variable to help predict or explain the second variable. In this situation, the first variable is called the **predictor variable** and the second variable (being explained or predicted) is called the **criterion variable.**

---

Describe how correlational studies can be used for prediction.

Learning Check

---

### Reliability and Validity

In Chapter 4 (page 86), the concepts of reliability and validity were introduced as the two basic criteria for evaluating a measurement procedure. In general terms, reliability evaluates the consistency or stability of the measurements, and validity evaluates the extent to which the measurement procedure actually measures what it claims to be measuring. Both reliability and validity are commonly defined by relationships that are established using the correlational research design.

For example, test-retest reliability is defined by the relationship between an original set of measurements and a follow-up set of measurements. If the same individuals are measured twice under the same conditions, and there is a consistent relationship between the two measurements, then the measurement procedure is said to be reliable. The concurrent validity of a measurement procedure can also be defined in terms of a relationship. If we develop a new test to measure intelligence, for example, we can demonstrate that we are really measuring intelligence by showing that our test scores are strongly related to scores obtained from an established IQ test. The following scenario demonstrates how correlational research can be used to determine reliability and validity.

Aptitude and personality tests are often administered to job applicants to determine how well their personal characteristics fit the demands of the job. The United States Air Force, for example, administers a battery of tests to help predict success for applicants to the aviation training program (Shanahan, 1984). One of the tests is a dot estimation task, used to measure compulsiveness versus decisiveness. Participants are shown very briefly a pattern of dots and asked to estimate the number of dots in the pattern. In theory, decisive people respond quickly, and compulsive people need more information and are slower to decide. In a correlational study, Lambirth, Gibb, and Alcorn (1986) evaluated the reliability and validity of the dot estimation task (the DOT). In the study, college students were administered the DOT and given one of two established tests for compulsiveness. Four weeks later, the students repeated the DOT and took the second compulsiveness test. The authors evaluated reliability by examining the relationship between the first and second attempts on the DOT. Also, validity was evaluated by examining the relationship between the DOT and the standard compulsiveness tests. The results showed a relatively poor relationship between scores on the first DOT and scores on the second DOT. In addition, the DOT had essentially no relation to either of the established compulsiveness measures. In everyday terms, the scores on the DOT appear to change randomly from one test to the next, and they are not consistently related to any known measure of compulsiveness. In measurement terms, the DOT appears to have poor reliability and poor validity as a measure of compulsiveness.

Learning Check

Describe how correlational studies can be used to determine reliability and validity.

## Evaluating Theories

Many theories generate research questions about the relationships between variables that can be addressed by the correlational research design. A good example comes from the age-old nature/nurture question as it applies to intelligence: Is intelligence primarily an inherited characteristic, or is it primarily determined by environment? A partial answer to this question comes from correlational studies examining the IQs of identical twins separated at birth and placed in different environments. Because these twins have identical heredity and different environments, they provide researchers with an opportunity to separate the two factors. The original work in this area, conducted by British psychologist Cyril Burt, showed a high relationship between the twins' IQs, suggesting that hereditary factors overwhelmed environment. However, later evidence showed that Burt probably falsified much of his data (Kamin, 1974). Nonetheless correlational results suggest a strong relationship between twins' IQs. Note the use of the correlational research design to address a theoretical issue.

What is the purpose of the correlational research design?

## STRENGTHS AND WEAKNESSES OF THE CORRELATIONAL RESEARCH STRATEGY

As is the case with the descriptive research strategy, the correlational research strategy is often used for the preliminary work in an area that has not received a lot of research attention. The correlational design can identify variables and describe relationships between variables that might suggest further investigation using the experimental strategy to determine cause-and-effect relationships. In addition, the correlational research design allows researchers an opportunity to investigate variables that would be impossible or unethical to manipulate. For example, a correlational study could investigate how specific behaviors or skills are related to diet deficiencies or brain injuries. Although it is possible and ethical to record diet deficiencies and brain injuries as they exist naturally, it would not be prudent to create these conditions in the laboratory. Countless other variables, such as family size, alcohol consumption, level of education, income, and color preferences, can be interesting topics for behavioral research but cannot be manipulated and controlled in an experimental research study. However, these variables can be easily measured and described in correlational research.

One of the primary advantages of a correlational study is that the researcher simply records what exists naturally. Because the researcher does not manipulate, control, or otherwise interfere with the variables being examined or with the surrounding environment, there is good reason to expect that the measurements and the relationships accurately reflect the natural events being examined. In research terminology, correlational studies tend to have high external validity. In general, a correlational study can establish that a relation exists, and it can provide a good description of the relationship. However, a correlational study usually does not produce a clear and unambiguous explanation for the relationship. In research terminology, correlational studies tend to have low internal validity. In particular, two limitations arise in explanations of results from a correlational study:

1.  The **third-variable problem.** Although a correlational study may establish that two variables are related, it does not necessarily mean that there is a *direct* relationship between the two variables. It is always possible that a third (unidentified) variable is controlling the two variables and is responsible for producing the observed relation. A recent TV news program, for example, reported that employees who participate in a company's fitness training program have higher productivity and lower rates of absenteeism than employees who do not participate. However, the company cannot conclude that their fitness program is causing benefits to the company; it may be that employees who chose to participate were already more fit and healthier than those who chose not to participate. Thus, a third variable (pre-existing health) may be controlling both participation and productivity, resulting in the observed relationship. See Figure 7.1.

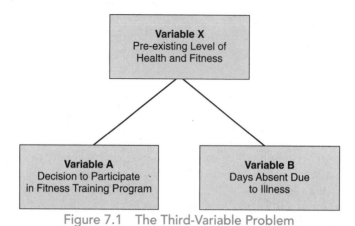

Figure 7.1    The Third-Variable Problem
Although participation in the fitness training program (Variable A) and absenteeism (Variable B) appear to vary together, there is no direct connection between these two variables. Instead, both are influenced by a third variable. In this example, an employee's level of health and fitness (Variable X) influences whether or not the employee chooses to participate in the fitness program. In addition, an employee's level of health influences the number of days that the employee is likely to be absent due to illness.

2.    The **directionality problem.** A correlational study can establish that two variables are related, that is, that changes in one variable tend to be accompanied by changes in the other variable. However, a correlational study does not determine which variable is the "cause" and which is the "effect." For example, many studies have demonstrated a relationship between exposure to television violence and aggressive or violent behavior in children. Given this relationship, it is tempting to conclude that watching TV violence "causes" children to behave violently. However, it is possible that the true "causal" relationship is in the opposite direction. Children who tend to be violent or aggressive may simply choose to watch TV programs that are consistent with their own behaviors. In this case, violent behavior causes the child to prefer violent TV. See Figure 7.2.

Table 7.4 summarizes the strengths and weaknesses of the correlational research design.

Learning
Check

Describe the third-variable problem and the directionality problem for correlational research designs.

Seeing violent acts on television causes
children to behave aggressively.

Children choose to watch TV shows with a level of
violence that matches their own level of aggression.

Figure 7.2   The Directionality Problem
Although a correlational study may show that viewing violence
on TV is directly related to aggressive behavior, the study cannot
determine which variable is responsible for changes in the other.
In this example, it is possible that viewing violence on TV causes
aggressive behavior, but it is equally possible that having an
aggressive personality causes people to prefer watching violent TV.

TABLE 7.4

**A Summary of the Strengths and Weaknesses
of the Correlational Research Design**

| Strengths | Weaknesses |
| --- | --- |
| • Describes relationships between variables | • Cannot assess causality |
| • Nonintrusive—natural behaviors | • Third-variable problem |
| • High external validity | • Directionality problem |
| | • Low internal validity |

## CHAPTER SUMMARY

The details of two nonexperimental research strategies, descriptive and correlational, were treated. The goal of the descriptive research strategy is to describe the variables being examined as they exist naturally. Three different types of descriptive research designs were discussed: observational research, survey research, and case study research. The goal of the correlational research strategy is to examine the relationship between two variables and to measure the strength of the relationship. The details of the correlational research strategy were considered as well.

In the observational research design, researchers observe and describe behaviors as they occur in natural settings. There are three kinds of observation. In *natural observation* a researcher tries as unobtrusively as possible to observe behavior in a natural setting. Although the results of natural observation have high external validity, a major weakness is the time it takes to conduct such research. *Participant observation* is used in situations where inconspicuous observation is not possible; instead the researcher interacts with the participants in order to observe and record behaviors. Participant observation allows researchers to observe behaviors not usually open to scientific observation; however, it, too, is time consuming. In *contrived observation* the observer sets up situations so that behaviors can be observed. A major strength of the observational research design is that the researcher observes and records actual behaviors.

In the survey research design we describe people's responses to questions about behaviors and attitudes. The three most common methods for administering a survey are mail surveys, phone surveys, and in-person surveys and interviews; each has strengths and weaknesses. Surveys are relatively easy to administer and can be used to obtain information about a wide variety of different variables. However, major weaknesses of survey research include low response rates, nonresponse bias, and the self-report nature of the design.

In case study research a single individual is described in great detail. Case studies can be used to provide information about rare and unusual behaviors and to demonstrate "exceptions to the rule." Further, case studies can suggest new variables that might account for a particular outcome and thereby generate hypotheses for future research. However, case studies tend to be weak in both internal and external validity.

In the correlational research strategy we describe the relationship between two variables. Correlational research can be used for prediction, to establish validity and reliability, and to evaluate theories. However, because of the third-variable and directionality problems, correlational research cannot be used to determine the causes of behavior.

Overall, the descriptive and correlational research strategies are extremely useful as preliminary research and valuable in their own right as sources of basic knowledge. However, both strategies simply describe behavior and do not examine causal factors.

## KEY WORDS

correlational research strategy
observational research design
naturalistic observation or
    nonparticipant observation

participant observation
contrived observation or
    structured observation
survey research design

case study design
case history
predictor variable
criterion variable

##  EXERCISES

1. In addition to the key words, you should also be able to define each of the following terms:
descriptive research strategy
nonresponse bias
idiographic approach
nomothetic approach
third-variable problem
directionality problem

2. What is the general characteristic that differentiates descriptive research designs from other types of research? For example, what differentiates the survey research design from other research that uses surveys to obtain measurements?

3. Why do the descriptive and correlational research strategies fall into the category of nonexperimental research strategies?

4. Describe each of the three types of descriptive research designs.

5. Compare and contrast the three types of observation.

6. Most descriptive research designs gather information from a group of participants. However, the case study design focuses on a single individual. What are the advantages and disadvantages of describing a single individual as compared to describing a group?

7.  For each of the following research goals, identify which of the nonexperimental research designs would be most appropriate:
    a.  To describe the relationship between alcohol consumption and grade point average for high school students
    b.  To describe how peer counseling affects a severely depressed teenager
    c.  To describe the social interactions among a group of preschool children while they are playing in a city park
    d.  To describe the study habits of students at a state college

## InfoTrac COLLEGE EDITION EXERCISE

1.  Using InfoTrac College Edition, locate at least one periodical article corresponding to each of the five descriptive research strategies discussed in this chapter. To help you in your search, we suggest that you consider the specific terminology used in each of the descriptive research strategies and the types of variables each one is likely to study. The terms and variable names can be used as subject terms or key words to help direct your search. A few examples are listed below for each research strategy. Keep in mind that you are likely to uncover hundreds of periodical articles, many of which will not be appropriate for your needs. Therefore, you will need to look closely at the titles of the articles and probably read the summary (abstract) at the beginning before you can decide which articles to keep and which to discard.

    For *observational research*, your best bet is to use subject terms that identify the types of behaviors that are most likely to be directly observed. Good examples would be terms like *aggression, social interaction, parenting,* or *helping behavior.* Try one of these, or think of your own examples.

*Survey research* consists of using surveys and questionnaires, so the terms *survey* and *questionnaire* might be good starting points (although you will also uncover a lot of material about geological and land surveys). Also, keep in mind that surveys are often used to measure *attitudes* and *opinions,* so these two terms would also be good choices for searching.

Because *case study research* is often used in clinical settings, you could try subject terms such as *therapy* or *treatment.* These will often lead to more specific categories such as behavior therapy or cognitive therapy. You might also try the direct approach and simply use the term *case study.*

The *correlational research strategy* is used for prediction as well as for describing the reliability and validity of measurements techniques. Thus, *prediction, reliability,* and *validity* are good choices for starting a search. In addition, the correlational strategy is often used to examine variables that cannot (or should not) be manipulated by a researcher. Therefore, variable names such as *alcohol consumption, self-esteem,* or *study habits* could be used to start a search.

# Experimental Research Strategy

## CHAPTER OVERVIEW

In this chapter we discuss details of the experimental research strategy. The goal of experimental research is to establish and demonstrate a cause-and-effect relationship between two variables. To accomplish this goal, an experiment must manipulate one of the two variables and isolate the two variables being examined from the influence of other variables. This manipulation and control are considered here.

## 8.1    CAUSE-AND-EFFECT RELATIONSHIPS

In Chapter 6 we identified four basic strategies for investigating variables and their relationships —descriptive, correlational, experimental, and quasi-experimental. In this chapter we discuss details of the experimental research strategy. (The descriptive and correlational strategies are discussed in Chapter 7, details of the quasi-experimental strategy are discussed in Chapter 9.)

The term *experiment* is often used as a generic label for any kind of scientific research; however, a research study must meet specific criteria to qualify as an experiment, and only a limited number of research studies actually deserve the label. This chapter introduces the characteristics that differentiate a true experiment from other kinds of research studies.

The goal of the experimental strategy is to establish the existence of a cause-and-effect relationship between two variables. That is, the method of observing variables is intended to show that changes in one variable are directly responsible for *causing* changes in the other variable. Although demonstrating a causal relationship may seem straightforward, it can be very difficult.

### CAUSATION AND THE THIRD-VARIABLE PROBLEM

One problem for researchers is that the variables they study rarely exist in isolation. In natural circumstances, changes in one variable are typically accompanied by changes in many other related variables. As a result, researchers are often confronted with a tangled network of interrelated variables. Although it is relatively easy to demonstrate that one variable is related to another, it is much more difficult to establish the underlying cause of the relationship. To determine the nature of the relationships among variables, particularly to establish the causal influence of one event on another, it is essential that a researcher separate and isolate the specific variables being studied. The task of teasing apart and separating a set of naturally interconnected variables is the heart of the experimental strategy. The following example illustrates one basic problem with interrelated variables.

Ronald Freedman and his colleagues examined trends in family planning and birth control through the 1960s and 1970s in Taiwan. In the course of their studies, they recorded data on a wide range of behavioral and environmental variables. The purpose of this research was to identify the factor or factors that determine how people set preferences for family size and whether or not they use birth control. The researchers evaluated the relationship between birth control practices and each of the individual variables. Although the research identified many variables related to family planning, the results clearly showed a strong relationship between television watching and birth control practices (Freedman, Coombs, Chang, & Sun, 1974).

Although the results of the study establish that television watching is related to contraception, you probably are not willing to conclude that it is a causal relationship; that is, having people watch more television probably will not cause the use of contraception to increase. Clearly, other variables such as age, household income, and education are involved. The existence of a relationship, even a strong one, is not sufficient to establish cause and effect.

This example is a demonstration of the **third-variable problem** introduced in Chapter 7. Although the researchers demonstrated a relation between contraception use and television watching, common sense suggests that this is not a causal relationship. A more reasonable interpretation of the results is that there is another, unidentified variable (or combination of variables) responsible for causing simultaneous increases in birth control and television watching.

## CAUSATION AND THE DIRECTIONALITY PROBLEM

A second problem for researchers attempting to establish cause and effect is demonstrated in the following example.

Many researchers have investigated the relationship between personality and success or failure in different occupations. One of the most consistent findings is that successful executives or entrepreneurs tend to be more assertive than their less successful counterparts (McClelland, 1976, 1987). Based on the consistency of the relationship and on common sense, it is tempting to conclude that there is a causal relation between assertiveness and executive success. For example, it is reasonable to assume that assertiveness is a necessary prerequisite for this kind of job; therefore, people who enter executive positions with an assertive personality will tend to be successful—that is, assertiveness *causes* success. However, it is equally reasonable to assume that executive positions require people to become assertive, so people who persist and are successful in the job tend to become assertive; that is, success *causes* assertiveness. This example is a demonstration of the **directionality problem,** introduced in Chapter 7. Although a research study may establish a relationship between two variables, the problem is determining which variable is the cause and which is the effect.

## CONTROLLING NATURE

The preceding examples demonstrated that we cannot establish a cause-and-effect relationship by simply measuring two variables. In particular, the researcher must actively unravel the tangle of relationships that exists naturally. To establish a cause-and-effect relation, an experiment must control nature, essentially creating an "unnatural" situation wherein the two variables being examined are isolated from the influence of other variables and wherein the exact character of a relationship can be seen clearly.

We acknowledge that it is somewhat paradoxical that experiments must interfere with natural phenomena to gain a better understanding of nature. How can observations made in an artificial, carefully controlled experiment reveal any truth about nature? One simple answer is that the contrived character of experiments is a necessity: To see beneath the surface, it is necessary to dig. A more complete answer, however, is that there is a difference between the conditions in which an experiment is conducted and the results of the experiment. Just because an experiment takes place in an unnatural environment does not necessarily imply that the results are unnatural.

For example, you are probably familiar with the law of gravity, which states that all objects fall at the same rate independent of mass. You are no doubt equally familiar with the "natural" fact that, if you drop a brick and a feather from the roof of a building, they will *not* fall at the same rate. Other factors in the natural world, such as air resistance, conceal the true effects of gravity. To demonstrate the law of gravity, we must create an artificial, controlled environment, specifically a vacuum, wherein forces such as air resistance have been eliminated. This fact does not invalidate the law of gravity; the law accurately describes the underlying force of gravity and explains the behavior of falling objects, even though natural conditions may conceal the basic principle. In the same way, the goal of any experiment is to reveal the natural underlying mechanisms and relationships that may be otherwise obscured. Nonetheless, there is always a risk that the conditions of an experiment will be so unnatural that the results are questionable. To use the terminology presented in Chapter 6, an experimenter can be so intent on ensuring internal validity that external validity is compromised. Researchers are aware of this problem and have developed techniques to increase the external validity (natural character) of experiments. We discuss some of these techniques in Section 8.6.

Learning Checks

It has been demonstrated that students with high self-esteem tend to have higher grades than students with low self-esteem. Does this relationship mean that higher self-esteem causes better academic performance? Does it mean that better academic performance causes higher self-esteem? Explain your answer, and identify the general problem that can preclude a cause-and-effect explanation.

A researcher would like to compare two methods for teaching math to third-grade students. Two third-grade classes are obtained for the study. Mr. Jones teaches one class using method A, and Mrs. Smith teaches the other class using method B. At the end of the year, the students from the method B class have significantly higher scores on a mathematics achievement test. Does this result indicate that method B causes higher scores than method A? Explain your answer, and identify the general problem that precludes a cause-and-effect explanation.

## 8.2    ELEMENTS OF AN EXPERIMENT

The general goal of the **experimental research strategy** is to establish a cause-and-effect relationship between two variables. That is, an experiment attempts to demonstrate that changes (or differences) in one variable are directly responsible for changes (or differences) in a second variable. This general goal can be broken down into two subgoals:

> More complex experiments may involve several variables. In its simplest form, however, an experiment focuses on only one variable that may cause changes in one other variable.

1.  It is not sufficient for an experiment to demonstrate that a relation exists between two variables. In addition, an experiment must demonstrate the character of the relationship. It must be shown that changes in one variable *cause* changes in the other variable.

2.  To establish that one specific variable is responsible for changes in another variable, an experiment must rule out the possibility that the changes are caused by some other variable.

These subgoals dictate the two characteristics that differentiate experiments from other research strategies:

1. Manipulation of one variable while measuring a second variable
2. Control of other, extraneous variables

The goal of the **experimental research strategy** is to establish the existence of a cause-and-effect relationship between two variables. To accomplish this goal, an experiment manipulates one variable while a second variable is measured and other variables are controlled.

## MANIPULATION AND MEASUREMENT

A distinguishing characteristic of the experimental strategy is that the researcher *manipulates* one of the variables under study. The primary purpose of manipulation is to allow researchers to determine the direction of a relationship. Figure 8.1 shows two situations in which there is a relationship between variables. In the top half of the figure, there is a direct relationship between the position of the switch and the brightness of the light. By manipulation, we can demonstrate that the switch causes changes in the light instead of the light causing changes in the switch. In general, whenever there is a relationship between two variables, a researcher can use manipulation to determine which variable is the cause and which is the effect. For example, a researcher could change the value of variable A (manipulation) and then observe what happens to variable B. If the manipulation produces changes in B, the researcher can conclude that variable A is the causal agent. But lack of change in variable B would indicate that variable A is not a causal agent.

For an example more closely related to psychology, consider the relationship between depression and insomnia. It has been observed repeatedly that people suffering from depression also tend to have problems sleeping. However, the observed relationship does not answer the causal question, Does depression cause sleep problems, or does the lack of sleep cause depression? Although it may be difficult to manipulate depression directly, it certainly is possible to manipulate the amount of sleep. One group of individuals, for example, could be allowed only 4 hours of sleep each night and a comparison group allowed 8 hours. After a week, depression scores could be obtained and compared for the two groups. If the 4-hour group is more depressed, this is evidence that sleep deprivation causes depression.

A second purpose of manipulation is to give the researcher command of one of the variables being studied. In the family planning study discussed earlier (Freedman, Coombs, Chang, & Sun, 1974), the researchers observed a higher use of birth control in homes where television was watched and a lower use in homes with no television. However, the researchers had no power to determine which households watched television and which did not. The lack of authority created two serious problems. First, other variables naturally related to television watching were allowed to intrude into the study. Second, the researchers had only vague definitions of watching television and not watching television. In an experiment, the researchers could manipulate the amount of television watching. For exam-

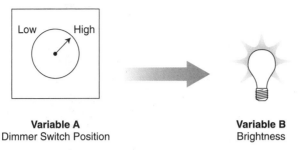

**Variable A**
Dimmer Switch Position

**Variable B**
Brightness

(a) Manipulating the position of the switch *causes* a change in the brightness of the light. However, manipulating the brightness of the light (change from a 60-watt to a 100-watt bulb) will *not* cause a change in the position of the switch.

**Variable B**
Brightness

**Variable C**
Air Temperature Surrounding the Bulb

(b) Manipulating the brightness of the light *causes* a change in the temperature around the bulb. However, manipulating the temperature around the bulb (with a fan or a hair dryer) will *not* cause a change in the brightness of the bulb.

Figure 8.1    Using Manipulation to Determine
the Direction of a Cause-and-Effect Relationship

ple, the researchers could remove all televisions from 100 households, allow another set of 100 households 10 hours per week of television, a third group 20 hours, etc. Once the groups are established, the researcher simply measures birth control practices within each household. By directly manipulating television watching, the researchers eliminate the problems with the original study. First, they disrupt any systematic relations between television and other variables; households in the zero-television group, for example, watch no television, irrespective of income level, educational background, and age. Second, the researchers can now precisely define the differences between the groups compared: One group has 0 hours of television, one group has 10 hours per week, etc. (Note: We acknowledge that manipulating television watching as described in this example would produce a somewhat senseless research study. Nonetheless, the study demonstrates the principle and the purpose of manipulation in an experiment.)

### Independent and Dependent Variables

Manipulation typically involves creating two or more different **treatment conditions** corresponding to selected values of the variable to be manipulated. For example, a researcher studying the relation between temperature and learning first identifies the room temperatures to be examined (e.g., 60°, 70°, and 80°).

Then the researcher creates a treatment condition, or environment, for each value (e.g., the room temperature is set at 60° for one condition, 70° for a second condition, and 80° for the third). The different values selected for the manipulated variable are called the **levels** of the variable. For this temperature-and-learning example, the researcher uses three levels of temperature.

The manipulated variable accounts for only one of the two variables examined in an experiment. Once the levels of the manipulated variable have been selected and the treatment conditions created, the researcher simply measures and records the second variable. For the example we are considering, the second variable is learning performance. The researcher measures learning performance for each individual in the 60° room and compares the scores with those obtained for individuals in the 70° room and the 80° room. Thus, an experiment examines the relationship between two variables: the manipulated variable, which is called the **independent variable,** and the measured variable, which is called the **dependent variable.** All other variables that exist in the study are called **extraneous variables.**

> An experiment must have at least two levels of the manipulated variable.

**Definitions**

In an experiment the **independent variable** is the variable manipulated by the researcher. In behavioral research, the independent variable usually consists of two or more treatment conditions to which participants are exposed.

The **dependent variable** is the variable that is observed for changes in order to assess the effects of manipulating the independent variable. The dependent variable is typically a behavior or a response measured in each treatment condition.

All variables in the study other than the independent and dependent variables are called **extraneous variables.**

In an experiment, a **treatment condition** is a situation or environment characterized by one specific value of the manipulated variable. An experiment contains two or more treatment conditions that differ according to the values of the manipulated variable.

The different values of the independent variable selected to create and define the treatment conditions are called the **levels** of the independent variable.

An essential characteristic of an experiment, then, is *comparison*. An experiment always compares measurements of the dependent variable across different levels of the independent variable—or in more familiar terms, an experiment compares behavior in one treatment condition with behavior in another treatment condition to establish whether the different treatments cause different behaviors.

## CONTROL AND EXTRANEOUS VARIABLES

The second distinguishing characteristic of an experiment is control of other variables. To accurately evaluate the relationship between two specific variables, a researcher must ensure that the observed relationship is not contaminated by the influence of other variables.

In general, the purpose of an experiment is to show that the manipulated variable is responsible for the changes observed in the dependent variable. To accomplish this, an experiment must rule out any other possible explanation for the observed changes—that is, eliminate all **confounding variables.** In Chapter 6 (page 141) we defined a confounding variable as a third variable that is allowed to change systematically along with the two variables being studied. In the context of an experiment, the particular concern is to identify and control any third variable that changes systematically along with the independent variable and has the potential to influence the dependent variable.

A confounding variable and the need for control are illustrated in a study examining the role of imagery in memory. Based on a long series of research studies, Alan Paivio developed a theory of memory that emphasizes the role of mental images in storing and retrieving information. The theory predicts that, when information can be easily transformed into images, it should be easy to store in memory, and that information that is not easily converted into images will not be easy to remember. To test this prediction, Paivio (1965) compared memory performance for high-imagery words (concrete nouns) and low-imagery words (abstract nouns). The results clearly demonstrated that memory performance is much better for high-imagery words than for low-imagery words. The structure of this experiment is shown in Figure 8.2. So far, Paivio's experiment appears relatively straightforward. However, this research contains a third, potentially confounding variable. Paivio also measured the "meaningfulness" of each word by asking a group of participants to list as many associations as possible for each of the words used in the memory study. The results showed that participants were able to generate many associations (high meaningfulness) for the high-imagery words but relatively few associations for the low-imagery words. Thus, the level of meaningfulness varied systematically with the imagery level and became a confounding variable. The confounding variable is included in Figure 8.2. In this experiment, it is impossible to determine whether the observed differences in memory performance were caused by imagery level (the independent variable) or by meaning level (confounding variable).

To establish an unambiguous causal relation between imagery level and memory, it is necessary to eliminate the possible influence of the confounding variable. For example, the level of meaningfulness could be balanced for the two lists. Words in the high-imagery list could be carefully selected for an average level of meaningfulness; similarly, the low-imagery list could be constructed with an average level of meaningfulness. The structure of the controlled experiment is shown in Figure 8.3. In the controlled experiment the confounding variable has been eliminated, and the true relation between imagery level and memory performance can be observed.

The Paivio study provides an opportunity to make another important point. Specifically, the independent variable in an experiment is determined by the research hypothesis. Because Paivio was studying the effects of imagery on memory, the independent variable was the imagery level of the words. On the other hand, if Paivio had been studying the effects of meaningfulness on memory, then the independent variable would be the meaning level of the words. In a

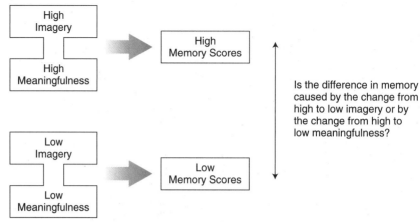

**Figure 8.2  Confounding Variables**
Because the level of imagery and the level of meaningfulness vary together systematically, they are confounded, and it is impossible to determine which variable is responsible for differences in memory scores.

study in which meaningfulness was the independent variable, the imagery level of the words risks being a confounding variable. The classification as an independent variable or a confounding variable depends on the research hypothesis.

Learning
Checks

Identify the two characteristics needed for a research study to qualify as an experiment.

In an experiment examining human memory, two groups of participants are used. One group is allowed 5 minutes to study a list of 40 words, and the second group is given 10 minutes of study time. Then, both groups are given a memory test, and the researcher records the number of words correctly recalled by each participant. For this experiment, identify the independent variable and the dependent variable.

## 8.3  DEALING WITH EXTRANEOUS VARIABLES

The intent of an experiment is to focus on two specific variables; the independent variable and the dependent variable. However, within every experiment there are thousands of other factors—variables—that are constantly changing and taking on different values. Different individuals enter the experiment with different backgrounds, ages, genders, heights, weights, IQs, personalities, etc. As time passes, room temperature and lighting fluctuate, weather changes, people get tired or bored or excited or happy, they forget things or remember things, develop itches, aches, and pains that distract from the task at hand. Beyond the independent and dependent variables, all these other variables are called *extraneous variables*, and every experiment is filled with them.

Figure 8.3   Eliminating a Confounding Variable
The level of meaningfulness does not change systematically with
the level of imagery, so the two variables are not confounded.
In this study you can be confident that the level of imagery (not
meaningfulness) is responsible for the differences in memory scores.

An experimental researcher must prevent any extraneous variable from becoming a confounding variable. This is the basic purpose of *control* within an experiment. With thousands of potentially confounding variables, however, the problem of controlling (or even monitoring) every extraneous variable appears insurmountable. Close inspection, however, reveals some hints.

We return to the definition of a *confounding variable*. Note that a confounding variable has two important characteristics:

1.  First, an extraneous variable becomes a confounding variable only if it influences the dependent variable. Something totally unrelated to the dependent variable is not a threat. In Paivio's imagery experiment, for example, individuals probably entered the experiment wearing different types of shoes (sneakers, flats, heels, loafers, sandals, etc.); however, it is unlikely that the type of shoe has any influence on memory performance. Thus, it was not necessary to take any steps to control the shoe variable (Paivio didn't even mention shoes in his report).

2.  Second, a confounding variable must vary *systematically* with the independent variable. Something that changes randomly, with no relation to the independent variable, is not a threat. The concept of *random* versus systematic change is an important part of control.

The first step in controlling extraneous variables is to identify those variables most likely to influence the dependent variable. This identification process is based primarily on common sense, simple logical reasoning, and past experience in controlling extraneous variables. For example, if you are measuring memory performance, IQ is a reasonable choice as a potentially confounding variable. If very young and/or very old participants are used, then age is also a variable that could reasonably affect memory performance. If memory performance is being measured in different settings or at different times, these variables also could influence performance. (A loud, busy room can create distractions that lower performance, as opposed to a quiet, empty room.) The variables you identify at this step merit special attention to ensure control. Other variables are not ignored, but are handled more casually. When identifying extraneous variables, note that they can be classified into two general categories:

1.  Participant variables: The individuals who participate in a research study differ from one another in a variety of ways—for example, gender, age, IQ, educational background, number of siblings.

2.  Environmental variables: Participants may be observed in different environments—for example, at different times of day, in different rooms, under different weather conditions, at different temperatures.

## CONTROL BY HOLDING CONSTANT OR MATCHING

Once a limited set of specific variables with real potential as confounding variables is identified, it is possible to exercise some control over them. There are three standard methods for controlling extraneous variables. Two involve actively intervening to control variables by

1.  holding the variable constant, or
2.  matching values across the treatment conditions.

The third method is randomization, which is discussed in the next section. For now, we will focus attention on the two active methods for controlling extraneous variables.

### Holding a Variable Constant

An extraneous variable can be eliminated completely by holding it constant. For example, all individuals in the experiment could be observed in the same room, at the same time of day, by the same researcher. Because these factors are the same for every observation, they are not variables and therefore cannot be confounding. By standardizing the environment and procedures, most environmental variables can be held constant. This technique can also be used with participant variables. For example, by selecting only 6-year-old males to participate in an experiment, age and gender are held constant.

Often it is unreasonable to hold a variable completely constant. For example, it would not be sensible to hold IQ constant by requiring all participants to have IQs of exactly 109. Similarly, it would be a bit overzealous to hold age constant by requiring all participants to have been born on June 13, 1983. Instead, researchers often choose to restrict a variable to a limited range instead of holding it absolutely constant. For example, a researcher may require participants to be between 18 and 21 years old and to have IQ scores between 100 and 110. Although age and IQ are not perfectly constant here, the restricted range should ensure that the participants in one treatment are not noticeably older or smarter than the participants in another treatment.

Although holding a variable constant eliminates its potential to become a confounding variable, this can limit the external validity of an experiment. For example, if an experiment is conducted exclusively with females (holding gender constant), the results cannot be generalized to males. Recall from Chapter 6 that any factor limiting the generalization of research results is a threat to external validity.

### Matching Values Across Treatment Conditions

Control over an extraneous variable can also be exercised by matching the levels of the variable across treatment conditions. For example, 10 males and 20 females could be assigned to each separate treatment condition. Gender still varies within treatment conditions, but it is now balanced and does not vary across treatments. Another common form of matching is to ensure that the average value is the same (or nearly the same) for all treatments. For example, participants could be assigned so that the average age is the same for all of the different treatment conditions. In this case, age is balanced across treatments and therefore cannot be a confounding variable. Matching can also be used to control environmental variables. For example, a study using two different rooms could match the rooms across treatment conditions by measuring one half of the participants in one room and half in the other room for every treatment condition.

Typically, controlling a variable by matching or holding constant requires some time and effort from the researcher and can intrude upon the experimental participants. Matching individuals for IQ, for example, requires the researcher to obtain an IQ score for each participant before the experiment can begin. Although it is possible to control a few variables by matching or holding constant, the demands of these control techniques make them impractical or impossible to use to control all extraneous variables. Therefore, active control by matching or holding constant is recommended for a limited set of specific variables identified as potentially serious threats to an experiment.

---

Identify the two active methods for preventing extraneous variables from becoming confounding variables.

Learning Check

---

## CONTROL BY RANDOMIZATION

Because it is essentially impossible to actively control the thousands of extraneous variables that can intrude on an experiment, researchers usually rely on a simpler, more passive control technique known as **randomization.** The principle underlying randomization is the disruption of any systematic relation between extraneous variables and the independent variable, thereby preventing the extraneous variables from becoming confounding variables.

Randomization involves using an unpredictable and unbiased procedure (such as a coin toss) to distribute different values of each extraneous variable across the treatment conditions. The procedure that is used must be a **random process,** which simply means that all the different possible outcomes are equally likely. For example, when we toss a coin, the two possible outcomes, heads and tails, are equally likely (see Chapter 5, page 118).

One common use of randomization is **random assignment,** in which a random process such as a coin toss or a random number table (see Appendix A) is used to assign participants to treatment conditions. For an experiment comparing two treatment conditions, a researcher could use a coin toss to assign participants to treatment conditions. Because the assignment of participants to treatments is based on a random process, it is reasonable to assume that individual participant variables (such as age, sex, height, IQ, etc.) are also distributed randomly across treatment conditions. Specifically, the use of random assignment should ensure that the participant variables do not change systematically across treatments and therefore cannot be confounding variables.

Definitions

**Randomization** is the use of a random process to help avoid a systematic relationship between two variables.

**Random assignment** is the use of a random process to assign participants to treatment conditions.

Alan Paivio's experiment, described earlier, also provides a concrete demonstration of randomization. Recall that Paivio compared memory performance for high-imagery words versus low-imagery words. One concern in a study like this one is that participants in one imagery condition might have higher IQ scores than individuals in the other condition; that is, there might be a systematic relation between IQ and the independent variable. Were this to occur, any differences observed in memory performance could be caused by IQ rather than the imagery level of the words. To minimize the possibility for IQ to become a confounding variable, a random process could be used to assign participants to imagery conditions. By using randomization, an individual with a high IQ would be equally likely to be assigned to the high-imagery or the low-imagery condition. As a result, both the high-IQ and low-IQ participants should be randomly distributed between the two conditions rather than clustered together in one condition. Again, the intent of randomization is to disrupt any systematic relation between extraneous variables and the independent variable and thereby prevent the extraneous variable from becoming a confounding variable.

This example discusses randomization in terms of IQ. However, random assignment will also produce random (nonsystematic) distributions for all other participant variables. For example, males are equally likely to be assigned to the high- or low-imagery conditions, so gender should also be randomly distributed between the two conditions. There are thousands of participant variables; rather than attempting to control each one individually, random assignment provides some control over all of these variables simultaneously.

Randomization can also be used to control environmental variables. If the research schedule requires some observations in the morning hours and some in the afternoon, a random process can be used to assign treatment conditions to the different times. A morning hour, for example, would be equally likely to be assigned to treatment condition 1 or treatment condition 2. Thus, time of day is randomly distributed across treatments and will not have a systematic effect on the outcome.

Randomization is a powerful tool for controlling extraneous variables. Its primary advantage is that it offers a method for controlling a multitude of variables simultaneously and does not require specific attention to each extraneous variable. However, randomization does not guarantee that extraneous variables are really controlled; rather, it uses *chance* to control variables. If you toss a coin 10 times, for example, you expect to obtain a random mixture of heads and tails. This random mixture is the essence of randomization. However, it is possible to toss a coin ten times and obtain heads every time; chance can produce a biased (or systematic) outcome. For example, a random process can result in assignment of all of the high IQ individuals to one treatment condition and all the low IQ participants to another. In the long run, with large numbers (i.e., a large sample) a random process will guarantee a balanced result, but in the short run, especially with small numbers (i.e., a small sample), there is a chance that randomization will not work. Because randomization can't be relied on to control extraneous variables, specific variables identified as having high potential for influencing results should receive special attention and be controlled by matching or holding constant. Then, other variables can be randomized, with the understanding that they probably will be controlled by chance, but with the risk that randomization may not succeed in providing adequate control.

---

Define a random process, and explain how this process is used for random assignment of participants to treatment conditions.

Learning Check

---

## COMPARING METHODS OF CONTROL

The goal of an experiment is to show that the scores obtained in one treatment condition are consistently different from the scores in another treatment and that the differences are caused by the treatments. In the terminology of the experimental design, the goal is to show that differences in the dependent variable are caused by the independent variable. In this context, the purpose of control is to ensure that no other variable (other than the independent variable) could be responsible for causing the scores to be different.

We have examined three different methods for controlling extraneous variables, and each is shown in Table 8.1. The table shows how participant gender can be a confounding variable and how the three methods are used to prevent confounding.

A.   Column A shows two treatment conditions with ten participants in each treatment. In this column, gender (M and F) is confounded with the treatments; 80% of the participants in treatment 1 are females, but in treatment 2 only 20% are females. If this study found differences between the scores in treatment 1 and treatment 2, the differences in scores could have been caused by the differences in gender.

B.   In column B, gender is held constant. All the participants in treatment 1 are female, and all the participants in treatment 2 are female. In this case, there is absolutely no gender difference between the two treatments, so gender cannot be responsible for causing differences in the scores.

| TABLE 8.1 |
| --- |

### A Confounding Variable and Three Methods to Prevent Confounding

In column A, participant gender (M and F) is confounded with the two treatments. Columns B, C, and D demonstrate how gender can be balanced across treatments by holding it constant, matching, or randomizing.

| (A) Gender Confounded | | (B) Gender Held Constant | | (C) Gender Matched | | (D) Gender Randomized | |
| --- | --- | --- | --- | --- | --- | --- | --- |
| Treatment | | Treatment | | Treatment | | Treatment | |
| 1 | 2 | 1 | 2 | 1 | 2 | 1 | 2 |
| M | M | F | F | M | M | M | F |
| M | M | F | F | M | M | F | M |
| F | M | F | F | M | M | F | F |
| F | M | F | F | M | M | M | F |
| F | M | F | F | F | F | F | M |
| F | M | F | F | F | F | M | M |
| F | M | F | F | F | F | M | F |
| F | M | F | F | F | F | F | F |
| F | F | F | F | F | F | M | M |
| F | F | F | F | F | F | F | M |

C. In column C, gender is matched across the treatments. In treatment 1 40% are males, and in treatment 2 40% are males. Again, the two groups are balanced with respect to gender, so any differences in scores for the two treatments cannot be caused by gender.

D. Finally, in column D, gender is randomized across treatments. By using a random process to assign males and females to the treatment conditions, it is reasonable to expect that gender will be balanced across treatments. If there are no substantial gender differences between treatments, then gender cannot cause the scores in one treatment to be different from the scores in the other treatment.

### ADVANTAGES AND DISADVANTAGES OF CONTROL METHODS

The two active methods of control (holding constant and matching) require some extra effort or extra measurement and therefore are typically used with only one or two specific variables identified as real threats for confounding. In addition, holding a variable constant has the disadvantage of limiting generalization (external validity). On the other hand, randomization has the advantage of controlling a wide variety of variables simultaneously. However, randomization is not guaranteed to be successful; chance is trusted to balance the variables across the different treatments. Nonetheless, randomization is the primary technique for controlling the huge number of extraneous variables that exist within any experiment.

## 8.4    CONTROL GROUPS

An experiment always involves comparison. The experimental strategy requires comparison of observations of the dependent variable across different levels of the independent variable. In general terms, an experiment compares observations across different treatment conditions. However, sometimes a researcher wishes to evaluate only one treatment rather than compare a set of different treatments. In this case it is still possible to conduct an experiment. The solution is to compare the treatment condition with a baseline "no-treatment" condition. In experimental terminology, the treatment condition is called the **experimental group,** and the no-treatment condition is called the **control group.** The term *group* is somewhat misleading: It is possible, for example, to observe the same set of individuals in both the treatment and the no-treatment conditions. In this type of design, only one "group" of subjects is used to generate two "groups" of scores for comparison. Although it might be less confusing to speak of a *control condition*, we use the more conventional term, *control group.*

The term **experimental group** refers to the treatment condition in an experiment.

The term **control group** refers to the no-treatment condition in an experiment.

The variety of different ways to construct a control group for an experiment can be classified into two general categories: no-treatment control groups and placebo control groups.

### NO-TREATMENT CONTROL GROUPS

As the name implies, a **no-treatment control group** is simply a treatment condition in which the participants do not receive the treatment being evaluated. The purpose of the no-treatment control is to provide a standard of normal behavior, or baseline, against which the treatment condition can be compared. To evaluate the effects of a drug, for example, an experiment could include one condition in which the drug is administered and a control condition in which there is no drug. To evaluate the effectiveness of a training procedure, the experimental group receives the training and the control group does not.

In an experiment, a **no-treatment control group** is a condition in which the participants do not receive the treatment being evaluated.

At first glance it may appear that a treatment-versus-no-treatment experiment eliminates the independent variable. However, the researcher still creates treatment conditions by manipulating different values of the treatment variable; the no-treatment condition is simply a zero-value of the independent variable. Thus, the experiment compares one condition having a "full amount" of the treatment with a second condition having a "zero amount" of the treatment.

The independent variable still exists, and its levels now consist of all and none or treatment and control.

## PLACEBO CONTROL GROUPS

A **placebo** is an inert or innocuous medication, a fake medical treatment such as a sugar pill or a water injection that by itself has absolutely no medicinal effect. Although there is no biological or pharmacological reason for a placebo to be effective, nonetheless a placebo can have a dramatic effect on health and behavior (Shapiro & Morris, 1978). The **placebo effect** is believed to be psychosomatic: The mind (psyche), rather than the placebo itself, has an effect on the body (somatic). The fact that an individual thinks or believes a medication is effective can be sufficient to cause a response to the medication.

---

Definition

The **placebo effect** refers to a response by a participant to an inert medication that has no real effect on the body. The placebo effect occurs simply because the individual thinks the medication is effective.

---

In psychotherapy, the term *nonspecific* is often used in place of *placebo* to refer to the elements of therapy that are *not specifically* therapeutic.

Although the concept of the placebo effect originated in medical research, it has been generalized to other situations where a supposedly ineffective "treatment" produces an effect. Common examples in behavioral research include the use of inactive drugs (especially when participants believe they are receiving psychotropic drugs), non-alcoholic beverages (when participants are expecting alcohol), and non-specific psychotherapy (therapy with the therapeutic components removed).

In the context of experimental research, the placebo effect can generate serious questions about the interpretation of results. When a researcher observes a significant difference between a treatment condition and a no-treatment control condition, can the researcher be sure that the observed effect is really caused by the treatment, or is part (or all) of the effect simply a placebo effect? The importance of this question depends on the purpose of the experimental research. Investigators often differentiate between *outcome* research and *process* research:

1. *Outcome research* simply investigates the effectiveness of a treatment. The goal is to determine whether or not a treatment produces a substantial or clinically significant effect. It is concerned with the general outcome of the treatment, rather than with isolation of the components that cause the treatment to be effective.

2. *Process research*, on the other hand, attempts to identify the active components of the treatment. In process research, it is essential that the placebo effect be separated from other, active components of the treatment.

To separate placebo effects from "real" treatment effects, researchers include one or more **placebo control groups** in an experiment. The placebo control is simply a treatment condition in which participants receive a placebo instead of the actual treatment. Comparison of the placebo control condition with the treatment condition reveals how much treatment effect exists beyond the placebo effect. It is also common to include a third, no-treatment control group. Comparison of the placebo control with the no-treatment condition reveals the magnitude of the placebo effect. In situations where it is possible to identify several different elements of a treatment, researchers may conduct a *component analysis* or *dismantling* of the treatment using multiple control groups in which selected elements (or combinations of elements) are included or excluded in each condition.

---

A **placebo control group** is a condition in which participants receive a placebo instead of the actual treatment.

Definition

---

What is the purpose of a control group?

Learning Check

---

## 8.5   MANIPULATION CHECKS

In the context of an experiment, a researcher always manipulates the independent variable and often manipulates and controls other variables. Although these manipulations and their results are obvious to the researcher, occasionally there is some question about the impact of the manipulations on the participants—specifically, are the participants even aware of the manipulation and, if so, how do they interpret it? Where these questions are important to the results or interpretation of an experiment, researchers often include a **manipulation check** as part of the study. A manipulation check directly measures whether the independent variable had the intended effect on the participant.

---

A **manipulation check** is an additional measure to assess how the participants perceived and interpreted the manipulation and/or to assess the direct effect of the manipulation.

Definition

---

There are two ways to check the manipulation. First, a manipulation check may be an explicit measure of the independent variable. Suppose, for example, a researcher wants to examine the effects of mood on performance. The study involves manipulating people's mood (i.e., mood is the independent variable). The researcher may include a mood measure to make sure that happy and sad moods were actually induced.

A second way to check the manipulation is to embed specific questions about the manipulation in a questionnaire that participants complete after their participation in the experiment. For example, participants may be given an exit questionnaire that asks for their responses to the experiment:

Did you enjoy participating?

How long did the experiment seem to take?

Were you bored?

What do you think was the purpose of the experiment?

Did you suspect that you were being deceived?

Embedded in the questionnaire are specific questions that address the manipulation. Participants can be asked directly whether or not they noticed a manipulation. For example, if the room lighting was adjusted during the experimental session, you could simply ask, "Did you notice that the lights were dimmed after the first 15 minutes?" Or, "Did you notice any change in the lights during the experiment?" In an experiment where the researcher manipulates "praise" versus "criticism" by making verbal comments to the participants, he or she might ask, "How did the researcher respond when you failed to complete the first task?" Notice that the intent of the manipulation-check questions is to determine whether the participants perceived the manipulation and/or how they interpreted the manipulation.

Although a manipulation check can be used with any study, it is particularly important in four situations:

1. Participant manipulations: Although researchers can be confident of the success of environmental manipulations (such as changing the lighting), there often is good reason to question the success of manipulations that are intended to affect participants. For example, a researcher who wanted to examine the effects of frustration on task performance might try to induce a feeling of frustration by giving one group of participants a series of impossible tasks to perform. To determine whether the participants actually are frustrated, the researcher might include a measure of frustration as a manipulation check.

2. Subtle manipulations: In some situations the variable being manipulated is not particularly salient and may not be noticed by the participants. For example, a researcher might make minor changes in the wording of instructions or in affect (smiling versus not smiling). Small changes from one treatment condition to another might be overlooked completely, especially when participants are not explicitly told that changes are being made.

3. Simulations: In simulation research the researcher attempts to create a real-world environment by manipulating elements within the experimental situation. The effectiveness of the simulation, however, depends on the participants' perception and acceptance. A manipulation check can be used to assess how participants perceive and respond to an attempted simulation.

4. Placebo controls: As with a simulation, the effectiveness of a placebo depends on its credibility. It is essential that participants believe that the placebo is real; they must have no suspicion that they are being deceived. A manipulation check can be used to assess the realism of the placebo.

 Learning Check

What is the general purpose of a manipulation check?

## 8.6 INCREASING EXTERNAL VALIDITY: SIMULATION AND FIELD STUDIES

Once again, the goal of the experimental strategy is to establish a cause-and-effect relationship between two variables. To do this, an experiment creates an artificial, controlled environment in which the two variables being studied are isolated from outside influences. As a result, experiments are commonly conducted in a laboratory setting. A controlled environment increases the internal validity of the research (see Chapter 6). However, by creating an artificial environment, experimenters risk obtaining results that do not accurately reflect events and relations that occur in a more natural, real-world environment. As we discussed in Chapter 6, in research terminology this risk is a threat to external validity. One example of this problem occurs when demand characteristics are present. Recall that demand characteristics are cues given to the participant that may influence the participant to behave in a certain way. Demand characteristics, as well as reactivity and other threats to external validity, are much more likely to be problems in experiments conducted in a laboratory setting.

For some research questions, a threat to external validity can be extremely serious. In particular, when research seeks cause-and-effect explanations for behavior in real-world situations, it is essential that the experimental results generalize outside the confines of the experiment. In these situations, researchers often attempt to maximize the realism of the experimental environment to increase the external validity of the results. Two standard techniques are used to accomplish this, simulation and field studies.

## SIMULATION

**Simulation** is the creation of conditions within an experiment that simulate or closely duplicate the natural environment being examined. The term *natural environment* is used in a very broad sense to mean not only the physical characteristics of the environment but, more important, its atmosphere or mood.

---

A **simulation** is the creation of conditions within an experiment that simulate or closely duplicate the natural environment in which the behaviors being examined would normally occur.

Definition

---

Researchers often differentiate between **mundane realism** and **experimental realism** in the context of simulation (Aronson & Carlsmith, 1968). Mundane realism refers to the superficial, usually physical, characteristics of the simulation, which probably have little positive effect on external validity. For example, converting a research laboratory into a mock singles bar probably would not do much to promote "natural" behavior of participants. In fact, most participants would probably view the situation as phony and respond with artificial behaviors. Experimental realism, on the other hand, concerns the psychological aspects of the simulation, that is, the extent to which the participants become immersed in the simulation and behave normally, unmindful of the fact that they are involved in an experiment. Obviously, a successful simulation is far more dependent on experimental realism than on mundane realism, and often the more mundane aspects of a simulation can be minimized or eliminated.

One of the most famous and most detailed simulation experiments was conducted in 1973 by researchers at Stanford University (Haney, Banks, & Zimbardo, 1973). The intent of the research was to study the development of interpersonal dynamics and relationships between guards and inmates in a prison. An actual prison, consisting of three barred cells, a solitary confinement facility, guards' quarters, and an interview room, was built in the basement of the psychology building. A sample of 24 normal, mature, emotionally stable male college students was obtained. On a random basis, half were assigned the role of "guard," and half were assigned the role of "prisoner." The guards were issued khaki uniforms, nightsticks, and sunglasses. The prisoners' uniforms were loose smocks with ID numbers on the front and back. The prisoners were publicly arrested, charged, searched, handcuffed, and led off to jail, where they were fingerprinted, photographed, stripped, sprayed with a delousing preparation, and finally given uniforms and locked up. Except for an explicit prohibition against physical punishment or aggression, little specific instruction was given to the guards or the prisoners. Almost immediately, the prisoners and guards became immersed in their roles. The interactions became negative, hostile, dehumanizing, and impersonal. Five prisoners had to be released because they developed extreme depression, crying, rage, and anxiety. When the experiment was stopped prematurely after only 6 days, the remaining prisoners were relieved, but the guards were distressed at the idea of giving up the control and power that had been part of their roles. Clearly the simulation was successful—perhaps too much so.

The Stanford prison study is an extreme example of a simulation experiment involving role playing and a detailed simulated environment. However, this degree of detail is not always necessary for a successful simulation. Bordens and Horowitz (1983) investigated the decision process by which trial jurors reach their verdicts by having college students participate as jurors in a mock trial. The study did not attempt to recreate a detailed simulation of a real criminal trial but rather had participants base their verdicts on an audiotaped summary of a trial. Although the study made some effort to duplicate a real courtroom environment, the emphasis was on experimental realism rather than mundane realism.

Both the prison study and the mock trial study attempted to simulate a specific real world situation, and both involved some degree of mundane realism. It is possible, however, for a simulation experiment to create a general atmosphere, rather than a specific situation, and completely ignore the concept of mundane realism. The many studies using the "prisoner's dilemma" game provide good examples of this type of simulation research. The prisoner's dilemma game is based on a hypothetical situation where two individuals have been arrested and are being interrogated by the police. Imagine that you and a partner have committed a crime and have both been arrested. The police have no real evidence against you and are relying on a confession to make their case. You and your partner are being held incommunicado, so you have no idea what your partner is saying or doing. The rules of the game are as follows: If both suspects confess, then both will be convicted. If both deny the crime, then both will be set free. However, if only one confesses and implicates his partner, then the confessor will be set free and will be rewarded for turning state's evidence. Note that your highest *personal gain* comes when you confess and your partner denies the crime. But the highest *mutual gain* comes when you both deny the crime. The dilemma is deciding what to do: Do you choose to behave in a cooperative manner and deny the crime, or do you behave in a conflicting manner and confess?

The prisoner's dilemma game is used in laboratory research to create a situation of interpersonal conflict, simulating real-life situations in which people must choose between cooperation and conflict based on the consequences of reward or punishment. In the laboratory, the two options of cooperation or conflict typically result in monetary consequences; for example, both players win $2 if both cooperate, both lose $2 if both conflict, and if they make opposite responses, the "conflictor" wins $5 while the "cooperator" loses $1. Notice that the prisoner's dilemma game is a *generic* simulation that is used to create a general atmosphere of competition. Nonetheless, it can be used to duplicate a variety of real-world conflict situations. For example, it has been used successfully to investigate racial prejudice (Tyson, Schlachter, & Cooper, 1987), gender stereotyping (Ferguson & Schmitt, 1988), and employee conflict/cooperation in the business world (Tomer, 1987).

---

Define and differentiate experimental realism and mundane realism.

Learning
Check

---

## FIELD STUDIES

A simulation experiment can be viewed as an effort to bring the real world into the laboratory to increase the external validity of experimental results. An alternative procedure that seeks the same goal is to take the laboratory into the real world. Research studies conducted in a real-world environment are called **field studies,** and researchers often speak of "going into the field" as a euphemism for taking research outside the laboratory. Field settings were discussed briefly in Chapter 6 and are detailed here.

---

A **field study** is an experiment conducted in a place that the participant or subject perceives as a natural environment.

Definition

---

Many of the more famous field studies involve the investigation of helping behavior or "bystander apathy" in emergency situations. In these studies the researchers create an emergency situation, then manipulate variables within the emergency and observe bystander responses. Research has used a variety of staged emergencies such as a flat tire (Bryan & Test, 1967), a lost wallet (Hornstein, Fisch, & Holmes, 1968), and a collapsed victim (Piliavin, Rodin, & Piliavin, 1969). A representative study involves a victim with a cane collapsing in a Philadelphia subway car (Piliavin & Piliavin, 1972). In one treatment condition the victim "bled" from the mouth; in the second condition there was no bleeding. The results show that help was significantly slower and less frequent for the bloody victim.

Cialdini, Reno, and Kallgren (1990) conducted a field experiment examining the natural phenomenon of littering and the theoretical issue of social conformity. They wanted to determine whether a person's tendency to litter depended on the "social norm" established by the amount of litter already in the area. Individuals were given a handbill as they entered a parking garage that already had either 1, 2, 4, or 8 handbills lying on the ground. The participants were then observed to determine whether or not they dropped their own handbills. The results indicated that behavior is influenced by social norms: People are significantly more likely to litter when a large amount of existing litter implies social acceptability.

Define and differentiate a simulation experiment and a field study.

## ADVANTAGES AND DISADVANTAGES OF SIMULATION AND FIELD STUDIES

Although simulation and field studies can be used to increase the realism of experiments, there are risks as well as advantages to these techniques. The obvious advantage of both procedures is that they allow researchers to investigate behavior in more lifelike situations and therefore should increase the chances that the experimental results will accurately reflect natural events. The disadvantage of both procedures is that allowing nature to intrude on an experiment means that the researcher often loses some control over the situation and risks compromising the internal validity of the experiment. This problem is particularly important for field experiments. In the "bloody victim" experiment, for example, the researchers had no control over *who* was riding in the subway car or *how many* passengers were present. Although it is reasonable that random variation of the "blood" versus "no-blood" conditions should have randomized participant variables across conditions, there is no guarantee. It is conceivable, for example, that the four o'clock subway was filled with business commuters but the five o'clock subway had only three or four street people. This type of unpredictable and uncontrolled variation could have significantly influenced the results. Simulation experiments, on the other hand, do provide researchers with the opportunity to control the assignment of participants to treatment conditions. However, simulation experiments are totally dependent on the participants' willingness to accept the simulation. No matter how realistic the simulation may be, participants still know that it is only an experiment, and they know that their behaviors are being observed. This knowledge could influence behavior and compromise the experimental results.

## CHAPTER SUMMARY

The goal of the experimental research strategy is to establish a cause-and-effect relationship between two variables. To accomplish this goal, an experiment must manipulate one of the two variables and create a situation in which the two variables being examined are isolated from the influence of other variables. In this chapter manipulation and control are considered.

In general, an experiment attempts to demonstrate that changes in one variable are directly responsible for changes in a second variable. The two

basic characteristics that distinguish the experimental research strategy from the descriptive research strategy are: (1) manipulation of one variable while measuring a second variable, and (2) control of extraneous variables. In an experiment, the independent variable is manipulated by the researcher, the dependent variable is measured for changes, and all other variables are controlled to prevent them from influencing the results.

To establish an unambiguous causal relationship between the independent and dependent variables, it is necessary to eliminate the possible influence of a confounding variable. Extraneous variables become confounds when they change systematically along with the independent variable. After identifying a short list of extraneous variables that have the potential to become confounding variables, it is possible to actively or passively control these variables. The two standard methods of active control are: (1) holding a variable constant, and (2) matching values across the treatment conditions. The method for passive control is to randomize these variables across the treatment conditions.

An experiment always involves comparison of measures of the dependent variable across different levels of the independent variable. To accomplish this, often a treatment condition (i.e., an experimental group) and a no-treatment condition (i.e., a control group) are created. The no-treatment condition serves as a baseline for evaluating the effect of the treatment. There are two general categories of control groups: (1) the no-treatment control group, a condition that involves no treatment whatsoever—participants receive a zero-level of the independent variable; (2) the placebo control group, a condition that involves the appearance of a treat-

ment but from which the active, effective elements have been removed.

In an experiment a researcher always manipulates the independent variable. Occasionally, a researcher may include a manipulation check to assess whether the participants are aware of the manipulation. A manipulation check is an additional measure to assess whether the manipulation was successful. It is particularly useful to use a manipulation check when participant manipulations, subtle manipulations, simulations, or a placebo control condition is used.

To establish a cause-and-effect relationship between two variables, an experiment necessarily creates an artificial, controlled environment in which the two variables being studied are isolated from outside influences. This high level of control required by an experiment can be a threat to external validity. To gain higher external validity, a researcher may use a simulation or a field study. A simulation involves creating a real-world atmosphere in a laboratory to duplicate a natural environment or situation; a field study involves moving an experiment from the laboratory into the real-world environment.

## KEY WORDS

experimental research strategy
treatment condition
levels
independent variable
dependent variable
extraneous variable

randomization
random assignment
experimental group
control group
no-treatment control group

placebo effect
placebo control group
manipulation check
simulation
field study

## EXERCISES

1. In addition to the key words, you should also be able to define the following terms:
   third-variable problem    placebo
   directionality problem     mundane realism
   confounding variable       experimental
   random process             realism

2. Define or describe the *third-variable problem* and the *directionality problem*. Explain the ac-

tions used in experiments to avoid these two problems.

3. Dr. Jones conducted a study examining the relationship between the amount of sugar in a child's diet and the activity level of the child. A sample of 30 4-year-old children from a local preschool was used in the study. Sugar consumption was measured by interviewing the

parents about each child's diet; and each child was then placed into one of two groups, high sugar consumption and low sugar consumption. Activity level was measured by observing the children during a regular preschool afternoon. Finally, Dr. Jones compared the activity level for the high sugar group with the activity level for the low sugar group. Explain why Dr. Jones' study is *not* an example of the experimental research strategy.

4. Which of the following is an example of the experimental research strategy?
   a. In a study examining the relationship between dietary fiber and cholesterol, a sample of 50-year-old men is randomly separated into two groups. Each group eats exactly the same diet for 2 months, except that one group also gets 2 cups of oatmeal every day. At the end of 2 months the cholesterol level is measured for each man. The researcher hopes to find a difference between the two groups.
   b. To evaluate the relationship between stress and general health, a researcher selects a random sample of 50-year-old men. For 2 months, each man is asked to keep a daily journal recording stressful events (such as a fight with his wife, an argument with his boss, or an automobile accident). After 2 months, a doctor examines each man and records an overall health rating. The goal of the study is to determine whether or not there is a relationship between the total amount of stress and overall health of the men.
   c. In a study examining the relationship between self-esteem and dishonest behavior, participants were first given a self-esteem questionnaire to classify them into high and low self-esteem groups. Then, cheating behavior was measured while the participants corrected their own exams. The goal of the study is to find a difference between the two groups.

5. Read the following example and answer the questions that follow it.

   Dr. Jones conducts a research study investigating the effects of a new drug that is intended to reduce the craving for alcohol. A group of alcoholics who are being treated at a clinic is selected for the study. One half of the participants are given the drug along with their regular treatment, and the other half receive a placebo. Dr. Jones records whether or not each individual is still sober after 6 months.
   a. Identify the independent variable and the dependent variable in this study.
   b. Identify the number of levels of the independent variable.
   c. Identify the dependent variable in this study.
   d. Assuming that the study includes participants ranging in age from 18 to 62 years old, participant age is a _____ variable in the study.
   e. If the participants in the drug group are noticeably older (on average) than the individuals in the placebo group, then participant age is a _____ variable.

6. Dr. Jones conducts an experiment investigating the effects of distraction on memory. A list of 40 two-syllable words is prepared. Dr. Jones obtains a sample of 50 students, all between the ages of 18 and 22, and presents the list of words to the entire group. Then each individual is randomly assigned to one of two groups. One group of participants is given a memory test for the list of words in a quiet room, and the second group is tested in a room with loud construction noises (hammering, sawing, etc.) in the background.
   a. Identify the independent variable and the dependent variable in this study.
   b. Explain why Dr. Jones can be reasonably confident that the participants' age is not a confounding variable. That is, explain why it is unlikely that one group does better on the memory task because they are substantially older than the other group.
   c. Although personality varies from one participant to another, Dr. Jones is probably not worried about personality as a confounding variable. Explain why not.

7. Define *extraneous variable* and *confounding variable*. Describe two methods used to prevent extraneous variables from becoming confounding variables.

8. In an experiment, subjects are usually assigned to treatments using a *random assignment* procedure. Explain why random assignment is used.

9. Describe and differentiate a no-treatment control group and a placebo control group.

10. Explain why simulations and field studies are used.

11. Describe the problems of simulations and field studies.

## InfoTrac COLLEGE EDITION EXERCISES

1. To qualify as a true experiment, a research study requires the manipulation of at least one variable. The fact that some variables cannot (or should not) be manipulated limits the topics that can be investigated easily with an experimental study. If you were conducting an InfoTrac College Edition search for each of the following subjects, indicate which subjects are more likely to produce examples of true experiments and which are less likely. In each case, explain your answer.
   a. adolescent self-esteem
   b. anorexia treatment
   c. mathematics instruction
   d. alcohol and academic performance

2. When we conducted an InfoTrac College Edition search using the subject term *self-esteem* and then limiting the search with the keyword *adolescent*, we found 14 periodical articles, including the following:
   a. Racial differences in adolescent coping and self-esteem (Chapman & Mullis, 2000)
   b. The effect of a physical activity intervention package on the self-esteem of pre-

adolescent and adolescent females (Boyd & Hrycaiko, 1997)
   c. A longitudinal study of self-esteem: implications for adolescent development (Zimmerman et al., 1997)
   Based on the titles of these articles, explain why you think that the study is (or is not) a true experiment. (Note: A longitudinal study examines how a group of individuals changes over time.)

3. Using InfoTrac College Edition, locate one periodical article reporting the results of a research study using the experimental research strategy. Provide a complete citation for your article (title, authors, journal, date, pages) and a brief description of the study that includes identifying the independent variable and the dependent variable. (Note: You may find a more complex study that includes several independent and/or dependent variables. In this case, identify one independent variable and one dependent variable, and focus on these two variables when you describe the study.)

# Quasi-Experimental Strategy: Nonequivalent Group, Time-Series, and Developmental Designs

## CHAPTER OVERVIEW

The goal of the quasi-experimental strategy is to show a causal relationship between two variables; however, quasi-experimental designs usually contain a confounding variable that is integral to the design and cannot be removed. In this chapter we discuss details of the quasi-experimental strategy, as well as different types of quasi-experimental designs. Developmental designs, which are closely related to quasi-experimental designs, are also presented.

## 9.1   INTRODUCTION

In the previous chapter we introduced the experimental research strategy as a means for establishing a cause-and-effect relationship between variables. Recall that the experimental strategy has two basic requirements:

1. Manipulation of one variable while a second variable is measured
2. Control of other, extraneous variables

In many research situations, however, it is difficult or impossible for a researcher to satisfy completely the rigorous requirements of an experiment. This is particularly true for applied research in natural settings, such as educational research in the classroom and clinical research with real clients. In these situations a researcher can often devise a research strategy (a method of collecting data) that is similar to an experiment but fails to satisfy at least one of the requirements of a true experiment. Such studies are generally called *quasi-experimental* research studies. Although quasi-experimental studies typically are intended to show causal relationships (for example, a clinician would like to show that the therapy causes patients to improve), they usually contain a confounding variable or other threat to internal validity that is an integral part of the design and simply cannot be removed. The existence of a confounding variable means that these studies cannot establish unambiguous cause-and-effect relationships and therefore are not true experiments. In this chapter we introduce several different quasi-experimental designs and some closely related nonexperimental designs. In each case we discuss the aspect of the design that prevents it from being a true experiment. The fact that quasi-experimental studies are not true experiments does not mean that they are useless or even second-class research studies. Quasi-experimental research serves a real purpose and in some cases is the only option available for certain questions.

At the end of this chapter we examine developmental research, which includes research designs intended to investigate how age is related to other variables. Because age is a variable that cannot be manipulated, developmental designs are not true experiments and can be included in other categories of nonexperimental or quasi-experimental research. However, developmental designs are generally presented as a separate group of research designs with their own terminology. As we introduce the basic developmental research designs, we discuss how they are related to other types of nonexperimental and quasi-experimental research.

Why aren't studies that examine the effects of aging considered true experiments?

Learning
Check

## 9.2   QUASI-EXPERIMENTAL STRATEGY

**Quasi-experimental research strategies** are used in studies that are almost, but not quite, true experiments. Quasi-experimental studies often look like experiments in terms of the general structure of the study. In an experiment, for example, a researcher typically creates treatment conditions by manipulating an independent variable and then measures participants to obtain a set of scores within each condition. If the scores in one condition are consistently different from the scores in another condition, the researcher can conclude that the two treatment conditions have different effects (see Figure 9.1). Similarly, a quasi-experimental study typically involves comparing groups of scores. One variable is used to create groups or conditions, and then a second variable is measured to produce a set of scores within each condition. In a quasi-experimental study, however, the different groups or conditions are not created by manipulating an independent variable. Instead, the groups are usually defined in terms of a pre-existing participant variable (for example, male/female) or in terms of time (for example, before and after treatment). These two methods of defining groups produce two general categories of quasi-experimental designs: nonequivalent group designs and time-series designs. The two general types of quasi-experimental research are shown in Figure 9.2 and are discussed in the following sections.

Definition

The **quasi-experimental research strategy,** like an experiment, typically involves a comparison of groups or conditions. However, a quasi-experimental study uses a nonmanipulated variable to define the groups or conditions being compared. The nonmanipulated variable is usually a participant variable (such as male versus female) or a time variable (such as before versus after treatment).

Figure 9.1    The Structure of an Experiment
An independent variable (in this case, temperature) is manipulated to create treatment conditions. Participants are then measured to obtain scores within each treatment condition. Here, a list of words is presented, and the score for each participant is the number of words recalled. If there is a consistent difference between the scores in one condition and the scores in another condition, the difference is attributed to the treatment. In this case, a consistent difference would indicate that room temperature has an effect on memory.

(a)

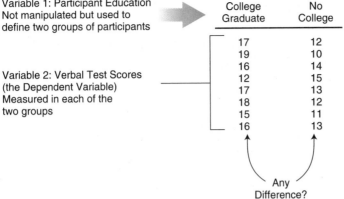

Variable 1: Participant Education
Not manipulated but used to
define two groups of participants

| College Graduate | No College |
|---|---|
| 17 | 12 |
| 19 | 10 |
| 16 | 14 |
| 12 | 15 |
| 17 | 13 |
| 18 | 12 |
| 15 | 11 |
| 16 | 13 |

Variable 2: Verbal Test Scores
(the Dependent Variable)
Measured in each of the
two groups

Any
Difference?

(b)

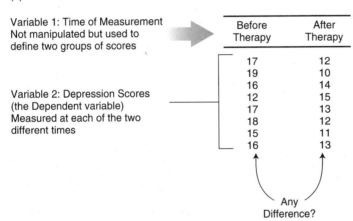

Variable 1: Time of Measurement
Not manipulated but used to
define two groups of scores

| Before Therapy | After Therapy |
|---|---|
| 17 | 12 |
| 19 | 10 |
| 16 | 14 |
| 12 | 15 |
| 17 | 13 |
| 18 | 12 |
| 15 | 11 |
| 16 | 13 |

Variable 2: Depression Scores
(the Dependent variable)
Measured at each of the two
different times

Any
Difference?

Figure 9.2    Two Examples of Quasi-Experimental Studies
(a) A pre-existing participant variable (education) is used to define
two groups, and then a dependent variable (verbal test score)
is measured in each group. (b) The two groups of scores
are defined by the time of measurement, and a dependent
variable (depression) is measured at each of the two times.

Explain why we cannot be as confident about causal relationships between variables when a quasi-experimental, instead of an experimental, design is used.

Learning
Check

## 9.3    NONEQUIVALENT GROUP DESIGNS

An element common to most experiments is the control of participant variables
by assigning participants to specific treatment conditions. The goal is to balance

or equalize participant variables across treatment conditions by using a random process or by deliberately matching participants. Note that the researcher attempts to create equivalent groups of participants by actively deciding which individuals go into which groups. There are occasions, however, where a researcher must examine pre-existing groups. For example, a researcher may want to evaluate a teen pregnancy prevention program by comparing the pregnancy rates in a high school where the program is used with pregnancy rates in a high school that does not use the program. In this study, the researcher does not have control over which individuals are assigned to which group; the two groups of participants already exist. Because the researcher cannot use random assignment or matching to balance participant variables across groups, there is no assurance that the two groups are equivalent. In this situation, the research study is called a **nonequivalent group design.**

| Definition | A **nonequivalent group design** is a research study in which the different groups of participants are formed under circumstances that do not permit the researcher to control the assignment of individuals to groups, and the groups of participants are therefore considered nonequivalent. |
| --- | --- |

## THREATS TO INTERNAL VALIDITY FOR NONEQUIVALENT GROUP DESIGNS

A general example of a nonequivalent group design is shown in Figure 9.3. Notice that the groups are differentiated by one specific factor that identifies the groups. In the teen pregnancy example, the differentiating factor was the pregnancy prevention program: One high school received the program and one did not. The purpose of the study is to show that the factor that differentiates the groups is responsible for causing the participants' scores to differ from one group to the other. For example, in the teen pregnancy study, the goal is to show that the pregnancy prevention program is responsible for the different pregnancy rates of the two schools.

However, a nonequivalent group design has a built-in threat to internal validity that precludes an unambiguous cause-and-effect explanation: **assignment bias.** As noted in Chapter 6, assignment bias occurs whenever the assignment procedure results in groups in which the participants in one have different characteristics from the participants in another group. For example, the two high schools in the teen pregnancy study may differ in terms of student IQs, socioeconomic background, racial mixture, student motivation, and so on. These variables are all potentially confounding variables because any one of them could explain the differences between the two groups. Because the selection and assignment of participants are not controlled in a study using nonequivalent groups, this type of research always is threatened by assignment bias.

In this section we consider three common examples of nonequivalent group designs: the differential research design, the posttest-only nonequivalent control group design, and the pretest–posttest nonequivalent control group design. The first two are research designs that make no attempt to control or minimize assignment bias and, as a result, do not approach the rigor of a true experiment;

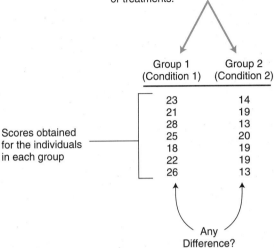

Nonequivalent groups (usually pre-existing). The researcher has no control over the assignment of individuals to groups. The groups may experience different conditions or treatments.

Group 1 (Condition 1)    Group 2 (Condition 2)

Scores obtained for the individuals in each group

| Group 1 | Group 2 |
|---------|---------|
| 23 | 14 |
| 21 | 19 |
| 28 | 13 |
| 25 | 20 |
| 18 | 19 |
| 22 | 19 |
| 26 | 13 |

Any Difference?

Figure 9.3   The General Structure of a Nonequivalent Group Study

they are referred to as **nonexperimental designs.** The third design is considered quasi-experimental because it does attempt to minimize the threat of assignment bias.

## DIFFERENTIAL RESEARCH DESIGN

One common example of nonequivalent group research involves no manipulation but simply attempts to compare pre-existing groups that are defined by a particular participant variable. For example, a researcher may want to compare self-esteem scores for children from two-parent households with children from single-parent households. Note that the researcher does not control the assignment of participants to groups; instead, the participants are automatically assigned to groups based on pre-existing characteristics. Although this type of study compares groups of participants (as an experiment does), the researcher does not manipulate the treatment conditions and does not have control over the assignment of participants to groups. Again, this is not a true experiment.

A research study that simply compares pre-existing groups is called a **differential research design** because its goal is to establish differences between the pre-existing groups. This type of study often is called *ex post facto* research because it looks at differences "after the fact"; that is, at differences that already exist between groups. For example, Updegraff, McHale, Crouter, and Kupanoff (2001) compared mothers' and fathers' involvement in the peer relationships of their adolescent children. Clearly, mothers and fathers form two pre-existing groups that were not manipulated or created by the researcher. (Incidentally, mothers were found to be more knowledgeable about their children's peer relationships, and both mothers and fathers spent more time with same-sex adolescents and their peers than with opposite-sex adolescents.) In a somewhat more bizarre study, DeGoede, Ashton-Miller, Liao, and Alexander (2001) swung a pendulum at their participants and measured how quickly the participants moved their hands to intercept the approaching object. This study examined gender differences and age differences, once again comparing pre-existing groups.

A research study that simply compares pre-existing groups is called a **differential research design.** A differential study uses a participant characteristic such as gender, race, or personality to automatically assign participants to groups. The researcher does not randomly assign individuals to groups. A dependent variable is then measured for each participant to obtain a set of scores within each group. The goal of the study is to determine whether the scores for one group are consistently different from the scores in another group.

### Differential Research and Correlational Research

Because differential research makes no attempt to control extraneous variables or to protect against the threat of assignment bias, it is usually classified as non-experimental. Many researchers place differential research in the same category as correlational research. Differential research is very similar to the correlational research discussed in Chapter 7. In a differential study a researcher simply observes two naturally occurring variables without any interference or manipulation, just as in a correlational study. The subtle distinction between differential research and correlational research is whether or not one of the variables is used to establish separate groups to be compared. In differential research, participant differences in one variable are used to create separate groups, and measurements of the second variable are made within each group. The researcher then compares the measurements for one group with the measurements for another group, typically looking at mean differences between groups (see Figure 9.4a). A correlational study, on the other hand, treats all the participants as a single group and simply measures the two variables for each individual (see Figure 9.4b). Although differential research and correlational research produce different kinds of data and involve different statistical analyses, their results should receive the same interpretation. Both designs allow researchers to establish the existence of relationships and to describe relationships between variables, but neither design permits a cause-and-effect explanation of the relationship.

Learning Check

A researcher measures personality characteristics of a group of participants who successfully lost weight in a diet program and compared their scores with a second group consisting of individuals who failed to lose weight in the program. Is this study a differential design? Explain your answer.

## POSTTEST-ONLY NONEQUIVALENT CONTROL GROUP DESIGN

Nonequivalent groups are commonly used in applied research situations in which the goal is to evaluate the effectiveness of a treatment administered to a pre-

(a) A differential study examining the relationship between self-esteem and academic performance.

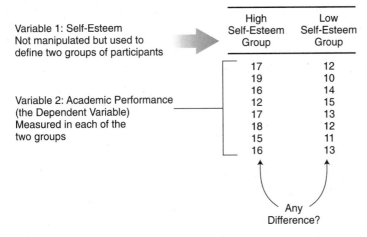

Variable 1: Self-Esteem
Not manipulated but used to
define two groups of participants

Variable 2: Academic Performance
(the Dependent Variable)
Measured in each of the
two groups

| High Self-Esteem Group | Low Self-Esteem Group |
|---|---|
| 17 | 12 |
| 19 | 10 |
| 16 | 14 |
| 12 | 15 |
| 17 | 13 |
| 18 | 12 |
| 15 | 11 |
| 16 | 13 |

Any Difference?

(b) A correlational study examining the relationship between self-esteem and academic performance.

| Participant | Variable 1 Self-Esteem | Variable 2 Academic Performance |
|---|---|---|
| A | 84 | 16 |
| B | 72 | 10 |
| C | 90 | 19 |
| D | 68 | 13 |
| E | 77 | 16 |
| F | 81 | 12 |
| G | 85 | 17 |
| H | 76 | 13 |

Figure 9.4    Comparison of Differential Research
and Correlational Research
(a) The structure of a differential study examining the relationship between self-esteem and academic performance. Note that one of the two variables (self-esteem) is used to create groups, and the other variable (academic performance) is measured to obtain scores within each group. (b) The structure of a correlational study examining the relationship between self-esteem and academic performance. Note that there is only one group of participants with two scores (self-esteem and academic performance) measured for each individual.

existing group of participants. A second group of similar but nonequivalent participants is used for the control condition. Note that the researcher uses pre-existing groups and does not control the assignment of participants to groups. In particular, the researcher does not randomly assign individuals to groups. For example, Skjoeveland (2001) used a nonequivalent group study to examine the effects of street parks on social interactions among neighbors. Parks were constructed in one area, and the people living in that neighborhood were compared with two control groups that did not get new parks. Similarly, Goldie, Schwartz,

McConnachie, and Morrison (2001) evaluated a new ethics course for medical students by comparing the group of students who took the new course with a nonequivalent group who did not take the course. This type of research is called a **nonequivalent control group design.**

Definition

A **nonequivalent control group design** uses pre-existing groups, one of which serves in the treatment condition and the other in the control condition. The researcher does not randomly assign individuals to the groups.

One common example of a nonequivalent control group design is called a **posttest-only nonequivalent control group design.** This type of study is also called a **static group comparison.** In this type of design, one group of participants is given a treatment and then is measured after the treatment (this is the posttest). The treated group is then compared with a nonequivalent group that has not received the treatment (this is the control group). This design can be represented schematically as follows:

$$X \quad O \quad \text{(treatment group)}$$

$$O \quad \text{(nonequivalent control group)}$$

In this notation system, developed by Campbell and Stanley (1963), the symbols represent events in the study. The letter X corresponds to the treatment, and the letter O corresponds to the observation or measurement. Each row of symbols corresponds to a separate group of participants and depicts the sequence of events in the study for that group. The symbols are presented in temporal order from left to right, with symbols on the left occurring before symbols to the right. Therefore, in the posttest-only design, one group is given a treatment and then is measured, and the other group is measured without receiving any treatment. This study compares the observations for the treatment group with the observations for the control group to determine whether there is any evidence for a treatment effect. If a design includes random assignment of participants to groups in the study, an R is placed as the first symbol in each line of notation. The absence of an R in this schematic reflects the use of pre-existing groups, as in a nonequivalent control group design.

Definition

A **posttest-only nonequivalent control group design** compares two nonequivalent groups of participants. One group is observed (measured) after receiving a treatment, and the other group is measured at the same time but receives no treatment.

The teen pregnancy program discussed earlier is a good example of a posttest-only nonequivalent control group study. The program is administered at one high school, and a second high school that does not receive the program serves as a nonequivalent control group. The purpose of the study is to show that the program has an effect by demonstrating a difference in pregnancy rates between the two schools.

Although this kind of research design appears to ask a cause-and-effect question, the research design does not protect against assignment bias. As we noted earlier, the students at the two schools could differ on a variety of variables (in addition to the pregnancy program), and any of these other variables could be responsible for the difference in pregnancy rates. Because the posttest-only nonequivalent control group design does not address the threat of assignment bias, it is considered a nonexperimental design.

Learning Check

Describe why the Skjoeveland (2001) study discussed above is a nonequivalent control group design.

## PRETEST–POSTTEST NONEQUIVALENT CONTROL GROUP DESIGN

A much stronger version of the nonequivalent control group design is often called a **pretest–posttest nonequivalent control group design** and can be represented as follows:

O    X    O    (treatment group)

O          O    (nonequivalent control group)

In this case, both groups are observed (measured) prior to the treatment. The treatment is then administered to one group, and following the treatment both groups are observed again.

Definition

A **pretest–posttest nonequivalent control group design** compares two nonequivalent groups. One group is measured twice—once before a treatment is administered and once after. The other group is measured at the same two times but does not receive any treatment.

The addition of the pretest measurement allows researchers to address the problem of assignment bias that exists with all nonequivalent groups research. Specifically, the researcher can now compare the observations before treatment to establish whether or not the two groups really are similar. If the groups are found to be similar before treatment, the researcher has evidence that the participants in one group are *not* substantially different from the participants in another group, and the threat of assignment bias is greatly reduced. Note that the pretest scores simply allow the researcher to ensure that the two groups are similar with respect to one specific variable. Other potentially important variables are not measured or controlled. Thus, the threat of assignment bias is reduced, but it is certainly not eliminated.

This type of design also allows a researcher to compare the pretest scores and posttest scores for both groups to help determine whether the treatment or some other factor is responsible for changes. For example, if the participants are similar before treatment but different after treatment, the researcher can be more confident that the treatment has an effect. On the other hand, if both groups show the same degree of change from the pretest to the posttest, then the researcher must conclude that some factor other than the treatment is responsible for the change. Thus, the pretest–posttest nonequivalent control group design minimizes the threat of assignment bias and can provide some evidence to support a cause-and-effect relationship. As a result, this type of research is considered quasi-experimental.

### Other Threats to a Pretest–Posttest Nonequivalent Control Group Design

Although the pretest–posttest design minimizes some threats to internal validity, the structure of the design creates the potential for other threats. This type of design involves repeated observations of participants over time (pretest observations and posttest observations), which allows other factors to threaten the internal validity of the study. These time-related threats to validity are discussed in detail in Chapter 11. We mention a few of them briefly here and explain how time-related threats are minimized by the pretest–posttest design.

1. *History:* Events that occur during the research study but outside it are called history. If the outside events can influence the participants' scores, then history becomes a threat to internal validity (a **history effect**). For example, a difference found between the pretest and posttest scores may have been caused by the treatment, or it may have been caused by some outside event (history). In the pretest–posttest nonequivalent control group design, however, the threat from history is minimized because both groups are observed over the same time period and presumably experience the same history.

2. *Instrumentation:* **Instrumentation** refers to changes in the measurement instrument that occur over time. For example, a teacher's grading standards may change such that two different grades are recorded at two different times even though the same exam or paper is graded. In a research study, a difference between pretest and posttest scores may be caused by instrumentation, not the treatment. However, the threat from instrumentation is minimized in the pretest–posttest nonequivalent control group design because any change in the measurement instrument should occur equally for the two groups.

3. *Practice/fatigue:* When the observation of participants involves some form of testing, it is possible that the testing experience during the first observation will change the participants and affect their scores during the second observation. Common examples are **practice effects** and **fatigue.** In either case, the difference between pretest and posttest scores may be explained by a factor other than the treatment. In the pretest–posttest nonequivalent control group design, however, both groups have the same pretest experience, so it is unlikely that practice or fatigue would cause a difference between groups.

4. *Maturation:* Any biological or psychological processes that change over time are called **maturation.** During the time between the first observation and the final observation, a participant may grow stronger (or weaker) or may develop new skills or abilities. These maturational changes provide an alternative explanation for any differences that may be found between the pretreatment and

the posttreatment observations. However, in the pretest–posttest nonequivalent control group design, both groups mature over the same time, so maturation should not cause a difference between groups.

5. *Regression Toward the Mean:* **Regression toward the mean** is a statistical phenomenon in which individuals who have extreme scores (either high or low) during the first observation tend to have less extreme (more average) scores during a later observation. In a study in which participants are selected because they have exceptionally high (or low) scores on the first observation, there is a risk that their scores will be different on a later observation because of regression, not because of the treatment. However, if regression effects exist in a pretest–posttest nonequivalent control group design, it is reasonable to expect that the effects would be equal for the two groups and would therefore not be an explanation for a difference between groups.

### Threats From Differential Effects

In the preceding discussion we said that both groups of participants are tested over the same time and that therefore the threats are not likely to cause a difference between groups. However, it is possible for a specific threat to affect the groups differently. For example, the history for one group could be different from that for the other group. History effects that differ from one group to another are called **differential history effects.** In a nonequivalent group design, there is always the possibility that differential history (and not the treatment) is causing the groups to be different. Because the different groups are not selected from the same source, they may be exposed to different environmental factors that can influence their scores. For example, one high school may be enjoying a winning football season, whereas students in another school may be depressed because they are losing every game. Thus, the difference between groups may be explained by differential history effects. In a similar fashion, the internal validity of a pretest–posttest nonequivalent control group design may be threatened by **differential instrumentation, differential practice/fatigue, differential maturation,** or **differential regression.**

Describe how differential history effects can threaten the internal validity of a pretest–posttest nonequivalent control group design.

Learning
Check

## 9.4    TIME-SERIES DESIGNS

The second general category of quasi-experimental studies consists of studies in which a series of observations is made over time. Collectively, such studies are known as **time-series designs** (Campbell & Stanley, 1963). A prototypical time-series study involves a series of observations that is followed by the introduction of a treatment or other event, which is then followed by another series of observations. The goal of a time-series design is to evaluate the influence of the intervening treatment or event by comparing the observations made before treatment with the observations made after treatment.

## THREATS TO INTERNAL VALIDITY FOR TIME-SERIES DESIGNS

As we noted earlier, whenever a research study involves repeated observations over time, time-related factors can threaten internal validity. History effects, instrumentation effects, practice/fatigue effects, maturation effects, and regression effects are five kinds of time-related threats. Clearly, time-series studies are vulnerable to these threats; any differences found between the pretreatment observations and the posttreatment observations could be explained by history, instrumentation, practice/fatigue, maturation, or regression.

In general, the internal validity of a time-series study is threatened by a variety of factors related to the passage of time. During the time between the first observation and the last observation, any one of these factors could influence the participants and cause a change in their scores. Unless these factors are controlled or minimized by the structure of the research design, a time-series study cannot approach the internal validity of a true experiment. In this section we introduce four examples of time-series studies: the one-group pretest–posttest design, the time-series design, the interrupted time-series design, and the equivalent time-samples design. The first of these designs makes no attempt to control the threats to internal validity and therefore is classified as nonexperimental. The other three manage to minimize most threats to internal validity and are classified as quasi-experimental.

## ONE-GROUP PRETEST–POSTTEST DESIGN

A simplified version of the time-series design consists of only one observation made before the treatment or event and only one observation made after it. Schematically, this simple form can be represented as follows:

$$O \quad X \quad O$$

The O represents an observation or measurement, and X represents the treatment. This type of study is not a real time-series design but rather is called a **one-group pretest posttest design,** or simply a pretest–posttest design. For example, a political consultant could evaluate the effectiveness of a new political TV commercial by assessing voters' attitude toward a candidate before and after they view the commercial. The results from this study may demonstrate a change in attitude; however, because it makes no attempt to control the many threats to internal validity, the study cannot conclude that the change was caused by the intervening commercial. Because the one-group pretest–posttest study precludes a cause-and-effect conclusion, this type of research is classified as nonexperimental.

| Definition | A **one-group pretest–posttest design** involves one measurement before treatment and one measurement after treatment for a single group of participants. This type of research is classified as a nonexperimental design. |
|---|---|

## TIME-SERIES AND INTERRUPTED TIME-SERIES DESIGNS

Once again, in a true time-series design, a *series* of observations is made before and after the treatment or event. It can be represented as follows:

$$O \quad O \quad O \quad X \quad O \quad O \quad O$$

The intervening treatment or event (X) may or may not be manipulated by the researcher. When the event that occurs in the middle of the series of observations is actually a treatment manipulated or administered by the researcher, the research study is simply called a **time-series design.** For example, a researcher may observe the number of fights at a school before and after administering an anger management program for the students. A time-series study can also be used to evaluate the influence of outside events that are not controlled or manipulated by the researcher. For example, a researcher may evaluate the impact of a natural disaster such as earthquake or flood on charitable contributions by recording the gifts received by human-service agencies for the months before and after the disaster. A study in which the intervening event is not manipulated by the researcher is called an **interrupted time-series design.**

A **time-series design** has a series of observations before a treatment and a series of observations after the treatment.

An **interrupted time-series design** consists of a series of observations before an event occurs and after the event occurs. The event is not a treatment or an experience that is created or manipulated by the researcher.

What characteristic differentiates an interrupted time-series design from a simple time-series design?

For both time-series designs, the pretest and posttest series of observations serve several valuable purposes. First, the pretest observations allow a researcher to see any trends that may already exist in the data before the treatment is even introduced. Trends in the data are an indication that the scores are influenced by some factor unrelated to the treatment. For example, practice or fatigue may cause the scores to increase or decrease over time. Similarly, instrumentation effects, maturation effects, or regression should produce a noticeable change in the observations before treatment. On the other hand, if the data show no trends or major fluctuations before the treatment, the researcher can be reasonably sure that these potential threats to internal validity are not influencing the participants. Thus, the series of observations allows a researcher to minimize most threats to internal validity. As a result, the time-series and interrupted time-series designs are classified as quasi-experimental.

Although the time-series and interrupted time-series designs minimize most threats to internal validity, it is still possible for some outside event (history) to influence the data. Suppose, for example, that a clinical researcher uses a time-series design to evaluate a treatment for depression. Observations are made for a group of depressed patients for a week before therapy begins, and a second series of observations is made for a week after therapy. The observations indicate significant improvement after therapy. However, suppose that, by coincidence, there is an abrupt change in the weather on the same day that therapy starts; after weeks of cold, dark, rainy days, it suddenly becomes bright, sunny, and unseasonably warm. Because the weather changed at the same time as the treatment, it is impossible to determine what caused the patients' improvement. Was the change caused by the treatment or by the weather?

External events (history) are also minimized as a potential threat to internal validity in time-series and interrupted time-series designs. If the outside event occurs at any time other than the introduction of the treatment, it should be easy to separate the history effects from the treatment effects. For example, if the participants are affected by an outside event that occurs before the treatment, the effect should be apparent in the observations that occur before the treatment. Figure 9.5 shows three possible outcomes in which the treatment has no effect but instead the participants are influenced by an outside event. Notice that the only problem occurs when the treatment and the outside event coincide perfectly. In this case, it is impossible to determine whether the change in behavior was caused by the treatment or by the outside event. Thus, history effects (outside events) are a threat to validity only when there is a perfect correspondence between the occurrence of the event and the introduction of the treatment.

The series of observations after the treatment or event also allows a researcher to observe any posttreatment trends. For example, it is possible that the treatment has only a temporary effect that quickly fades. Such a trend would be seen in the series of posttreatment observations. Figure 9.6 demonstrates how a series of observations can be more informative than single observations made before and after treatment. The figure shows a series of scores that are consistently increasing before treatment and continue to increase in an uninterrupted pattern after treatment. In this case, it does not appear that the treatment has any impact on the scores. However, if the study included only one observation before treatment and only one observation after treatment ($O_3$ and $O_4$), the results would indicate a substantial increase in scores following the treatment, suggesting that the treatment did have an effect.

## EQUIVALENT TIME-SAMPLES DESIGN

One way of minimizing the threat of coincidence in a time-series design is to expand the simple time series into an **equivalent time-samples design.** In an equivalent time-samples study, the treatment is repeatedly administered and removed during the series of observations. That is, the study begins with a series of observations, which is followed by a period of treatment, another series of observations, and a period of no-treatment; then the sequence is repeated, with observation, treatment, observation, no treatment. This series of events can be extended as long as the researcher wants. In symbols, this strategy can be represented as:

O O O X O O O N O O O X O O O N O O O X O O O N O O O …

where O = Observation, X = Treatment, and N = No Treatment (treatment withdrawn).

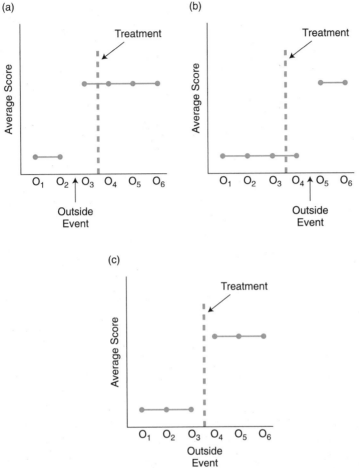

Figure 9.5   How Data in a Time-Series Study
Might Be Affected by an Outside Event
(a) The event influences scores before the treatment is introduced.
(b) The event occurs and influences scores after the treatment.
(c) The event and the treatment occur simultaneously, and it is
impossible to determine which is influencing the scores.

If the treatment actually causes a change, then the data should show a change in the observations following each treatment and a return to regular behavior when the treatment is withdrawn. If this pattern occurs repeatedly, the researcher can be reasonably confident that the treatment is responsible for the change. There is still a possibility that coincidental outside events are responsible for the observed changes, but this possibility is improbable. A coincidence may happen once, but it is very unlikely that a coincidence will occur again and again in a consistent way. Thus, the equivalent time-samples design effectively eliminates history as a threat to internal validity. The equivalent time-samples

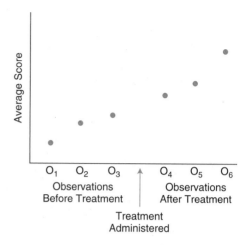

Figure 9.6    A Time-Series Study With Multiple Observations Before and After Treatment
The series of observations makes it possible to see the trend in the data that existed before the treatment was administered and that continues after the treatment.

design is usually classified as quasi-experimental; however, it has a level of internal validity that approximates that of most true experiments.

Definition

An **equivalent time-samples design** consists of a long series of observations during which a treatment is alternately administered and then withdrawn. By repeatedly applying and withdrawing the treatment, this design reduces the likelihood that some coincidental outside event, and not the treatment, is responsible for observed changes in behavior.

The equivalent time-samples design is best used when the treatment effect is expected to be temporary. With a temporary effect, the participants will show a response after each treatment but should revert to their old behaviors during the no-treatment periods. If the treatment effect is permanent, on the other hand, a response will be seen only after the first treatment, and the data will not show the repeating pattern that helps to establish the credibility of a causal treatment effect.

Learning Check

Describe how the equivalent time-samples design may be a more internally valid research design than other time-series designs.

## 9.5   DEVELOPMENTAL RESEARCH STRATEGY

The **developmental research strategy** is another type of nonexperimental (or quasi-experimental) research that can be used to study changes in behavior that relate to age. The purpose of developmental research designs is to describe the relationship between age and other variables. For example, if a researcher is interested in how language ability changes with age, a developmental research design would be appropriate.

The **developmental research strategy** is used to examine changes in behavior related to age.

Two basic types of developmental research designs are the cross-sectional design and the longitudinal design. Each has its strengths and weaknesses.

## CROSS-SECTIONAL RESEARCH DESIGN

The **cross-sectional research design** involves measuring a variable for individuals of different ages all at the same time. Specifically, groups of individuals are compared, in which each group represents a different age. For example, a researcher who wants to examine the relationship between IQ and aging could select three different groups of people—40-year-olds, 60-year-olds, and 80-year-olds—and could then measure IQ for each group. See Figure 9.7.

The **cross-sectional research design** uses different groups of individuals, each group representing a different age. The different groups are measured at one point in time and then compared.

For example, Saitoh, Karns, and Courchesne (2001) examined brain development in groups of people ranging in age from 29 months to 42 years. Magnetic resonance imaging (MRI) was used to measure hippocampal formation

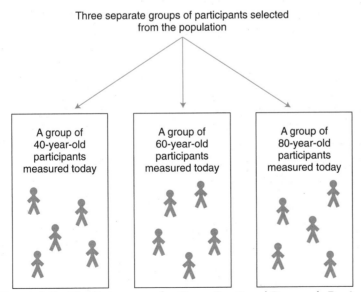

Figure 9.7    The Structure of a Cross-Sectional Research Design
Three separate groups of participants are
selected to represent three different ages.

within the brains of autistic patients and in a control group of healthy patients. By looking at individuals across a wide range of ages, the researchers were able to establish that abnormalities existed in the autistic patients from their earliest years and persisted throughout adolescence and adulthood.

A cross-sectional design can be viewed as a nonequivalent group design. The different groups of participants are not created by manipulating an independent variable; instead, the groups are defined by a pre-existing participant variable (age). Earlier in this chapter we defined this kind of study as *differential* research. However, when a study evaluates differences related to age, the design is typically called a cross-sectional study.

### Strengths and Weaknesses of the Cross-Sectional Design

One obvious advantage of the cross-sectional design is that the researcher need not wait for the participants to age but can examine the effects of 40 years of aging in one day. In the example in Figure 9.7, we do not need to follow a group of people over the next 40 years. With the cross-sectional design, data can be collected in a short period of time. In addition, cross-sectional research does not require long-term cooperation between the researchers and the participant; that is, the researcher doesn't have to incur the time and expense of tracking people down for 40 years and encouraging them to continue in the research.

The cross-sectional research design is not without its weaknesses. One weakness is that a researcher cannot say anything about how a particular individual develops over time, because individuals are not followed over years. Further, the design's major problem is that factors other than age may differentiate the groups. For example, 40-year-old women not only are younger than 80-year-old women, but they also grew up in very different environments. Opportunities for education and employment and social expectations were very different for the two groups of women. Individuals who are the same age and have lived in similar environments are called **cohorts.** The environmental changes that differentiate one age group from another are called **generation effects** or **cohort effects,** and they may be responsible for differences observed between the groups, instead of age. Generation effects are a type of third-variable problem (discussed in Chapter 8). In a cross-sectional study the generation of the participants changes from one group to another so that the apparent relationship between age and other variables may actually be caused by generation differences.

---

**Definitions**

Individuals who were born at roughly the same time and grew up under similar circumstances are called **cohorts.**

The terms **cohort effect** and **generation effect** refer to a difference between age groups (or cohorts) due to unique characteristics or experiences other than age.

---

A great example of how cohort effects can influence the results of research comes from studies on the relationship between IQ and age (Horn, 1978). Many research studies show that IQ declines between the ages of 20 and 50. On the other hand, a separate group of studies shows little or no decline in IQ between the ages of 20 and 50. How can these two sets of data be so completely different? One answer lies in the designs of the studies. The data that show IQ declining with age are generally obtained with cross-sectional studies. The problem with cross-sectional designs is that the results may be influenced by cohort effects; the groups compared are not only different in age but also may be different because they lived in different decades. The fact that the groups grew up and lived in different environments could affect their IQ scores and could be the source of the IQ differences between the groups. Cohort effects are more problematic the more years there are between the groups. The second group of studies, showing stable IQ, monitored the same set of people over a long period of time. This type of research design is called the longitudinal research design and is discussed next.

Why is the cohort effect a problem in the cross-section design?

Learning
Check

## LONGITUDINAL RESEARCH DESIGN

The **longitudinal research design** involves measuring a variable in individuals over a period of time (typically every few months or every few years). Several measures of a particular variable are made in the same individuals at 2 or more times in their lives to investigate the relationship between age and that variable. For example, to examine IQ and age using the longitudinal approach, a researcher might measure IQ in a group of 40-year-olds and then measure the same individuals again at ages 60 and 80. See Figure 9.8.

The **longitudinal research design** examines development by making a series of observations or measurements over time. Commonly the same group of individuals is followed and measured at different points in time.

Definition

One group of participants selected
from the population

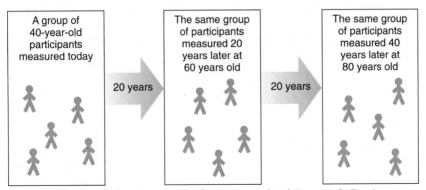

Figure 9.8   The Structure of a Longitudinal Research Design
One group of participants is measured at different times as they age.

Longitudinal studies are very similar to the time-series studies discussed earlier in this chapter. In a longitudinal design, however, no treatment is administered; instead, the "treatment" is age. That is, a longitudinal study can be described as a set of observations followed by a period of development or aging and then another series of observations. The differences between the initial observations and the final observations define the effects of development. Thus, longitudinal studies can be viewed as a kind of time-series study. However, when this type of research is used to evaluate development or the effects of age, the design is typically called a longitudinal study.

The distinction between longitudinal designs and time-series designs is not always clear. For example, Sun (2001) examined the well-being of a group of adolescents for an extended period before and after their parents' divorces. This can be viewed as a longitudinal study because it examined the changes that occur over time for a group of participants. However, it also can be viewed as a time-series study that compared a series of observations made before an event (the divorce) with a series of observations made after the event.

### Atypical Longitudinal Designs

We define *longitudinal design* rather broadly to include research that examines the development of phenomena other than individual aging. For example, Pope, Ionescu-Pioffia, and Pope (2001) examined how drug use and lifestyle have changed over the past 30 years by returning to the same college every 10 years to measure freshman attitudes and behaviors. Because Pope and his colleagues measured different individuals every 10 years, many researchers would not place this study in the category of longitudinal research. That is, for many people, the designation *longitudinal research* should be reserved for studies that observe developmental changes in a single group of individuals over time. However, the Pope study does examine the development of a social phenomenon by making repeated observations over a 30-year period. Although this study is not a typical longitudinal design, it is an example of research that examines development (or social evolution) over time. Therefore, we allow this type of study to be classified as longitudinal, but we hedge a little by calling them "atypical" longitudinal designs.

Learning Check

For each of the following, indicate whether it is a typical or atypical longitudinal study. In each case, a researcher examines changes in child discipline.

a. Every three years the researcher contacts the local schools to obtain a sample of newly registered kindergarten students. The students' families are contacted and asked to complete a questionnaire describing the kinds of discipline they use and how often they discipline their children.

b. The researcher contacts the local schools to obtain a sample of newly registered kindergarten students. The students' families are contacted and asked to complete a questionnaire describing the kinds of discipline they use and how often they discipline their children. Every 3 years, the researcher returns to the families and asks them to complete the questionnaire again.

## Strengths and Weaknesses of the Longitudinal Design

Because the typical longitudinal design involves observing a single group of individuals over an extended period, we focus our discussion of strengths and weaknesses on this type of design. In this context, a major strength of the longitudinal research design is the absence of cohort effects, because the researcher examines one group of people over time rather than comparing groups of different ages. Second, with longitudinal research, a researcher can discuss how a single individual's behavior changes with age. However, longitudinal research is extremely time consuming both for the participants (it requires a big commitment to continue in the study) and the researchers (the researcher must stay interested in the research for years and wait for years to see the final results). In addition, these designs are very expensive to conduct because researchers need to track people down and persuade them, when necessary, to come back to participate in the study. If the study spans many years, there is the additional expense of repeatedly training experimenters to conduct the study. Further, these designs are subject to high dropout rates of participants. People lose interest in the study, move away, and die. When participants drop out of a study, it is known as **participant attrition** (or participant mortality), and it may weaken the internal validity of the research. Specifically, if the participants who drop out are systematically different from those who stay, the group at the end of the study may have different characteristics from the group at the beginning. For example, if the less motivated individuals drop out, then the group at the end will be more motivated than the group at the beginning. The higher level of motivation (rather than age) may explain any changes that are observed over time. (The issue of participant attrition is discussed in more detail in Chapter 11.) A final weakness of the longitudinal research design is that the same individuals are measured repeatedly. It is possible that the scores obtained late in the study are partially affected by the participants' having been exposed to the test. (In Chapter 6 we discussed practice effects and fatigue and their effects on internal validity.)

Table 9.1 summarizes the strengths and weaknesses of each of the developmental research designs.

TABLE 9.1

**Strengths and Weaknesses of Cross-Sectional and Longitudinal Developmental Research Designs**

|  | Longitudinal Research | Cross-Sectional Research |
| --- | --- | --- |
| Strengths | • No cohort or generation effects<br>• Assesses individual behavior changes | • Time efficient<br>• No long-term cooperation required |
| Weaknesses | • Time consuming<br>• Participant dropout may create bias<br>• Potential for practice effects | • Individual changes not assessed<br>• Cohort or generation effects |

Learning Check

Describe the strengths and weaknesses of the longitudinal research design.

## 9.6 TERMINOLOGY IN QUASI-EXPERIMENTAL AND DEVELOPMENTAL DESIGNS

In a true experiment, the researcher manipulates an independent variable to create treatment conditions and then measures a dependent variable (scores) in each condition; scores in one condition are compared with the scores obtained in another condition. In quasi-experimental research, no independent variable is manipulated. Nonetheless, quasi-experimental studies do involve comparing groups of scores. In nonequivalent group studies, for example, the scores from one group of participants are compared with the scores from a different group. In time-series studies, the scores obtained before the treatment are compared with the scores obtained after the treatment. In general, the variable that differentiates the groups (or sets of scores) is similar to the independent variable in an experiment and is called a **quasi-independent variable.** As in an experiment, the score obtained for each participant is called the **dependent variable.**

Definitions

Within the context of quasi-experimental research, the variable that is used to differentiate the groups of participants or the groups of scores being compared is called the **quasi-independent variable,** and the variable that is measured to obtain a score for each individual is called the **dependent variable.**

In nonequivalent control group studies, for example, one group receives the treatment and one does not. The group difference, treatment versus no-treatment, determines the quasi-independent variable. In time-series studies the researcher compares one set of observations (scores) before treatment with a second set of observations after treatment. For these studies, the quasi-independent variable is defined as "before versus after treatment."

This same terminology is often extended to research studies that are not officially classified as quasi-experimental. In differential research, for example, the participant variable used to differentiate the groups is called the quasi-independent variable. In a differential study comparing self-esteem scores for children from two-parent and single-parent homes, the number of parents is the quasi-independent variable, and self-esteem is the dependent variable. In a developmental study (either longitudinal or cross-sectional) examining changes in memory that occur with aging, the participants' ages are the quasi-independent variable, and the memory scores are the dependent variable.

Learning Check

Suppose that a researcher compares personality scores for people who were successful in a diet program with the scores for people who were not successful. Identify the quasi-independent variable and the dependent variable for this study.

## CHAPTER SUMMARY

In many research situations it is difficult or impossible for a researcher to satisfy completely the rigorous requirements of an experiment, particularly applied research in natural settings. In these situations a researcher may use the quasi-experimental research strategy, the goal of which is to show a causal relationship between two variables. Quasi-experimental studies often look like experiments in terms of the general structure of the study, for example, comparing groups of scores. However, quasi-experimental designs usually contain a confounding variable that is integral to the design and cannot be removed. The different groups or conditions are not created by manipulating an independent variable; instead, the groups are usually defined in terms of a pre-existing participant variable (for example, male/female) or defined in terms of time (for example, before and after treatment). These two methods for defining groups produce two general categories of quasi-experimental designs: nonequivalent group designs and time-series designs.

In nonequivalent group designs the researcher does not control the assignment of individuals to groups because the two groups already exist. Therefore, there is no assurance that the two groups are equivalent in terms of extraneous and therefore potentially confounding variables. Three types of nonequivalent group designs are discussed: (1) the differential research design, (2) the posttest–only nonequivalent control group design,

and (3) the pretest–posttest nonequivalent control group design.

The second general category is the time-series design. The goal of a time-series design is to evaluate the influence of the intervening treatment or event by comparing the observations before treatment with the observations made after treatment. Four examples of time-series designs are considered: (1) the one-group pretest–posttest design, (2) the time-series design, (3) the interrupted time-series design, and (4) the equivalent time-samples design.

The developmental research strategy is another type of nonexperimental (quasi-experimental) research. The purpose of the developmental strategy is to describe the relationship between age and other variables. There are two types of developmental research designs. In the cross-sectional research design groups of individuals are compared where each group represents a different age. The obvious advantage of this design is that the researcher need not wait for participants to age to examine the relationship between a variable and age. However, the cohort or generation effect is a major weakness. In the longitudinal research design the same group of individuals is followed and measured at different points in time; hence cohort effects are not a problem. However, longitudinal research is extremely time consuming for participants and researchers, and participant dropout may create a biased sample.

## KEY WORDS

quasi-experimental research
  strategy
nonequivalent group design
differential research design
nonequivalent control group
  design
posttest-only nonequivalent
  control group design or static
  group comparison

pretest–posttest nonequivalent
  control group design
one-group pretest–posttest
  design
time-series design
interrupted time-series design
equivalent time-samples design

developmental research strategy
cross-sectional research design
cohort
cohort effect or generation effect
longitudinal research design
quasi-independent variable
dependent variable

## EXERCISES

1. In addition to the key words, you should also be able to define the following terms:
   assignment bias
   nonexperimental designs
   history effects
   instrumentation
   practice effects
   fatigue
   maturation
   regression toward the mean
   differential history effects
   differential instrumentation
   differential practice/fatigue
   differential maturation
   differential regression
   participant attrition

2. Experimental studies and quasi-experimental studies are similar because they both compare groups of scores. Describe the major difference between the experimental and quasi-experimental research strategy.

3. Give an example of a situation (aside from gender) in which a researcher must examine *pre-existing groups*.

4. Describe the two basic problems that threaten internal validity for nonequivalent group designs.

5. Describe the two basic categories of quasi-experimental designs.

6. Describe the major difference between the simple and interrupted time-series designs.

7. How can history threaten the internal validity of a time-series design?

8. What is the purpose of developmental research designs?

9. Describe each of the types of developmental research designs.

10. For each of the following research goals, identify which quasi-experimental research design is most appropriate.
    a. Describe how infants' fine-motor skills change between 12 months and 18 months of age.
    b. Describe the relationship between alcohol consumption and grade point average for college students.
    c. Describe possible gender differences between social interactions among a group of preschool children while they play in a city park.
    d. Describe the effectiveness on high school students of a new teaching program for reading.

## InfoTrac COLLEGE EDITION EXERCISES

1. Use InfoTrac College Edition to find a quasi-experimental research study. (Note: Try using specific terms such as *quasi-experimental* or *time series* or *nonequivalent control group* as key terms. Or look for a topic that involves comparing different populations of participants. For example, using *gender differences* as a key word should lead you to studies comparing males and females.). Once you have located an article, answer each of the following:
   a. Describe the structure of the research study. (For example, what variables are measured? How many groups are involved?

   Are the participants measured several times or only once?)
   b. Does your study fit into one of the general categories of quasi-experimental research discussed in this chapter? If so, which one? (Warning: You may find that your study is much more complex than the examples discussed in the text. In this case, it may be that a simple quasi-experimental study is one small part of a more complicated design. If you have a complex design, try to identify the part of the study that corresponds to a quasi-experimental design.)

c. Identify one factor in the study that prevents the study from being a true experiment. That is, why can't the researchers say that changes in one variable are unquestionably responsible for changes in another variable?

2. Use InfoTrac College Edition to find a developmental research study. (Again, you can try key words such as *longitudinal* or search subject areas such as *human development* or *aging*.) Once you have located an article, answer each of the following:

   a. Describe the structure of the research study. (For example, what variables are measured? How many groups are involved? Are the participants measured several times or only once?)

   b. Does your study qualify as a cross-sectional design or a longitudinal design? If so, which one? (Warning: You may find that your study is much more complex than the examples discussed in the text. In this case, it may be that a simple cross-sectional or longitudinal design is one small part of a more complicated study. See if you can identify the part of the study that corresponds to a simple developmental design.)

   c. Identify one factor in the study that prevents the study from being a true experiment. That is, why can't the researchers say that changes in one variable are unquestionably responsible for changes in another variable?

# Experimental Designs: Between-Subjects Design

## CHAPTER OVERVIEW

Step 6 of the research process involves selecting a research design. In this chapter we discuss in detail one type of experimental research design—the between-subjects design. The advantages, disadvantages, and different versions of between-subjects designs are considered.

## 10.1   INTRODUCTION

### REVIEW OF EXPERIMENTAL RESEARCH STRATEGY

In Chapter 6 we identified four basic strategies: descriptive, correlational, experimental, and quasi-experimental. In Chapter 8 we discussed the experimental research strategy in detail, as well as its major goal, demonstration of cause-and-effect relationships between two variables. The two basic characteristics of the experimental research strategy are (1) manipulation of one variable while a second is measured, and (2) control of extraneous variables. Thus, in an experiment the independent variable is manipulated by the researcher, the dependent variable is measured for changes, and all other variables are controlled to prevent them from influencing the results.

A common strategy in behavioral research for investigating causal relationships between two variables is to compare different groups of scores. A researcher may compare mathematics achievement scores for students taught by one method with scores for students taught by a different method. Another researcher may measure the activity level for a group of rats and compare the scores obtained under different temperature conditions. By showing that there are consistent differences between the groups of scores, a researcher can demonstrate that one teaching method is better than another (i.e., teaching methods cause differences in mathematics achievement scores) or that rats really do slow down as temperature goes up (i.e., changing temperature causes changes in activity). Two basic research designs are used to obtain the groups of scores:

1. The different groups of scores are all obtained from the same sample of participants. For example, one sample of individuals is given a memory test using a list of one-syllable words, and then the same set of individuals is tested again using a list of two-syllable words. Thus, the researcher gets two sets of scores, both obtained from the same sample. This strategy is called a **within-subjects design** and is discussed in Chapter 11.

2. An alternative strategy is to obtain each of the different groups of scores from a separate group of participants. For example, one group of students is assigned to teaching method A and a separate group to method B. This type of design, comparing scores from separate groups, is called a **between-subjects design.** We examine the characteristics of a between-subjects research design in this chapter.

### CHARACTERISTICS OF BETWEEN-SUBJECTS DESIGNS

The defining characteristic of a between-subjects design is that it compares separate groups of individuals. In the context of an experiment, a researcher manipulates the independent variable to create different treatment conditions. A separate group of participants is assigned to each of the different conditions using an assignment procedure that attempts to produce equivalent groups. The dependent variable is then measured for each individual, and the researcher examines the data, looking for differences between the groups (see Figure 10.1).

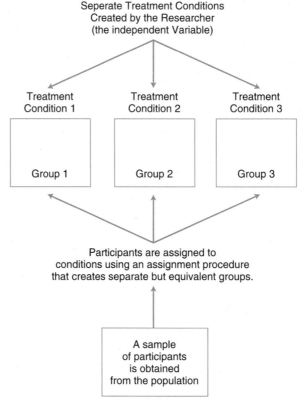

Figure 10.1   The Structure of a Between-Subjects Experiment
The key element is that separate but equivalent groups of
participants are used for the different treatment conditions.

This chapter focuses on the between-subjects design as it is used in experimental research. However, between-subjects designs are commonly used for other types of research as well, where the goal is also to compare different groups of individuals. In Chapter 9, for example, we introduced several research designs that compare nonequivalent groups, including the cross-sectional developmental design that is used to compare people of different ages. See Box 10.1 for more information about the terminology used to describe different research designs.

One characteristic of between-subjects designs deserves special mention: A between-subjects design allows only one score per participant. Every individual score represents a separate, unique participant. If a between-subjects experiment produces 30 scores in treatment A and 30 scores in treatment B, then the experiment must have employed a group of 30 individuals in treatment A and a separate group of 30 individuals in treatment B. Occasionally a researcher may combine several measurements for each individual into a single score. In particular, when the variable being measured is not particularly stable (for example, reaction time), a researcher may choose to measure the variable several times and average the measurements to produce a single, more reliable score. However, the net result is always one score per individual participant. Because each

In 1994, the fourth edition of *The Publication Manual of the American Psychological Association* recommended that humans who participate in a research study be called *participants* and that nonhumans be called *subjects*. Prior to 1994, the term *subject* was used for all individuals, human and nonhuman, who participated in research. This change in terminology has created some confusion for those of us who write and talk about research. In particular, there are many well-established terms that use the word *subjects*. In this chapter we introduce *between-subjects* designs—a good example of the confusion. A between-subjects design uses separate groups of individuals and therefore looks for differences between groups of subjects (or participants); hence the term *between-subjects design*. We have elected to continue with the established terminology rather than create unfamiliar terms such as *between-participants designs*. Perhaps the terminology issues will resolve themselves in a few years, but for now please remember that the term *subjects* simply refers to the individuals who participate (are treated, observed, and measured) in a research study.

score represents a separate participant, a between-subjects design is often called an **independent-measures design**.

A **between-subjects experimental design** requires a separate, independent group of individuals for each treatment condition compared. Individuals are assigned to groups using a procedure that attempts to create equivalent groups. Additionally, the data for a between-subjects design allow only one score for each individual participant.

The general goal of a between-subjects experiment is to determine whether differences exist between two or more treatment conditions. For example, a researcher may want to compare two teaching methods (two treatments) to determine whether one is more effective than the other. In this case, two separate groups of individuals would be used, one for each of the two teaching methods.

Identify the basic features of a between-subjects research design.

Learning Check

## ADVANTAGES AND DISADVANTAGES OF BETWEEN-SUBJECTS DESIGNS

A main advantage of a between-subjects design is that each individual score is independent of the other scores. Because each participant is measured only once, the researcher can be reasonably confident that the resulting measurement is relatively clean or uncontaminated by other treatment factors. In an experiment comparing performance under different temperature conditions, for example, each participant is exposed to only one treatment condition. Thus, the participant's score is not influenced by such factors as:

- Practice or experience gained in other treatments
- Fatigue or boredom from participating in a series of different treatments
- Contrast effects that result from comparing one treatment to another (A 60-degree room might feel cold after a 70-degree room, but the same 60-degree room might feel warm after 50 degrees.)

Between-subjects designs can be used for a wide variety of research questions. To compare two (or more) treatment conditions, different groups can always be assigned to the different conditions; thus, a between-subjects design is always possible. It may not always be the best choice, but it is always an option.

One disadvantage of between-subjects designs is that they require a relatively large number of participants. Remember, each participant contributes only one score to the final data. To compare three different treatment conditions with 30 scores in each treatment, the between-subjects design requires 90 participants. This can be a problem for research involving special populations in which the number of potential participants is relatively small. For example, a researcher studying preschool children with a specific learning disability might have trouble finding a large number of individuals to participate.

### Individual Differences

The primary disadvantage of a between-subjects design stems from the fact that each score is obtained from a unique individual who has different personal characteristics from all of the other participants. Consider the following descriptions of two individuals participating in the same research study:

**John**

John is an 21-year-old White male. He is 5' 10" tall, weighs 180 pounds, and has blue eyes, blonde hair, and an IQ of 110. He comes from a middle-class family with one older sister. John is a chemistry major and was awake until 2 a.m. this morning after celebrating his success on a chemistry exam. He comes to the experiment with only 4 hours of sleep, suffering from a mild hangover.

**Mary**

Mary is a 20-year-old Black female. She is 5' 3" tall and has brown eyes, black hair, and an IQ of 142. Her mother and father are both doctors, and she is an only child. Mary is a history major with a minor in psychology. She had a head cold yesterday and went to bed at 8 p.m. She arrived at the experiment well rested and feeling much better. However, she skipped breakfast and is hungry.

Clearly, these two individuals differ on a variety of dimensions. It should also be clear that we have identified only a few of the countless variables that differentiate the two people. Differences (such as gender, age, personality, and family background) that exist between participants at the beginning of an experiment are called **pre-existing individual differences** or simply **individual differences.**

Definition

Characteristics that differ from one participant to another are called **individual differences.**

Occasionally research is designed with the intention of examining a specific individual difference; for example, a study may be designed to compare behavior or attitudes for males and females. (This type of research was discussed in Chapter 9.) Most of the time, however, individual differences are simply extraneous variables that are not directly addressed in the research design. For a between-subjects design, individual differences are a particular concern, and can create serious problems. The two major concerns are:

1. Individual differences can become confounding variables (see Chapter 6). Suppose that a researcher finds that the participants in treatment A have higher scores than the participants in treatment B. The researcher would like to conclude that the higher scores were caused by the treatment. However, individual differences between groups may have produced the difference in the scores. For example, perhaps the participants in treatment A are generally older than the participants in treatment B. In this case, it may be that pre-existing age differences, rather than the treatments, are responsible for the higher scores.

2. Individual differences can produce high variability in the scores, making it difficult to determine whether or not the treatment has any effect. The unpredictable variability caused by individual differences can obscure patterns in the data and cloud a study's results.

The problems of confounding variables and high variability are discussed in detail in the following sections. However, one more look at our two hypothetical participants, John and Mary, may further illustrate the problems that individual differences can cause. Suppose John is assigned to treatment A, where he produces a score of 45. Mary is assigned to treatment B, and her score is 51. The researcher has found a 6-point difference between the two scores. The researcher must determine what caused the 6-point difference. Is the 6-point difference in scores caused by the different treatment conditions? By pre-existing individual differences? Partially due to treatment differences and partially due to individual differences?

---

In a between-subjects design each individual score is obtained from a separate participant.

Learning Check

a. Briefly explain why this is an advantage.
b. Briefly explain why this is a disadvantage.

---

## 10.2  INDIVIDUAL DIFFERENCES AS CONFOUNDING VARIABLES

In a between-subjects design, each level of the independent variable (each treatment condition) is represented by a separate group of participants. The primary concern is to ensure that the different groups are as similar as possible, except for the independent variable used to differentiate the groups. Any extraneous variable that systematically differentiates the groups is a confounding variable. For example, in a between-subjects experiment comparing two treatments (A and B), one group of participants would be assigned to treatment A and a separate group to treatment B. If the participants in one group are generally older (or smarter, or taller, or faster, etc.) than the participants in the other group, then the experiment has a confounding variable (see Figure 10.2). In this example, the two groups of participants are differentiated by:

1.  Treatment (A versus B)
2.  Age (one group is older than the other)

Now suppose the researcher measures the dependent variable for each individual and finds a difference between groups. It would be impossible to determine whether the obtained difference had been caused by the treatment or by the age difference. Because the experiment is confounded, it is impossible to draw any clear conclusions.

Although confounding variables present a threat to any research design, they pose a particular problem for between-subjects designs. In a between-subjects design, potential confounding variables fall into two categories:

1.  *Individual differences:* Individual differences are any participant characteristics that differ from one group to another. For example, the participants in one group may be older, smarter, taller, or have higher socio-economic status than the participants in another group. One group may have a higher proportion of males or a higher proportion of divorced individuals than another group. Any of these variables may produce differences between groups that can compromise the research results.

2.  *Environmental variables:* These are any characteristics of the environment that differ between groups. For example, one group may be tested in a large room and another group in a smaller room. Or one group may be measured

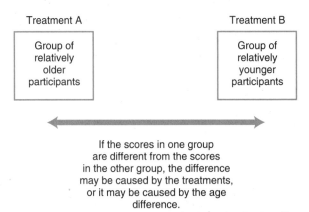

Figure 10.2    An Experiment in Which Individual Difference (Participant Age) Is a Confounding Variable

primarily during the morning and another group during the afternoon. Any such variable may cause differences between groups that cannot be attributed to the independent variable.

## EQUIVALENT GROUPS

In Chapter 9 we examined several research designs that use nonequivalent groups of participants. The defining characteristic of these designs is that the researcher has no control over the assignment of individuals to groups. This lack of control creates a confounded variable and prevents these studies from being true experiments. Specifically, if a researcher finds a difference between groups at the end of the study, there are two possible explanations:

1.  The difference between groups may have been caused by the different treatments administered to the groups.

2.  The groups may simply have been different at the beginning of the study before any treatments were introduced. The researcher did not control the formation of the groups and has no assurance that they were ever equivalent.

But with a between-subjects experimental design, the researcher does have control over the assignment of individuals to groups. With this design a researcher has both the ability and the responsibility to create groups that are equivalent. The separate groups must be:

1.  *Created equally:* The process used to obtain participants should be as similar as possible for all of the groups.

2.  *Treated equally:* Except for the treatment conditions that are deliberately varied between groups, the groups of participants should receive exactly the same experiences.

3.  *Composed of equivalent individuals:* The characteristics of the participants in any one group should be as similar as possible to the characteristics of the participants in every other group.

The techniques available for establishing equivalent groups of participants are discussed in the following section.

---

Briefly explain how a participant characteristic such as personality could be a confounding variable in a between-subjects experiment.

Learning Check

---

## 10.3 LIMITING CONFOUNDING BY INDIVIDUAL DIFFERENCES

The first step in conducting a between-subjects research study is to establish the separate groups of participants to be compared. In a between-subjects experiment, each group of participants is assigned to a specific treatment condition representing one value (i.e., one level) of the independent variable. The goal of this research is to identify differences in the dependent variable between groups and to demonstrate that the observed differences are caused by the different treatments. If the differences in the dependent variable between groups can be attributed to any other factor, the research is confounded, and the results cannot be interpreted without some ambiguity. Therefore, the initial groups must be as similar as possible. To accomplish this, researchers typically use one of the following three procedures to set up groups for a between-subjects study. The three procedures are the same methods that were identified for controlling potentially confounding variables in an experiment (Chapter 8).

## RANDOM ASSIGNMENT (RANDOMIZATION)

Probably the commonest method of establishing groups of participants is random assignment. Recall from Chapter 8 that the term *random assignment* simply means that a random process (such as a coin toss) is used to assign participants to groups. The goal is to ensure that all individuals have the same chance of being assigned to a group. Because group assignment is based on a random process, it is reasonable to expect that characteristics such as age, IQ, and gender will also be distributed randomly across groups. Thus, we minimize the potential for confounding because it is unlikely that any group will be systematically older, or smarter, or more feminine than another.

For an experiment comparing different treatment conditions, researchers typically use a specified sampling method (see Chapter 5) to obtain a large sample of participants. Then, random assignment is used to divide the sample into smaller, separate groups for each of the treatments. As with random selection, some simple random process (e.g., a coin toss) is used to determine the group assignment for each participant. Suppose a researcher wants to separate 90 individuals into three separate groups. The numbers 1, 2, and 3 could be written on separate slips of paper and placed in a hat. Drawing one slip of paper for each participant would determine the group assignment for that participant.

It should be obvious that a simple random process such as a coin toss or drawing numbers out of a hat is likely to create groups of different sizes. If it is desirable to have all groups the same size (equal $n$'s), the process can be modified to guarantee equal-size groups. To divide 90 participants into three equal groups, for example, the researcher could start with 90 slips of paper, 30 with #1, 30 with #2, and 30 with #3, and then draw one slip for each individual to determine the group assignment. In this case, the process is a **restricted random assignment;** the restriction is that the groups must be equal in size.

---

Definition    In **restricted random assignment,** the group assignment process is limited to ensure predetermined characteristics (such as equal size) for the separate groups.

---

The advantage of using a random process to establish groups is that it is fair and unbiased. Just as football teams use a coin toss to determine who receives the opening kickoff, random assignment eliminates prejudice from the decision process. However, random processes do not guarantee perfectly balanced outcomes. When tossing a coin, for example, we can expect an equal, 50-50, distribution of heads and tails *in the long run* (with a large sample). However, in the short run (with a small sample), there are no guarantees. A sample of only $n = 10$ tosses, for example, can easily contain 8 or 9 heads and only 1 or 2 tails. With any random process we trust chance to create a balanced outcome. In the long run chance will prove to be fair, but in the short run *anything* can happen by chance. Because pure chance is not a dependable process for obtaining balanced and equivalent groups, researchers often modify random processes by placing some limitations on or exerting some control over the outcomes. One such modification, restriction of equal group sizes, has been discussed; two additional techniques follow.

Learning Check

Briefly explain how random assignment attempts to keep participant characteristics, such as age or gender, from becoming confounding variables in a between-subjects experiment.

## MATCHING GROUPS (MATCHED ASSIGNMENT)

In many situations a researcher can identify a few specific variables that are likely to influence the participants' scores. In a learning experiment, for example, it is reasonable to expect that intelligence is a variable that can influence learning performance. In this case, it is important that the researcher not allow intelligence to become a confounding variable by allowing one group of participants to be noticeably more intelligent than another group. In this situation, a researcher can use **matching** to ensure that the different groups of participants are equivalent (or nearly equivalent) with respect to intelligence.

For example, a researcher comparing two different methods for teaching 5th-grade math wants to be sure that the two groups of participants are roughly equivalent in terms of IQ. School records are used to determine the IQs of the participants, and each student is classified as high IQ, medium IQ, or low IQ. The high-IQ participants are distributed equally between the two groups; one-half assigned to one group and one-half assigned to the second group. The medium-IQ participants and the low-IQ participants are likewise evenly distributed between the two groups. The result is two separate groups of participants with roughly the same level of intelligence on average.

A similar matching process can be used to equate groups in terms of proportions. If a sample consists of 60% males and 40% females, restricted random assignment could be used to distribute the males equally among the different groups. The same process is then used to distribute the females equally among the groups. The result is that the groups are matched in terms of gender, with each group containing exactly 60% males and 40% females.

Notice that the matching process requires three steps:

1. Identification of the variable (or variables) to be matched across groups
2. Measurement of the matching variable for each participant
3. Assignment of participants to groups by means of a restricted random assignment that ensures a balance between groups

Definition

**Matching** involves assigning individuals to groups so that a specific variable is balanced or matched across the groups. The intent is to create groups that are equivalent (or nearly equivalent) with respect to the variable matched.

This section and Chapter 8 discuss methods of creating matched groups—that is, constructing groups so that, overall, one group of participants is equivalent to another group. Chapter 11 discusses an alternative matching process in which each participant in one group is matched one-to-one with an "equivalent" participant in another group. The process of matching individuals is called *matching subjects* (as opposed to matching groups). **Matched-subjects designs** are discussed in Chapter 11.

Matching groups of participants provides researchers with a relatively easy way to ensure that specific variables do not become confounding variables. However, there is a price to pay for matching, and there are limitations that restrict the usefulness of this process. In order to match groups with respect to a specific variable, the researcher first must measure the variable. The measurement procedure can be tedious or costly and always adds another level of work to the study. In addition, it can be difficult or impossible to match groups on several different variables simultaneously. To match groups in terms of intelligence, and age, and gender could require some fairly sophisticated juggling to achieve the desired balance of all three variables. Finally, groups cannot be matched on every single variable that might differentiate participants. Therefore, researchers typically use matching only for variables that are judged to have strong potential for confounding. In a learning experiment, for example, intelligence is a variable that is likely to affect learning performance, but eye color is a variable that probably has little to do with learning. In this case, it would make sense to match groups for intelligence but not for eye color.

## HOLDING VARIABLES CONSTANT OR RESTRICTING RANGE OF VARIABILITY

Another method for preventing individual differences from becoming confounding variables is simply to hold the variable constant. For example, if a researcher suspects that gender differences between groups might confound a research study, one solution is to eliminate gender as a variable. By using only female participants, a researcher can guarantee that all of the groups in a study are equivalent with respect to gender; all groups are all female.

An alternative to holding a variable completely constant is to restrict its range of variation. For example, a researcher concerned about potential IQ differences between groups could restrict participants to those with IQs between 100 and 110. Because all groups have the same narrow range of IQs, it is reasonable to expect that all groups would be roughly equivalent in terms of IQ.

Although holding a variable constant (or restricting its range) can be an effective way to prevent the variable from confounding a research study, this method has a serious drawback. Whenever a variable is prevented from reaching its natural range of variation, the external validity of the research is limited. A research study that uses only females, for example, cannot be generalized to the entire population of males *and* females. Similarly, results obtained for participants within a narrow range of IQ cannot be generalized to the whole population. As we noted in Chapter 6, the process of exercising control within a research study can threaten the external validity or generalizability of the results.

## SUMMARY AND RECOMMENDATIONS

Individual differences (or group differences) are always a potential source of confounding variables in a between-subjects design. Therefore, it is important for researchers to create groups of participants that are as equivalent as possible at the beginning of a research study. Most of the time researchers attempt to create equivalent groups by using random assignment, because it is relatively easy and does not require any measurement or direct control of extraneous variables. The number of variables (individual differences) that could produce differences between groups is essentially infinite, and random assignment provides a simple method of balancing them across groups without addressing each individual variable. However, random assignment is not perfect and cannot guarantee equivalent groups, especially when a small sample is used. Pure chance is not a dependable process for obtaining balanced equivalent groups.

When one or two specific variables can be identified as likely to influence the dependent variable, these variables can be controlled either by matching groups with respect to the variable(s) or by holding the variable constant. However, matching requires pretesting to measure the variable(s) being controlled, and it can become difficult to match several variables simultaneously; holding a variable constant guarantees that the variable cannot confound the research, but this process limits the external validity of the research results.

Briefly explain how holding a variable constant attempts to keep participant characteristics from becoming confounding variables in a between-subjects experiment.

Learning Check

## 10.4    INDIVIDUAL DIFFERENCES AND VARIABILITY

In addition to becoming confounding variables, individual differences have the potential to produce high variability in the scores within a research study. As we noted earlier, high variability can obscure any treatment effects that may exist and therefore can undermine the purpose of the study (i.e., threaten or limit internal validity). To demonstrate this phenomenon, we present a hypothetical research study that uses two distinct populations, one in which the individual differences are relatively small and one in which the individual differences are large. The two populations are shown in Table 10.1. In the table, each number represents the response for a single individual. Notice that in population A the numbers are all very similar, indicating that the individual differences (the differences from one person to another) are relatively small. In population B the differences among the numbers are large, indicating large individual differences.

Our hypothetical research study proceeds as follows:

1.  We select a random sample of 20 individuals (numbers) from population A and randomly divide the sample into two groups with 10 in each group.

2.  One group is then assigned to a control condition that has no effect whatsoever on the participants' scores. The second group is assigned to a treatment that increases each participant's score by 8 points. To simulate this treatment effect, we simply add 8 points to the original score for each individual.

The results of this hypothetical research study are shown as a table and as a graph in Figure 10.3. From either the numbers in the table or the piles of scores

### TABLE 10.1

**Two Simulated Populations**

In population A the individual differences are relatively small, and in population B the individual differences are relatively large.

| | | Population A | | | | | | Population B | | |
|---|---|---|---|---|---|---|---|---|---|---|
| 42 | 39 | 41 | 39 | 39 | | 30 | 40 | 20 | 20 | 20 |
| 41 | 38 | 41 | 41 | 38 | | 20 | 30 | 50 | 60 | 40 |
| 40 | 38 | 38 | 40 | 40 | | 40 | 60 | 60 | 50 | 60 |
| 42 | 39 | 38 | 41 | 42 | | 40 | 30 | 30 | 40 | 60 |
| 42 | 42 | 40 | 38 | 39 | | 30 | 50 | 50 | 50 | 20 |
| 38 | 41 | 40 | 39 | 38 | | 50 | 30 | 60 | 20 | 20 |
| 38 | 42 | 41 | 42 | 39 | | 30 | 50 | 40 | 50 | 20 |
| 41 | 38 | 42 | 39 | 42 | | 40 | 20 | 60 | 60 | 60 |
| 40 | 39 | 41 | 40 | 40 | | 60 | 40 | 30 | 20 | 40 |
| 41 | 40 | 40 | 42 | 39 | | 50 | 30 | 30 | 40 | 50 |

in the graph it is easy to see the 8-point difference between the two conditions. Remember, in population A the individual differences are small, which means that the variability of the scores is small. When variability within each group is small, treatment effects tend to show up clearly.

Next, we repeat the study using participants (numbers) selected from population B. The results of this simulation are shown in Figure 10.4. This time, it is very difficult to see any difference between the two conditions. With the large individual differences in population B, the variability is high, and the 8-point treatment effect is completely obscured.

It may be helpful to think of variability within each group as analogous to the background noise or static on a radio. When there is a lot of background noise, it is difficult to get a clear signal. Similarly, when a research study has a lot of variability, it is difficult to see a real treatment effect. In between-subjects research, much of the variability is caused by individual differences. Remember, each individual score represents a different individual. Whenever there are large differences between individuals, there will be large variability.

## DIFFERENCES BETWEEN TREATMENTS AND VARIABILITY WITHIN TREATMENTS

In general, the goal of a between-subjects research study is to establish the existence of a treatment effect by demonstrating that the scores obtained in one treatment condition are significantly different (higher or lower) than the scores in another treatment condition. For example, if we can demonstrate that people in a bright yellow room are consistently happier and have more positive moods than people in a dark brown room, then we have reason to conclude that room color (the treatment) has an effect on mood. Thus, big differences *between* treatments

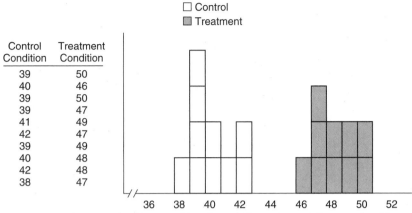

| Control<br>Condition | Treatment<br>Condition |
|:---:|:---:|
| 39 | 50 |
| 40 | 46 |
| 39 | 50 |
| 39 | 47 |
| 41 | 49 |
| 42 | 47 |
| 39 | 49 |
| 40 | 48 |
| 42 | 48 |
| 38 | 47 |

Figure 10.3   Results From a Simulated Experiment Comparing Two
Conditions Using Participants Selected from a Population Where
Individual Differences Are Relatively Small
When the individual differences are small, the variability
is also small, and it is easy to see the 8-point treatment effect.

are good because they provide evidence of differential treatment effects. On the other hand, big differences *within* treatments are bad. Differences that exist inside the treatment conditions determine the variability of the scores and, as we demonstrated in Figure 10.4, large variability can obscure patterns in the data.

Notice that we are distinguishing differences *between treatments* and variability (differences) *within treatments*. Researchers typically try to increase the differences between treatments and to decrease the variability within treatments. For example, if we were examining the effects of room color on mood, it would not be wise to compare two rooms that were slightly different shades of green. With only a subtle difference between the two colors, we would be unlikely to find a noticeable difference in mood. Instead, the best strategy would be to maximize the difference between room colors to increase our chances of finding a large difference in mood between treatments. Again, the goal is to increase the difference between treatments. At the same time, however, we would like to decrease the variability within treatments. In the following section we examine some of the methods that can be used to reduce or minimize the variability within treatments. In addition, we consider some of the design decisions that a researcher must make when developing a between-subjects research study and look at how those decisions affect variability within treatments.

## MINIMIZING VARIABILITY WITHIN TREATMENTS

As we have noted, large individual differences can lead to large variability within treatment conditions, which can undermine the potential success of a between-subjects research study. Therefore, researchers are well advised to take whatever steps are possible to reduce the variability inside each of the treatment conditions. The following options provide some ways to accomplish this.

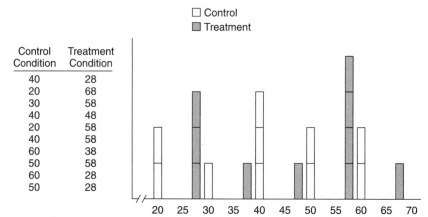

| Control<br>Condition | Treatment<br>Condition |
|:---:|:---:|
| 40 | 28 |
| 20 | 68 |
| 30 | 58 |
| 40 | 48 |
| 20 | 58 |
| 40 | 58 |
| 60 | 38 |
| 50 | 58 |
| 60 | 28 |
| 50 | 28 |

Figure 10.4    Results From a Simulated Experiment Comparing
Two Conditions using Participants Selected From a Population
Where Individual Differences are Relatively Large
When the individual differences are large, the variability is also
large, and it is not at all easy to see the 8-point treatment effect.

### Standardize Procedures and Treatment Setting

In a between-subjects design each group of participants represents a single treatment condition. One obvious way to help minimize the variability within a group is to be sure that all participants within a group are treated exactly the same. Although existing individual differences are not reduced, at least care is taken not to *increase* them. Thus, researchers should avoid making any changes in the treatment setting or the procedures that are used from one individual to another. Whenever two individuals are treated differently, there is a chance that differences between their scores will be increased, thus increasing the variability within the group. In general, when two participants are in the same group (the same treatment condition), a researcher should not do anything that might cause their scores to be different.

### Limit Individual Differences

In Section 10.3 we suggested that holding a participant variable constant or restricting its range could be used as effective techniques for limiting the differences between groups of participants (see page 250). This technique also reduces the variability within a group of participants. If it is known, for example, that gender is a variable related to the participants' scores (e.g., females tend to have higher scores than males), then a mixed group of males and females will have higher variability than a group consisting of only males. In the mixed group the gender differences (male versus female) will contribute to the variability within the group. By holding gender constant (males only), gender differences are eliminated and variability within the group is reduced.

In the same way, restricting a participant variable to a narrow range of values eliminates much of the variability in scores that is caused by that variable.

For example, if the participants within a group are limited to those between the ages of 18 and 20, then age differences between participants contribute little to the variability of scores within the group. In general, any attempt to minimize the differences between participants within a group tends to reduce the variability within the group.

### Random Assignment and Matching

In Section 10.3 we also suggested that random assignment or matching groups could be used to help minimize differences between groups. However, these techniques do not affect the variability within groups. If we randomly assign males and females to each group, for example, then we can expect relatively little gender difference between groups, but we still have a mixture of males and females (gender differences) within groups. In the same way, matching groups so that each group has exactly 50% males does not eliminate or reduce the gender differences within each group.

### Sample Size

Although sample size does not affect individual differences or variability directly, using a large sample can help minimize the problems associated with high variability. Sample size exerts its influence in the statistical analyses such that some of the negative effects of high variability can be statistically overcome by use of a very large sample. However, this technique has limitations because the influence of sample size occurs in relation to the *square root* of the sample size. The square-root relationship means that it takes a dramatic increase in sample size to have a real effect. To reduce the effects of high variability by a factor of four, for example, the sample size must be increased by a factor of sixteen; a sample of 20 would need to be increased to a sample of 320. Usually it is much more efficient to control variability by either standardizing procedures or directly limiting individual differences.

## SUMMARY AND RECOMMENDATIONS

The best techniques for minimizing the negative consequences of high variability are to standardize treatments and to minimize individual differences between participants. Both of these techniques help eliminate factors that can cause differences between scores and thereby increase the variability within treatments. The technique of minimizing individual differences by holding a variable constant or restricting its range has two advantages:

1. It helps reduce differences between groups which reduces the threat of confounding variables.
2. It helps reduce the variability within groups, which makes treatment effects easier to see.

As we noted earlier, however, limiting individual differences has the serious disadvantage of limiting external validity. (An alternative method for reducing individual differences without threatening external validity is presented in Chapter 12 when we introduce factorial research designs.)

Learning
Check

Briefly explain why large variability within treatments is a problem in a between-subjects experiment.

## 10.5 OTHER THREATS TO INTERNAL VALIDITY OF BETWEEN-SUBJECTS DESIGNS

Remember that the goal of the between-subjects experimental design is to look for differences between groups on the dependent variable and to demonstrate that the observed differences are caused by the different treatments (i.e., by the manipulation of the independent variable). If the differences between the groups can be attributed to any additional factors, the research is confounded, and the results cannot be interpreted without some ambiguity. Also recall from Chapter 6 that any factor that allows for an alternative explanation for the research results is a threat to internal validity. In Chapter 6 we discussed some general threats that can undermine the internal validity of a study; now we consider the threats to internal validity that are specific to between-subjects designs and how to avoid or minimize each of these threats. In addition to individual differences and any characteristic of the environment that may differ between groups, there are six potential confounds for between-subjects designs; each is discussed in this section.

### ASSIGNMENT BIAS

Earlier in the chapter we introduced the idea that individual differences such as age, gender, IQ, or personality can mean that one group of participants differs from another group. If the groups of participants are different *before* the treatments are administered, then the research is confounded, and its internal validity is threatened. Specifically, any differences in the dependent variable that are found after the treatments may have been caused by the treatments or by the pre-existing group differences. **Assignment bias** (see Section 6.3) is the term used to describe situations where the group assignment process produces groups with noticeably different characteristics. To avoid or minimize this problem, the different groups of participants must be as similar as possible. Section 10.3 discussed the three procedures commonly used to establish equivalent groups of participants for a between-subjects study—random assignment, matched assignment, and holding variables constant.

### DIFFERENTIAL ATTRITION

The term *attrition* refers to participant withdrawal from a research study before it is completed. As long as the rate of attrition is fairly consistent from one group to another, it usually is not a threat to internal validity. However, big differences in attrition rates between groups can create problems. The different groups are initially created to be as similar as possible; if large numbers of individuals leave one group, the group may no longer be similar to the others. Again, whenever the groups of participants are noticeably different, the research is confounded.

**Differential attrition** refers to differences in attrition rates from one group to another and can threaten the internal validity of a between-subjects experiment.

For example, a researcher may want to test the effectiveness of a dieting program. Using a between-subjects design, the researcher forms two groups of participants with approximately equal characteristics (i.e., weight, gender, dieting history, etc.). Next, one group of participants is exposed to the 10-week dieting program, and the other group receives no treatment (this group, recall from Chapter 8, is the no-treatment control group). At the end of the 10 weeks the weights of the two groups are compared. During the course of the 10 weeks, however, it is likely that some participants will drop out of the study. If more participants drop out of one group than the other, then there is a risk that the two groups will no longer be similar. For example, maybe only the most motivated participants stay in the diet program. At the end of 10 weeks, the individuals who are left in the program will have a higher level of motivation than those in the control group. In this case, the difference in dropout rate between the groups may account for the obtained differences in mean weight. Differential attrition is a threat to internal validity because we do not know whether the obtained differences between treatment conditions are caused by the treatments or by differential attrition. Whenever participants drop out of a study, a researcher must be concerned about differential attrition as an alternative explanation for treatment effects.

## DIFFUSION OR IMITATION OF TREATMENT

In the course of an experiment, it is sometimes possible for the treatment given to one group of participants to be provided accidentally to all or some of the participants in the control group as well. **Diffusion** refers to the spread of the treatment effects from the experimental group to the control group. Therefore, rather than comparing a treatment condition with a no-treatment condition, the researcher actually compares conditions that are more similar than intended. The primary cause of diffusion is simply that participants talk to one another.

For example, a researcher may want to test the effectiveness of a new treatment for depression. Using a between-subjects design, the researcher randomly assigns half the clients of an in-patient facility to receive the new treatment and half to receive the standard treatment for depression. If the participants talk to each other, however, then those individuals receiving the old treatment may learn about the new treatment and may begin to use some elements from the new treatment. Thus, the difference between the two treatment conditions is reduced. Diffusion is a threat to the internal validity of a between-subjects design because it can mask or wipe out the true effects of the treatment (make it look like there is no difference between the groups on the dependent variable). The best way to minimize diffusion effects is to keep the groups of participants as separate from or unaware of one another as possible.

## COMPENSATORY EQUALIZATION

**Compensatory equalization** occurs when an untreated group learns about the treatment being received by another group and demands the same or equal treatment. For example, in comparing the effects of violent television viewing on boys in a residential facility, one team of researchers faced this problem: The boys in the nonviolent TV group learned that those in the violent TV group were allowed to watch the television series *Batman* and demanded the right to watch *Batman* too. This threat commonly occurs in medical and clinical studies when one group receives a treatment drug and another does not. A similar problem arises when researchers try to assess the effectiveness of large-scale educational enrichment programs (involving such improvements as computers in the classrooms). Parents and teachers of the classes or schools that do not receive the enrichment (the control group) hear about the special program other classes or schools (the experimental group) receive and demand that their children receive the same program or something equal in value. If the demand is met, the comparison is no longer between treatment and no-treatment but between treatment and same or equally good treatment instead. Compensatory equalization is a threat to the internal validity of a between-subjects design because it can wipe out the true effects of the treatment (make it look like there is no differences between the groups on the dependent variable). The best way to minimize this threat is to keep the groups of participants as separate from or unaware of one another as possible.

### COMPENSATORY RIVALRY

**Compensatory rivalry** occurs when an untreated group learns about the treatment received by another group and then works extra hard to show that they can perform just as well as the individuals receiving the special treatment. This threat is also called the *John Henry effect.* (John Henry was a folklore railroad worker who attempted to outperform a machine designed to take over his job.) Once again consider a research study evaluating the effectiveness of an enrichment program in a school. The teachers in the control classrooms that do not receive the enrichments (for example, computers) may become especially motivated to do well and to show that their students can do just as well as those who receive the special treatment. When this happens, the level of motivation triggered by compensatory rivalry has become a confounding variable. As a result, compensatory rivalry is a threat to the internal validity of a between-subjects design because it can wipe out the true effects of the treatment (make it look like there is no difference between the groups on the dependent variable). The best way to minimize this threat is to keep the groups of participants as separate from or unaware of one another as possible.

### RESENTFUL DEMORALIZATION

Resentful demoralization can be considered the opposite of compensatory rivalry. **Resentful demoralization** occurs when an untreated group learns about the treatment received by another group and is less productive and less motivated because they resent the expected superiority of the treated group. As a result, the treatment looks like it was effective. This threat commonly occurs in medical and clinical studies, where one group receives a treatment drug and another does not. Resentful demoralization is a threat to the internal validity of a between-subjects design because it can make it look like there is a difference between the groups on the dependent variable. As with the last four threats, the best way to minimize this threat is to separate the groups of participants as much as possible and keep them from being aware of one another.

Describe how each of the following factors threatens the internal validity of between-subjects designs: assignment bias, differential attrition, and diffusion.

## 10.6   APPLICATIONS AND STATISTICAL ANALYSES OF BETWEEN-SUBJECTS DESIGNS

### TWO-GROUP MEAN DIFFERENCE

The simplest version of a between-subjects design involves comparing only two groups of participants—the researcher manipulates one independent variable with only two levels. This design is often referred to as the **single-factor two-group design** or simply the **two-group design.** This type of design can be used to compare treatments or to evaluate the effect of one treatment by comparing a treatment group and a control group. When the measurements consist of numerical scores, typically a mean is computed for each group of participants, and then an independent-measures *t* test is used to determine whether there is a significant difference between the means (see Chapter 14).

The primary advantage of a two-group design is its simplicity. It is easy to set up a two-group study, and there is no subtlety or complexity to interpreting the results; either the two groups are different or they are not. In addition, a two-group design provides the best opportunity to maximize the difference between the two groups; that is, you may select opposite extreme values for the independent variable. For example, in comparing two types of therapy, the two therapies can be structured to maximize or even exaggerate the differences between them. Or, in a research study comparing a treatment and a no-treatment control, the treatment group can be given the full-strength version of the treatment. This technique increases the likelihood of obtaining noticeably different scores from the two groups and thereby demonstrating a significant mean difference.

The primary disadvantage of a two-group design is that it provides relatively little information. With only two groups, a researcher obtains only two real data points for comparison. Although two data points are sufficient to establish a difference, they often are not sufficient to provide a complete or detailed picture of the full relationship between an independent and a dependent variable. Figure 10.5 shows a hypothetical relation between dosage levels for a drug (independent variable) and activity (dependent variable). Notice that the complete set of five data points, representing five different drug doses, gives a good picture of how drug dosage affects behavior. Now consider the limited data that would be available if the researcher had used only two different drug doses. If, for example, the researcher had used only a 0-dose and a 1-dose group (points A and B in the figure), the data would seem to indicate that increasing the drug dose produces an increase in activity. However, a researcher comparing a 2-dose versus a 4-dose group (points C and E) would reach exactly the opposite conclusion. Although both of the two-group studies are accurate, neither provides a complete picture. In general, several groups (more than two) are

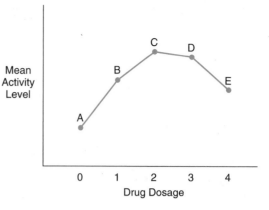

Figure 10.5 Hypothetical Data Showing a Relationship Between Activity Level and Drug Dosage for Five Different Levels of Drug Dosage

necessary to obtain a good indication of the functional relation between an independent and a dependent variable.

A two-group study also limits the options when a researcher wishes to compare a treatment group and a control group. Often, it is necessary to use several control groups to obtain a complete picture of a treatment's effectiveness. As we noted in Chapter 8, two common controls that often are used together are a no-treatment control and a placebo control. With these two control groups, researchers can separate the real treatment effects from the placebo effects that occur simply because participants think that they are receiving treatment. We should note that there is some ethical concern regarding the use of no-treatment or placebo groups in clinical research. Rather than denying treatment to some participants, it is suggested that an established, standard therapy be used for the control comparison (LaVaque & Rossiter, 2001).

Learning Check

Describe the advantages of a two-group design.

## COMPARING MEANS FOR MORE THAN TWO GROUPS

As noted in the previous section, research questions often require more than two groups to evaluate the functional relation between an independent and a dependent variable or to include several different control groups in a single study. In these cases, a **single-factor multiple group design** may be used. For example, a researcher may want to compare memory scores for a list of 1-syllable words with the scores from lists of 2-syllable words and 3-syllable words. Another researcher may want to examine five different dosages of a drug to evaluate the relation between dosage and activity level for laboratory rats. In the first example, the independent variable is the number of syllables, with three levels compared. In the second example, the researcher compares five levels of drug dosage. For either study, the mean is computed for each group of participants, and a single-factor analysis of variance (independent measures) would be used to determine whether there are any significant differences among the means (see Chapter 14). When the analysis of variance (ANOVA) concludes that significant differences exist, some form of post hoc test or posttest is used to determine exactly which groups are significantly different from each other.

### A Word of Caution About Multigroup Designs

Although a research study with more than two groups can give a clearer picture of the relationship between an independent and a dependent variable, it is possible to have too many groups in a research design. One advantage of a simple, two-group design is that it allows the researcher to maximize the difference between groups by selecting opposite extremes for the independent variable. The mirror image of this argument is that a design with more than two groups tends to reduce or minimize the difference between groups. At the extreme, there is a risk of reducing the differences between groups so much that the differences are no longer significant.

Therefore, when designing a single-factor multiple group research study, be sure that the levels used for the independent variable are sufficiently different to allow for substantial differences for the dependent variable. Consider, for example, a researcher examining the relation between room temperature (independent variable) and problem-solving performance (dependent variable). Figure 10.6 shows hypothetical results from such an experiment. Notice that the data show a general decline in performance as the room gets hotter.

If the researcher had used only two groups of participants to compare temperature levels of 70 and 90 degrees (opposite extremes on the temperature scale), the data would show a large difference between groups: On average, the 90-degree group scored 10 points lower than the 70-degree group. The 10-point difference is relatively large and likely to be significant.

However, if the researcher added an intermediate group tested at 80 degrees, the mean differences between groups become smaller: Although there is still a

Figure 10.6   Hypothetical Data Showing a Relationship Between Temperature and Problem-Solving Performance

10-point difference between the 70- and 90-degree groups, there is only a 6-point difference between 80 and 90, and only a 4-point difference between 70 and 80 degrees. On average, the obtained difference between groups is now *less than* 10 points. Because the three-group experiment results in smaller differences between treatments, there is a risk that the mean differences are no longer large enough to be statistically significant.

Obviously, this problem would become even worse if the researcher uses six groups of participants tested at temperature levels of 70, 74, 78, 82, 86, and 90 degrees. In general, adding extra groups to a research study tends to reduce the differences between groups. Although there are definite advantages to comparing several groups (more than two) in the same study, be careful that the groups do not become so similar that they are no longer significantly different.

Identify the advantages of a between-subjects experiment with multiple groups.

## COMPARING PROPORTIONS FOR TWO OR MORE GROUPS

Often the dependent variable in a research study is measured on a nominal or ordinal scale. In this case, the researcher does not have a numerical score for each participant and cannot calculate and compare averages for the different groups. Instead, each individual is simply classified into a category, and the data consist of a simple frequency count of the participants in each category on the scale of measurement.

Examples of nominal scale measurements are:

- Gender (male, female)
- Academic major for college students
- Success or failure on a performance task

Examples of ordinal scale measurements are:

- College class: (freshman, sophomore, etc.)
- Birth order: (first born, second born, etc.)
- High, medium, low performance on a task

Because you cannot compute means for these variables, you cannot use an independent-measures *t* test or an analysis of variance (*F* test) to compare means between groups. However, it is possible to compare proportions between groups using a chi-square test for independence (see Chapter 14, page 388). As with other between-subjects experiments, the different groups of participants represent different treatment conditions (manipulated by the researcher). For example, a researcher could manipulate different training methods and then compare the proportions of success and failure for the group in one method with those of the group in another. In this case, the structure of the design can be represented by a matrix with the independent variable (different groups) determining the rows of the matrix, and the classification categories for the dependent variable determining the columns. Figure 10.7 shows the basic structure of the example design mentioned earlier. The number in each cell of the matrix is simply the frequency count showing how many participants are classified in that cate-

|  | Succeed | Fail |
|---|---|---|
| Training Method A | 19 out of 25 participants succeed | 6 out of 25 participants fail |
| Training Method A | 12 out of 25 participants succeed | 13 out of 25 participants fail |
| Training Method A | 21 out of 25 participants succeed | 4 out of 25 participants fail |

Figure 10.7   Hypothetical Results From an Experiment Comparing Three Training Methods With 25 Participants Assigned to Each Method
The dependent variable is the success or failure of the participant. Note that the dependent variable is not a numerical score so you cannot compute a mean score for each training method.

gory. The chi-square test compares the proportions across one row of the matrix (one group of participants) with the proportions across other rows. A significant outcome means that the proportions in one row are different from the proportions in another row, and the difference is more than would be expected from chance.

## CHAPTER SUMMARY

In this chapter we examine the characteristics of the between-subjects research design. The general goal of a between-subjects experiment is to determine whether differences exist between two or more treatment conditions. The defining characteristic of a between-subjects design is that different but equivalent groups of individuals are compared. The primary advantage of a between-subjects design is the fact that each individual score is independent of the other scores because each participant is measured only once. The primary disadvantage of a between-subjects design is individual differences. In between-subjects designs, individual differences can become confounding variables and can produce high variability.

The potential confounding influence of individual differences is a particular problem for between-subjects designs. Because a between-subjects design compares different groups of individuals, there is always the possibility that the characteristics of one group will be substantially different from the characteristics of another group. Techniques for establishing equivalent groups of participants include random assignment, matched assignment, and holding variables constant. Individual differences also have the potential to produce high variability in the scores within a research study. High variability can obscure any treatment effects that may exist. Several methods that can be used to minimize the differences within treatments are discussed.

In addition to individual differences, there are other threats to the internal validity of between-subjects designs. Each of these potential confounds is also discussed in this chapter. Finally, different versions of the between-subjects design are considered.

## KEY WORDS

between-subjects experimental
    design or independent-
    measures design

individual differences
restricted random assignment
matching

## EXERCISES

1. In addition to the key words, you should also be able to define the following terms:
   within-subjects design
   matched-subjects design
   assignment bias
   differential attrition
   diffusion
   compensatory equalization
   compensatory rivalry or John Henry effect
   resentful demoralization
   single-factor two-group design or two-group design
   single-factor multiple-group design

2. Describe the major difference between within-subjects and between-subjects designs.

3. Describe the advantages of the between-subjects design.

4. Describe the disadvantages of the between-subjects design.

5. How can individual differences create problems in a between-subjects design?

6. Why is it so important in between-subjects designs to keep the different groups of participants as similar as possible?

7. Explain how the process of matching attempts to keep participant characteristics from becoming confounding variables in a between-subjects design.

8. Describe how holding variables constant as a way to keep participant characteristics from becoming confounding variables in between-subjects designs can limit the external validity of the results.

9. What steps can a researcher take to limit the variability within treatments?

10. Describe how each of the following factors threatens the internal validity of between-subjects designs: compensatory equalization, compensatory rivalry, and resentful demoralization.

11. Describe the disadvantages of the single-factor two-group design.

12. Describe the disadvantages of the single-factor multiple-group design.

## InfoTrac COLLEGE EDITION EXERCISES

1. The list of journals covered by InfoTrac College Edition does not include most of the experimental research journals in psychology; as a result you will probably find it difficult to locate an example of an experimental between-subjects study. Following is a list of research topics that you may find on InfoTrac College Edition. In each case, briefly explain why the study would probably *not* involve an experimental between-subjects design.

   a. a study examining gender differences or racial differences

   b. a study examining the effects of divorce

   c. a study examining preferences for different types of automobile seats

2. Although it is likely to be difficult, use InfoTrac College Edition to locate an experimental between-subject study. We suggest that you limit your search to specific journals such as *Behavioral Medicine*, *Human Factors*, or the *Journal of Social Psychology*. (Note: Click on *PowerTrac* instead of regular search, and select "journal" from the list of options. Then enter the journal name.) Even with this limitation, you will probably need to sort through a long list of article titles to find one or two that sound like they might be between-subjects experiments. When you find some likely candidates, locate the Method section of the report to verify that it is a true experiment and that the researchers did

assign participants to different conditions. Then answer the following questions:

a. What process was used to assign participants to conditions? Was it a simple random process, or was it restricted in some way?

b. What attempts did the researchers make to ensure that the different groups were equivalent (matching or holding a variable constant)?

c. Did the study compare one group with another? What was reported to indicate that the groups were similar?

3. Locate an experimental study in which one group of participants was tested in two (or more) different conditions. (This kind of study is called a "within-subjects design" and is discussed in the next chapter. The journal *Human Factors* is a good source for this type of study.)

a. Briefly describe what was done in the study. (How many participants were there and what were the different conditions?)

b. Explain how the study could have been conducted using a between-subjects design.

# 11

# Experimental Designs: Within-Subjects Design

## CHAPTER OVERVIEW

Step 6 of the research process involves selecting a research design. In this chapter we discuss in detail another type of experimental research design—the within-subjects design. The advantages, and disadvantages, and different versions of within-subjects designs are considered.

## 11.1   INTRODUCTION

### CHARACTERISTICS OF WITHIN-SUBJECTS DESIGNS

In the preceding chapter we described the basic elements of the between-subjects experimental research design. Recall that the defining characteristic of a between-subjects experiment is that it requires separate but equivalent groups of participants for the different treatment conditions compared. In this chapter we introduce an alternative research procedure, the **within-subjects design.** The defining characteristic of a within-subjects design is that it uses a single group of participants and tests or observes each individual in all of the different treatments being compared. Thus, in a within-subjects study, the sample is not separated into several groups but rather exists as a single group that participates in every treatment condition. In one sense, a within-subjects study is the ultimate in equivalent groups because the group in one treatment condition is absolutely identical to the group in every other condition. In the context of statistical analysis, a within-subjects design is often called a **repeated-measures design** because the research study repeats measurements of the same individuals under different conditions (see Figure 11.1).

Definition

A **within-subjects experimental design** compares two or more different treatment conditions (or compares treatment and control) by observing or measuring the same group of individuals in all of the treatment conditions being compared. Thus, a within-subjects design looks for differences between treatment conditions within the same group of participants.

In this chapter we examine the within-subjects design as it is used in experimental situations comparing different treatment conditions. This type of design is also well suited to other types of research that investigate changes occurring over time. In Chapter 9, for example, we introduced several time-series designs and the longitudinal developmental design as methods for investigating progressive changes that occur in a single group of individuals.

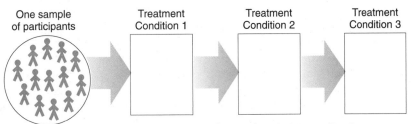

Figure 11.1   The Structure of a Within-Subjects Design
The same sample of individuals participates in all of the treatment conditions. Because each participant is measured in each treatment, this design is sometimes called a repeated-measures design. Note: All participants go through the entire series of treatments but not necessarily in the same order.

Identify the basic features of a within-subjects research design.

## ADVANTAGES OF WITHIN-SUBJECTS DESIGNS

One advantage of a within-subjects design is that it requires relatively few participants, in comparison to between-subjects designs. For example, to compare three different treatment conditions with 30 participants in each treatment, a between-subjects design requires a total of 90 participants (three separate groups with 30 in each). A within-subjects design, however, requires only 30 participants (the same group of 30 is used in all three conditions). Because a within-subjects study requires only one group, it is particularly useful in situations where participants are rare or difficult to obtain.

The primary advantage of a within-subjects design, however, is that it essentially eliminates all of the problems based on individual differences that are the primary concern of a between-subjects design. Recall from Chapter 10 that, in a between-subjects design, individual differences can create two major problems for research:

1.  Differences between groups can become a confounding variable. If the individuals in one treatment condition are noticeably different from the individuals in another treatment (for example, smarter, faster, bigger, or older), the individual differences, rather than the treatments, may explain any observed differences.

2.  The individual differences within each treatment condition can create high variability, which can obscure any differences between treatments.

These problems are reduced or eliminated in a within-subjects design. First, obviously a within-subjects design has no differences between groups; because there is only one group of participants, the group in treatment 1 is exactly the same as the group in treatment 2, and hence there are no individual differences between groups to confound the study. Second, because each participant appears in every treatment condition, each individual serves as his or her own control or baseline. This makes it possible to measure and remove the variability caused by individual differences. The following example demonstrates how the problems associated with individual differences are reduced in a within-subjects design.

Table 11.1 shows two sets of hypothetical data. The first set is from a typical between-subjects experiment, and the second set represents a within-subjects experiment. Each score is labeled with the participant's name so that we can examine the effects of individual differences. For the between-subjects data, every score represents a different person. For the within-subjects data, on the other hand, the same people are measured in all three treatment conditions.

The difference between the two designs has some important consequences:

1.  Both research studies have exactly the same scores, and both show the same differences between treatments. In each case, the researcher would like to conclude that the differences between treatments were caused by the treatments. However, with the between-subjects design (Table 11.1a), the participants in treatment 1 could have different characteristics from the

TABLE 11.1

**Hypothetical Data Showing the Results From a Between-Subjects Experiment and a Within-Subjects Experiment. The two sets of data use exactly the same numerical scores.**

(a) Between-Subjects Experiment—Three Separate Groups

| Treatment 1 | | Treatment 2 | | Treatment 3 | |
|---|---|---|---|---|---|
| (John) | 20 | (Sue) | 24 | (Beth) | 28 |
| (Mary) | 30 | (Tom) | 35 | (Bob) | 39 |
| (Bill) | 40 | (Dave) | 43 | (Don) | 47 |
| (Kate) | 50 | (Ann) | 54 | (Zoe) | 58 |
| Mean = 35 | | Mean = 39 | | Mean = 43 | |

(b) Within-Subjects Experiment—One Group in All Three Treatments

| Treatment 1 | | Treatment 2 | | Treatment 3 | |
|---|---|---|---|---|---|
| (John) | 20 | (John) | 24 | (John) | 28 |
| (Mary) | 30 | (Mary) | 35 | (Mary) | 39 |
| (Bill) | 40 | (Bill) | 43 | (Bill) | 47 |
| (Kate) | 50 | (Kate) | 54 | (Kate) | 58 |
| Mean = 35 | | Mean = 39 | | Mean = 43 | |

participants in treatment 2. For example, the four individuals in treatment 2 may be more intelligent than the participants in treatment 1, and their higher intelligence may have caused their higher scores. This problem disappears in the within-subjects design (Table 11.1b); the participants in one treatment cannot differ from the participants in another treatment, because the same individuals are used in all the treatments.

2. Although the two sets of data contain exactly the same scores, they differ greatly in the way that the individual differences contribute to the variability. For the between-subjects experiment, the individual differences and the treatment effects are tied together and cannot be separated. To measure the difference between treatments, we must also measure the differences between individuals. For example, John scored 4 points lower than Sue, but it is impossible to determine whether this 4-point difference is caused by the treatments or is simply a matter of individual differences (John is different from Sue). Individual differences are an integral part of a between-subjects design, and they are automatically a part of the variability in the scores.

Now consider the within-subjects experiment (Table 11.1b). Once again, individual differences are part of the variability in the data (for example, John's scores are different from Mary's scores). This time, however, we can separate the individual differences from the rest of the variability in the data. Specifically, the individual differences within treatment 1 are exactly the same as the individual differences within treatment 2 and within treatment 3; for example, there is a consistent difference of about 10 points between John and Mary in each of the three treatments. Because the individual differences are the same in each of the treatment conditions, they can be measured and separated from the rest of the variability. Thus, in a within-subjects design:

1. It is possible to measure the differences between treatments without involving any individual differences. Because the same participants are in every treatment condition, the treatment effects and the individual differences are not linked.

2. It is possible to measure the differences between individuals. Because the individual differences are consistent across all treatments, they can be separated from the rest of the variability shown in the data.

To demonstrate the actual process of separating the individual differences from the rest of the variability, consider once again the within-subjects data in Table 11.1b. For example, John's score increases by 4 points from treatment 1 to treatment 2 and increases an additional 4 points from treatment 2 to treatment 3. John starts with a score of 20 in treatment 1, but this starting value is not as important as the changes from one treatment to the next. In fact, we can reset John's starting score to 0 (like zeroing the odometer in a car) and then simply measure how much his score changes from one treatment to another. The results of this zeroing process are presented in Table 11.2. Notice that we start John (and all the other participants) with a score of zero but preserve the same *amount of change* from treatment to treatment that existed in the original data. The newly created scores preserve all of the important characteristics of the original scores. That is, the changes that occur for the participants, individually and collectively, are the same as in the original data. However, the process of zeroing the data eliminates all of the individual differences. Specifically, the big differences from one participant to another in Table 11.1b are now gone, and the resulting scores show only a 1- or 2-point difference between individuals. Removing the individual differences drastically reduces the variability of the scores and makes the 4-point differences from treatment to treatment much easier to see. Figure 11.2 shows the original within-subjects data from Table 11.1b and the adjusted data from Table 11.2. When the individual differences are removed, the treatment effects are much easier to see.

As we have noted, the within-subjects design reduces variability and reveals differences between treatments that might not be apparent in a between-subjects design. In statistical terms, a within-subjects design is generally more powerful than a between-subjects design. This is one reason that a within-subjects design can use fewer participants than a between-subjects design.

In the preceding example, we removed the individual differences by equalizing all the participants with the same starting score of zero. In a normal research situation, this equalizing process is accomplished by the statistical analysis (instead of manipulation of the data). However, the net result is the same: The variability caused by individual differences is removed. This cannot be done with data from a between-subjects design; with between-subjects data every score is from a separate individual and an attempt to zero the scores as in Table 11.2 would simply change *all* the scores to zero.

TABLE 11.2

## Removing Individual Differences From Within-Subjects Data

This table shows the same data from Table 10.1b, except that we have started each individual with a score of zero in treatment 1 and then recorded how much the individuals' scores change from one treatment to the next. This process eliminates the individual differences from the data and makes the differences between treatments much easier to see.

| Treatment 1 | | Treatment 2 | | Treatment 3 | |
|---|---|---|---|---|---|
| (John) | 0 | (John) | 4 | (John) | 8 |
| (Mary) | 0 | (Mary) | 5 | (Mary) | 9 |
| (Bill) | 0 | (Bill) | 3 | (Bill) | 7 |
| (Kate) | 0 | (Kate) | 4 | (Kate) | 8 |
| Mean = 0 | | Mean = 4 | | Mean = 8 | |

(a) Within-subjects data from Table 11.1

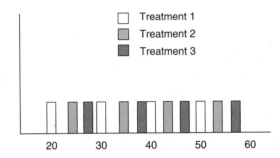

(b) Within-subjects data from Table 11.2

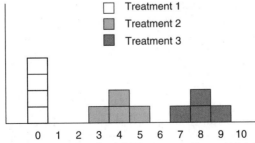

Figure 11.2   Removing Individual Differences From Within-Subjects Data
(a) The original data, which include the individual
differences among the four participants.
(b) The individual differences have been removed by adjusting each
participant's score to zero in treatment 1. When the individual differences
are removed, it is much easier to see the differences between treatments.

Learning
Check

In a within-subjects design, problems stemming from individual differences are eliminated. Briefly explain how.

## DISADVANTAGES OF WITHIN-SUBJECTS DESIGNS

Caution: In Chapter 10 we discussed *differential attrition* as a threat to internal validity. The *attrition* discussed here simply means the loss of participants from a research study.

Although a within-subjects design has some definite advantages relative to a between-subjects design, it also has some disadvantages. One potential problem is **participant attrition.** In simple terms, some of the individuals who start the research study may be gone before the study is completed. Because a within-subjects design requires repeated measurements under different conditions for each individual, some participants may be lost between the first measurement and the final measurement. This problem is especially serious when the study extends over a period of time and participants must be called back for additional observation. Participants may forget appointments, lose interest, quit, move away, or even die. In addition to shrinking the sample size, the attrition problem may exaggerate volunteer bias if only the most dedicated volunteers continue from start to finish. As noted in Chapter 6, volunteer bias can threaten both the internal and external validity of a research study.

In situations where participant attrition is anticipated, it is advisable to begin the research study with more individuals than are actually needed. In this way, the chances are increased of having a reasonable number of participants left when the study ends.

### Time-Related Problems

A more serious concern with within-subjects designs comes from the fact that the design requires a series of measurements made over time. During the time between the first measurement and the final measurement, the participants may be influenced by a variety of factors other than the treatments investigated, and these other factors may affect the participants' scores. If this occurs, then the internal validity of the study is threatened; a change in a participant's score from one treatment to the next could be caused by the different treatments or by some outside factor. In Section 11.2 we consider a number of time-related factors that can threaten the internal validity of a within-subjects experimental design.

### Order-Effect Problems

Another concern is that, in within-subjects designs, the scores obtained in one treatment condition are directly related to scores in every other condition. In Chapter 10 we note that an advantage of a between-subjects design is that all of the scores are *independent* measurements; that is, the scores all come from separate participants. Obviously, this independence does not exist in a within-subjects study, where each participant undergoes a series of treatments and measurements. In this situation, there is always the potential that the measurement obtained in one treatment condition has been influenced by previous treatments or measurements—by factors other than the treatment itself. Once again, a threat to internal validity or a case of confounding variables exists when variables other than the treatment may affect the results. In a within-subjects design, each participant receives the series of treatments in a particular order. Confounding by a treatment condition or measurement occurring earlier in the order is referred to as an *order effect*, discussed in detail in Section 11.3.

In a within-subjects design, independence of scores does not occur. Briefly explain why this is considered a disadvantage of the within-subjects design.

Learning Check

## 11.2   TIME-RELATED THREATS TO THE INTERNAL VALIDITY OF WITHIN-SUBJECTS DESIGNS

The goal of the within-subjects experimental design is to look for differences between treatment conditions within the same group of participants and to demonstrate that the observed differences are caused by the different treatments (by the manipulation of the independent variable). If the differences between the different treatment conditions can be attributed to additional factors, the research is confounded, and the results cannot be interpreted without some ambiguity. Recall from Chapter 6 that any factor allowing an alternative explanation for the research results is a threat to internal validity. In Chapter 6 we discussed some general threats that can undermine the internal validity of a research study. Here we consider some specific threats to the internal validity of within-subjects designs.

In a within-subjects design, research takes place over time. Each participant undergoes a series of treatment conditions. During the time between the first treatment condition and the final treatment condition, individual participants or their scores may be influenced by factors other than the treatments—and any factor affecting the data other than the treatment is a confounding variable and a threat to the internal validity of the study. In this section we consider four factors related to the passage of time that present a threat to the internal validity of a within-subjects research design.

### HISTORY

The term **history** refers to environmental events other than the treatment that occur between the first treatment condition and the last treatment condition of a within-subjects experiment and may affect the results. Events that occur in participants' lives at home, in school, or at work may affect their performance or behavior in later sections of the experiment. For example, suppose a college professor uses a within-subjects experiment to examine human memory under a variety of different treatment conditions. A sample of students serves as participants in the study. Each day the professor changes the treatment condition and gives the students another memory test. Now suppose that in the middle of this study a fire alarm sounds in the main campus dormitory just after midnight, and the students are left standing outdoors for hours. When the students are tested later in the day, they are likely to show poor memory scores, not because of the treatment condition but because they are all exhausted from missing sleep the night before.

---

The term **history** refers to any outside event(s) that occurs during the time that a within-subjects experiment is being conducted and has an influence on the participants' scores. History is a threat to internal validity because any differences that are observed between treatment conditions may be caused by history instead of by the treatments.

---

In general, history threatens the internal validity of a research study because it creates the possibility that observed changes in a dependent variable are caused by outside events instead of by the treatments. The threat of outside events (history) increases whenever it takes a long period of time to complete the series of treatments in a within-subjects study.

Note that *history effects* are defined as events that occur during the course of the research study. In most cases, this is correct. However, a study can be influenced by an event that occurs prior to it. Earlier, we discussed the effect of a midnight fire alarm on the participants' performance the following day. If the fire alarm sounded on the night before the study started, then it could affect performance on the first day of the study but not on subsequent days. In this case, the event is still a threat to internal validity, even though it occurred prior to the start of the study. History effects must influence at least one treatment condition differently. Suppose, for example, that an individual suffers a brain injury one year before participating in a research study. This event will probably affect the individual's performance, but it should not threaten internal validity. In this situation, any deficits from the injury appear equally in all treatment conditions, and therefore the injury does not constitute a history effect.

### MATURATION

Any systematic changes in an individual's physiology or psychology occurring over time and unrelated to the independent variable are referred to as **maturation.** Maturation effects are of particular concern when the research participants are young children or elderly adults. Young children, for example, can gather new knowledge and skills or simply grow bigger and stronger in a relatively short time. As a result, their performance at the end of a series of treatment conditions may be very different from their performance at the beginning, and the change in performance may not have been caused by the treatments but instead by maturation. With elderly participants, maturation effects are often negative. As people age, they may experience losses in vision or hearing that could affect their performance in a research study. In general, maturation threatens the internal validity of a within-subjects design because it weakens our confidence that the independent variable is responsible for observed changes in the dependent variable. Maturation is a particular concern in research situations where the series of treatments extends over a relatively long time.

The term **maturation** refers to any physiological or psychological changes that occur in a participant during the time a within-subjects experiment is conducted and that can influence the participant's scores. Maturation is a threat to internal validity because observed differences between treatment conditions may be caused by maturation instead of by the treatments.

Definition

## INSTRUMENTATION

The terms **instrumentation** and **instrumental bias** refer to changes in the measuring instrument that occur over time. For example, a scale used to weigh participants may gradually wear out over the course of the study. Then the measurements change during the study not because of the different treatments but because the scale changes.

Behavioral observation measures (discussed in Chapters 4 and 7) are much more subject to instrumentation than other types of measures. For example, from one testing to the next the researcher doing the observing may become more proficient in making the observations, may change the standards on which the observations are based, may become more skilled, or may become fatigued—and as a result may judge the same behavior differently at different times. Notice that the change in the measurement is not caused by the treatment but instead by a change in the measurement instrument (the researcher). Like history and maturation, instrumentation is a particular concern in research situations where the series of treatments extends over a relatively long time.

**Instrumentation** refers to changes in the measurement instrument that occur over time. Instrumentation is a threat to internal validity because any observed differences between treatment conditions may be caused by changes in the measuring instrument instead of the treatments.

Definition

## STATISTICAL REGRESSION

**Statistical regression** or **regression toward the mean** refers to the tendency of extreme scores on any measurement to revert to or regress toward the mean when the measurement procedure is readministered. Individuals who score extremely high on a measure during the first testing are likely to score lower on the second testing, and, conversely, individuals who score extremely low on a measure during the first testing are likely to score higher on the second testing. Statistical regression occurs because an individual's score on a measure is a function both of stable factors such as skill and of unstable factors such as chance. Although the stable factors remain constant from one measurement to another, the unstable factors can change substantially. Your grade on an exam, for example, is based on a combination of knowledge and luck. Some of the answers you really know; others you guess. The student who gets the highest score on the first exam probably combines knowledge and good luck. On the second exam, this student's knowledge will still be there, but luck is likely to change; thus, the student will probably score lower on the second exam. This is regression toward the mean.

In research, regression is a concern whenever participants are selected for their exceptionally high (or low) scores. Suppose a clinical psychologist uses a within-subjects design to examine the social skills of autistic children. A sample of autistic children is selected because they show exceptionally poor social skills. The psychologist administers a treatment and then once again measures social skills. Because of the children's extremely low scores on social skills at the beginning of the study, it is possible that the children's scores improve and that they appear less withdrawn at future testings, not because of the treatment condition but because their scores regress toward the mean. In general, statistical regression threatens the internal validity of a research study because it creates the possibility that the observed changes in a dependent variable are caused by this regression instead of by the treatments. Statistical regression is especially a problem when participants are selected for their extreme scores.

| Definition | **Statistical regression** or **regression toward the mean** is a mathematical phenomenon in which extreme scores (high or low) on one measurement tend to be less extreme on a second measurement. Regression is a threat to internal validity because changes that occur in participants' scores from one treatment to the next may be caused by regression instead of the treatments. |

Learning Check | Describe how history and maturation each threaten the internal validity of within-subjects designs.

## 11.3 ORDER EFFECTS: CARRYOVER EFFECTS AND PROGRESSIVE ERROR

In a within-subjects design, each individual participates in a series of different treatment conditions and is measured in each of the conditions. In this situation participation in one treatment condition may produce a lasting change that carries over into the next treatment, where it affects the participant's performance or behavior. Such a change is called a **carryover effect.**

| Definition | **Carryover effects** are changes in behavior or performance that are caused by participation in an earlier treatment condition. Carryover effects exist whenever one treatment condition produces a change in the participants that affects their scores in subsequent treatment conditions. |

Consider the following examples:

- A drug administered in treatment 1 lingers in a participant's system when the individual enters treatment 2. In this case, the drug (treatment 1) could influence the participant's behavior in treatment 2.

- Participants learn specific skills in one treatment condition and continue to use the skills in later conditions. A memory experiment intended to compare different rehearsal strategies introduces one strategy in condition 1 and then asks participants to use a different strategy in condition 2. The participants, however, find the first strategy easier or more efficient and continue to use it despite the instructions.

For each of these examples a researcher observes a change in the participant from one treatment condition to the next; however, the change is not caused by the different treatments but instead by carryover. Carryover effects are another threat to the internal validity of a within-subjects design.

Similarly, a participant's behavior may change during the course of a research study, not because of previous treatments but simply as a function of experience over time. Such changes are called **progressive error.** In a within-subjects design, each participant is measured over and over again; when repeated measurement experience influences the participants and produces progressive error, the changes are sometimes called **testing effects.** Common kinds of progressive error are **fatigue** (progressive decline in performance over time) and **practice effects** (progressive improvement in performance over time). Again, the results are confounded because the researcher does not know whether performance changes are caused by the different treatments or by fatigue or practice.

**Progressive error** refers to changes in a participant's behavior or performance that are related to experience over time in a research study but not related to a specific treatment or treatments. Common kinds of progressive error are practice effects and fatigue.

Technically, carryover effects and progressive error are two different phenomena. Carryover effects are changes in a participant that can be attributed directly to a preceding treatment; the lingering aftereffects of a treatment carry over into the next treatment (or treatments) and alter behavior. On the other hand, progressive error is any change in the participant that can be attributed to experience over time. Thus, progressive error is caused by general experience or participation in a research study, and carryover effects are caused by specific experience or participation in a particular treatment condition. However, both progressive error and carryover effects can be viewed as aspects of the same basic problem: Participants' scores are influenced by factors other than the immediate treatment. To simplify future discussion, we combine carryover effects and progressive error into the general category of **order effects.**

Whenever individuals participate in a series of treatment conditions and experience a series of measurements, their behavior or performance at any point in the series may be influenced by events or experience that occurred earlier in the sequence. Such influences are called **order effects** and include carryover effects and progressive error.

## ORDER EFFECTS AS A CONFOUNDING VARIABLE

Order effects can produce changes from one treatment condition to another that are not caused by the treatments and thus can confound the results of a research study. To demonstrate this confounding effect, we examine a hypothetical experiment in which a researcher uses a within-subjects design to compare two treatment conditions with a sample of eight participants. We also assume that there is no difference between the two treatments; on the average, the scores in treatment 1 are the same as the scores in treatment 2. Results for this hypothetical study are shown in Table 11.3a. Notice that some individual participants show a small increase or decrease between treatment conditions, representing error that can occur in any measurement process (see the discussion of reliability in Chapter 4). However, on the average, there is no difference between the treatment conditions; both produce an average score of 20.

Now consider the data shown in Table 11.3b. For these data, we assume that each participant started the experiment in treatment 1 and then was moved to treatment 2. In addition, we assume that participation in treatment 1 changes each participant so that subsequent measurements show higher scores—a 5-point order effect. Thus, for each participant measured again in treatment 2, the data show 5 points added to each individual's score. The 5-point increase is not caused by the second treatment but is rather an order effect resulting from earlier participation in treatment 1. The resulting data in Table 11.3b illustrate two important points:

1.  The order effect varies *systematically* with the treatments; that is, it always contributes to the second treatment but never to the first. Whenever something

### TABLE 11.3

**Hypothetical Data Showing How Order Effects Can Distort the Results of a Research Study**

| (a) Original Scores With No Order Effect | | (b) Modified Scores With a 5-Point Order Effect | |
|---|---|---|---|
| Treatment 1 | Treatment 2 | Treatment 1 | Treatment 2 |
| 20 | 21 | 20 | 26 (21 + 5) |
| 23 | 23 | 23 | 28 (23 + 5) |
| 25 | 23 | 25 | 28 (23 + 5) |
| 19 | 20 | 19 | 25 (20 + 5) |
| 26 | 25 | 26 | 30 (25 + 5) |
| 17 | 16 | 17 | 21 (16 + 5) |
| 14 | 14 | 14 | 19 (14 + 5) |
| 16 | 18 | 16 | 23 (18 + 5) |
| Mean = 20 | Mean = 20 | Mean = 20 | Mean = 25 |

changes systematically with the independent variable, it is a confounding variable. Thus, the results of this study are confounded by the order effects.

2.  In this example the confounding from the order effects makes the data look like there is a 5-point difference between the treatments. With the help of order effects, the individual participants and the group mean show consistently higher scores in the second treatment. These data could lead the researcher to conclude that there is a significant difference between the treatments when in fact no such difference exists (remember, we constructed the data so there is no difference between treatments). Thus, order effects, like any confounding variable, can distort the results of a research study. In this example, the order effect seems to create a treatment effect where none really exists. In other situations, order effects can diminish or exaggerate a real effect, thereby posing a real threat to the internal validity of the research.

Briefly explain how order effects can be a confounding variable in a within-subjects design.

Learning Check

## 11.4  DEALING WITH TIME-RELATED THREATS AND ORDER EFFECTS

Because within-subjects designs can have significant advantages in comparison to between-subjects designs, they are often preferred as a method for addressing research questions. At the same time, however, order effects and time-related threats to internal validity can be serious problems whenever a within-subjects design is selected. Therefore, researchers have developed a variety of ways to control these potential threats. In this section we examine some of the methods for dealing with order effects and time-related threats to gain the full benefit of within-subjects designs.

### CONTROLLING TIME

The possibility that a research study will be affected by a time-related threat such as history or maturation is directly related to the length of time required to complete the study. For example, if participants go through a series of two or three treatment conditions in a single 45-minute laboratory session, it is very unlikely that time-related threats will have any influence on the results. On the other hand, if the different treatment conditions are scheduled over a period of weeks, the chances greatly increase that the results will be influenced by some outside event (history) or maturation or change in the measurement instrument. By controlling the time from one treatment condition to the next, a researcher has some control over time-related threats to internal validity.

Although shortening the time between treatments can reduce the risk of time-related threats, this technique can often increase the likelihood that order effects will influence the results. For example, in situations where order effects are expected to be temporary, one strategy is to increase the time between treatment conditions so the order effects can dissipate. Fatigue, for example, is less likely to be a problem if participants are allowed ample opportunity to rest and recover between treatments. As we have noted, however, increasing the time between treatments increases the risk of time-related threats to internal validity.

## WHEN A WITHIN-SUBJECTS DESIGN IS NOT A GOOD IDEA

Often researchers begin a research study with some knowledge or expectation of the existence and magnitude of order effects. For example, if the study involves measuring skill or performance over a series of treatment conditions, it is reasonable to assume that practice gained in the early treatments is likely to affect performance in later treatments. If the study involves a tedious or boring task repeated under different conditions, the researcher can expect fatigue or boredom to develop during the course of the study. In some situations, order effects are so strong and so obvious that a researcher probably would not even consider using a within-subjects design. For example, a within-subjects design is a poor choice for a study comparing two methods of teaching reading to first-grade children. It would be foolish to teach the children how to read with method 2 after they have already learned with method 1. In this extreme case, the obvious strategy for avoiding order effects is to use a between-subjects design. Usually a between-subjects design (with a separate group for each treatment) is available as an alternative and will completely eliminate any threat of confounding from order effects. Although the potential for order effects is not always as severe as with learning to read, a between-subjects design is often the best strategy whenever a researcher has reason to expect substantial order effects.

## COUNTERBALANCING

The most frequently used strategy for dealing with time-related threats and order effects is **counterbalancing.** In counterbalancing, different participants undergo the treatment conditions in different order. With two treatments, for example, one half the participants begins in treatment 1, then moves to treatment 2. The other half begins in treatment 2, then receives treatment 1. This procedure disrupts any systematic relationship between time and the order of treatment conditions and thereby eliminates potential confounding from time-related threats or order effects.

| Definition | **Counterbalancing** a within-subjects design involves changing the order in which treatment conditions are administered from one participant to another. The goal is to use every possible order of treatments with an equal number of individuals participating in each sequence. The purpose of counterbalancing is to eliminate the potential for confounding by disrupting any systematic effects from factors related to time or the order of treatments. |
|---|---|

To better understand the effects of counterbalancing, first consider a situation in which the order of treatments is not counterbalanced. Without counterbalancing, all the participants begin in treatment 1 and then move to treatment 2.

Note that treatment 2 always occurs after treatment 1. In this case, a time-related threat such as history or instrumentation will influence only the scores in treatment 2. An order effect, too, will influence only the scores in treatment 2. Thus, without counterbalancing, the scores in treatment 2 may be influenced by factors other than the treatment, and the study is confounded. With counterbalancing, however, a time-related threat would affect the scores in treatment 2 for half of the participants, but it would affect the scores in treatment 1 for the other half. Thus, the effect is distributed evenly, balanced between the two treatments. Because the outside factor does not cause a difference between the two treatments, it is no longer a threat to internal validity.

You may have noticed that counterbalancing requires separate groups of participants, with each group going through the series of treatments in a different order. The existence of separate groups may appear to contradict the basic definition of a within-subjects design. The solution to this apparent contradiction is based on the observation that, although the groups go through the treatments in different orders, they all receive the full set of treatments. Thus, we still have a within-subjects design, with one combined group of individuals participating in all of the different treatment conditions. In Chapter 12 (page 315) we return to this issue when we re-examine a counterbalanced study as a combination of a within-subjects design (with one group in all the treatments) and a between-subjects design (with different groups receiving the treatments in different orders).

### Counterbalancing and Order Effects

Although counterbalancing has exactly the same effect on time-related threats and order effects, the process of counterbalancing is usually discussed in terms of order effects. Therefore, throughout the rest of this section, we focus on counterbalancing and order effects. Keep in mind, however, that counterbalancing is just as effective for controlling factors such as history and maturation as for controlling order effects.

The hypothetical data in Table 11.4 provide a numerical demonstration of counterbalancing and how it controls threats to validity. The table shows the results from an experiment in which a researcher uses a within-subjects design to compare two treatments. The design is counterbalanced with four of the eight participants starting in treatment 1 and ending with treatment 2, and the other four participants receiving the treatments in the reverse order.

Table 11.4a shows scores as they would appear if there were no order effects. The data have been constructed to produce a 6-point difference between the two treatment conditions (Mean$_1$ = 20 versus Mean$_2$ = 26). The modified scores in Table 11.4b show how order effects influence the data. For this example, we assume that experience in one treatment condition produces an order effect that causes a 5-point increase in scores for the next treatment.

Because the design is counterbalanced, the first 4 participants begin the experiment in treatment 1, and the 5-point order effect adds to their scores in treatment 2. The remaining 4 participants receive the treatments in the opposite order, so the order effect adds to their scores in treatment 1. Notice that the result of the counterbalancing is to distribute the order effects evenly between the two treatments; that is, the order effects are balanced across the treatment conditions. Although the treatment means are affected by the order effects, they are

TABLE 11.4

**Hypothetical Data Showing How Counterbalancing Distributes Order Effects Evenly Between the Treatment Conditions**

| (a) Original Scores With No Order Effect | | (b) Modified Scores With a 5-Point Order Effect | | |
|---|---|---|---|---|
| Treatment 1 | Treatment 2 | Treatment 1 | | Treatment 2 |
| 20 | 27 | 20 | — order → | 32 (27 + 5) |
| 23 | 29 | 23 | ———→ | 34 (29 + 5) |
| 25 | 29 | 25 | ———→ | 34 (29 + 5) |
| 19 | 26 | 19 | ———→ | 31 (26 + 5) |
| 26 | 31 | (26 + 5) 31 | ← order — | 31 |
| 17 | 22 | (17 + 5) 22 | ←——— | 22 |
| 14 | 20 | (14 + 5) 19 | ←——— | 20 |
| 16 | 24 | (16 + 5) 21 | ←——— | 24 |
| Mean = 20 | Mean = 26 | Mean = 22.5 | | Mean = 28.5 |

affected equally. As a result, there is still a 6-point difference between the two treatment means, exactly as it was without any order effects. The point of this demonstration is to show that order effects can change individual scores and can change means but, when a design is counterbalanced, the changes do not influence the differences between treatments. Because the treatment differences are not affected, the order effects do not threaten the internal validity of the study.

In Chapter 12 (page 315) we will present a method that allows researchers to measure and evaluate order effects.

The value of counterbalancing a within-subjects design is that it prevents any order effects from accumulating in one particular treatment condition. Instead, the order effects are spread evenly across all the different conditions so that it is possible to make fair, unbiased comparisons between treatments (no single treatment has any special advantage or disadvantage). On the other hand, counterbalancing does not eliminate the order effects; they are still embedded in the data. Furthermore, the order effects are hidden in the data so that a researcher cannot see whether they exist or how large they are. In Table 11.4 we identify and expose hypothetical order effects to demonstrate how they influence a counterbalanced design. In real life, however, all you see are the final scores, which may or may not include order effects.

Learning
Check

Describe the process of counterbalancing and the benefits of using it in a within-subjects design.

## LIMITATIONS OF COUNTERBALANCING

As demonstrated in Table 11.4, counterbalancing can be used to prevent order effects (or other time-related effects) from confounding the results of a within-subjects research study. In the same way that random assignment is a routine technique for maintaining validity in between-subjects research, counterbalancing is a routine technique used in within-subjects research. However, this apparently simple and effective technique has some limitations.

## Counterbalancing and Variability

The purpose of counterbalancing is to distribute order effects evenly across the different treatment conditions. However, this process does not *eliminate* the order effects. In particular, the order effects are still part of the data, and they can still create problems. One is that they can distort the treatment means. In Table 11.4, the order effects are present in both treatments and inflate both of the treatment means. Usually this kind of distortion is not important because researchers typically are interested in the amount of difference between treatments rather than the absolute magnitude of any specific mean. When counterbalancing works as intended, the differences between means will not be changed. However, in situations where the absolute level of performance (the true mean) is important, the process of counterbalancing can disguise the true value of a treatment mean.

A more serious problem is that counterbalancing adds order effects to some of the individuals within each treatment but not to all of the individuals. In the example shown in Table 11.4, some of the individuals in treatment 1 receive an extra 5 points and some do not. As a result, the differences between scores are increased within each treatment, which adds to the variability. Recall from Chapter 10 (page 251) that large variability within treatments can obscure treatment effects. In statistical terms, high variability decreases the likelihood that a research study will obtain significant differences between treatments. Thus, in situations where order effects are relatively large, the process of counterbalancing can undermine the potential for a successful experiment.

## Asymmetrical Order Effects

In Table 11.4 we use exactly the same 5-point order effect whether participants started in treatment 1 or in treatment 2. That is, we assume that the order effects are symmetrical. This assumption of symmetry is not always justified. It is definitely possible that one treatment might produce more of an order effect than another treatment. For example, one treatment condition might provide more opportunity for practice than the other conditions. Or one treatment might be more demanding and create more fatigue than the other treatment conditions. In such situations, the order effects are not symmetrical, and counterbalancing the order of treatments does not balance the order effects.

## Counterbalancing and the Number of Treatments

In order to completely counterbalance a series of treatments, it is necessary to present the treatments in every possible sequence. The idea behind **complete counterbalancing** is that a particular series of treatment conditions may create its own unique order effect. For example, treatments 2 and 3, in sequence, may produce a unique effect that carries over into the next treatment. Treatments 1 and 3, in sequence, may produce a different order effect. To completely balance these combined effects, the research design should use every possible ordering of treatment conditions.

With only two treatment conditions, complete counterbalancing is easy: There are only two possible sequences. However, as the number of treatments increases, complete counterbalancing becomes more complex. If the number of different treatment conditions is identified as $n$, then the number of different sequences is $n!$ ($n$ factorial).

$$n! = n (n-1)(n-2)(n-3)...\quad(1)$$

For example, with four treatment conditions, there are $4! = 4 \times 3 \times 2 \times 1 = 24$ different sequences. If the four treatments are identified as A, B, C, and D, the 24 sequences are

| | | | |
|---|---|---|---|
| ABCD | BACD | CABD | DABC |
| ABDC | BADC | CADB | DACB |
| ACBD | BCAD | CBAD | DBAC |
| ACDB | BCDA | CBDA | DBCA |
| ADBC | BDAC | CDAB | DCAB |
| ADCB | BDCA | CDBA | DCBA |

To completely counterbalance a within-subjects experiment with four treatment conditions, the researcher must divide the participants into 24 equal-sized groups and assign one group to each of the 24 different sequences. Obviously, this study would require at least 24 participants (one per group), which may be more than the researcher needs or wants. With even more treatments, the demands of complete counterbalancing can become outrageous. With $n = 6$ treatments, for example, there are $6! = 720$ different treatment sequences, which means that the study would require a minimum 720 participants.

One solution to this problem is to use what is known as **partial counterbalancing.** Instead of every possible sequence, partial counterbalancing simply uses enough different orderings to ensure that each treatment condition occurs first in the sequence for one group of participants, occurs second for another group, third for another group, and so on. With four treatments, for example, this requires only four different sequences, such as: ABCD, CADB, BDAC, DCBA. To conduct a partially counterbalanced study with four treatments, a researcher needs to divide the participants into four equal-sized groups and assign one group to each of the four sequences. One group of participants receives treatment A first, one group has A second, one has A third, and one has A fourth. Similarly, each of the other treatments appears once in each ordinal position.

Because partial counterbalancing does not use every possible sequence of treatment conditions, one problem is to decide exactly which sequences will be selected. A simple and unbiased procedure for selecting sequences is to construct a **Latin square.** To create a Latin square for four treatment conditions, start with a $4 \times 4$ matrix and fill it in with the letters A, B, C, and D, as follows:

> List the letters ABCD in order. This line of letters forms the first row of the matrix. To create the next row, simply move the last letter in line to the beginning. This creates DABC for the second row. Continue moving the last letter to the beginning of the line to create each new row. The result is the following Latin square:

A B C D          By definition a Latin square
D A B C          is a matrix of $n$ elements (letters)
C D A B          where each element appears exactly
B C D A          once in each column and in each row.

Each row in the square provides a sequence of treatment conditions for one group of participants. For this example, the first group receives the four treatments in the order ABCD. A second group receives the order DABC, and so on.

The Latin square in the preceding paragraph is not a particularly good example, because it does not balance every possible sequence of treatment conditions. For example, the first three groups all receive treatment A followed immediately by treatment B. On the other hand, no one receives treatment B followed by treatment A. Whenever possible, a Latin square should ensure that every possible sequence of treatments is represented. One method for improving the square is to use a random process to rearrange the columns (for example, a coin toss to decide whether or not each column is moved), then use a random process to rearrange the rows. The resulting rows in the square should provide a better set of sequences for a partially counterbalanced research study.

Briefly describe some of the problems of counterbalancing.

Learning
Check

## 11.5    APPLICATIONS AND STATISTICAL ANALYSES OF WITHIN-SUBJECTS DESIGNS

Within-subjects designs are used most often to evaluate mean differences between treatment conditions. In an experiment, the researcher manipulates an independent variable to create two or more treatment conditions and then observes the same group of individuals in all of the conditions. The mean score for the group is then computed for each treatment condition, and the means are compared for significant differences.

Commonly a within-subjects design is selected in preference to a between-subjects design to take advantage of one or more of the special characteristics of this type of research. For example:

1.  Because the within-subjects design requires only one group, it often is used when obtaining a large group of research participants is difficult or impossible. If a researcher studies a population with a rare characteristic (such as Olympic athletes, people with multiple-personality disorder, or women over 7 feet tall) then a within-subjects design is more efficient because it requires fewer participants.

2.  We have noted repeatedly that one big advantage of a within-subjects design is that it reduces or eliminates variability caused by individual differences. Whenever a researcher anticipates that the data will show large variability caused by differences between participants, a within-subjects design is the preferred choice.

## TWO-TREATMENT DESIGNS

The simplest application of a within-subjects design is to evaluate the difference between two treatment conditions. The two-treatment within-subjects design has many of the same advantages and disadvantages as the two-group between-subjects design discussed in Chapter 10 (see pages 259–260). On the positive side, the design is easy to conduct and the results are easy to understand. With only two treatment conditions, a researcher can easily maximize the difference between treatments by selecting two treatment conditions that are clearly different. This usually increases the likelihood of obtaining a significant difference. In addition, with only two treatment conditions, it is very easy to counterbalance the design to minimize the threat of confounding from time-related factors or order effects. On the negative side, a study with only two treatments provides only two data points. In this situation it is possible to demonstrate a difference between conditions, but the data do not provide any indication of the functional relationship between the independent and dependent variables. That is, we cannot determine how the dependent variable would respond to small, gradual changes of the independent variable.

With data measured on an interval or ratio scale, the most common strategy for data analysis is to compute a mean score for each treatment condition. The means are used to describe (summarize) the individual treatments, and the difference between means is used to describe the differential effects of the treatments. With two treatment conditions, a repeated-measures $t$ or an analysis of variance can be used to evaluate the statistical significance of the mean difference; that is, to determine whether the obtained mean difference is greater than what would be reasonably expected from sampling error (see Chapter 14). If the data do not permit the calculation of treatment means, there are alternative methods for statistically evaluating the difference between treatments. If the data are measured on an ordinal scale (or can be rank ordered), a Wilcoxon test can be used to evaluate significant differences. Occasionally a within-subjects study comparing two treatments will produce data that show only the direction of difference between the two treatments. For example, a therapist may be able to classify individual clients as showing improvement or showing decline after treatment. In this situation, the data can be statistically evaluated using a sign test to determine whether or not the changes are consistently in one direction (enough to satisfy statistical significance).

## MULTIPLE-TREATMENT DESIGNS

As we discussed in Chapter 10, the primary advantage of using more than two treatment conditions is that the data are more likely to reveal the functional relationship between the two variables being studied (see Figure 10.5, page 260). A researcher can create a series of conditions (independent variable), and then observe how the participants' behavior (dependent variable) changes as they move through the series of treatments.

The disadvantages of using multiple treatments with a within-subjects design include the same basic problem introduced in Chapter 10 (see pages 261-262). If a researcher creates too many treatment conditions, the distinction between treatments may become too small to generate significant differences in behavior. In addition, multiple treatments for a within-subjects design typically increase the amount of time required for each participant to complete the full series of treatments. This can increase the likelihood of participant attrition. Finally, the ability to completely counterbalance a design becomes more difficult as the number of treatment conditions increases.

With data measured on an interval or ratio scale, the typical statistical analysis consists of computing a mean for each treatment condition and then using a repeated-measures analysis of variance to test for any significant differences among the treatment means (see Chapter 14). For more complex within-subjects designs, consult an advanced statistics text to verify that an appropriate analysis technique exists before beginning the research study.

---

Describe the advantages of a two-treatment design.

 Learning Check

---

## 11.6   MATCHED-SUBJECTS DESIGNS

By now it should be clear that a within-subjects design has some distinct advantages and some unique disadvantages compared to a between-subjects design. It should also be clear that the advantages of one design are essentially the same as the disadvantages of the other. The two major concerns for both designs are:

1.  *Individual differences:* The prospect that individual differences may become confounding variables or increase variability is a major disadvantage of between-subjects designs, but these problems are eliminated in a within-subjects design.

2.  *Time-related factors and order effects:* There is always the potential for factors that change over time to distort the results of within-subjects designs, but this problem is eliminated in a between-subjects design, where each individual participates in only one treatment and is measured only once.

Occasionally, researchers attempt to approximate the advantages of both types of designs by using a technique known as a **matched-subjects design.** A matched-subjects design uses a separate group for each treatment condition, but each individual in one group is matched one-to-one with an individual in every other group. The matching is based on a variable considered to be particularly relevant to the specific study. Suppose, for example, that a researcher wants to compare different methods for teaching mathematics in the third grade. For this study, the researcher might give a mathematics achievement test to a large sample of students and then match individuals based on their test scores. Thus, if Tom and Bill have identical math achievement scores, then these two students can be treated as a matched pair, with Tom assigned to one teaching method and Bill assigned to the other. If the study compares three treatments, then the researcher needs to find triplets of matched individuals. Although a matched-subjects study does not have exactly the same individuals in each treatment condition (like a within-subjects design), it does have equivalent (matched) individuals in each treatment.

In Chapter 10 (page 249) we discussed *matching groups* as a technique for ensuring that one group has essentially the same characteristics as another group. Now, we are *matching subjects,* one to one, as an attempt to simulate a within-subjects design.

| Definition | In a **matched-subjects design,** each individual in one group is matched with a participant in each of the other groups. The matching is done so that the matched individuals are equivalent with respect to a variable that the researcher considers to be relevant to the study. |
|---|---|

Because the individuals in one group are matched one-to-one with the individuals in each other group, a matched-subjects design reduces the problems caused by individual differences. For example, a researcher does not need to worry that the participants in one group have better math skills than the participants in another group, because the two groups are matched. In addition, the statistics used to evaluate a matched-subjects design are the same as those used for within-subjects designs. As part of the statistical analysis, the variability caused by individual differences is measured and subtracted from in both designs. Finally, the matched-subjects design uses a separate group for each treatment condition, with each individual measured only once. Thus, there is no chance for the scores to be influenced by time-related factors or order effects. Thus, a matched-subjects design maintains all the advantages of between-subjects and within-subjects designs without the limitations of either.

It is possible to match participants on more than one variable. For example, a researcher could match participants on the basis of age, gender, race, and IQ. In this case, for example, a 22-year-old White female with an IQ of 118 who was in one group would be matched with another 22-year-old White female with an IQ of 118 in another group. Note, however, that matching can become extremely difficult as the number of matched variables increases and the number of different groups increases.

In general, the goal of a matched-subjects design is to simulate a within-subjects design and remove the threat of confounding from time-related factors or order effects. In a within-subjects study, the matching is perfect because the same individuals are used in all treatment conditions. In a matched-subjects design, however, the best we can get is a degree of match that is limited to the variable(s) used for the matching process. Matching on only one or two variables is only a rough approximation to the perfect match that exists in a real within-subjects design. Simply because two individuals have the same IQ is no guarantee that they are also the same or even similar on other variables. Thus, matched-subjects designs are not nearly as effective at removing individual differences as are within-subjects designs.

## CHAPTER SUMMARY

This chapter examines the characteristics of the within-subjects design. The general goal of a within-subjects experiment is to determine whether differences exist between two or more treatment conditions. The defining characteristic of a within-subjects design is that it uses a single group of individuals and tests or observes each individual in all of the different treatments being compared.

The primary advantage of a within-subjects design is that it essentially eliminates all the problems based on individual differences that are the primary concern of a between-subjects design.

First, a within-subjects design will have no individual differences between groups. There is only one group of participants, so the group of individuals in treatment 1 is exactly the same as the group of individuals in treatment 2; hence there are no individual differences between groups to confound the study. Second, because each participant appears in every treatment condition, each individual serves as his or her own control or baseline. This makes it possible to measure and remove the variability caused by individual differences.

The primary disadvantage of a within-subjects design is that the scores obtained in one treatment condition are directly related to scores in every other condition. The relationship between scores across treatments creates the potential for the scores in one treatment to be influenced by previous treatments, previous measurements, or previous experience. This general problem is called an *order effect* because the current scores may have been affected by events that occurred earlier in the order of treatments. Order effects can be a confounding variable in a within-subjects design. Two kinds of order effects are *carryover effects* and *progressive error*. A technique for dealing with such problems is to *counterbalance* the conditions.

In addition to order effects, other threats to the internal validity of within-subjects designs are discussed, as are different versions of the within-subjects design.

## KEY WORDS

within-subjects experimental
   design or repeated-measures
   design
history
maturation

instrumentation or instrumental
   bias
statistical regression or
   regression toward the mean
carryover effects

progressive error
order effects
counterbalancing
matched-subjects design

## EXERCISES

1. In addition to the key words, you should also be able to define the following terms:
   participant attrition
   testing effects
   fatigue
   practice effects
   complete counterbalancing
   partial counterbalancing
   Latin square
2. Describe the major difference between within-subjects and between-subjects designs.
3. Describe the advantages of the within-subjects design.
4. Describe the disadvantages of the within-subjects design.

5. Explain how order effects can create problems in a within-subjects design.
6. Explain how the process of counterbalancing attempts to keep order effects from becoming a confounding variable in a within-subjects design.
7. Explain how statistical regression and instrumental bias threaten the internal validity of within-subjects designs.
8. Describe the disadvantages of the multiple-treatment design.
9. Describe the advantages of a matched-subjects design.

1. Use InfoTrac College Edition to locate an example of an experimental study using a within-subjects design. As in the previous chapter, we suggest that you focus your search in journals such as *Human Factors*, *Behavioral Medicine*, and the *Journal of Social Psychology*. Also, you can simply try using *within subjects* as a key word. When you locate a potential article, check that it really is an experiment (that a variable was manipulated) and that it really uses a within-subjects design (that one sample was measured in all conditions).

    a. Describe how the different treatments or conditions compared.

    b. Did the study use counterbalancing? If so, was it complete or partial? If not, is there reason to suspect that order effects may have influenced the results?

    c. Identify the research question this study is trying to answer.

    d. Could the research question for this study have been answered using a between-subjects design? If so, how? If not, why not?

2. Using the same research article you located for Exercise 1, determine whether you think that the internal validity of the study is threatened by history, maturation, instrumentation, or regression. In each case, explain why or why not.

# Factorial Designs

## CHAPTER OVERVIEW

Step 6 of the research process involves selecting a research design. In this chapter we discuss in detail research designs that include more than one independent variable—factorial designs. The unique information they provide is considered, as well as different types and various applications of factorial designs.

## 12.1   INTRODUCTION TO FACTORIAL DESIGNS

In most research situations the goal is to examine the relationship between two variables by isolating those variables within the research study. The idea is to eliminate or reduce the influence of any outside variables that may disguise or obscure the specific relationship under investigation. For example, experimental research (discussed in Chapter 8) typically focuses on one independent variable (which is expected to influence behavior) and one dependent variable (which is a measure of the behavior). In real life, however, variables rarely exist in isolation. That is, behavior usually is influenced by a variety of different variables acting and interacting simultaneously. To examine these more complex, real-life situations, researchers often design research studies that include more than one independent variable. Consider the following example:

> It is common practice for a host to serve coffee at the end of a party where the guests have been drinking alcohol. Presumably, the caffeine will counteract some of the effects of the alcohol so that the guests will be more mentally alert when they head out for the trip home. Most of us believe that we have a good understanding of the effects of caffeine and alcohol on mental alertness. For many people, the first cup of coffee each morning is necessary to get started; on the other hand, many people have a glass of wine in the evening to help them relax and unwind at the end of a busy day. But do we really know how these substances influence our ability to react in an emergency situation? Does that cup of coffee at the end of the party really improve reaction time? These questions were addressed in a study by Liguori and Robinson (2001). They designed an experiment in which both alcohol and caffeine consumption were manipulated within the same study. They observed how quickly participants with different levels of alcohol and caffeine could apply the brakes in a simulated driving test. Figure 12.1 shows the general structure of this experiment. Notice that the study involves two independent variables: Alcohol consumption is varied from no alcohol to enough to create dizziness or a "high"; caffeine consumption is varied from no caffeine to 200 mg to 400 mg. The two independent variables create a matrix, with the different values of caffeine defining the columns and the different levels of alcohol defining the rows. The resulting $2 \times 3$ matrix shows six different combinations of the variables, producing six treatment conditions to be examined. The dependent variable for the study is a measure of reaction time in a simulated driving emergency situation for people observed in each of the six conditions.

To simplify further discussion of this kind of research study, some basic terminology and definitions are in order. When two or more independent variables are combined in a single study, the independent variables are commonly called **factors.** For the study in our example, the two factors are alcohol consumption and caffeine consumption. A research study involving two or more factors is called a **factorial design.** This kind of design is often referred to by the number of its factors, as a **two-factor design** or a **three-factor design.**

| | No Caffeine | 200 Mg Caffeine | 400 Mg Caffeine |
|---|---|---|---|
| Alcohol | Reaction time scores for a group of participants who received alcohol and a 0-mg dose of caffeine | Reaction time scores for a group of participants who received alcohol and a 200-mg dose of caffeine | Reaction time scores for a group of participants who received alcohol and a 400-mg dose of caffeine |
| No Alcohol | Reaction time scores for a group of participants who received no alcohol and a 0-mg dose of caffeine | Reaction time scores for a group of participants who received no alcohol and a 200-mg dose of caffeine | Reaction time scores for a group of participants who received no alcohol and a 400-mg dose of caffeine |

Figure 12.1    The Structure of a Two-Factor Experiment Where Alcohol Consumption (Factor 1) and Caffeine Consumption (Factor 2) Are Manipulated in the Same Study
The purpose of the experiment is to examine how different combinations of alcohol and caffeine affect reaction time in a simulated emergency driving situation.

Our example is a two-factor design. A research study with only one independent variable is often called a **single-factor design.**

Generically, each factor is denoted by a letter (A, B, C, etc.). In addition, factorial designs use a notation system that identifies both the number of factors and the number of values or **levels** that exist for each factor (see Ch. 8, page 194). The previous example has two levels for the alcohol factor (factor A) and three for the caffeine factor (factor B) and can be denoted as a 2 × 3 (read as "two by three") factorial design, with 2 indicating two levels of the first factor (alcohol) and 3 symbolizing three levels of the second factor (caffeine). The number of treatment conditions can be determined by multiplying the levels for each factor. Additional examples: a 2 × 2 factorial design (the simplest factorial design) would represent a two-factor design with two levels of the first factor and two levels of the second, with a total of four treatment conditions; and a 2 × 3 × 2 design would represent a three-factor design with two, three, and two levels of each of the factors, respectively, for a total of twelve conditions. Factorial designs including more than two independent variables are discussed in Section 12.4.

It is possible to have a factor that is not a manipulated variable and therefore is not a true independent variable but rather a quasi-independent variable. For example, a researcher could examine work proficiency for males and females (factor 1) under different temperature conditions (factor 2). In this case, gender is a factor, but it is not manipulated. This kind of factorial study is discussed in Section 12.4.

In an experiment, an independent variable is often called a **factor,** especially in experiments that include two or more independent variables.

A research design that includes two or more factors is called a **factorial design.**

As we have noted, one advantage of a factorial design is that it creates a more "realistic" situation than can be obtained by examining a single factor in isolation. Because behavior is influenced by a variety of factors usually acting together, it is sensible to examine two or more factors simultaneously in a single study. At first glance it may appear that this kind of research is unnecessarily complicated. Why not do two separate, simple studies looking at each factor by itself? The answer to this question is that combining of factors within one study provides researchers with a unique opportunity to examine not only how the factors influence behavior but also how the factors influence or interact with each other. Returning to the alcohol/caffeine example, a researcher who manipulated only alcohol consumption would observe how alcohol affects behavior. Similarly, manipulating only caffeine consumption would demonstrate how caffeine affects behavior. However, combining the two variables permits researchers to examine how changes in caffeine consumption can influence the effects of alcohol on behavior. The idea that two factors can act together, creating unique conditions that are different from either factor acting alone, underlies the value of a factorial design.

Learning
Check

Suppose a researcher is interested in examining the effects of mood and food deprivation on eating. Females listen to one of two types of music to induce either a happy or a sad mood, following either 19 hours of food deprivation (breakfast and lunch are skipped) or no deprivation. In a feeding laboratory setting, the amount of food consumed is measured in all participants.

a. How many independent variables or factors does this study have? What are they?

b. Describe this study using the notation system that indicates factors and numbers of levels of each factor.

In addition to a separate group for each cell (a between-subjects design), the same group can participate in all of the different cells (a within-subjects design). These two designs can also be mixed, for example, using separate groups for one factor but having each group participate in all the different conditions defined by the second factor. These different versions of a two-factor study are discussed in Section 12.4.

## 12.2    MAIN EFFECTS AND INTERACTIONS

The primary advantage of a factorial design is that it allows researchers to examine how unique combinations of factors, acting together, influence behavior. To explore this feature in more detail, we focus on designs involving only two factors; that is, the simplest possible example of a factorial design. In Section 12.4, we look briefly at more complex situations involving three or more factors.

The structure of a two-factor design can be represented by a matrix in which the levels of one factor determine the columns and the levels of the second factor determine the rows (see Figure 12.1). Each cell in the matrix corresponds to a specific combination of the factors; that is, a separate treatment condition. The research study would involve observing and measuring a group of individuals under the conditions described by each cell.

Learning
Check

With a matrix, diagram the example study examining the effects of mood and food deprivation on eating.

The data from a two-factor study provide three separate and distinct sets of information describing how the two factors independently and jointly affect behavior. To demonstrate the three kinds of information, the general structure of the alcohol/caffeine study is repeated in Table 12.1, with hypothetical data added showing the mean reaction time (in milliseconds) for participants in each of the cells. The data provide the following information:

1.  Each column of the matrix corresponds to a specific level of caffeine consumption. For example, all of the participants tested in the first column (both sets of scores) were measured with no caffeine. By computing the mean score for each column, we obtain an overall mean for each of the three different caffeine conditions. The resulting three column means provide an indication of how caffeine consumption (factor 1) affects behavior. The differences among the three column means are called *the main effect for caffeine*. In more general terms, the mean differences among the columns determine the **main effect** for one factor. Notice that the calculation of the mean for each column involves averaging both levels of alcohol consumption. (Half the scores were obtained with alcohol and half were obtained with no alcohol.) Thus, the alcohol consumption is balanced or matched across all three caffeine levels, which means that any differences obtained between the columns cannot be explained by differences in alcohol.

    > We use hypothetical data throughout the chapter to demonstrate different patterns of results. If you are curious about the real results, see the Liguori and Robinson (2001) article.

    For the data in Table 12.1, the participants in the no-caffeine condition have an average score of 250. This column mean was obtained by averaging the two groups (Mean = 290 and Mean = 210) in the no-caffeine column. In a similar way, the other column means are computed as 225 and 200. These three means show a general tendency for faster reaction times as caffeine consumption increases. This relationship between caffeine consumption and reaction time is the main effect for caffeine. Finally, note that the mean differences among columns simply describe the main effect for caffeine. A statistical test is necessary to determine whether or not the mean differences are significant.

    > For reaction time, smaller numbers indicate faster reaction times.

2.  Just as we determine the overall main effect for caffeine by calculating the column means for the data in Table 12.1, we can determine the overall effect of alcohol consumption by examining the rows of the data matrix. For example, all of the participants in the top row were tested with alcohol. The mean score for these participants (all three sets of scores) provides a measure of reaction time under that level of alcohol. Similarly, the overall mean for the bottom row describes reaction time when no alcohol is given. The difference between these two means is called the *main effect for alcohol*. As before, notice that the process of obtaining the row means involves averaging all three levels of caffeine. Thus, each row mean includes exactly the same caffeine conditions such that caffeine is matched across rows and cannot explain the mean differences between rows. In general terms, the differences between the column means define the main effect for one factor, and the differences between the row means define the main effect for the second factor.

    For the data shown in Table 12.1, the overall mean for the first row (alcohol) is 250. This mean is obtained by averaging the three treatment means in the top row (290, 250, and 210). Similarly, the overall mean reaction time for participants in the no-alcohol condition is 200. The 50-point difference between the two row means (250 and 200) describes the main effect for alcohol. In this study, alcohol consumption decreases (slows) reaction time by 50 points.

3. A factorial design allows researchers to examine how combinations of factors, working together, affect behavior. Although the effects of each independent variable, and hence, each main effect, can be examined in its own separate study, a factorial design provides an opportunity to explore potential interaction between the two variables as well. For the data in Table 12.1, this means looking at the effects of caffeine and alcohol that are different from the effect of caffeine alone or the effect of alcohol alone. In the data matrix, each cell corresponds to a specific combination of the two factors, and the mean differences between cells indicate differential treatment effects. The question is whether the differences between cells can be explained by the overall main effects of the two factors, or whether the cell differences show effects that are separate and distinct from the overall main effects.

For example, the data in Table 12.1 show a 50-point main effect for alcohol. However, in the first column, where the caffeine level is 0, the change in alcohol produces an 80-point effect on reaction time (means of 290 versus 210). Also, in the third column (where the caffeine level is 400 mg), the two alcohol conditions show only a 20-point mean difference in reaction time, from a mean of 210 to a mean of 190. In each case, the mean difference between cells is *not explained* by the overall 50-point effect of alcohol. For these data, individual combinations of caffeine and alcohol appear to have effects that are different from the overall effects of caffeine or alcohol acting alone. The "extra" mean differences between cells that are not explained by the main effects are called an **interaction between factors.** In this example, the alcohol has a large effect on reaction time (more than 50 points) when there is no

TABLE 12.1

**Hypothetical Data Showing the Treatment Means for a Two-Factor Study Examining How Different Combinations of Alcohol and Caffeine Affect Reaction Time (in Milliseconds) in a Simulated Emergency Driving Situation**

The data are structured to create main effects for both factors and an interaction.

|  | No Caffeine | 200 Mg Caffeine | 400 Mg Caffeine |  |
|---|---|---|---|---|
| Alcohol | $M = 290$ | $M = 250$ | $M = 210$ | Overall $M = 250$ |
| No Alcohol | $M = 210$ | $M = 200$ | $M = 190$ | Overall $M = 200$ |
|  | Overall $M = 250$ | Overall $M = 225$ | Overall $M = 200$ |  |

caffeine but a small effect (less than 50 points) when combined with 400 mg of caffeine. The special advantage of combining two factors within the same study is the ability to examine the unique effects caused by an interaction between factors.

Thus, the results from a two-factor design reveal how each factor independently affects behavior (the main effects) and how the two factors operating together (the interaction) can affect behavior. For the data in Table 12.1, the main effect for alcohol consumption describes how reaction time in a simulated driving test is influenced by alcohol independent of caffeine consumption. The main effect for caffeine consumption describes how reaction time is affected by changes in caffeine independent of alcohol. Finally, the interaction describes how combinations of alcohol and caffeine consumption influence reaction time in a simulated driving test in ways that are different from alcohol acting alone or from caffeine acting alone.

In general, when the data from a two-factor study are organized in a matrix as in Table 12.1, the mean differences between the columns describe the main effect for one factor and the mean differences between rows describe the main effect for the second factor. The main effects reflect the results that would be obtained if each factor were examined in its own separate experiment. The extra mean differences that exist between cells in the matrix (differences that are not explained by the overall main effects) describe the interaction and represent the unique information that is obtained by combining the two factors in a single study.

Definitions

The mean differences among the levels of one factor are called the **main effect** of that factor. When the research study is represented as a matrix with one factor defining the rows and the second factor defining the columns, then the mean differences among the rows define the main effect for one factor, and the mean differences among the columns define the main effect for the second factor.

An **interaction between factors** occurs whenever the mean differences between individual treatment conditions, or cells, are different from what is predicted from the overall main effects of the factors.

Learning Check

Use the data presented in Table 12.1 to determine what numbers are compared to assess:

    a. the main effects for caffeine
    b. the main effects for alcohol
    c. the interaction between caffeine and alcohol

## 12.3    MORE ABOUT INTERACTIONS

The previous section introduced the concept of interaction as the unique effects produced by two factors working together. Now we define interaction more formally and look in detail at this unique component of a factorial design. For simplicity, we continue to examine two-factor designs and postpone discussion of more complex designs (and more complex interactions).

As noted, the data in Table 12.1 show an 80-point difference between alcohol consumption and no alcohol consumption when there is no caffeine. This value is different from the 50-point difference shown as the main effect for alcohol and therefore indicates an interaction. In a similar fashion, the main effects for caffeine show that reaction times speed up from a mean 225 to a mean of 200 when caffeine level is increased from 200 mg to 400 mg. However, this 25-point main effect does not explain the mean differences between individual cells. For example, when the alcohol is high, increasing caffeine from 200 mg to 400 mg results in a 40-point change in performance, not the 25-point change predicted from the main effect. Again, the main effects do not explain the cell differences, which indicates an interaction.

As a counterexample, consider the data in Table 12.2. To construct this new set of data, the same column means and row means that appeared in Table 12.1 are used. Thus, the new data show exactly the same main effects as the original set of data. However, the individual cell means have been adjusted to eliminate the interaction. Notice, for example, that the 50-point main effect for alcohol (row means of 250 versus 200) now explains the individual cell differences for every caffeine condition. When the caffeine level is 0, there is a 50-point difference between the alcohol and no-alcohol conditions. This 50-point difference (the main effect) exists for all three caffeine levels. Similarly, the main effect for caffeine shows a 25-point change in reaction time when the caffeine level is increased from 200 mg to 400 mg (overall reaction times speed up from a mean of 225 to a mean of 200). This 25-point main effect explains the individual cell differences for no alcohol (a 25-point drop from 200 to 175) and for alcohol (a 25-point drop from

| TABLE 12.2 |

**Hypothetical Data Showing the Treatment Means for a Two-Factor Study Examining How Different Combinations of Alcohol and Caffeine Affect Reaction Time (in Milliseconds) in a Simulated Emergency Driving Situation**

The data are structured to create the same main effects as in Table 12.1 but without an interaction.

|  | No Caffeine | 200 Mg Caffeine | 400 Mg Caffeine |  |
|---|---|---|---|---|
| Alcohol | $M = 275$ | $M = 250$ | $M = 225$ | Overall $M = 250$ |
| No Alcohol | $M = 225$ | $M = 200$ | $M = 175$ | Overall $M = 200$ |
|  | Overall $M = 250$ | Overall $M = 225$ | Overall $M = 200$ |  |

250 to 225). For these data, there are no "extra" unexplained mean differences among the cells; all the mean differences are accounted for by the main effects, and there is no interaction.

## ALTERNATIVE DEFINITIONS OF INTERACTION

A slightly different perspective on the concept of interaction focuses on the notion of interdependency between the factors, as opposed to independence. More specifically, if the two factors are independent so that the effect of either one is not influenced by the other, then there is no interaction. On the other hand, if the two factors are interdependent so that one factor does influence the effect of the other, then there is an interaction. The notion of interdependence is consistent with our earlier discussion of interactions; if one factor does influence the effects of the other, then unique combinations of the factors produce unique effects.

---

When the effects of one factor depend on the different levels of a second factor, then there is an **interaction between the factors.**

Definition

---

This second definition of an interaction uses different terminology but is equivalent to the first definition (page 297). When the effects of a factor vary depending on the levels of another factor, the two factors are combining to produce unique effects. Returning to the data in Table 12.1, notice that the size of the alcohol effect (top row versus bottom row) *depends on* the caffeine. At no caffeine, for example, the alcohol effect is 80 points. However, the alcohol effect decreases to 50 points at 200 mg and decreases further to 20 points when the caffeine level is 400 mg. Again, the effect of one factor (alcohol) depends on the levels of the second factor (caffeine), which indicates an interaction. By contrast, the data in Table 12.2 show that the effect of alcohol is independent of caffeine. For these data, the change in alcohol shows the same 50-point effect for all three levels of caffeine. Thus, the alcohol effect does not depend on caffeine, and there is no interaction.

When the results of a two-factor study are presented in a graph, the concept of interaction can be defined in terms of the pattern displayed in the graph. Figure 12.2 shows the original data from Table 12.1 that were used to illustrate the existence of an interaction. To construct this figure, one of the factors was selected as the independent variable to appear on the horizontal axis; in this case, the different levels of caffeine are displayed. The dependent variable, reaction time, is shown on the vertical axis. Notice that the figure actually contains two separate graphs; the top line shows the relationship between caffeine and reaction time when alcohol is given, and the bottom line shows the relationship when no alcohol is given. In general, the graph matches the structure of the data matrix; the columns of the matrix appear as values along the X-axis, and each row of the matrix appears as a separate line in the graph.

For this particular set of data (Figure 12.2), notice that the lines in the graph are not parallel. The distance between the lines decreases from left to right. For these data, the distance between the lines corresponds to the alcohol effect, that

Figure 12.2    A Line Graph of the Data From Table 12.1
The hypothetical data are structured to show main
effects for both factors and an interaction.

is, the mean difference in reaction times for alcohol and no alcohol. The fact
that this difference depends on caffeine indicates an interaction between factors.

<table>
<tr><td>**Definition**</td><td>When the results of a two-factor study are graphed, the existence of nonparallel lines (lines that cross or converge) is an indication of an **interaction** between the two factors. (Note that a statistical test is needed to determine whether or not the interaction is significant.)</td></tr>
</table>

To demonstrate the pattern that appears in a graph when there is no interaction, the data from Table 12.2 are presented in Figure 12.3. Notice that the
two lines in this figure are parallel; that is, the distance between lines is constant. In this case, the distance between lines reflects the 50-point difference in
reaction time between alcohol and no alcohol, and this 50-point difference is
the same for all three caffeine conditions.

**Learning Check**    Evaluate the means in the following matrix.

|  | Treatment 1 | Treatment 2 |
|---|---|---|
| Males | $M = 10$ | $M = 30$ |
| Females | $M = 20$ | $M = 50$ |

a.   Is there evidence of a main effect for the treatment factor?

b.   Is there evidence of a main effect for the gender factor?

c.   Is there evidence of an interaction? (Hint: Sketch a graph of the data.)

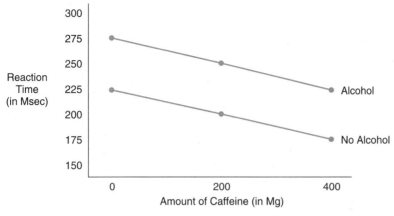

Figure 12.3    A Line Graph of the Data From Table 12.2
The hypothetical data are structured to show
main effects for both factors but no interaction.

## INTERPRETING MAIN EFFECTS AND INTERACTIONS

As we have noted, the mean differences between columns and between rows describe the main effects in a two-factor study, and the extra mean differences describe the interaction. However, you should realize that these mean differences are simply *descriptive* and must be evaluated by a statistical hypothesis test before they can be considered *significant*. That is, the obtained mean differences may not represent a real treatment effect but rather may be simply due to chance or error. Until the data are evaluated by a hypothesis test, be cautious about interpreting any results from a two-factor study.

When a statistical analysis does indicate significant effects, you must still be careful about interpreting the outcome. In particular, if the analysis results in a significant interaction, then the main effects, whether significant or not, may present a distorted view of the actual outcome. Remember, the main effect for one factor is obtained by averaging all the different levels of the second factor. Because each main effect is an *average*, it may not accurately represent any of the individual effects that were used to compute the average. To illustrate this point, Figure 12.4 presents two hypothetical outcomes from a two-factor experiment.

Figure 12.4a shows a data matrix and a graph presenting one set of data from a two-factor study examining the effects of a drug intended to reduce arthritis pain. The first factor in the study is drug versus no drug (placebo), and the second factor is administration of the drug on a full stomach versus an empty stomach. The dependent variable is a measure of arthritis pain. Looking first at the data matrix, recognize that these results show a 10-point main effect for the drug factor; the overall mean with the drug (second column) is 10 points lower than the overall mean for participants with no drug (first column). However, looking at the graph, recognize that these data show an interaction. One interpretation of the interaction is that the drug effect *depends on* stomach fullness; that is, the effect of the drug is different for a full stomach than for an empty stomach. Specifically, the drug seems to have no effect on an empty stomach, but it has a

(a) Data showing how an overall main effect can be distorted by an interaction

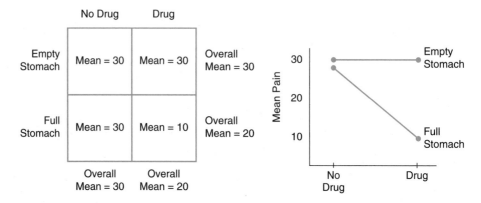

(b) Data showing how an interaction can disguise main effects

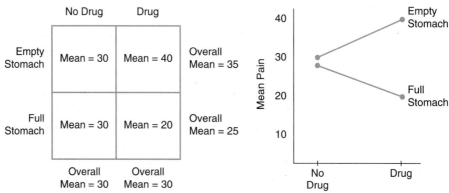

Figure 12.4   Hypothetical Results for a Two-Factor Study
Examining the Effect of a Drug Intended to Reduce Arthritis Pain
One factor is drug dosage (drug versus no drug), and the second
factor is the state of the participant (empty stomach versus full stomach).

20-point effect on a full stomach. The 10-point main effect was obtained by averaging these two values (0 and 20), but in truth the 10-point main effect does not accurately describe the influence of the drug for anyone. In this example, concluding that the drug has a 10-point effect on behavior (based on the main effect) would be misleading.

Now consider the second set of data shown in Figure 12.4b. Starting with the data matrix, these data show no main effect for the drug factor; participants with the drug and participants without the drug both show a mean of 30. However, the data once again show an interaction, suggesting that the effect of the drug is different for empty stomach than it is for full stomach. Specifically, the drug appears to increase pain scores by 10 points for empty stomach and to decrease scores by 10 points for full stomach. Averaging these two values (+10 and −10) results in the zero difference for the main effect. However, the main effect does not accurately describe the results. In particular, it would be incorrect to conclude that the drug has no effect.

In general, the presence of an interaction can obscure or distort the main effects of either factor. Whenever a statistical analysis produces a significant interaction, you should take a close look at the data before giving any credibility to the main effects.

## INDEPENDENCE OF MAIN EFFECTS AND INTERACTIONS

The two-factor study allows researchers to evaluate three separate sets of mean differences: (1) the mean differences from the main effect of factor 1, (2) the mean differences from the main effect of factor 2, and (3) the mean differences from the interaction between factors. The three sets of mean differences are not only separate, they are also completely independent. Thus, it is possible for the results from a two-factor study to show any possible combination of main effects and interaction. The data sets in Figure 12.5 show several possibilities. To simplify discussion, the two factors are labeled A and B, with factor A defining the rows of the data matrix and factor B defining the columns.

Figure 12.5a shows data with mean differences between levels of factor A but no mean differences for factor B and no interaction. To identify the main effect for factor A, notice that the overall mean for the top row is 10 points higher than the overall mean for the bottom row. This 10-point difference is the main effect for factor A, or simply the A effect. To evaluate the mean effect for factor B, notice that both columns have exactly the same overall mean, indicating no difference between levels of factor B; hence, no B effect. Finally, the absence of an interaction is indicated by the fact that the overall A effect (the 10-point difference) is constant within each column; that is, the A effect *does not depend* on the levels of factor B. (Alternatively, the data indicate that the overall B effect is constant within each row.)

Figure 12.5b shows data with an A effect and a B effect but no interaction. For these data, the A effect is indicated by the 10-point mean difference between rows, and the B effect is indicated by the 20-point mean difference between columns. The fact that the 10-point A effect is constant within each column indicates no interaction.

Finally, Figure 12.5c shows data that display an interaction but no main effect for factor A or for factor B. For these data, note that there is no mean difference between rows (no A effect) and no mean difference between columns (no B effect). However, within each row (or within each column) there are mean differences. The "extra" mean differences within the rows and columns cannot be explained by the overall main effects and therefore indicate an interaction.

## 12.4    TYPES OF FACTORIAL DESIGNS

Thus far, we have examined only one version of all the many different types of factorial designs. In particular,

- All of the designs that we have considered use a separate group of participants for each of the individual treatment combinations or cells. In research terminology, we have looked exclusively at *between-subjects* designs.

(a) Data showing a main effect for factor A but no main effect for factor B and no interaction

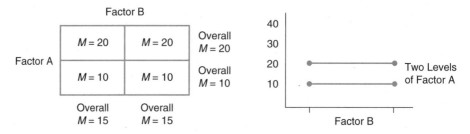

(b) Data showing main effects for both factor A and factor B but no interaction

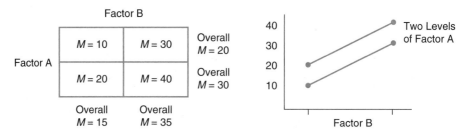

(c) Data showing no main effect for either factor, but an interaction

Figure 12.5  Three Possible Combinations of Main Effects and Interactions in a Two-Factor Experiment

- All of the previous examples use factors that are true independent variables. That is, the factors are manipulated by the researcher so that the research study is an example of the *experimental* strategy.

  Although it is possible to have a separate group for each of the individual cells (a between-subjects design), it is also possible to have the same group of individuals participate in all of the different cells (a within-subjects design). In addition, it is possible to construct a factorial design where the factors are not manipulated but rather are quasi-independent variables (see Chapter 9, page 236). Finally, a factorial design can use any combination of factors. As a result, a factorial study can combine elements of experimental and nonexperimental designs, and it can combine elements of between-subjects and within-subjects designs within a single research study. A two-factor design, for example, may include one between-subjects factor (with a separate group for each level of the factor) and one within-subjects factor (with each group measured in several different treatment conditions). The same study could also include one experimental factor (with a manipulated independent variable) and one nonexperimental factor (with a pre-existing, nonmanipulated variable). The ability to mix designs within a single research study provides researchers with the potential to blend several different research strategies within one study. This potential allows researchers to develop studies that address scientific questions that could not be answered by any single strategy. In the following sections we examine some of the possibilities for mixed or blended factorial designs.

## BETWEEN-SUBJECTS AND WITHIN-SUBJECTS DESIGNS

It is possible to construct a factorial study that is purely a between-subjects design; that is, in which there is a separate group of participants for each of the treatment conditions. As we noted in Chapter 10, this type of design has some definite advantages as well as some disadvantages. A particular disadvantage for a factorial study is that a between-subjects design can require a large number of participants. For example, a 2 × 4 factorial design has eight different treatment conditions. A separate group of 30 participants in each condition requires a total of 240 (8 × 30) participants. As noted in Chapter 10, another disadvantage of between-subject designs is that individual differences (characteristics that differ from one participant to another) can become confounding variables and can increase the variability of the scores. On the positive side, a between-subjects design completely avoids any problem from order effects because each score is completely independent of every other score. In general, between-subjects designs are best suited to situations where a lot of participants are available, where individual differences are relatively small, and where order effects are likely.

At the other extreme, it is possible to construct a factorial study that is purely a within-subjects design. In this case, a single group of individuals participates in all of the separate treatment conditions. As we noted in Chapter 11, this type of design has some definite advantages and disadvantages. A particular disadvantage for a factorial study is the number of different treatment conditions that each participant must undergo. In a 2 × 4 design, for example, each participant must be measured in eight different treatment conditions. The large number of different treatments can be very time consuming, which increases the chances that participants will quit and walk away before the study is ended (participant attrition). In addition, having each participant undergo a long series of treatment conditions can increase the potential for order effects (such as fatigue or practice effects) and can make it more difficult to counterbalance the design to control for order effects. Two advantages of within-subjects designs are: (1) they require only one group of participants and (2) they eliminate or greatly reduce the problems associated with individual differences. In general, within-subjects designs are best suited for situations where individual differences are relatively large and where there is little reason to expect order effects to be large and disruptive.

### Mixed Designs: Within and Between Subjects
Very often a researcher encounters a situation in which the advantages or convenience of a between-subjects design apply to one factor but a within-subjects design is preferable for a second factor. For example, a researcher may prefer to

use a within-subjects design to take maximum advantage of a small group of participants. However, if one factor is expected to produce large order effects, then a between-subjects design should be used for that factor. In this situation it is possible to construct a **mixed design** with one between-subjects factor and one within-subjects factor. If the design is pictured as a matrix with one factor defining the rows and the second factor defining the columns, then the mixed design has a separate group for each row with each group participating in all of the different columns.

A factorial study that combines two different research designs is called a **mixed design.** A common example of a mixed design is a factorial study with one between-subjects factor and one within-subjects factor.

Figure 12.6 shows a mixed factorial design in a study examining the relationship between mood and memory. The typical result in this research area is that people tend to recall information that is consistent with their current mood. Thus, people remember happy things when they are happy and remember sad things when they are sad. In a study like the one shown in Figure 12.6, Teasdale and Fogarty (1979) manipulated mood by instructing one group of participants to read a series of increasingly depressing statements (such as "Looking back on my life, I wonder if I have accomplished anything really worthwhile") and another group to read a series of increasingly euphoric statements (such as "Life is so full and interesting, it is great to be alive"). Thus, the researchers created a between-subjects factor consisting of a happy mood group and a sad mood group. In Figure 12.6, the two groups correspond to the two rows in the matrix. All participants were then presented a list of words that contained some words with positive/pleasant associations and some words with negative/unpleasant associations. For each participant, the researchers recorded how many pleasant words were recalled and how many unpleasant words were recalled. Thus, the researchers created a within-subjects factor consisting of pleasant words and unpleasant words. The within-subjects factor corresponds to the columns in Figure 12.6.

Learning
Checks

For a two-factor research study with three levels for factor A and two levels for factor B, how many participants are needed to obtain five scores in each treatment condition for each of the following situations?

a. Both factors are between subjects.

b. Both factors are within subjects.

c. Factor A is a between-subjects factor, and factor B is within subjects.

A researcher would like to use a factorial study to compare two different strategies for solving problems. Participants will be trained to use one of the strategies and then tested on three different types of problems. Thus, the two strategies make up one factor, the three types of problems make up the second factor, and problem-solving scores are the dependent variable. For this study, which factor(s) should be between-subjects and which should be within subjects? Explain your answer.

Two separate groups of participants

| | Positive Words | Negative Words |
|---|---|---|
| Happy Mood | Mean recall $M = 70$ | Mean recall $M = 23$ |
| Sad Mood | Mean recall $M = 48$ | Mean recall $M = 35$ |

**Figure 12.6**   Hypothetical Results From a Mixed Two-Factor Study That Combines One Between-Subjects Factor and One Within-Subjects Factor The researchers induced a feeling of happiness in one group of participants and a feeling of sadness in another group to create the between-subjects factor (happy/sad). For each group, memory was tested for a set of words with positive connotations and a set of words with negative connotations to create a within-subjects factor (positive/negative).

## EXPERIMENTAL AND NONEXPERIMENTAL DESIGNS

As we demonstrated with the alcohol-and-caffeine example at the beginning of this chapter, it is possible to construct a factorial study that is a purely experimental research design. In this case, both factors are true independent variables that are manipulated by the researcher. It also is possible to construct a factorial study that is purely nonexperimental. In a two-factor study, for example, a purely nonexperimental design simply means that both factors are nonmanipulated, quasi-independent variables. For example, Bahrick and Hall (1991) examined the permanence of memory by testing recall for high school algebra and geometry. The study compared two groups of participants, those who had taken college-level math courses and those who had no advanced math courses in college. Note that these groups were not created by manipulating an independent variable; instead, they are pre-existing, nonequivalent groups, and therefore they form a nonexperimental factor. The second factor in the study was time. The researchers tested recall at different time intervals ranging from 3 years up to 55 years after high school. Again, note that time is a nonmanipulated variable and hence another nonexperimental factor. Thus, the study contains no manipulated variables and is a purely nonexperimental design. Incidentally, the group with no advanced college math showed a systematic decline in mathematics knowledge over time, but the group with college math showed excellent recall of mathematics even decades after their high school courses.

### Mixed Designs: Experimental and Nonexperimental

In the behavioral sciences it is very common for a factorial design to mix an experimental design for one factor and a nonexperimental design for another factor. This type of study is another example of a **mixed design.** Typically, this kind of study involves one factor that is a true independent variable consisting of a set of manipulated treatment conditions, and a second factor that is a quasi-independent variable falling into one of the following categories:

1.  The second factor is a pre-existing participant characteristic such as age or gender. In this case, the researcher wants to examine whether the treatment conditions have the same impact on males as on females, or the question is whether the treatment effects change as a function of age. Note that pre-existing characteristics create nonequivalent groups; thus this is a quasi-experimental factor.

2.  The second factor is time. In this case, the research question concerns how the different treatment effects persist over time. For example, two different therapy techniques may be equally effective immediately after the therapy is concluded, but one may continue to have an effect over time, while the other loses effectiveness as time passes. Note that time is not controlled or manipulated by the researcher, so this is a quasi-experimental factor.

| Definition | A factorial study that combines two different research strategies is called a **mixed design.** A common example of a mixed design is a factorial study with one experimental factor and one nonexperimental factor. |
| --- | --- |

For example, Shrauger (1972) examined how the presence or absence of an audience can influence people's performance. Half of the research participants worked alone (no audience) on a concept-formation task, and half of the participants worked with an audience of people who claimed to be interested in observing the experiment. Note that the audience-versus-no-audience variable is manipulated by the researcher, so this is an experimental factor. The second factor in Shrauger's study was self-esteem. In each of the audience groups, participants were divided into high self-esteem and low self-esteem groups. Note that the second factor, self-esteem, is a pre-existing participant variable and therefore a nonexperimental factor. The structure of this study, including results similar to Shrauger's actual data, is shown in Figure 12.7. Notice that the results show an interaction between the two factors. Specifically, the presence of an audience had a large effect on participants with low self-esteem, but the audience has essentially no effect on those with high self-esteem.

 Learning Checks

A researcher would like to compare two therapy techniques for treating depression. One technique is suspected to have only temporary effects, and the other is expected to produce permanent or long-lasting effects. Describe a factorial research study that would compare the effectiveness of the two techniques and answer the question about the duration of their effectiveness. Identify which factor is experimental and which is nonexperimental.

A researcher would like to compare two therapy techniques for treating depression. One technique is expected to be very effective for patients with relatively mild depression, and the other is expected to be more effective for treating moderate to severe depression. Describe a factorial research study that would compare the effectiveness of the two techniques and answer the question about which is better for different levels of depression. Identify which factor is experimental and which is nonexperimental.

**Figure 12.7** Hypothetical Results From a Mixed Two-Factor Study That Combines One Experimental Factor and One Quasi-Experimental Factor. To create the experimental factor (audience versus no audience), the researchers manipulated whether or not the participants performed in front of an audience. Within each experimental condition, to create a quasi-experimental factor, two nonequivalent groups of participants were observed (high versus low self-esteem). The dependent variable is the number of errors committed by each participant.

## PRETEST–POSTTEST CONTROL GROUP DESIGNS

In Chapter 9 we introduced a quasi-experimental design known as the pretest–posttest nonequivalent control group design (page 223). This design involves two separate groups of participants. One group, called the treatment group, is measured before and after receiving a treatment. A second group, the control group, also is measured twice (pretest and posttest) but does not receive any treatment between the two measurements. Using the notation introduced in Chapter 9, this design can be represented as follows:

$$\text{O} \quad \text{X} \quad \text{O} \quad \text{(treatment group)}$$

$$\text{O} \quad\quad\quad \text{O} \quad \text{(control group)}$$

Each O represents an observation or measurement, and the X indicates a treatment. Each row corresponds to the series of events for one group.

You should recognize this design as an example of a two-factor mixed design. One factor, treatment/control, is a between-subjects factor. The other factor, pre/post, is a within-subjects factor. Figure 12.8 shows the design using the matrix notation customary for factorial designs.

Finally, the design introduced in Chapter 9 was classified as quasi-experimental because it used nonequivalent groups (for example, students from two different high schools or patients from two different clinics). On the other hand, if a researcher has one sample of participants and can randomly assign them to the two groups, then the design is classified as a true experiment. The experimental version of the pretest–posttest control group design can be represented as follows:

$$\text{R} \quad \text{O} \quad \text{X} \quad \text{O} \quad \text{(treatment group)}$$

$$\text{R} \quad \text{O} \quad\quad\quad \text{O} \quad \text{(control group)}$$

|              | Pretest | Posttest |
|--------------|---------|----------|
| Treatment Group | Pretest scores for participants who receive the treatment | Posttest scores for participants who receive the treatment |
| Control Group | Pretest scores for participants who do not receive the treatment | Posttest scores for participants who do not receive the treatment |

Figure 12.8    The Structure of a Pretest–Posttest Control Group Study Organized as a Two-Factor Research Design Notice that the treatment/control factor is a between-subjects factor and the pre/post factor is a within-subjects factor.

The letter R symbolizes random assignment, which means that the researcher has control over assignment of participants to groups and therefore can create equivalent groups.

## HIGHER-ORDER FACTORIAL DESIGNS

The basic concepts of a two-factor research design can be extended to more complex designs involving three or more factors; such designs are referred to as **higher-order factorial designs.** A three-factor design, for example, might look at academic performance scores for two different teaching methods (factor A), for boys versus girls (factor B), and for first-grade versus second-grade classes (factor C). In the three-factor design, the researcher would evaluate main effects for each of the three factors, as well as a set of two-way interactions: A × B, B × C, and A × C. In addition, the extra factor introduces the potential for a three-way interaction, A × B × C.

The logic for defining and interpreting higher-order interactions follows the pattern set by two-way interactions. For example, a two-way interaction, A × B, indicates that the effect of factor A depends on the levels of factor B. Extending this definition, a three-way interaction, A × B × C, indicates that the two-way interaction between A and B depends on the levels of factor C. For example, two teaching methods may be equally effective for boys and girls in the first grade (no two-way interaction between method and gender), but in the second grade one of the methods works better for boys and the other method works better for girls (an interaction between method and gender). Because the method by gender pattern of results is different for the first-graders and the second-graders, there is a three-way interaction. Although the general idea of a three-way interaction is easily grasped, most people have great difficulty comprehending or interpreting a four-way (or higher) interaction. Although it is possible to add factors to a research study without limit, studies that involve three or more factors can produce very complex results that are difficult to understand and thus often have limited practical value.

## 12.5    APPLICATIONS OF FACTORIAL DESIGNS

Factorial designs provide researchers with a tremendous degree of flexibility and freedom for constructing research studies. As noted earlier, the primary advantage of factorial studies is that they allow researchers to observe the influence of two (or more) variables acting and interacting simultaneously. Thus, factorial designs have an almost unlimited range of potential applications. In this section, however, we focus on three specific situations where adding a second factor to an existing study answers a specific research question or solves a specific research problem.

### ADDING A SECOND FACTOR TO A PREVIOUS STUDY

Often factorial designs are developed when researchers plan studies that are intended to build on previous research results. For example, a published report may compare a set of treatment conditions or demonstrate the effectiveness of a particular treatment by comparing the treatment condition with a control condition. The critical reader asks questions such as

Would the same treatment effects be obtained if the treatments were administered under different conditions?

Would the treatment outcomes be changed if individuals with different characteristics had participated?

Developing a research study to answer these questions would involve a factorial design. Answering the first question, for example, requires administering the treatments (one factor) under a variety of different conditions (a second factor). The primary prediction for this research is to obtain an interaction between factors; that is, the researcher predicts that the effect of the treatments *depends on* the conditions under which they are administered. (See Figure 12.9 as an example.) Similarly, the second question calls for a factorial design involving the treatments (factor one) and different types of participants (factor two). Again, the primary prediction is for an interaction.

Because current research tends to build on past research, factorial designs are fairly common and very useful. In a single study, a researcher can replicate and expand previous research. The replication involves repeating the previous study by using the same factor or independent variable exactly as it was used in the earlier study. The expansion involves adding a second factor in the form of new conditions or new participant characteristics to determine whether or not the previously reported effects can be generalized to new situations or new populations.

One example of adding a new factor to an existing study comes from the area of human memory. Psychologists have demonstrated repeatedly that the ability to remember a list of items is determined in large part by the method used to study the items. If studying consists of shallow and superficial activity, then memory will be poor. On the other hand, deeper, more substantial processing produces better memory. A common demonstration of this phenomenon involves presenting the same list of words to two groups of participants. One group is instructed to perform a rhyming task requiring relatively superficial attention to the sound of each word. The second group is assigned a more substantial task requiring that

(a) The original study simply compares two treatments (A and B) using participants who are reasonably well rested.

| Treatment A | Scores for a group of participants in treatment A who are measured when well rested |
| Treatment B | Scores for a group of participants in treatment B who are measured when well rested |

(b) The new study adds a second factor by manipulating the participants' state of rest. The new question is whether the difference between the two treatments depends on the participants' degree of rest.

Degree of Rest
(the New Factor)

|  | Well Rested | Fatigued |
|---|---|---|
| Treatment A | Scores for a group of participants in treatment A who are measured when well rested | Scores for a group of participants in treatment A who are measured when fatigued |
| Treatment B | Scores for a group of participants in treatment B who are measured when well rested | Scores for a group of participants in treatment B who are measured when fatigued |

Figure 12.9   Creating a New Research Study by Adding a Second Factor to an Existing Study

they analyze the meaning of each word. As expected, the task of analyzing meaning results in better memory performance. This outcome should not be surprising, but it does not necessarily mean that the best way to study a list of words is to analyze their meaning. For example, if you were preparing for a spelling test, you would probably do better by studying the sounds and letter patterns of each word than you would by analyzing its meaning. To test the notion that the "best" way to study depends on the type of test, a two-factor experiment was created (Bransford, Franks, Morris, & Stein, 1979). The first factor simply repeated the standard experiment comparing a rhyming task and a meaning task. The second factor consisted of two different types of memory test. For one test, participants were simply asked to recall as many words as possible (replicating the previous research). The second memory test focused on rhymes. Participants were asked, for example, "Was there a word in the list that rhymes with *boat*?" When the memory test was based on rhymes, the data show that the participants who studied by rhyming outperformed those who studied by analyzing meaning. Thus, the results produced an interaction: The effectiveness of a study method depends on the type of test.

A researcher has demonstrated that a new noncompetitive physical education program significantly improves self-esteem for children in a kindergarten program.

    a. What additional information can be obtained by introducing participant gender as a second factor to the original research study?

    b. What additional information can be obtained by adding participant age (third grade, fifth grade, and so on) to the original study?

## REDUCING VARIABILITY IN BETWEEN-SUBJECTS DESIGNS

In Chapter 10 we noted that individual differences such as age or gender can create serious problems for between-subjects research designs. One such problem is the simple fact that differences between participants can result in large variability for the scores within a treatment condition. Recall that large variability can make it difficult to establish any significant differences between treatment conditions (see page 251). Often a researcher has reason to suspect that a specific participant characteristic such as age is a major factor contributing to the variability of the scores. In this situation, it often is tempting to eliminate or reduce the influence of the specific characteristic by holding it constant or by restricting its range. For example, suppose that a researcher compares two treatment conditions using a separate group of children for each condition. Within each group, the children range in age from 5 to 10 years old. The researcher is concerned that the older children may have higher scores than the younger children simply because they are more mature. If the scores really are related to age, then there will be big differences and high variability within each group. In this situation, the researcher may be tempted to restrict the study by holding age constant (for example, using only 10-year-old participants). This will produce more homogeneous groups with less variability, but it will also limit the researcher's ability to generalize the results. Recall that limiting generalization reduces the external validity of the study. Fortunately, there is a relatively simple solution to this dilemma that allows the researcher to reduce variability within groups without sacrificing external validity. The solution involves using the specific variable as a second factor, thereby creating a two-factor study.

    Consider the between-subjects design shown in Figure 12.10a. The design involves a comparison of two treatment conditions (A and B) with a group of 12 participants in each condition. Suppose that the dependent variable for this design is performance on a memory task, and the researcher suspects that the participants' age is a variable that will influence memory performance. Because age varies within each group, this variable is likely to cause increased variability for the memory scores within each group. To eliminate this problem, the researcher

(a) A study comparing two treatments with large age differences among the participants in each group

|  | Treatment A | Treatment B |
| --- | --- | --- |
|  | A group of 12 participants ranging in age from 5 to 15 years old | A group of 12 participants ranging in age from 5 to 15 years old |

(b) Using participant age as a second factor, the participants have been separated into smaller, more homogeneous groups. The smaller age differences within each group should reduce the variability of the scores.

|  | Treatment A | Treatment B |
| --- | --- | --- |
| Younger (5–8 Years Old) | A group of 4 participants ranging in age from 5 to 8 years old | A group of 4 participants ranging in age from 5 to 8 years old |
| Middle (9–11 Years Old) | A group of 4 participants ranging in age from 9 to 11 years old | A group of 4 participants ranging in age from 9 to 11 years old |
| Older (12–15 Years Old) | A group of 4 participants ranging in age from 12 to 15 years old | A group of 4 participants ranging in age from 12 to 15 years old |

**Figure 12.10    A Participant Characteristic (Age) used as a Second Factor to Reduce the Variability of Scores in a Research Study**
(a) Each treatment condition contains a wide range of ages, which probably produces large variability among the scores. (b) The participants have been separated into more homogeneous age groups, which should reduce the variability within each group.

simply regroups the participants within each treatment. Instead of one group in each treatment, the researcher uses age, as a second factor, to divide the participants into three groups within each treatment: a younger age group (5–8 years), a middle age group (9–11 years), and an older group (12–15 years). The result is the two-factor experiment shown in Figure 12.10b, with one factor consisting of the two treatments (A and B) and the second factor consisting of the three age groups (younger, middle, older).

By creating six groups of participants instead of only two, the researcher has greatly reduced the individual differences (age differences) within each group while still keeping the full range of ages from the original study. In the new, two-factor design, age differences still exist, but now they are differences *between groups* rather than variability *within groups.* The variability has been reduced without sacrificing external validity. Furthermore, the researcher has gained all of the other advantages that go with a two-factor design: In addition to examining how the different treatment conditions affect memory, the researcher can now examine how age (the new factor) is related to memory and can determine whether there is any interaction between age and the treatment conditions.

---

Under what circumstances would a researcher reduce the variability of the scores by adding gender as a second factor in a between-subjects study comparing two treatments?

Learning Check

---

## EVALUATING ORDER EFFECTS IN WITHIN-SUBJECTS DESIGNS

In Chapter 11 we noted that order effects can be a serious problem for within-subjects research studies. Specifically, in a within-subjects design each participant goes through a series of treatment conditions in a particular order. In this situation, it is possible that treatments that occur early in the order may influence a participant's scores for treatments that occur later in the order. Because order effects can alter and distort the true effects of a treatment condition, they are generally considered a confounding variable that should be eliminated from the study. In some circumstances, however, a researcher may want to investigate the order effects (where and how big they are). In some situations, a researcher may be specifically interested in how the order of treatments influences the effectiveness of treatments. (Is treatment A more effective if it comes before treatment B or after it?) Or a researcher may simply want to remove the order effects to obtain a clearer view of the data. In any of these situations, it is possible to create a research design that actually measures the order effects and separates them from the rest of the data.

### Using Order of Treatments as a Second Factor

To measure and evaluate order effects, it is necessary to use counterbalancing (as discussed in Chapter 11). Remember that counterbalancing requires separate groups of participants, with each group going through the set of treatments in a different order. The simplest example of this procedure is a within-subjects design comparing two treatments, A and B. The design is counterbalanced so that half of the participants begin with treatment A and then move to treatment B. The other half of the participants start with treatment B and then receive treatment A. The structure of this counterbalanced design can be presented as a matrix, with the two treatment conditions defining the columns and the order of treatments defining the rows (see Figure 12.11).

You should recognize the matrix structure in Figure 12.11 as a two-factor research design and that this is an example of a mixed design. In particular, the treatment factor (A and B) is a within-subjects factor, and the order factor (AB and BA) is a between-subjects factor. By using the order of treatments as a second factor, it is possible to evaluate any order effects that may exist in the data. There are three possible outcomes that can occur, and each produces its own pattern of results.

Treatment A        Treatment B

X ⟶ X                Group 1
X ⟶ X                Half the participants
X ⟶ X                get treatment A first and
X ⟶ X                treatment B second.

X ⟵ X                Group 2
X ⟵ X                Half the participants
X ⟵ X                get treatment B first and
X ⟵ X                treatment A second.

|  | | Treatment A | Treatment B |
|---|---|---|---|
| Order of Treatments | Group 1<br>A ⟶ B | Mean score in treatment A for participants who had treatment A first | Mean score in treatment B for participants who had treatment B second |
|  | Group 2<br>B ⟶ A | Mean score in treatment A for participants who had treatment A second | Mean score in treatment B for participants who had treatment B first |

**Figure 12.11    Order of Treatments Added as a Second Factor to a Within-Subjects Study**
The original study uses a counterbalanced design to compare two treatment conditions (A and B). Thus, half of the participants have treatment A first, and half have treatment B first. Similarly, half of the participants have treatment A second, and half have treatment B second.

1. *No order effects:* When there are no order effects, it does not matter whether a treatment is presented first or second. An example of this type of result is shown in Figure 12.12. For these data, when treatment A is presented first (group 1), the mean is 20, and when treatment A is presented second (group 2), the mean is still 20. Similarly, the order of presentation has no effect on the mean for treatment B. As a result, the difference between treatments is 10 points for both groups of participants. Thus, the treatment effect (factor 1) does not depend on the order-of-treatments (factor 2). You should recognize this pattern as an example of data with no interaction. When there are no order effects, the data show a pattern with no interaction. It makes no difference whether a treatment is presented first or second; the mean is the same in either case.

2. *Symmetrical order effects:* When order effects exist, the scores in the second treatment are influenced by participation in the first treatment. An example of this outcome is shown in Figure 12.13. To create these data a 5-point order effect was added to the data in Figure 12.12. Thus, when treatment B

Figure 12.12    Treatment Effects and Order Effects Revealed in a Two-Factor Design Using Order of Treatments as a Second Factor
A 10-point difference between the two treatment conditions is assumed, with the mean score for treatment A equal to $M = 20$ and the mean score for treatment B equal to $M = 30$. No order effects is also assumed. Thus, participating in one treatment has no effect (0 points) on an individual's score in the following treatment. In the two-factor analysis, the treatment effect shows up as a 10-point main effect for the treatment factor, and the absence of any order effects is indicated by the absence of an interaction between treatments and order of treatments.

occurs second (after A), the mean score is raised by 5 points. This occurs for the participants in group 1. Also, when treatment A is second (after B), the mean is raised by 5 points. This occurs for the individuals in group 2.

In this situation, the treatment effect (A versus B), depends on the order of treatments. Thus, the effect of one factor depends on the other factor. You should recognize this as an example of interaction. When order effects exist, they show up in the two-factor analysis as an interaction between treatments and the order of treatments.

For these data, a symmetrical order effect was created; that is, the second treatment always gets an extra 5 points, whether it is treatment A or treatment B. This symmetry appears in the data as a symmetrical interaction. In the graph of the data, for example, the two lines cross exactly at the

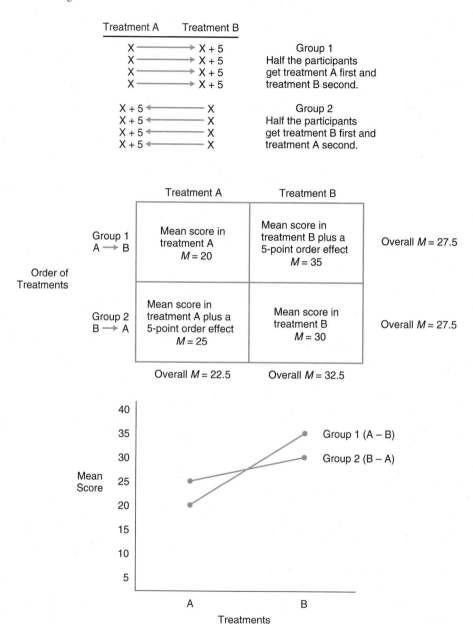

Figure 12.13  Symmetrical Order Effects Revealed in a Two-Factor Design Using Order of Treatments as a Second Factor
A 10-point difference between the two treatment conditions is assumed, with the mean score for treatment A equal to $M = 20$ and the mean score for treatment B equal to $M = 30$. A symmetrical 5-point order effect is added. After participating in one treatment, the order effect adds 5 points to each participant's score in the second treatment. In this situation, the order effect appears as an interaction between treatments and the order of treatments.

center. Also, the 5-point difference between the two groups in treatment A (left-hand side of the graph) is exactly equal to the 5-point difference between the groups in treatment B (right-hand side of the graph). This symmetry only exists in situations where the order effects are symmetrical.

3. *Asymmetrical order effects:* Figure 12.14 shows data where the order effects are not symmetrical. To create these data we started with the original means in Figure 12.12, and then added order effects as follows:

   a. The participants in group 1 received the treatments in the order AB. For these participants, we added a 10-point order effect. Thus, the mean for treatment B is increased by 10 points.
   b. The participants in group 2 receive the treatments in the order BA. For these participants, we added a 5-point order effect. Thus, the mean for treatment A is increased by 5 points.

   Notice that the graph in Figure 12.14 shows an interaction, just as with symmetrical order effects. Again, the existence of an interaction in this analysis is an indication that order effects exist. For these data, however, the interaction is not symmetrical; in the graph, the two lines do intersect at their midpoints. Also, the difference between groups in treatment A is much smaller than the difference in treatment B. In general, asymmetrical order effects produce a lopsided or asymmetrical interaction between treatments and orders as seen in Figure 12.14.

   In the preceding examples, we created order effects and added them into the data. In this artificial situation, we knew that order effects existed and how big they were. In an actual experiment, however, a researcher cannot see the order effects. However, as we have demonstrated in the three examples, using order of treatments as a second factor makes it possible to examine any order effects that exist in a set of data; their magnitude and nature are revealed in the interaction. Thus, researchers can observe the order effects in their data and can separate them from the effects of the different treatments.

---

What does it mean to say that order effects are "symmetrical" or "asymmetrical"?

If order effects exist in a research study, how do they show up in a two-factor analysis where order of treatments has been added as a second factor?

Learning Checks

---

## CHAPTER SUMMARY

To examine more complex, real-life situations, researchers often design research studies that include more than one independent variable. These designs are called factorial designs. Factorial designs are commonly described with a notation system that identifies not only the number of factors in the design but also the number of values or levels that exist for each factor. For example, a 2 × 3 factorial design is a design with two independent variables, two levels of the first factor, and three levels of the second factor.

The results from a factorial design provide information about how each factor individually affects

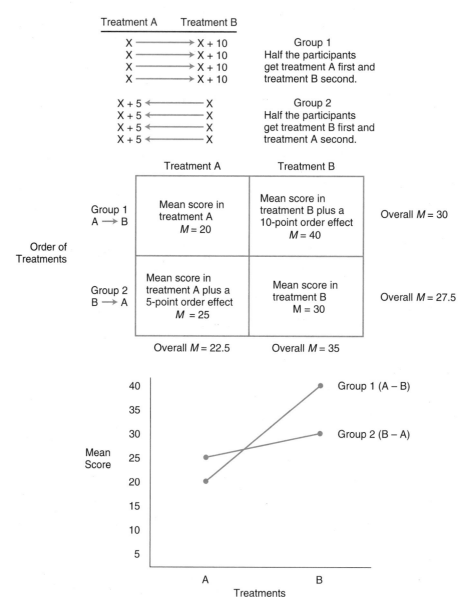

Figure 12.14   Asymmetrical Order Effects Revealed in a
Two-Factor Design Using Order of Treatments as a Second Factor
A 10-point difference between the two treatment conditions is assumed,
with the mean score for treatment A equal to $M = 20$ and the mean score
for treatment B equal to $M = 30$. An asymmetrical order effect is added.
After participating in treatment A, the order effect adds 10 points to each
participant's score, and after participating in treatment B the order effect
adds 5 points to each participant's score. In this situation, the order
effects appear as an interaction between treatments and order of
treatments. Because the order effects are not symmetrical, the
structure of the interaction is also not symmetrical.

behavior (main effects) and how the factors jointly affect behavior (interaction). The value of a factorial design is that it allows a researcher to examine how unique combinations of factors, acting together, influence behavior. When the effects of a factor vary depending on the levels of another factor, it means that the two factors are combining to produce unique effects and that there is an interaction between the factors.

In factorial designs, it is possible to have a separate group for each of the conditions (a between-subjects design) and to have the same group of individuals participate in all of the different conditions (a within-subjects design). In addition, it is possible to construct a factorial design where the factors are not manipulated but rather are quasi-independent variables. Finally, a factorial design can use any combination of factors to create a variety of mixed designs. As a result, a factorial study can combine elements of experimental and quasi-experimental designs, and it can combine elements of between-subjects and within-subjects designs within a single research study.

Although factorial designs can be used in a variety of situations, three specific applications were discussed: (1) Often a new study builds on existing research by adding another factor to an earlier research study; (2) using a participant variable such as age or gender as a second factor can separate participants into more homogeneous groups and thereby reduce variability in a between-subjects design; and (3) when the order of treatments is used as a second factor in a counterbalanced within-subjects design, it is possible to measure and evaluate the order effects.

## KEY WORDS

| | | |
|---|---|---|
| factor | main effect | mixed design |
| factorial design | interaction between factors | |

## EXERCISES

1. In addition to the key words, you should also be able to define the following terms:
   two-factor design    single-factor design
   three-factor design    levels
   higher-order factorial design
2. Describe the major advantage of using a factorial design.
3. Explain why it is better to use a factorial design in research than to conduct two separate studies.
4. How many independent variables are there in a $4 \times 2 \times 2$ factorial design?
5. What is a *main effect*?
6. How many main effects are there in a study examining the effects of treatment (behavioral versus psychoanalytic versus cognitive) and experience of the therapist (experienced versus not experienced) on depression?
7. Use the values in the following matrix to answer questions a, b, and c:

| | Before Treatment | After Treatment | |
|---|---|---|---|
| Males | $M = 20$ | $M = 24$ | overall $M = 22$ |
| Females | $M = 22$ | $M = 32$ | overall $M = 27$ |
| | overall $M = 21$ | overall $M = 28$ | |

   a. What numbers are compared to evaluate the main effect for the treatment?
   b. What numbers are compared to evaluate the main effect for gender?
   c. What numbers are compared to evaluate the interaction?
8. The following matrix represents the results (the means) from a $2 \times 2$ factorial study. One mean is not given.
   a. What value for the missing mean would result in no main effect for factor A?
   b. What value for the missing mean would result in no main effect for factor B?

c. What value for the missing mean would result in no interaction?

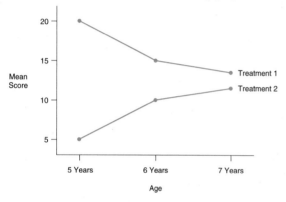

|     | A1 | A2 |
|-----|-----|-----|
| B1  | 40 | 20 |
| B2  | 30 |    |

9. Examine the data in the following graph.

a. Is there a main effect for the treatment factor?
b. Is there a main effect for the age factor?
c. Is there an interaction between age and the treatment?

10. Explain the issue of interdependence and independence of factors and how it is related to interaction.

11. Under what circumstances will the main effects in a factorial study not provide an accurate description of the results?

12. A researcher conducts a 2 × 3 × 2 factorial study with 20 participants in each treatment condition.
   a. If the researcher uses an exclusively between-subjects design, how many individuals participate in the entire study?
   b. If the researcher uses an exclusively within-subjects design, how many individuals participate in the entire study?

13. A researcher would like to compare two therapy techniques for treating depression in both adolescents and adults. Identify which factor is experimental and which is quasi-experimental.

14. Suppose a researcher has demonstrated that a particular treatment is effective in reducing stress in adults. Describe some ways to add a second factor to expand these results.

15. Under what circumstances would adding gender as a second factor in a between-subjects study *not* reduce variability?

---

 InfoTrac COLLEGE EDITION EXERCISES

1. Use InfoTrac College Edition to locate a research study using a factorial design. Note: You can try a subject term based on an area of interest, but the most direct path to finding factorial designs is to use a key word such as 2 × 2 or 2 × 3. Once you find a factorial study, do the following:
   a. Identify each factor and the specific levels that are used for each factor.
   b. Specify whether each factor is an experimental or a quasi-experimental factor.
   c. Specify whether each factor is a between-subjects or a within-subjects factor.
   d. Describe the results of the study in terms of main effects and interactions (Which main effects were significant? Was the interaction significant?) Then describe the results of the study in terms of the variables studied. (How did the independent variables affect the dependent variable? What pattern of results was obtained?)

2. Retrieve the between-subjects study you used for the InfoTrac College Edition exercise in Chapter 10 and the within-subjects study you used in Chapter 11. In each case, explain how the study could be expanded by adding a second factor. What new information might be obtained from your proposed two-factor studies?

# Single-Subject Research Designs

## CHAPTER OVERVIEW

In this chapter we discuss in detail another type of experimental research design, the single-subject design. The characteristics of this design are discussed, as well as evaluation of the data from it. Different types of single-subject designs are considered, followed by the general strengths and weaknesses of this type of design.

## 13.1   INTRODUCTION

As the name implies, **single-subject designs** are research designs that can be used with only one participant (or subject) in the entire research study. Single-subject designs are also commonly called **single-case designs.** Although these designs can be used with groups of participants, their particular advantage is that they provide researchers with an option for data collection and interpretation in situations where a single individual is being treated, observed, and measured. This option is especially valuable in clinical psychology because it allows clinicians to conduct experimental research without seriously disrupting the normal therapist/client interaction. This option is also valuable in developmental and school psychology. We use the term *experimental* to describe these single-subject designs because the designs presented in this chapter also allow researchers to relatively unambiguously identify cause-and-effect relationships between variables.

<table>
<tr><td>Definition</td><td>**Single-subject designs** or **single-case designs** are research designs that use the results from a single participant or subject to establish the existence of cause-and-effect relationships.</td></tr>
</table>

Historically, most single-subject designs were developed by behaviorists examining operant conditioning. The behavior of a single subject (usually a laboratory rat) was observed, and changes in behavior were noted while the researcher manipulated the stimulus or reinforcement conditions. Although the designs have been adopted by clinicians, their application is still largely behavioral, especially to the field of behavior modification. Despite this strong association with behaviorism, however, single-subject research is not tied directly to any single theoretical perspective and is available as a research tool for general application.

The goal of single-subject research, as with other experimental designs, is to identify cause-and-effect relationships between variables. In common application, this means demonstrating that a *treatment* (variable 1) that is implemented or manipulated by the researcher causes a change in the participant's *responses* (variable 2). As you will see, the general methodology of single-subject research incorporates elements of case studies and time-series designs (see Chapters 7 and 9). Like a case study, single-subject research focuses on a single individual and allows a detailed description of the observations and experiences related to that unique individual. Like time-series research, the single-subject approach typically involves a series of observations made over time. Usually, a set of observations made before treatment is contrasted with a set of observations made during or after treatment.

Learning Check

What is the goal of a single-subject research study?

### EVALUATING THE RESULTS FROM A SINGLE-SUBJECT STUDY

Unlike other experimental methods, the results of a single-subject design do not provide researchers with a set of scores from a group of subjects that can be used to compute means and variances and conduct traditional tests for statistical significance. Instead, the presentation and interpretation of results from a single-subject experiment are based on a simple graph of the data. Figure 13.1, for example, shows hypothetical results from a study examining the effects of a behavior modification program on the classroom disruption behavior of a single student. The student's behavior (number of disruptions) was observed and recorded for five days prior to implementing the behavior modification. In the graph, each day's observation is recorded as a single point, with the series of days presented on the horizontal axis and the magnitude of the behavior (number of disruptions) on the vertical axis. The behavior modification program was implemented on day 6, and behavior during the program was recorded for five additional days (days 6 through 10 in the graph). The vertical line in the graph between days 5 and 6 indicates when the treatment was started; the five points to the left of the line are before treatment, and the five points to the right are during treatment. Also notice that the individual data points are connected by straight lines to help emphasize the pattern of behavior before treatment and the change in the pattern that occurred with treatment.

Because the results of a single-subject study do not involve any traditional statistical methods, researchers must rely on the visual inspection of a graph to convey the meaning of their results. The graph in Figure 13.1, for example, appears to indicate that a substantial change in behavior occurred when the behavior modification was started. However, the graph by itself is not a convincing demonstration that the behavior modification treatment actually has *caused* a change in behavior. In fact, there are two reasons for skepticism concerning the results:

1.  The results as presented do not represent a true experiment because there is no control over extraneous variables. In particular, it is possible that factors other than the treatment are responsible for the apparent change in behavior. Variables outside the study, such as the weather, changes in the student's family situation, or changes in the student's relationships with peers, may be responsible for causing the change in behavior. Because the study cannot measure or control all these potentially confounding variables, it is impossible to interpret the results as a clear, unambiguous demonstration of the treatment's effectiveness. To demonstrate cause-and-effect relationships,

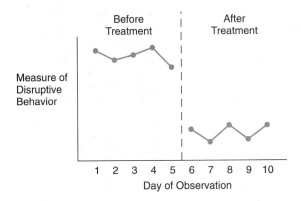

Figure 13.1    Data Obtained From a Single-Subject Research Study

single-subjects designs must convincingly demonstrate that it is the treatment, not coincidental extraneous variables, causing the changes in behavior.

2. The second problem with interpreting results such as those shown in Figure 13.1 is that the apparent difference between the before-treatment observations and the after-treatment observations may simply be due to *chance*. Notice that there is variability in the day-to-day observations; this variability is a natural part of behavior and measurement. Although the results appear to suggest a pattern of higher scores before treatment and lower scores after treatment, the "pattern" may be nothing more than normal variability. You may recognize this problem as the traditional question of statistical significance.

In a traditional group design (for example, a between-subjects or a within-subjects design), a researcher is able to obtain a precise measure of how much difference is reasonable to expect by chance. A hypothesis test can then be used to determine whether the pattern of differences found in the data is significantly greater than chance. In single-subject research, however, there is no group of scores that allows a researcher to compute a measure of chance. Instead, a researcher must rely on the appearance of the graph to convince others that the treatment effect is "significant." Hence, it is essential that the obtained data be unquestionably clear so that an observer can "see" the treatment effect by visually inspecting a graph of the results. (Guidelines for visual inspection of single-subject graphs are presented later in the chapter; see page 332.)

**Learning Check**    What is the role of traditional statistics (means, variances, and hypothesis tests) in the evaluation of the results from a single-subject study?

## 13.2 PHASES AND PHASE CHANGES

Before beginning discussion of specific single-subject experimental designs, we introduce and define the general concept of a **phase**, which is the basic building block used to construct most single-subject designs. A phase is a series of observations made under the same conditions. The results shown in Figure 13.1, for example, consist of two phases: The series of five observations before treatment constitutes one phase (before treatment), and the final five observations constitute a second phase (during treatment). In the terminology of single-subject research, observations made in the absence of a treatment are called **baseline observations**, and a series of baseline observations is called a **baseline phase**. Similarly, observations made during treatment are called **treatment observations**, and a series of treatment observations is called a **treatment phase.** By convention, a baseline phase is identified by the letter *A*, and a treatment phase is usually identified by the letter *B*. Designating different phases by different letters allows researchers to describe the sequence of phases in a study by using a sequence of letters. For example, the study producing the results shown in Figure 13.1 would be described as an AB design; that is, the study consists of a baseline phase, A, followed by a treatment phase, B.

A **phase** is a series of observations of the same individual under the same conditions.

When no treatment is being administered, the observations are called **baseline observations.** A series of baseline observations is called a **baseline phase** and is identified by the letter *A*.

When a treatment is being administered, the observations are called **treatment observations.** A series of treatment observations is called a **treatment phase** and is identified by the letter *B*.

Although the treatment phase of a single-subject study is usually identified by the letter B, there are situations where other letters may be used. Specifically, when a study contains two or more distinct treatments, the first treatment condition is identified by B, and other treatments are identified by C, D, etc. Also, when a study contains modifications of a basic treatment, the basic treatment is identified by B, and the different modifications are called $B_1$, $B_2$, etc. Thus, a single-subject research design might be described as an $ABB_1AC$ design. This letter sequence indicates that the researcher first made a series of baseline observations, then implemented a treatment, B, while continuing to make observations. Next, the researcher tried a modification of the treatment (perhaps treatment B was not effective), followed by withdrawal of all treatment (back to baseline), and finally administration of a different treatment, C.

## LEVEL, TREND, AND STABILITY

The purpose of a phase within a single-subject experiment is to establish a clear picture of the participant's behavior under the specific conditions that define the phase. That is, the series of observations that make up the phase should show a clear pattern that describes the behavior. Ultimately, the researcher will change phases by implementing or withdrawing a treatment, and the goal is to show that the pattern of behavior changes from one phase to the next. Before it is possible to demonstrate a change in patterns, however, it is essential that the pattern within a phase be clearly established.

One way to define a pattern within a phase is in terms of the **level** of behavior. The term *level* simply refers to the magnitude of the participant's responses. If all of the observations within a phase indicate approximately the same magnitude or level of behavior, then the data have demonstrated a consistent or stable level of behavior within the phase. Figure 13.2a shows data demonstrating a stable level of behavior. Although there are minor differences in magnitude from one observation to another, the data points generally line up at the same level of magnitude. Notice that the concept of a "stable level" simply means that the data points within a phase tend to form a horizontal line on the graph.

An alternative way to define a pattern within a phase is in terms of a **trend.** The term *trend* refers to a consistent increase (or a consistent decrease) in the magnitude of behavior across the series of observations that make up the phase. Figure 13.2b shows data demonstrating a consistent or stable trend in behavior.

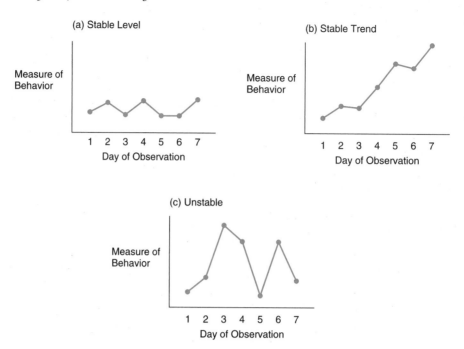

Figure 13.2   Three Patterns of Results for the Data From
One Phase in a Single-Subject Research Study
(a) A stable level. (b) A stable trend. (c) Unstable data.

Again, notice that the data points tend to form a relatively straight line, but now the line slopes upward to the right, indicating a consistent increase in the magnitude of behavior over time.

Thus, the pattern within a phase can be described in terms of level or trend. In either case, however, the critical factor is the consistency of the pattern. Remember that single-subject research does not use statistical analysis to summarize or interpret the results, but depends on the visual appearance of the data in a graph. It is essential that the graph show a clear picture that establishes an unambiguous level or trend within each phase. In the terminology of single-subject research, the critical factor is the **stability** of the data. When the data points form a straight line with only minor deviations, the data are said to be "stable," and the pattern is easy to see. Although there is no simple definition of stability, the idea is that the deviations from a consistent level or a consistent trend are relatively small. Note that the data points do not have to form a perfectly straight line to be considered stable; some variability is allowed, but it should be relatively small.

On the other hand, if there are large differences (high variability) from one observation to the next, so that no obvious pattern emerges, the data are said to be "unstable." Figure 13.2c shows unstable data. Unstable data are disastrous to the goals of single-subject research. When the data points vary wildly, it is impossible to define any pattern within a phase, and therefore it is impossible to determine whether changing the phase (for example, implementing a treatment) produces any change in the pattern.

A consistent **level** occurs when a series of measurements are all approximately the same magnitude. In a graph, the series of data points cluster around a horizontal line.

A consistent **trend** occurs when the differences from one measurement to the next are consistently in the same direction and are approximately of the same magnitude. In a graph the series of data points cluster around a sloping line.

The **stability** of a set of observations refers to the degree to which the observations show a pattern of consistent level or consistent trend. Stable data may show minor variations from a perfectly consistent pattern, but the variations should be relatively small and the linear pattern relatively clear.

Why is it necessary to have a stable pattern within a phase?

### Dealing With Unstable Data

Usually behavior is fairly consistent over time, which means that a series of observations shows a consistent pattern (either a consistent level or consistent trend in behavior). Where data appear to be unstable, however, researchers can employ several techniques to help uncover a consistent pattern:

1. First, you can simply wait; that is, keep making observations and hope that the data will stabilize and reveal a clear pattern. Occasionally, a participant will react unpredictably to the novelty of being observed. When this happens, the first few days of observation are distorted by the participant's reactivity and may appear unstable. After several days, however, the novelty wears off and the participant returns to normal, consistent behavior.

2. A second method for stabilizing data is simply to average over a set of two (or more) observations. Figure 13.3a shows a set of observations made over a ten-day period. Notice that the large, day-to-day differences produce a relatively unstable set of data. Figure 13.3b shows the same data after they have been "smoothed" by averaging over two-day periods. To create Figure 13.3b the first two days' observations were averaged to produce a single data point. Similarly, days three and four were averaged, and so on. Notice that the averaging process tends to reduce the variability of the data points and produce a more stable set of data in which the "pattern" of behavior is easier to see.

3. A final strategy for dealing with unstable data is to look for patterns within the inconsistency. For example, a researcher examining disruptive classroom behavior may find that a student exhibits very high levels of disruption on some days and very low levels on other days. Although the data appear to be very unstable, closer examination reveals that the high levels tend to occur on Mondays, Wednesdays, and Fridays, and the low levels are observed on Tuesdays and Thursdays. The obvious question is, Why are Tuesdays and Thursdays different? Checking the class schedule reveals that

Figure 13.3 Stabilizing Data by Averaging Over Successive Data Points
(a) The original unstable data. (b) The results of averaging over 2–day periods.

the student is in gym class immediately prior to the Tuesday/Thursday observation periods. Perhaps the exercise in gym allows the student to burn off excess energy and results in more subdued behavior. The researcher could try changing the time of observation to early morning to eliminate the influence of the gym class. Or the researcher could simply limit the data to observation made on the non-gym days. In general, unstable data may be caused by extraneous variables; it is often possible to stabilize the data by identifying and controlling them.

### Length of a Phase

To establish a pattern (level or trend) within a phase and to determine the stability of the data within a phase, a phase must consist of a minimum of three observations. You may have noticed that the graphs in Figure 13.2 were constructed so that the first two data points are identical in all three graphs. In Figure 13.2a the difference between the first two observations is simply minor variation that eventually becomes part of a consistent level. In Figure 13.2b the difference signifies the beginning of a consistent trend, and in Figure 13.2c the difference between the two points is part of an unstable set of data. Our point is that the first two observations, by themselves, do not provide enough information to determine a pattern. Additional observations beyond the first two are essential to establish level, trend, and stability. Although three data points are the absolute minimum for determining a phase, typically five or six observations are necessary to determine a clear pattern. However, when high variability exists in the data points, additional observations should be made.

## CHANGING PHASES

After a researcher has obtained the necessary data points to establish a clear and stable pattern within a phase, it is possible to initiate a **phase change.** A phase change is essentially a manipulation of the independent variable and is accomplished by implementing a treatment, withdrawing a treatment, or changing a treatment. This process begins a new phase, during which the researcher will collect a series of observations under a new set of conditions.

A phase consists of a series of observations of the same individual under the same conditions. A **phase change** involves changing the conditions, usually by administering or stopping a treatment.

The purpose of a phase change is to demonstrate that adding a treatment (or removing a treatment) produces a noticeable change in behavior. This goal is accomplished when the data show a clear difference between the pattern that exists before the phase change and the pattern that exists after the phase change. For example, a dramatic drop in the level of behavior when the treatment is started (phase change) is evidence that the treatment has an effect on behavior.

### Deciding When to Change Phases

As we have discussed, the primary factor determining when a new phase should be started is the emergence of a clear pattern within the preceding phase. However, there are several other factors that can influence the decision concerning when and if a phase change is appropriate.

The first consideration involves changing from a baseline phase to a treatment phase. When the data in a baseline phase show a trend indicating improvement in the client's behavior, a researcher should not intervene by introducing a treatment phase. There are two good reasons for this no-action strategy, one clinical and one experimental. From a clinical point of view, if the client is already showing improvement, the simplest and safest decision is to stand back and let the improvement run its course. The client's improvement indicates that there is no need for immediate intervention. From an experimental perspective, initiating a treatment when the participant is already showing a trend toward improvement can only result in ambiguous results. Specifically, if a treatment is started and the participant continues to improve, the researcher cannot determine whether the continued improvement is caused by the treatment or is simply the continuation of an established trend. Because the results cannot be interpreted as a clear demonstration of the treatment's effect, the experiment is compromised.

Another possibility is that the baseline data indicate a seriously high level of dangerous or threatening behavior. In this case, a researcher probably should not wait for the full set of five or six observations necessary to establish a clear pattern. Instead, the researcher/clinician has an ethical obligation to begin treatment immediately (after one or two observations). After the behavior is brought under control during a treatment phase, the researcher can consider resuming the experiment by changing back to a baseline (no-treatment) phase or by introducing a different treatment phase.

It also is possible that the data within a treatment phase can dictate a premature phase change. If, for example, a treatment appears to produce an immediate and severe deterioration in behavior, the researcher/clinician should stop, change, or modify the treatment immediately without waiting for a clear pattern to emerge.

In general, the decision to make a phase change is based on the participant's responses. If the responses establish a clear pattern, then a change is appropriate. If the responses indicate a serious problem, then a change is necessary. In either case, the step-by-step progress of the experiment is controlled by the participant and does not necessarily follow a predetermined plan developed by the researcher. This aspect of single-subject research creates a very flexible and adaptive research strategy that is particularly well suited to clinical application. We return to this point later when the strengths and weaknesses of single-subject designs are discussed in Section 13.8.

**Learning Checks**

What is the primary factor that determines when it is time to change phases?

What pattern of results is needed to provide convincing evidence that behavior changed when the phase was changed?

### VISUAL INSPECTION TECHNIQUES

In very general terms the goal of single-subject research is to demonstrate that manipulation of one variable (the treatment) causes a change in a second variable (the participant's behavior). More specifically, the goal is to demonstrate that the pattern of behavior established in a baseline phase changes to a different pattern when the researcher switches to a treatment phase. Because the interpretation of the experimental results depends entirely on the visual appearance of a graph, it is important that the change in pattern from baseline to treatment be easy to see when the results are presented in a graph. The most convincing results occur when the change in pattern is immediate and large.

Unfortunately, there are no absolute, objective standards for determining how much of a change in pattern is sufficient to provide a convincing demonstration of a treatment effect. The visual inspection of single-subject data is very much a subjective task, and different observers often interpret data in different ways (DeProspero & Cohen, 1979). Nonetheless, there are guidelines that focus attention on specific aspects of the data and help observers decide whether or not a phase change produced a real change in pattern. Kazdin (1998) has identified four specific characteristics of single-subject data that help determine whether there is a meaningful change between phases:

1.  *Change in mean level:* Although statistical means and variances are typically not computed for single-subject data, the mean level of behavior during a phase provides a simple and understandable description of the behavior within the phase. Figure 13.4 shows hypothetical data from a single-subject design where the mean for each phase is indicated by a dashed line. Notice that the data show substantial mean differences from one phase to another. In general, large differences in mean level are a good indication that there is a real difference between phases.

2.  *Immediate change in level:* Another indicator of a difference between phases is the initial response of the participant to the change. This involves comparing the last data point in one phase with the first data point in the following phase. A large difference between these two points is a good indication that the participant showed an immediate response to the addition (or removal) of the treatment. In Figure 13.4, for example, the data show a large difference between the final score in the first baseline phase

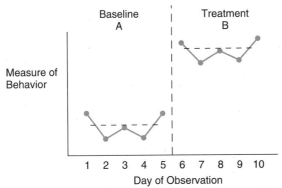

Figure 13.4    Data Showing a Change in Mean Level
From One Phase to the Next
The horizontal dashed lines in each phase correspond to the mean level.
A clear difference between means is a good indication of a real difference
between phases. Also note the large difference between the final point in
the baseline phase and the first point in the treatment phase. This
difference also indicates that the participant's behavior was changed
when the treatment was introduced.

and the first score in the first treatment phase. Apparently the participant
showed an immediate reaction when the treatment was introduced.

3.  *Change in trend:* When the trend observed in one phase is noticeably differ-
    ent from the trend in the previous phase, it is a clear indication of a differ-
    ence between phases. Figure 13.5 demonstrates changes in trend. Figure
    13.5a shows a change from no trend (consistent level) to a clear, increasing
    trend. The data in Figure 13.5b are even more convincing. Here the trends
    change direction from increasing to decreasing. Again, clear changes in
    trend are evidence of a real difference between phases.

4.  *Latency of change:* The most convincing evidence for a difference between
    phases occurs when the data show a large, immediate change in pattern. A
    delay between the time the phase is changed and the time behavior begins
    to change undermines the credibility of a cause-and-effect explanation. Fig-
    ure 13.6 shows two examples of a baseline-to-treatment phase change. In
    Figure 13.6a, the data show an immediate change in behavior when the treat-
    ment is introduced, providing clear evidence that the treatment is affecting
    behavior. In Figure 13.6b, however, there is no immediate change in behav-
    ior. Although there is an eventual change in behavior, it does not occur until
    several sessions after the treatment starts. In this case, the data do not pro-
    vide unambiguous evidence that the treatment is affecting behavior.

## 13.3    THE ABAB REVERSAL DESIGN

We have introduced the concept of a phase as the basic building block of most
single-subject experiments. A specific research design, therefore, consists of a

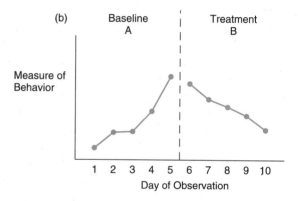

Figure 13.5   Two Examples of a Clear Change in Trend From One Phase to the Next (a) A clear change from no trend (consistent level) to an increasing trend. (b) A reversal in trend from increasing to decreasing.

sequence of phases that can be represented by a sequence of letters, for example, $ABB_1AC$. Because each unique sequence of letters represents a unique experimental design, the number of potential designs is essentially unlimited. We address the issue of complex designs in Section 13.4. For now, however, we focus on one design that is extremely common and probably accounts for the majority of single-subject research studies, the **ABAB design** or **reversal design.**

As the letters indicate, the ABAB design consists of four phases: a baseline phase (A), followed by treatment (B), then a return to baseline (A), and finally a repeat of the treatment phase (B). The goal of the ABAB design is to demonstrate that the treatment causes a change in behavior by showing that:

- The pattern of behavior in each treatment phase is clearly different from the pattern in each baseline phase. This demonstration is necessary to establish a relation between the treatment and the behavior.
- The changes in behavior from baseline to treatment and from treatment to baseline are the same for each of the phase-change points in the experiment. This demonstration is necessary to establish a *causal* relation between treatment and behavior. That is, the results demonstrate that the researcher can turn the behavior on and off at will simply by starting and stopping the treatment.

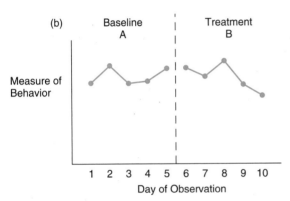

Figure 13.6    Latency of Change Affects Interpretation (a) An immediate change in trend when the treatment is introduced. This pattern provides good evidence that the treatment is influencing behavior. (b) The behavior remains at the baseline level for several days after the treatment is introduced. Although the behavior does eventually show a decreasing trend, it is not clear that the decrease occurs as a result of the treatment.

---

An **ABAB design,** also known as a **reversal design,** is a single-subject phase-change design consisting of four phases: a baseline phase, a treatment phase, a return to baseline phase, and a second treatment phase. The goal of the design is to demonstrate that the treatment causes changes in the participant's behavior.

Definition

---

Figure 13.7 shows two sets of hypothetical data representing optimal out-comes from an ABAB experiment. Close examination of these graphs reveals the elements that make it possible to infer a causal relation between the treatment and the behavior:

1.  In each case, the first phase change (baseline to treatment) shows a clear change in the pattern of behavior. This first change by itself simply demonstrates that a behavior change accompanies the treatment. At this point we cannot conclude that the treatment has caused the change in behavior because some extraneous variable that changed coincidentally with the treatment may be responsible for changing the behavior.

2.  The second phase change in each graph (treatment to baseline) shows the participant's behavior returning to the same pattern observed during the initial baseline phase. This component of the experiment is often called the

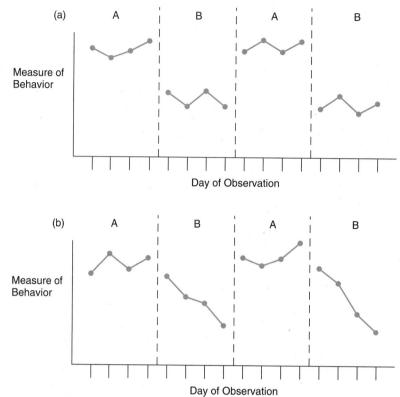

**Figure 13.7   Two Examples of Optimal Results from an ABAB Reversal Design**
(a) A clear change in level when the treatment is introduced, a clear return to baseline when the treatment is withdrawn, and a clear replication of the treatment effect when the treatment is reintroduced. (b) A similar pattern, except that the treatment produces a change in trend rather than a change in level.

"reversal" or "return to baseline." The reversal component is important because it begins to establish the causal relation between the treatment and behavior. Although the participant's behavior may have been influenced by extraneous variables at the first phase change, it now appears more likely that the treatment (not extraneous variables) is responsible for the change. Behavior changed when the treatment was introduced, and behavior reverted back to baseline when the treatment was withdrawn.

3.   The final phase change (baseline back to treatment) shows the same treatment effect that was observed in the initial phase change. This component of the experiment, the second AB in the sequence, provides a replication of the first AB. This replication clinches the argument for a causal interpretation of the results. By showing that behavior changes repeatedly when the treatment is implemented, the results minimize the likelihood that a coincidence (extra-

neous variables) is responsible for the changes in behavior. Although it is possible that coincidence is responsible for the first change in behavior, it is very unlikely that another coincidence occurred when the second treatment was introduced. By using replication, the ABAB design maximizes the likelihood that the observed changes in behavior are caused by the treatment.

Although the ABAB design is typically used to show that a treatment does have an effect, it also can provide convincing evidence that a treatment is not effective. Craig and Kearns (1995) used an ABAB design to evaluate the effectiveness of acupuncture as a treatment for stuttering. Hypothetical results similar to those obtained in the study are shown in Figure 13.8. Notice that stuttering frequency remains at baseline levels throughout both of the treatment phases. These results provide a fairly strong demonstration that the acupuncture treatment has no effect on stuttering.

Identify the four phases that make up an ABAB reversal design, and describe how the participant's behavior is expected to change each time the phase is changed if the treatment is to be shown to cause changes in behavior.

Learning
Check

## LIMITATIONS OF THE ABAB DESIGN

Like other experimental designs, the ABAB research design can establish, with good credibility, the existence of a cause-and-effect relationship between a treatment and corresponding changes in behavior. However, the credibility of this causal interpretation depends in large part on the reversal (return to baseline) that is a part of the design. Withdrawing treatment in the middle of the experiment

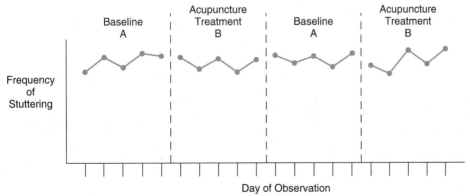

Figure 13.8   Hypothetical Data Similar to Results
Obtained by Craig and Kearns (1955)
The graph shows results from an ABAB study where the treatment
is clearly not effective. The frequency of stuttering remains at
baseline levels throughout the entire study. The data indicate
that the acupuncture treatment has no effect.

can create some practical and ethical problems that can limit the application and success of this specific design.

The first issue related to the withdrawal of treatment focuses on the participant's response; withdrawing treatment may not result in a change in behavior. That is, although the researcher may return to baseline by removing the treatment, the participant's behavior may not return to baseline. From a purely clinical point of view this phenomenon is not a problem; in fact it is an excellent outcome. The clinician has implemented a treatment that has corrected a problem behavior, and when the treatment is removed, the correction continues. In simple terms, the patient is cured. From an experimental perspective, however, the credibility of the treatment effect is seriously compromised if the participant's behavior does not respond to removal of the treatment. If a manipulation of the treatment fails to produce any response in the participant, the researcher is left with doubts about the treatment effect. One obvious consequence of this problem is that an ABAB design is not appropriate for evaluating treatments that are expected to have a permanent or long-lasting effect.

Thus far we have discussed the failure to return to baseline as an absolute, all-or-none phenomenon. Degrees of failure are also possible. That is, the participant may show some response to the withdrawal of treatment but not a complete or immediate return to the original baseline behavior. As long as there is some noticeable response when the treatment is removed, the experiment is not severely compromised. However, the degree of credibility generally depends on the degree of the response; large responses close to the original baseline are more convincing than small responses. In addition, the final phase of the experiment (reimplementation of the treatment) provides an opportunity to reestablish the credibility of the treatment effect. If the second application of the treatment produces another clear change in behavior, the problem of a less-than-perfect return to baseline becomes less critical.

A second problem with an ABAB design concerns the ethical question of withdrawing a successful treatment. The ABAB design asks a clinician to withdraw a treatment that has been shown to be effective. Furthermore, the treatment is withdrawn with the intention of having the client's behavior revert to its original problem condition. Although this reversal component is an integral part of the ABAB design, it appears to be contrary to good clinical practice. The ethical question is compounded by the practical problem of convincing the client, therapist, and family members to agree to stop treatment. Although this problem cannot be eliminated completely, two considerations help to minimize (or rationalize) its impact. First, everyone can be reassured that the withdrawal of treatment is a temporary event; the treatment will be returned. Second, the eventual withdrawal of treatment is often a practical necessity. Eventually, the client must be released to return to a normal life. In this sense, the return-to-baseline phase can be viewed as a trial period to assess the permanence or long-term effectiveness of the treatment.

Learning Check

Explain why an ABAB reversal design is inappropriate for a treatment that has a permanent or long-lasting effect.

## 13.4   MORE COMPLEX PHASE-CHANGE DESIGNS

The ABAB design discussed in the previous section is only one example of a single-subjects design that can be built from a sequence of phases. The sequence of baseline and treatment phases can be modified by adding new treatments, and the sequence can be extended far beyond four phases to create an essentially unlimited number of different designs. Occasionally a researcher may plan a specific sequence of phases, but often the sequence evolves during the course of the study as the clinician/researcher reacts to the participant's responses. For example, a researcher may plan for an ABAB design but switch to a new treatment (C) when the participant fails to respond to the first treatment phase.

Although the number of potential phase sequences is unlimited, not every sequence qualifies as an experimental design. Remember, a true experiment should produce a reasonably unambiguous cause-and-effect explanation for the relation between treatment and behavior. In single-subject research, the experiment must show a clear change in behavior when the treatment is introduced, and it must provide at least one replication of the change. These two criteria can produce some interesting consequences in a study with two or more different treatment phases. Consider the following example.

Suppose that a researcher begins with the traditional baseline phase, then moves to a specific treatment, B. However, the participant's responses indicate that the treatment has little or no effect, so the researcher modifies the treatment, creating a new phase, $B_1$. Again, there is little or no response, so a completely different treatment, C, is started. Finally, the data show a clear change in pattern, indicating that treatment C may be effective. Thus far, the sequence of phases can be described as $ABB_1C$, and the pattern of results we have described is presented as a graph in Figure 13.9a. Although the data seem to suggest that treatment C has produced a change in behavior, there are several alternative explanations for the observed data:

- It is possible that the change in behavior is simply a coincidence caused by some extraneous variable that coincided with the beginning of treatment C.
- The change in behavior may be a delayed effect from one of the previous treatments, B or $B_1$. That is, treatment B or $B_1$ really was effective, but the effect did not become visible until several days after the treatment was administered.
- It is possible that the observed change is not due to treatment C by itself. Instead, treatment C may be effective only when it is preceded by B and/or $B_1$. That is, either treatment B or treatment $B_1$ is a necessary "catalyst" that made the participant more receptive to treatment C.

To qualify as an experiment, the study must consider these alternatives and eventually produce one unambiguous explanation for the results. The problem for the researcher is to decide what to do next. One course of action is to begin a second baseline phase, hoping that the participant's behavior returns to baseline, and then to try repeating treatment C. In symbols, the sequence of phases would become: $ABB_1CAC$. If the observed behavior replicates the patterns seen in the original A and C phases (see Figure 13.9b), you can be reasonably confident that treatment C is causing the changes. However, failure to replicate the original effects of treatment C would suggest that this treatment by itself is not the causal

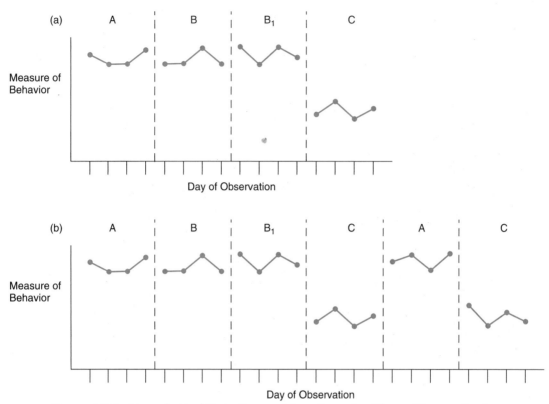

Figure 13.9   Hypothetical Data From a More Complex Phase-Change Design
(a) The first treatment B and its modification $B_1$ appear to have no effect;
however, treatment C produces a change in level.
(b) An extension of the study by addition of a return-to-baseline phase
and a replication of treatment C.

agent. In this case the study would need to be extended to evaluate the potential of a delayed effect from one of the preceding treatments, or the potential of a catalyst effect. For example, the researcher could attempt another return to baseline followed by a $B_1C$ sequence to determine whether the presence of treatment $B_1$ is a necessary prerequisite for the effectiveness of treatment C.

As you can see, a single-subject design can easily grow into a sequence of 10 to 12 phases before a clear cause-and-effect relationship emerges. At any time during the study, the researcher's decision concerning the next phase is determined by the pattern of responses observed during the preceding phases.

Learning Check

In general, how does a phase-change design demonstrate that the treatment (rather than chance or coincidence) is responsible for changes in behavior?

## DISMANTLING OR COMPONENT-ANALYSIS DESIGN

When a treatment consists of several well-defined, distinct elements, it is possible to use a phase-change design to evaluate the extent to which each separate element contributes to the overall treatment effect. The general strategy is to use a series of phases, where each phase adds or eliminates one component of the treatment. Additional baseline phases or full-treatment phases are interspersed in the series so researchers can observe how a participant's behavior changes when each treatment component is added or removed. This type of design, where a treatment is broken down into its separate parts, is called a **dismantling design** or a **component-analysis design.**

A **dismantling design,** also called a **component-analysis design,** consists of a series of phases where each phase adds or subtracts one component of a complex treatment to determine how each component contributes to the overall treatment effectiveness.

The following example demonstrates this type of design.

Individuals with severe developmental disabilities or autism often have great difficulty communicating their needs and desires. Frustration from this inability to communicate often results in inappropriate behaviors such as aggression, self-injury, and tantrums. One method of treating this problem is functional communication training. This training typically involves two components: (a) an intervention or punishment for the inappropriate behavior, and (b) training a communicative response (usually a sign or signal) to request a reinforcement. Wacker et al. (1990) conducted a component-analysis study to evaluate the relative contribution of the two components of functional communication training. One participant in the study was identified as Bobby, a 7-year-old boy with autism who was nonverbal and also did not communicate with signs or gestures. The problem behavior for Bobby was hand biting; he bit his own hand several times an hour, often drawing blood. The treatment package for Bobby consisted of two elements:

1. Reinforcement of signing: Bobby was trained to sign by touching his chin with one finger to indicate a request for play items. When he made this sign, he was given a selection of items.
2. Punishment for hand biting: The play items were immediately taken away when Bobby started biting his hand.

Hypothetical results similar to those obtained in the study are shown in Figure 13.10. We have simplified the data and eliminated other measures in order to show only the hand-biting data. Note that, during the first phase when the total treatment package is administered, hand biting stays near zero. During the next stage, signing is still reinforced, but the punishment component is removed. When this component is eliminated, hand-biting behavior increases. In the third phase, the total treatment is returned, and hand biting drops back toward zero. In the next stage, Bobby is still punished for hand biting, but the reinforcement component is removed (signs are ignored). Once again hand biting increases. Finally,

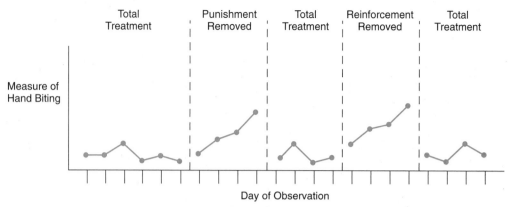

Figure 13.10   Hypothetical Data Showing a Component-Analysis
Design Similar to Results Obtained by Wacker et al. (1990)
The total treatment includes a punishment component and a reinforcement
component. Note that when either component is removed from
the treatment, hand-biting behavior increases.

the total package is administered again, and the problem behavior decreases toward zero. The general conclusion from these data is that both treatment components are important; when either one is removed, behavior deteriorates.

## 13.5   MULTIPLE-BASELINE DESIGNS

One basic problem with the single-subject designs considered thus far is the reversal or return-to-baseline component that is essential to provide a replication
of the initial treatment effect. Specifically, reversal designs require that the participant's behavior revert to baseline as soon as the treatment is removed. In addition to the ethical dilemma created by withdrawing treatment, these studies
are also limited to evaluation of treatments with only a temporary effect. The
**multiple-baseline design** provides an alternative technique that eliminates the
need for a return to baseline and therefore is particularly well suited for evaluating treatments with long lasting or permanent effects.

A multiple-baseline design requires only one phase change, from baseline to
treatment, and establishes the credibility of the treatment effect by replicating the
phase change for a second participant or for a second behavior. The general plan
for a multiple-baseline study is shown in Figure 13.11. The figure shows hypothetical results for a study involving two different participants, both of whom are
exhibiting the same problem behavior; the top half of the figure presents data for
one participant, and the bottom half shows the results for the second participant.
Notice that the study begins with a baseline phase with simultaneous observations, beginning at the same time, for both participants. After a baseline pattern is
established for both participants, the treatment phase is initiated for one participant only. Meanwhile, the baseline phase is continued for the second participant.
Finally, the treatment phase is initiated for the second participant, but at a differ-

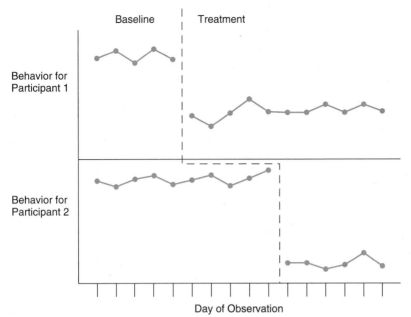

Figure 13.11    Hypothetical Data Showing the
Results From a Multiple-Baseline Design
The baseline phase begins for two participants simultaneously
but continues for one participant after the treatment phase
has been started for the other participant.

ent time from that at which treatment is begun for the first participant. Thus, this study consists of simultaneous observations of two participants during a baseline phase and a treatment phase but uses two different baseline periods for the two different participants. Figure 13.11 shows the data from a multiple-baseline design using two separate participants, each with the same problem behavior. This kind of design is called a **multiple-baseline across subjects.**

As we noted earlier, however, it also is possible to conduct a multiple-baseline study using two or more different behaviors for a single participant. The key to the single-subject version of the design is that the different behaviors are independent (one does not influence another) and can be treated separately by focusing a treatment on one behavior at a time. For example, a student may show disruptive behavior (speaking out and interrupting) and aggressive behavior (picking on other students). Each of these problem behaviors can be treated using a behavior modification program directed specifically at the problem behavior. Or a clinical client may have several different phobias, each of which can be treated with a specific desensitization program. Note that the same treatment is being used for each of the different behaviors. After clear baseline patterns are established for both behaviors, the treatment is started for one of the behaviors, and baseline observations continue for the second behavior. After a short period, the treatment is started for the second behavior. The single-subject design follows exactly the same pattern that was shown in Figure 13.11, however, the top half of the figure now corresponds to one behavior, and the bottom half represents the second behavior. This type of design, using two behaviors for a single participant, is called a **multiple-baseline across behaviors.**

Finally, the multiple-baseline design can be used to evaluate the treatment of one behavior that is exhibited in two different situations. For example, a child may exhibit disruptive behavior at school and at home. When it is possible to treat the two situations separately, you can begin baseline measurements for both situations simultaneously and then administer treatment at two different times for the two different situations. In this case, the design is called a **multiple-baseline across situations.**

---

Definitions

A **multiple-baseline design** begins with two simultaneous baseline phases. A treatment phase is initiated for one of the baselines while baseline observations continue for the other. At a later time, the treatment is initiated for the second baseline.

When the initial baseline phases correspond to two separate participants, the design is called a **multiple-baseline across subjects.**

When the initial baseline phases correspond to two separate behaviors for the same participant, the design is called a **multiple-baseline across behaviors.**

When the initial baseline phases correspond to the same behavior in two separate situations, the design is called a **multiple-baseline across situations.**

---

### RATIONALE FOR THE MULTIPLE-BASELINE DESIGN

The goal of a multiple-baseline design is to show that the treatment causes a change in behavior. The data in Figure 13.11 provide an ideal example of how this goal is accomplished. Notice that the following criteria for a successful multiple-baseline experiment are essentially identical to the criteria described earlier to define the success of an ABAB design:

- The pattern of behavior in each treatment phase is clearly different from the pattern in each baseline phase. This demonstration is necessary to establish a relation between the treatment and the behavior; that is, a change in behavior accompanies the manipulation of the treatment.
- The change from baseline to treatment occurs at two different times, but the change in behavior is essentially the same for both of the participants in the study. This replication is necessary to establish a causal relation between treatment and behavior. Although it might be argued that the change observed for the first participant is simply a coincidental effect caused by extraneous variables, the fact that the change is replicated for a second participant at a different time undermines the coincidence argument. By minimizing the potential confounding from extraneous variables, the multiple-baseline design maximizes the likelihood that the observed changes are caused by the treatment. Because the design uses at least two different

baseline periods, the results demonstrate that the researcher is able to control the participants' behavior by simply starting the treatment.

The following example demonstrates the multiple-baseline design. Ludwig and Geller (1991) used a multiple-baseline design to evaluate the effectiveness of a safe-driving program for pizza delivery drivers. The participants in this study were employees of three pizza stores. During an initial baseline phase, the authors observed safety belt use for drivers at all three stores. After several weeks, a driver safety program was initiated at one store. Three weeks later the program was started at a second store. The third store served as a control, with no driver safety program. Hypothetical results similar to those obtained in the study are presented in Figure 13.12. Notice that there is an immediate and substantial change in safety belt use at both treatment stores when the treatment is initiated. Because the

**Figure 13.12   Hypothetical Data Showing a Multiple-Baseline Design With Results Similar to Those Obtained by Ludwig and Geller (1991)**
The study evaluated the effectiveness of a seat-belt training program at three pizza shops. The training was started at two different times at two stores, and the third store served as a no-training control.

change in behavior (initiation of treatment) occurs at different times for the two stores, the authors can be confident that the safety program is responsible for the change. The control store provides additional evidence that extraneous variables (for example, a police crackdown on seat belt use) are not responsible for the changes in behavior.

Under what circumstances would you use a multiple-baseline design instead of an ABAB reversal design?

### STRENGTHS AND WEAKNESSES OF THE MULTIPLE-BASELINE DESIGN

The primary strength of the multiple-baseline design is that it eliminates the need for a reversal or return-to-baseline phase and therefore is well suited for evaluating treatment effects that are permanent or long-lasting. However, when this design is used with a single participant to examine two or more behaviors, the problem is identifying similar but independent behaviors. The risk is that a treatment applied to one behavior may generalize and produce changes in the second behavior. Once again, this problem illustrates a general conflict between clinical goals and experimental goals. From a clinical perspective, it is valuable to have a single treatment that produces a general effect, producing improvement in a variety of different problem behaviors. For the multiple-baseline experiment, however, it is essential that the treatment affect only the specific behavior to which it is applied. If both behaviors show a response to the initiation of treatment, the credibility of the treatment effect is undermined. That is, the observed changes may be due to the treatment, or they may be caused by outside variables that are changing coincidentally with the treatment.

In addition, the clarity of the results can be compromised by individual differences either between participants or between behaviors. For example, one participant may be more (or less) responsive to treatment than another. One participant may show an immediate, large change in level of behavior but the second participant only a minor change in level or a gradual change that appears as a trend in the graph. When this happens, the pattern of behavior is different from one participant to another and therefore creates doubts about the consistency of the treatment effect. The same problem can occur with research involving different behaviors for a single participant. Although the behaviors are similar, they may not be equally responsive to treatment and therefore result in different patterns when the treatment is administered.

How does a multiple-baseline design rule out chance or coincidence as the explanation for changes in behavior that occur when the treatment is started?

## 13.6    THE CHANGING-CRITERION DESIGN

Occasionally a clinician or a researcher encounters a problem behavior that can be quantified into a set of different magnitudes or levels that are clearly defined and easily understood by both the client and the clinician. A good example is cigarette smoking, which can be quantified by the number of packs or number of cigarettes smoked per day. In these situations the treatment can involve a series of target levels or criteria that can be arbitrarily set and changed by the researcher. For example, a clinician might set a criterion of 2 packs per day for the first week, then change the criterion to 1 pack per day for the next 2 weeks, and continue lowering the criterion over the course of treatment. During treatment the participant's behavior is continuously observed and recorded. If the behavior repeatedly and closely follows the criteria, the researcher can be reasonably confident that the criteria (treatment) are responsible for the observed changes in behavior. This type of research study is called a **changing-criterion design.**

A **changing-criterion design** consists of a series of phases where each phase is defined by a specific criterion that determines a target level of behavior. The criterion level is changed from one phase to the next. Evidence for a successful treatment effect is obtained when the participant's level of behavior changes in accord with the changing criterion levels.

Definition

Fitterling et al. (1988) conducted a study showing that aerobic exercise can be effective in the treatment of vascular headaches. Because aerobic exercise programs are notorious for high drop-out rates and general nonadherence, the authors used a changing criterion design to assess the relationship between the treatment program and the participants' exercise behavior. Participants exercised at home using a standardized exercise program with well-defined criteria. At the beginning of each week, each individual was given a personalized exercise prescription, including a specific criterion. After several weeks at one criterion, the researchers changed the exercise criterion, generally upward, and the participant entered a new phase in the study. Hypothetical data representing the exercise activity of an average participant are shown in Figure 13.13. During the baseline period, exercise equipment was made available, but the participant was not given any instructions or criteria for exercising. During aerobic training, the criteria levels are noted by the shading in the figure, and the participant's exercise activity is noted by the series of connected data points. Note that, with a few exceptions, the participant's exercise performance closely follows the changing criterion levels, indicating that the criteria were effective in controlling behavior. Also note that the pattern of changing criteria is bidirectional (one decrease in a series of increasing criteria), and that the participant's behavior tracks the criteria in both directions.

The most compelling evidence for a causal relation between the treatment criteria and the participant's behavior occurs when the data consistently and closely track the criteria levels. The greater the discrepancy between the data and the criteria, the weaker the argument for a cause-and-effect interpretation. One specific problem for a changing-criterion design is differentiating between data showing a general trend and data that track the criteria levels. For example, if a researcher continuously lowers the criterion value and the participant's behavior continuously decreases, it can be difficult to determine whether the data show a continuous trend or a stepwise tracking of the criteria. One solution to this problem is to incorporate one or more backward steps into the series of criteria. For example, a researcher can arbitrarily introduce one increasing criterion

Figure 13.13    Hypothetical Data Showing a Changing-Criterion Design With Results
Similar to Those Obtained by Fitterling et al. (1988)
Notice how the participant's behavior follows the criteria set by the researcher.

into a sequence of decreasing criterion values. If the participant's behavior follows this blip in the pattern, the argument for a causal effect is enhanced. An alternative technique is to arbitrarily vary the duration of each criterion phase. A random sequence of short phases and long phases will create a pattern that is clearly different from a continuous linear trend.

Learning
Check

Under what circumstances is a changing-criterion design an appropriate method for evaluating the effectiveness of a treatment?

## 13.7    THE ALTERNATING-TREATMENTS DESIGN

Each of the single-subject designs discussed thus far has involved comparisons between phases, where a phase is defined by a specific block of time. The responses within one time block are grouped together to create a pattern that is then compared with the pattern within another time block. These designs require that each treatment condition (or baseline condition) be administered continuously for an extended period. The **alternating-treatments design,** on the other hand, allows a researcher to switch back and forth between treatments rapidly without waiting for a long series of observations to reveal a level, trend, or stability in the data. This type of design is also called a **discrete-trials design** because each trial or data point can be a separate, individual treatment condition.

The procedure for an alternating-treatments design involves using a random process to determine which of two treatment conditions will be administered for each observation. Thus, the series of observations corresponds to a randomly alternating series of treatment conditions. The basic requirements for an alternating treatments design are:

1. It must be possible for the researcher/clinician to switch rapidly between treatment conditions.
2. The participant's behavior must show an immediate response to the treatment being administered. There is no time for a response to evolve over a series of observations.

---

In an **alternating-treatments design,** also called a **discrete-trials design,** two treatment conditions are randomly alternated from one observation to the next. The result is a series of observations that represent a corresponding series of alternating treatment conditions.

---

The data from an alternating-treatments study are grouped by treatment conditions rather than grouped into blocks of time. In a graph of the results, a line is used to connect all the data points from one condition. A separate line is used for each separate condition. The following example presents a demonstration of an alternating-treatments study and shows how the results are presented in a graph.

Rolider, Cummings, and Van Houten (1991) used an alternating-treatments design to examine the effects of punishment on academic performance. In this study, two therapists, identified as therapist A and therapist B, administered a functional teaching program to developmentally disabled individuals. One participant, Billy, was taught a receptive labeling task. The task involved presenting Billy with four animal pictures and asking him to "give me the picture of the _____." Both therapists were present during the teaching, with one acting as teacher and the other standing close by. The two therapists alternated roles as teacher, with a 30-minute break separating the two teaching sessions each day. However, only one of the therapists administered punishment for inappropriate behavior. For Billy, therapist A always administered punishment, whether she was teaching or simply observing. Thus, the study alternated between two treatment conditions (teacher as punisher versus external punisher) within each session. Figure 13.14 shows hypothetical data similar to the results obtained for Billy. During the baseline sessions no punishment was administered, and during the treatment sessions, therapist A punished inappropriate behavior. The solid circles indicate performance while therapist A was teaching, and the open circles show performance while therapist B was teaching. Notice that the data show a general trend toward improved performance when punishment is initiated. Comparison of the two lines, however, indicates that Billy performed better when the teacher controlled the punishment than when punishment was delivered by a nonteaching third party.

## APPLICATION OF THE ALTERNATING-TREATMENTS DESIGN

One advantage of the alternating-treatments design is that it allows an immediate and essentially simultaneous evaluation of two different treatments. This strategy can be useful in situations where a clinician has two (or more) treatment options but is unsure which is better for a particular client. With an alternating-treatments design, differences between treatments will emerge after a relatively short series of observations, and the clinician can then switch to the more effective treatment.

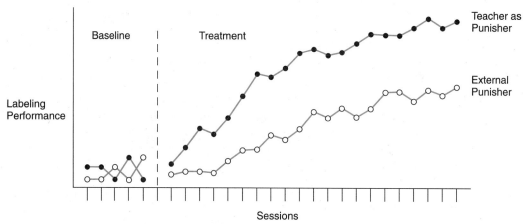

Figure 13.14 Hypothetical Data Showing an Alternating-Treatments Design With Results Similar to Those Obtained by Rolider, Cummings, and Van Houten (1991) The solid circles show the participant's behavior when therapist A teaches and administers punishment for inappropriate behavior. The open circles show behavior when therapist B teaches and therapist A only administers punishment.

The fact that this design permits rapid alternation between conditions allows a researcher to examine the effects of different strategies within a single therapy session. For example, a clinician could divide a 1-hour session into a series of 5-minute observation periods. The therapist could then modify aspects of the therapy from one period to another and observe the effects of this alternation on the client's behavior. For example, a therapist could alternate between "personal involvement" and "personal detachment" by leaning forward, smiling, and appearing interested during some periods but leaning back and appearing relatively cold and neutral during other periods. Finally, the alternating-treatments design can be used to compare different treatment techniques in situations where alternation between therapists or treatment conditions occurs naturally. In a school or residential program, for example, a client may routinely encounter two or more different counselors or supervisors. In this situation, the two counselors may adopt different treatment strategies. For example, one counselor may be sympathetic to tantrums, while a second counselor simply ignores the outbursts. Although this type of study is inherently confounded (different counselors are confounded with different strategies), the results may provide some insight into determining which strategy is more effective in dealing with the problem behavior.

Learning Check

Is an alternating-treatments design effective if one or both of the treatments has a permanent or long-lasting effect? Explain why or why not.

## 13.8    GENERAL STRENGTHS AND WEAKNESSES OF SINGLE-SUBJECT DESIGNS

There are three fundamental differences between single-subject designs and traditional group designs:

1. The first and most obvious distinction is that single-subject research is conducted with only one participant or occasionally a very small group.
2. Single-subject research also tends to be much more flexible than a traditional group study. A single-subject design can be modified or changed completely in the middle of a study without seriously affecting the integrity of the design, and there is no need to standardize treatment conditions across a large set of different participants.
3. Single-subject designs require continuous assessment. In a traditional group design, an individual subject typically is observed and measured only once or twice. A single-subject design, however, normally involves a series of 10 to 20 observations for each individual.

As a consequence of these differences, single-subject designs have some advantages and some disadvantages in comparison with group designs. In this section we identify and discuss the general strengths and weaknesses of single-subject research, beginning with the strengths.

### ADVANTAGES OF SINGLE-SUBJECT DESIGNS

The primary strength of single-subject designs is that they make it possible for a researcher to establish a cause-and-effect relationship between treatment and behavior using only a single participant. This simple fact makes it possible to integrate experimental research into applied clinical practice. As we noted in Chapters 8 and 9, the demands and restrictions of traditional group experiments are often at odds with good clinical practice. As a result, clinicians tend to prefer alternative strategies such as case studies or quasi-experimental research. However, these alternative strategies do not permit clinicians to establish causal relations between the treatments they use and the resulting behaviors. As a result, clinical psychologists are often left in the unenviable position of using treatments that have not been "scientifically demonstrated" to be effective. Single-subject designs provide a solution to this dilemma. By employing single-subject designs, a clinician who typically works with individual clients or small groups can conduct experimental research and practice therapy simultaneously without seriously compromising either activity. By recording and graphing observations during the course of treatment, a clinician can demonstrate a cause-and-effect relation between a treatment and the effects of the treatment. This scientific demonstration is an important part of establishing accountability in the field of clinical psychology. That is, clinicians should be able to demonstrate unambiguously that the treatments they use are effective.

A second major advantage of single-subject designs comes from their flexibility. Although a researcher may begin a single-subject experiment with a preconceived plan for the design, the ultimate development of the design depends on the participant's responses. If a participant fails to respond to treatment, for example, the researcher is free to modify the treatment or change to a new treatment without compromising the experiment. Once again, this characteristic of single-subject research makes these designs extremely well suited to clinical research. In routine clinical practice, a therapist monitors a client's responses and makes clinical decisions based on those responses. This same flexibility is an integral part of most single-subject research. That is, the clinical decision to begin a new treatment and the experimental decision to begin a new phase are both determined by observing the participant's response to the current treatment or current phase. In addition, single-subject designs allow a clinician/researcher to individualize treatment to meet the needs of a specific client. Because these designs typically employ only one participant, there is no need to standardize a treatment across a group of individuals with different needs, different problems, and different responses.

In summary, the real strength of single-subject designs is that they make experimental clinical research compatible with routine clinical practice. These designs combine the clinical advantages of case study research with the rigor of a true experiment. In particular, single-subject research allows for the detailed description and individualized treatment of a single participant and allows a clinician/researcher to establish the existence of a cause-and-effect relation between the treatment and the participant's responses.

## DISADVANTAGES OF SINGLE-SUBJECT DESIGNS

Earlier we noted that one of the strengths of a single-subject design is that it can establish the presence of a cause-and-effect relation using only one participant. At the same time, however, a weakness of these designs is that the relationship is demonstrated only for one participant. This simple fact leaves researchers with some question as to whether or not the relation can or should be generalized to other individuals. You should recognize this problem as the general concern of external validity. However, the problem of limited external validity is mitigated by the fact that single-subject research seldom exists in isolation. Usually the researcher or clinician has observed the treatment effect in multiple cases before one individual case is selected for the single-subject research project. Also, the relationship between the treatment and outcome is commonly demonstrated in other nonexperimental research such as case studies or quasi-experimental studies. These other studies provide support for generalizing the treatment effect (external validity), and the single-subject study demonstrates the causal nature of the effect (internal validity).

A second potential weakness of single-subject designs comes from the requirement for multiple, continuous observations. If the observations can be made unobtrusively, without constantly interrupting or distracting the participant, there is little cause for concern. However, if the participant is aware that observations are continuously being made, this awareness may result in reactivity or sensitization that could affect the participant's responses (see Chapter 11). As a result, there is some risk that the participant's behavior may be affected not only by the treatment conditions but also by the assessment procedures. In experimental terminology, the continuous assessment can be a threat to internal validity.

Another concern for single-subject designs is the absence of statistical controls. With traditional group designs, researchers can use standard inferential statistical techniques to quantify the likelihood that the results show a real treatment effect versus the likelihood that the results simply reflect chance behavior. Single-subject designs, on the other hand, rely on the visual impact of a graph to convince others that the treatment effects are real. Problems can arise if there is any ambiguity at all in the graphed results. One observer, for example, may see clear indications of a treatment effect, while other observers may not. On the positive side, reliance on graphed results helps to ensure that researchers report only results that are substantial; that is, the treatment effects must be sufficiently large that they are obvious to a casual observer when presented in a graph. Researchers often make a distinction between **statistical significance** and **practical significance.** Practical significance means that the treatment effect is substantial, large enough to have practical application. Statistical significance, on the other hand, simply means that the observed effect, whether large or small, is very unlikely to have occurred by chance. Using this terminology, the results from a single-subject study tend to have practical significance, although they typically are not evaluated in terms of statistical significance.

The reliance on a graph to establish the significance of results places additional restrictions on the application of single-subject designs. Specifically, the treatment effects must be large and immediate to produce a convincing graph. Treatments that produce small effects or effects that are slow to develop will generate ambiguous graphs and therefore are unlikely to appear in published reports. As a result, single-subject research is likely to fail to detect such effects. From a research perspective, this tendency is unfortunate because many real treatments will be overlooked. From the clinician's point of view, however, this aspect of single-subject research simply means that marginally effective treatments are weeded out, and only those treatments that are truly effective are reported.

---

Briefly explain why a clinical psychologist might prefer doing research with a single-subject design instead of traditional group design.

Learning Check

---

## CHAPTER SUMMARY

In this chapter we examine the characteristics of single-subject designs. The general goal of single-subject research, like other experimental designs, is to establish the existence of a cause-and-effect relationship between variables. The defining characteristic of a single-subject study is that it can be used with a single individual, testing or observing the individual before and during or after the treatment is implemented by the researcher.

The basic building block of most single-subject designs is the phase, a series of observations all made under the same conditions. Observations are made in a baseline phase (i.e., in the absence of a treatment) and in a treatment phase (i.e., during treatment). The series of observations that make up any phase should show a clear pattern that describes the behavior. The pattern within a phase can be described in terms of level or trend, but in either case the critical factor is the consistency or stability of the pattern. Ultimately, the researcher changes phases by implementing or withdrawing a treatment. The purpose for a phase change is to demonstrate that adding or removing a treatment produces a noticeable change in the pattern of behavior from one phase to the next.

Unlike other experimental designs, the results of a single-subject design are not evaluated with traditional tests for statistical significance. Instead, researchers must rely on graphs to convey the meaning of their results. The graph must show a clear change in behavior when the treatment is introduced. Also, the change in behavior must be replicated at least one more time to demonstrate that the first change was not due to coincidence or chance. Because the interpretation of the results depends entirely on the visual appearance of a graph, it is important that the change in pattern from baseline to treatment be easy to see when the results are presented in a graph. Visual inspection of single-subject data is unfortunately a very subjective task. However, four specific characteristics help determine whether there is a meaningful change between phases: (1) change in mean level of behavior, (2) immediate change in level of behavior, (3) change in trend of behavior, and (4) latency of change of behavior.

Different types of single-subject designs were discussed: the ABAB or reversal design, more complex phase-change designs, dismantling or component-analysis design, variations of the multiple-baseline design, changing-criterion design, and the alternating-treatments design. The strengths and weaknesses of each of these designs, as well as the general strengths and weaknesses of single-subject designs, are also considered.

## KEY WORDS

single-subject designs or single-case designs
phase
baseline observations
baseline phase
treatment observations
treatment phase
level

trend
stability
phase change
ABAB design or reversal design
dismantling design or component-analysis design
multiple-baseline design
multiple-baseline across subjects

multiple-baseline across behaviors
multiple-baseline across situations
changing-criterion design
alternating-treatments design or discrete-trials design

## EXERCISES

1. In addition to the key words, you should also be able to define the following terms:
   statistical significance
   practical significance
2. Describe the similarity between single-subject designs, case studies, and time series designs.
3. Explain why single-subject designs are often preferred to traditional group designs for clinical research.
4. Describe the major difference between single-subject designs and other experimental designs.
5. Describe how extraneous variables can threaten the internal validity of the results presented in Figure 13.1.

6. Describe how the level and trend of behavior can be used to define a pattern of behavior in a graph of data from a single-subject design.
7. Describe the three techniques that can be used to show a consistent pattern of behavior in situations where the data appear to be unstable.
8. What is the purpose of a phase change?
9. Describe how changes in mean, level, trend, and latency can each be used to evaluate data in a single-subject design.
10. Describe the importance of the reversal phase in the ABAB design.
11. Draw a graph for an ABAB research design showing the data that would be obtained from

a treatment with a permanent or long-lasting effect. Explain why the data you have drawn are not considered to be clear evidence for a cause-and-effect relationship between the treatment and the behavior.

12. Describe the strengths and weaknesses of the ABAB design.

13. Describe the purpose of a dismantling design.

14. Suppose that a complex therapy procedure contains one component that has absolutely no effect on behavior.
    a. Explain how a dismantling design could be used to demonstrate that the component has no effect.
    b. Draw a graph showing data that demonstrate that the component has no effect.

15. Describe the advantages of the multiple-baseline design over the ABAB design.

16. Describe how the multiple-baseline design can be used to evaluate the treatment of one behavior in two participants.

17. Suppose a researcher uses a multiple-baseline design to evaluate a therapy to treat two different problem behaviors for the same individual. Draw a graph showing the data that would be obtained if the therapy affected both behaviors simultaneously even though the therapy was directed at only one behavior. Explain why the data you have drawn would not be considered to be clear evidence for a cause-and-effect relationship between the therapy and the behaviors.

18. Describe the strengths and weaknesses of the multiple-baseline design.

19. Describe the strengths and weaknesses of the changing-criterion design.

20. Describe the strengths and weaknesses of the alternating-treatments design.

21. Describe the general strengths and weaknesses of single-subject designs.

 InfoTrac COLLEGE EDITION EXERCISES

1. Use InfoTrac College Edition to find a research study using an ABAB reversal design. (Hint: Try key words or subject terms such as *single subject*, *reversal design*, or *ABAB reversal*.) Once you have found your study, answer each of the following:
   a. What behavior is being measured, and how is it measured?
   b. What treatment is being evaluated, and how is the treatment expected to affect the behavior?
   c. Does the study include a graph of the results? If so, print out a copy of the graph, and ask 10 people whether or not they think that the graph provides convincing evidence that the treatment actually has an effect on behavior.

2. Use InfoTrac College Edition to find a research study using a multiple-baseline design. (Hint: Try key words or subject terms such as *single-subject* or *multiple-baseline*.) Once you have found your study, answer each of the following:
   a. Does the study explain why this specific design was used? If so, what is the reason? If not, why do you think a multiple-baseline design was used?
   b. Does the design use separate participants or separate behaviors for one participant?
   c. If the study includes a graph of the results, print out a copy of the graph, and ask 10 people whether or not they think that the graph provides convincing evidence that the treatment actually has an effect on behavior.

# Statistical Evaluation of Data

## CHAPTER OVERVIEW

In this chapter we consider Step 8 of the research process—evaluating the data. Both descriptive and inferential statistics are described in detail. In addition, special statistical analyses for research are considered.

## 14.1    THE ROLE OF STATISTICS IN THE RESEARCH PROCESS

When the data collection phase of the research process is completed, a researcher typically is confronted with pages of data—the scores, measurements, and observations recorded during the research study. The next step, Step 8 in the research process, is to use statistical methods to help make sense of the data. (The exception is single-subject research, in which statistical techniques usually are not used.) Statistical methods serve two principal purposes:

1. Statistics help to organize and summarize the data so the researcher can see what happened in the study and communicate the results to others.
2. Statistics help the researcher to answer the general questions that initiated the research by determining exactly what conclusions are justified based on the results.

These two general purposes correspond to the two general categories of statistical techniques: descriptive statistics and inferential statistics. **Descriptive statistics** are techniques that help to describe a set of data. Examples of descriptive statistics include organizing a set of scores into a graph or a table and calculating a single value, such as the average score, that describes the entire set. The goal of descriptive statistics is to organize, summarize, and simplify data.

**Inferential statistics,** on the other hand, are methods that use the limited information from samples to answer general questions about populations. Recall from Chapter 5 that research questions concern a population, but research studies are conducted with relatively small samples. Although the sample is selected from the population and is intended to represent the population, there is no guarantee that a sample will provide a perfectly accurate picture of the population. Thus researchers must be cautious about assuming that the results obtained from a sample will generalize to the entire population. Inferential statistics help researchers determine when it is appropriate to generalize from a sample to a population.

Definitions

**Descriptive statistics** are methods that help researchers to organize, summarize, and simplify the results obtained from research studies.

**Inferential statistics** are methods that use the results obtained from samples to help make generalizations about populations.

### PLANNING AHEAD

Although using statistics to evaluate research results appears as Step 8 in the research process, you should think about statistics long before you begin the research study. In particular, you should decide how to describe your results and exactly which descriptive statistics will be needed. This task includes an evaluation of your planned measurement procedure to be sure that the scores you obtain are compatible with the statistics you plan to use. For example, if you plan to compute mean scores, you will need to have numerical data.

You also need to anticipate the inferential statistics you will use. This involves deciding exactly what kind of conclusion you would like to make and then ensuring that there is an appropriate inferential procedure to make your point.

In general, as soon as you begin to make decisions about how to define and measure the variables in your research study, you should also make decisions about the statistical analysis of your data. You should anticipate the appearance of your research data, plan the descriptive statistics that will allow you to present your data so that others can see and understand your results, and plan the inferential statistics that will allow you to interpret your results.

## STATISTICS TERMINOLOGY

Before we discuss descriptive and inferential statistical techniques, two additional terms should be introduced. The most commonly used descriptive technique is to compute one or two numerical values that summarize an entire set of data. When the set of data is a sample, the summary values are called **statistics.**

**Definition**

A summary value that describes a sample is called a **statistic.** A common example of a statistic is the average score for a sample.

Sample statistics serve a dual purpose:

1. They describe or summarize the entire set of scores in the sample. For example, the average IQ score for a sample of $n = 100$ people provides a summary description of the intelligence level of the entire sample.
2. They provide information about the corresponding summary values for the entire population. For example, the average reading score for a sample of $n = 25$ first-grade students provides information about the general reading level for the entire population of first-graders.

Once again, summary values computed for a sample are called statistics. The corresponding summary values for a population are called **parameters.**

**Definition**

A summary value that describes a population is called a **parameter.** A common example of a parameter is the average score for a population.

Each statistic (computed for a sample) has a corresponding parameter (for the entire population). As you will see later in this chapter, most inferential statistical techniques use sample statistics as the basis for drawing general conclusions about the corresponding population parameters.

 Learning Checks

Describe the two general purposes of statistics and the two corresponding general categories of statistical techniques.

Explain the difference between a statistic and a parameter.

## 14.2   DESCRIPTIVE STATISTICS

As noted earlier, the general goal of descriptive statistics is to organize or summarize a set of scores. The two general techniques for accomplishing this goal are:

1.   To organize the entire set of scores into a table or a graph that allows researchers (and others) to see the whole set of scores
2.   To compute one or two summary values (such as the average) that describe the entire group

Each of these techniques is discussed in the following sections.

### FREQUENCY DISTRIBUTIONS

One method of simplifying and organizing a set of scores is to group them into an organized display that shows the entire set. The display is called a **frequency distribution** and consists of a tabulation of the number of individuals in each category on the scale of measurement. Thus, a frequency distribution consists of two parts:

1.   A display showing the set of categories that make up the scale of measurement
2.   A display showing how many individuals had scores in each of the categories

Depending on the method used to display the scale of measurement and the frequencies, a frequency distribution can be a table or a graph. The advantage of a frequency distribution is that it allows a researcher to view the entire set of scores. The disadvantage is that constructing a frequency distribution can be somewhat tedious, especially with large sets of data.

#### Frequency Distribution Tables

A frequency distribution table consists of two columns of information. The first column presents the scale of measurement or simply lists the set of categories into which individuals have been assigned. The second column lists the frequency, or the number of individuals, located in each category. Table 14.1 is a frequency distribution table summarizing the scores from a 6-point quiz given to a class of $n = 15$ students. The first column lists all the possible quiz scores (categories of measurement) in order from 6 to 1; it is headed $X$ to indicate that these are the potential scores. The second column shows the frequency of occurrence for each score. In this example, one person had a perfect score of $X = 6$ on the quiz, three people had scores of $X = 5$, and so on.

#### Frequency Distribution Graphs

The same information that is presented in a frequency distribution table can be presented in a graph. The graph shows the scale of measurement (set of categories) along the horizontal axis and the frequencies on the vertical axis. Recall from Chapter 4 that there are four different scales of measurement: nominal, ordinal, interval, and ratio. When the measurement scale (scores) consist of numerical values (interval or ratio scale of measurement), there are two options for graphing the frequency distribution:

| TABLE 14.1 |
| --- |

**A Frequency Distribution Table**

The table shows the distribution of scores from a 6-point quiz.

| X | f |
| --- | --- |
| 6 | 1 |
| 5 | 3 |
| 4 | 4 |
| 3 | 3 |
| 2 | 2 |
| 1 | 2 |

1. A **histogram** shows a bar above each score such that the height of the bar indicates the frequency of occurrence for that particular score. The bars for adjacent scores touch each other.

2. A **polygon** shows a point above each score such that the height of the point indicates the frequency. Straight lines connect the points, and additional straight lines are drawn down to the horizontal axis at each end to complete the figure.

Figure 14.1 shows two histograms and a polygon presenting the same data as Table 14.1. Figure 14.1a is a traditional histogram with a bar above each category. In Figure 14.1b we have modified the histogram slightly by changing each bar into a stack of blocks. The modification helps emphasize the concept of a frequency distribution: Each block represents one individual, and the graph shows how the individuals are distributed (piled up) along the scale of measurement. Finally, Figure 14.1c presents the same data in a polygon. Each of the graphs gives an organized picture of the entire set of scores so you can tell at a glance where the scores are located on the scale of measurement.

When the categories on the scale of measurement are not numerical values (nominal or ordinal scales), the frequency distribution is presented as a **bar graph.** A bar graph is like a histogram, except that a space is left between adjacent bars. Figure 14.2 is a bar graph that presents a frequency distribution of academic majors in an introductory college course. Notice that the height of each bar indicates the frequency associated with that particular category. In this example, the class contains 10 psychology majors, six biology majors, and so on.

Frequency distributions, especially graphs, can be a very effective method for gathering information about a set of scores. The distribution shows whether the scores are clustered together or spread out across the scale. You can see at a glance whether the scores are generally high or generally low, that is, where the distribution is centered. Also, if there are one or two extreme scores (very different from the rest of the group), these values are easy to see in the graph. However, a frequency distribution is generally considered to be a preliminary method of statistical analysis. As a result frequency distributions are rarely shown in published research reports. Nonetheless, a frequency distribution graph is an excellent first step in examining a set of data. As soon as you finish

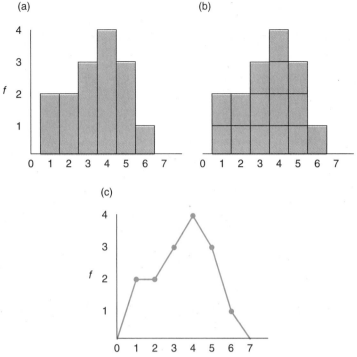

Figure 14.1    Frequency Distribution Graphs
The same set of scores is shown in a traditional histogram (a), in a modified histogram (b), and in a polygon (c). In the modified histogram (b) each score is represented by a block, so there is no need for a vertical axis to show the frequency for each score.

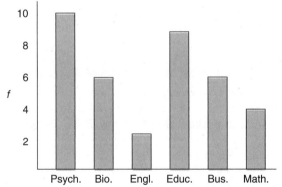

Figure 14.2    A Bar Graph Showing the Frequency Distribution of Academic Majors in an Introductory Psychology Class
Notice the space between adjacent bars.

data collection, constructing a frequency distribution graph will give you a clear picture of the results. In addition, a frequency distribution graph is probably the single best method for thinking about a set of data. Whenever you encounter the concept of a "sample" or a "set of scores," we suggest that you visualize the scores in a frequency distribution graph. The image of a frequency distribution graph gives you a concrete representation of all the individual scores as well as the appearance of the entire set of data.

Learning Checks

What are the advantages and disadvantages of using a frequency distribution to organize data?

What type of data should be presented in a histogram, and what type of data should be presented in a bar graph?

## MEASURES OF CENTRAL TENDENCY

Although frequency distribution tables and graphs have the advantage of presenting a complete picture of a set of data, there are simpler methods for describing the scores in a sample. Perhaps the most commonly used descriptive statistic involves computing the average score for a set of data. In statistical terms, this process is called measuring **central tendency.** The purpose of measuring central tendency is to locate the center of the distribution of scores by finding the single score that best represents the entire set. The goal is to find the average score or the most typical score for the entire set.

Definition

**Central tendency** is a statistical measure that identifies a single score that defines the center of a distribution. The goal of central tendency is to identify the value that is most typical or most representative of the entire group.

Measures of central tendency can be used to describe or summarize a group of individuals. For example, if a research report states that the children who participated in the study had an average IQ of 124, you should recognize that these children are definitely smarter than average (IQs average 100). In addition, measures of central tendency are the most commonly used measures for comparing two (or more) different sets of data. For example, a research report might state that the students who received special tutoring had exam scores that averaged 12 points higher than the scores of students who did not receive tutoring.

Although the concept of central tendency is fairly straightforward, a few concerns arise in implementing the concept. The goal is to use an objective, clearly defined procedure for determining the center of a set of scores so that other researchers will know exactly how the average score for a sample was computed and so be able to duplicate the process. Unfortunately, no single procedure always works. As a result, researchers have developed three different procedures for measuring central tendency, each suited to a specific situation or type of data. The three measures of central tendency are the mean, the median, and the mode.

### The Mean

When individual scores are numerical values obtained from an interval or a ratio scale of measurement, the **mean** is the most commonly used measure of central tendency. The mean is computed by summing scores and dividing the sum by the number of individuals. Conceptually, the mean is the amount each individual would receive if the total were divided equally. In research reports, the convention is to use the letter $M$ to represent a sample mean. The mean for a population is represented by the symbol μ, the Greek letter *mu*. As noted earlier, the mean is the most commonly used measure of central tendency. However, there are situations where the mean does not provide a good measure of central tendency or where it is impossible to compute a mean. Usually these situations fall into one of the following categories:

> In statistics textbooks the symbol $\bar{X}$ is commonly used for a sample mean.

- When a sample contains a few extreme scores—unusually high or unusually low values—the mean tends to be distorted by the extreme values so that it is not a good central, representative value. For example, one or two exceptionally large scores can raise the mean so that it is not located in the center of the distribution.
- Often sample data consist of measurements from a nominal scale and are not numerical values. For example, a researcher might measure variables such as gender, occupation, academic major, or eye-color for a sample of students. Because no numerical values are involved, it is impossible to compute a mean value for such data. Occasionally, nominal measurements are coded with numerical values. For example, a researcher may use the value 0 for a male and the value 1 for a female. In this situation it is possible to compute a mean; however, the result is a meaningless number.

When it is impossible to compute a mean, or when the mean does not produce a good representative value, one of the alternative measures of central tendency should be used: the median or the mode.

### The Median

The **median** is the score that divides a distribution exactly in half. Exactly 50% of the individuals in a distribution have scores greater than or equal to the median, and exactly 50% of the individuals have scores less than or equal to the median. The median also is called the 50th percentile. Usually the median is used for data sets where the mean does not provide a good representative value. In a distribution with a few extreme scores, for example, the extreme values can displace the mean so that it is not a central value. In this situation, the median often provides a better measure of central tendency. Thus, you can think of the median as a back-up measure of central tendency that is used in situations where the mean does not work well.

Often demographic data, such as family income or prices of new single-family homes, contain a few extreme values. In these situations, the median income or the median price is typically used to describe the average.

### The Mode

The **mode** is the score or category with the greatest frequency. In a frequency distribution graph, the mode identifies the location of the peak (highest point) in the distribution. When the scores consist of classifications that are not numerical values (for example, measurements from a nominal scale of measurement), it is impossible to compute the mean or the median. In this case, the mode is the only available measure of central tendency. When the scores are numerical values, the mode is often reported along with the mean because it helps describe the shape of the distribution. Although a distribution of scores can have only one mean and only one median, it is possible to have multiple peaks and therefore multiple modes. A distribution with two distinct peaks is said to be **bimodal.** A distribution with more than two modes is **multimodal.**

---

The **mean** is a measure of central tendency obtained by summing the individual scores and then dividing the sum by the number of scores. The mean is the arithmetic average.

The **median** measures central tendency by identifying the score that divides the distribution exactly in half. If the scores are listed in order, exactly 50% of the individuals have scores above the median and 50% have scores below the median.

The **mode** measures central tendency by identifying the most frequently occurring score in the distribution.

---

Examples demonstrating calculation of the mean, the median, and the mode are presented in Appendix B, page 430.

---

Learning
Checks

What is the purpose of measuring central tendency?

In what situations would it be best to use the mean as a measure of central tendency? In what situations should you use an alternative method?

Describe a situation in which the median provides a better measure of central tendency than the mean.

---

## MEASURES OF VARIABILITY

**Variability** describes the spread of the scores in a distribution. When variability is small, it means that the scores are all clustered close together. Large variability means that the scores are spread across a wide range of values. As with central tendency, there are several different ways to measure or describe variability; however, the most common are the standard deviation and its associated measure, variance.

### Standard Deviation and Variance

Whenever the mean is used as the measure of central tendency, the standard deviation is used as the measure of variability. Standard deviation uses the mean of the distribution as reference point and measures variability by measuring the distance between each score and the mean. Conceptually, **standard deviation** measures the average distance from the mean: When the scores are clustered close to the mean, the standard deviation is small; when the scores are scattered widely around the mean, the standard deviation is large.

Although the concept of the standard deviation is fairly straightforward, its actual calculation is somewhat more complicated. First, the calculations require computation of the average squared distance from the mean. This average squared value is called **variance.** Although variance is not an intuitively meaningful concept, it is an important statistical measure, especially in the context of inferential statistics. In summary, the calculation of variance and standard deviation can be viewed as a series of steps:

1. For each score, measure the distance away from the mean. This distance is often called a deviation. For example, if the mean is 80 and you have a score of 84, then the distance (or deviation) is 4 points.
2. Square each of the distances and compute the average of the squared distances. This is variance.
3. Because the variance measures the average squared distance from the mean, simply take the square root to obtain the standard deviation. Thus, variance and standard deviation are directly related by a squaring or square root operation.

$$\text{Standard deviation} = \sqrt{\text{Variance}}$$

$$\text{Variance} = (\text{Standard deviation})^2$$

In statistics textbooks the sample standard deviation is usually identified by the letter $s$, and the sample variance is $s^2$. In published reports the sample standard deviation is identified as $SD$.

---

**Variability** is a measure of the spread of scores in a distribution.

**Variance** measures variability by computing the distance from the mean for each score, then squaring the distances and finding the average squared distance. Variance is the average squared distance from the mean.

**Standard deviation** is the square root of the variance and provides a measure of variability by describing the average distance from the mean.

---

Because the standard deviation is a measure of distance, it is a fairly easy concept to understand. Therefore, the standard deviation is considered the best way to describe variability. Once again, standard deviation provides a measure of the standard distance from the mean. A small value for standard deviation indicates that the individual scores are clustered close to the mean, and a large value indicates that the scores are spread out relatively far from the mean. You can also think of standard deviation as describing the distance between scores; a small standard deviation, for example, indicates that the differences or distances from one score to another are relatively small.

Variance, on the other hand, measures squared distance. Because squared distance is not a simple concept, variance is not usually used to describe variability. However, variance does provide a measure of distance. A small variance indicates that the scores are clustered close together; a large variance means that the scores are widely scattered.

### Variance and Degrees of Freedom

Variance is defined as the average squared distance from the mean. For a sample of 5 scores, for example, this definition would seem to imply that variance is computed by the following process:

1. Measure the distance from the mean for each of the 5 scores.
2. Square each of the 5 distances.
3. Add up the 5 squared distances to obtain the sum.
4. Divide the sum by 5 to obtain the average squared distance.

In fact, this procedure is correct except for the final step. Instead of dividing by 5, you should divide by 4. In general, if the number of scores in a sample is identified by $n$, then the final step in computing sample variance is to divide by $n - 1$.

The value of $n - 1$ is called the **degrees of freedom** (or simply $df$) for the sample variance. Dividing by $n - 1$ (instead of dividing by $n$) is a necessary adjustment to ensure that the sample variance provides an accurate representation of its population variance. Without the adjustment, the sample variance would tend to underestimate the actual variance in the population. With the adjustment the sample variance, on average, gives an accurate and unbiased picture of the population variance.

It is not critical to understand the concept of degrees of freedom; however, degrees of freedom ($df$) are encountered in nearly every situation where statistics are computed or reported. In most cases, you should be able to find a relationship between the structure of the study and the value for degrees of freedom. For example, a research study with 20 participants will have a sample variance with $df = 19$. The topic of degrees of freedom occurs again later in the context of hypothesis tests (Section 14.4).

Examples demonstrating the calculation of standard deviation and variance are presented in Appendix B, pages 430–431.

**Learning Checks**

Describe the relationship between variance and standard deviation.

Describe the relationship between the standard deviation and the mean.

## DESCRIBING INTERVAL AND RATIO DATA (NUMERICAL SCORES)

Earlier in this chapter we introduced the frequency distribution as the best method of visualizing a set of scores. When the scores are measured on an interval or a ratio scale, the mean and the standard deviation are the best methods of describing a set of scores. In fact, all three of these statistical concepts (distribution, mean, and standard deviation) are interrelated.

In a frequency distribution graph, the mean can be represented by a vertical line drawn through the center of the set of scores. By definition, the mean identifies the location of the center. In the same way, the standard deviation can be represented by two arrows that point out from the mean toward the opposite extremes of the frequency distribution. The two arrows should be the same length (equal to the standard deviation), and the length should be about one half of the distance from the mean to the most extreme scores. Figure 14.3 is a

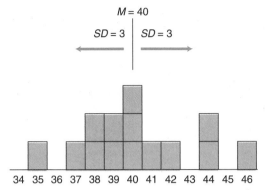

Figure 14.3   A Distribution of Scores with a Mean of $M = 40$ and a
Standard Deviation of $SD = 3$
Notice that the mean is shown with a vertical line positioned
at a value of 40. The standard deviation (standard distance
from the mean) is shown with arrows that extend 3 points
above the mean and 3 points below the mean.

frequency distribution graph with the mean and standard deviation displayed as described. Notice that the standard deviation is shown as a distance from the mean and is intended to represent the standard distance: Some of the scores are closer to the mean, and some are farther away from the mean, but the arrows represent the standard or average distance.

As you examine Figure 14.3, also notice that the values for the mean and the standard deviation provide information about the location of the scores in the distribution. Specifically, the value of the mean identifies the numerical score in the center of the distribution, and the standard deviation specifies how far the scores are distributed to the right and to the left of the mean. In Figure 14.3, the mean is 40 and the standard deviation is 3. Thus, the mean is located at a value of 40, and the arrows extend to 43 on the right and 37 on the left. For this distribution, most of the scores are located between 37 and 43.

Figure 14.4a is a frequency distribution for a set of scores. This is the kind of distribution you might prepare after collecting data in a research study. Just by looking at the distribution, you should be able to make reasonably accurate estimates of the mean and the standard deviation. Try it. For this set of scores the actual mean is 16.88, and the standard deviation is 2.23. How close were your estimates?

In the literature, the mean is identified by the letter $M$, and the standard deviation is identified by $SD$. These two values are probably the most commonly reported descriptive statistics, and they should provide enough information to construct a good picture of the entire set of scores. For example, suppose that a research report describes a set of scores by stating that $M = 45$ and $SD = 6$. Based on this information you should be able to visualize (or sketch) a frequency distribution graph showing the set of scores. Try it; your distribution should look like the graph in Figure 14.4b.

(a)

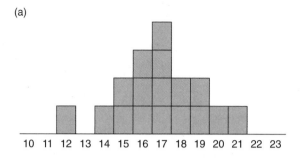

10  11  12  13  14  15  16  17  18  19  20  21  22  23

(b)

32  34  36  38  40  42  44  46  48  50  52  54  56  58

Figure 14.4   (a) A Distribution of Scores with a Mean of $M = 16.88$
and a Standard Deviation of $SD = 2.23$.
(b) A Distribution with a Mean of $M = 45$
and a Standard Deviation of $SD = 6$.

## DESCRIBING NOMINAL AND ORDINAL DATA

Occasionally the measurements or observations made by a researcher are not numerical values. Instead, a researcher may simply classify participants by placing them in separate nominal or ordinal categories. Examples of this kind of measurement include:

- classification of people by gender: male or female
- classification of attitude: agree or disagree
- classification of self-esteem: high, medium, or low

In each case the data will not consist of numerical values—there are no numbers with which to compute a mean or a standard deviation. In this case the researcher must find some other method of describing the data.

One of the simplest ways to describe nominal and ordinal data is to report the proportion or percentage in each category. These values can be used to describe a single sample or to compare separate samples. For example, a report might describe a sample of voters by stating that 43% prefer candidate Green, 28% prefer candidate Brown, and 29% are undecided. A research report might compare two groups by stating that 80% of the 6-year-old children were able to successfully complete the task, but only 34% of the 4-year-olds were successful.

In addition to percentages and proportions, you also can use the mode as a measure of central tendency for data from a nominal scale. Remember, the mode simply identifies the most commonly occurring category and therefore describes the most typical member of a sample. For example, if the modal response to a survey question is "no opinion," you can probably conclude that the people surveyed do not care much about the issue.

## USING GRAPHS TO SUMMARIZE DATA

When a research study compares several different treatment conditions (or several different populations), it is common to use a graph to display the summary statistics for all the different groups being compared. The value of a graph is that it allows several different statistics to be displayed simultaneously so an observer can easily see the differences (or similarities) between them. For example, it is possible to list the means from eight different treatment conditions, but it probably is easier to compare the eight means if they are all presented in a single picture.

The most common statistics to present in a graph are sample means, but it is possible to present sample medians or sample proportions. In each case the graph is organized with the same basic structure:

1.  The different groups or treatment conditions are listed on the horizontal axis. Usually this involves the different levels of an independent variable or different values for a quasi-independent variable.
2.  The values for the statistics are listed on the vertical axis. Usually this involves values for the sample means that are being compared.

The graph can be constructed as either a **line graph** or a bar graph. Figure 14.5 shows each type of graph displaying the means from four different treatment conditions. To construct the line graph, we placed a point above each value on the horizontal axis (each treatment) such that the vertical position of the point corresponds to the mean for that treatment condition, and then connected the points by straight lines. The bar graph simply uses a bar above each of the treatment conditions such that the height of the bar corresponds to the mean for the treatment. By convention, line graphs are used when the values on the horizontal axis are measured on an interval or a ratio scale; bar graphs are used when the values are from a nominal or ordinal scale.

Similar graphs are used to display sample medians or sample proportions. Two examples are shown in Figure 14.6. The first graph shows the median incomes for three samples of 30-year-old men. The samples represent three different levels of education. The second graph shows the results from a study examining how preferences for wristwatch styles are related to age. Participants in three samples (representing three age groups) were asked whether they preferred a digital watch or a traditional analog watch. The graph shows the proportion preferring digital watches for each of the three samples.

Factorial research studies (Chapter 12) include two or more independent variables (or quasi-independent variables). For example, a researcher may want to examine the effects of heat and humidity on performance. For this study, both the temperature (variable 1) and the humidity (variable 2) would be manipulated, and performance would be evaluated under a variety of different temperature and humidity conditions. The structure of this type of experiment can be represented as a matrix, with one variable determining the rows and the second variable defining the columns. Each cell in the matrix corresponds to a specific combination of treatments. Figure 14.7 presents hypothetical data for the temperature-and-humidity experiment just described. The figure includes a matrix showing the mean level of performance for each treatment condition and demonstrates how the means would be displayed in a graph. To construct the graph, we listed the values for one of the independent variables (temperature) along the

(a)

(b)

Figure 14.5   A Line
Graph (a) and a Bar
Graph (b) Showing
Treatment Means
Obtained from a
Research Study

horizontal axis. Values for the dependent variable (mean level of performance)
are listed on the vertical axis. Then, a separate line is used to present the means
for each level of the second independent variable; in this case there is a separate
line for each of the two levels of humidity. Notice that the top line presents the
means in the top row of the data matrix, and the bottom line shows the means
from the bottom row. The result is a graph that displays all six means from the
experiment and allows comparison of means and mean differences.

Learning
Check

What are the ways to describe nominal and ordinal data?

## CORRELATIONS

Thus far, all of the statistics we have considered are intended to describe a group
of scores and to permit a researcher to look for differences between groups.
For example, a researcher interested in examining the relationship between

(a)

(b)

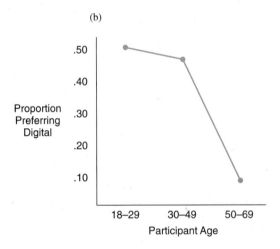

Figure 14.6   Graphs
Showing Medians (a)
and Proportions (b)

| | Temperature (in °F) | | |
|---|---|---|---|
| | 70 | 80 | 90 |
| Low Humidity | $M = 30$ | $M = 28$ | $M = 24$ |
| High Humidity | $M = 28$ | $M = 20$ | $M = 12$ |

Figure 14.7   A Matrix and a Graph Showing the
Means From a Two-Factor Study

self-esteem and task performance could select a sample of high self-esteem participants and a sample of low self-esteem participants. Each individual is given a task, and performance is measured. An example of the data resulting from this type of study is shown in Table 14.2a. Notice that the researcher has two sets of scores. The mean would be computed for each set to describe the scores, and the difference between the two means would describe the relationship between self-esteem and performance.

---

**TABLE 14.2**

**Two Different Strategies for Evaluating the Relationship Between Self-Esteem and Performance**
One study (a) uses a quasi-experimental strategy and evaluates the mean difference between two groups of participants. The other study (b) uses a correlational strategy, measuring two variables for each participant, and will compute a correlation to evaluate the relationship between variables.

(a)

| High Self-Esteem Group | Low Self-Esteem Group | |
|:---:|:---:|:---|
| 19 | 12 | |
| 23 | 14 | |
| 21 | 10 | |
| 24 | 17 | ← Performance Scores |
| 17 | 13 | |
| 18 | 20 | |
| 20 | 13 | |
| 22 | 11 | |
| $M = 20.50$ | $M = 13.75$ | |

(b)

| Participant | Self-Esteem Scores | Performance Scores | |
|:---:|:---:|:---:|:---|
| A | 62 | 13 | |
| B | 84 | 20 | |
| C | 89 | 22 | |
| D | 73 | 16 | ← Two Separate Scores |
| E | 66 | 11 | for Each Participant |
| F | 75 | 18 | |
| G | 71 | 14 | |
| H | 80 | 21 | |

An alternative research approach is to use a correlational design in which self-esteem and performance are measured for each participant (see Chapter 7). In this case, the researcher has one sample (instead of two) and obtains two scores for each individual. The kind of data that result from this type of study are shown in Table 14.2b. For this type of data, the researcher computes a **correlation** that measures and describes the relationship between the two variables. For this example, the correlation would measure and describe the relationship between self-esteem and performance.

The data for a correlation always consist of two scores for each individual. By convention, the scores are identified as $X$ and $Y$ and can be presented in a table or in a graph called a **scatterplot.** Figure 14.8 shows the same set of data in both representations. The table simply lists the $X$ and $Y$ values for each participant; notice that there is a pair of scores for each individual. In the scatterplot, each individual is represented by a point in the graph; the horizontal position of the point corresponds to the value of $X$, and the vertical position is the value of $Y$. A scatterplot can be a great aid in helping you to see the nature of a relationship between two variables.

A correlation measures and describes three aspects of the relationship between two variables:

1. the direction of the relationship
2. the form of the relationship
3. the degree or strength of the relationship

The sign of the correlation (positive or negative) identifies the direction of the relationship. A positive correlation indicates that the two variables, $X$ and $Y$, tend to change in the same direction; as the $X$ values increase, the $Y$ values also tend to increase, and as the $X$ values decrease, the $Y$ values also decrease. A negative correlation indicates that $X$ and $Y$ change in opposite directions; increases in $X$ are accompanied by decreases in $Y$.

Different kinds of correlations are available to measure different kinds of relationships, but most are derived from the **Pearson correlation,** which evaluates

| Person | X | Y |
|--------|---|---|
| A | 1 | 1 |
| B | 1 | 3 |
| C | 3 | 2 |
| D | 4 | 5 |
| E | 6 | 4 |
| F | 7 | 5 |

Figure 14.8    X and Y Values for Six People
Shown in a Table and in a Scatterplot

linear (straight-line) relationships. The Pearson correlation is the most commonly used correlation by far, and a straight line is the form of relationship that is usually measured. In the literature, the Pearson correlation is identified by the letter $r$.

Finally, the magnitude of a correlation measures how well the data points fit the specified form. The Pearson correlation, for example, measures how well the data points fit on a straight line. A value of $r = 1.00$ indicates a perfect fit. No correlation can exceed $+1.00$ (or $-1.00$). At the other extreme, a value of 0 indicates no fit at all. Figure 14.9 shows several different degrees of relationship. Notice that the sign of the correlation and the magnitude of the correlation are independent. For example, correlations of $r = +0.85$ and $r = -0.85$ are equally strong, and correlations of $r = +1.00$ and $r = -1.00$ both indicate a perfect linear relationship. Also note that a correlation of $-0.80$ indicates a stronger relationship than a correlation of $+0.70$.

---

Definition

A **correlation** is a statistical value that measures and describes the direction and degree of relationship between two variables.

---

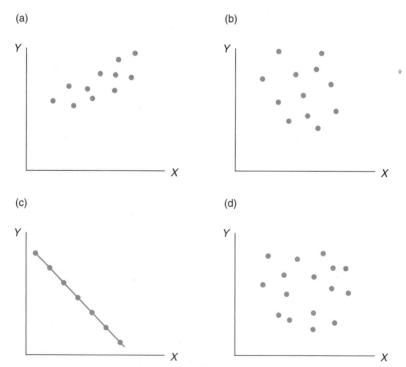

Figure 14.9   Data Showing Different Degrees of Relationship
(a) A strong positive relationship, approximately $r = +.90$. (b) A weak negative relationship, approximately $r = -.40$. (c) A perfect negative relationship, $r = -1.00$. (d) No evidence of a linear relationship, $r = 0$.

An example demonstrating the calculation of the Pearson correlation is presented in Appendix B, pages 431–432.

Learning Check

A researcher obtains a correlation of $r = -.72$ between grade point average and amount of time spent watching TV for a sample of college students. For this sample, who tends to get the better grades, the students who watch a lot of TV or the students who watch only a little TV? Explain your answer.

## 14.3   INFERENTIAL STATISTICS

The general goal of inferential statistics is to use the limited information from samples as the basis for reaching general conclusions about the populations from which the samples were obtained. Notice that this goal involves making a generalization or an inference from limited information (a sample) to a general conclusion (a population). The basic difficulty with this process is centered around the concept of **sampling error**. In simple terms, sampling error means that a sample does not provide a perfectly accurate picture of its population; that is, there is some discrepancy or error between the information available from a sample and the true situation that exists in the general population.

Earlier we defined a *parameter* as a characteristic of a population, and we defined a *statistic* as a characteristic of a sample. Obviously it is possible to select many different samples from the same population. Each of the samples will have its own individuals and its own scores, and each sample will have its own statistics. For example, if we take two different samples from one population, we probably will obtain two different sample means. The population, however, has only one mean. This general situation is shown in Figure 14.10. Notice that the sample statistics vary from one sample to another, and the sample statistics are generally different from the corresponding population parameters. The natural discrepancy between a sample statistic and a population parameter is called *sampling error*.

**Sampling error** is the naturally occurring difference between a sample statistic and the corresponding population parameter.

Definition

The fundamental problem for inferential statistics is to differentiate between research results caused by a treatment and those that are due simply to sampling error. Figure 14.11 shows a prototypical research situation. In this case the research study is examining the relationship between violence on TV and aggressive behavior for preschool children. Two groups of children (two samples) are selected from the population. One sample watches TV programs containing violence for 30 minutes, and the other sample watches nonviolent programs. Both groups are observed during a play period, and the researcher records the amount of aggression displayed by each child. The researcher then calculates a sample mean (a statistic) for each group and compares the two sample means. In Figure 14.11, there is a 4-point difference between the two sample means. The problem for the researcher is to decide whether the 4-point difference was caused

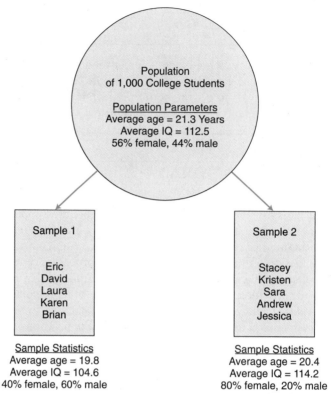

Figure 14.10   A Demonstration of Sampling Error
Two samples are selected from the same population.
Notice that the sample statistics are different from one
sample to another, and all of the sample statistics are
different from the corresponding population parameters.

by the treatments (the different TV programs) or is just a case of sampling error
(like the differences that are shown in Figure 14.10). That is, does the 4-point
difference provide convincing evidence that viewing TV violence has an effect
on behavior, or is the 4-point difference due simply to chance? The purpose of
inferential statistics is to help researchers answer this question.

## HYPOTHESIS TESTS

In Chapter 1 we presented an overview of the research process, and we have
followed the research process step by step throughout this book. Recall that the
second step in the process was to form a specific, testable research hypothesis—
a tentative statement describing the relationship between variables. The suc-
ceeding steps involved planning and conducting a research study to determine
whether or not the hypothesis is correct. Now the data have been collected, and
it is time to use the data to test the credibility of the original hypothesis.

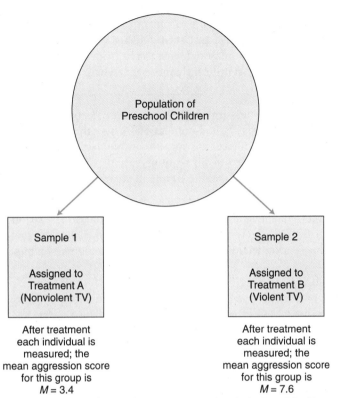

Figure 14.11   A Research Study Examining the Relationship Between TV
Violence and Aggressive Behavior for Preschool Children
Two groups of children (two samples) receive two different treatments
and produce different means. The problem is to determine whether
the mean difference was caused by the treatments or is simply
an example of sampling error (as in Figure 14.10).

As we have noted, the original research question and the hypothesis concern the population. The research results, however, come from a sample. Thus the task of evaluating a research hypothesis involves using the information from samples as the basis of general conclusions about populations. This is the task of inferential statistics. One of the most commonly used inferential procedures is the **hypothesis test.** In very general terms, a hypothesis test is a systematic procedure that determines whether the sample data provide enough evidence to conclude that the original research hypothesis is correct.

A hypothesis test can be viewed as a technique to help ensure the internal validity of a research study. Recall that internal validity is threatened whenever there is an alternative explanation for the results obtained in a research study. Because it is always possible that the results from a study are due simply to chance (sampling error), it is always possible that chance is an alternative explanation. In Figure 14.11, for example, the 4-point difference between the two sample means could have been caused by the treatments, but it also could be due to chance.

The goal of a hypothesis test is to rule out chance as a plausible explanation for the results. The hypothesis test accomplishes this goal by first determining what kind of results can be reasonably expected from chance and then ensuring that the actual results are significantly more than chance.

---

Definition

A **hypothesis test** is a statistical procedure that uses sample data to evaluate the credibility of a hypothesis about a population. A hypothesis test attempts to distinguish between two explanations for the sample data: (1) that the patterns in the data represent real relationships among variables in the population, and (2) that the patterns in the data are due simply to chance.

---

Although the details of a hypothesis test vary from one situation to another, the different tests all use the same basic logic and consist of the same basic elements. In this section we introduce the five basic elements of a hypothesis test.

### 1. The Null Hypothesis

The **null hypothesis** is a statement about the population or populations being examined that always states that there is no effect, no change, or no relationship. In general, the null hypothesis says that nothing happened. In a study comparing two treatments, for example, the null hypothesis states that there is no difference between the treatments. In a study examining a correlation, the null hypothesis states that the correlation for the population is zero (no relationship). According to the null hypothesis, any patterns in the sample are nothing more than chance (sampling error). For the research situation shown in Figure 14.11, the null hypothesis states that the type of TV program has no effect on behavior and therefore the 4-point difference between the two sample means is simply sampling error.

In Chapter 1 (page 23) we introduced the idea of developing a good research hypothesis as Step 2 in the research process. At that time, we noted that one characteristic of a good hypothesis is that it must make a positive statement about the existence of a relationship or the existence of a treatment effect. The null hypothesis is exactly the opposite of the research hypothesis: The null hypothesis says that the treatment has no effect, and the research hypothesis says that the treatment does have an effect. The goal of the research study is to gather enough evidence to demonstrate convincingly that the treatment really does have an effect. The purpose of the hypothesis test is to evaluate the evidence. The test determines whether the results of the research study are sufficient to reject the null hypothesis and justify a conclusion that the treatment has an effect.

### 2. The Sample Statistic

The data from the research study are used to compute a sample statistic (or statistics). Common examples of sample statistics are sample means, sample mean differences, and sample correlations.

### 3. The Standard Error

Earlier we introduced the concept of sampling error as the natural difference between a sample statistic and the corresponding parameter. Figure 14.10, for example, shows several sample means (statistics) that are all different from the population mean (parameter). In most research situations it is possible to calculate the average amount of sampling error, that is, the average difference between a statistic and a parameter. This average distance is called the **standard error.**

Definition

**Standard error** is a measure of the average or standard distance between a sample statistic and the corresponding population parameter.

The advantage of computing the standard error is that it provides a measure of how much difference can reasonably be expected between a statistic and a parameter. Notice that this distance is a measure of the natural discrepancy that occurs just by chance. Samples are intended to represent their populations, but they are not expected to be perfect. Typically, there will be some discrepancy between a sample statistic and the population parameter, and the standard error tells you how much discrepancy to expect.

### 4. The Test Statistic

A **test statistic** is a mathematical technique for comparing the sample statistic and the standard error (elements 2 and 3). In many hypothesis tests, the test statistic is a ratio with the following structure:

$$\text{Test statistic} = \frac{\text{Sample statistic}}{\text{Standard error}} = \frac{\text{Actual result}}{\text{Result expected by chance}}$$

The null hypothesis states that the results of the research study are due to nothing more than chance. If this is true, then the actual results (the numerator) and the chance results (the denominator) should be very similar, and the test statistic will have a value near 1.00. Thus, when the test statistic produces a value near 1.00, it is an indication that there is no treatment effect, no difference, or no relationship; that is, the results are consistent with the null hypothesis.

On the other hand, if there is a real treatment effect or a real relationship, the actual results should be noticeably bigger than chance. In this case, the test statistic should produce a value much larger than 1.00. Thus, a large value for a test statistic (much greater than 1.00) is an indication that the null hypothesis should be rejected.

Definition

In the context of a hypothesis test, a **test statistic** is a summary value that measures the degree to which the sample data are in accord with the null hypothesis. Typically, a large value for the test statistic indicates a large discrepancy between the sample and the hypothesis and leads to rejecting the null hypothesis.

### 5. The Alpha Level (Level of Significance)

The final element in a hypothesis test is the **alpha level** or **level of significance.** The alpha level provides a criterion for interpreting the test statistic. As we noted earlier, a test statistic with a value greater than 1.00 indicates that the obtained result is greater than expected from chance. However, researchers typically demand research results that are not just greater than chance but *significantly* greater than chance. The alpha level provides a criterion for significance.

Remember, the goal of a hypothesis test is to rule out chance as a plausible explanation for the results. To achieve this, researchers attempt to show that it is extremely unlikely or almost impossible that their results can be explained by chance. The alpha level is a probability value that defines "extremely unlikely" and determines the maximum probability that the sample result can be explained simply by chance. That is, the alpha level is the probability that the sample results would be obtained even if the null hypothesis were true. By convention, alpha levels are very small probabilities, usually .05, .01, or .001. An alpha level of .01, for example, means that there is a maximum probability of .01 (1 in 100) that the sample result is simply chance. From another perspective, an alpha level of .01 means that the probability is .99 (99%) that the result really is greater than chance.

> With rare exceptions, a value of .05 is the largest acceptable alpha level.

---

Definition

The **alpha level** or **level of significance** for a hypothesis test is the maximum probability that the research result was obtained simply by chance. A hypothesis test with an alpha level of .01, for example, means that the test demands that there is less than a 1% (.01) probability that the results are due only to chance.

---

## REPORTING RESULTS FROM A HYPOTHESIS TEST

The goal of a hypothesis test is to establish that the results from a research study are very unlikely to have occurred by chance. "Very unlikely" is defined by the alpha level. When the results of a research study satisfy the criterion imposed by the alpha level, the results are said to be **significant** or **statistically significant.** For example, when the difference between two sample means is so large that there is less than a 1% probability that the difference occurred by chance, it is said to be a significant difference at the .01 level of significance. Notice that a smaller level of significance means that you have more confidence in the result. A result that is significant at the .05 level means that there is a 5% risk that the result is just due to chance. Significance at the .01 level, on the other hand, means that there is only a 1% probability that the result is due to chance. On the other hand, if the research results do not satisfy the criterion established by the alpha level, the results are said to be *not significant.*

In the literature, significance levels are reported as $p$ values. For example, a research paper may report a significant difference between two treatments with $p < .05$. The expression $p < .05$ simply means that there is less than a .05 probability that the result is due to chance.

When statistics are computed on a computer, the printouts usually report exact values for $p$. For example, a computer-based hypothesis test evaluating the mean difference between two treatments may report $p = .028$. In this case, the computer has determined that there is a .028 probability that the mean difference is due to chance. Based on this outcome and using an alpha level of .05, the researcher would:

1. Reject the null hypothesis. In other words, the researcher rejects chance as an explanation for the research results.

2.  Report a significant result with $p < .05$ or $p = .028$. In the past, research reports identified the probability of chance in relation to standardized alpha levels. In this example, $p = .028$ is less than the standard alpha level of .05, so the researcher would report $p < .05$, indicating that it is very unlikely (probability less than .05) that the results can be explained by chance. More recent studies report the exact level of probability. In this case, $p = .028$.

If the computer reported a value of $p = .067$, the researcher would have to conclude that the result is not statistically significant. Again using an alpha level of .05, the researcher would

1.  Fail to reject the null hypothesis. In other words, the researcher must accept chance as a plausible explanation for the research results.
2.  Report the result as not significant, with $p > .05$. The actual probability of chance ($p = .067$) is greater than the maximum acceptable alpha level, .05.

---

A **significant result** or a **statistically significant result** means that it is extremely unlikely that the research result was obtained simply by chance. A significant result is always accompanied by an alpha level that defines the maximum probability that the result is due only to chance.

Definition

---

What is the goal of a hypothesis test?

Learning
Checks

What does it mean when a result is found to be significant at the .01 level?

Suppose that a researcher obtains a computed value of $p = .03$ for a hypothesis test.

  a.  With an alpha level of .05, does the researcher reject or fail to reject the null hypothesis?

  b.  With an alpha level of .01, does the researcher reject or fail to reject the null hypothesis?

---

## ERRORS IN HYPOTHESIS TESTING

Because a hypothesis test is an inferential process (using limited information to reach a general conclusion), there is always a possibility that the process will lead to an error. Specifically, a sample always provides limited and incomplete information about its population, and a sample can provide misleading information. If a researcher is misled by the results from the sample, it is likely that the researcher will reach an incorrect conclusion. Two kinds of errors can be made in hypothesis testing.

### Type I Errors
One possibility for error occurs when the sample data appear to show a significant effect but in fact there is no effect in the population. By chance the researcher has selected an unusual or extreme sample and, based on the sample data, incorrectly concludes that there is a significant effect. This kind of mistake is called a **Type I error.**

Definition

A **Type I error** occurs when a researcher finds evidence for a significant result when in fact there is no effect (no relationship) in the population. The error occurs because the researcher has by chance selected an extreme sample that appears to show the existence of an effect when there is none.

Note that the consequence of a Type I error is a false report. This is a serious mistake. Fortunately, the likelihood of a Type I error is very small, and the exact probability of this kind of mistake is known to everyone who sees the research report. Recall that a significant result means that the result is very unlikely to have occurred by chance. It does not mean that it is impossible for the result to have occurred by chance. In particular, a significant result is always accompanied by an alpha level or an exact $p$ value (for example, $p < .01$ or $p = .006$). By reporting the $p$ value, researchers are acknowledging it is possible that their result is due to chance. More precisely, the $p$ value identifies the probability that the result is chance, or the probability of a Type I error.

### Type II Errors

The second possibility for error occurs when the sample data do not show a significant effect when in fact there is a real effect in the population. This often occurs when an effect is very small and does not show up in the sample data. In this case, the researcher concludes that there is no significant effect when a real effect actually exists. This is a **Type II error.**

Definition

A **Type II error** occurs when sample data do not show evidence of a significant effect when in fact a real effect does exist in the population. This often occurs when the effect is so small that it does not show up in the sample.

The consequence of a Type II error is that a researcher fails to detect a real effect. In this case, the researcher may choose to repeat the study with some refinements in an attempt to find a significant result. The researcher also may abandon the research project under the assumption that either there is no effect or the effect is too small to be of any consequence.

Learning Checks

Describe the relationship between alpha level and Type I errors.

Describe the consequences of each type of error.

## MEASURES OF EFFECT SIZE

By now it should be very clear that most researchers conduct a hypothesis test with the hope that its conclusion will be to reject the null hypothesis. Specifically, the goal is to demonstrate that a treatment has a significant effect or to show that there is a significant relationship between two variables. However, be very cautious about interpreting the concept of statistical significance or the idea of rejecting a null hypothesis. When the conclusion from a hypothesis test is that there is a significant effect (reject $H_0$), it simply means that it is very unlikely that the result from the study can be explained by chance.

In Chapter 13, while discussing single-subject research, we noted a distinction between statistical significance and **practical** or **clinical significance.** It seems appropriate to repeat part of that discussion here. As we have noted, when research results are found to be statistically significant, it means that the obtained results are greater than would be expected from chance alone. Notice that this is a relative statement and does not necessarily have any implications about the absolute size of the results. For example, if the results expected from chance are very small, then the research results can also be very small and still be greater than chance. Thus, it is possible for a treatment to have a very small effect that is statistically significant (greater than chance). Practical or clinical significance, on the other hand, is concerned with whether or not the treatment effect is large enough to have a practical or clinical application.

Suppose, for example, that a researcher is testing a new drug for lowering cholesterol. Also, suppose that the drug really works, lowering cholesterol levels for most people by about 6 points. If the drug effect is consistent (small variability) and the researcher uses a large sample, then a hypothesis test will probably conclude that the drug has a statistically significant effect. At the same time, however, you should realize that a drug that lowers cholesterol by only 6 points does not have practical significance.

The general point of this argument is that statistical significance does not necessarily provide any information about the magnitude of the treatment effect. To try to avoid this problem, it is often recommended that, when researchers report a statistically significant effect, they also include a report of **effect size** (see the guidelines presented by the APA Task Force on Statistical Inference; Wilkinson, 1999).

The simplest and most direct way to report the size of a treatment effect is simply to report the actual results of the research study. For example, in the cholesterol study just described, the results showed that the drug lowered cholesterol by 6 points. However, in some situations a 6-point difference may be relatively large, and in other situations a 6-point difference may be relatively small. For example, two men who differ in weight by 6 pounds would be considered to weigh essentially the same. On the other hand, if two men differ in height by 6 inches, it is considered to be a relatively large difference. Therefore, statisticians have developed several different methods for computing a standardized measure of effect size. We consider two examples that are representative of the most commonly used methods.

### Cohen's *d*

Cohen (1969) recommended that the expression of effect size be standardized by measuring the mean difference between two treatments in terms of the standard deviation. The resulting measure of effect size is defined as **Cohen's *d*** and is computed as

$$d = \frac{\text{Sample mean difference}}{\text{Sample standard deviation}}$$

For example, a value of $d = 2.00$ indicates that the mean difference is twice as big as the standard deviation. On the other hand, a value of $d = 0.5$ indicates that the mean difference is only half as large as the standard deviation. Examples demonstrating the calculation of Cohen's $d$ are presented in Appendix B, pages 434–435.

Cohen also provided objective criteria for evaluating the size of an effect:

| Magnitude of $d$ | Evaluation of Effect Size | |
|---|---|---|
| $0 < d < 0.2$ | Small effect | (mean difference less than 0.2 standard deviation) |
| $0.2 < d < 0.8$ | Medium effect | (mean difference around 0.5 standard deviation) |
| $d > 0.8$ | Large effect | (mean difference more than 0.8 standard deviation) |

### Percentage of Variance Accounted For ($r^2$ and $\eta^2$)

When there is a consistent difference between two treatment conditions, it is possible to predict whether a participant's score will be relatively high or relatively low if you know which treatment the participant receives. For the cholesterol study discussed earlier, we know that people who receive the drug tend to have lower cholesterol levels than people who do not receive the drug. The ability to predict differences forms the basis of another method of calculating effect size, one that measures the degree to which one variable can be predicted from another. Typically, the calculation involves measuring the percentage of variance for one variable that can be predicted by knowing a second variable. For example, the participants in the cholesterol study all have different cholesterol levels. In statistical terms, their scores are variable. However, some of this variability can be predicted by knowing which group the scores come from; participants in the drug condition score lower than participants in the no-drug condition. By measuring exactly how much of the variability is predictable, we can obtain a measure of how big the effect actually is. Measures of the percentage of variance accounted for include $r^2$ and $\eta^2$ (the Greek letter *eta* squared). Examples demonstrating the calculation of $r^2$ and $\eta^2$ are presented in Appendix B, pages 434–435, 440, and 444–445.

## 14.4   EXAMPLES OF HYPOTHESIS TESTS

In this section we discuss some of the different kinds of hypothesis tests that are used for different research situations. We present only a small selection of the many different tests that exist; however, those described here are most of the statistical tests needed for student research projects or class assignments. We classify the different types of hypothesis tests and briefly describe each one. Our goal is to help you determine which test is appropriate for a particular research situation and help you interpret the results of the test. This information should be sufficient if you use a computer to perform the hypothesis test.

If you perform the calculations yourself, you can consult Appendix B, where we present numerical examples for many different hypothesis tests; or refer to a statistics textbook for a detailed description of each test.

### TESTS FOR MEAN DIFFERENCES

All of the hypothesis tests covered in this section use the means obtained from sample data as the basis for testing hypotheses about population means. The goal of each test is to determine whether the observed sample mean differences are more than chance; that is, whether the sample data provide enough evidence for the conclusion that some factor other than chance (for example, a treatment effect) has caused the means to be different.

## Two-Group Between-Subjects Test

The **independent-measures $t$ test** is the appropriate hypothesis test to compare the two means obtained from a two-group between-subjects research design (see page 259). The two groups of participants represent two different treatment conditions (for example, in an experimental research design) or two different populations (for example, in a quasi-experimental design comparing males and females). The mean is calculated for each group, and the sample mean difference is used to test a hypothesis about the corresponding population mean difference. The null hypothesis states that the population mean difference is zero.

The $t$ statistic is a direct ratio comparing the actual difference between the sample means with the amount of difference that would be expected by chance. For example, a $t$ statistic of $t = 3.00$ indicates that the obtained difference between sample means is 3 times greater than would be expected from chance. A large value for the $t$ statistic (either positive or negative) indicates a significant difference.

In a research report, the results of an independent-measures $t$ test are reported in the following format:

$$t(28) = 4.00, p = .01$$

This report indicates that the researcher obtained a $t$ statistic with a value of 4.00, which is very unlikely to have occurred by chance (probability equal to .01). The number in parentheses is the value of degrees of freedom ($df$) for the test. For this test, $df = (n_1 - 1) + (n_2 - 1)$ where $n_1$ is the number of participants in one group and $n_2$ is the number in the second group.

An example demonstrating the independent-measures $t$ test is in Appendix B, pages 432–433.

## Two-Treatment Within-Subjects Test

The **repeated-measures $t$ test** is the appropriate hypothesis test for a within-subjects research design comparing two treatment conditions (see page 286). In this situation, the same group of participants is measured in two different treatment conditions. The sample mean is computed for each treatment condition, and the sample mean difference is used to test a hypothesis about the corresponding population mean difference. The null hypothesis states that the population mean difference is zero.

Once again, the $t$ statistic is a direct ratio comparing the obtained sample mean difference with the amount of difference that would be expected from chance. As with the independent-measures $t$, a large value for the $t$ statistic indicates a significant difference.

In a research report, the results of a repeated-measures $t$ test are reported in the following format:

$$t(19) = 2.40, p = .04$$

This report indicates that the researcher obtained a $t$ statistic with a value of 2.40, which is very unlikely to have occurred by chance (probability equal to .04).

The number in parentheses is the value of degrees of freedom $(df)$ for the test. For this test, $df = n - 1$, where $n$ is the number of participants in the study.

An example demonstrating the repeated-measures $t$ test is in Appendix B, pages 433–434.

### More-Than-Two-Groups Single-Factor Tests

When a research study obtains means from more than two groups or more than two treatment conditions, the appropriate hypothesis test is an analysis of variance, commonly referred to as an ANOVA. When the groups are defined by a single factor with more than two levels (such as 3 age groups or 3 temperature conditions), the test is called a **single-factor analysis of variance** or a **one-way analysis of variance** (see page 260). The mean is computed for each group of participants or for each treatment condition, and the differences among the means from the sample data are used to evaluate a hypothesis about the differences among the corresponding population means. The null hypothesis states that there are no differences among the population means.

A variance is computed for the set of sample means to measure the size of the mean differences. A second variance, called **error variance,** is computed to measure the magnitude of the differences that would be expected from chance. The $F$ ratio is a ratio of the two variances. A large $F$-ratio indicates that the actual mean differences are greater than would be expected from chance.

Note that the single-factor analysis of variance can be used with data from either a between-subjects or a within-subjects design. However, the calculation of the error variance is different for the two designs, so you must specify which design is being used.

In a research report, the results of a single-factor analysis of variance are reported as follows:

$$F(2, 36) = 5.00, p = .025$$

The report indicates that the researcher obtained an $F$-ratio with a value of 5.00, which is very unlikely to have occurred by chance (probability equal to .025). The two numbers in parentheses are the degrees of freedom $(df)$ values for the $F$-ratio. The first of the two number is the degrees of freedom for the numerator of the $F$-ratio and is determined by $(k - 1)$, where $k$ is the number of treatment conditions being compared. The second number is the degrees of freedom for the error variance in the denominator of the $F$-ratio. For a between-subjects design, the error degrees of freedom is determined by $(n_1 - 1) + (n_2 - 1) + (n_3 - 1) + \ldots$, where $n_1$ is the number of participants in the first group, $n_2$ is the number in the second group, and so on. For a within-subjects design, the degrees of freedom for the error variance are determined by $(k - 1)(n - 1)$ where $k$ is the number of treatment conditions and $n$ is the number of participants.

Examples demonstrating the single-factor analysis of variance (between-subjects and within-subjects) are in Appendix B, pages 435–440.

### Factorial Tests

When a research design includes more than one factor (a factorial design), you must use a hypothesis test to evaluate the significant of the mean differences (see Chapter 12, page 301). The simplest case, a two-factor design, requires a **two-**

**way analysis of variance** or **two-factor analysis of variance.** The two-factor analysis of variance consists of three separate hypothesis tests. One test evaluates the main effects for the first factor, a second test evaluates the main effects for the second factor, and a third test evaluates the interaction. The significance of any one test has no relationship to the significance of any other test.

The data from a two-factor design can be displayed as a matrix, with the levels of one factor defining the rows and the levels of the second factor defining the columns. The mean is computed for each cell in the matrix, and the overall mean is computed for each row and for each column. The differences among the sample means are used to evaluate the three hypotheses about the differences among the corresponding population means. For all three tests, the null hypothesis states that there are no differences among the population means.

A variance is computed for the set of column means to measure the size of the mean differences for one factor. A second variance, called *error variance*, is computed to measure the magnitude of the differences that would be expected from chance. The *F*-ratio evaluating the main effect for the factor is a ratio of the two variances. A large *F*-ratio indicates that the actual mean differences are greater than would be expected from chance, and there is a significant main effect for the factor.

The main effect for the second factor is evaluated using the set of row means from the data matrix.

The interaction is evaluated by computing a variance for the set of cell means and then subtracting the variance that is accounted for by the mean differences among the row means and the column means. This variance is then compared with the error variance in an *F*-ratio to determine whether the mean differences from the interaction are significantly greater than would be expected from chance. A research report for a two-factor analysis of variance includes three separate *F*-ratios.

The two-factor analysis of variance can be used with either a between-subjects or a within-subjects design; however, the calculation of the error variance is different for the two designs. An example of the two-factor analysis of variance for between-subjects designs is given in Appendix B, pages 440–444.

## TESTS FOR CORRELATIONS

In many research situations the relationship between two variables is evaluated by simply measuring the variables for each individual and then computing a correlation (see page 373). In the same way that there is sampling error between a sample mean and a population mean, there also is sampling error between a sample correlation and the corresponding population correlation. Thus, a sample correlation ($r$) is expected to be representative of the population correlation, but it is not expected to be perfectly accurate. In particular, a nonzero correlation for a sample does not necessarily mean that there is a real nonzero correlation in the population. The problem for researchers is deciding when a correlation obtained for a sample provides enough evidence to justify a conclusion that there is a corresponding correlation in the population.

The hypothesis test for a correlation begins with a null hypothesis stating that there is no correlation in the population; that is, that the population correlation is zero. The hypothesis test uses either a $t$ statistic or an $F$-ratio. The *test for the significance of a correlation* computes a $t$ statistic that is a ratio of the actual sample correlation and the magnitude of correlation that would be expected from chance. A large value of $t$ indicates that the sample correlation is greater than expected from chance. If an $F$-ratio is used, it simply squares the $t$ statistic ($F = t^2$).

In a research report, the results of a test for the significance of a correlation are reported as follows:

$$r = 0.65, N = 40, p < .01$$

The report indicates that the correlation is $r = 0.65$ for a group of $N = 40$ participants, which is very unlikely to have occurred by change (probability less than .01.) Note that the report does not identify the exact test ($t$ or $F$) that was used to evaluate the significance of the correlation.

An example demonstrating the test for the significance of a correlation is presented in Appendix B, page 445.

## TESTS FOR PROPORTIONS

In many research situations the data are not numerical scores, so it is impossible to compute sample means or sample correlations. Instead, the data consist of frequencies or proportions (see page 262). For example, a researcher may find that, in a group of 50 young women diagnosed with an eating disorder, only 12% have high self-esteem. By comparison, in a control group of 50 women who have no diagnosed disorder, 48% have high self-esteem. Although the data consist entirely of proportions, it is still possible to determine whether there is a significance difference between the two groups using a **chi-square test for independence.** Equivalently, the chi-square test will determine whether there is a significant relationship between eating disorders and self-esteem. (Note: *Chi* is a Greek letter, $\chi$, and the symbol for chi-square is $\chi^2$.)

The rationale behind the chi-square test is that sample proportions, just like sample means, are not expected to provide perfectly accurate representations of their corresponding population values. Thus, there naturally will be some discrepancy or error between the proportions obtained for sample data and the actual proportions in the population. The question is whether the patterns observed in the sample data can be explained by chance or are caused by real relationships in the population.

The null hypothesis for the chi-square test says that in the population the two variables are independent (there is no relationship between them). The chi-square statistic is computed by first calculating a set of expected frequencies that represent an ideal sample that is in perfect agreement with the null hypothesis. These expected frequencies are then compared with the actual observed frequencies to determine the degree to which the sample fits the hypothesis. A large value for the chi-square statistic indicates a big discrepancy between the sample and the hypothesis and suggests that the null hypothesis should be rejected.

In a research report, the results from a chi-square test for independence are reported as follows:

$$\chi^2(3, N = 40) = 8.70, p = .02$$

The report indicates that the researcher obtained a chi-square statistic with a value of 8.70, which is very unlikely to occur by chance (probability is equal to .02). The numbers in parentheses indicate that the chi-square statistic has degrees of freedom ($df$) equal to 3 and that there were 40 participants ($N = 40$) in the study. The degrees of freedom for chi-square is determined by the number of categories for the two variables: $df = (C_1 - 1)(C_2 - 1)$, where $C_1$ is the number of categories for the first variable and $C_2$ is the number of categories for the second variable.

An example demonstrating the chi-square test is in Appendix B, pages 446–447.

Learning
Check

The purpose of an independent-measures $t$ test is to determine whether the mean difference obtained between two groups in a between-subjects study is greater than could reasonably be expected by chance. In other words, do the data provide enough evidence to show that the mean difference was caused by something other than chance? Briefly describe the purpose of each of the following hypothesis tests:

a.  single-factor analysis of variance

b.  test for the significance of a correlation

c.  chi-square test for independence

## 14.5    SPECIAL STATISTICS FOR RESEARCH

In addition to the traditional statistical techniques that are used for data analysis, several special mathematical procedures have been developed to help evaluate and interpret research results. Most of these special techniques address questions concerning measurement procedures, specifically the reliability of measurements. Recall from Chapter 4 that reliability refers to the stability or consistency of measurements. Specifically, reliability means that when the same individuals are measured under the same conditions, you should obtain nearly identical measurements.

Notice that reliability refers to the relationship between two sets of measurements. Often the relationship is measured by computing a correlation. However, there are situations where a simple correlation may not be completely appropriate. To deal with these special situations, researchers have developed several techniques that produce a correction or an adjustment to the correlation. In this section we examine four statistical techniques for adjusting or correcting measures of reliability: the Spearman-Brown formula, the Kuder-Richardson formula 20, Cronbach's coefficient alpha, and Cohen's kappa.

### THE SPEARMAN-BROWN FORMULA

When a single variable is measured with a test that consists of multiple items, it is common to evaluate the internal consistency of the test by computing a **split-half reliability.** The concept behind split-half reliability is that all the different items on the test measure the same variable, and therefore the measurement obtained from each individual item should be related to every other item. Specifically, if you split the test in half, then the score obtained from one half of the test should be related to the score obtained from the other half.

There are a number of ways to split a test in half. For a 20-item test, for example, you could compute one score for the first 10 items and a second score for the last 10 items. Alternatively, you could compute one score for the odd-numbered items and a second score for the even-numbered items. In any case, you obtain two scores for each participant, and you can compute a correlation to measure the degree of relationship between the scores. The higher the correlation, the better the split-half reliability.

Although computing a correlation appears to be a straightforward method for measuring the relationship between two halves of a test, this technique has a problem. In particular, the two split-half scores obtained for each participant are based on only half of the test items. In general, the score obtained from half of a test is less reliable than the score obtained from the full test. (With a smaller number of items there is a greater chance for error or chance to distort the participant's score.) Therefore, a measure of split-half reliability (based on half the test) tends to underestimate the true reliability of the full test. A number of procedures have been developed to correct this problem, but the most commonly used technique is the **Spearman-Brown formula.** The formula adjusts the simple correlation between halves as follows:

$$\text{Spearman-Brown } R = \frac{2r}{1 + r},$$

where $r$ is the simple correlation between the two halves of the test.

For a test consisting of 20 items, for example, each participant receives two scores, with each score based on 10 items. If the split-half correlation between the two scores was $r = 0.80$, then the corrected correlation from the Spearman-Brown formula would be

$$R = \frac{2(0.80)}{1 + 0.80} = \frac{1.60}{1.80} = 0.89$$

Notice that the effect of the correction is to increase the size of the correlation.

## THE KUDER-RICHARDSON FORMULA 20

As we noted earlier, there are many different ways to split a test in half to obtain the two scores necessary to calculate a split-half reliability. Depending on how the test is split, you are likely to obtain different measures of reliability. To deal with this problem, Kuder and Richardson (1937) developed a formula that estimates the average of all the possible split-half correlations that can be obtained from all of the possible ways to split a test in half. The formula is the twentieth and best one they tried and is therefore called the **Kuder-Richardson formula 20** (often shortened to K-R 20).

The Kuder-Richardson formula 20 is limited to tests in which each item has only two possible answers, such as true/false, agree/disagree, or yes/no, and the two responses are assigned numerical values of 0 and 1. Each participant's score is the total, summed over all the items. The Kuder-Richardson measure of reliability is obtained by

$$\text{K-R 20} = \left(\frac{n}{n-1}\right)\left(\frac{SD^2 - \Sigma pq}{SD^2}\right)$$

The elements in the formula are defined as follows:

$n$ is the number of items on the test

$SD$ is the standard deviation for the set of test scores

For each item, $p$ is the proportion of the participants whose response is coded 0

$q$ is the proportion of the participants whose response is coded 1

(note that $p + q = 1$ for each item)

$\Sigma pq$ is the sum of the $p$ times $q$ products for all items

The Kuder-Richardson formula 20 produces values ranging from 0 to 1.00, with higher values indicating a higher degree of internal consistency or reliability.

## CRONBACH'S ALPHA

One limitation of the Kuder-Richardson formula is that it can only be used for tests in which each item has only two response alternatives. Cronbach (1951) developed a modification of the K-R 20 formula that can be used when test items have more than two alternatives, such as a Likert scale that has five response choices (see page 100). **Cronbach's alpha** has a structure similar to the K-R 20 formula and is computed as follows:

$$\text{Cronbach's alpha} = \left(\frac{n}{n-1}\right)\left(\frac{SD^2 - \Sigma \text{variance}}{SD^2}\right)$$

The elements in Cronbach's formula are identical to the elements in the K-R 20 formula except for $\Sigma$variance. To compute this new term, first calculate the variance of the scores for each item separately. With 20 participants, for example, you would compute the variance for the 20 scores obtained for item 1, and the variance for the 20 scores on item 2, and so on. Then sum the variances across all the test items.

Like the K-R 20 formula, Cronbach's alpha is intended to measure split-half reliability by estimating the average correlation that would be obtained by considering every possible way to split the test in half. Also, like the K-R 20 formula, Cronbach's alpha produces values between 0 and 1.00, with a higher value indicating a higher degree of internal consistency or reliability.

## COHEN'S KAPPA

When measurements are obtained by behavioral observation, it is customary to evaluate the measurement procedure by determining inter-rater reliability (see page 105). Inter-rater reliability is the degree of agreement between two observers who have independently observed and recorded behaviors at the same time. The simplest technique for determining inter-rater reliability is to compute the percentage of agreement as follows:

$$\text{Percent agreement} = \frac{\text{Number of observations in agreement}}{\text{Total number of observations}} \times 100$$

For example, if two observers agree on 46 out of 50 observations, their percent agreement is $(46/50)100 = 92\%$.

The problem with a simple measure of percent agreement is that the value obtained can be inflated by chance. That is, the two observers may record the same observation just by chance. As an extreme example, consider two observers who are supposed to be watching the same child but by mistake are actually watching two different children. Even though the two observers are watching different children, it is possible that from time to time they will still record the same behaviors. Thus, the two observers will "agree," but their agreement is just chance.

**Cohen's kappa** is a measure of agreement that attempts to correct for chance (Cohen, 1961). Cohen's kappa is computed as follows:

$$\text{Cohen's kappa} = \frac{P_A - P_C}{1 - P_C},$$

where the elements in the formula are defined as follows:

$P_A$ is the observed percent agreement.

$P_C$ is the percent agreement expected from chance.

We use the data in Table 14.3 to demonstrate the calculation of Cohen's kappa. The data show the recorded observations of two observers watching a child over 25 observation periods. For every observation period, each observer records yes or no, indicating whether or not an example of aggressive behavior was observed. The number of agreements is obtained by counting the number of periods in which both observers record the same observation. For the data in Table 14.3, there are 21 agreements out of the 25 observation periods. Thus, the percent agreement is

$$P_A = \frac{21}{25} = 84\%$$

To determine the percentage agreement expected from chance ($P_C$), we must call upon a basic law of probability. The law states:

Given two separate events, $A$ and $B$, with the probability of $A$ equal to $p$ and the probability of $B$ equal to $q$, then the probability of $A$ and $B$ occurring together is equal to the product of $p$ and $q$.

For example, if two coins are tossed simultaneously, the probability of each one coming up heads is 0.50 ($p = q = 0.50$). According to the rule, the probability that both coins will come up heads is $p \times q = (0.50)(0.50) = 0.25$.

Applying the probability rule to the data in Table 14.3, we can calculate the probability that both observers will say yes just by chance and the probability that both will say no just by chance. For the data in the table, the probability that observer 1 says yes is 20 out of 25, which equals 0.80. The probability that observer 2 says yes is 18 out of 25, or 0.72. According to the probability rule, the probability that both will say yes just by chance is

TABLE 14.3

**Data That Can Be Used to Evaluate Inter-Rater Reliability Using Either the Percentage of Agreement or Cohen's Kappa**
Two observers record behavior for the same individual over 25 observation periods and record whether or not they observe aggressive behavior during each period.

| Observation Period | Observer 1 | Observer 2 | Agreement |
|---|---|---|---|
| 1 | Yes | Yes | Agree |
| 2 | Yes | Yes | Agree |
| 3 | Yes | No | Disagree |
| 4 | No | No | Agree |
| 5 | Yes | Yes | Agree |
| 6 | Yes | Yes | Agree |
| 7 | Yes | Yes | Agree |
| 8 | Yes | Yes | Agree |
| 9 | Yes | Yes | Agree |
| 10 | No | No | Agree |
| 11 | No | No | Agree |
| 12 | No | No | Agree |
| 13 | Yes | No | Disagree |
| 14 | Yes | Yes | Agree |
| 15 | Yes | Yes | Agree |
| 16 | Yes | Yes | Agree |
| 17 | Yes | Yes | Agree |
| 18 | No | Yes | Disagree |
| 19 | Yes | Yes | Agree |
| 20 | Yes | Yes | Agree |
| 21 | Yes | Yes | Agree |
| 22 | Yes | No | Disagree |
| 23 | Yes | Yes | Agree |
| 24 | Yes | Yes | Agree |
| 25 | Yes | Yes | Agree |

probability that both say yes = (0.80)(0.72) = 0.576 or 57.6%

Similarly, the probability that both will say no just by chance is

probability that both say no = (0.20)(0.28) = 0.056 or 5.6%

Combining these two values, we obtain an overall probability that the two observers will agree by chance:

$$P_C = 57.6\% + 5.6\% = 63.2\%$$

The value for Cohen's kappa can now be computed as follows:

$$\text{Kappa} = \frac{P_A - P_C}{1 - P_C} = \frac{84\% - 63.2\%}{1 - 63.2\%} = \frac{20.8\%}{36.8\%} = 56.5\%$$

Notice that correcting for chance dramatically reduces the percentage of agreement—from 84% without correction to 56.5% with Cohen's correction.

**Learning Checks**

Briefly explain why a split-half correlation is likely to underestimate the true reliability for the full set of test items. (Note: The Spearman-Brown formula attempts to correct this problem.)

Briefly explain why the percentage of agreement between two observers is likely to overestimate the real degree of agreement. (Note: Cohen's kappa is intended to correct this problem.)

## CHAPTER SUMMARY

This chapter examines the statistical techniques that researchers use to help describe and interpret the results from research studies. Statistical methods are classified into two broad categories: descriptive statistics that are used to organize and summarize research results, and inferential statistics that help researchers generalize the results from a sample to a population.

Descriptive statistical methods include constructing frequency distribution tables or graphs that provide an organized view of an entire set of scores. Commonly, a distribution of numerical scores is summarized by computing measures of central tendency and variability. The mean is the most commonly used measure of central tendency, but the median and the mode are available for situations where the mean does not provide a good representative value. Variability is commonly described by the standard deviation, which is a measure of the average distance from the mean. Variance measures the average squared distance from the mean. The relationship between two variables can be measured and described by a correlation. The Pearson correlation measures the direction and degree of linear relationship.

In behavioral science research, the most commonly used inferential statistical method is the hypothesis test. A hypothesis test begins with a null hypothesis that states that there is no treatment effect or no relationship between variables for the population. According to the null hypothesis, any treatment effect or relationship that appears to exist in the sample data is really just chance or sampling error. The purpose of the hypothesis test is to rule out chance as a plausible explanation for the obtained results. A significant result is one that is very unlikely to have occurred by chance alone. The alpha level, or level of significance, defines the maximum probability that the results are due to chance. Hypothesis tests that evaluate the significance of mean differences, correlations, and proportions are discussed.

The final section of the chapter introduces special statistical procedures used to evaluate the reliability of measurements. Three techniques (the Spearman-Brown formula, the Kuder-Richardson formula 20, and Cronbach's alpha) are used to measure split-half reliability. All three techniques address the general problem that split-half reliability is based on only half the test items and therefore underestimates the true level of reliability. Cohen's kappa provides a measure of inter-rater reliability. Cohen's kappa is intended to correct for inter-rater agreements that are due simply to chance.

## KEY WORDS

descriptive statistics
inferential statistics
statistic
parameter
central tendency
mean
median

mode
variability
standard deviation
variance
correlation
sampling error
hypothesis test

standard error
test statistic
alpha level or level of
    significance
statistically significant result
Type I error
Type II error

## EXERCISES

1. In addition to the key words, you should also
   be able to define each of the following terms:
   frequency distribution
   histogram
   polygon
   bar graph
   bimodal distribution
   multimodal distribution
   degrees of freedom
   line graph
   scatterplot
   Pearson correlation
   null hypothesis
   practical significance or clinical significance
   effect size
   Cohen's *d*
   independent-measures *t* test
   repeated-measures *t* test
   single-factor analysis of variance or one-way
       ANOVA
   error variance
   two-way analysis of variance or two-factor
       ANOVA
   chi-square test for independence
   split-half reliability
   Spearman-Brown formula
   Kuder–Richardson formula 20
   Cronbach's alpha
   Cohen's kappa

2. Explain why it is important to consider statistical analyses before you conduct a study and
   collect data.

3. Construct a frequency distribution graph for
   the set of scores presented in the following frequency distribution table:

   | X | f |
   |---|---|
   | 5 | 2 |
   | 4 | 3 |
   | 3 | 5 |
   | 2 | 1 |
   | 1 | 1 |

4. Statistical techniques are classified into two
   major categories, descriptive and inferential.
   Explain the basic purpose of the statistics in
   each category.

5. In a distribution with a mean of 70 and a standard deviation of 4, would a score of 82 be
   considered an extreme value or an average
   score near the center of the distribution?
   (Hint: Use the mean and standard deviation to
   sketch a frequency distribution graph, and
   then find the location for a score of 82.)

6. In a distribution with a mean of 70 and a standard deviation of 20, would a score of 82 be
   considered an extreme value or an average
   score near the center of the distribution?

7. Make up a set of 10 scores such that the set of
   scores has a mean approximately equal to 30
   and a standard deviation approximately equal
   to 5. (Hint: Sketch a frequency distribution
   graph with the correct mean and standard deviation, then list the scores as they appear in
   your sketch.)

8. Define the term *sampling error.* Be sure to include the terms *statistic* and *parameter* in your definition.

9. A national reading achievement test is standardized such that the mean score for the population of seventh-grade students is equal to 100. A researcher selects a sample of 25 seventh-grade students and enrolls them in a special reading course. After six weeks, the students in the sample take the standardized test. The mean for the sample is 112. Based on the sample results, can the researcher conclude that the special training has an effect on reading achievement? Explain your answer. (Hint: If the course has no effect, how can you explain the 12-point difference between the sample mean and the population mean?)

10. Briefly explain what is meant when a researcher reports "a significant mean difference between two treatment conditions."

11. Dr. Jones reports a significant result with $p < .05$, and Dr. Smith reports a significant result with $p < .01$. Who should be more confident that their result is real and not simply due to chance? Explain your answer.

12. Identify the appropriate hypothesis test for each of the following research situations:
    a. A researcher conducts a cross-sectional developmental study to determine whether there is a significant difference in vocabulary skills between 8-year-old and 10-year-old children.
    b. A researcher determines that 8% of the males enrolled in Introductory Psychology have some form of colorblindness, compared to only 2% of the females. Is there a significant relationship between colorblindness and gender?
    c. A researcher records the daily sugar consumption and the activity level for each of 20 children enrolled in a summer camp program. The researcher would like to determine whether there is a significant relationship between sugar consumption and activity level.
    d. A researcher would like to determine whether a 4-week therapy program produces significant changes in behavior. A group of 25 participants is measured before therapy, at the end of therapy, and again 3 months after therapy.
    e. A researcher would like to determine whether a new program for teaching mathematics is significantly better than the old program. It is suspected that the new program will be very effective for small-group instruction but probably will not work well with large classes. The research study involves comparing four groups of students: a small class taught by the new method, a large class taught by the new method, a small class taught by the old method, and a large class taught by the old method.

13. Each of the following special statistical techniques was developed to deal with a particular problem. In each case, identify the problem that the technique attempts to solve.
    a. the Spearman-Brown formula
    b. the Kuder-Richardson formula 20
    c. Cronbach's coefficient alpha
    d. Cohen's kappa

## InfoTrac COLLEGE EDITION EXERCISES

1. Use InfoTrac College Edition to locate two journal articles that report the results from research studies. Your articles must include participants, measurements, and, most important, statistics.
    a. Identify the descriptive statistics that are reported in the results section of each article (for example, means, standard deviations, correlations, or proportions).
    b. Locate the report of inferential statistics in the results sections. Identify what kind of test (*t* test, analysis of variance, etc.) was used and what alpha level was used. (Note: You may need to refer to the method sec-

tion to obtain a more complete description of the study. For example, the results section may simply report mean differences but may not identify whether the means are from a between-subjects or a within-subjects design.)

c. Try to locate the word *significant* (or *not significant*) in the abstract or the first few para-graphs of the discussion section of the articles. Usually a research report includes one or two sentences that summarize the results of the study by describing exactly what was found to be significant (or not). Find one of these sentences and, in your own words explain what it means.

chapter

# 15

# Writing a Research Report

## CHAPTER OVERVIEW

In this chapter, we consider Step 9 of the research process—preparing a research report. A few general elements of APA style are considered. In addition, the details of the contents of each part of the research report are provided. Finally, the processes of submitting a manuscript for publication and writing a research proposal are discussed.

## 15.1   THE GOAL OF A RESEARCH REPORT

Preparing a **research report** is Step 9 in the overall research process. When the study is completed and the data are in and analyzed, it is time to share your work with others who are interested in the topic. Ideally, this means preparing a written report for future publication in a scientific journal. Perhaps your report will be presented as a paper at a professional conference. Possibly your report will simply be a personal record of your research project to be filed away for future reference. In any case, the research report fulfills one of the basic tenets of scientific investigation: Science is public. Thus, your research is not finished until you have made it available to the rest of the scientific community.

The basic purpose of a good research report is to provide three kinds of information about the research study:

1.  *What was done.* The report should describe in some detail the step-by-step process you followed to complete the research project.
2.  *What was found.* The report should contain an objective description of the outcome. Typically, this involves the measurements that were taken and the statistical summary and interpretation of those measurements.
3.  *How your research study is related to other knowledge in the area.* As we noted in Chapter 2, a good research study does not stand alone, but rather grows out of an existing body of knowledge and adds to that body of knowledge. The research report should show the connections between the present study and past knowledge.

Although the prospect of writing an entire research report may appear overwhelming at first glance, several factors make this task more manageable. First, throughout the research process you have read and consulted many journal articles, each of which can be viewed as a good model of how your report should look. Second, if you have kept notes or maintained a journal of your research, you have an excellent foundation for preparing a formal report. Simply noting what background literature you consulted, how you used each journal article, how you obtained a sample for your study, what was done to individuals in your study, what each subject or participant actually did, and so on, should give you a very complete outline for the written report. Finally, you should realize that a research report is a very structured document. It is subdivided into separate, well-defined segments, and each segment has a specified content. You simply need to describe your own study, piece by piece, in each segment.

In the following sections of this chapter we examine the formal style and structure that have become the accepted convention for writing research reports in the behavioral sciences. This style and structure have evolved over the years, and the current guidelines are presented in the **Publication Manual of the American Psychological Association** (5th edition, 2001; henceforth referred to as the *Publication Manual*). Incidentally, you probably will find that writing a research report is very different from any other writing you have done.

**Definition**

A **research report** is a written description of a research study that includes a clear statement of the purpose of the research, a review of the relevant background literature that led to the research study, a description of the methods used to conduct the research, a summary of the research results, and a discussion and interpretation of the results.

**Learning Check**

What is the purpose of a research report?

## 15.2 GENERAL APA GUIDELINES FOR WRITING STYLE AND FORMAT

Although your research report may eventually be published in a professionally formatted, two- or three-column journal, everyone must start with a typed or word-processed manuscript. The *Publication Manual* provides detailed information on the proper method of preparing a manuscript to be submitted for publication. The methods it presents are generally accepted and appropriate for most scientific writing.

### SOME ELEMENTS OF WRITING STYLE

A research report is not the same as creative writing. You are not trying to amuse, entertain, challenge, confuse, or surprise your reader. Instead, the goal is to provide a simple, straightforward description and explanation of your research study. The *Publication Manual* contains hundreds of guidelines and suggestions to help create a clear and precise manuscript, and we will not attempt to repeat all of them here. Note that here we present some of the general guidelines; when you actually write a research report, you would be wise to consult the *Publication Manual* directly. In addition, you can access some of the manual's information at www.apastyle.org. In the meantime, this discussion of four general elements of style will help you get a good start.

#### Impersonal Style

A research report is not a personal story and should be written in an objective and impersonal style. A simple rule is to minimize using first-person pronouns such as I, me, my, or we. Do not include phrases like "I think . . . ," "I believe . . . ," "I did . . . ," "this is important to me." Instead of saying "I tested the children," use the passive form, "The children were tested," or let the participants become the subject of your sentence, "The children completed the questionnaire." Although the latest edition of the *Publication Manual* does allow increased use of first-person pronouns and active sentences (as opposed to passive), keep in mind that you are writing a research report, not a personal journal.

#### Verb Tense

When describing or discussing past events, use the past tense (for example, "They demonstrated . . .") or the present perfect tense ("It has been demonstrated . . .")

when you present background material to introduce your study and when you describe the procedures you used to conduct the study. When you present your results, always use the past tense ("the scores increased . . ."). After you have described the study and presented the results, switch to the present tense to discuss the results and present your conclusions ("the data suggest . . .").

### Biased Language

Scientific writing should be free of implied or irrelevant evaluation of groups. Therefore, when describing or discussing characteristics of participants, avoid implying bias against people on the basis of gender, sexual orientation, racial or ethnic group, disability, or age. The *Publication Manual* gives three guidelines for avoiding biased language. First, describe people with a level of specificity that is accurate. For example, when describing ethnic groups, instead of general terms such as *Asian* or *Hispanic*, use *Korean* or *Dominican*. Second, be sensitive to labels; call people what they prefer to be called. For example, *Asian, Black*, and *African American* are preferred to the older terms *Oriental, Negro*, and *Afro-American*. And keep in mind that, over time, preferences change. Third, acknowledge people's participation in your study. For example, instead of "the participants were run in the study," write "the students completed the survey," or "participants completed the study." The *Publication Manual* provides the details of these guidelines, as well as further information about avoiding biased language.

### Citations

Throughout your manuscript you will cite the published research of other scientists. Other research results are cited as background for your hypothesis, to establish a basis for any claims or "facts" you assert, and to credit those who prepared the foundation for your own work. Recall from Section 3.4 that using someone else's ideas or words as your own is **plagiarism**—a serious breach of ethics.

Whenever you state a fact that may be questionable or refer to a previous research finding, you must provide a **citation** that identifies your source. The convention for citation requires that you identify the author(s) and the year of publication. Although there are a variety of methods for accomplishing this goal, two formats are commonly used for citation:

1.  State a fact or make a claim in the text; then cite your source in parentheses within the same sentence. For example:

    > It has been demonstrated that immediate recall is extremely limited for 5-year-old children (Jones, 1998).

    > Previous research has shown that response to an auditory stimulus is much faster than response to a visual stimulus (Smith & Jones, 1999).

    Note that both the author(s) last name(s) and the date of publication appear outside the body of the sentence (i.e., all within parentheses). Also note that the ampersand (&) is used before the last author's name when you cite your source in parentheses.

2.  You may want to use the source as the subject of your sentence. In this case, only the year of publication is noted in parentheses. For example:

In a related study, Jones (1998) found that . . .

In a related study, Smith and Jones (1999) found that . . .

Note that the author(s) name(s) appear within the body of the sentence and only the date of publication appears in parentheses outside the body of the sentence. Also note that the word *and* is used before the last author's name when your source is the subject of your sentence.

In either case, the citation should provide enough information for the reader to find the complete reference in your list of references at the end of the paper. It also is customary to distinguish between citations of empirical results and citations of theory or interpretation. To report an empirical result, for example, you could use

Jones (1998) demonstrated . . .

To cite a theory or speculation you might use

Jones (1998) argued . . .

---

**Definition**

A **citation** identifies the author(s) and the year of publication of the source of a specific fact or idea mentioned in a research report. The citation provides enough information for a reader to locate the full reference in the list of references at the end of the report.

---

As a general rule, be conservative about the number of references you include in a research report, especially a report of an empirical study. Select only those references that are truly useful and contribute to your arguments. Also, it is better to summarize a point using your own words than to quote extensively from another work. Direct quotes can be useful, but they should be used only when it is necessary to preserve the whole essence of the original statements. Thus, direct quotes should be used sparingly. Remember that, whenever you paraphrase someone else's work or use direct quotes, you need to give them credit.

---

Learning Check

What is the *Publication Manual*?

---

## GUIDELINES FOR TYPING OR WORD-PROCESSING

The general APA guidelines require that manuscript be double spaced with no more than 27 lines of text per page (8½ × 11-inch page), with at least a one-inch margin on all sides. In addition, the text should have a straight left-hand margin but an uneven or ragged right-hand margin without hyphenation breaking words at the ends of lines. Indent the first line of each paragraph 5 to 7 spaces; indentation should be consistent throughout the manuscript. The preferred typefaces are 12-point Times Roman or 12-point Courier. This uniform format serves several purposes. First, it ensures lots of blank space on every page to allow editors, reviewers, or professors space to make comments or corrections. In addition, uniform spacing makes it possible for editors to estimate the length of a printed article from the number of pages in a manuscript.

## MANUSCRIPT PAGES

In addition to the body of the manuscript (the basic text that describes the research study), a research report consists of several other parts that are necessary to form a complete manuscript. In Section 15.3 we discuss each of these parts in much more detail, but for now, note that they are organized in the following order, with each part starting on its own separate page:

*Title Page:* Title, author's name, and other identifying information. Page 1.

*Abstract:* Page 2.

*Text:* This is the body of the research report (containing four sections—introduction, method, results, and discussion) beginning on page 3.

*References:* Listed together, starting on a separate page.

*Appendixes* (if any): Each appendix starts on its own separate page.

*Author Note* (if any): Listed together, starting on a separate page.

*Tables:* Each starts on its own separate page.

*Figure Captions:* Listed together, starting on a separate page.

*Figures:* Each on its own separate page.

## PAGE NUMBERS AND PAGE HEADERS

Each page of the manuscript, except for the figures, is numbered and identified with a page header. The page number should be positioned in the upper right corner of the page, above the text and at least one inch from the right-hand edge. The **page header** is simply the first two or three words from the title of the paper; it is printed either above or 5 spaces to the left of the page number. The pages are numbered consecutively, starting with the title page, so the manuscript can be reassembled if the pages become mixed and to allow editors and reviewers to refer to specific items by their page number. The page header is used to identify the manuscript.

You may have noticed that individual identification (such as your name) appears only on the title page. This allows editors to create a completely anonymous manuscript by simply removing the title page. The anonymous manuscript can then be mailed to reviewers who will not be influenced by the author's reputation but can give an unbiased review based solely on the quality of the research study.

## 15.3  THE ELEMENTS OF AN APA-STYLE RESEARCH REPORT

In the previous section we identified the components of a complete manuscript. In this section we look in more detail at the contents of each part, dividing the body of the manuscript into additional subsections that make up the majority of a research report.

Throughout this chapter we use a series of figures to illustrate different parts of a manuscript. The figures were adapted from an early draft of a real research manuscript published by Downs and Abwender (2002).

## TITLE PAGE

The **title page** is the first page of the manuscript and contains four pieces of identifying information: the title, the author name(s), the author's institutional affiliation, and a running head for publication.

The title should be a concise statement of the content of your paper. It should identify the main variables or theories and the relationships being investigated. Avoid unnecessary words, and try to describe your study as accurately and completely as possible. Keep in mind that the words used in the title will often be the basis for indexing and referencing your paper. Also remember that the title gives the first impression of your paper and often determines whether or not an individual reads the rest of the article. (Recall that in Section 2.4 we discussed using the title of an article as a first basis for deciding whether or not to read the rest of the article.) The title is centered between the left and right margins and positioned in the upper half of the page. It is recommended that a title be 10–12 words in length.

Immediately following the title, on the next double-spaced lines, are the author's name(s), followed by the institution(s) where the research was conducted (without the words *by* or *from*). If there are multiple authors, the order of the names is usually significant; the first author listed is typically the individual who made the primary contribution to the research, and the remaining authors are listed in descending order of their contributions.

The **running head** for publication is an abbreviated title that contains a maximum of 50 characters, including spaces and punctuation. In a published article the running head appears at the top of the pages to identify the article for the readers. On the title page the running head is printed at the top of the page on the next double-spaced line beneath the page header and page number. The running head begins at the left margin, and all letters are capitalized. Note that the running head for publication and the page header for the manuscript are not the same. The page header is the first few words from the title and identifies the pages of the typed manuscript. The running head is a complete but abbreviated title that will appear in the published paper. Also note that the running head appears only once in your manuscript—on the title page.

A title page from an APA-style manuscript, illustrating all of these elements, is shown in Figure 15.1.

Definitions

The **title page** is the first page of a research report manuscript and contains the title of the paper, the author names and affiliations, and the running head.

A **running head** is an abbreviated title for a research report, containing a maximum of 50 characters. The running head appears on the title page of the manuscript and at the top of the pages in a published article.

Learning
Check

Describe the difference between a page header and a running head.

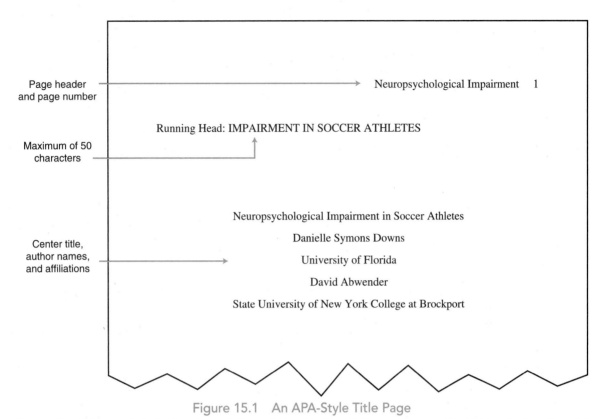

Page header
and page number

Neuropsychological Impairment    1

Maximum of 50
characters

Running Head: IMPAIRMENT IN SOCCER ATHLETES

Center title,
author names,
and affiliations

Neuropsychological Impairment in Soccer Athletes

Danielle Symons Downs

University of Florida

David Abwender

State University of New York College at Brockport

Figure 15.1   An APA-Style Title Page

## ABSTRACT

The **abstract** is a concise summary of the paper that focuses on what was done and what was found. The abstract appears alone on page 2 of the manuscript. The word *Abstract* is centered at the top of page 2, and the one-paragraph summary starts on the next double-spaced line, with no paragraph indentation. Although the abstract appears on page 2 of your manuscript, the abstract typically is written last, after the rest of the paper is done. It is considered the most important section you will write. With the possible exception of the title, the abstract is the section that most people will read and use to decide whether or not to seek out and read the entire article. (In Section 2.4, we discussed using the abstract of an article as a second screening device, after the title, for deciding whether or not to read the rest of the article.)

For an empirical research study, the abstract should not exceed 120 words. It should be a self-contained report that does not add to or evaluate the body of the paper. In a mere 120 words, the abstract of an empirical study should include the following elements, although not necessarily in this order:

1. A one-sentence statement of the problem or research question
2. A brief description of the subjects or participants (identifying how many and any relevant characteristics)

3. A brief description of the research method and procedures
4. A report of the results
5. A statement about the conclusions or implications

The abstract of an APA-style manuscript is shown in Figure 15.2.

| Definition | The **abstract** is a brief summary of the research study, totaling no more than 120 words. The abstract focuses on what was done and what was found in the study. |

|  Learning Check | Describe the elements of an abstract. |

## INTRODUCTION

The first major section of the body or text of a research report is the **introduction.** The introduction provides the background and orientation that introduces the reader to your research study. The introduction should identify the question or problem that your study addresses, and it should explain how you arrived at the question, why the question is important, and how the question is related to existing knowledge in the area. The introduction begins on page 3 of your manuscript. It is identified by centering the title of the article (exactly as it appears on the title page) at the top of the page. The first paragraph of the introduction begins with a paragraph indentation on the next double-spaced line.

An introduction typically consists of the following five parts, although not necessarily in this order; the parts are not labeled:

1. Typically, this section begins with a general introduction to the topic of the paper. In a few sentences or paragraphs, describe the issue investigated and why this problem is important.

2. Next is a review of the relevant literature. You do not need to review and discuss everything that has been published in the area, only the articles that are directly relevant to your research question. Discuss only relevant sections of previous work. Identify and cite the important points along the way, but do not provide detailed descriptions. The literature review should not be an article-by-article description of one study after another; instead, the articles should be presented in an integrated manner. Taken together, your literature review should provide a rationale for your study. Remember, you are taking your readers down a logical path that leads to your research question.

3. Ultimately the introduction reaches the specific problem or question that the research study addresses. State the problem or purpose of your study, and clearly define the relevant variables. The review of the literature should lead directly to the purpose of or the rationale for your study.

4. Explain briefly what you did to obtain an answer to your research problem. Briefly outline the methodology used for the study (the details of which will be provided in the next section of the report, the method section). At this

Begin a new page

Center

No indent

Statement of problem

Describe participants

Describe method

Report results

Conclusions or Implications

Neuropsychological Impairment    2

Abstract

Soccer reportedly places participants at risk for neuropsychological impairment, although it is unknown if the risk is associated primarily with concussion, subconcussive blows from heading the ball, or some combination thereof. We evaluated the risk of impairment by examining the neuropsychological test performance for soccer players and a comparable group of swimmers. Participants were 32 soccer players (26 college and 6 professional) and 29 swimmers (22 college and 7 masters level). All participants underwent neuropsychological tests assessing motor speed, attention, concentration, reaction time, and conceptual thinking. The soccer athletes performed worse than swimmers on measures of conceptual thinking. The older soccer group in particular performed poorly on measures of conceptual thinking, reaction time, and concentration. The results provide additional evidence that participation in soccer may be associated with poorer neuropsychological performance, although the observed pattern of findings does not specifically implicate heading as the cause.

Figure 15.2    An APA-Style Abstract

point simply provide a snapshot of how the study was conducted so the reader is prepared for the upcoming details.

5. Introductions typically end with a statement of the hypothesis (or hypotheses) concerning the relationship between the variables. (The details of developing a hypothesis were discussed in Chapter 1, Step 2 of the research process.)

If the introduction is well written, your readers will finish the final paragraphs with a clear understanding of the problem you intend to address, the rationale that led to the problem, a basic understanding of how you answered the problem, and your hypothesis regarding the results of the study.

Figure 15.3 shows the introduction of an APA-style manuscript.

Figure 15.3   An APA-Style Introduction

The following text appears within the figure:

Begin a new page → Neuropsychological Impairment   3

Center title → Neuropsychological Impairment in Soccer Athletes

General introduction → A growing body of evidence suggests that soccer may present a risk for neuropsychological (NP) compromise, including deficits in attention, mental processing efficiency, memory, planning, and visual perception function (Matser, Kessels, Jordan, Lezak, & Troost, 1998; Matser, Kessels, Lezak, Jordan, & Troost, 1999; Tysvaer & Lochen, 1991). Several issues remain unresolved, however. First, although NP impairment has been documented more consistently in older soccer athletes, the extent to which it can be detected in younger athletes remains unclear. Second, it is not known by what mechanism(s), if any, brain injury is caused during participation in soccer. Acute traumatic brain injury (i.e., concussion) is roughly as

Relevant literature → common in soccer as in American football (Green & Jordan, 1998), and repeated concussions are known to produce chronic NP impairment (Gronwall & Wrightson, 1975). Some authors suggest that heading the soccer ball may also contribute to soccer-related NP dysfunction (Tysvaer & Lochen, 1991). No study has been has been able to clearly disentangle the potential deleterious effects of heading from the effects of concussions, and researchers disagree as to whether heading itself presents a serious risk of brain injury (Abreau, Templer, Schuyler, & Hutchison, 1990; Asken & Schwartz, 1998; Baroff, 1998; Green & Jordan, 1998; Jordan, Green, Galanty, Mandelbaum, & Jabour, 1996; Tysvaer & Lochen, 1991).

Heading, which professionals typically do thousands of times in an average career (Tysvaer & Storli, 1981), may lead to microscopic diffuse axonal injury (DAI). DAI is maximal in fronto-temporal brain regions and the gray-white matter junction, and is often a consequence of rotational forces on the brain (Levin, Eisenberg, & Benton, 1989; Lezak, 1995), such as might occur in heading. DAI is not always evident on neuroimaging (Gean, 1994), but its functional

Neuropsychological Impairment   4

correlates (e.g., reduced concentration, slowed reaction time, inefficient mental processing) can be reliably detected by NP testing (Levin et al., 1989; Lezak, 1995). No previous studies have

Purpose → explored NP performance as an interactive function of participant age and sport. Therefore, we

Method and hypothesis → used a battery of tests designed to detect NP impairment in order to test the hypothesis that soccer athletes, especially older ones, would show poorer NP test performance than comparison groups of swim athletes (who are less likely to sustain sport-related brain injury).

The **introduction** is the first major section of text in a research report. The introduction presents a logical development of the research question, including a review of the relevant background literature, a statement of the research question or hypothesis, and a brief description of the methods used to answer the question or test the hypothesis.

Describe the major elements of an introduction.

## METHOD

The second major section of the body or the text of a research report is the **method section.** The method section provides a relatively detailed description of exactly how the research study was conducted. Other researchers should be able to read your method section and obtain enough information to duplicate all of the essential elements of your research study. The method section immediately follows the introduction. That is, do not start a new page. Instead, after the last line of the introduction, drop to the next double-spaced line and center the word *Method*. Usually a method section is divided into three subsections: subjects or participants, apparatus or materials, and procedure. Each subsection heading is presented at the left margin in italics, and only the first letter of the heading is capitalized.

The first subsection of the method section is either the **subjects subsection** or the **participants subsection.** This subsection describes the sample that participated in the study. For nonhumans, this subsection is entitled *Subjects*, and for humans, *Participants*. For nonhumans, describe (1) the number of animals used in the study, (2) their genus, species, and strain, (3) the supplier, (4) how the animals were housed and handled, and (5) their specific characteristics, including, sex, weight, and age. For humans it is customary to report (1) the number of participants, (2) how they were selected, (3) basic demographic characteristics of the group, including, age, gender and ethnicity, and (4) any other characteristics relevant to the study (e.g., IQ or psychopathology diagnosis).

The second subsection of the method section is entitled either *Apparatus* or *Materials*. This second subsection describes any apparatus (i.e., equipment) or materials (i.e., questionnaires, etc.) used in the study. Occasionally both subsections are included in a research report. In an **apparatus subsection,** common items such as chairs, tables, and stopwatches are mentioned without a lot of detail. The more specialized the equipment is, the more detail is needed. For custom-made equipment, a figure or picture is required as well. The apparatus subsection is occasionally omitted (if there is no apparatus) or may be blended into other subsections of the method section if the apparatus deserves only brief mention. For studies that use questionnaires, the second subsection of the method section is a **materials subsection.** Each questionnaire used in the study requires a description, a citation for it, and an explanation of its function in the study (i.e., what was it used to measure). For a new questionnaire that you developed for the purposes of your study, it is also necessary to provide a copy of the measure in an appendix.

Typically the third subsection of the method section is the **procedure subsection.** The procedure subsection provides a description of the step-by-step process used to complete the study. Include any methods used to divide/assign subjects or participants into groups, a description of instructions given to participants, and any unusual testing or assessment procedures. For experiments, also describe in detail the manipulation and the precautions against confounds.

Figure 15.4 shows the method section of an APA-style manuscript.

---

Definition

The **method section** of a research report describes how the study was conducted, including the subjects or participants, the apparatus or materials, and the procedures used.

---

Learning Check

Describe the contents of each subsection of the method section.

---

## RESULTS

The third major section of the body or text of the research report is the **results section.** The results section presents a summary of the data and the statistical analyses. The results section immediately follows the method section. That is, do not start a new page. Instead, after the last line of the method section, drop down to the next double-spaced line and center the word *Results.* The first paragraph in the results section is indented and begins on the next double-spaced line.

Usually a results section begins with a statement of the primary outcome of the study, followed by the basic descriptive statistics (usually means and standard deviations), then the inferential statistics (usually the results of hypothesis tests), and finally the measures of effect size. If the study was relatively complex, it may be best to summarize the data in a table or a figure. However, with only a few means and inferential tests, it usually is more economical to report the results as text. Note that figures and tables are not included in the results section of a manuscript but are placed at the end of the manuscript. Figures and tables are numbered (for example, Table 1 or Figure 1) and are referred to by number in the text.

Reports of statistical significance should be made in a statement that identifies (1) the type of test used, (2) the degrees of freedom, (3) the outcome of the test, and (4) the level of significance. When reporting the level of significance, you are encouraged to use the exact probability value (as provided by most computer programs), or you may use a traditional alpha level (.05, .01, .001) as a point of reference. Using an exact probability, for example, a report might state:

The results indicated a significant difference between groups, $F(2, 36)$ = 4.37, $p$ = .006.

With a traditional alpha level, the same result would be reported as:

The results indicated a significant difference between groups, $F(2, 36)$ = 4.37, $p$ < .01.

Figure 15.5 shows the results section of an APA-style manuscript.

End of introduction; no new page → soccer athletes, especially older ones, would show poorer NP test performance than comparison groups of swim athletes (who are less likely to sustain sport-related brain injury).

Center → Method

Italics and flush left → *Participants*

Describe participants or subjects → Thirty-two soccer players participated, including 26 (15 males, 11 females) drawn from an upstate New York college ($M$ age = 19.81, $SD$ = 1.50). Also studied were six older male soccer players ($M$ age = 41.5, $SD$ = 9.77), all current or former professionals. Age-matched comparison groups consisted of 22 swim athletes (7 males, 15 females) from the same college ($M$ age = 19.50, $SD$ = 1.22), and seven adult male swimmers ($M$ age = 42.86, $SD$ = 15.90). None participated in diving, giving a predicted low rate of sports-related head injury but with similar levels of exertion.

*Materials*

Describe apparatus or materials used → Three neuropsychological tests were used. The Paced Auditory Serial Addition Test (PASAT) is a measure of ability to focus attention (Gronwall, 1977). The examinee hears a sequence of digits presented at speeds ranging from 1 digit/2.4 sec. to 1 digit/1.2 sec and must sum each pair of successive digits. The score represents the number of correctly added digits (maximum = 240). The Continuous Performance Test (CPT) assesses reaction time and capacity

Neuropsychological Impairment   5

for sustained concentration (Conners, 1995). It is presented in a computer game-like fashion, in which the examinee presses the space bar as quickly as possible following the appearance on the screen of any letter except "X." The Wisconsin Card Sorting Test (WCST) measures conceptual thinking ability and mental flexibility (Heaton, Chelune, Talley, Kay, & Curtiss, 1993). It is a problem-solving task in which the examinee must determine the criteria for sorting cards featuring stimuli of various shape, color, and number, based on examiner feedback following each sorting attempt.

*Procedure*

Describe the process of conducting the study → Participants were tested individually. After giving informed consent, each participant completed a general demographic/personal history questionnaire to collect information such as age, gender, details of sport participation, history of head injuries, neurologic and psychiatric history, and learning disabilities. Following the questionnaire, the three neuropsychological tests were administered.

Figure 15.4   An APA-Style Method Section

End of method section;
no new page

Center

Descriptive statistics
in a table placed at
the end of the
manuscript

Inferential statistics

history, and learning disabilities. Following the questionnaire, the three neuropsychological tests were administered.

Results

A series of 2 × 2 (sport × age category) analyses of variance (ANOVA) were conducted on the neuropsychological test variables, descriptive statistics for which are shown in Table 1. Goaltenders ($n = 4$), who are believed to have a lower risk of soccer-related head injury, were excluded from these analyses. A significant effect for age category was found on the PASAT, with the older groups outperforming the younger groups, $F(1, 53) = 11.13$, $p < .001$. A main effect for sport (swimmers outperforming soccer athletes) was observed for the total errors score

Neuropsychological Impairment    6

on the WCST, $F(1, 53) = 5.28$, $p < .025$. An interaction between sport and age was found for the reaction time scores for the CPT, $F(1, 53) = 11.10$, $p < .001$; post-hoc tests indicated that the older soccer group significantly underperformed all other groups, $F(1, 53) = 5.30$, $p < .025$.

Discussion

Results partially supported the hypothesis that soccer athletes, especially older ones, would demonstrate poorer NP test performance than comparable swimmers. Similar to other

Figure 15.5    An APA-Style Results Section

---

**Definition**

The **results section** of a research report presents a summary of the data and the statistical analysis.

---

## DISCUSSION

The fourth and final major section of the body or text of a research report is the **discussion section.** In the discussion section, you offer interpretation, evaluation, and discussion of the implications of your findings. The discussion section immediately follows the results section. Do not start a new page; instead, after the last line of the results section, drop down to the next double-spaced line and center the word *Discussion*. The first paragraph of the discussion section is indented and begins on the next double-spaced line.

The discussion section should begin with a restatement of the hypothesis. (Recall that your hypothesis is first presented at the end of the introduction.) Next, briefly restate your major results, and indicate how they either support or fail to support your primary hypothesis. Next, relate your results to the work of others, explaining how your outcome fits into the existing structure of knowledge of the area. It is also common to identify any limitations of the research, especially factors that may affect the generalization of the results.

It can be helpful to think of the discussion section as a mirror image of the introduction. Remember, the introduction moved from general to specific, using items from the literature to focus on a specific hypothesis. Now, in the discussion section, you begin with a specific hypothesis (your outcome) and relate it back to the existing literature. Do not simply repeat statements from the introduction; but you may find it useful to mention some of the same references you used earlier to make new points relating your results to the other work.

### Refine or Reformulate Your Research Idea
In the last paragraphs of the discussion section you may reach beyond the actual results and begin to consider their implications and/or applications. This corresponds to Step 10 in the research process, refining or reformulating a research idea (see Chapter 1, page 28). Your results may support or challenge existing theories, suggest changes in practical, day-to-day interactions, or indicate new interpretations of previous research results. Any of these is an appropriate topic for a discussion section and each can lead to new ideas for future research. If your results support your original hypothesis, it is now possible to test the boundaries of your findings by extending the research to new environments or different populations. If the research results do not support your hypothesis, then more research is needed to find out why. This never-ending process of asking questions, gathering evidence, and asking new questions is part of the general scientific method. The "answer" to a research question is always open to challenge.

Figure 15.6 shows the discussion section of an APA-style manuscript.

---

The **discussion section** of a research report restates the hypothesis, summarizes the results, and then presents a discussion of the interpretation, implications, and possible applications of the results.

Definition

---

Describe how the discussion section of a research report brings us full circle and provides a mirror image of the introduction.

Learning Check

---

### REFERENCES

Beginning on a new page, with the centered title, *References*, the **reference section** provides complete information about each item cited in the manuscript. Notice that there is a precise one-to-one relationship between the items listed in the references and the items cited in the paper: Each item cited must appear in the references, and each item in the references must have been cited. The references are listed alphabetically by the last name of the first author. One-author reaction time scores for the CPT, $F(1, 53) = 11.10$, $p < .001$; post-hoc tests indicated that the older soccer group significantly underperformed all other groups, $F(1, 53) = 5.30$, $p < .025$.

**End of results; no new page**

**Center** → Discussion

**Restate hypothesis** Results partially supported the hypothesis that soccer athletes, especially older ones, would demonstrate poorer NP test performance than comparable swimmers. Similar to other

**Restate results** studies (Matser et al., 1998; Tysvaer & Lochen, 1991), our data indicated that older soccer athletes seem to be at risk for problems with concentration, reaction time, and conceptual thinking. This pattern of performance is consonant with, but not specific to, frontal lobe damage and does not unequivocally implicate heading rather than concussion as the causative

**Relate to other research** mechanism. Green and Jordan (1998) have argued that heading is a relatively safe activity, except perhaps for those with a history of concussion. If so, then the longer one's career, and the more likely one is to sustain concussion, the greater the potential risk associated with heading. The fairly consistent findings, from our own as well as other studies (Baroff, 1998; Tysvaer & Lochen, 1991) of significantly poorer NP performance confined primarily to older soccer athletes, supports this possibility. Nonetheless, no study has yet indicated that NP impairments demonstrated on formal testing lead to practical difficulties in daily living.

In light of the accumulating findings implicating soccer participation as a risk factor for NP impairment (Matser et al., 1998; Matser et al., 1999; Tysvaer & Lochen, 1991), careful prospective studies of the combinatory effects of heading, concussions, and normal aging appear warranted. Most importantly, the precautions suggested by previous authors (e.g., use of proper

**Implications or applications**

Neuropsychological Impairment    7

size soccer balls, coaching of correct heading technique, availability of adequate on-site care, return-to-play guidelines, annual NP screenings for athletes in head-contact sports) must be implemented (Asken & Schwartz, 1998; Baroff, 1998; Green & Jordan, 1998; Tysvaer, 1992).

Figure 15.6   An APA-Style Discussion Section

entries precede multiple-author entries beginning with the same first author. References with the same author or authors in the same order are listed chronologically from earliest to most recent publication date. Figure 15.7 shows the reference section of an APA-style manuscript.

Begin a new page

Center

Neuropsychological Impairment　8

References

Abreau, F., Templer, D. I., Schuyler, B. A., & Hutchison, H. T. (1990). Neuropsychological assessment of soccer players. *Neuropsychology, 4,* 175–181.

Asken, M. J., & Schwartz, R. C. (1998). Heading the ball in soccer: What's the risk of brain injury? *The Physician and Sportsmedicine, 26,* 37–44.

Baroff, G. S. (1998). Is heading a soccer ball injurious to brain function? *Journal of Head Trauma Rehabilitation,* 13, 45–52.

Conners, C. K. (1995). *Conners' Continuous Performance Test.* North Tonawanda, NY: Multi-Health Systems.

Gean, A. D. (1994). *Imaging of head trauma.* New York: Raven Press.

Green, G. A., & Jordan, S. E. (1998). Are brain injuries a significant problem in soccer? *Clinics in Sports Medicine, 17,* 795–809.

Gronwall, D. M. A. (1977). Paced auditory serial-addition task: A measure of recovery from concussion. *Perceptual and Motor Skills, 44,* 367–373.

Gronwall, D. M. A., & Wrightson, P. (1975). Cumulative effect of concussion. *Lancet, 2,* 995–997.

Heaton, R. K., Chelune, G. J., Talley, J. L., Kay, G. G., & Curtiss, G. (1993). *Wisconsin Card Sorting Test (WCST) manual: Revised and expanded.* Odessa, FL: Psychological Assessment Resources.

Jordan, S. E., Green, G. A., Galanty, H. L., Mandelbaum, B. R., & Jabour, B. A. (1996). Acute and chronic brain injury in United States national team soccer players. *American Journal of Sports Medicine, 24,* 205–210.

Figure 15.7　An APA-Style References Section

Table 15.1 presents examples of proper formatting of the most commonly used types of references. Note that the *Publication Manual* provides formats for close to 100 types of references.

The **reference section** of a research report is a listing of complete references for all sources of information cited in the report, organized alphabetically by the last name of the first author.

Definition

TABLE 15.1

## Common Reference Formats and Examples

### Journal Article With One Author

Begin with the author's last name and initials, followed by the year of publication in parentheses. Then list the title of the journal article, the name of the journal (in italics), volume number (in italics), and the pages for the article.

**Example**

Miller, R. J. (2001). Gender differences in illusion response: The influence of spatial strategy and sex ratio. *Sex Roles, 44,* 209–225.

### Journal Article With Multiple Authors

Listing each author's last name and initials, with authors separated by commas. An ampersand (&) is used instead of the word "and" before the final author. Next, list the year of publication in parentheses, the title of the journal article, the name of the journal (in italics), volume number (in italics), and the pages for the article.

**Example**

Birch, S. L., Albrecht, J. E., & Myers, J. L. (2000). Syntactic focusing structures influence discourse processing. *Discourse Processes, 30,* 285–304.

### Entire Book

Begin with the author's last name and initials; if there are multiple authors, list exactly as in a journal article. Follow with the book title (in italics), the city and state of the publisher, and the name of the publisher. (The state name is usually not identified for a major city such as New York or Chicago.)

**Example**

Gravetter, F. J., & Forzano, L. B. (2003). *Research methods for the behavioral sciences.* Belmont, CA: Wadsworth.

### Chapter or Article in an Edited Book

This reference consists of two parts: a reference for the chapter and a reference for the edited book. The reference for the chapter or article consists of the author's (or authors') names listed exactly as in a journal article, the year of publication in parentheses, and the title of the chapter or article. The reference for the edited book begins with the word *In,* followed by the name (or names) of the editors (initials first, then last name) followed by *(Ed.)* for a single editor or *(Eds.)* for multiple editors. Then list the name of the book (in italics), the page numbers of the article or chapter, the city and state of the publisher, and the name of the publisher.

**Example**

Brennan, K. A., Clark, C. L., & Shaver, P. R. (1998). Self-report measurement of adult romantic attachment: An integrative overview. In J. A. Simpson & W. S. Roles (Eds.), *Attachment theory and close relationships* (pp. 46–76). New York: Guilford.

## APPENDIX

An **appendix** may be included as a means of presenting detailed information that is useful but would interrupt the flow of text if it were presented in the body of the paper. Examples of items that might be presented in an appendix are a copy of a new measure, a computer program, a detailed description of an unusual or complex piece of equipment, and detailed instructions to participants. Appendixes each start on their own separate page with the centered title *Appendix* and are identified by consecutive letters (A, B, C, etc.) if there is more than one (for example, *Appendix A*).

## AUTHOR NOTE

The author note, which also starts on a separate page with the centered title *Author Note*, simply provides details about the authors, including:

1. Departmental affiliation
2. Sources of financial support for the research
3. Acknowledgment of others who contributed or assisted with the study
4. Identification of a contact person if a reader wants further information

## TABLES, FIGURE CAPTIONS, AND FIGURES

The final sections of the manuscript present any tables and figures used to illustrate points or present results. As a general rule, tables and figures supplement the text; they should not duplicate information that has already been presented in text form, and they should not be completely independent of the text. Instead, any table or figure should be mentioned in the text by number, and the text should point out some of the more important aspects of the figure or table.

Tables, formatted according to APA specifications, are each typed separately on its own page. The table number and title, respectively, are displayed at the top of the page, each at the left margin. The title or header for the table should describe what information is included in the table. Figure 15.8 shows a table from an APA-style manuscript.

Figure captions (titles or descriptions of figures), in contrast to table titles, are not displayed at the top of each figure. Instead, they are listed together and presented separate from the figures, beginning on a new page, with the centered title *Figure Captions*. Each figure caption is numbered (for example, Figure 1) and formatted with the word *Figure* and the number at the left margin in italics. Only the *F* in *Figure* is capitalized, and the figure number is followed by a period. The figure title immediately follows on the same line. See the following example.

*Figure 1.* Mean reaction time for each treatment condition.

The figures are included last, prepared according to APA specification, each on its own separate page, as final artwork or photographs and should be identified by penciling the figure number and partial caption on the back.

## 15.4    SUBMITTING A MANUSCRIPT FOR PUBLICATION

After you have prepared your research report, you are ready to submit the manuscript for publication in a scientific journal. Recall that communicating your research to the scientific community makes your finding public, which is necessary in the realm of science. The *Publication Manual* provides detailed information for

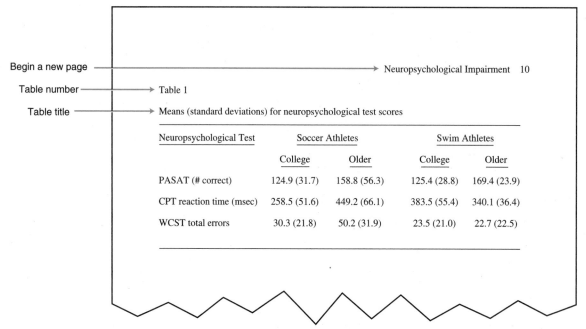

Begin a new page — Neuropsychological Impairment   10

Table number — Table 1

Table title — Means (standard deviations) for neuropsychological test scores

| Neuropsychological Test | Soccer Athletes | | Swim Athletes | |
| --- | --- | --- | --- | --- |
| | College | Older | College | Older |
| PASAT (# correct) | 124.9 (31.7) | 158.8 (56.3) | 125.4 (28.8) | 169.4 (23.9) |
| CPT reaction time (msec) | 258.5 (51.6) | 449.2 (66.1) | 383.5 (55.4) | 340.1 (36.4) |
| WCST total errors | 30.3 (21.8) | 50.2 (31.9) | 23.5 (21.0) | 22.7 (22.5) |

Figure 15.8    An APA-Style Table

preparation and submission of a manuscript for publication. However, the following three steps will help you get a good start.

1. First, select a journal that is appropriate for the topic of your research report. Most journals focus on a few special topics. The inside front cover of the most recent issue of a journal or a journal's Web site describes what kinds of manuscripts are appropriate for that journal (see Figure 15.9). In addition, there are a few journals that exclusively publish undergraduate research papers. *Modern Psychological Studies* is one such journal.

2. Consult the journal's instructions to authors for specific submission requirements. Instructions to authors are typically printed in the journal or can be found on the journal's Web site. Information on the inside front cover of each issue of the journal should lead you to specific instructions. Some journals print these instructions once a year; therefore, you may need to find the correct issue of a particular journal for this information. For the journal described in Figure 15.9, for example, the information on the inside cover directs authors to a detailed set of instructions printed elsewhere in the journal and to a detailed discussion of the journal's content that is printed in an earlier issue. When you are ready to mail your manuscript, be sure to include the number of additional photocopies required by the journal.

3. Enclose a cover letter along with the manuscript to the journal editor. Section 5.26 of the *Publication Manual* details the contents of this letter.

The **Journal of Experimental Psychology: Learning, Memory, and Cognition**

publishes original experimental studies on basic processes of cognition, learning, memory,

imagery, concept formation, problem solving, decision making, thinking, reading, and

language processing. The journal emphasizes empirical reports but may include specialized

reviews and other nonempirical reports, called Observations, which are theoretical notes,

commentary, or criticism on topics appropriate to the journal's content area. For further

information on content, authors should refer to the editorial in the January 2000 issue of the

*Journal* (Vol. 26, No. 1, pp. 253–255).

**Manuscripts:** Submit manuscripts in quintuplicate to the Editor, Thomas O. Nelson,

Department of Psychology, University of Maryland, College Park, MD 20742, according to

the Instructions to Authors published elsewhere in this issue (see the table of contents). The

opinions and statements published are the responsibility of the authors, and such opinions and

statements do not necessarily represent the policies of APA or the views of the Editor.

Figure 15.9    Inside Front Cover of a 2002 Issue of the *Journal of Experimental Psychology: Learning, Memory, and Cognition*
The two paragraphs provide authors with information about the kinds of papers and the content areas that are appropriate for this journal, and information about submitting manuscripts to be considered for publication.

When a manuscript is received by a journal editor, the editor usually informs the author of its receipt and distributes copies of the manuscript to reviewers. The reviewers are selected on the basis of their expertise in the research area of your manuscript. Reviewers provide the editor with an evaluation of the manuscript, but ultimately the editor makes the decision to accept it, reject it, or request its revision. Note that most manuscripts are rejected for publication—only the best of the best manuscripts get published.

## 15.5    WRITING A RESEARCH PROPOSAL

Although we have identified writing a research report as Step 9 in the research process, researchers often do some writing earlier. Before conducting a study, most researchers write a **research proposal.** A research proposal is basically a plan for a new study. As outlined in the research process (see Chapter 1), before data are collected, you must (1) find a research idea, (2) convert your idea into a specific testable hypothesis, (3) define and choose your measures, (4) identify and select the individuals for your study, (5) select a research strategy, (6) select a research design, and (7) make a plan for analyzing and interpreting the data (as discussed in Chapter 14).

## WHY WRITE A RESEARCH PROPOSAL?

Research proposals are commonly used in the following situations:

- Researchers submit research proposals to government and local funding agencies to obtain financial support for their research.
- Researchers develop proposals for their own use to help develop and refine their thinking and to remind themselves to attend to details they might otherwise overlook.
- Undergraduate honors thesis and graduate students submit proposals to their thesis and dissertation committees for approval.
- Undergraduate students are asked to write research proposals for the purposes of research methods classes (even when they are not required to conduct the actual study).

In each case the research proposal is evaluated, feedback is provided, and suggestions for modification are made.

Like the research report, the basic purpose of a good research proposal is to provide three kinds of information about the research study:

1. *What will be done.* The proposal should describe in some detail the step-by-step process you will follow to complete the research project.

2. *What may be found.* The proposal should contain an objective description of the possible outcomes. Typically, this involves a description of the measurements that will be taken and the statistical summary and interpretation of those measurements that will be used.

3. *How your planned research study is related to other knowledge in the area.* The research proposal should show the connections between the planned study and past knowledge.

| Definition | A **research proposal** is a written report presenting the plan and underlying rationale of a future research study. A proposal includes a review of the relevant background literature, an explanation of how the proposed study is related to other knowledge in the area, a description of how the planned research will be conducted, and a description of the possible results. |
|---|---|

 Learning Check

Describe a situation in which writing a research proposal may be useful.

## HOW TO WRITE A RESEARCH PROPOSAL

Writing a research proposal is very much like writing a research report. First, the general APA style guidelines discussed in Section 15.2 are identical, with the exception of verb tense. In a research proposal, always use the future tense when you describe your study. You will need to do this (1) at the end of the introduction when you introduce your study (for example, "The purpose of this study will be . . ."); (2) in the method section (for example, "The participants will be . . .," "Participants will complete . . ."); and in the results/discussion (for example, "It is expected that the scores will increase . . ."). Unlike in a research report, in a research proposal your study has not been conducted yet, and therefore it doesn't make sense to refer to it in the past tense.

Second, the content of each part of the manuscript body discussed in Section 15.3 is identical, with these exceptions:

1. An abstract is optional in a research proposal.
2. The literature review in the introduction is typically more extensive than the review in a research report.
3. The results and discussion sections are typically replaced either by a combined results/discussion section or a section entitled *Expected Results and Statistical Analysis* or *Data Analysis and Expected Results*. Regardless of its heading, this final section of the body of the research proposal should describe (1) how the data will be collected and analyzed, (2) the expected or anticipated results, (3) other plausible outcomes, and (4) implications of the expected results.

Describe the ways in which a research proposal is similar to and different from a research report.

Learning Check

---

Your research is not finished until you have made it available to the rest of the scientific community. Therefore, when the study is completed and the data are in and analyzed, it is time to prepare a research report (Step 9 in the overall research process). Briefly, a research report describes what was done, what was found, and how your research study is related to other knowledge in the area.

The current guidelines for the formal style and structure that are the convention for research reports in the behavioral sciences are presented in the *Publication Manual of the American Psychological Association* (5th edition, 2001). The *Publication Manual* provides detailed information on properly preparing a manuscript to be submitted for publication.

Although the *Publication Manual* contains hundreds of guidelines and suggestions for creating a clear, precisely written manuscript, four elements of writing style will help you get a good start: using an impersonal writing style, past-tense verbs, unbiased language, and appropriate citations. We also describe three elements of format: general guidelines for word processing, headings and order of manuscript pages, and pagination and page headings.

The contents of each part of a research report are described in detail. Submitting a manuscript for publication and writing a research proposal are briefly discussed as well.

## KEY WORDS

research report
citation
title page
running head

abstract
introduction
method section
results section

discussion section
reference section
research proposal

## EXERCISES

1. In addition to the key words, you should be able to define each of the following terms:
   *Publication Manual of the American Psychological Association* (5th ed., 2001)
   plagiarism
   page header
   subjects subsection
   participants subsection
   apparatus subsection
   materials subsection
   procedure subsection
   appendix
2. What are the four items of information that appear on the title page of a research manuscript?
3. Which section of a research manuscript is usually written last? Why?

4. Which section of a research manuscript usually contains most of the citations? Why?
5. To learn why a particular research study was done, which section of the research manuscript should you read?
6. To find out if the results of the study have any practical applications, what section of the research manuscript should you read?
7. Which section of the research report provides step-by-step instructions for replicating the study?
8. In 1994, Steven Schmidt published a research report demonstrating that humor has a positive effect on human memory. Write a sentence that presents this result as a statement of fact and cites the 1994 publication.

## InfoTrac COLLEGE EDITION EXERCISES

1. Most journals in psychology use APA style for their research reports. You should know where to look in an article to find specific information about the research study. Use InfoTrac College Edition to find a psychology journal and a report of an empirical research study. [Hint: Use the PowerTrac (advanced) search with the Journal Name List option. Then enter *journal of psychology* after the jn= prompt. This should lead you to a set of journals that all have the words *journal of* and *psychology* in the title (such as *Journal of Abnormal Child Psychology*). Check some articles until you find an empirical study

that appears to use APA style.] Once you have found your study, do the following:
   a. Find a statement of the hypothesis or the purpose for the research study. Where should you look for this piece of information?
   b. Find a suggestion for future research. Where are the authors likely to put such a suggestion?
   c. Find out how many individuals participated in the study, and describe their characteristics (age, gender, and so on). Where is this information located in the report?

2. Psychology journals and medical journals tend to use very different formats for citations.
   a. Locate a report in a medical journal such as *Lancet* or the *American Journal of Drug and Alcohol Abuse*, and describe how the references are cited in the text. (Hint: Use the PowerTrac search with the Journal Name or the Journal Name List option to find medical journals.)
   b. Check another category of journal (such as economics, philosophy, or sports) and describe the format they use for citations.

# Appendix A

# Random Number Table
## and Instructions

In the text we often discuss using a random process, such as a coin toss, to randomly select participants from a population or to randomly assign participants to groups. Instead of tossing a coin, many researchers prefer to use a table of random numbers. A table of random numbers is simply a huge list of randomly generated digits (0 to 9) grouped into 5-digit sequences and organized into rows and columns. A table of random numbers is included on page 427 (RAND, 1983).

The process of using a table of random numbers is demonstrated in the following two examples.

## Example A

For this example we use the table of random numbers to randomly select a sample of 20 individuals from a population of 197 people. Each individual in the population is assigned a number from 1 to 197. The goal is to randomly pick a set of 20 numbers between 1 and 197 to identify the 20 individuals in the sample. To use the random number table, follow these steps:

1.  Because you want to generate numbers from 001 to 197, limit the selections to 3-digit numbers. However, each column consists of 5-digit values; therefore, you need to decide how to identify three digits within each group. For example, you can use the first three digits, the middle three digits, the last three digits, or some other 3-digit sequence.

2.  Begin in a random spot; close your eyes and place your finger or a pen anywhere in the table. If your pen falls on one of the digits, you are ready to begin. Otherwise, try again.

3.  The number on which your pen falls determines the first value. For example, if you have decided to use the final three digits in each sequence, and your pen lands on the 4 in the number 14225 in row 19, column 3, then the first number to consider is 225.

4.  Numbers outside the range of the population are skipped. In our example, any value greater than 197 is outside the range. Therefore, 225 is not a usable number and is skipped.

5.  The next number is determined by continuing down the column of numbers. In our example, 479, 940, and 157 are the next 3 numbers to consider. The first two are outside our range and are skipped. However, 157 is usable, and the participant numbered 157 is selected for the sample.

6.  Continue down the column of numbers until you have selected the designated number of participants. Skip any number that you have already selected. When you cannot go any further down a column, go to the top of the next column.

### Example B

For this example we use the table of random numbers to assign participants to four different treatment conditions. Each treatment condition is assigned a number from 1 to 4, and the participants are organized sequentially—first, second, third, and so on. The goal is to randomly pick a number between 1 and 4 to determine the treatment condition for each of the participants. To use the random number table, follow these steps:

1.  Because you want to generate numbers from 1 to 4, limit the selections to 1-digit numbers. Decide how to identify one digit within each group of five digits. For example, you can use the first digit, the second digit, the third digit, and so on.

2.  Begin in a random spot; close your eyes and place your finger or a pen anywhere in the table. If your pen falls on one of the digits, you are ready to begin. Otherwise, try again.

3.  The number on which your pen falls determines the first value. For example, if you have decided to use the first digit in each sequence, and your pen lands on the 4 in the number 14225 in row 19, column 3, then the first number to consider is 1.

4.  Numbers outside the range are skipped. In our example, the range is values from 1 to 4. Therefore, the value 1 is a usable number. The first participant is assigned to treatment condition 1.

5.  The next number to consider is determined by continuing down the column of numbers. In our example, numbers 6, 2, and 8 are the next three numbers to consider. The first and third numbers are outside our range and are skipped. However, 2 is a usable value, and the participant second is assigned to treatment condition 2.

6.  Continue down the column of numbers until you have selected a treatment condition for each participant. When you cannot go any further down a column, go to the top of the next column.

A portion of a table of random numbers (from RAND Corporation, 1983) follows.

## A Page of Random Numbers

| Row/Col | (1) | (2) | (3) | *(4) | (5) | (6) | (7) | (8) | (9) | (10) |
|---|---|---|---|---|---|---|---|---|---|---|
| 00000 | 10097 | 32533 | 76520 | 13586 | 34673 | 54876 | 80959 | 09117 | 39292 | 74945 |
| 00001 | 37542 | 04805 | 64894 | 74296 | 24805 | 24037 | 20636 | 10402 | 00822 | 91665 |
| 00002 | 08422 | 68953 | 19645 | 09303 | 23209 | 02560 | 15953 | 34764 | 35080 | 33606 |
| 00003 | 99019 | 02529 | 09376 | 70715 | 38311 | 31165 | 88676 | 74397 | 04436 | 27659 |
| 00004 | 12807 | 99970 | 80157 | 36147 | 64032 | 36653 | 98951 | 16877 | 12171 | 76833 |
| 00005 | 66065 | 74717 | 34072 | 76850 | 36697 | 36170 | 65813 | 39885 | 11199 | 29170 |
| 00006 | 31060 | 10805 | 45571 | 82406 | 35303 | 42614 | 86799 | 07439 | 23403 | 09732 |
| 00007 | 85269 | 77602 | 02051 | 65692 | 68665 | 74818 | 73053 | 85247 | 18623 | 88579 |
| 00008 | 63573 | 32135 | 05325 | 47048 | 90553 | 57548 | 28468 | 28709 | 83491 | 25624 |
| 00009 | 73796 | 45753 | 03529 | 64778 | 35808 | 34282 | 60935 | 20344 | 35273 | 88435 |
| 00010 | 98520 | 17767 | 14905 | 68607 | 22109 | 40558 | 60970 | 93433 | 50500 | 73998 |
| 00011 | 11805 | 05431 | 39808 | 27732 | 50725 | 68248 | 29405 | 24201 | 52775 | 67851 |
| 00012 | 83452 | 99634 | 06288 | 98083 | 13746 | 70078 | 18475 | 40610 | 68711 | 77817 |
| 00013 | 88685 | 40200 | 86507 | 58401 | 36766 | 67951 | 90364 | 76493 | 29609 | 11062 |
| 00014 | 99594 | 67348 | 87517 | 64969 | 91826 | 08928 | 93785 | 61368 | 23478 | 34113 |
| 00015 | 65481 | 17674 | 17468 | 50950 | 58047 | 76974 | 73039 | 57186 | 40218 | 16544 |
| 00016 | 80124 | 35635 | 17727 | 08015 | 45318 | 22374 | 21115 | 78253 | 14385 | 53763 |
| 00017 | 74350 | 99817 | 77402 | 77214 | 43236 | 00210 | 45421 | 64237 | 96286 | 02655 |
| 00018 | 69916 | 26803 | 66252 | 29148 | 36936 | 87203 | 76621 | 13990 | 94400 | 56418 |
| 00019 | 09893 | 20505 | 14225 | 68514 | 46427 | 56788 | 96297 | 78822 | 54382 | 14598 |
| 00020 | 91499 | 14523 | 68479 | 27686 | 46162 | 83554 | 94750 | 89923 | 37089 | 20048 |
| 00021 | 80336 | 94598 | 26940 | 36858 | 70297 | 34135 | 53140 | 33340 | 42050 | 82341 |
| 00022 | 44104 | 81949 | 85157 | 47954 | 32979 | 26575 | 57600 | 40881 | 22222 | 06413 |
| 00023 | 12550 | 73742 | 11100 | 02040 | 12860 | 74697 | 96644 | 89439 | 28707 | 25815 |
| 00024 | 63606 | 49329 | 16505 | 34484 | 40219 | 52563 | 43651 | 77082 | 07207 | 31790 |
| 00025 | 61196 | 90446 | 26457 | 47774 | 51924 | 33729 | 65394 | 59593 | 42582 | 60527 |
| 00026 | 15474 | 45266 | 95270 | 79953 | 59367 | 83848 | 82396 | 10118 | 33211 | 59466 |
| 00027 | 94557 | 28573 | 67897 | 54387 | 54622 | 44431 | 91190 | 42592 | 92927 | 45973 |
| 00028 | 42481 | 16213 | 97344 | 08721 | 16868 | 48767 | 03071 | 12059 | 25701 | 46670 |
| 00029 | 23523 | 78317 | 73208 | 89837 | 68935 | 91416 | 26252 | 29663 | 05522 | 82562 |
| 00030 | 04493 | 52494 | 75246 | 33824 | 45862 | 51025 | 61962 | 79335 | 65337 | 12472 |
| 00031 | 00549 | 97654 | 64051 | 88159 | 96119 | 63896 | 54692 | 82391 | 23287 | 29529 |
| 00032 | 35963 | 15307 | 26898 | 09354 | 3351 | 35462 | 77974 | 50024 | 90103 | 39333 |
| 00033 | 59808 | 08391 | 45427 | 26842 | 83609 | 49700 | 13021 | 24892 | 78565 | 20106 |
| 00034 | 46058 | 85236 | 01390 | 92286 | 77281 | 44077 | 93910 | 83647 | 70617 | 42941 |
| 00035 | 32179 | 00597 | 87379 | 25241 | 05567 | 07007 | 86743 | 17157 | 85394 | 11838 |
| 00036 | 69234 | 61406 | 20117 | 45204 | 15956 | 60000 | 18743 | 92423 | 97118 | 96338 |
| 00037 | 19565 | 41430 | 01758 | 75379 | 40419 | 21585 | 66674 | 36806 | 84962 | 85207 |
| 00038 | 45155 | 14938 | 19476 | 07246 | 43667 | 94543 | 59047 | 90033 | 20826 | 69541 |
| 00039 | 94864 | 31994 | 36168 | 10851 | 34888 | 81553 | 01540 | 35456 | 05014 | 51176 |

## A Page of Random Numbers (*continued*)

| Row/Col | (1) | (2) | (3) | (4) | (5) | (6) | (7) | (8) | (9) | (10) |
|---|---|---|---|---|---|---|---|---|---|---|
| 00040 | 98086 | 24826 | 45240 | 28404 | 44999 | 08896 | 39094 | 73407 | 35441 | 31880 |
| 00041 | 33185 | 16232 | 41941 | 50949 | 89435 | 48581 | 88695 | 41994 | 37548 | 73043 |
| 00042 | 80951 | 00406 | 96382 | 70774 | 20151 | 23387 | 25016 | 25298 | 94624 | 61171 |
| 00043 | 79752 | 49140 | 71961 | 28296 | 69861 | 02591 | 74852 | 20539 | 00387 | 59579 |
| 00044 | 18633 | 32537 | 98145 | 06571 | 31010 | 24674 | 05455 | 61427 | 77938 | 91936 |
| 00045 | 74029 | 43902 | 77557 | 32270 | 97790 | 17119 | 52527 | 58021 | 80814 | 51748 |
| 00046 | 54178 | 45611 | 80993 | 37143 | 05335 | 12969 | 56127 | 19255 | 36040 | 90324 |
| 00047 | 11664 | 49883 | 52079 | 84827 | 59381 | 71539 | 09973 | 33440 | 88461 | 23356 |
| 00048 | 48324 | 77928 | 31249 | 64710 | 02295 | 36870 | 32307 | 57546 | 15020 | 09994 |
| 00049 | 69074 | 94138 | 87637 | 91976 | 35584 | 04401 | 10518 | 21616 | 01848 | 76938 |

# Appendix B

## Statistics Demonstrations and Statistical Tables

## DESCRIPTIVE STATISTICS

### THE MEAN

To compute the mean, first find the sum of the scores (represented by $\Sigma X$) and then divide by the number of scores (represented by $n$).

Scores: 4, 2, 1, 5, 2, 2, 3, 4, 3, 2, 3, 1

$\Sigma X = 32$ and $n = 12$   The mean is $M = 32/12 = 2.67$.

### THE MEDIAN

To compute the median, first list the scores in order. With an odd number of scores the median is the middle value. With an even number of scores, the median is the average of the middle two scores.

Scores: 4, 2, 1, 5, 2, 2, 3, 4, 3, 2, 3, 1

Listed in order: 1, 1, 2, 2, 2, 2, 3, 3, 3, 4, 4, 5

The middle two scores are 2 and 3. The median is 2.5.

### THE MODE

The mode is simply the most frequently occurring score.

Scores: 4, 2, 1, 5, 2, 2, 3, 4, 3, 2, 3, 1

There are more scores $X = 2$ than any other value. The mode is 2.

### VARIANCE AND SS (Sum of Squared Deviations)

Variance is the average squared distance from the mean and is usually identified with the symbol $s^2$. The calculation of variance involves two steps:

*Step 1:*
Compute the distance from the mean, or the deviation, for each score, then square each distance, then sum the squared distances. The result is called *SS* or the sum of the squared deviations.

| Score | Distance from M | Squared Distance |
|-------|-----------------|------------------|
| 5 | 1 | 1 |
| 6 | 2 | 4 |
| 1 | −3 | 9 |
| 5 | 1 | 1 |
| 3 | −1 | 1 |

For these scores:
$n = 5$ and $\Sigma X = 20$
$M = 20/5 = 4$.

$16 = SS$ (The sum of the squared deviations)

Note: The value for *SS* can also be completed using a computational formula:

$$SS = \Sigma X^2 - \frac{(\Sigma X)^2}{n}$$

For these scores:

| X | X² | | |
|---|----|---|---|
| 5 | 25 | $\Sigma X = 20$ | $SS = 96 - \dfrac{(20)^2}{5}$ |
| 6 | 36 | | $= 96 - 80$ |
| 1 | 1 | $\Sigma X^2 = 96$ | $= 16$ |
| 5 | 25 | | |
| 3 | 9 | | |
| 20 | 96 | | |

*Step 2:*
Variance is obtained by dividing *SS* (the sum of squared deviations) by $n - 1$. The value of $n - 1$ is also called *degrees of freedom* or simply *df.*

For the scores we have been using

$$\text{Variance} = s^2 = \frac{SS}{n-1} = \frac{16}{4} = 4$$

## STANDARD DEVIATION (*SD*)

Standard deviation is the square root of the variance and measures the standard distance from the mean.

In the demonstration of variance, we computed a variance of 4 for a set of $n = 5$ scores. For these scores, the standard deviation is

$$SD = \sqrt{4} = 2$$

## PEARSON CORRELATION

The Pearson correlation measures and describes the direction and degree of linear relationship between two variables. The data consist of two different measurements (two different variables) for each individual in the sample. The following data are used to demonstrate the calculation of the Pearson correlation. (Note that the two variables are labeled *X* and *Y* and that we have already computed the sum of squared deviations, *SS*, for the *X* values and the *Y* values.)

| X | Y | |
|---|---|---|
| 3 | 1 | For the *X* scores, $M = 2$ and $SS = 10$. |
| 4 | 2 | |
| 0 | 5 | For the *Y* scores, $M = 4$ and $SS = 40$. |
| 2 | 3 | |
| 1 | 9 | |

In addition to the *SS* for the *X* scores and *SS* for the *Y* scores, the calculation of the Pearson correlation requires the sum or the products of the deviations, or *SP*. The value of *SP* can be computed directly by

1.  Finding the distance from the mean for the *X* score and the distance from the mean for the *Y* score for each individual
2.  Multiplying the two distances to obtain the product for each individual
3.  Summing the products

This process is demonstrated:

| X | Y | Distance for X | Distance for Y | Products |
|---|---|---|---|---|
| 3 | 1 | 1 | −3 | −3 |
| 4 | 2 | 2 | −2 | −4 |
| 0 | 5 | −2 | 1 | −2 |
| 2 | 3 | 0 | −1 | 0 |
| 1 | 9 | −1 | 5 | −5 |
| | | | | −14 = SP |

Note: The value for $SP$ can also be found using a computational formula:

$$SP = \Sigma XY - \frac{(\Sigma X)(\Sigma Y)}{n}$$

| X | Y | XY |
|---|---|---|
| 3 | 1 | 3 |
| 4 | 2 | 8 |
| 0 | 5 | 0 |
| 2 | 3 | 6 |
| 1 | 9 | 9 |
| | | 26 = $\Sigma XY$ |

$$SP = 26 - \frac{(10)(20)}{5}$$

$$= 26 - 40$$

$$= -14$$

The Pearson correlation, identified by the letter $r$, can now be computed as follows:

$$r = \frac{SP}{\sqrt{(SS \text{ for } X)(SS \text{ for } Y)}}$$

For our data,

$$r = \frac{-14}{\sqrt{(10)(40)}} = \frac{-14}{\sqrt{400}} = -0.70$$

## INFERENTIAL STATISTICS

### INDEPENDENT-MEASURES $t$ TEST

The independent-measures $t$ test is a hypothesis test used to evaluate the mean difference between two separate groups. The test involves computing a $t$ statistic and then consulting a statistical table to determine whether the obtained value of $t$ is large enough to indicate a significant mean difference. The following sample data are used to demonstrate the independent-measures $t$ test. [Note that each group is described by the number of scores ($n$), the mean ($M$), the sum of squared deviations ($SS$), and the degrees of freedom ($df = n - 1$).]

| Group 1 | Group 2 |
|---|---|
| $n_1 = 10$ | $n_2 = 5$ |
| $M_1 = 44$ | $M_2 = 40$ |
| $SS_1 = 280$ | $SS_2 = 110$ |
| $df_1 = 9$ | $df_2 = 4$ |

The calculation of the $t$ statistic involves the following three steps.

## Step 1: Pool the Two Sample Variances

$$\text{Pooled variance} = s_p^2 = \frac{SS_1 + SS_2}{df_1 + df_2} = \frac{280 + 110}{9 + 4} = \frac{390}{13} = 30$$

## Step 2: Compute the Standard Error (Denominator of the $t$ Statistic)

$$\text{Standard error} = \sqrt{\frac{s_p^2}{n_1} + \frac{s_p^2}{n_2}} = \sqrt{\frac{30}{10} + \frac{30}{5}} = \sqrt{3 + 6} = \sqrt{9} = 3$$

## Step 3: Compute the $t$ Statistic

$$t = \frac{M_1 - M_2}{\text{Standard error}} = \frac{44 - 40}{3} = \frac{4}{3} = 1.33$$

Consult a $t$ distribution table to determine whether or not the obtained $t$ statistic, $t = 1.33$, is large enough to indicate a significant difference. The $t$ statistic has degrees of freedom equal to the sum of the $df$ values for the two groups.

$$df \text{ for the } t \text{ statistic} = df_1 + df_2$$

For these data, $df = 9 + 4 = 13$. The $t$ distribution table shows that a minimum value of $t = 2.160$ is needed for significance with an alpha level of .05. Our $t$ value does not meet this criterion, so we must conclude that there is no significant difference between the two means.

## REPEATED-MEASURES T TEST

The repeated-measures $t$ test is a hypothesis test used to evaluate the mean difference between two sets of scores obtained from a single group of participants. The test involves computing a $t$ statistic and then consulting a statistical table to determine whether the obtained value of $t$ is large enough to indicate a significant mean difference. The following sample data are used to demonstrate the repeated-measures $t$ test. Notice that we have computed the difference between the first and second score for each participant by subtracting the first score from the second. Note that the signs (+/−) are important.

| Participant | Score in Condition 1 | Score in Condition 2 | Difference |
|---|---|---|---|
| A | 20 | 22 | +2 |
| B | 24 | 23 | −1 |
| C | 18 | 24 | +6 |
| D | 21 | 24 | +3 |
| E | 26 | 28 | +2 |
| F | 19 | 25 | +6 |

The calculation of the $t$ statistic involves three steps.

**Step 1: Compute the Mean and the Variance for the Set of Difference Scores**

For these data, there are $n = 6$ difference scores with a mean of $M = 3.00$ and a variance of $s^2 = 7.2$.

**Step 2: Compute the Standard Error (Denominator of the $t$ Statistic)**

$$\text{Standard error} = \sqrt{\frac{s^2}{n}} = \sqrt{\frac{7.2}{6}} = \sqrt{1.20} = 1.10$$

**Step 3: Compute the $t$ Statistic**

$$t = \frac{M}{\text{Standard error}} = \frac{3.00}{1.10} = 2.73$$

Consult a $t$ distribution table to determine whether or not the obtained $t$ statistic, $t = 2.73$, is large enough to indicate a significant difference. The $t$ statistic has degrees of freedom equal to $n - 1$.

For these data, $df = 5$. The $t$ distribution table shows that a minimum value of $t = 2.571$ is needed for significance with an alpha level of .05. Our $t$ value exceeds this criterion, so we conclude that there is a significant mean difference between the two treatment conditions.

## MEAURES OF EFFECT SIZE FOR INDEPENDENT- AND REPEATED-MEASURES $t$

In addition to reporting the statistical significance of a mean difference, it is also recommended that you provide a report of the size of the mean difference. There are two commonly used methods for measuring effect size following a hypothesis test with a $t$ statistic. The first technique involves computing a standardized measure of the mean difference, and the second technique involves computing the proportion (or percentage) of variance that is accounted for by the mean difference. We demonstrate each of these using the data and results from the preceding demonstrations of the independent- and repeated-measures $t$ tests.

Cohen's $d$ is a standardized measure of mean difference that is computed by

$$d = \frac{\text{Mean difference}}{\text{Standard deviation}}$$

For the independent-measures $t$, the standard deviation is obtained by taking the square root of the pooled variance. Using the data from the previous demonstration,

$$d = \frac{M_1 - M_2}{\sqrt{s_p^2}} = \frac{44 - 40}{\sqrt{30}} = \frac{4}{5.48} = 0.73$$

For the repeated-measures $t$, the standard deviation is simply the square root of the variance. Using the data from the previous demonstration,

$$d = \frac{M}{\sqrt{s^2}} = \frac{3}{\sqrt{7.2}} = \frac{3}{2.68} = 1.12$$

The proportion of variance accounted for is represented by $r^2$ and is computed by

$$r^2 = \frac{t^2}{t^2 + df}$$

For the data from the independent-measures $t$ demonstration, we obtained $t = 1.33$ with $df = 13$. For these data,

$$r^2 = \frac{(1.33)^2}{(1.33)^2 + 13} = \frac{1.77}{14.77} = 0.12$$

For the data from the repeated-measures $t$ demonstration, we obtained $t = 2.73$ with $df = 5$. For these data,

$$r^2 = \frac{(2.73)^2}{(2.73)^2 + 5} = \frac{7.45}{12.45} = 0.60$$

## SINGLE-FACTOR ANALYSIS OF VARIANCE (INDEPENDENT MEASURES)

The single-factor analysis of variance is a hypothesis test used to evaluate the mean differences among two or more separate groups where the groups are defined by separate values of the same variable or factor. The test involves computing an $F$-ratio and then consulting a statistical table to determine whether the value obtained for the $F$-ratio is large enough to indicate significant mean differences. The following sample data are used to demonstrate the single-factor analysis of variance. [Note that each group is described by the number of scores ($n$), the mean ($M$), the sum of squared deviations ($SS$), and the degrees of freedom ($df = n - 1$). Also note that we have computed $\Sigma X$ and $\Sigma X^2$ for the entire set of $N = 15$ scores.]

| Treatment 1 Group 1 | Treatment 2 Group 2 | Treatment 3 Group 3 | |
|---|---|---|---|
| 0 | 1 | 2 | $N = 15$ |
| 2 | 5 | 5 | |
| 1 | 2 | 6 | $\Sigma X = 60$ |
| 5 | 4 | 9 | |
| 2 | 8 | 8 | $\Sigma X = 354$ |
| $n = 5$ | $n = 5$ | $n = 5$ | |
| $M = 2$ | $M = 4$ | $M = 6$ | |
| $SS = 14$ | $SS = 30$ | $SS = 30$ | |
| $df = 4$ | $df = 4$ | $df = 4$ | |

The $F$-ratio for the analysis is a ratio of two variances:

$$F = \frac{\text{Variance between treatments}}{\text{Variance within treatments}}$$

where each variance is computed as

$$\text{Variance} = \frac{SS}{df}$$

The *SS* values and the *df* values for the two variances are obtained by an analysis process that first computes *SS* and *df* for the total set of scores and then separates the total into the two components: between treatments and within treatments. The analysis for *SS* and *df* can be pictured as follows:

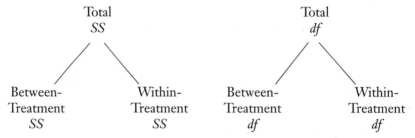

We demonstrate the analysis of variance in three steps, first analyzing the *SS* values, then analyzing the *df* values, and finally using the *SS* and *df* values to compute the two variances and the *F*-ratio.

### Step 1: Analyze *SS* (Sum of Squared Deviations)

Using the computational formula, *SS* for the total set of scores is

$$SS\ \text{total} = \Sigma X^2 - \frac{(\Sigma X)^2}{n}$$

$$= 354 - \frac{(60)^2}{15}$$

$$= 354 - 240$$

$$= 114$$

The value for *SS* within treatments is obtained directly from the *SS* values that were computed inside each treatment.

$$SS\ \text{within treatments} = \Sigma SS = 14 + 30 + 30 = 74$$

Finally, the value for *SS* between treatments is obtained by subtraction.

$$SS\ \text{between treatments} = SS\ \text{total} - SS\ \text{within treatments}$$

$$= 114 - 74$$

$$= 40$$

### Step 2: Analyze *df* (Degrees of Freedom)

Degrees of freedom for the total set of scores is simply

$$df\ \text{total} = N - 1 = 14$$

The value for *df* within treatments is obtained directly from the *df* values that were computed inside each treatment.

$$df \text{ within treatments} = \Sigma df = 4 + 4 + 4 = 12$$

Finally, the value for *df* between treatments is obtained by subtraction.

$$df \text{ between treatments} = df \text{ total} - df \text{ within treatments}$$
$$= 14 - 12$$
$$= 2$$

### Step 3: Compute the Two Variances and the *F*-Ratio

$$\text{Variance between treatments} = \frac{SS \text{ between}}{df \text{ between}} = \frac{40}{2} = 20$$

$$\text{Variance within treatments} = \frac{SS \text{ within}}{df \text{ within}} = \frac{74}{12} = 6.17$$

For these data, the *F*-ratio is

$$F = \frac{\text{Variance between treatments}}{\text{Variance within treatments}} = \frac{20.00}{6.17} = 3.24$$

Consult an *F* distribution table to determine whether or not the obtained *F*-ratio, *F* = 3.24, is large enough to indicate a significant difference. The *F*-ratio has two values for degrees of freedom, one for the variance in the numerator and one for the denominator. For our example, the *F*-ratio has *df* = 2 for the numerator and *df* = 12 for the denominator. Together, the *F*-ratio has *df* = 2, 12.

The *F* distribution table shows that a minimum value of *F* = 3.88 is needed for significance with an alpha level of .05. Our *F*-ratio does not meet this criterion, so we must conclude that the mean differences among the three groups are not significant.

## SINGLE-FACTOR ANALYSIS OF VARIANCE (REPEATED-MEASURES)

The repeated-measures analysis of variance serves exactly the same purpose as the independent-measures analysis in the previous demonstration. However, the repeated-measures analysis is used when the different sets of scores are all obtained from a single group of participants. To demonstrate the single-factor, repeated-measures analysis of variance, we use the same numerical scores that were used for the independent-measures demonstration. Notice that the data are now presented as scores from one group of participants with each individual measured three times. Also note that we have computed the mean score for each of the five participants.

| Participant | Treatment 1 | Treatment 2 | Treatment 3 | Participant Means | |
|:---:|:---:|:---:|:---:|:---:|:---:|
| A | 0 | 1 | 2 | *M* = 1 | *N* = 15 |
| B | 2 | 5 | 5 | *M* = 4 | |
| C | 1 | 2 | 6 | *M* = 3 | $\Sigma X = 60$ |
| D | 5 | 4 | 9 | *M* = 6 | |
| E | 2 | 8 | 8 | *M* = 6 | $\Sigma X^2 = 354$ |
| | *n* = 5 | *n* = 5 | *n* = 5 | | |
| | *M* = 2 | *M* = 4 | *M* = 6 | | |
| | *SS* = 14 | *SS* = 30 | *SS* = 30 | | |
| | *df* = 4 | *df* = 4 | *df* = 4 | | |

Most of the repeated-measures analysis uses exactly the same computations that were used for the independent-measures analysis of variance. With repeated-measures, however, we can use the participant means to measure the magnitude of the individual differences and then subtract these differences from the denominator before computing a final $F$-ratio. Thus, the $F$-ratio for the repeated-measures analysis has the following structure:

$$F = \frac{\text{Variance between treatments}}{\text{Error variance (individual differences removed)}}$$

Each variance is computed as

$$\text{Variance} = \frac{SS}{df}$$

The $SS$ values and the $df$ values for the two variances are obtained by a two-stage analysis. The first stage is identical to the independent-measures analysis and can be pictures as follows:

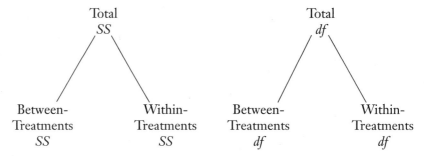

The second stage analyzes the within-treatment components by measuring and subtracting the differences between subjects.

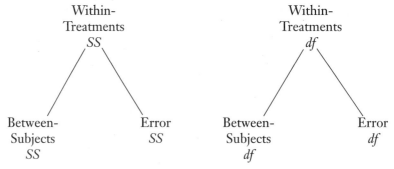

The first stage of this analysis is identical to the independent-measures analysis in the previous demonstration and produces exactly the same values.

| | |
|---|---|
| $SS$ total = 114 | $df$ total = 14 |
| $SS$ between treatments = 40 | $df$ between treatments = 2 |
| $SS$ within treatments = 74 | $df$ within treatments = 12 |

The second stage involves computing $SS$ and $df$ between subjects and then subtracting these values from the corresponding $SS$ and $df$ within treatments. The results provide the $SS$ and $df$ for the error variance in the denominator of the $F$-ratio.

Using the symbol $k$ to represent the number of treatment conditions, the $SS$ between subjects can be computed as follows:

$$SS \text{ between subjects} = k(SS \text{ for the participant means})$$

First we compute $SS$ for the set of means. The means and squared means are presented in the following table, and the computational formula is used to obtain $SS$.

| X | X² | | |
|---|---|---|---|
| 1 | 1 | $\Sigma X = 20$ | $SS = 98 - \dfrac{(20)^2}{5}$ |
| 4 | 16 | | |
| 3 | 9 | $\Sigma X^2 = 98$ | $= 98 - 80$ |
| 6 | 36 | | |
| 6 | 36 | | $= 18$ |
| 20 | 98 | | |

For these data we have $k = 3$ treatments, so

$$SS \text{ between subjects} = 3(18) = 54$$

With a group of $n = 5$ participants,

$$df \text{ between subjects} = n - 1 = 4$$

Completing the second stage of the analysis, we obtain

$$SS \text{ error} = SS \text{ within treatments} - SS \text{ between subjects}$$
$$= 74 - 54$$
$$= 20$$

$$df \text{ error} = df \text{ within treatments} - df \text{ between subjects}$$
$$= 12 - 4$$
$$= 8$$

Finally, the two variances and the $F$-ratio are

$$\text{Variance between treatments} = \frac{SS \text{ between treatments}}{df \text{ between treatments}} = \frac{40}{2} = 20$$

$$\text{Error variance} = \frac{SS \text{ error}}{df \text{ error}} = \frac{20}{8} = 2.50$$

For these data, the $F$-ratio is

$$F = \frac{\text{Variance between treatments}}{\text{Error variance}} = \frac{20.00}{2.50} = 8.00$$

Consult an $F$ distribution table to determine whether or not the obtained $F$-ratio, $F = 8.00$, is large enough to indicate a significant difference. The $F$-ratio has two values for degrees of freedom, one for the variance in the numerator and one for the denominator. For our example, the $F$-ratio has $df = 2$ for the numerator and $df = 8$ for the denominator. Together, the $F$-ratio has $df = 2, 8$.

The $F$ distribution table shows that a minimum value of $F = 4.46$ is needed for significance with an alpha level of .05, and a minimum value of 8.65 is needed with an alpha level of .01. Our $F$-ratio, $F = 8.00$, is large enough to conclude that there are significant differences at the .05 level of significance.

## MEASURES OF EFFECT SIZE FOR THE SINGLE-FACTOR ANALYSIS OF VARIANCE

In addition to reporting the statistical significance of mean differences, it is also recommended that you provide a report of the size of the mean differences. Following a single-factor analysis of variance, the common technique for measuring effect size is to compute the proportion of variance accounted for by the mean differences. The resulting value is called $\eta^2$ (the Greek letter *eta* squared). We demonstrate the calculation of $\eta^2$ using data from the previous demonstrations of the single-factor analysis of variance.

For the independent-measures analysis, with separate groups of participants, $\eta^2$ is computed by

$$\eta^2 = \frac{SS \text{ between treatments}}{SS \text{ between} + SS \text{ within}} = \frac{40}{40 + 74} = 0.35$$

For the repeated-measures analysis, using the same group of participants in all treatment conditions, $\eta^2$ is computed by,

$$\eta^2 = \frac{SS \text{ between treatments}}{SS \text{ between} + SS \text{ error}} = \frac{40}{40 + 20} = \frac{40}{60} = 0.67$$

## TWO-FACTOR ANALYSIS OF VARIANCE (INDEPENDENT MEASURES)

The two-factor analysis of variance is a hypothesis test used to evaluate the mean differences in a research study with two factors. The different groups in the study can be represented as cells in a matrix, with the levels of one factor determining the rows and the levels of the second factor determining the columns. The test involves computing three separate $F$-ratios: one to evaluate the main effects of the first factor, one to evaluate the main effects of the second factor, and one to evaluate the interaction. The following sample data are used to demonstrate the two-factor analysis of variance. [Note that each group is described by the number of scores ($n$), the mean ($M$), the sum of squared deviations ($SS$), and the degrees of freedom ($df = n - 1$). Also note that we have computed the overall mean for each row in the matrix (each level of factor A) and the overall mean for each column (each level of factor B). Finally, note that we have computed $\Sigma X$ and $\Sigma X^2$ for the entire set of $N = 30$ scores.]

Factor B

|   | B1 | B2 | B3 |   |
|---|---|---|---|---|

Factor A

|   | B1 | B2 | B3 |   |
|---|---|---|---|---|
| A1 | $n = 5$<br>$M = 10$<br>$SS = 400$<br>$df = 4$ | $n = 5$<br>$M = 20$<br>$SS = 500$<br>$df = 4$ | $n = 5$<br>$M = 30$<br>$SS = 400$<br>$df = 4$ | $M = 20$ |
| A2 | $n = 5$<br>$M = 10$<br>$SS = 300$<br>$df = 4$ | $n = 5$<br>$M = 10$<br>$SS = 300$<br>$df = 4$ | $n = 5$<br>$M = 10$<br>$SS = 500$<br>$df = 4$ | $M = 10$ |
|   | $M = 10$ | $M = 15$ | $M = 20$ | Overall<br>$N = 30$<br>$\Sigma X = 450$<br>$\Sigma X^2 = 10,900$ |

The two-factor analysis of variance can be viewed as a two-stage process. The first stage is identical to the single-factor analysis of variance with each cell of the matrix considered as a separate treatment condition. In this stage, we first compute $SS$ and $df$ for the total set of scores and then separate the total into the two components, between treatments and within treatments. This stage of the analysis for $SS$ and $df$ can be pictured as follows:

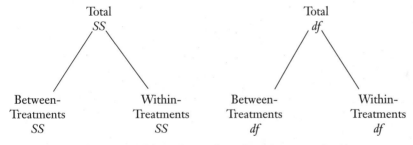

In the second stage of the analysis, the values for $SS$ and $df$ between treatments are further analyzed into the main effect for factor A, the main effect for factor B, and the interaction. This stage can be pictured as follows:

We demonstrate the two-factor analysis of variance in three steps. The first two steps correspond to the two stages of the analysis, and the third step involves computing the variances and the $F$-ratios.

**Step 1: Analyze the Total *SS* and *df* Values Into a Between-Treatments Component and a Within-Treatments Component**

*SS* total measures the *SS* for the entire set of $N = 30$ scores. Using the computational formula, *SS* for the total set of scores is

$$SS \text{ total} = \sum X^2 - \frac{(\sum X)^2}{n}$$

$$= 10{,}900 - \frac{(450)^2}{30}$$

$$= 10{,}900 - 6750$$

$$= 4150$$

The value for *SS* within treatments is obtained directly from the *SS* values that were computed inside each treatment (each cell of the matrix).

$$SS \text{ within treatments} = \sum SS = 400 + 500 + 400 + 300 + 300 + 500$$

$$= 2400$$

Finally, the value for *SS* between treatments is obtained by subtraction.

$$SS \text{ between treatments} = SS \text{ total} - SS \text{ within treatments}$$

$$= 4150 - 2400$$

$$= 1750$$

Degrees of freedom for the total set of scores is simply

$$df \text{ total} = N - 1 = 29$$

The value for *df* within treatments is obtained directly from the *df* values that were computed inside each treatment ( each cell of the matrix).

$$df \text{ within treatments} = \sum df = 4 + 4 + 4 + 4 + 4 + 4 = 24$$

Finally, the value for *df* between treatments is obtained by subtraction.

$$df \text{ between treatments} = df \text{ total} - df \text{ within treatments}$$

$$= 29 - 24$$

$$= 5$$

**Step 2: Analyze the Between-Treatments *SS* and *df* Values Into Three Separate Components**

These components should correspond to the main effect for factor A, the main effect for factor B, and the interaction.

The *SS* for factor A can be computed using the overall means for A1 and A2 (the means for the two rows). Each of these means was computed from a set of 15 scores (three groups, each with $n = 5$), so the *SS* for factor A can be computed as follows:

$$SS \text{ factor A} = 15(SS \text{ for the A1 and A2 means})$$

The first step is to compute *SS* for the set of means. The means and squared means are presented in the following table, and the computational formula is used to obtain *SS*.

| X | X² |
|---|---|
| 20 | 400 |
| 10 | 100 |
| 30 | 500 |

$\Sigma X = 30$

$\Sigma X^2 = 500$

$SS = 500 - \dfrac{(30)^2}{2}$

$= 500 - 450$

$= 50$

Multiplying by 15 give us

$$SS \text{ factor A} = 15(50) = 750$$

The *SS* for factor B can be found using the means for B1, B2, and B3. Each of these means is based on 10 scores (2 groups, each with $n = 5$), so the *SS* for factor B can be computed as follows:

$$SS \text{ factor B} = 10(SS \text{ for the B1, B2, and B3 means})$$

The first step is to compute *SS* for the set of means. The means and squared means are presented in the following table, and the computational formula is used to obtain *SS*.

| X | X² |
|---|---|
| 10 | 100 |
| 15 | 225 |
| 20 | 400 |
| 45 | 725 |

$\Sigma X = 45$

$\Sigma X^2 = 725$

$SS = 725 - \dfrac{(45)^2}{3}$

$= 725 - 675$

$= 50$

Multiplying by 10 give us

$$SS \text{ factor B} = 10(50) = 500$$

Finally, we compute *SS* for the interaction by subtraction:

$$SS \text{ interaction} = SS \text{ between treatments} - SS \text{ factor A} - SS \text{ factor B}$$
$$= 1750 - 750 - 500$$
$$= 500$$

There were only two means for factor A, so

$$df \text{ factor A} = 2 - 1 = 1$$

There were three means for factor B, so

$$df \text{ factor B} = 3 - 1 = 2$$

*df* for the interaction is found by subtraction:

$$df \text{ interaction} = df \text{ between treatments} - df \text{ factor A} - df \text{ factor B}$$
$$= 5 - 1 - 2$$
$$= 2$$

## Step 3: Compute the Variances and the *F*-Ratios

$$\text{Variance for factor A} = \frac{SS \text{ for factor A}}{df \text{ for factor A}} = \frac{750}{1} = 750$$

$$\text{Variance for factor B} = \frac{SS \text{ for factor B}}{df \text{ for factor B}} = \frac{500}{2} = 250$$

$$\text{Variance for the interaction} = \frac{SS \text{ for the interaction}}{df \text{ for the interaction}} = \frac{500}{2} = 250$$

The variance within treatments will be the denominator for each *F*-ratio.

$$\text{Variance within treatments} = \frac{SS \text{ within treatments}}{df \text{ within treatments}} = \frac{2400}{24} = 100$$

Finally, the three *F*-ratios are

$$F\text{-ratio for factor A} = \frac{\text{Variance for factor A}}{\text{Variance within treatments}} = \frac{750}{100} = 7.50$$

$$F\text{-ratio for factor B} = \frac{\text{Variance for factor B}}{\text{Variance within treatments}} = \frac{250}{100} = 2.50$$

$$F\text{-ratio for the interaction} = \frac{\text{Variance for the interaction}}{\text{Variance within treatments}} = \frac{250}{100} = 2.50$$

Consult an *F* distribution table to determine whether or not the obtained *F*-ratios are large enough to indicate significant differences. Each *F*-ratio has two values for degrees of freedom, one for the variance in the numerator and one for the denominator. For our example, the *F*-ratio for factor A has $df = 1$ for the numerator and $df = 24$ for the denominator. With $df = 1, 24$, the *F* distribution table shows that a minimum value of $F = 4.26$ is needed for significance with an alpha level of .05 and a value of $F = 7.82$ for an alpha level of .01. Our *F*-ratio exceeds the .05 value (but not the .01 value), so we conclude that the mean difference between the two levels of factor A is significant at the .05 level of significance. That is, the main effect for factor A is significant.

The *F*-ratios for factor B and for the interaction both have $df = 2, 24$. For these degrees of freedom, the *F* distribution table shows that a minimum value of $F = 3.40$ is needed for significance with an alpha level of .05. Both of our *F*-ratios fail to meet this criterion, so we must conclude that there is no significant main effect for factor B and no significant interaction between factors.

## MEASURES OF EFFECT SIZE FOR A TWO-FACTOR ANALYSIS OF VARIANCE

In addition to reporting the statistical significance of mean differences, it is also recommended that you provide a report of the size of the mean differences. Following a two-factor analysis of variance, the common technique for measuring effect size is to compute the proportion of variance accounted for by the mean differences in both main effects and in the interaction. The resulting values are each called $\eta^2$ (the Greek letter *eta* squared). We demonstrate the calculation of the $\eta^2$ values using the data from the previous demonstration of the two-factor analysis of variance.

The $\eta^2$ corresponding to the main effect for factor A is computed by

$$\eta^2 = \frac{SS \text{ for factor A}}{SS \text{ for A} + SS \text{ within}}$$

For the data from the two-factor demonstration,

$$\text{Effect size for factor A} = \eta^2 = \frac{750}{3150} = 0.24$$

Similarly, the $\eta^2$ corresponding to the main effect for factor B is computed by

$$\text{Effect size for factor B} = \eta^2 = \frac{SS \text{ for factor B}}{SS \text{ for B} + SS \text{ within}} = \frac{500}{2900} = 0.17$$

Finally, the $\eta^2$ corresponding to the interaction is computed by

$$\text{Effect size for interaction} = \eta^2 = \frac{SS \text{ for interaction}}{SS \text{ interaction} + SS \text{ within}} = \frac{500}{2900} = 0.17$$

## SIGNIFICANCE OF A CORRELATION

The significance test for a correlation is used to determine whether or not a sample correlation is sufficiently  large to justify concluding that there is a real, nonzero correlation in the population. To demonstrate the test for significance of a correlation, we assume that a researcher has obtained a correlation of $r = +0.41$ for a sample of $n = 25$ individuals.

The significance test is based on a $t$ statistic that is computed as follows:

$$t = \frac{r}{\sqrt{(1 - r^2)/df}} \quad \text{where the degrees of freedom are } df = n - 2.$$

Note: If all the terms in the $t$ formula are squared, the calculation produces an $F$-ratio with degrees of freedom determined by $df = 1, n - 2$.

For the sample in this demonstration, $r = 0.41$, $r^2 = 0.17$, and $df = 23$. With these values,

$$t = \frac{0.41}{\sqrt{(1 - 0.17)/23}} = 2.16$$

Consult a $t$ distribution table to determine whether or not the obtained $t$ statistic is large enough to indicate a significant correlation . With $df = 23$, the table shows that a minimum value of $t = 2.069$ is needed to be significant with an alpha level of .05. Our sample exceeds this criterion, so we can conclude that there is a significant correlation between the two variables.

## CHI-SQUARE TEST FOR INDEPENDENCE

The chi-square test for independence is a hypothesis test that is used to evaluate the relationship between two variables measured on nominal or ordinal scales, or the difference in proportions between separate groups of participants. The following data are used to demonstrate the chi-square test for independence. The data represent a frequency distribution for a sample of 200 people. Each person is classified on two variables, personality (introvert or extrovert) and favorite color (red, yellow, green, or blue). The number in each cell is the number of individuals with the corresponding personality and color preference. For example, 10 people were classified as introverts and selected red as their favorite color. The frequency values found in the data are called *observed frequencies* or $F_O$ values.

Favorite Color

|  | Red | Yellow | Green | Blue | |
|---|---|---|---|---|---|
| Introvert | 10 | 3 | 15 | 22 | 50 |
| Extrovert | 90 | 17 | 25 | 18 | 150 |
|  | 100 | 20 | 40 | 40 | |

For these data, the null hypothesis can be stated two ways:

1. There is no relationship between personality and color preference.
2. The distribution of color preferences (the set of proportions) is the same for introverts and extroverts.

### Step 1

The first step in the chi-square test is to compute a hypothetical set of frequencies that represent how the sample would appear if it were in perfect accord with the null hypothesis. The hypothetical frequencies are called *expected frequencies* or $f_E$ values. For each cell in the matrix, the expected frequency can be computed by

$$f_E = \frac{(\text{Row total})(\text{Column total})}{\text{Total number}}$$

For example, the upper left-hand cell in the matrix is in the first row (with a total of 50) and in the first column (with a total of 100). The total number of participants in the entire study is 200, so this cell would have an expected frequency of

$$f_E = \frac{(50)(100)}{200} = 25$$

The complete set of expected frequencies is shown in the following matrix.

Favorite Color

|  | Red | Yellow | Green | Blue | |
|---|---|---|---|---|---|
| Introvert | 25 | 5 | 10 | 10 | 50 |
| Extrovert | 75 | 15 | 30 | 30 | 150 |
|  | 100 | 20 | 40 | 40 | |

## Step 2

The second step in the chi-square test is to compute the value of the chi-square ($\chi^2$), which provides a measure of how well the observed frequencies (the data) fit the expected frequencies (the hypothesis). The formula for chi-square is

$$\chi^2 = \Sigma \frac{(f_O - f_E)^2}{f_E}$$

The step-by-step calculation for our data is shown in the following table.

a. For each cell in the matrix, find the difference between the expected and the observed frequency.
b. Square the difference.
c. Divide the squared difference by the expected frequency.
d. Sum the resulting values for each category.

| $f_O$ | $f_E$ | $(f_O - f_E)$ | $(f_O - f_E)^2$ | $(f_O - f_E)^2/f_E$ |
|---|---|---|---|---|
| 10 | 25 | 15 | 225 | 9.00 |
| 3 | 5 | 2 | 4 | 0.80 |
| 15 | 10 | 5 | 25 | 2.50 |
| 22 | 10 | 12 | 144 | 14.40 |
| 90 | 75 | 15 | 225 | 3.00 |
| 17 | 15 | 2 | 4 | 0.27 |
| 25 | 30 | 5 | 25 | 0.83 |
| 18 | 30 | 12 | 144 | 4.80 |
| | | | | $35.60 = \chi^2$ |

Consult a chi-square distribution table to determine whether or not the obtained chi-square value, $\chi^2 = 35.60$, is large enough to be statistically significant. The chi-square statistic has degrees of freedom given by

$$df = (C_1 - 1)(C_2 - 1)$$

where $C_1$ is the number of categories for the first variable and $C_2$ is the number of categories for the second variable. For our data,

$$df = (2 - 1)(4 - 1) = 3$$

With $df = 3$, the table shows that a minimum value of $\chi^2 = 11.34$ is needed for significance with an alpha level of .01. Our data exceed this criterion, so, depending on which version of the null hypothesis was used, we can conclude that either

a. there is a significant relationship between personality and color preference, or
b. the distribution of color preferences for introverts is significantly different from the distribution for extroverts.

## STATISTICAL TABLES

### The *t* Distribution

Table entries are the minimum values of *t* that are necessary for a *t* statistic to be significant at the alpha level specified. To be significant, a calculated *t* statistic must be greater than or equal to the value in the table.

| | Alpha Level for a Directional (One-Tailed) Test | | | | | |
|---|---|---|---|---|---|---|
| | 0.25 | 0.10 | 0.05 | 0.025 | 0.01 | 0.005 |
| | Alpha Level for a Nondirectional (Two-Tailed) Test | | | | | |
| df | 0.50 | 0.20 | 0.10 | 0.05 | 0.002 | 0.01 |
| 1 | 1.000 | 3.078 | 6.314 | 12.706 | 31.821 | 63.657 |
| 2 | 0.816 | 1.886 | 2.920 | 4.303 | 6.965 | 9.925 |
| 3 | 0.765 | 1.638 | 2.353 | 3.182 | 4.541 | 5.841 |
| 4 | 0.741 | 1.533 | 2.132 | 2.776 | 3.747 | 4.604 |
| 5 | 0.727 | 1.476 | 2.015 | 2.571 | 3.365 | 4.032 |
| 6 | 0.718 | 1.440 | 1.943 | 2.447 | 3.143 | 3.707 |
| 7 | 0.711 | 1.415 | 1.895 | 2.365 | 2.998 | 3.499 |
| 8 | 0.706 | 1.397 | 1.860 | 2.306 | 2.896 | 3.355 |
| 9 | 0.703 | 1.383 | 1.833 | 2.262 | 2.821 | 3.250 |
| 10 | 0.700 | 1.372 | 1.812 | 2.228 | 2.764 | 3.169 |
| 11 | 0.697 | 1.363 | 1.796 | 2.201 | 2.718 | 3.106 |
| 12 | 0.695 | 1.356 | 1.782 | 2.179 | 2.681 | 3.055 |
| 13 | 0.694 | 1.350 | 1.771 | 2.160 | 2.650 | 3.012 |
| 14 | 0.692 | 1.345 | 1.761 | 2.145 | 2.624 | 2.977 |
| 15 | 0.691 | 1.341 | 1.753 | 2.131 | 2.602 | 2.947 |
| 16 | 0.690 | 1.337 | 1.746 | 2.120 | 2.583 | 2.921 |
| 17 | 0.689 | 1.333 | 1.740 | 2.110 | 2.567 | 2.898 |
| 18 | 0.688 | 1.330 | 1.734 | 2.101 | 2.552 | 2.878 |
| 19 | 0.688 | 1.328 | 1.729 | 2.093 | 2.539 | 2.861 |
| 20 | 0.687 | 1.325 | 1.725 | 2.086 | 2.528 | 2.845 |
| 21 | 0.686 | 1.323 | 1.721 | 2.080 | 2.518 | 2.831 |
| 22 | 0.686 | 1.321 | 1.717 | 2.074 | 2.508 | 2.819 |
| 23 | 0.685 | 1.319 | 1.714 | 2.069 | 2.500 | 2.807 |
| 24 | 0.685 | 1.318 | 1.711 | 2.064 | 2.492 | 2.797 |
| 25 | 0.684 | 1.316 | 1.708 | 2.060 | 2.485 | 2.787 |
| 26 | 0.684 | 1.315 | 1.706 | 2.056 | 2.479 | 2.779 |
| 27 | 0.684 | 1.314 | 1.703 | 2.052 | 2.473 | 2.771 |
| 28 | 0.683 | 1.313 | 1.701 | 2.048 | 2.467 | 2.763 |
| 29 | 0.683 | 1.311 | 1.699 | 2.045 | 2.462 | 2.756 |
| 30 | 0.683 | 1.310 | 1.697 | 2.042 | 2.457 | 2.750 |
| 40 | 0.681 | 1.303 | 1.684 | 2.021 | 2.423 | 2.704 |
| 60 | 0.679 | 1.296 | 1.671 | 2.000 | 2.390 | 2.660 |
| 120 | 0.677 | 1.289 | 1.658 | 1.980 | 2.358 | 2.617 |
| ∞ | 0.674 | 1.282 | 1.645 | 1.960 | 2.326 | 2.576 |

## The *F* Distribution

Table entries in lightface type are the minimum values that are necessary for an *F*-ratio to be significant at an alpha level of .05. Boldface entries are the minimum values that are necessary for an *F*-ratio to be significant at an alpha level of .01. To be significant, a calculated *F*-ratio must be greater than or equal to the value in the table.

| Degrees of Freedom: Denominator | Degrees of Freedom: Numerator | | | | | | | | | | | | | | |
|---|---|---|---|---|---|---|---|---|---|---|---|---|---|---|---|
| | 1 | 2 | 3 | 4 | 5 | 6 | 7 | 8 | 9 | 10 | 11 | 12 | 14 | 16 | 20 |
| 1 | 161 | 200 | 216 | 225 | 230 | 234 | 237 | 239 | 241 | 242 | 243 | 244 | 245 | 246 | 248 |
| | **4052** | **4999** | **5403** | **5625** | **5764** | **5859** | **5928** | **5981** | **6022** | **6056** | **6082** | **6106** | **6142** | **6169** | **6208** |
| 2 | 18.51 | 19.00 | 19.16 | 19.25 | 19.30 | 19.33 | 19.36 | 19.37 | 19.38 | 19.39 | 19.40 | 19.41 | 19.42 | 19.43 | 19.44 |
| | **98.49** | **99.00** | **99.17** | **99.25** | **99.30** | **99.33** | **99.34** | **99.36** | **99.38** | **99.40** | **99.41** | **99.42** | **99.43** | **99.44** | **99.45** |
| 3 | 10.13 | 9.55 | 9.28 | 9.12 | 9.01 | 8.94 | 8.88 | 8.84 | 8.81 | 8.78 | 8.76 | 8.74 | 8.71 | 8.69 | 8.66 |
| | **34.12** | **30.92** | **29.46** | **28.71** | **28.24** | **27.91** | **27.67** | **27.49** | **27.34** | **27.23** | **27.13** | **27.05** | **26.92** | **26.83** | **26.69** |
| 4 | 7.71 | 6.94 | 6.59 | 6.39 | 6.26 | 6.16 | 6.09 | 6.04 | 6.00 | 5.96 | 5.93 | 5.91 | 5.87 | 5.84 | 5.80 |
| | **21.20** | **18.00** | **16.69** | **15.98** | **15.52** | **15.21** | **14.98** | **14.80** | **14.66** | **14.54** | **14.45** | **14.37** | **14.24** | **14.15** | **14.02** |
| 5 | 6.61 | 5.79 | 5.41 | 5.19 | 5.05 | 4.95 | 4.88 | 4.82 | 4.78 | 4.74 | 4.70 | 4.68 | 4.64 | 4.60 | 4.56 |
| | **16.26** | **13.27** | **12.06** | **11.39** | **10.97** | **10.67** | **10.45** | **10.27** | **10.15** | **10.05** | **9.96** | **9.89** | **9.77** | **9.68** | **9.55** |
| 6 | 5.99 | 5.14 | 4.76 | 4.53 | 4.39 | 4.28 | 4.21 | 4.15 | 4.10 | 4.06 | 4.03 | 4.00 | 3.96 | 3.92 | 3.87 |
| | **13.74** | **10.92** | **9.78** | **9.15** | **8.75** | **8.47** | **8.26** | **8.10** | **7.98** | **7.87** | **7.79** | **7.72** | **7.60** | **7.52** | **7.39** |
| 7 | 5.59 | 4.47 | 4.35 | 4.12 | 3.97 | 3.87 | 3.79 | 3.73 | 3.68 | 3.63 | 3.60 | 3.57 | 3.52 | 3.49 | 3.44 |
| | **12.25** | **9.55** | **8.45** | **7.85** | **7.46** | **7.19** | **7.00** | **6.84** | **6.71** | **6.62** | **6.54** | **6.47** | **6.35** | **6.27** | **6.15** |
| 8 | 5.32 | 4.46 | 4.07 | 3.84 | 3.69 | 3.58 | 3.50 | 3.44 | 3.39 | 3.34 | 3.31 | 3.28 | 3.23 | 3.20 | 3.15 |
| | **11.26** | **8.65** | **7.59** | **7.01** | **6.63** | **6.37** | **6.19** | **6.03** | **5.91** | **5.82** | **5.74** | **5.67** | **5.56** | **5.48** | **5.36** |
| 9 | 5.12 | 4.26 | 3.86 | 3.63 | 3.48 | 3.37 | 3.29 | 3.23 | 3.18 | 3.13 | 3.10 | 3.07 | 3.02 | 2.98 | 2.93 |
| | **10.56** | **8.02** | **6.99** | **6.42** | **6.06** | **5.80** | **5.62** | **5.47** | **5.35** | **5.26** | **5.18** | **5.11** | **5.00** | **4.92** | **4.80** |
| 10 | 4.96 | 4.10 | 3.71 | 3.48 | 3.33 | 3.22 | 3.14 | 3.07 | 3.02 | 2.97 | 2.94 | 2.91 | 2.86 | 2.82 | 2.77 |
| | **10.04** | **7.56** | **6.55** | **5.99** | **5.64** | **5.39** | **5.21** | **5.06** | **4.95** | **4.85** | **4.78** | **4.71** | **4.60** | **4.52** | **4.41** |
| 11 | 4.84 | 3.98 | 3.59 | 3.36 | 3.20 | 3.09 | 3.01 | 2.95 | 2.90 | 2.86 | 2.82 | 2.79 | 2.74 | 2.70 | 2.65 |
| | **9.65** | **7.20** | **6.22** | **5.67** | **5.32** | **5.07** | **4.88** | **4.74** | **4.63** | **4.54** | **4.46** | **4.40** | **4.29** | **4.21** | **4.10** |
| 12 | 4.75 | 3.88 | 3.49 | 3.26 | 3.11 | 3.00 | 2.92 | 2.85 | 2.80 | 2.76 | 2.72 | 2.69 | 2.64 | 2.60 | 2.54 |
| | **9.33** | **6.93** | **5.95** | **5.41** | **5.06** | **4.82** | **4.65** | **4.50** | **4.39** | **4.30** | **4.22** | **4.16** | **4.05** | **3.98** | **3.86** |
| 13 | 4.67 | 3.80 | 3.41 | 3.18 | 3.02 | 2.92 | 2.84 | 2.77 | 2.72 | 2.67 | 2.63 | 2.60 | 2.55 | 2.51 | 2.46 |
| | **9.07** | **6.70** | **5.74** | **5.20** | **4.86** | **4.62** | **4.44** | **4.30** | **4.19** | **4.10** | **4.02** | **3.96** | **3.85** | **3.78** | **3.67** |
| 14 | 4.60 | 3.74 | 3.34 | 3.11 | 2.96 | 2.85 | 2.77 | 2.70 | 2.65 | 2.60 | 2.56 | 2.53 | 2.48 | 2.44 | 2.39 |
| | **8.86** | **6.51** | **5.56** | **5.03** | **4.69** | **4.46** | **4.28** | **4.14** | **4.03** | **3.94** | **3.86** | **3.80** | **3.70** | **3.62** | **3.51** |
| 15 | 4.54 | 3.68 | 3.29 | 3.06 | 2.90 | 2.79 | 2.70 | 2.64 | 2.59 | 2.55 | 2.51 | 2.48 | 2.43 | 2.39 | 2.33 |
| | **8.68** | **6.36** | **5.42** | **4.89** | **4.56** | **4.32** | **4.14** | **4.00** | **3.89** | **3.80** | **3.73** | **3.67** | **3.56** | **3.48** | **3.36** |
| 16 | 4.49 | 3.63 | 3.24 | 3.01 | 2.85 | 2.74 | 2.66 | 2.59 | 2.54 | 2.49 | 2.45 | 2.42 | 2.37 | 2.33 | 2.28 |
| | **8.53** | **6.23** | **5.29** | **4.77** | **4.44** | **4.20** | **4.03** | **3.89** | **3.78** | **3.69** | **3.61** | **3.55** | **3.45** | **3.37** | **3.25** |
| 17 | 4.45 | 3.59 | 3.20 | 2.96 | 2.81 | 2.70 | 2.62 | 2.55 | 2.50 | 2.45 | 2.41 | 2.38 | 2.33 | 2.29 | 2.23 |
| | **8.40** | **6.11** | **5.18** | **4.67** | **4.34** | **4.10** | **3.93** | **3.79** | **3.68** | **3.59** | **3.52** | **3.45** | **3.35** | **3.27** | **3.16** |

*(continued)*

## TABLE B2 (continued)

| Degrees of Freedom: Denominator | 1 | 2 | 3 | 4 | 5 | 6 | 7 | 8 | 9 | 10 | 11 | 12 | 14 | 16 | 20 |
|---|---|---|---|---|---|---|---|---|---|---|---|---|---|---|---|
| 18 | 4.41 | 3.55 | 3.16 | 2.93 | 2.77 | 2.66 | 2.58 | 2.51 | 2.46 | 2.41 | 2.37 | 2.34 | 2.29 | 2.25 | 2.19 |
|    | **8.28** | **6.01** | **5.09** | **4.58** | **4.25** | **4.01** | **3.85** | **3.71** | **3.60** | **3.51** | **3.44** | **3.37** | **3.27** | **3.19** | **3.07** |
| 19 | 4.38 | 3.52 | 3.13 | 2.90 | 2.74 | 2.63 | 2.55 | 2.48 | 2.43 | 2.38 | 2.34 | 2.31 | 2.26 | 2.21 | 2.15 |
|    | **8.18** | **5.93** | **5.01** | **4.50** | **4.17** | **3.94** | **3.77** | **3.63** | **3.52** | **3.43** | **3.36** | **3.30** | **3.19** | **3.12** | **3.00** |
| 20 | 4.35 | 3.49 | 3.10 | 2.87 | 2.71 | 2.60 | 2.52 | 2.45 | 2.40 | 2.35 | 2.31 | 2.28 | 2.23 | 2.18 | 2.12 |
|    | **8.10** | **5.85** | **4.94** | **4.43** | **4.10** | **3.87** | **3.71** | **3.56** | **3.45** | **3.37** | **3.30** | **3.23** | **3.13** | **3.05** | **2.94** |
| 21 | 4.32 | 3.47 | 3.07 | 2.84 | 2.68 | 2.57 | 2.49 | 2.42 | 2.37 | 2.32 | 2.28 | 2.25 | 2.20 | 2.15 | 2.09 |
|    | **8.02** | **5.78** | **4.87** | **4.37** | **4.04** | **3.81** | **3.65** | **3.51** | **3.40** | **3.31** | **3.24** | **3.17** | **3.07** | **2.99** | **2.88** |
| 22 | 4.30 | 3.44 | 3.05 | 2.82 | 2.66 | 2.55 | 2.47 | 2.40 | 2.35 | 2.30 | 2.26 | 2.23 | 2.18 | 2.13 | 2.07 |
|    | **7.94** | **5.72** | **4.82** | **4.31** | **3.99** | **3.76** | **3.59** | **3.45** | **3.35** | **3.26** | **3.18** | **3.12** | **3.02** | **2.94** | **2.83** |
| 23 | 4.28 | 3.42 | 3.03 | 2.80 | 2.64 | 2.53 | 2.45 | 2.38 | 2.32 | 2.28 | 2.24 | 2.20 | 2.14 | 2.10 | 2.04 |
|    | **7.88** | **5.66** | **4.76** | **4.26** | **3.94** | **3.71** | **3.54** | **3.41** | **3.30** | **3.21** | **3.14** | **3.07** | **2.97** | **2.89** | **2.78** |
| 24 | 4.26 | 3.40 | 3.01 | 2.78 | 2.62 | 2.51 | 2.43 | 2.36 | 2.30 | 2.26 | 2.22 | 2.18 | 2.13 | 2.09 | 2.02 |
|    | **7.82** | **5.61** | **4.72** | **4.22** | **3.90** | **3.67** | **3.50** | **3.36** | **3.25** | **3.17** | **3.09** | **3.03** | **2.93** | **2.85** | **2.74** |
| 25 | 4.24 | 3.38 | 2.99 | 2.76 | 2.60 | 2.49 | 2.41 | 2.34 | 2.28 | 2.24 | 2.20 | 2.16 | 2.11 | 2.06 | 2.00 |
|    | **7.77** | **5.57** | **4.68** | **4.18** | **3.86** | **3.63** | **3.46** | **3.32** | **3.21** | **3.13** | **3.05** | **2.99** | **2.89** | **2.81** | **2.70** |
| 26 | 4.22 | 3.37 | 2.98 | 2.74 | 2.59 | 2.47 | 2.39 | 2.32 | 2.27 | 2.22 | 2.18 | 2.15 | 2.10 | 2.05 | 1.99 |
|    | **7.72** | **5.53** | **4.64** | **4.14** | **3.82** | **3.59** | **3.42** | **3.29** | **3.17** | **3.09** | **3.02** | **2.96** | **2.86** | **2.77** | **2.66** |
| 27 | 4.21 | 3.35 | 2.96 | 2.73 | 2.57 | 2.46 | 2.37 | 2.30 | 2.25 | 2.20 | 2.16 | 2.13 | 2.08 | 2.03 | 1.97 |
|    | **7.68** | **5.49** | **4.60** | **4.11** | **3.79** | **3.56** | **3.39** | **3.26** | **3.14** | **3.06** | **2.98** | **2.93** | **2.83** | **2.74** | **2.63** |
| 28 | 4.20 | 3.34 | 2.95 | 2.71 | 2.56 | 2.44 | 2.36 | 2.29 | 2.24 | 2.19 | 2.15 | 2.12 | 2.06 | 2.02 | 1.96 |
|    | **7.64** | **5.45** | **4.57** | **4.07** | **3.76** | **3.53** | **3.36** | **3.23** | **3.11** | **3.03** | **2.95** | **2.90** | **2.80** | **2.71** | **2.60** |
| 29 | 4.18 | 3.33 | 2.93 | 2.70 | 2.54 | 2.43 | 2.35 | 2.28 | 2.22 | 2.18 | 2.14 | 2.10 | 2.05 | 2.00 | 1.94 |
|    | **7.60** | **5.42** | **4.54** | **4.04** | **3.73** | **3.50** | **3.33** | **3.20** | **3.08** | **3.00** | **2.92** | **2.87** | **2.77** | **2.68** | **2.57** |
| 30 | 4.17 | 3.32 | 2.92 | 2.69 | 2.53 | 2.42 | 2.34 | 2.27 | 2.21 | 2.16 | 2.12 | 2.09 | 2.04 | 1.99 | 1.93 |
|    | **7.56** | **5.39** | **4.51** | **4.02** | **3.70** | **3.47** | **3.30** | **3.17** | **3.06** | **2.98** | **2.90** | **2.84** | **2.74** | **2.66** | **2.55** |
| 32 | 4.15 | 3.30 | 2.90 | 2.67 | 2.51 | 2.40 | 2.32 | 2.25 | 2.19 | 2.14 | 2.10 | 2.07 | 2.02 | 1.97 | 1.91 |
|    | **7.50** | **5.34** | **4.46** | **3.97** | **3.66** | **3.42** | **3.25** | **3.12** | **3.01** | **2.94** | **2.86** | **2.80** | **2.70** | **2.62** | **2.51** |
| 34 | 4.13 | 3.28 | 2.88 | 2.65 | 2.49 | 2.38 | 2.30 | 2.23 | 2.17 | 2.12 | 2.08 | 2.05 | 2.00 | 1.95 | 1.89 |
|    | **7.44** | **5.29** | **4.42** | **3.93** | **3.61** | **3.38** | **3.21** | **3.08** | **2.97** | **2.89** | **2.82** | **2.76** | **2.66** | **2.58** | **2.47** |
| 36 | 4.11 | 3.26 | 2.86 | 2.63 | 2.48 | 2.36 | 2.28 | 2.21 | 2.15 | 2.10 | 2.06 | 2.03 | 1.98 | 1.93 | 1.87 |
|    | **7.39** | **5.25** | **4.38** | **3.89** | **3.58** | **3.35** | **3.18** | **3.04** | **2.94** | **2.86** | **2.78** | **2.72** | **2.62** | **2.54** | **2.43** |
| 38 | 4.10 | 3.25 | 2.85 | 2.62 | 2.46 | 2.35 | 2.26 | 2.19 | 2.14 | 2.09 | 2.05 | 2.02 | 1.96 | 1.92 | 1.85 |
|    | **7.35** | **5.21** | **4.34** | **3.86** | **3.54** | **3.32** | **3.15** | **3.02** | **2.91** | **2.82** | **2.75** | **2.69** | **2.59** | **2.51** | **2.40** |
| 40 | 4.08 | 3.23 | 2.84 | 2.61 | 2.45 | 2.34 | 2.25 | 2.18 | 2.12 | 2.07 | 2.04 | 2.00 | 1.95 | 1.90 | 1.84 |
|    | **7.31** | **5.18** | **4.31** | **3.83** | **3.51** | **3.29** | **3.12** | **2.99** | **2.88** | **2.80** | **2.73** | **2.66** | **2.56** | **2.49** | **2.37** |
| 42 | 4.07 | 3.22 | 2.83 | 2.59 | 2.44 | 2.32 | 2.24 | 2.17 | 2.11 | 2.06 | 2.02 | 1.99 | 1.94 | 1.89 | 1.82 |
|    | **7.27** | **5.15** | **4.29** | **3.80** | **3.49** | **3.26** | **3.10** | **2.96** | **2.86** | **2.77** | **2.70** | **2.64** | **2.54** | **2.46** | **2.35** |
| 44 | 4.06 | 3.21 | 2.82 | 2.58 | 2.43 | 2.31 | 2.23 | 2.16 | 2.10 | 2.05 | 2.01 | 1.98 | 1.92 | 1.88 | 1.81 |
|    | **7.24** | **5.12** | **4.26** | **3.78** | **3.46** | **3.24** | **3.07** | **2.94** | **2.84** | **2.75** | **2.68** | **2.62** | **2.52** | **2.44** | **2.32** |

| Degrees of Freedom: Denominator | Degrees of Freedom: Numerator | | | | | | | | | | | | | | |
|---|---|---|---|---|---|---|---|---|---|---|---|---|---|---|---|
| | 1 | 2 | 3 | 4 | 5 | 6 | 7 | 8 | 9 | 10 | 11 | 12 | 14 | 16 | 20 |
| 46 | 4.05 | 3.20 | 2.81 | 2.57 | 2.42 | 2.30 | 2.22 | 2.14 | 2.09 | 2.04 | 2.00 | 1.97 | 1.91 | 1.87 | 1.80 |
| | **7.21** | **5.10** | **4.24** | **3.76** | **3.44** | **3.22** | **3.05** | **2.92** | **2.82** | **2.73** | **2.66** | **2.60** | **2.50** | **2.42** | **2.30** |
| 48 | 4.04 | 3.19 | 2.80 | 2.56 | 2.41 | 2.30 | 2.21 | 2.14 | 2.08 | 2.03 | 1.99 | 1.96 | 1.90 | 1.86 | 1.79 |
| | **7.19** | **5.08** | **4.22** | **3.74** | **3.42** | **3.20** | **3.04** | **2.90** | **2.80** | **2.71** | **2.64** | **2.58** | **2.48** | **2.40** | **2.28** |
| 50 | 4.03 | 3.18 | 2.79 | 2.56 | 2.40 | 2.29 | 2.20 | 2.13 | 2.07 | 2.02 | 1.98 | 1.95 | 1.90 | 1.85 | 1.78 |
| | **7.17** | **5.06** | **4.20** | **3.72** | **3.41** | **3.18** | **3.02** | **2.88** | **2.78** | **2.70** | **2.62** | **2.56** | **2.46** | **2.39** | **2.26** |
| 55 | 4.02 | 3.17 | 2.78 | 2.54 | 2.38 | 2.27 | 2.18 | 2.11 | 2.05 | 2.00 | 1.97 | 1.93 | 1.88 | 1.83 | 1.76 |
| | **7.12** | **5.01** | **4.16** | **3.68** | **3.37** | **3.15** | **2.98** | **2.85** | **2.75** | **2.66** | **2.59** | **2.53** | **2.43** | **2.35** | **2.23** |
| 60 | 4.00 | 3.15 | 2.76 | 2.52 | 2.37 | 2.25 | 2.17 | 2.10 | 2.04 | 1.99 | 1.95 | 1.92 | 1.86 | 1.81 | 1.75 |
| | **7.08** | **4.98** | **4.13** | **3.65** | **3.34** | **3.12** | **2.95** | **2.82** | **2.72** | **2.63** | **2.56** | **250** | **2.40** | **2.32** | **2.20** |
| 65 | 3.99 | 3.14 | 2.75 | 2.51 | 2.36 | 2.24 | 2.15 | 2.08 | 2.02 | 1.98 | 1.94 | 1.90 | 1.85 | 1.80 | 1.73 |
| | **7.04** | **4.95** | **4.10** | **3.62** | **3.31** | **3.09** | **2.93** | **2.79** | **2.70** | **2.61** | **2.54** | **2.47** | **2.37** | **2.30** | **2.18** |
| 70 | 3.98 | 3.13 | 2.74 | 2.50 | 2.35 | 2.23 | 2.14 | 2.07 | 2.01 | 1.97 | 1.93 | 1.89 | 1.84 | 1.79 | 1.72 |
| | **7.01** | **4.92** | **4.08** | **3.60** | **3.29** | **3.07** | **2.91** | **2.77** | **2.67** | **2.59** | **2.51** | **2.45** | **2.35** | **2.28** | **2.15** |
| 80 | 3.96 | 3.11 | 2.72 | 2.48 | 2.33 | 2.21 | 2.12 | 2.05 | 1.99 | 1.95 | 1.91 | 1.88 | 1.82 | 1.77 | 1.70 |
| | **6.96** | **4.88** | **4.04** | **3.56** | **3.25** | **3.04** | **2.87** | **2.74** | **2.64** | **2.55** | **2.48** | **2.41** | **2.32** | **2.24** | **2.11** |
| 100 | 3.94 | 3.09 | 2.70 | 2.46 | 2.30 | 2.19 | 2.10 | 2.03 | 1.97 | 1.92 | 1.88 | 1.85 | 1.79 | 1.75 | 1.68 |
| | **6.90** | **4.82** | **3.98** | **3.51** | **3.20** | **2.99** | **2.82** | **2.69** | **2.59** | **2.51** | **2.43** | **2.36** | **2.26** | **2.19** | **2.06** |
| 125 | 3.92 | 3.07 | 2.68 | 2.44 | 2.29 | 2.17 | 2.08 | 2.01 | 1.95 | 1.90 | 1.86 | 1.83 | 1.77 | 1.72 | 1.65 |
| | **6.84** | **4.78** | **3.94** | **3.47** | **3.17** | **2.95** | **2.79** | **2.65** | **2.56** | **2.47** | **2.40** | **2.33** | **2.23** | **2.15** | **2.03** |
| 150 | 3.91 | 3.06 | 2.67 | 2.43 | 2.27 | 2.16 | 2.07 | 2.00 | 1.94 | 1.89 | 1.85 | 1.82 | 1.76 | 1.71 | 1.64 |
| | **6.81** | **4.75** | **3.91** | **3.44** | **3.14** | **2.92** | **2.76** | **2.62** | **2.53** | **2.44** | **2.37** | **2.30** | **2.20** | **2.12** | **2.00** |
| 200 | 3.89 | 3.04 | 2.65 | 2.41 | 2.26 | 2.14 | 2.05 | 1.98 | 1.92 | 1.87 | 1.83 | 1.80 | 1.74 | 1.69 | 1.62 |
| | **6.76** | **4.71** | **3.88** | **3.41** | **3.11** | **2.90** | **2.73** | **2.60** | **2.50** | **2.41** | **2.34** | **2.28** | **2.17** | **2.09** | **1.97** |
| 400 | 3.86 | 3.02 | 2.62 | 2.39 | 2.23 | 2.12 | 2.03 | 1.96 | 1.90 | 1.85 | 1.81 | 1.78 | 1.72 | 1.67 | 1.60 |
| | **6.70** | **4.66** | **3.83** | **3.36** | **3.06** | **2.85** | **2.69** | **2.55** | **2.46** | **2.37** | **2.29** | **2.23** | **2.12** | **2.04** | **1.92** |
| 1000 | 3.85 | 3.00 | 2.61 | 2.38 | 2.22 | 2.10 | 2.02 | 1.95 | 1.89 | 1.84 | 1.80 | 1.76 | 1.70 | 1.65 | 1.58 |
| | **6.66** | **4.62** | **3.80** | **3.34** | **3.04** | **2.82** | **2.66** | **2.53** | **2.43** | **2.34** | **2.26** | **2.20** | **2.09** | **2.01** | **1.89** |
| ∞ | 3.84 | 2.99 | 2.60 | 2.37 | 2.21 | 2.09 | 2.01 | 1.94 | 1.88 | 1.83 | 1.79 | 1.75 | 1.69 | 1.64 | 1.57 |
| | **6.64** | **4.60** | **3.78** | **3.32** | **3.02** | **2.80** | **2.64** | **2.51** | **2.41** | **2.32** | **2.24** | **2.18** | **2.07** | **1.99** | **1.87** |

Table A14 of *Statistical Methods*, 7th ed., by George W. Snedecor and William G. Cochran. Copyright © 1980 by the Iowa State University Press. Used with permission.

## TABLE B3

### The Chi-Square Distribution

Table entries are the minimum values of chi-square ($\chi^2$) that are necessary for a chi-square statistic to be significant at the alpha level specified. To be significant, a calculated $\chi^2$ statistic must be greater than or equal to the value in the table.

| df | Proportion in Critical Region | | | | |
| --- | --- | --- | --- | --- | --- |
| | 0.10 | 0.05 | 0.025 | 0.01 | 0.005 |
| 1 | 2.71 | 3.84 | 5.02 | 6.63 | 7.88 |
| 2 | 4.61 | 5.99 | 7.38 | 9.21 | 10.60 |
| 3 | 6.25 | 7.81 | 9.35 | 11.34 | 12.84 |
| 4 | 7.78 | 9.49 | 11.14 | 13.28 | 14.86 |
| 5 | 9.24 | 11.07 | 12.83 | 15.09 | 16.75 |
| 6 | 10.64 | 12.59 | 14.45 | 16.81 | 18.55 |
| 7 | 12.02 | 14.07 | 16.01 | 18.48 | 20.28 |
| 8 | 13.36 | 15.51 | 17.53 | 20.09 | 21.96 |
| 9 | 14.68 | 16.92 | 19.02 | 21.67 | 23.59 |
| 10 | 15.99 | 18.31 | 20.48 | 23.21 | 25.19 |
| 11 | 17.28 | 19.68 | 21.92 | 24.72 | 26.76 |
| 12 | 18.55 | 21.03 | 23.34 | 26.22 | 28.30 |
| 13 | 19.81 | 22.36 | 24.74 | 27.69 | 29.82 |
| 14 | 21.06 | 23.68 | 26.12 | 29.14 | 31.32 |
| 15 | 22.31 | 25.00 | 27.49 | 30.58 | 32.80 |
| 16 | 23.54 | 26.30 | 28.85 | 32.00 | 34.27 |
| 17 | 24.77 | 27.59 | 30.19 | 33.41 | 35.72 |
| 18 | 25.99 | 28.87 | 31.53 | 34.81 | 37.16 |
| 19 | 27.20 | 30.14 | 32.85 | 36.19 | 38.58 |
| 20 | 28.41 | 31.41 | 34.17 | 37.57 | 40.00 |
| 21 | 29.62 | 32.67 | 35.48 | 38.93 | 41.40 |
| 22 | 30.81 | 33.92 | 36.78 | 40.29 | 42.80 |
| 23 | 32.01 | 35.17 | 38.08 | 41.64 | 44.18 |
| 24 | 33.20 | 36.42 | 39.36 | 42.98 | 45.56 |
| 25 | 34.38 | 37.65 | 40.65 | 44.31 | 46.93 |
| 26 | 35.56 | 38.89 | 41.92 | 45.64 | 48.29 |
| 27 | 36.74 | 40.11 | 43.19 | 46.96 | 49.64 |
| 28 | 37.92 | 41.34 | 44.46 | 48.28 | 50.99 |
| 29 | 39.09 | 42.56 | 45.72 | 49.59 | 52.34 |
| 30 | 40.26 | 43.77 | 46.98 | 50.89 | 53.67 |
| 40 | 51.81 | 55.76 | 59.34 | 63.69 | 66.77 |
| 50 | 63.17 | 67.50 | 71.42 | 76.15 | 79.49 |
| 60 | 74.40 | 79.08 | 83.30 | 88.38 | 91.95 |
| 70 | 85.53 | 90.53 | 95.02 | 100.42 | 104.22 |
| 80 | 96.58 | 101.88 | 106.63 | 112.33 | 116.32 |
| 90 | 107.56 | 113.14 | 118.14 | 124.12 | 128.30 |
| 100 | 118.50 | 124.34 | 129.56 | 135.81 | 140.17 |

Table 8 of E. Pearson and H. Hartley, *Biometrika Tables for Statisticians*, 3d ed. New York: Cambridge University Press, 1966. Adapted and reprinted with permission of the *Biometrika* Trustees.

# Glossary

**ABAB design** A single-subject design consisting of four phases: a baseline phase, a treatment phase, a return-to-baseline phase, and a second treatment phase. Also known as a *reversal design*.

**Abstract** A brief summary of the research study, totaling no more than 120 words.

**Accessible population** The easily available segment of a target population. Researchers typically select their samples from this type of population.

**Active deception** The intentional presentation of misinformation about a study to its participants. The most common form of active deception is misleading participants about the specific purpose of the study. Also known as *commission*.

**Alpha level** In a hypothesis test, the criterion for statistical significance that defines the maximum probability that the research result was obtained simply by chance. Also known as *level of significance*.

**Alternating-treatments design** A single-subject design in which two treatment conditions are randomly alternated from one observation to the next. Also known as a *discrete-trials design*.

**Anchors** On a rating scale question, the opposite extremes, identified with verbal labels, that establish the endpoints of the scale.

**Anonymity** The practice of ensuring that an individual's name is not directly associated with the information or measurements obtained from that individual.

Keeping records anonymous is a way to preserve the confidentiality of research participants.

**APA Ethics Code** A common set of values upon which psychologists build their professional and scientific work. This Code is intended to provide both the general principles and the decision rules to cover most situations encountered by psychologists. Its primary goal is the welfare and protection of the individuals and groups with whom psychologists work.

**Apparatus subsection** In a research report, the portion of the method section that describes any apparatus or materials used in the study.

**Appendix** The section of a research report which presents detailed information that is useful but would interrupt the flow of information if presented in the body of the paper.

**Apprehensive subject role** In a study, a participant's tendency to respond in a socially desirable fashion rather than truthfully.

**Archival research** Looking at historical records (archives) to measure behaviors or events that occurred in the past.

**Argument** In the rational method, a set of premise statements that are logically combined to yield a conclusion.

**Assessment sensitization** See *sensitization*.

**Assignment bias** A threat to internal validity that occurs when the process used to assign different participants to different treatments produces groups of individuals with noticeably different characteristics.

---

**Bar graph**      A frequency distribution graph in which a vertical bar indicates the frequency of each score from a nominal or ordinal scale of measurement.

**Baseline observations**      In a single-subject research study, a series of observations or measurements made while no treatment is being administered.

**Baseline phase**      In a single-subject research study, a series of baseline observations identified by the letter A.

**Behavior categories**      Categories of behavior to be observed (such as group play, play alone, aggression, social interaction.) A set of behavior categories and a list of exactly which behaviors count as examples of each are developed before observation begins.

**Between-subjects experimental design**      An experimental design using separate but equivalent groups of individuals for each treatment condition being compared. Also known as an *independent-measures design*.

**Biased sample**      A sample with different characteristics from those of the population.

**Bimodal distribution**      In a frequency distribution graph, a distribution of scores with two modes or two distinct peaks.

---

**Carryover effects**      Changes in the scores observed in one treatment condition that are caused by participation in an earlier treatment condition.

**Case history**      A case study that does not include a treatment or intervention.

**Case study design**      An in-depth study and detailed description of a single individual (or a very small group). A case study may involve an intervention or treatment administered by the researcher.

**Ceiling effect**      The clustering of scores at the high end of a measurement scale, allowing little or no possibility of increases in value; a type of range effect.

**Central tendency**      A statistical measure that identifies a single score that defines the center of a distribution. It provides a representative value for the entire group.

**Changing-criterion design**      A single-subject design consisting of a series of phases, each phase defined by a specific criterion that determines a target level of behavior. The criterion level is changed from one phase to the next.

**Chi-square test for independence**      A hypothesis test that evaluates the statistical significance of the differences between proportions for two or more groups of participants.

**Citation**      An identification of the author(s) and year of publication of the source of a specific fact or idea mentioned in a research report.

**Clinical significance**      See *practical significance*.

**Cluster sampling**      A probability sampling technique involving random selection of groups, instead of individuals, from a population.

**Cohen's *d***      A standard measure of effect size computed by dividing the sample mean difference by the sample standard deviation.

**Cohen's kappa**      A calculation that corrects for chance agreement when inter-rater reliability is measured.

**Cohort effect**      A difference between age groups that is due to a characteristic or experience other than age. Also called *generation effect*.

**Cohorts**      Individuals who were born at roughly the same time and grew up under similar circumstances.

**Commission**      See *active deception*.

**Compensatory equalization**      A threat to internal validity that occurs when an untreated group demands to receive a treatment that is the same as or equivalent to the treatment received by another group in the research study.

**Compensatory rivalry**      A threat to internal validity that occurs when an untreated group learns about special treatment received by another group and then works extra hard to show they can perform just as well as that group. Occasionally called the *John Henry effect*.

**Complete counterbalancing**      In within-subjects design, using a separate group of participants for every possible order of the treatment conditions. With *n* different treatment conditions, there are *n*! (*n* factorial) different orders.

**Component-analysis design**    See *dismantling design*.

**Concurrent validity**    The type of validity demonstrated when scores obtained from a new measure are directly related to scores obtained from a more established measure of the same variable.

**Confidentiality**    The practice of keeping strictly secret and private the information or measurements obtained from an individual during a research study. APA ethical guidelines require researchers to ensure the confidentiality of their research participants.

**Confounding variable**    An extraneous variable (usually unmonitored) that is allowed to change systematically along with the two variables being studied.

**Consent form**    A written statement by the researcher containing all of the elements of informed consent and a line for the participant's signature. The consent form is provided prior to the study so that potential participants have all the information they need in order to make an informed decision regarding participation.

**Construct**    A hypothetical attribute or mechanism that helps explain and predict behavior in a theory. Also known as a *hypothetical construct*.

**Construct validity**    The type of validity demonstrated when scores obtained from a measure are directly related to the variable itself.

**Content analysis**    Using the techniques of behavioral observation to measure the occurrence of specific events in literature, movies, television programs, or similar media that present replicas of behaviors.

**Contrived observation**    Observation in settings arranged specifically for observing and recording behavior. Also known as *structured observation*.

**Control group**    In a research study, the group that receives no treatment or a placebo treatment.

**Convenience sampling**    A nonprobability sampling method involving selection of individuals on the basis of their availability and willingness to respond—that is,

because they are easy to get. Occasionally called *accidental sampling* and *haphazard sampling*.

**Convergent validity**    The type of validity demonstrated by a strong relationship between the scores obtained from two different methods of measuring the same construct.

**Correlation**    A statistical value that measures and describes the direction and degree of relationship between two variables.

**Correlational research strategy**    A general approach to research that involves measuring two variables for each individual in order to describe the relationship between the variables. Two variables are measured and recorded for each individual; the measurements are then reviewed to identify any patterns of relationship that exist between the two variables and to measure the strength of the relationship.

**Cost-restrictive sampling**    See *subject selection bias*.

**Counterbalancing**    In a within-subjects design, a procedure to minimize order effects and threats from time-related factors by using separate groups so that each group receives the series of treatment conditions in a different order. The goal is to use every possible order of treatments with an equal number of individuals participating in each sequence.

**Criterion variable**    In a correlational study, a researcher often is interested in the relationship between two variables in order to use knowledge about one variable to help predict or explain the second variable. In this situation, the second variable (being explained or predicted) is called the *criterion variable*.

**Cronbach's alpha**    A generalization of the Kuder-Richardson formula that computes a corrected measure of split-half reliability when each test item has more than two responses.

**Cross-sectional research design**    A developmental design comparing different groups of individuals, each group representing a different age.

**Database**    A computerized cross-referencing tool that focuses on an individual topic area (such as psychology); used for searching the literature for articles relevant to your topic.

**Debriefing**    A postexperimental explanation of the purpose of the study. A debriefing is given after a participant completes a study, especially if deception was used.

**Deception**    The purposeful withholding of information or misleading of participants about a study. There are two forms of deception, passive and active.

**Deduction**    The use of a general statement as the basis for reaching a conclusion about specific examples. Also known as *deductive reasoning*.

**Deductive reasoning**    See *deduction*.

**Degrees of freedom**    The value $n - 1$ when the variance for a sample of $n$ scores is computed; in general, the number of independent elements when a sample statistic is computed.

**Demand characteristics**    Potential cues or features of a study that make obvious to the participants what the purpose and hypothesis are and influence the participants to respond or behave in a certain way. Demand characteristics threaten external validity.

**Dependent variable**    In a research study that compares different groups or different treatment conditions, the variable that is measured for each individual. In an experiment, the dependent variable is observed to determine whether or not it changes in response to manipulation of the independent variable.

**Descriptive research strategy**    A general approach to research that involves measuring a variable or set of variables as they exist naturally, with the purpose of describing the variables as they exist.

**Descriptive statistics**    Statistical methods used to organize, summarize, and simplify the results obtained from research studies.

**Desynchrony**    Lack of agreement between two measures.

**Developmental research strategy**    A research strategy used to examine changes in an individual that are related to age.

**Differential attrition**    A threat to internal validity that occurs when the rate of attrition in one group is not the same as the rate of attrition for another group.

**Differential history effects**    In a research study, a threat to internal validity that occurs when the history effects for one group are not the same as the history effects for another group.

**Differential instrumentation**    In a research study, a threat to internal validity that occurs when the instrumentation effects for one group are not the same as the instrumentation effects for another group.

**Differential maturation**    In a research study, a threat to internal validity that occurs when the maturation effects for one group are not the same as the maturation effects for another group.

**Differential practice/fatigue**    In a research study, a threat to internal validity that occurs when the practice or fatigue effects for one group are not the same as the practice or fatigue effects for another group.

**Differential regression**    In a research study, a threat to internal validity that occurs when the regression toward the mean for one group is not the same as the regression toward the mean for another group.

**Differential research design**    A research study that compares pre-existing groups rather than randomly assigning individuals to groups. Usually the groups are defined by a participant characteristic such as gender, race, or personality.

**Diffusion**    A threat to internal validity that occurs when a treatment effect spreads from the treatment group to the control group, usually from participants talking to each other.

**Directionality problem**    A correlational study can establish that two variables are related, that is, that changes in one variable tend to be accompanied by changes in the other variable. However, a correlational study does not determine which variable is the "cause" and which is the "effect."

**Discrete-trials design**    See *alternating-treatments design*.

**Discussion section**    The portion of a research report that restates the hypothesis, summarizes the results, and presents a discussion of the interpretation, implications, and possible applications of the results.

**Dismantling design**    A single-subjects design consisting of a series of phases where each phase adds or subtracts one component of a complex treatment. Also known as *component-analysis design*.

**Divergent validity**    A type of validity demonstrated by using two different methods to measure two different constructs; convergent validity must be shown for each of the two constructs and that there is little or no relationship between the scores obtained for the two different constructs when they are measured by the same method.

**Double-blind research**    A research study in which both the researcher and the participants are unaware of the predicted outcome.

**Duration method**    In behavioral observation, a technique for converting observations into numerical scores that involves recording how much time an individual spends engaged in a specific behavior during a fixed-time observation period.

---

**Effect size**    The measured magnitude of the effect of an experimental treatment.

**Equivalent time-samples design**    A quasi-experimental time-series design that consists of a long series of observations during which a treatment is alternately administered and then withdrawn.

**Error variance**    A variance computed to measure the magnitude of differences that are due to chance. The denominator of the $F$-ratio computed in an analysis of variance.

**Ethics**    The study of proper action.

**Event sampling**    A technique of behavioral observation that involves observing and recording one specific event or behavior during the first interval, then shifting to a different event or behavior during the second interval, and so on for the full series of intervals.

**Expectancy**    See *experimenter bias*.

**Experimental group**    The treatment condition in an experiment.

**Experimental realism**    In simulation research, the extent to which the psychological aspects of the research environment duplicate the real-world environment that is being simulated.

**Experimental research strategy**    A research strategy that attempts to establish the existence of a cause-and-effect relationship between two variables by manipulating one variable while measuring the second variable and controlling all other variables. Also known as the *manipulative research strategy*.

**Experimenter bias**    Influence of the experimenter's expectations or personal beliefs on the findings of a study. Also known as *expectancy*.

**External validity**    The extent to which we can generalize the results of a research study to people, settings, times, measures, and characteristics other than those used in that study.

**Extraneous variable**    Any variable that exists within a study other than the variables being studied. In an experiment, any variable other than the independent and dependent variables.

---

**Face validity**    An unscientific form of validity that concerns whether or not a measure superficially appears to measure what it claims to measure.

**Factor**    A variable that differentiates a set of groups or conditions being compared in a research study. In an experimental design, a factor is an independent variable.

**Factorial design**    A research design that includes two or more factors.

**Faithful subject role**    In a study, a participant's attempt to follow experimental instructions to a tee and to avoid acting on the basis of any suspicions about the purpose of the experiment.

**Fatigue**    A threat to internal validity that occurs when prior participation in a treatment condition or measurement procedure tires the participants, lowering their performance on subsequent measurements.

**Field**    A research setting that the participant or subject perceives as a natural environment.

**Field study**    A research study conducted in a setting that the participant or subject perceives as a natural environment.

**Floor effect** The clustering of scores at the low end of a measurement scale, allowing little or no possibility of decreases in value; a type of range effect.

**Fraud** The explicit efforts of a researcher to deceive and misrepresent data. Fraud is unethical.

**Frequency distribution** An organized display of a set of scores that shows how many scores are located in each category on the scale of measurement.

**Frequency method** In behavioral observation, a technique for converting observations into numerical scores that involves counting the instances of each specific behavior that occur during a fixed-time observation period.

**Generation effect** See *cohort effect.*

**Good subject role** In a study, a participant's tendency to respond in a way that corroborates the investigator's hypothesis.

**Habituation** In behavioral observation, repeated exposure of participants to the observer's presence until it is no longer a novel stimulus.

**Higher-order factorial design** A research design with more than two factors.

**Histogram** A frequency distribution graph in which a vertical bar indicates the frequency of each score from an interval or ratio scale of measurement.

**History** Any outside event that occurs during a within-subjects experiment and influences participants' scores.

**History effect** A threat to internal validity from any outside event(s) that occurs during the time that a research study is being conducted and has an influence on the participants' scores.

**Hypothesis** A statement describing the relationship between two variables.

**Hypothesis test** An inferential statistical procedure that uses sample data to evaluate the credibility of a hypothesis about a population. A hypothesis test determines whether research results are statistically significant.

**Hypothetical construct** See **construct.**

**Idiographic approach** The study of individuals, in contrast to the study of groups.

**Independent-measures design** See *between-subjects experimental design.*

**Independent-measures *t* test** In a between-subjects design, a hypothesis test that evaluates the statistical significance of the mean difference between two separate groups of participants.

**Independent variable** In an experiment, the variable manipulated by the researcher. In behavioral research, the independent variable usually consists of two or more treatment conditions to which participants are exposed.

**Individual differences** Characteristics that differ from one participant to another.

**Individual sampling** A technique of behavioral observation involving identifying one participant to be observed during the first interval, then shifting attention to a different individual for the second interval, and so on.

**Induction** The use of a relatively small set of specific observations as the basis for forming a general statement about a larger set of possible observations. Also known as *inductive reasoning.*

**Inductive reasoning** See *induction.*

**Inferential statistics** Statistical methods used to determine when it is appropriate to generalize the results from a sample to an entire population.

**Informed consent** The ethical principle requiring the investigator to provide all available information about a study so that a participant can make a rational, informed decision regarding whether to participate in the study.

**Institutional Animal Care and Use Committee (IACUC)** A committee that examines all proposed research with respect to its treatment of nonhuman subjects.

**Institutional Review Board (IRB)** A committee that examines all proposed research with respect to its treatment of human participants.

**Instrumental bias**     See *instrumentation*.

**Instrumentation**     A threat to internal validity from changes in the measurement instrument that occur during the time a research study is being conducted. Also known as *instrumental bias*.

**Interaction between factors**     In a factorial design, the mean differences between individual treatment conditions, or cells that are not consistent with the main effects. Also, when the effects of one factor depend on the different levels of a second factor. Indicated by the existence of nonparallel (converging or crossing) lines in a graph showing the means for a two-factor design.

**Internal validity**     The extent to which a research study produces a single, unambiguous explanation for the results.

**Inter-rater reliability**     The degree of agreement between two observers who simultaneously record measurements of a behavior.

**Interrupted time-series design**     A time-series design consisting of a series of observations before and after an event that is not a treatment or an experience created or manipulated by the researcher.

**Interval method**     In behavioral observation, a technique for converting observations into numerical scores that involves dividing the observation period into a series of intervals and then recording whether or not a specific behavior occurs during each interval.

**Interval scale**     A scale of measurement in which the categories are organized sequentially and all categories are the same size. The zero point of an interval scale is arbitrary.

**Introduction**     The first major section of a research report, which presents a logical development of the research question, including a review of the relevant background literature, a statement of the research question or hypothesis, and a brief description of the methods used to answer the question or test the hypothesis.

**Key word**     A term used to identify and describe a variable in a study. Key words are used to search through publications.

**Kuder-Richardson formula 20**     A formula for computing split-half reliability that corrects for the fact that individual scores are based on only half of the total test items.

**Laboratory**     A research setting that is obviously devoted to the discipline of science. It can be any room or space that the subject or participant perceives as artificial.

**Latin square**     An $N \times N$ matrix where each of $N$ different items appears exactly once in each column and exactly once in each row. Used to identify sequences of treatment conditions for partial counterbalancing.

**Level**     In a single-subject research study, the overall magnitude for a series of observations. A consistent level occurs when measurements in a series are all approximately the same magnitude.

**Level of significance**     See *alpha level*.

**Levels**     In an experiment, the different values of the independent variable selected to create and define the treatment conditions. In other research studies, the different values of a factor.

**Line graph**     A display in which points connected by straight lines show several different means obtained from different groups or treatment conditions.

**Literature search**     The process of gaining a general familiarity with the current research conducted in your subject area and finding a small set of journal articles that will serve as the basis for your research idea and will provide the justification or foundation for your new research.

**Longitudinal research design**     A research design that examines development by making a series of observations or measurements over time. Typically, the same group of individuals is measured at different points in time.

**Main effect**     In a factorial study, the mean differences among the levels of one factor.

**Manipulation check**     In a research study, an additional measure used to assess how the participants perceived and interpreted the manipulation and/or to assess the direct effect of the manipulation.

**Manipulative research strategy**     See *experimental research strategy*.

**Matched-subjects design**     A research design comparing separate groups of individuals where each individual in one group is matched with a participant in each of the other groups. The matching is done so that the matched individuals are equivalent with respect to a variable that the researcher considers to be relevant to the study.

**Matching**     The assignment of individuals to groups so that a specific variable is balanced or matched across the groups.

**Materials subsection**     See *apparatus subsection*.

**Maturation**     A threat to internal validity from any physiological or psychological changes that occur in a participant during the time that research study is being conducted and that can influence the participant's scores.

**Mean**     A measure of central tendency obtained by summing the individual scores and dividing the sum by the number of scores.

**Median**     A measure of central tendency that identifies the score that divides the distribution exactly in half. Exactly 50% of the individuals have scores above the median, and 50% have scores below the median.

**Method of authority**     A method of inquiry in which a person relies on information or answers from an expert in the subject area.

**Method of empiricism**     A method of inquiry in which observation and direct sensory experience are used to obtain knowledge.

**Method of faith**     A variant of the method of authority in which people have unquestioning trust in the authority figure and therefore accept information from the authority without doubt or challenge.

**Method of intuition**     A method of inquiry in which information is accepted on the basis of a hunch or "gut feeling."

**Method of tenacity**     A method of inquiry in which information is accepted as true because it has always been believed or because superstition supports it.

**Method section**     The section of a research report that describes how the study was conducted, including the subjects or participants, the apparatus or materials, and the procedures used.

**Methods of inquiry**     The variety of ways in which a person can acquire knowledge or find answers to questions.

**Mixed design**     A factorial study that combines two different research strategies, such as between-subjects and within-subjects, or combines an experimental factor and a nonexperimental factor.

**Mode**     A measure of central tendency that identifies the most frequently occurring score in the distribution.

**Multimodal distribution**     In a frequency distribution graph, a distribution of scores with more than two modes or distinct peaks.

**Multiple-baseline across behaviors**     A multiple-baseline design in which the initial baseline phases correspond to two separate behaviors for the same participant.

**Multiple-baseline across situations**     A multiple-baseline study in which the initial baseline phases correspond to the same behavior in two separate situations.

**Multiple-baseline across subjects**     A multiple-baseline study in which the initial baseline phases correspond to two separate participants.

**Multiple-baseline design**     A single-subject design that begins with two simultaneous baseline phases, then initiates a treatment for one baseline and at a later time initiates the treatment for the second baseline.

**Multiple-treatment interference**     A threat to external validity that occurs when participants are exposed to more than one treatment and their responses are affected by an earlier treatment.

**Mundane realism**     In simulation research, the extent to which the superficial, usually physical, characteristics of the research environment duplicate the real-world environment that is being simulated.

---

**Naturalistic observation**     A type of observation in which a researcher observes behavior in a natural setting as unobtrusively as possible.

**Negativistic subject role**    In a study, a participant's tendency to respond in a way that will refute the investigator's hypothesis.

**Nominal scale**    A scale of measurement in which the categories represent qualitative differences in the variable being measured. The categories have different names but are not related to each other in any systematic way.

**Nomothetic approach**    The study of groups, in contrast to the study of individuals.

**Nonequivalent control group design**    A research design in which the researcher does not randomly assign individuals to groups but rather uses pre-existing groups, with one group serving in the treatment condition and another group serving in the control condition.

**Nonequivalent group design**    A research study in which the different groups of participants are formed under circumstances that do not permit the researcher to control the assignment of individuals to groups, and the groups of participants are therefore considered nonequivalent.

**Nonexperimental design**    A research design in which little or no attempt is made to minimize or eliminate threats to internal validity. Occasionally called *pre-experimental design*.

**Nonexperimental research**    A category of research that does not seek to establish the existence of cause-and-effect relationships. Also called *nonmanipulative research*.

**Nonmanipulative research**    See *nonexperimental research*.

**Nonparticipant observation**    See *naturalistic observation*.

**Nonprobability sampling**    A category of sampling method in which the population is not completely known, individual probabilities cannot be known, and the sampling method is based on factors such as common sense or ease, with an effort to maintain representativeness and avoid bias.

**Nonresponse bias**    In survey research involving mailed surveys, individuals who return the survey are not usually representative of the entire group who received the survey. Nonresponse bias is a threat to external validity.

**No-treatment control group**    A group or condition in which the participants do not receive the treatment being evaluated.

**Novelty effect**    A threat to external validity that occurs when individuals participating in a research study (a novel situation) perceive and respond differently than they would in the normal, real world.

**Null hypothesis**    In a hypothesis test, a statement about the population(s) or treatments being studied that says there is no change, no effect, no difference, or no relationship.

**Nuremberg Code**    A set of 10 guidelines for the ethical treatment of human participants in research. The Nuremberg Code, developed from the Nuremberg Trials in 1947, laid the groundwork for the current ethical standards for medical and psychological research.

---

**Observational research design**    Descriptive research in which the researcher observes and systematically records the behavior of individuals in order to describe the behavior.

**Omission**    See *passive deception*.

**One-group pretest–posttest design**    A nonexperimental design involving one measurement before treatment and one measurement after treatment for a single group of participants.

**One-way ANOVA**    See *single-factor analysis of variance*.

**Operational definition**    A procedure for measuring and defining a construct. An operational definition specifies a measurement procedure (a set of operations) for measuring an external, observable behavior and uses the resulting measurements as a definition and a measurement of the hypothetical construct.

**Order effect**    A change in the scores observed in one treatment condition, caused by participation in earlier treatments (carryover effects) or experience over time in a research study (progressive error).

**Ordinal scale**    A scale of measurement on which the categories have different names and are organized sequentially (for example, first, second, third).

**Page header**       In a research report, the first two or three words of the title, printed with the page number on each page of the manuscript.

**Parameter**       A summary value that describes a population.

**Partial counterbalancing**       A system of counterbalancing that ensures that each treatment condition occurs first for one group of participants, second for one group, third for one group, and so on but does not require that every possible order of treatment conditions be used.

**Participant**       A human who takes part in a research study.

**Participant attrition**       The loss of participants that occurs during the course of a research study conducted over time. Attrition can be a threat to internal validity.

**Participant observation**       A type of observation in which the researcher engages in the same activities as the people being observed, in order to observe and record their behavior.

**Participants subsection**       In a research report, the portion of the method section that describes the humans who participated in the study.

**Passive deception**       The intentional withholding or omitting of information whereby participants are not told some information about the study. Also known as *omission*.

**Pearson correlation**       A correlation used to evaluate linear (straight-line) relationships.

**Peer review**       The editorial process that many articles undergo when a researcher submits a research report for publication. In a typical peer review process, the editor of the journal and a few experts in the field of research review the paper in extreme detail. The reviewers critically scrutinize every aspect of the research, with the primary purpose of evaluating the quality of the study and its contribution to scientific knowledge. Reviewers are also likely to detect anything suspect about the research or the findings.

**Phase**       In a single-subject research design, a series of observations of the same individual under the same conditions.

**Phase change**       In a single-subjects research study, a change in the conditions from one phase to another, usually involving administering or stopping a treatment.

**Placebo**       An ineffective, inert substitute for a treatment or medication.

**Placebo control group**       A group or condition in which the participants receive a placebo instead of the actual treatment.

**Placebo effect**       A participant's response to an inert medication or treatment that has no real effect on the body but which occurs simply because the individual thinks it is effective.

**Plagiarism**       Presenting someone else's ideas or words as one's own. Plagiarism is unethical.

**Polygon**       A frequency distribution graph in which a series of points connected by straight lines indicates the frequency of each score from an interval or ratio scale of measurement.

**Population**       The entire set of individuals of interest to a researcher. Although the entire population usually does not participate in a research study, the results from the study will be generalized to the entire population. Also known as *target population*.

**Posttest-only nonequivalent control group design**       A nonexperimental design in which one group is observed (measured) after receiving a treatment and a second, nonequivalent, group is measured at the same time but receives no treatment. Also known as *static group comparison*.

**Practical significance**       In a research study, a result or treatment effect that is large enough to have value in a practical application. Also known as *clinical significance*.

**Practice effects**       A threat to internal validity that occurs when prior exposure to a measurement procedure provides participants with additional skills that produce improved scores.

**Predictive validity**       The type of validity demonstrated when scores obtained from a measure accurately predict behavior according to a theory.

**Predictor variable**       In a correlational study, a researcher often is interested in the relationship between two variables in order to use knowledge about one variable to help predict or explain the second variable. In this situation, the first variable is called the *predictor variable*.

**Premise statements**     Sentences used in logical reasoning that describe facts or assumptions.

**Pretest–posttest nonequivalent control group design**     A quasi-experimental research design comparing two nonequivalent groups; one group is measured twice—once before treatment is administered and once after. The other group is measured at the same two times but receives no treatment.

**Pretest sensitization**     A form of assessment sensitization that occurs when measurement of participant behavior prior to treatment affects a participant's response to the treatment.

**Primary source**     A first-hand report of observations or research results written by the individual(s) who actually conducted the research and made the observations.

**Probability sampling**     A sampling method in which the entire population is known, each individual in the population has a specifiable probability of selection, and sampling is done using a random process based on the probabilities.

**Procedure subsection**     In a research report, the portion of the method section that describes the step-by-step process used to complete the study.

**Progressive error**     In a research study, changes in the scores observed in one treatment condition that are related to experience over time but not to a specific treatment or treatments. Common kinds of progressive error are practice effects and fatigue.

**Proportionate stratified random sampling**     A probability sampling technique that involves identifying specific subgroups to be included, determining what proportion of the population corresponds to each group, and randomly selecting individual samples from each subgroup such that the proportion in the sample exactly matches the proportion in the population.

*Psychological Abstracts*     A series of bound volumes containing abstracts or summaries, a subject index, and an author index; a noncomputerized tool for searching the psychology literature for articles relevant to your research topic.

**PsycINFO**     A computerized database that provides the same information as *Psychological Abstracts*.

**PsycLIT**     A computerized database that provides the same information as *Psychological Abstracts*.

*Publication Manual of the American Psychological Association* (5th ed., 2001)     A manual that describes conventions for style and structure of written research reports in the behavioral sciences.

---

**Quasi-experimental research strategy**     A research strategy that attempts to minimize threats to internal validity and produce cause-and-effect conclusions (like an experiment) but lacks one of the critical components, either manipulation or control, that is necessary for a true experiment. Typically compares pre-existing groups or defines the conditions with a time variable.

**Quasi-independent variable**     In a quasi-experimental or nonexperimental research study, the variable that differentiates the groups or conditions being compared. Similar to the independent variable in an experimental study.

**Quota sampling**     A nonprobability sampling method; a type of convenience sampling involving identifying specific subgroups to be included in the sample and then establishing quotas for individuals to be sampled from each group.

---

**Random assignment**     A procedure in which a random process is used to assign participants to treatment conditions.

**Randomization**     The use of a random process to help avoid a systematic relationship between two variables. The intent is to disrupt any systematic relationship that may exist.

**Random process**     A procedure that produces one outcome from a set of possible outcomes. The outcome must be unpredictable each time, and the process must guarantee that each of the possible outcomes is equally likely to occur.

**Range effect**     The clustering of scores at one end of a measurement scale. Ceiling effects and floor effects are types of range effects.

**Rational method**     A method of inquiry that involves seeking answers by the use of logical reasoning.

**Ratio scale**     A scale of measurement in which the categories are sequentially organized, all categories are the same size, and the zero point is absolute or nonarbitrary.

**Reactivity**     Participants' modification of their natural behavior in response to the fact that they are participating in a research study or the knowledge that they are being measured.

**Reference section**     The section of a research report that lists complete references for all sources of information cited in the report, organized alphabetically by the last name of the first author.

**Refutable hypothesis**     A hypothesis that can be demonstrated to be false. That is, the hypothesis allows the possibility that the outcome will differ from the prediction.

**Regression toward the mean**     A statistical phenomenon in which extreme scores (high or low) on a first measurement tend to be less extreme on a second measurement; considered a threat to internal validity because changes in participants' scores may be caused by regression rather than by the treatments. Also known as *statistical regression*.

**Reliability**     The degree of stability or consistency of measurements. If the same individuals are measured under the same conditions, a reliable measurement procedure will produce identical (or nearly identical) measurements.

**Repeated-measures design**     See *within-subjects experimental design*.

**Repeated-measures *t* test**     In a within-subjects or matched-subjects design, a hypothesis test that evaluates the statistical significance of the mean difference between two sets of scores obtained from the same group of participants.

**Replication**     Repetition of a research study with the same basic procedures used in the original study. The intent of replication is to test the validity of the original study. Either the replication will support the original study by duplicating the original results, or it will cast doubt on the original study by demonstrating that the original result is not easily repeated.

**Representativeness**     The extent to which the characteristics of the sample accurately reflect the characteristics of the population.

**Representative sample**     A sample with the same characteristics as the population.

**Research design**     A general plan for implementing a research strategy. A research design specifies whether the study will involve groups or individual subjects, whether the study will make comparisons within a group or between groups, and how many variables will be included in the study.

**Research ethics**     The responsibility of researchers to be honest and respectful to all individuals who may be affected by their research studies or their reports of the studies' results. Researchers are usually governed by a set of ethical guidelines that assist them to make proper decisions and choose proper actions. In psychological research, the American Psychological Association maintains a set of ethical principles for research (APA, 1992).

**Research procedure**     The exact, step-by-step description of a specific research study.

**Research proposal**     A written report presenting the plan and underlying rationale for a future research study. A proposal includes a review of the relevant background literature, an explanation of how the proposed study is related to other knowledge in the area, a description of how the planned research will be conducted, and a description of the possible results.

**Research report**     A written description of a research study that includes a clear statement of the purpose of the research, a review of the relevant background literature that led to the research study, a description of the methods used to conduct the research, a summary of the research results, and a discussion and interpretation of the results.

**Research strategy**     A general approach to research determined by the kind of question that the research study hopes to answer.

**Resentful demoralization**     A threat to internal validity that occurs when an untreated group learns of special treatment given to another group and becomes less productive and less motivated because they resent the other group's expected superiority.

**Response set**    On a rating-scale question, a participant's tendency to answer all (or most) of the questions the same way.

**Restricted random assignment**    A random process for assigning individuals to groups that has a limitation to ensure predetermined characteristics (such as equal size) for the separate groups.

**Results section**    The section of a research report that presents a summary of the data and the statistical analysis.

**Reversal design**    See *ABAB design*.

**Running head**    The abbreviated title of a research report, containing a maximum of 50 characters, that appears on the title page of the manuscript and at the top of the pages in a published article.

**Sample**    A set of individuals selected from a population, usually intended to represent the population in a research study.

**Sampling**    The process of selecting individuals to participate in a research study. Also known as *sampling procedures* or *sampling techniques*.

**Sampling bias**    See *selection bias*.

**Sampling error**    The naturally occurring difference between a sample statistic and the corresponding population parameter.

**Sampling procedures**    See *sampling*.

**Sampling techniques**    See *sampling*.

**Scale of measurement**    The set of categories used for classification of individuals. The four types of measurement scales are nominal, ordinal, interval, and ratio.

**Scatterplot**    A graph that shows the data from a correlational study. The two scores for each individual appear as a single point in the graph, with the vertical position of the point corresponding to one score and the horizontal position corresponding to the other.

**Scientific method**    An approach to acquiring knowledge that uses observations to develop a hypothesis and then empirically tests the hypothesis by making additional, systematic observations. Typically, the new observations lead to a new hypothesis, and the cycle continues.

**Secondary source**    A description or summary of another person's work, written by someone who did not participate in the research or observations being discussed.

**Selection bias**    A form of experimental bias in which participants or subjects are selected in a manner that increases the probability of obtaining a biased sample.

**Semantic differential**    A type of rating-scale question that presents a list of adjectives (such as *helpful, hostile, devious*) and asks each participant to use the scale to rate how well each adjective describes a particular individual.

**Sensitization**    A threat to external validity that occurs when the assessment procedure alters participants so that they react differently to treatment than they would in the real world when the treatment is used without assessment. Also known as *assessment sensitization* or *pretest sensitization*.

**Significant result**    See *statistically significant result*.

**Simple random sampling**    A probability sampling technique in which each individual in the population has an equal and independent chance of selection.

**Simulation**    In a research study, the creation of conditions that simulate or closely duplicate the natural environment in which the behaviors being examined would normally occur.

**Single-blind research**    A research study in which the researcher does not know the predicted outcome.

**Single-case designs**    See *single-subject designs*.

**Single-factor analysis of variance**    A hypothesis test that evaluates the statistical significance of the mean differences among two or more sets of scores obtained from a single-factor multiple group design. Also known as *one-way ANOVA*.

**Single-factor multiple group design**    A research design comparing more than two groups of participants (or groups of scores) representing more than two levels of the same factor.

**Single-factor two-group design**    A research design comparing two groups of participants or two groups of scores representing two levels of a factor. Also known as the *two-group design.*

**Single-subject designs**    Research designs that use the results from a single participant or subject to establish the existence of a cause-and-effect relationship. Also known as *single-case designs.*

**Spearman-Brown formula**    A formula for computing split-half reliability that corrects for the fact that individual scores are based on only half of the total test items.

**Split-half reliability**    A measure of the consistency of scores from separate items on a test or questionnaire consisting of multiple items.

**Stability**    The degree to which a series of observations shows a consistent level or trend.

**Standard deviation**    A measure of variability that describes the average distance from the mean, obtained by taking the square root of the variance.

**Standard error**    A measure of the average or standard distance between a sample statistic and the corresponding population parameter.

**Static group comparison**    See *posttest-only nonequivalent control group design.*

**Statistic**    A summary value that describes a sample.

**Statistically significant result**    In a research study, a result that is extremely unlikely (as defined by an alpha level or level of significance) to have occurred simply by chance. Also known as a *significant result.*

**Statistical regression**    See *regression toward the mean.*

**Stratified random sampling**    A probability sampling technique involving identifying specific subgroups to be included in the sample and then selecting equal random samples from each pre-identified subgroup.

**Structured observation**    See *contrived observation.*

**Subject**    A nonhuman who takes part in a research study.

**Subject role**    The different ways that participants respond to experimental cues based on whatever they judge to be appropriate in the situation. Also known as *subject role behavior.*

**Subject role behavior**    See *subject role.*

**Subject selection bias**    A threat to external validity that occurs when selection of participants is based on who is convenient rather than on an unbiased procedure.

**Subjects subsection**    In a research report, the portion of the method section that describes the nonhumans who participated in the study.

**Survey research design**    A research study that uses a survey to obtain a description of a particular group of individuals.

**Systematic sampling**    A probability sampling technique in which a sample is obtained by selecting every $n$th participant from a list containing the total population, after a random start.

---

**Target population**    A group defined by a researcher's specific interests; see *population.*

**Testable hypothesis**    A hypothesis in which all of the variables, events, and individuals are real and can be defined and observed.

**Testing effects**    A type of progressive error resulting from the influence of repeated measurement experience on participants.

**Test-retest reliability**    The type of reliability established by comparing the scores obtained from two successive measurements and calculating a correlation between the two sets of scores.

**Test statistic**    A summary value computed in a hypothesis test to measure the degree to which the sample data are in accord with the null hypothesis.

**Third-variable problem**    The possibility that two variables appear to be related when in fact they are both influenced by a third variable that causes them to vary together.

**Threat to external validity**     Any characteristic of a study that limits the generality of the results.

**Threat to internal validity**     Any factor that allows for an alternative explanation for the results of a study.

**Threat to validity**     Any component of a research study that introduces questions or raises doubts about the quality of the research process or the accuracy of the research results.

**Three-factor design**     A research study involving three factors.

**Time sampling**     A technique of behavioral observation that involves observing for one interval, then pausing during the next interval to record all the observations. The sequence of observe-record-observe-record is continued through the series of intervals.

**Time-series design**     A quasi-experimental research study consisting of a series of observations before the treatment and a series of observations after the treatment.

**Title page**     The first page of a research report manuscript, containing the title of the paper, the author names and affiliations, and the running head.

**Treatment condition**     In an experiment, a situation or environment characterized by one specific value of the manipulated variable. An experiment contains two or more treatment conditions that differ according to values of the manipulated variable.

**Treatment observations**     In a single-subject research study, observations or measurements made while a treatment is being administered.

**Treatment phase**     In a single-subject research study, a series of treatment observations, identified by the letter B.

**Trend**     In a single-subject research study, a consistent difference in direction and magnitude from one measurement to the next in a series.

**Two-group design**     See *single-factor two-group design.*

**Two-factor ANOVA**     See *two-way analysis of variance.*

**Two-factor design**     A research study involving two factors.

**Two-way analysis of variance**     A hypothesis test that evaluates the statistical significance of the mean differences (both main effects and interaction) obtained in a two-factor research study. Also known as *two-factor ANOVA.*

**Type I error**     The conclusion, based on a hypothesis test, that a result is statistically significant when in fact the result is simply due to chance.

**Type II error**     The conclusion, based on a hypothesis test, that a result is not statistically significant when in fact a real effect or relationship does exist in the population.

---

**Validity (of a measurement procedure)**     The degree to which the measurement process measures the variable it claims to measure.

**Validity (of a research study)**     The degree of truth or accuracy of the results. Validity is determined by the quality of the research process and the accuracy of the results.

**Variability**     A measure of the size of the differences between scores in a distribution.

**Variance**     A measure of variability obtained by computing the average squared distance from the mean.

**Volunteer bias**     A threat to external validity that occurs because volunteers are not perfectly representative of the general population.

---

**Within-subjects experimental design**     An experimental design in which the same group of individuals participates in all of the different treatment conditions. Also known as *repeated-measures design.*

# References

Allport, G. W. (1961). *Pattern and growth in personality*. New York: Holt, Reinhart, & Winston.

American Psychological Association. (1992). Ethical principles of psychologists and code of conduct. *American Psychologist, 47*, 1597–1611.

American Psychological Association. (2001). *Publication manual of the American Psychological Association* (5th ed.). Washington, DC: Author.

Aronson, E., & Carlsmith, J. M. (1968). Experimentation in social psychology. In G. Lindzey & E. Aronson (Eds.), *Handbook of social psychology* (2nd ed.), (Vol. 2, pp. 1–79). Reading, MA: Addison-Wesley.

Bahrick, H. P., & Hall, L. K. (1991). Lifetime maintenance of high school mathematics content. *Journal of Experimental Psychology: General, 120*, 20–33.

Baldwin, E. (1993). The case for animal research in psychology. *Journal of Social Issues, 49*, 121–131.

Barnard, N. D., & Kaufman, S. R. (1997). Animal research is wasteful and misleading. *Scientific American, 276*, 80–82.

Baumrind, D. (1985). Research using intentional deception: Ethical issues revisited. *American Psychologist, 40*, 165–174.

Bordens, K. S., & Horowitz, I. A. (1983). Information processing in joined and severed trials. *Journal of Applied Social Psychology, 13*, 351–370.

Botting, J. H., & Morrison, A. R. (1997). Animal research is vital to medicine. *Scientific American, 276*, 83–85.

Bowd, A. D., & Shapiro, K. J. (1993). The case against laboratory animal research in psychology. *Journal of Social Issues, 49*, 133–142.

Bransford, J. D., Franks, J. J., Morris, C. D., & Stein, B. S. (1979). Some general constraints on learning and memory research. In L. S. Cermak & F. I. M. Craik (Eds.), *Levels of processing in human memory* (pp. 331–354). Hillsdale, NJ: Erlbaum.

Broadhead, W. E., Kaplan, B. H., James, S. A., Wagner, E. H., Schoenbach, V. I., Grimson, R., Heyden, S., Tibblin, G., & Gehlbach, S. H. (1983). The epidemiologic evidence for a relationship between social support and health. *American Journal of Epidemiology, 117*, 521–537.

Bryan, J. H., & Test, M. A. (1967). Models and helping: Naturalistic studies in aiding behavior. *Journal of Personality and Social Psychology, 6*, 400–407.

Campbell, D. T., & Stanley, J. C. (1963). *Experimental and quasi-experimental designs for research*. Chicago: Rand McNally.

Cialdini, R. B., Reno, R. R., & Kallgren, C. A. (1990). A focus theory of normative conduct: Recycling the concept of norms to reduce littering in public places. *Journal of Personality and Social Psychology, 58*, 1015–1026.

Cohen, J. (1961). A coefficient of agreement for nominal scales. *Educational and Psychological Measurement, 20*, 37–46.

Cohen, J. (1969). *Statistical power analysis for the behavioral sciences*. New York: Academic Press.

Converse, J. M., & Presser, S. (1986). *Survey questions: Handcrafting the standardized questionnaire*. Newbury Park, CA: Sage.

Craig, A. R., & Kearns, M. (1995). Results of a traditional acupuncture intervention for stuttering. *Journal of Speech & Hearing Research, 38*, 572–578.

Craik, F. I. M., & Lockhart, R. S. (1972). Levels of processing: A framework for memory research. *Journal of Verbal Learning and Verbal Behavior, 11*, 671–684.

Cronbach, L. J. (1951). Coefficient alpha and the internal structure of tests. *Psychometrika, 16*, 297–334.

DeGoede, K. M., Ashton-Miller, J. A., Liao, J. M., & Alexander, N. B. (2001). How quickly can healthy adults move their hands to intercept an approaching object? Age and gender effects. *Journals of Gerontology:*

*Series A: Biological Sciences and Medical Sciences, 56,* 584–588.

DeProspero, A., & Cohen, S. (1979). Inconsistent visual analyses of intrasubject data. *Journal of Applied Behavior Analysis, 12,* 573–579.

Dillman, D.A. (1978). *Mail and telephone surveys: The total design method.* New York: Wiley.

Downs, D. S., & Abwender, D. (2002). Neuropsychological impairment in soccer athletes. *Journal of Sports Medicine and Physical Fitness, 42,* 103–107.

Dremen, S. (Ed.). (1997). *The family on the threshold of the 21st century: Trend and implications.* Mahway, NJ: Erlbaum.

Ferguson, E. D., & Schmitt, S. (1988). Gender linked stereotypes and motivation affect performance in the Prisoner's Dilemma game. *Perceptual and Motor Skills, 66,* 703–714.

Fisher, C. B., & Fyrberg, D. (1994). Participant partners: College students weigh the costs and benefits of deceptive research. *American Psychologist, 49,* 417–425.

Fitterling, J. M., Martin, J. E., Gramling, S., Cole, P., & Milan, M. (1988). Behavioral management of exercise training in vascular headache patients: An investigation of exercise adherence and headache activity. *Journal of Applied Behavior Analysis, 21,* 9–19.

Freedman, R., Coombs, L. C., Chang, M., & Sun, T. (1974). Trends in fertility, family size preferences, and practice of family planning: Taiwan, 1965–1973. *Studies in Family Planning, 5,* 270–288.

Goldie, J., Schwartz, L., McConnachie, A., & Morrison, J. (2001). Impact of a new course on students' potential behavior on encountering ethical dilemmas. *Medical Education, Special Issue, 35,* 295–302.

Goodall, J. (1971). *In the shadow of man.* Boston: Houghton Mifflin.

Goodall, J. (1986). *The chimpanzees of Gombe: Patterns of behavior.* Cambridge: University Press.

Haney, C., Banks, C., & Zimbardo, P. (1973). Interpersonal dynamics in a simulated prison. *International Journal of Criminology and Penology, 1,* 69–97.

Harmon, T. M., Nelson, R. O., & Hayes, S. C. (1980). Self-monitoring of mood versus activity by depressed clients. *Journal of Consulting and Clinical Psychology, 48,* 30–38.

Holmes, D. S. (1976a). Debriefing after psychological experiments I: Effectiveness of post-deception dehoaxing. *American Psychologist, 31,* 858–867.

Holmes, D. S. (1976b). Debriefing after psychological experiments I: Effectiveness of post-deception desensitizing. *American Psychologist, 31,* 868–875.

Horn, J. L. (1978). The nature and development of intellectual abilities. In R. T. Osborne, C. T. Noble, &

N. Weyl (Eds.), *Human variation.* New York: Academic Press.

Hornstein, H. A., Fisch, E., & Holmes, M. (1968). Influence of a model's feeling about his behavior and his relevance as a comparison on other observers' helping behavior. *Journal of Personality and Social Psychology, 10,* 222–226.

Huck, S. W., & Sandler, H. M. (1979). *Rival hypotheses: Alternative explanations of data based conclusions.* New York: Harper & Row.

Jones, J. H. (1981). *Bad blood: The Tuskegee syphilis experiment.* New York: Free Press.

Kaczmarek, M., & Franco, J. N. (1986). Sex differences in prediction of academic performance by the Graduate Record Exam. *Psychological Reports, 59,* 1197–1198.

Kamin, L. J. (1974). *The science and politics of IQ.* Potomac, MD: Erlbaum.

Katz, J. (1972). *Experimentation with human beings.* New York: Sage.

Kazdin, A. E. (1998). *Research design in clinical psychology* (4th ed.). Boston: Allyn & Bacon.

Kent, R. N., Wilson, G. T., & Nelson, R. (1972). Effects of false heart-rate feedback on avoidance behavior: An investigation of cognitive desensitization. *Behavior Therapy, 3,* 1–6.

Kuder, G. F., & Richardson, M. W. (1937). The theory of estimation of test reliability. *Psychometrika, 2,* 151–160.

LaVaque, T. J., & Rossiter, T. (2001). The ethical use of placebo controls in clinical research: The Declaration of Helsinki. *Psychophysiology & Biofeedback, 26,* 23–37.

Lambirth, T. T., Gibb, G. D., & Alcorn, J. D. (1986). Use of a behavior-based personality instrument in aviation selection. *Educational and Psychological Measurement, 46,* 973–978.

Liguori, A., & Robinson, J. H. (2001). Caffeine antagonism of alcohol-induced driving impairment. *Drug & Alcohol Dependence, 63,* 123–129.

Likert, R. (1932). A technique for the measurement of attitude. *Archives of Psychology, 140,* 55.

Logue, A.W. (1991). *The psychology of eating and drinking: An introduction* (2nd ed.). New York: W.H. Freeman.

Ludwig, T. D., & Geller, E. S. (1991). Improving the driving practices of pizza deliverers: Response generalization and moderating effects of driving history. *Journal of Applied Behavior Analysis, 24,* 31–44.

Maloney, D. M. (1984). *Protection of human research subjects: A practical guide to federal laws and regulations.* New York: Plenum Press.

McClelland, D. C. (1958). Risk taking in children with high and low need for achievement. In Atkinson,

J. W. (Ed.), *Motives in fantasy, action, and society.* New York: Van Nostrand.

McClelland, D. (1976). *The achieving society* (2nd ed.). New York: Irvington.

McClelland, D. (1987). *Human motivation.* New York: Cambridge University Press.

McMahon, S. R., Rimsza, M. E., & Bay, R. C. (1997). Patients can dose liquid medication accurately. *Pediatrics, 100,* 330–333.

Milgram, S. (1963). Behavioral study of obedience. *Journal of Abnormal and Social Psychology, 67,* 371–378.

Melton, G. B., Levine, R. J., Koocher, G. P., Rosenthal, R., & Thompson, W. C. (1988). Community consultation in socially sensitive research: Lessons from clinical trials in treatments for AIDS. *American Psychologist, 43,* 573–581.

Myers, A., & Hansen, C. (1997). *Experimental psychology.* Pacific Grove, CA: Brooks Cole.

Nagi, J. L. (1975). Predictive validity of the Graduate Record Examination and the Miller Analogies Test. *Educational & Psychological Measurement, 35,* 471–472.

National Research Council. (1996). *Guide for the care and use of laboratory animals.* Washington, DC: National Academy Press.

Page, R. M., Hammermeister, J. J., & Scanlan, A. (2000). Everybody's not doing it: Misperception of college students' sexual activity. *American Journal of Health Behavior, 24,* 387–394.

Paivio, A. (1965). Abstractness, imagery, and meaningfulness in paired-associate learning. *Journal of Verbal Learning & Verbal Behavior, 4,* 32–38.

Piliavin, I. M., Rodin, J., & Piliavin, J. A. (1969). Good samaritanism: An underground phenomenon. *Journal of Personality and Social Psychology, 13,* 289–299.

Piliavin, J. A., & Piliavin, I. (1972). Effects of blood on reactions to a victim. *Journal of Personality and Social Psychology, 23,* 353–361.

Pope, H. G., Ionescu-Pioggia, M., & Pope, K. W. (2001). Drug use and life style among college undergraduates: A 30-year longitudinal study. *American Journal of Psychiatry, Special Issue, 158,* 1519–1521.

Rahe, R. H., & Arthur, R. J. (1978). Life change and illness studies: Past history and future directions. *Journal of Human Stress, 4,* 3–15.

Ray, W. J. (2000). *Methods: Toward a science of behavior and experience* (6th ed.). Belmont, CA: Wadsworth.

Reich, W. T. (Ed.). (1995). *Encyclopedia of bioethics* (Rev. ed., Vol. 3). New York: Simon & Schuster.

Ring, K., Wallston, K., & Corey, M. (1970). Mode of debriefing as a factor affecting subjective reaction to a Milgram-type obedience experiment: An ethical inquiry. *Representative Research in Social Psychology (University of North Carolina, Department of Psychology), 1,* 67–88.

Rolider, A., Cummings, A., & Van Houten, R. (1991). Side effects of therapeutic punishment on academic performance and eye contact. *Journal of Applied Behavior Analysis, 24,* 763–773.

Rosenhan, D. L. (1973). On being sane in insane places. *Science, 179,* 250–258.

Rosenthal, R., & Fode, K. L. (1963). The effect of experimenter bias on the performance of the albino rat. *Behavioral Science, 8,* 183–189.

Rosenthal, R., & Rosnow, R. L. (1975). *The volunteer subject.* New York: Wiley.

Rosnow, R., & Rosenthal, R. (1997). *People studying people: Artifacts and ethics in behavioral research.* New York: W. H. Freeman.

Rubin, Z. (1985). Deceiving ourselves about deception: Comment on Smith and Richardson's "Amelioration of deception and harm in psychological research." *Journal of Personality & Social Psychology, 48,* 252–253.

Saitoh, O., Karns, C. M., & Courchesne, E. (2001). Development of the hippocampal formation from 2 to 42 years: MRI evidence of smaller area dentate in autism. *Brain, Special Issue, 124,* 1317–1324.

Sales, B. D., & Folkman, S. (2000). *Ethics in research with human participants.* Washington, DC: American Psychological Association.

Schwartz, D., Dodge, K., & Coie, J. (1993). The emergence of chronic peer victimization in boys' play groups. *Child Development, 64,* 1755–1772.

Scoville, W. B., & Milner, B. (1957). Loss of recent memory after bilateral hippocampal lesions. *Journal of Neurology, Neurosurgery, & Psychiatry, 20,* 11–21.

Sears, D. (1986). College sophomores in the laboratory: Influences of a narrow data base on social psychology's view of human nature. *Journal of Personality & Social Psychology, 51,* 515–530.

Shanahan, F. (1984, October). *BAT overview and preliminary results of selected subtests.* Paper presented at the annual meeting of the Human Factors in Aviation Screening and Performance Prediction Sub-Technical Advisory Group of the Human Factors Engineering Technical Advisory Group, San Antonio, Texas.

Shapiro, A. K., & Morris, L. A. (1978). The placebo effect in medical and psychological therapies. In S. L. Garfield & A. E. Bergin (Eds.), *Handbook of psychotherapy and behavior change: An empirical analysis* (2nd ed.). New York: Wiley.

Shrauger, J. S. (1972). Self-esteem and reactions to being observed by others. *Journal of Personality & Social Psychology, 23,* 192–200.

Siegel, J. M. (1990). Stressful life events and use of physician services among the elderly: The moderating role of pet ownership. *Journal of Personality & Social Psychology, 58,* 1081–1086.

Skjoeveland, O. (2001). Effects of street parks on social interactions among neighbors. *Journal of Architectural & Planning Research, Special Issue, 18,* 131–147.

Smith, S. S., & Richardson, D. (1983). Amelioration of deception and harm in psychological research: The important role of debriefing. *Journal of Personality & Social Psychology, 44,* 1075–1082.

Stanley, B., Sieber, J., & Melton, G. (1996). *Research ethics: A psychological approach.* Lincoln: University of Nebraska Press.

Strack, F., Martin, L. L., & Stepper, S. (1988). Inhibiting and facilitating conditions of the human smile: A nonobtrusive test of the facial feedback hypothesis. *Journal of Personality & Social Psychology, 54,* 768–777.

Sun, Y. (2001). Family environment and adolescents' well-being before and after parents' marital disruption: A longitudinal analysis. *Journal of Marriage & Family, 63,* 697–713.

Teasdale, J. D., & Fogarty, S. J. (1979). Differential effects of induced mood on retrieval of pleasant and unpleasant events from episodic memory. *Journal of Abnormal Psychology, 88,* 248–257.

Thigpen, C. H., & Cleckley, H. M. (1954). A case of multiple personality. *Journal of Abnormal & Social Psychology, 49,* 135–151.

Thigpen, C. H., & Cleckley, H. M. (1957). *Three faces of Eve.* New York: McGraw-Hill.

Tomer, J. F. (1987). Productivity through intra-firm cooperation: A behavioral economic analysis. *Journal of Behavioral Economics, 16,* 83–95.

Tversky, A., & Kahneman, D. (1973). Availability: A heuristic for judging frequency and probability. *Cognitive Psychology, 5,* 207–232.

Tyson, G. A., Schlachter, A., & Cooper, S. (1987). Game playing strategy as an indicator of racial prejudice among South African students. *Journal of Social Psychology, 128,* 473–485.

Updegraff, K. A., McHale, S. M., Crouter, A. C., & Kupanoff, K. (2001). Parents' involvement in adolescents' peer relationships: A comparison of mothers' and fathers' roles. *Journal of Marriage & Family, 63,* 655–668.

Valins, S., & Ray, A. A. (1967). Effects of cognitive desensitization on avoidance behavior. *Journal of Personality & Social Psychology, 7,* 345–350.

Wacker, D. P., Steege, M. W., Northup, J., Sasso, G., Berg, W., Reimers, T., Cooper, L., Cigrand, K., & Donn, L. (1990). A component analysis of functional communication training across three topographies of severe behavior problems. *Journal of Applied Behavior Analysis, 23,* 417–429.

Weber, S. J., & Cook, T. D. (1972). Subject effects in laboratory research: An examination of subject roles, demand characteristics, and valid inferences. *Psychological Bulletin, 77,* 273–295.

Wilkinson, L., & Task Force on Statistical Inference. (1999). Statistical methods in psychology journals. *American Psychologist, 54,* 594–604.

# Index